Public Administration
of Recreational Services

Public Administration
of Recreational Services

GEORGE HJELTE, B.S., M.S., M.H. (Hon.)

Consultant for Recreational and Youth Services
Planning Council of Los Angeles;
Formerly General Manager, Recreation and Park Department,
City of Los Angeles,
Los Angeles, California

JAY S. SHIVERS, Ph.D.

Professor of Physical Education,
Supervisor, Recreational Service Education,
The School of Education,
The University of Connecticut,
Storrs, Connecticut

Foreword by
JOSEPH HALPER

Chief Deputy Director of the Los Angeles County
Department of Parks and Recreation
Los Angeles, California

SECOND EDITION

Lea & Febiger · *Philadelphia 1978*

HEALTH EDUCATION, PHYSICAL EDUCATION, AND RECREATION

Ruth Abernathy, Ph.D., Editorial Adviser
Professor Emeritus, School of Physical and Health Education
University of Washington
Seattle, Washington 98105

1st Edition, 1972
Reprinted, 1975

Library of Congress Cataloging in Publication Data

Hjelte, George.

Public administration of recreational services.
Bibliography: p.
Includes index.
1. Recreation—Administration. I. Shivers, Jay Sanford, 1930- joint author.
II. Title.
GV182.15.H55 1978   658.91'79   78-2530
ISBN 0-8121-0639-3

Published in Great Britain by Henry Kimpton Publishers, London

PRINTED IN THE UNITED STATES OF AMERICA

Print Number 3 2 1

Ratio sine exercitatione inutilis, exercitatio sine ratione caeca est.

Foreword

At this time of rapidly changing social priorities, those of us engaged in the administration of recreational services and facilities are faced with the need for updated information on the technologies and strategies available for dealing effectively with the social and administrative problems that confront us in the performance of our mission. This publication combines the wisdom and expertise of both town and gown by bringing together the collective knowledge of an eminent scholar and a nationally recognized public administrator. The perspective reflected in this text melds the pragmatism of the public arena and the creative thought process of academia.

This combination gives us a creative approach to resolving the problems of this specialized area of public administration. The administrative concepts and techniques advanced in this publication are leavened by the interaction of the separate perspectives of the authors. I commend the text to both the student and the veteran administrator for use as a resource in the field of the administration of public recreational services.

Joseph W. Halper
Chief Deputy Director
County of Los Angeles
Department of Parks and Recreation

Acknowledgments

We appreciate the information, willingly provided, from the leaders in recreational service throughout the United States. Particular thanks are due Joseph Curtis, Commissioner of Human Services, New Rochelle, New York, and Jack Foley, Superintendent of Recreational Services, Culver City, California, for information concerning human services. Attorney Joseph Triarsi furnished case material dealing with an example of public liability; Dr. Harry Hartley, Vice President for Financial Affairs of the University of Connecticut, provided information concerning Planning, Programming, Budgeting Systems and Zero Based Budgeting analyses.

We owe special recognition to Joseph Halper, Chief Deputy Director of the Department of Parks and Recreation for the County of Los Angeles, who furnished information dealing with policy development as well as his generously written and well thought-out Foreword.

The presses, publishing houses, and professional journals mentioned specifically in the footnotes graciously consented to allow reproduction of quotations from their pages and publications. For these permissions we express our gratitude.

Finally, we owe much to Mary Lou Nye, who translated rough copy into a clean manuscript. Her dedication to the task demands deep appreciation.

G. H.
J. S. S.

Preface

This book is intended primarily as a text for use in universities offering professional courses for the preparation of recreational service personnel at the administrative level. Although public recreational services are administered by jurisdictions other than local governments, and some recreational services are offered by private and commercial agencies, courses for the professional education of recreationists are related to the field of municipal administration. Recreational services administered by federal and state governments, which are expanding rapidly, are a subject of special study that should be treated independently.

The text deals with administrative techniques and practices pertaining to public administration of recreational services. Therefore, it covers every facet of public administration as it concerns recreational service including organization, operation, planning, development, and managerial procedures. It describes the basic elements of the public field; liability factors and legal framework of operation; community structure; political practices; social implications and typical municipal setting of the recreational service agency. An investigation of other social agencies which may have direct or indirect influence on the amount and degree of recreational services offered within the community is included. The text treats the internal structure of a public recreational service department and the administrative functions that are based on daily operations of the agency. Emphasis is placed on fundamental principles and practices of administering public recreational service departments.

The work is oriented to a consideration of administration from the standpoint of departmental problems. Departmental administration derives its form largely from uniform practice within the municipal government as a whole and, to a large extent, is governed by state and municipal laws. Problems of administering the particular program and facilities of the unit center or other public recreational place are not included except as they illustrate or are related to universal problems involved in the administration of all types of public recreational sites.

The book is organized into six major parts: Administrative Foundations —dealing with legal establishment and policy making; External Influences on Administration—dealing with other than municipally based agencies, liability, and public relations; Organizational Functions—dealing with organizational conditions, line and staff arrangements, computer technology, systems management, and office management; Personnel Administration—dealing with recruitment, examination, probation, deployment, management-employee relations, employee organizations, management by objectives, and supervision; Fiscal Administration—dealing with financial management, budgeting, budget formats; Administrative Responsibility—dealing with public planning, maintenance management, program administration, and evaluation.

The advantage of this organization is logical progression. The sequence of chapters is in the exact order which might arise in the establishment, development, and operation of a public agency providing community recreational services. There have also been included the impinging forces which create or alleviate problems for the operation of the agency. The reader is introduced to each topic by definition and narrative discussion. Each chapter, although it may stand alone and be perused independently of the others, is authoritative in itself and has been placed to supplement and complement preceding chapters. Thus, the reader is able to follow the complete development and day-to-day administrative practices of the public recreational service system from its inception to operational problems and methods for their resolvement.

A secondary purpose of this book is to discuss problems that are the concern of administrators and lay board members or commissioners. Principles that have been formulated and that have borne the test of experience have been set forth. On some unresolved questions, dogmatic and premature generalizations have been avoided. Sound administrative practice is not subordinated to the uniqueness of recreational service, but the management of the department and its professional and auxiliary personnel illustrates how scientific principles may be applied so that maximum effectiveness and comprehensive services ensue. Basically, the book approaches the science and art of public administration in recreational service with logic and sound data to supply concepts that will be of use to administrators every day on the job.

New trends in the organization of public recreational services, as presented here, conform with the best thinking in municipal government. Lines of authority and responsibility are clearly set forth for large or small legal units. Legal and other provisions and suggestions are made for a rich cooperative program including municipal, county, special district, and school units as well as private and quasi-public groups.

The term *recreational service* has been deliberately used in the title and throughout the text. This use denotes our conviction and acceptance of the functional fact that municipal agencies of whatever designation which supply or provide for the public's demand for recreational programming and places are performing recreational service. Since functional names are usually preferred in designating departments of governmental services, it may well develop that *recreational services administration* will comprehend all that is now connoted by other existing titles.

Although this text is based upon previously published works by both of us (*The Administration of Public Recreation*, Macmillan, 1940; *Public Administration of Park and Recreational Services*, Macmillan, 1963; *Public Administration of Recreational Services*, Lea & Febiger, 1972) it contains both updated material as well as many new chapters not offered before. Moreover, it provides the latest administrative techniques as well as illustrative case studies. The work combines the pragmatic outlook of the agency executive and the theoretical orientation of a university professor. The synthesis of these viewpoints and analyses has resulted in a more complete and useful text that tells how to administer. It offers crystalized and acceptable methods for handling current operational problems and for resolving them successfully. The text should meet a vital need of practicing administrators and provide definite information for teachers of higher education.

Los Angeles, California
Storrs, Connecticut

GEORGE HJELTE
JAY S. SHIVERS

Contents

PART I

ADMINISTRATIVE FOUNDATIONS

CHAPTER 1

Introduction to Public Administration of Recreational Services

This book is directed to the processes of administration which are relevant to the public sector of society. Of necessity, all forms of human association require some aspect of administration. Whenever there is a need to mobilize material, fiscal, natural, or human resources in order to accomplish some set purpose, administrative procedures are called into play. Administration is certainly a cooperative undertaking, the net result of which is to gain a specific objective. While the goals of organizations vary considerably, depending upon their differing environments, ideology, confronted problems, and assumed risks undergone in consequence of mandated functions, there are techniques held in common. The precise form of administration differs because of local conditions and the nature of the organization in question.

SCOPE OF PUBLIC ADMINISTRATION

Public administration is understood to denote all governmental activities concerned with operation as distinct from adjudication or legislation. However, with the complexities and interrelationships of government on every level, actual administrative functions overlap the purely judicial and legislative areas. Typically, all administration is similar whether carried out in the public or private sector of society. Public administration is restricted only by the government under which it functions. Therefore, the public administrator is vitally concerned with what may be achieved within the legislative enactments or policy statements passed by those in authority, and by the available resources. The chief purposes of administration are cooperation, coordination and control. It has been closely identified with management and, to a great extent, relies on devising and keeping records.

Performance of public administration is implicit in the state of the art. All efforts to establish a set of generally applicable principles to all situations have thus far failed. Therefore, any claim that public administration is a science is bound to be received with some skepticism. Nevertheless, students of administration must continue to attempt to apply scientific principles to administration. In an increasingly complex society, the only logical administrative approach to problems is the scientific method. Although scientific approaches and certain technical devices, may be utilized within public administration processes, administration, in either the public or private sector, is not as yet a science. A great body of knowledge concerning the field has been accumulated through research into the way outcomes are generated, why interactions between people are significant to administration, and the purely mechanical aspects of regulating material goods (storage, distribution, allocation, purchase) for efficiency, economy, and speed. But public administration is not susceptible to science in the true sense of the word. The art of administration confirms that, while a tremendous portion of the work may be learned, transmitted, recorded, and filed, crucial decisions are based neither on scientifically acquired research nor on obvious fact. Much decision making critical to public administration at the policy level is still romanticized or made "by feel." The individual administrator's experience, knowledge, and sensitivity to situations and prevailing conditions remain the critical factors from which value judgments and systems are derived and defined. The last best opinion, regardless of its basis, is still opinion.

Scientific management principles may be successfully utilized in organizations, but in recent years people have come to be recognized as being quite different from the machines or materials they operate or manipulate. Scientific managers view administration as essentially devoted to technical features of division of labor and specialization. However, concentration on mechanical features to the exclusion of the human factors involved has come to be regarded as a primary error. Technology can be applied wherever repetitive movements are required or where facts alone constitute the basis for making decisions. However, when the human element is a component of the work situation, another important facet must be understood. Men are not susceptible to manipulation as are inert items; they are much too unpredictable, even on the basis of probability tests and surveys, to be subjects for precise calculations, for they are subject to whims, fancies, subjective influences, and varying beliefs. Their actions or behaviors are not completely predictable nor reliable. Thus, from scientific management practices has come a realization that administration is not a science when it deals with people.

The unalterable view of administration as a pure science has not gained wide acceptance. Even the technological advances made in computer processing, data analysis, cybernetics, and automation have not convinced students of this field that administration is, can be, or should be a science. Certainly, scientific principles should be applied wherever they are feasible, but this does not make a discipline a science. Individuals who stubbornly revel in this approach rarely can visualize the social contexts of which economic and technical units comprise but one segment. People are seen as pinpoints on impersonal organizational charts or diagrams. Writing about those whose attitude reflects this concept, Robert Tannenbaum states that:

> While the effective manager must, without question, be able to understand and deal with economic and technological phenomena, he must *also* be able to deal with interpersonal phenomena. Managerial problems involving motivation, morale, teamwork, creativity, introduction of change, demand creation, public relations, etc., can adequately be solved only through a keen understanding of human-relations variables and an ability to behave appropriately in light of such understanding.[1]

Scientific principles and practices greatly aid public administration in organizational analysis and efficient production, but the field itself relies on the art of administration because interpersonal relations are integral throughout its processes. Cooperative or collective endeavor is the touchstone of administration. Public administration encompasses every area and enterprise under the aegis of public policy and should not be thought of as mere policy execution. In the most restricted view this is precisely the outcome of administrative effort. Administrative adroitness is found in the enactment of legislation, the adjudication of legislation, and the shaping or molding of value judgments that become policy statements.

Public administration is often thought to be concerned with the organization, policy execution, and management of personnel, finances, and other practices fundamental to the effective operation of agencies charged with carrying out the specific functions of government. It is all of this, but, by asserting its cooperative significance in recognizing that human behavior of a collective type is vital to it, its scope becomes much broader. Among its characteristics are the necessity for cooperative group effort for or toward some goal; an overt influence on the formulation of policy and, therefore, on politics; its involvement in all aspects of government whether of the legislative, judicial, or executive branches;

[1]Robert Tannenbaum, "Some Current Issues in Human Relations," *California Management Review,* II, No. 1 (Fall, 1959), p. 53. Originally published by the University of California Press; reprinted by permission of The Regents of the University of California.

and, its impact on private persons and organizations by providing a variety of services.

NATURE OF PUBLIC ADMINISTRATION

Administration is formed of three components: (1) the determination of policy, because policy is essential to direct the activities of the institution or agency; (2) the policies must be translated into substantive operations to achieve the prescribed ends; and (3) the operations must be put into action. Therefore, administrative achievement comes from sound interpersonal relationships: first, between the administrator and those who set the policy; second, between the administrator and his chief subordinates in managing, motivating, leading, and supervising the personnel who will execute the policy of the agency; and third, among the operating personnel, because production (whether of goods or services) depends on cooperative relations.

Although there is a blurring of distinct spheres of interest between policy making and administration, owing to the strong influence exerted on policy makers by the administrator and the realities of administration, a discrete function may be clearly observed. Administration is always subordinate to policy. Despite the reliance of executives, political leaders, and legislators on administrators to supply them with relevant facts on which to base decisions (thereby permitting the administrator to subtly influence policy decisions), policy making is not a responsibility of administration. Execution of policy by operable means to reach desired ends is the essence of administration.

The primary purpose of public administration is to manage the public's business in the most competent manner possible. Administration is a highly complex process which has evolved gradually with the maturation of society and is a direct outgrowth of the division of labor, requiring special learning and skills. The administrator requires an ever-expanding body of knowledge, both formal and informal, to equip himself for competency. Whether the process of administration is a science or an art, the administrative practitioner will have a much restricted role within the social milieu unless he brings a scientific orientation to his work.

A science is fundamentally defined in terms of universally applicable principles having precise and demonstrable consequences on application. Outstanding authorities are attempting to determine basic principles for public administration.

CULTURAL INFLUENCES ON PUBLIC ADMINISTRATION

Public administration in any society is a reflection of that society's complexity. As the social order becomes more complicated, the range and variety of all public services increase. Furthermore, as environmental and human relationships are modified, emphasis is laid on the need to redirect public programs appropriate to such changes. Among the significant factors that influence adaptations in public administration are demographic changes; technological improvements; environmental pollution; educational innovations; social movements and ideologies; the political system; the interrelationships of public, quasi-public, and private sectors on each other; social problems and disintegration; and economic resources and their utilization.

Demographic changes are typically reflected in the kinds, numbers, and degrees of services rendered by public agencies. When population increases or decreases, an analogous movement in the fiscal position of the public service occurs. Thus, increases in population require a corresponding increase in governmental budgets. In municipalities more money must be expended on police and fire protection, health services, garbage collection, public works, low- and middle-income public housing, and public recreational services. Simultaneously, states must increase their support of school systems, public welfare payments, highways, recreational areas, and penal, custodial, rehabilitation, and learning institutions. Federally, more grants to state governments are allocated, interstate highways and mass transportation receive increased attention and funding, national parks, forests, and monuments are afforded additional financial support, institutions of higher education receive federal grants in greater proportion, and a larger amount of money is spent on such facilities and services as social security, urban renewal, acquisition of open space, and similar programs.

As population increases, usually covert problems become all too apparent in urban centers: congestion, crime, racism, ecological destruction, plethora of traffic, violence, and other conditions created by an enigmatic and complex social structure require assistance at higher and higher governmental levels. Therefore, public administration must assume the burden, and, of even more importance, must undertake such stresses in the most expeditious way possible. Actions that can cope with a changing social fabric are vital. Any social system in transition is characterized by its complexity and requires a public service that can adjust to and arrange its procedures in conformity to rapid change.

Technology

The late 1970s will witness a more rapid advance in all forms of automation. Automation, both in governmental services and private enterprise, is one of the major forces for change in American society today. Many of the manifestations of automation will have a significant impact on public administration. Technological advances make possible massive leisure, mobility, affluence, and an entire complex of permutations with enormous influence on the American way of life.[2] Jet aircraft provide an example. With the advent of faster transport, people travel throughout the world on business and recreational activity. Americans have literally caused a negative balance of payments simply because so many of them now take vacations in foreign lands. Increased travel has caused a growing demand for more airports capable of handling bigger aircraft. The supersonic transports or SST are capable of flying higher and traveling at speeds above that of sound. If they become common carriers, present airport accommodations must be expanded, putting greater strain on the region in which the jetport is situated. Such installations require major highways, transit systems, police protection, fire-fighting apparatus, large numbers of personnel, all-weather performance, location within a metropolitan area and yet distant enough so that the noise level does not cause disruption. Airport facilities have become so large that they represent vast management enterprises in themselves.

People of this era are witnesses to history as it is being made through instant mass communication, primarily television. Although newspapers still provide the detailed information necessary for thorough understanding of news events, television carries the initial impact to millions of people all over the world. With instant communication and rapid transportation, greater knowledge about other peoples, and, in return, a concurrent demand for the "better life" that is seen so clearly through visual communication occur. Technological progress in transportation and communication ultimately results in the widespread interchange of ideas, ideals, values, and it is hoped, human understanding.

Educational techniques have not lagged behind the development of communications media. Teaching machines, video tape for instant replay of lectures and lessons, and exposure to great artists, scientists, lawyers, historians, and other resource personnel are at the fingertips of the child in the modern classroom. The whole concept of language instruction has been modified by laboratories in which the student may hear and compare his progress with experts in the language of his choice. The advances and rewards heaped on the educated person have created a demand for more and better education for all. Once only the wealthy could afford any kind of education, today education from kindergarten to university is considered to be the birthright of every child. More and better education produces an individual whose value judgments are not the same as those of his elders. He is a more knowledgeable, aware, and sophisticated person than men of previous generations. He is skeptical about platitudes and asks questions basic to governmental establishment and function. This, too, tends to modify the social structure of society.

[2] F. A. Nigro and L. G. Nigro, *Modern Public Administration,* 4th ed. (New York: Harper & Row, 1973), pp. 33–39.

Politics and Economic Pressure

Political ideology and economic philosophy play an extremely important role in decision making in the public sector. Increasingly, the politician's influence on public administration is felt in terms of political appointment to high office as well as employment of personnel in administrative, technical, and menial positions. If the political official believes in a "spoils system" or patronage approach to public administration, his election to office may mean the demise or a considerable hampering of the merit system of employment. In many instances, political rewards for assisting individuals to gain some high office actually mean the placement of party figures in public office, spelling the decline of public service.

When patronage payoffs are permitted to interfere with the employment of professionally and technically prepared personnel, the entire merit system or civil service program becomes suspect. Usually, the politician sends his personnel requirements to the public administrator and the public administrator must comply, particularly if his own position is within the executive branch of government. However, the public administrator will accede only so far. When the administrator feels that political appointments to his staff are impairing the organization's effectiveness and efficiency, he will protest to the politician. A good politician does not want his administration to be tainted by poor service, for he realizes that the public has a long memory for service slights. Thus he will probably refrain from causing further slippage since he has fulfilled his contract with party workers. The politician therefore permits the career administrator to operate his agency and no longer requires that unqualified or partially qualified persons be hired.[3] The department must succeed with the professionally and technically competent employees that it has retained, despite having to carry "deadweight" personnel. Of course, political appointees may have the talent and skill necessary to perform competently, but this usually is not the case.

Governmental agencies saddled with political appointees develop bureaucratic tendencies, are less efficient than organizations in which each employee must prove his technical worth, and are less likely to have a favorable cost-benefit relationship between the financial needs of agency and the expectations of public service. Political influence and orientation of elected officials invariably have repercussions on the administration of any public agency within the level of government in question. Thus policy decisions pertaining to personnel practices, pressure brought to bear on the agency for specific services or favors for particular groups, favorable consideration for some practices as opposed to others,

---

[3] James C. Charlesworth, *Governmental Administration* (New York: Harper & Brothers, Publishers, 1951), pp. 172–175.

all these intimately connected, sometimes subtle other times overt, pressures have a decided impact on the proper administration and execution of prescribed functions of a single agency or the government at large.

The economic philosophy of the chief administrator or executive, or his political superior, also influences agency responsibility and function. A conservatively oriented political official may view the function of government as purely status quo. A conservative economic outlook may oppose social services, require a lowering or holding of current tax lines, or attempt to discontinue the social welfare functions of government. Economic philosophy also may color the role of the public agency by pushing forward certain aspects at the expense of others. A park administrator may view the development of park, playground, or other recreational areas and facilities from a rigidly conservative economic stance. These facilities and areas are then constructed or developed to reflect inexpensive maintenance instead of functional utility. Thus, the administrator's economic conservatism is reflected in more durable recreational facilities with less expenditure for maintenance. Unfortunately, recreational places that are, or have been, developed for easy and inexpensive maintenance are seldom attractive and functional. They may even promote vandalism, which can be more expensive in the long run. This does not mean to imply that expensive maintenance automatically provides highly attractive and functional recreational facilities. Far from it! Nevertheless, the typical low-maintenance playground facility has not lent itself to attractive design or even to safety for the users.

Economic philosophy is reflected in the services a government offers. In fact, nothing is more significant to public administration and the operation of public services than the economic ideology that elected public officials hold. Whatever the economic philosophy, it is translated into functions and services or diverted to maintaining the particular public posture the officeholder believes his constituents desire him to have. Within this framework public policy is made, and public administrators either abide by decisions rendered or take their leave of public service. Indeed, public administrators may attempt to influence policy decisions, but once policy is decided they must carry it out.

Governmental Structure

The structure of governmental organization can, by itself, either alleviate or instigate many of the problems that often beset major metropolitan areas. On the rare clear day, observers at the highest level of the World Trade Center towers in New York City can see an area that is under the jurisdictional control of 1,400 political entities: city, state, county, township and special-purpose districts. All are governmental in nature. The special-purpose district operates everything from garbage collection to airports, seaports, or public auditoriums. The United States has approximately 81,000 special-purpose districts. Many of these governments (for that is what they legally are) have been established to focus on particular problems. Unfortunately, the special-purpose government's interest and intent are so narrow that they frequently have caused many more problems than they have solved, often worsening existing problems or creating new ones. Thus, environmental pollution (smog, festering rivers, noise, sewage disposal) that runs across political boundaries is often heightened by these autonomous governments. Responsibility is scattered in a labyrinth of independent, unequal, and duplicating jurisdictions.

Some political theorists state that the problem of overlapping jurisdictions may be resolved by the development of regional governments essentially designed to abolish environmental, social, political, and other violations on a wide-ranging, logical basis.[4] Provided the typical jealousies, pride, and somewhat inflexible outlooks currently held by the political entities involved, regional government may seem to be rather utopian. However, it may be correct to assume that the American public will eventually tire of political abuses and the ills they perpetuate and seek a governmental organization that can satisfactorily handle the complex problems of environmental need, public service, and growing bureaucracy with imagination, efficiency, and effectiveness.

The Balkanization of power plaguing the great metropolitan areas of the United States has given rise to disagreements on the ways to deal with pressing problems. Industrial plants spew millions of tons of pollutants into the air, subdivisions spread the "slurb" over a formerly spectacular landscape, traffic congestion on the ground and in the air mounts to strangling proportions. The most serious ecological imbalances are impotable water for domestic purposes, air pollution of inescapable magnitude, and discharge of domestic effluent and industrial waste into once clean waterways. Even with imminent danger to life and property, autonomous jurisdictions will not give up their precious positions to control the probability of a disintegrating environment.[5]

The solution lies in regional government with the power to control regional problems. Thus, water and air pollution, sewage treatment, transportation systems, construction of highways, planning of recreational space, preservation of open space, conservation practices, and interstate criminal activity would come under the province of the regional govern-

[4] Charles Frankel, "Out of Touch in Washington," *Saturday Review* (November 1, 1969), p. 22.

[5] Betty D. Hawkins, "Cities and the Environmental Crisis," in *Perspectives on Urban America*, M. I. Urovsky, ed. (New York: Anchor Press/Doubleday, 1973), pp. 164–184.

ment. Perhaps all governmental matters, as they pertain to intermunicipal and interstate boundaries, may one day be resolved at the regional level.[6]

Surge of Leisure

A crucial point has been reached in the cultural history of Western society. Civilization is undergoing both a quiet and a not-so-quiet social revolution. Everybody is a part of this rapid change. Recreational service must be removed from its present niche of merely being tolerated as a frill to a position of status in society. If recreationists are to do the job that massive leisure will demand of them, professionalization must be achieved, as it is both the means and the end for successfully accomplishing the chief objective of recreational service—the provision of complete recreational opportunities for all people.

For good or bad, people have always managed their own leisure. If the public is secure in the knowledge that such an entity as recreational service exists, then there is every likelihood that recreationists will be called on to assist in guiding the manner in which people utilize their leisure. Recreational service must achieve a reputation that will enable its practitioners to offer positive advice to those who soon will or now have a great deal of leisure. Leisure may be spent in many ways. The recreationist's function is to guide the use of leisure in the ways that are most beneficial to the individual and society as a whole.

MEANING OF PUBLIC RECREATIONAL SERVICE ADMINISTRATION

Public recreational service administration is immediately concerned with the methods of providing effective recreational opportunities to citizens of a community at the least possible cost and without duplicating functions of other agencies. Organization, implementation, operation, and maintenance of all recreational services within any given system on any governmental level are part of administration, as are the methods and practices of management. Consequently, administration emphasizes what the agency does and how it carries out the obligations assigned to it. Beyond these factors are those that attempt to stimulate the public through a dynamic program. The interrelationships existing between the recreational agency, other municipal institutions, and the political and personal facets that duly represent the agency to the public are important also.

Public recreational service administration is composed of three general categories:

[6] Charles Abrams, "Regional Planning in an Urbanizing World: Problems and Potentials," *Taming Megalopolis*, H. W. Eldredge, II, Ed. (New York: Frederick A. Praeger, Publishers, 1967), pp. 1030–1041.

1. Policy making: Local interest groups and political influence, legal establishment of the department; scope of agency function; and determination of purposes, policy, and plans.
2. Operations: Internal structure, administrative organization, fiscal management and support, personnel recruitment and direction, program planning and administration.
3. Supervision: Leadership, authority, responsibility, cooperation, co-ordination, conditions of work, morale, internal communications, in-service education, professionalization, policy compliance.

There is no clear delineation of one area from another. Each segment of the major divisions influences the others as they are interdependent for a most satisfying program of services.

Effective recreational service is achieved by:

1. Initiation, administration, and retention of a legally constituted public recreational service system through permissive state legislation, enactment provisions in the municipal charter, or establishment by local ordinances.
2. Activation, execution, and responsiveness of recreational policies through investigation of community recreational needs, financial posture, and balancing sound administrative concepts and principles with the expediency of public demand and political reality.
3. Administration of public funds in the operation of the recreational system. Instigation of sound fiscal policy clearly understood by local governmental authorizing powers for the financial support of the agency. Reportorial obligation through standard public accountancy methods accepted by the system for receipt and disbursement of public funds.
4. Administration of personnel practices and policies. Codes of conduct clearly established and explained in order to recruit and retain the best possible personnel. Line and staff functions precisely defined with the necessary authority and responsibility for performing the assigned functions.
5. Promotion of recreational experiences in the greatest variety and broadest possible range to assure the satisfaction of each actual and potential participant within the system's program. Continuous initiation of new activities designed to stimulate participation to fulfill personal needs and assure public support. (Properly conceived program administration is the main function of the recreational service agency—the essential reason for the agency's creation. There is no justification for a recreational service agency other than to provide recreational services to the people of the community.)

6. Acquisition of land and development of facilities within the prescribed authority of enabling legislation, charter grant, local ordinance and by due process. (Unless such acquisition and development are implemented and conscientiously carried out in terms of conservation and protection of such property, the program of service is greatly reduced and may be completely immobilized.)

7. Administration of public relations. Transmitting and interpreting information to the public, analyzing the recreational needs of citizens within the community, and maintaining internal and external communications for the enlightenment and motivation of the staff.

8. Public planning administration. Providing the required spaces and facilities at logical places. Coordination of master planning with community growth to establish priority in the development of a comprehensive physical plant enabling optimum use by the greatest number without impairing ecological balance or destroying traditional values.

NATURE OF PUBLIC RECREATIONAL SERVICE ORGANIZATION

Social needs require individual assignment to a particular role in order to function. This division of labor stems the tide of modern complexity. Although such arrangements will begin to change during the next few decades, individual relationships are now developed this way so that maximum output is gained with minimum expenditure of resources.

Organization is inseparable from administration. Organization involves the arrangements of personnel, materials, and money; administration deals with the management of these resources. Both suggest cooperation. Administration is impossible unless or until organization is established. Within the structure of the agency, administrative objectives guide the organization. The purpose of the public recreational service system determines the structure of the agency. The organization of recreational services refers to all community resources; the process directing and channeling such resources and structure is administration.

Because administration is concerned with all patterns of organized effort, any participant in a cooperative endeavor with some set goal is engaged in administration. This implies establishing the method by which cooperative effort can be facilitated and the arrangements required to initiate and sustain cooperation.

Organization also means agency; i.e., a formally designed agency created for some specified purpose or purposes and requiring the services of technically competent personnel to achieve that purpose. If organizations are to attain their purpose and if the intricate relationships among individuals operating within the agency, those operating within related agencies, and those operating outside any agency are not to shatter under the pressures of modern life, then organization—in terms of both agency and arrangement—urgently needs to be understood. People who take part in and conduct the formal agencies need to know just what induces cooperative behavior and what disrupts it.

ESTABLISHMENT OF THE RECREATIONAL AGENCY

Recreational service agencies are created because individuals feel that such organizations are desirable. The nature, structure, and operation of the agency are determined by the concepts of its initiators. Usually legislative action precedes the creation of a new agency. Either legislation exists permitting the community to create a new municipal department or the city has the power to perform all of those functions that it deems necessary to insure the health, safety, and welfare of its citizens. Local charter provisions may be spelled out in great detail or consist only of a short generalized statement granting authority to operate. If the municipal charter grant is not available, the general welfare authority and the home rule principle may be utilized and an ordinance for the creation of a recreational service agency passed. In any case, the legality of the municipal department rests squarely on the firm foundation of state legislation or local code. Then only the formality of precisely defining the functions and responsibilities of the agency and providing it with the jurisdictional and financial power to carry them out remain.

Structure of the recreational service department will also be determined by tradition or the established pattern of organization within the local legal subdivision. If lay commissions operate other administrative or advisory departments, a commission will probably be formed for the recreational service agency. If the single executive plan is in use, it is likely to be the adopted pattern of organization for recreational service.

Where is the newly created municipal function to be fitted into the existing structure of government? Most recreational service proponents advocate that an independent department be established. Some specialists believe that the school system or another established department should be selected to administratively house and operate the service. Many points are debatable about the placement of the recreational service system in the municipal setting. The fundamental question remains: Where can the most efficient and effective service be obtained and performed? Community agencies must be coordinated and utmost cooperation achieved if maximum recreational service is to be offered. Past experiences assume that the most effective agency is one set up independently and charged with the sole responsibility of providing public

and more responsibility is devolving on public recreational service systems.[7]

Priorities in Allocation of Resources

Neighborhoods, districts, and communities with special problems, such as changing population, low economic levels, interracial tensions, inferior housing, and other social deprivations, require an intensification of services. In middle and upper economic neighborhoods and communities, homes provide normal recreational spaces, outdoors and indoors, for children. Neighborhood playgrounds are essential in every neighborhood, but they are imperative in crowded, poor sections of the city where homes and yards do not permit normal play.

All four recreational functions should be provided on a high level in these problem areas, and special emphasis should be placed on the last two (special leadership for groups and guidance for maladjusted groups), because of prevalent social difficulties.

All city areas need and have the right to such opportunities for recreational activity and group living. Areas with greater social problems need more opportunities under superior professional guidance, leadership, and personal dedication to human welfare, including identification with the people in the locale and the cumulative experience in their type of community living.

Priorities in Facilities

1. Neighborhood playgrounds and play centers for children of kindergarten, elementary, and junior high school age should be provided at their respective public schools, with supervised programs after school hours, on vacation days, and during the summer. Well distributed in geographic centers throughout the city, schools should have ample sites adaptable as recreational centers. Public schools should be supplemented by parochial schools, when situated in neighborhoods of need. Non-school public recreational service agencies should provide neighborhood playgrounds in areas incapable of being served by the schools for lack of sufficient space and facilities, or for other reasons (pedestrian barriers presenting hazards in travel to and from the school). Full use of the neighborhood school should be exhausted before providing other neighborhood facilities, public or private.

2. District facilities should be provided for teen-agers, adults, and senior citizens. This is a joint responsibility of the municipal recreational service department and of the system of high schools and junior or community colleges, supplemented by voluntary agency centers.

[7] Richard G. Kraus, *Recreation Today Program Planning and Leadership,* 2nd ed. (Santa Monica, Calif.: Goodyear Publishing Company, Inc., 1977), pp. 19–20, 23–24.

3. Outdoor play fields and large city-wide and sometimes regional areas are necessary for all types of physical activity games and sports, for outdoor education and environmental experience also need to be provided by the local city and county governments.

4. Indoor recreational facilities are needed for social, cultural, and educational programs. Attractive lounges, meeting rooms, social rooms, and game rooms are necessary for youth, young adult, and older adult programs. Active physical play can be carried on out-of-doors most of the time, but the social, cultural, and educational activities of the community require informal indoor facilities throughout the year. These community, as distinguished from neighborhood, facilities can best be provided by the schools, by buildings located in public parks, and by centers maintained by voluntary agencies.

5. Gymnasiums are basically a school responsibility to provide for the schools' curricular and extracurricular athletic programs. At other times they can be used by the community non-school athletic groups organized under the auspices of the school system, if it has espoused the community recreational responsibility, or by the municipal agency operating city-wide recreational programs. This sometimes extra-school use can also be accorded to voluntary agencies conducting community programs in sports and related activities. Outdoor gymnasiums provide similar facilities for less sophisticated play and should be maintained for use throughout the year and be equipped with lights for use in the evening.

6. Swimming pools for recreational use and instruction are provided by the public. Instruction is a prime concern of the school system and facilities for this purpose should be provided. When provided, pools can, of course, serve for recreational swimming, whether operated by the school system or by the community or municipal agency. The school pools need to be supplemented by conveniently located community pools in public parks, in which case they are advisably outdoor pools, since recreational swimming, for the bulk of the population, is essentially an outdoor summer activity.

7. Sites for day camping are important facilities in appropriate publicly owned parks or park-like places. They should be made available for school and other publicly supported youth-serving and voluntary agencies. A local recreational service department which frequently has park lands suitable for the purpose can best provide these sites. Overnight camping, requiring travel away from the city, is a proper service for county recreational service departments, state and national park systems, and state and national forest systems.

Comparison of School and City Facilities and Services

In the foregoing analysis of the overall responsibility of schools and city, great dependence is placed on the public school system, especially to provide local centers and neighborhood services, because usually there are about three times as many schools as there are parks. Secondly, schools have many of the facilities required for a city-wide program of community recreational service and these are not regularly required for the educational function of the schools at all times. Any plan to duplicate centers and facilities already present must be dismissed as impractical, consequently the city must accept a complementary role, even though a school is not ideally suited to all parts of a desirable community program. In some places an effort has been made to augment the facilities of each school in order to more adequately fulfill the neighborhood function. In doing so, care must be taken that clientele are not attracted and activities are not accommodated which would interfere with the education of the children attending each school.

On casual observation it might appear that the recreational areas, facilities, and programs of a public school and a city park are quite similar, but there are important differences. The following paragraphs highlight some limitations on the scope and extent of the services provided by each.

Elementary school ground equipment is limited in kind, being selected for the physical education program of the school. Usually there are no slides, swings, teeter-totters, nor apparatus of unusual design; neither is there equipment designed for the teen-age youth over the age of those attending the school. On the other hand, parks are equipped with a variety of apparatus, sometimes of exotic design and presenting a variety of challenges. Since attendance at parks is wholly voluntary, it is advisable to provide inducements to attend. Consequently, the criteria of novelty, attraction, diversity, and dimension influence design of the park and selection of equipment.

Parks more often are lighted for evening activities and have grassed areas that are necessary for some activities, whereas most elementary school yards in cities are paved from fence to fence and gates often are locked when school supervision is not assigned. Parks are fenced only where safety of players and others may so require, and, with few exceptions, are open at all hours. School security and particular legal liability related to the public schools' custodial responsibility for pupils dictate the extra-precautionary measures. Municipal liability is less restrictive.

Elementary school recreational programs and supervised activities usually occur from about 3 to 5 p.m. on weekdays and 10 a.m. to 5 p.m. on vacation days, with no planned use of the grounds on weekends or holidays. Of course, there are many exceptions, especially in smaller cities and neighborhoods of greater need. City parks and recreational programs extend through all the days, including Sundays and holidays.

Although the use of elementary school grounds is not officially limited to children of the age regularly attending the school, in practice older children and youth are reluctant to attend. Equipment is specifically adapted to the younger age group and older youths view the school from which they have graduated as a place where restraints on their behavior are more restrictive than in public parks. School personnel often discourage the attendance of former pupils; they are regarded as a discordant element and are not made particularly welcome. The "free wheeling" operation of a park is more suited to their fancy.

Interagency Policy

The impingement of school and municipal services in providing recreational experiences is such that public understanding and smooth operation require mutual adoption of policies and procedures, as well as priorities. Such an understanding of "division of the field" will conduce to the fullest possible utilization of the resources of both agencies and will set the pattern for the future development of a sound system of public service.

PUBLIC RECREATIONAL SERVICE AS A SYSTEM

When the purposes of the newly established agency have been formulated and the administrative policies and plans appearing most likely to achieve these purposes have been determined, organization, staff, and monetary support are required.

If recreational service is seen as a system by which opportunities are delivered to the public rather than as a special agency actually providing recreational experiences per se, the organizational pattern will be quite different from extant agency types. The best possible recreational service will be constituted by a coordinating, instead of a performing, department. Under such circumstances the entire resource potential of the community, in terms of sectors of interest, personal, natural, financial, and artificial means, will be mobilized to afford the most effective service that can be made available. As a system, the most significant feature may be one of coordinating diverse community resources rather than of having a permanent performing staff to instruct or supervise recreational activities. Some combined form of specialized department with a permanent staff acting as coordinator of community resources for recreational purposes may be most effective. This concept will be developed further in Chapter 10, page 212.

The administrative process can best facilitate recreational service only when full use is made of individual capacities and an environment conducive to coordinated effort is created. All personnel must be interrelated as members of a unified team whose purpose is clearly defined, and each worker must be allowed to exercise his initiative to the fullest, with each contributing cooperative endeavor directed toward achieving the goal of the organization.

The appropriate structural organization for any agency is the one most conducive to its established purpose. The basic factor to be considered in structure is size, but the need for and availability of specialized personnel, adequate finances, possible pressure from political or local interest groups, and tradition also are important. Often it is not a single factor but a combination of several that finally decides the organizational structure.

Typically, the structure of the agency is settled long before an administrator is employed. If the administrator has a strong sense of organizational value he may attempt to alter what he finds. Insofar as he has a choice, the administrator must determine the most important factors and proceed to organize along the lines that offer the best possibilities. Responsibility for creating a structure that will prove most effective in carrying out the purpose of the agency is a continuing one. The administrator must be prepared to move patiently, as well as definitively, and to introduce modifications in a manner such as to make them palatable to all concerned.

Although the concept of structure may seem to be adverse to the idea of a system, there is still the need to maintain some kind of organizational frame of reference as far as agency responsibility and performance are involved. Even though the term "structure" connotes formalized lines of authority, some representational form is necessary if a system is to produce effective results.

Widening the scope of the agency and diversifying the positions are usually the main reasons for structural changes in the organization. The one-man department has no problem of this nature, because the executive performs all necessary services insofar as he is able. In the larger agencies, however, there is permanency of structure, operations analysis, and the components must be divided and assigned to insure cooperation and coordination for optimum service. Such provisions are secured at the lowest level of the organization. Each higher level is integrated for maximum productivity and facilitation of operation. Each level is provided with operational personnel with ability appropriate to their assignments. In this way the quantity and quality of work performed are improved.

Selected References

Beuchele, R. B.: *The Management of Business and Public Organizations* (New York: McGraw-Hill Book Company), 1977.

Browne, W. P. and M. E. Dillon, Eds.: *The Politics of Bureaucracy* (Woodbury, N.Y.: Barron's Educational Series, Inc.), 1976.

Golembiewski, R. T., and others, Eds.: *Public Administration, 3rd ed.* (Chicago, Ill.: Rand McNally Company), 1976.

Janowitz, M. and D. Wright: *Public Administration and the Public—Perspectives Toward Government in a Metropolitan Community* (Westport, Conn.: Greenwood Press, Inc.), 1977.

Kraus, R. G. and J. E. Curtis,: *Creative Administration in Recreation and Parks, 2nd ed.* (St. Louis, Mo.: The C. V. Mosby Company), 1977.

Lorch, R. S.: *Public Administration* (St. Paul, Minn.: West Publishing Co.), 1977.

Lutzin, S. G. and E. H. Storey, Eds.: *Managing Municipal Leisure Services* (Washington, D.C.: International City Management), 1973.

Nigro, F. A.: *Modern Public Administration, 4th ed.* (New York: Harper & Row Publishers, Inc.), 1977.

Rapp, B. and F. Patitucci: *Managing Local Government for Improved Performance: A Practical Approach* (Boulder, Col.: Westview Press), 1977.

Reekie, W. D. and N. C. Hunt, Eds.: *Management in the Social and Safety Services* (Scranton, Pa.: Barnes & Noble, Inc.), 1975.

CHAPTER 2

Legal Foundations for Public Recreational Service

Most thinking people who are products of Western Culture believe that recreational activity is necessary for a better quality of life. Such activity may be more important to the individual's self-expression and growth than any other social factor. People everywhere engage in recreational activities—though these activities may be vastly different in nature, quality, setting, and outcome. The implications and results of recreational experiences for people are so vital that governmental support of recreational service has come to be expected. This recognition and attention begins with control of anti-social forms of leisure activity and extends to measures designed to provide all people with the benefits of wholesome, developmental activity. A sovereign representative government, dedicated to the general welfare, cannot be oblivious to the meaning of recreational experience, nor can it remain content with a negativistic or restrictive stance acting only when people choose to use their leisure in ways that disturb domestic tranquility, are degrading to themselves, or interfere with the peaceful pursuit of worthy activities by the law-abiding public.

The developmental and cultural implications and consequences of qualitative recreational experience motivate most governments to take positive positions in offering the public competently administered recreational services. But governmental enterprise in this field need not, nor can it, preempt private endeavor. On the contrary, it only exists where and when individuals, either alone or in voluntary association with others, are thwarted in securing the recreational experiences they need and should enjoy as a human right. Thus, recreational service ranks with education, public health, and safety as a necessary concern of government.

24

SOVEREIGNTY AND POLICE POWER

The rationale for all recreational service under governmental auspice may be found in the Declaration of Independence in terms of each man's unquestioned right to "the pursuit of happiness." This philosophical basis justifies governmental activity in public recreational service. Since governments are instituted with the express aim of ensuring the domestic tranquility and enhancing the public welfare, no further justification is needed for establishing a public recreational service.

Sovereignty is complete authority without subjugation to any other jurisdiction.[1] It is the supreme power which any autonomous country possesses and which the United States possesses under the Constitution.[2] Through enactment of the Constitution, the federal system, with its component states, was brought into being and exercises sovereignty implying the right to administer internal affairs without interference. Thus, the federal government of the United States is a sovereign power. The several states, being a part of the United States and established by Constitutional compact, may be said to be semi-sovereign because, while retaining sovereign powers in certain areas, they have yielded and are subject to higher authority, the federal government. This doctrine was confirmed in the aftermath of the Civil War. Yet within the limitations of its sovereignty each state exercises supreme power, in effect, complete authority and jurisdiction over the internal affairs of government. This holds true to the extent that such authority has not been specifically delegated by the state to the federal government and that such power does not come into conflict with the rights of other states, the national government, or the constitutional rights of the citizens.

Such sovereignty establishes a rule, termed *police power*, by which a state can control the behavior of its people and provide for their welfare. Police power is that authority vested in state governments to establish laws and ordinances of reasonable and wholesome content, with or without penalties, and not in conflict with the Constitution, for the security and the enhancement of the general health, safety, morals, education, welfare, and prosperity of its people. This power is specifically reserved to the states; the national government does not have it, except in the District of Columbia and various overseas territories.

Recent governmental activities in recreational service have not been undertaken for the purpose of interfering with the rights of individual citizens; on the contrary, they have been initiated to expand the scope of recreational experience of all the people and to complement the opportunities for recreational experience provided by the states. Certain activ-

---

[1] John Austin, *Lectures on Jurisprudence* (London: J. Murray, 1811), p. 221.
[2] A. T. Mason and W. M. Beaney, *American Constitutional Law*. 3rd ed. (Englewood Cliffs, N.J.: Prentice-Hall, Inc., 1964), p. 11.

ities require collective effort beyond the capability of individual citizens. Some activities do not lend themselves to commercial enterprise but are still of such value that a beneficent government can ill afford to neglect them. Still other activities cannot be wholly entrusted to commercial agencies, which frequently disregard the needs and concerns of individuals. Some activities are of such general concern that public taxation appears to be the most economical and expeditious way of making them available to all. While recreational activity must remain largely a matter of individual initiative and a proper field for commercial enterprise as well, in many respects it becomes a legitimate field for governmental activity, not only in the regulatory and prohibitory sense, but in a positive sense to promote a state of general well-being and human development.

GOVERNMENTAL CONCERN

Since recreational service is now closely embraced by government at all levels the recreationist must be familiar with the history of the American system of government and the various traditions of governmental relationships. Regardless of his position in the hierarchy of agency organization, the recreationist must have a sound knowledge of the legal foundations for his agency and of local ordinances and codes if he is to conform to the law, cooperate with governmental units, utilize their public resources, and advance recreational service to the greatest possible degree. Understanding governmental relationships and the attention that various levels of government focus on recreational service in terms of legislation, finance, regulation, and promotion is indispensable to intelligent, proper, and effective action in the planning, organization, and administration of public recreational service.

Governmental Relationships

The United States is a federal government. The Constitution divides the powers of government between federal and state levels, and neither may upset the established equilibrium. This does not imply that the initial division of jurisdiction is irrevocable and can never be changed to meet the dynamics of social conditions. Constitutional amendments may be proposed and adopted by the Congress and thereafter ratified by the legislatures of two thirds of the states.

The Constitution specifically states the powers of the federal government and allows all others, or residual powers, to be exercised by the states unless expressly denied to them.[3] Therefore, the federal government may only exercise those powers specifically enumerated by the Constitution and no others. However, the federal government—through an extremely liberal interpretation of its implied powers under the Constitu-

---

[3] United States Constitution, Article X.

tion—may legislate for the health, safety, welfare, education, and promotion of the general well-being of the people.

As the country has grown, the authority of the federal government has increased while the authority of the states has diminished. This shift of balance has been largely the result of the aftermaths of several wars and the increased pressure of national and international affairs. Various laws and constitutional amendments approved by the states have also increased the scope of federal power. Called on to interpret the precise and implicit meaning of the Constitution, the Supreme Court of the United States has profoundly affected the balance of power between the federal government and the states. In the last decade, for example, the Supreme Court has struck down a variety of traditional activities that were long held to be within the purview of the several states, among which are voting rights, desegregation of all public schools, interpretation of free speech, separation of church and state, censorship of pornography and obscenity, and others.

Federal financial aid to the states also has contributed to the increased power and influence of the national government. Although not enumerated in the Constitution, federal grants (which the states must match, equally or in some percentage) permit the federal government to inspect and influence certain state processes. Under such subsidies, administration remains in the hands of the state with the federal government acting in a supervisory capacity. The amount of state funds, the plans, and, in some cases, even the personnel are subject to federal approval. Thus the federal government establishes minimum standards to which the state must adhere if it is to receive its share of grants. All states do not have to conform to identical specifications, but they must subscribe to minimum criteria established by the federal authority.

The only limitation on a state's option to regulate the general welfare is *due process*. As interpreted by the judiciary, due process implies a degree of equity or reasonableness. Therefore, the power of the state almost always conflicts with the Fourteenth Amendment which states that "No State shall make or enforce any law which shall abridge the privileges or immunities of citizens of the United States; nor shall any State deprive any person of life, liberty, or property, without due process of law . . ." Each question of police power must be decided on its own merits. The reluctance of the courts to make any decision concerning such controversy imposes a restraint on the police power of the states.

Recreational services directly espoused by state governments have largely been such as may be rendered in state parks and other natural preserves. Forests, rivers, lakes, bays, sounds, or oceans may also come under state jurisdiction when used to render regional services of a recreational nature. These services are usually referred to as being regional in character, because they are enjoyed by people other than purely local inhabitants, and because the facilities are nearly always in areas beyond city boundaries. States sometimes permit local legal subdivisions to undertake responsibility for such service. In few states has there been any direct subvention from the state to local agencies for recreational purposes. Several states (North Carolina, California, Vermont, Washington, Indiana, and Georgia) have created recreational service commissions or similar agencies to coordinate state and local recreational functions and to provide consultative services to local jurisdictions. In other states (Florida, Wisconsin, New York, Pennsylvania, Tennessee, New Hampshire, Kansas, Missouri, and Michigan), authorization for employing recreationists to promote standards and provide consultative services has been effected. In the latter-named states specialists report to agencies in which recreational services are only one of several functions. In most instances the main function of such state agencies is industrial development and/or the promotion of tourism.

Legally, a city is defined as a municipal corporation. Its very existence is derived from the state, which either chartered it or granted it certain privileges. With these privileges certain obligations are imposed. Incorporation is an act of the legislature by which citizens of the city, organized in their municipal government, are constituted a single legal entity— the municipal corporation. The corporation has standing in court and can sue or be sued. Thus, when a city is sued in court it is not the individual citizens who are defendants, but the corporate body of the city. The corporation may acquire and hold property in perpetuity and may execute contracts. The city continues its life until dissolved, even though its individual citizens come and go. Thus the municipality is largely a creature of the state and has only such powers as the state confers on it. Unless there are constitutional provisions to the contrary, the state legislature has great power over the organization and functions of the municipal government.

Counties, school districts, villages, townships, and special districts also are creatures of the state. Unless constitutional limitations restrict or prohibit state legislative control, most counties and legal subdivisions are not even accorded corporate status but are designated quasi-corporations. Thus the state may create, rearrange, or eliminate legal subdivisional boundaries at will.

Probably one of the most significant definitions of municipal and quasi-corporations is found in a decision by the Supreme Court of Illinois:

> Municipal corporations are those called into existence either at the direct request or by consent of the persons composing them. Quasi-municipal corporations, such as counties and townships, are at most but local organizations, which are created by general law, without the consent of the inhabitants thereof, for the purpose of the civil and political administration of government, and they are invested with but few characteristics

of corporate existence. They are, in other words, local subdivisions of the state created by the sovereign power of the state of its own will, without regard to the wishes of the people inhabiting them. A municipal corporation is created principally for the advantage and convenience of the people of the locality. County and Township organizations are created in this state with a view to carry out the policy of the state at large for the administration of matters of political government, finance, education, taxing, care of the poor, military organization, means of travel, and the administration of justice.[4]

In the past, legislators have sometimes used their power capriciously, arbitrarily imposing special laws on municipalities—often at the behest of local pressure groups. In consequence, municipalities have demanded a larger share in the management of their local affairs. Through constitutional amendments, the authority of state legislatures has been restricted. But it was not until the historic Missouri Enactment of 1875 that protection against legislative abuse was granted to municipal corporations. The new constitution provided new freedom for the city: "Any city having a population of more than one hundred thousand inhabitants may frame a charter for its own government . . ."[5] For the first time, the principle of municipal home rule was recognized and put into effect.

Home rule essentially is the power to make and amend the municipal charter and to do those things necessary for the continued beneficial operation of the city for its constituents. Several states have provided for home rule in more or less complete fashion. In other states the powers of cities are exercised under state statutes universally applicable to all cities of specified classes other than cities exercising the right to adopt individual charters. The right of any city to organize, promote, conduct, and otherwise provide for recreational service rests on the powers granted to the city by the general state laws, the city charter, or through the general provisions of home rule.

Strictly speaking, a municipal corporation "possesses and can exercise, the following powers, and no others: first, those granted in express words; second, those necessarily or fairly implied in, or incident to, the powers expressly granted; third, those essential to the accomplishment of the declared objects and purposes of the corporation, not simply convenient but indispensable."[6] Although a tendency in recent years has been to liberalize the phraseology thus given, this rule generally has been uniformly and strictly followed.

Nevertheless, even where home rule has been granted to municipalities, the states manage to retain some control over various city affairs through variations in phraseology and implementation, particularly through finan-

[4] *Cook County v. City of Chicago,* 142 N.E. 512 (1924).
[5] Constitution of the State of Missouri (Article IX, sec. 16–17).
[6] J. F. Dillon, *Commentaries in the Law of Municipal Corporations* (Boston: Little Brown & Co., 1927), Vol. I, Sec. 33.

cial support. If a state constitution specifically provides that cities shall have power to exercise all functions of local self-government or all municipal authority, it becomes a matter for the court to decide what comprises matters of local concern. The courts have often been called on to disentangle the disputes that have arisen from state interference with internal municipal operations.

Municipality-County Relations

As municipalities grow in area and population, they find it expedient to increase the number and extent of functions over which they have jurisdiction. Often such extension of power and function brings the city into conflict with the county, particularly in duplication of services. Moreover, city and county officials appear disinclined to accept easy solutions through consolidation of functions, or through cooperation and coordination of efforts.

Several remedial measures would seem to satisfy this relationship. There should be a complete separation of and distinction between city and county government. City-county mergers, county expansion, county-city cooperation, and, finally, special regions or districts could be established. These districts may be granted complete autonomy over all aspects of government or they may be organized to perform special activities, i.e., sanitation, flood control, park, or recreational functions. By providing the special districts with clear-cut authority to act, many jurisdictional disputes, wasted time, and inefficient use of money are avoided, if not prohibited.

Local cooperation and creation of districts have been particularly effective in alleviating city-county conflicts. In some cases in which city and county officials have collaborated, excellent results have been obtained. However, unless such cooperation is legally defined and implemented, it is very haphazard and offers only partial satisfaction of the problem. By creating a special district, granting it the power formerly enjoyed by both the city and the county, and assigning it explicit functions for designated services, much conflict is resolved and more efficient operation is generated. Many special districts have already been established which effectively serve the needs of large metropolitan areas. Normally, their boundaries are determined without regard to city or county lines. Special districts are created by state legislatures or by county boards. They are initiated as separate governments within a particular area having corporate identity and are granted official designation, perpetual succession, popularly elected or appointed officials, a high degree of public accountability, rights to sue and to be sued, to acquire and to dispose of property, to tax, and to make contracts. They are instigated in order to provide services that are not or have not been provided adequately by either city or county governments. District officials are often appointed by the governor of the state. For maximum effectiveness, the district must coincide exactly with the economic area it has been created to serve, disregarding all other political boundaries, and all district problems must be placed under district jurisdiction. The economic area of a given community usually refers to the trade or market area that the city provides, not only within its corporate limits, but also the unincorporated regions surrounding it. Thus, the economic area of a large centrally located city may encompass hundreds of square miles outside the city proper.

Unfortunately, the proliferation of special districts has created a new series of problems. Typically, special districts perform their respective functions very well, perhaps too well. So intent are these governmental entities in carrying out their narrow tasks that they fail to observe the effects that their total disregard of other functions promotes. Thus, a sanitation district may rid the involved communities of garbage by incineration, thereby causing increased air pollution by burning thousands of tons of refuse leading to greater air pollution. The same effects may be shown for airport, sewage, mosquito control, road, and other special districts. They do an excellent job, but their tunnel vision does not permit them to see or understand that such parochial performance also causes environmental disaster. A regional government that can incorporate the functions of special districts and other interpolitical governments must be created with a broader, coordinating view of the services to be rendered and their effects on the entire area in question.

Of necessity, and usually after considerable public prodding and concerted demand for action, the state legislature must pass an act establishing some form of regional government designed to plan and control the orderly physical, social, and economic growth of the concerned area. Under such legislation, the regional body controls regional matters pertaining to pollution, sewage, open space preservation, and the like. Appointments to the regional body are made by the governor of the state from the population of the regional area. Since appointments are at large, they are not influenced by short-sighted municipalities. The regional body has financial independence because it can levy taxes. Regional governments are free to plan for wide services and instigate plans that are mutually beneficial because coordination is effectively implemented. They have all the powers of districts but not their myopia.[7]

Federal Interest in Recreational Service

More than 40 units in several different departments in the federal government are engaged in promoting programs affecting citizens' use of leisure. These programs include conservation of national resources to be

[7] Robert Reinhold, "Move to Regional Planning Is Led By a Minneapolis-St. Paul Agency," *The New York Times* (Tuesday, March 8, 1977), pp. 1, 18.

used for recreational purposes; maintenance and administration of recreational areas within national parks, forests, and other land preserves; surveys of recreational needs and facilities within the several states; provision of professional leadership in communities that are distinctly under federal control in local matters (Indian reservations, the District of Columbia, and military bases); furnishing information about recreational service through correspondence, publications, and conferences; provision of federal funds for construction of state, regional, or local facilities of a recreational nature. The larger part of the permanent activity of the federal government in recreational service is in providing national and regional opportunities for recreational activity as distinguished from local recreational facilities and programs.

Recreational service activities of the federal agencies are largely incidental to the performance of the function for which the agency was originally created. The Department of Agriculture offers advisory recreational service to state departments of agriculture through its extension division, which employs specialists in rural organization, recreational service, home economics, and 4-H Club activities, and through the United States Forest Service. Soil Conservation Service efforts have also had a coincidental effect on the preservation of natural resources for recreational usage. Other federal agencies providing recreational services in a consultative manner are the Departments of Labor, Commerce, and Transportation. Divisions of federal agencies offering direct program, facility, or financial support at state and local levels are the Department of Health, Education, and Welfare through the Office of Education, Children's Bureau, Vocational Rehabilitation Administration, and the Bureau of Mental Retardation; the Department of the Interior through its Bureau of Outdoor Recreation, Bureau of Public Roads, Bureau of Indian Affairs, Bureau of Reclamation, National Park Service, and Fish and Wildlife Service; the Department of Defense through the U.S. Corps of Army Engineers, which administers federal flood control lands that can be used for recreational purposes; and the Department of Housing and Urban Affairs, which offers many functions related to recreational service.

The federal government also holds several national conferences with important implications for recreational service, among them are the decennial White House Conferences on Children and Youth and the Conference on Aging. The establishment of the President's Council on Youth Fitness has focused attention on the physical fitness of young people through recreational activities. The President's Council on Recreation and Natural Beauty has called attention to the fast-disappearing heritage of natural phenomena and resources which have significance for the general public's utilization of these natural places for recreational purposes.

Bills have been introduced into the Congress to create a federal recreational service agency which would coordinate the recreational functions of the several federal agencies, compile and publish statistics related to recreational activity, promote adherence to high standards of service, and otherwise assist in the development of more adequate recreational services. Thus far these bills have made little headway and have not been reported out of committee.

Recently, a spate of federal agency activity has had distinct recreational overtones. A number of national organizations including the Job Corps, Vista, the Peace Corps, Office of Economic Opportunity, and legislative enactments through Titles I-III of the federal educational bills have been inaugurated. Each of these agencies or enactments has general or specific ramifications for recreational service. Some are concerned with the development of recreational programs in low-end socioeconomic neighborhoods within urban areas, others deal with the planning and construction of recreational facilities and places, others are directed to the education or technical upgrading of recreational service personnel. In all, hundreds of separate programs and millions of dollars are directed to the provision of recreational affairs and function by the federal government.

Municipal Interest in Recreational Service

Municipalities mainly have concerned themselves with the establishment of local areas and facilities for frequent utilization by the residents of their constituent urban neighborhoods and communities. Cities have given considerable attention to the development of recreational programs and have been more cognizant of the importance of organizing and supervising recreational pursuits of people by professional leadership. Some indication of the extent to which cities have adopted community recreational service may be inferred from the fact that over 3,600 cities in America report some organized public activities in this field.

Community recreational service has been considered largely a matter of local prerogative, as has education. The federal government has not assumed direct responsibility for local community recreational service except in rare instances (see p. 31), although it has offered financial support to states for local recreational service. New functions are assumed by local governments in response to public demand. Sometimes the demand is expressed in unmistakable form through an initiative or referendum vote of the electorate. Sometimes it is expressed no less forcefully, albeit illegally, by riot. More frequently, it is expressed by a group of more or less influential citizens who insist that the government take steps to meet an obvious public need.

In many cities the inauguration of certain recreational activities, which gave rise to the subsequent establishment of a department to administer them, took place in response to an expressed demand by individual citizens and civic groups. Frequently the specific act that launched the municipality on the recreational venture consisted of the purchase of a piece of land for a park or playground, the improvement of already owned land for recreational activity, or the employment of a recreationist for a public park. Establishment—by ordinance or by amendment to the city charter—of a supervisory bureau in an already existing department, or the establishment of a separate department for the administration of parks, playgrounds, or recreational service, usually followed in due course.

Thus, municipalities have come to be associated with the most extensive operation and administration of all those services of a recreational nature which require the pooling of tax resources in order to provide a wide variety of indoor and outdoor programs, on a full-time basis, for the benefit of all citizens of the community.

LEGISLATIVE AUSPICES

Most states now recognize the right of each city to organize, promote, and otherwise exercise power for the operation and administration of public recreational services. However, some states are still reluctant to relinquish any of their prerogatives. Fortunately, many state supreme court decisions have interpreted quite liberally the right of municipalities to conduct recreational service operations and to operate parks, playgrounds, and other recreational facilities and spaces. Many decisions upheld municipal efforts to establish, build, or develop facilities that could and would be used for public recreational services. Courts have consistently interpreted, in the broadest possible manner, the right of the city to purchase playground property, stadiums, campgrounds, auditoriums, and other land or water areas and structures for recreational activities.

The inauguration of children's playground and field areas in the larger urban centers did not originally require special legislation by the state. In many cases municipalities exerted pressure on their state legislatures to pass special laws applicable to themselves alone. However, such special legislation also had many negative applications and as a result the clamor for municipal home rule was instigated. Politically powerful individuals or groups lobbied for legislation that would favor them at the expense of the city as a whole. In some instances, special legislation granted access right or other concessions to private persons which resulted in their being able to control vast properties to the detriment of the city government. Such inequity paved the way for much abuse of power, particularly in districts that later became the slums of cities.

The power of local legal subdivisions to conduct recreational services is usually implied in various general powers granted to them. Thus many incorporated cities have taken steps to provide for community recreational service even in the absence of special enabling legislation. Such steps rarely have been seriously challenged. In many cases however, local governments have deferred action in the absence of specific legislation. The failure of a few state legislatures to pass enabling acts for recreational service has often furnished reluctant local authorities with a convenient excuse for not yielding to public pressure to provide public recreational service. Fortunately this handicap to more rapid growth of community recreational service as a universal function is gradually being removed.

Legislation for Parks

The liberalizing of park legislation has permitted park officials to extend and broaden their functions in order to provide a more comprehensive recreational program. Through extremely liberal court interpretation of what the terms *park* and *park purposes* mean, community recreational services were established in many cities. Historically, the acquisition, improvement, and maintenance of parks are more traditionally a function of local government than is recreational service. State enabling legislation for parks included recreational-type operations insofar as the nature of the recreational service function was not inconsistent with "park purposes." However, courts have consistently held that land deeded to municipalities for park purposes may be utilized for swimming pools, recreational centers, and similar facilities. Recognition that parks are established essentially for recreational purposes has come from such interpretations. If the primary use of an area is not recreational, then such an area should not be considered a park.[8] However, the function of recreational service includes, in addition to the establishment and operation of facilities, the promotion and organization of a balanced program of activities. Consequently, to avoid any question as to whether the recreational service function in all of its ramifications was included in the authority to establish parks, legislatures were persuaded to enact special legislation for recreational service implementation.

Recreational Service and School Codes

In the past, school legislation was usually considered distinct from legislation affecting cities because school districts are not separate corporations but legal subdivisions of the state (see p. 28). Thus uncertainty existed concerning the power of the local school system to provide recreational activities on a city-wide basis. The distinction between corporate and quasi-corporate entities, e.g., city versus school district, also explains why municipal and school service recreational programs are difficult to coordinate and probably impossible to consolidate.

Since 1900 all states have passed legislation permitting school buildings and grounds to be utilized for cultural, educational, recreational, civic, and, in some instances, religious and political activities. Legislative enactments of this kind have generally implied that the school board

---

[8] Charles E. Doell and Louis F. Twardzik, *Elements of Park and Recreation Administration*, 3rd ed. (Minneapolis: Burgess Publishing Company, 1973), p. 55.

might assume no more responsibility than to tolerate such uses under certain regulatory provisions. Some, however, have authorized the assumption of more complete responsibility for promotion, organization, and supervision of recreational activities on school premises. Almost all these acts have stipulated that recreational uses shall not interfere with the primary "educational purposes" of the schools.

Authority to provide recreational service to the community was first conferred on the schools by Indiana in 1859. The law specifically permitted the utilization of school buildings and property for recreational purposes, but no expenditure of school funds was authorized. In 1924, Massachusetts enacted more liberal legislation that authorized schools to function in the sphere of community recreational service:

> *Public uses of school property.* For the purposes of promoting the usefulness of public school property the school committee of any town may conduct such educational activities in or upon school property under its control, and subject to such regulation as it may establish and constantly and without interference with the use of the premises for school purposes, shall allow the use thereof by individuals and associations for such educational, recreational, social, civic, philanthropic, and like purposes as it deems for the interest of the community. The use of such property as a place of assemblage for citizens to hear candidates for public office shall be considered a civic purpose within the meaning of this section. (This section shall not apply to Boston.)[9]

Those school boards and/or systems providing sole or extensive recreational service within the community usually derive their power from broadened school codes, specific court decisions, or particular state legislation.

State Enabling Legislation for Recreational Service

All too often, state enabling legislation is not broad enough in scope or intent to encompass all of the necessities required by local legal subdivisions. Much of the enabling legislation has embodied only the following authorizations or provisions:

1. Authorization for the local governments to exercise the powers conferred.
2. Authorization for establishment of a particular agency within the local governmental structure to exercise the powers conferred.
3. Specification of particular powers that may be exercised.
4. Provision of the means to be employed in financing the powers to be performed.
5. Provision of the means whereby the powers authorized to be performed may be initiated.

[9] Massachusetts, *General Laws* (1927), C, 71, Sec. 71.

6. Authorization of certain joint exercise of powers by two or more or combination of local agencies, and cooperation between certain authorities.

To be effective, legislation should include the following authorizations and provisions:

1. Authorization for *all* local legal subdivisions to exercise the powers conferred, without hindrance or specification as to where such authority will originate in the structure of the government.
2. Provision for two or more subdivisional recreational service authorities to combine and otherwise coordinate the operation, administration, finance, and leadership of such recreational service.
3. Authorization for local recreational service authorities to acquire, build, construct, or otherwise develop such land and water areas or spaces as the local authorities deem adequate for the satisfactory provision of recreational service, as long as such measures are not inconsistent with public use or welfare.
4. Authorization for the expenditures of any funds, consistent with public welfare and local policy, which the local recreational service agency deems necessary for the most comprehensive recreational offerings and incidental services for the benefit of the public; and permission for said agency to receive any bequest, grant, or endowment of money, goods, services, equipment, or other real property which is in keeping with local policy and not inconsistent with any prescription as provided by law, as long as acceptance of such valuables does not require additional expenditures by the locality as a whole.
5. Authorization for the appropriation of funds from the general tax funds for the establishment and continued adequate operation of the most comprehensive recreational service program within the corporate or quasi-corporate boundaries, with provision for issuance of bonds for the purchase of any real property, buildings, structures, or other facilities for recreational purposes within or outside of the boundaries of the local legal subdivision.
6. Permission for the local recreational service authority to utilize any of the buildings, grounds, structures, or facilities of other local legal subdivisions, agencies, bureaus, departments, or systems with the consent and agreement of said parties, or to utilize private property on mutually agreeable terms between the negotiating parties.
7. Authorization for the local recreational service system to conduct and otherwise operate activities, property, structures, and other facilities within or without the legal boundaries of the local subdivision for the maximum recreational services which might then be afforded to the citizens and public at large.

8. Authorization of metropolitan recreational districts or regions where the cooperation of local legal subdivisions proves inoperable so that such special governments, established to coincide with economic areas rather than with existing political boundaries, can provide comprehensive recreational services without regard to urban or rural lines of demarcation. Such governments are then empowered to organize, operate, and administer a complete program of recreational services with all the resources of land, water, real estate, structures, facilities, funds, and leadership necessary for the execution of this mandate.

It must be clearly understood that state enabling legislation of any type does not necessitate the compliance of local legal subdivisions. Such enabling legislation merely serves as the stimulus and authority for local execution. Enabling legislation does not require action on the part of local authorities; it simply gives them the right to pursue courses of action that will benefit their respective constituents through the provision of local recreational services. Even with the broadest powers granted from the state legislature, local authorities are sometimes hesitant about providing recreational services until they have a clear mandate from their constituency. Therefore, enabling legislation should provide for public referenda to allow the voting citizens of the community to express their desire for a recreational service system. In addition, such acts should empower the recreational service agency to use special fund-raising measures, such as millage levies, property surtax, or other effective devices, to support such a system.

Local Recreational Service Legislation

Local ordinances provide for the legal establishment of a specific managing authority with well-defined powers, responsibilities, and functions for the organization, administration, supervision, personnel recruitment, personnel selection, finance, and maintenance of a system whose sole function is the widest dissemination of adequate recreational opportunities to the constituency of the community. Such local legislation must conform to state enabling enactments, to the charter of the municipality, and/or to the principle of home rule.

If local authorities contemplate legally establishing a recreational service system, the municipal attorney or the attorney general of the state usually determines the measures that will be in conformity with the state laws and whether there are legal provisions for the establishment of a recreational service authority through home rule powers or enabling acts. An analysis of the existing local authorization for the establishment of a recreational service system is necessary to determine the structure and administrative form the agency will take.

City Charter and Ordinances

Provisions for recreational service should be incorporated in the city charter, which can be amended only by vote of the people and approval of the state legislature. On the other hand, ordinances may be amended or rescinded by the local legislative body which passed them.

If the charter lacks suitable provision for recreational service, which is extremely rare, the city may provide for recreational service enactment by an appropriate ordinance. The content of either charter or ordinance will be substantially the same and should:

1. Establish by name a department for the exercise of the recreational service function. The name should be descriptive of the work the agency is to perform. Heretofore the tendency has been to designate departments by the places they operate; recent tendency has been to add the functional term *recreational service* to the name or to substitute it for all the other names as an inclusive term covering all operations and functions performed or rendered.

2. Create a board or commission of public recreational service as the local public representative body legally responsible for policy making and appraising the local recreational service system. It is important to note that the department or agency is the entity that carries on the work incidental to the performance of the recreational service function. The commission or board, if any, is the governing body of the department. This distinction has not always been made clearly, but it is fundamental if legislative and policy-making jurisdiction is to be kept separate from management. In creating a commission, the charter should state the manner by which members are appointed and dismissed, the terms they serve, and remuneration or per diem allowance (if any). The organization of the commission and its powers and duties should also be stated so as to make clear that the commission is responsible for governing the department and determining its policies, but that the duties of management are reserved to the executive or superintendent. The increasing size and complexity of the recreational program and the technical and professional development of its leaders, supervisors, and administrators have made it desirable, from a functional aspect, to have recreational service boards or commissions delegate administrative responsibility completely to their chief executive and to act for the public as a policy-making and appraising body.

3. Enumerate the extent of services to be provided by the department of public recreational service. Many of the older charters limited the department to the operation of property and omitted reference to recreational programs. (This was due to a lack of under-

standing of the true function of the recreational service system which, in effect, has to do with the organization of recreational activities, opportunities, and leadership of people.) The charter should authorize the department to organize, promote, supervise, and conduct any and all recreational activities it deems advisable, either on property owned by the municipality or elsewhere. (In the past, some recreational service departments were inconveniently hampered in the free development of program by being restricted to the city-owned properties.)

4. Assign to the superintendent the creation of necessary positions to carry out the work of the department and to fix salary schedules unless these duties are already assigned to the city council. In such instances, the commission should be given authority to recommend the selection, appointment, discharge, and suspension of employees. The classification of positions and determination of salaries and wages are matters of policy which should be assigned to the commission or board or to the local managing authority.

5. Authorize the commission to enter into written agreements (between school system and/or board and municipality or other public bodies) providing for coordination of recreational programs, facilities, and the conditions under which school recreational service will be made available to the general public.

6. Provide for uniform administration throughout the city government. All provisions in the charter affecting the recreational service department may not be contained in the sections relating specifically and exclusively to the department. Some provisions vitally affecting the operation of the recreational service system are mentioned below.

    a. Certain uniform personnel practices are usually set forth. Many cities have personnel departments organized under a civil service system which prescribes policy and procedure governing examination, exemptions, appointments, discharge, separation or suspension pending investigation, vacations, leaves of absence, sick leaves, and retirement and/or pension privileges. Charters often restrict political activities of city employees and almost always require residence within the city.

    b. Definite procedure for the guidance of all departments is set forth concerning preparation and approval of the budget and budgetary control following adoption. Procedures are specified for safeguarding and collecting money as are accounting measures. Borrowing money by bond issue, for either recreational or other purposes, and periodic reports also are covered by appropriate provisions.

7. Authorize the establishment of rules and regulations governing

public conduct in parks and other publicly operated recreational places, and for the control and management of the recreational program. These rules have the same effect, in theory, as do ordinances passed by the local civil authorities, but they are not as easily enforced in practice because they do not include penalties for violation. They may carry more moral force than ordinances, and they have the additional advantage of being easily passed, rescinded, or amended.

8. Authorize the acquisition of real and personal property deemed to be necessary for public recreational purposes by purchase, condemnation, gift in fee simple or in trust, bequest, lease, transfer, and grant. The title to any property acquired should be owned by the city and not by a department. The power to acquire park property should be vested in the recreational service system or commission, if there is one, and if it is granted control of its own funds. If there is no commission, the legislative body will perform this function. Property set aside for recreational purposes should be dedicated in perpetuity to be used solely for park and recreational purposes. It should be specified that property may be acquired inside or outside of the city limits. (Although as a general rule the park and other recreational properties will be within the municipal boundaries, situations sometimes arise in which it is altogether desirable to acquire properties wholly or partly outside the legal limits of the city.)

9. Authorize the city authorities to designate for recreational purposes any lands, buildings, or other structures owned by the city regardless of the original purposes for which they might have been acquired.

10. In cities with separate park and recreational service department, or where there are commissions for both agencies, authorize each to permit the use of portions of its lands by the other. For example, it might be desirable for a portion of a park to be operated as a playground under the jurisdiction of the recreational service department; or landscape areas on certain playgrounds might be cared for by the park department. Permits granted by one department to another under such provisions should either be for stated periods or until revoked by mutual consent of the departments and/or commissions in question.

11. Authorize the department to improve lands and to construct buildings or other facilities in a manner deemed necessary or convenient for recreational purposes. This applies only where the commission controls its own funds and the agency is large enough. In any event, the commission should be granted authority to approve or reject plans for such improvement.

12. Authorize the department to establish, construct, maintain, operate, control, and supervise specific types of recreational places, but not to the exclusion of any others. These may include playgrounds, recreational centers, athletic fields, gymnasiums, parks, auditoriums, community centers, golf courses, museums, beaches, and camps. Some inclusive phrase, such as "and any other place deemed advisable or necessary for the purpose of public recreational service," should be made.

13. Authorize the legislative body to make annual appropriation of funds for the support of the recreational service system, and such emergency or additional appropriations as may be necessary. Financial support other than taxes may consist of fees or charges assessed for special services or under certain extraordinary circumstances. Although not generally favored by public administrative authorities in municipal government, the establishment of a special recreational service fund by charter or ordinance is highly advantageous. The main advantage derives from the fact that fees and/or charges collected may then be deposited to this fund and may serve to augment the tax monies appropriated for recreational service operations. Without a special fund for recreational service operations under the control of the department, all fees and charges are deposited in the general fund of the city. In such cases the incentive to raise more revenue through legitimate fees is weakened, for the right of the department to use the revenue from recreational services is lost. The revenue from recreational service fees and charges in relation to the entire revenue budget of the municipality is almost inconsequential. Adoption of an annual budget of estimated revenues and expenditures is one of the duties of the department which should be specified in the charter or ordinance.

Control of Civil Disturbance

The social upheavals and insecurities of recent years have resulted in outbreaks of civil disturbance and violence. Some of this disorder touches the recreational settings where people gather in large numbers. Acts of lawlessness and riotous conduct at amusement parks, beaches, swimming pools, playgrounds, baseball stadiums, and other recreational facilities have increased.[10] Although control of riots and civil disturbances is essentially a responsibility of law enforcement agencies, good administration of park and recreational service systems can alleviate and often prevent such occurrences. If appropriate measures are not taken, the consequences are often the closing of many facilities and a disinclination on the part

[10] Mary Breasted, "Police Added After the Rampage By Turnaways at Rock Concert," *The New York Times* (October 12, 1977), p. A 22.

of the public to organize and promote worthy recreational opportunities. For example, teen-age dances have been banned; in others, swimming pools, golf courses, parks, and playgrounds have been closed to the public. Public behavior may be controlled by a system of permits and fees for the use of facilities. Permits regulate the size of groups, specify facilities to be used at stated times, set forth regulations in general, and fix responsibility for compliance with regulations. The collection of fees usually requires that patrons be checked at a central control point.

Preventive measures include planning the physical environment: decentralizing places where people assemble to participate in activities, lighting areas adequately, controlling ingress and egress, and regulating automobile traffic. They also include planning the program: arranging activities for groups of limited size, and assigning times for holding events.

Also important in public control is the presence of well-prepared and experienced recreationists whose leadership qualities are recognized. Such personnel are capable of sensing trouble in its incipient stage and are alert to ways of ameliorating problems of human conflict. Furthermore, recreationists may be able to instill a sense of group responsibility for behavior in individual members and for behavior toward other groups. All these measures recognize the role of leadership and the principle that whatever is accomplished in human behavior by force is but a temporary expedient that eventually will have to be reaccomplished through moral force.

Nevertheless, it may be necessary to resort to law enforcement to preserve the peace and curb persons who are amenable only to police control. The content of regulatory ordinances usually is recommended by the governing board or the superintendent of the recreational service system to the local city managing authority. The ordinances are prepared by the legal department and adopted by the legislative body of the city. Prescribed procedure for enacting ordinances requires serving notice of intention to pass them, advertising their contents, allowing an interval between the first and final reading, and providing opportunity for the public to express its reactions to them. Deliberation should be free from hysteria and unenforceable rules should be avoided. Among the items usually covered by ordinances regulating conduct in parks and other recreational places are:

1. Prohibited:
    a. Posting of signs, commercial advertising, and the use of public address systems without permit
    b. Parades and demonstrations without police permit
    c. Removal of trees, shrubs, plants, and flowers
    d. Destruction, defacement, or willful damage to structures or facilities

    e. Misuse of equipment with intent to damage or destroy
    f. Use of explosives, firearms, fireworks, and fires except at duly authorized and designated facilities or areas
    g. Entrance to certain areas except during specified hours
    h. Disorderly conduct, annoying women and children, loitering
    i. Gambling and solicitation of funds
    j. Hawking and merchandising in, or within a stated distance of, the public facility except at designated areas
    k. Bringing animals into the area, unless otherwise permitted
    l. Molesting birds, fish, or other fauna
    m. Disposing of refuse except in designated containers, littering
    n. Inciting to riot
    o. Use of vile or abusive language
    p. Disregarding posted notices
    q. Causing hazardous conditions.

2. Permitted, subject to regulations:
    a. Picnicking at stated areas, usually under permit
    b. Bathing, boating, swimming, and winter sports at specified places and under stated conditions
    c. Meetings, rallies, exhibitions, parade, and/or demonstrations
    d. Automobiles, bicycles, and motorcycle traffic
    e. Camping, use of tents and shelters, sleeping in areas at night.

3. Specified penalties for violations:
    a. Fine, not to exceed a particular amount in accordance with civic codes
    b. Imprisonment, in accordance with terms set by courts having jurisdiction in such matters
    c. Both of the above when warranted.

Selected References

Adrian, C. R. and E. S. Griffith: *A History of American City Government: The Formation of Traditions, 1775–1870* (New York: Praeger Publishers), 1975.

Adrian, C. R. and C. Press: *Governing Urban America, rev. 4th ed.* (New York: McGraw-Hill Book Company, Inc.), 1972.

Bent, A. E. and R. A. Rossum, Eds.: *Urban Administration: Management, Politics, and Change* (Port Washington, N.Y.: Kennikat Press Corporation), 1976.

Caraley, D.: *City Government and Urban Problems: A New Introduction to Urban Politics* (Englewood Cliffs, N.J.: Prentice-Hall, Inc.), 1977.

Claude, R. P., Ed.: *Comparative Human Rights* (Baltimore, Md.: Johns Hopkins University Press), 1976.

Freund, E.: *The Police Power: Public Policy and Constitutional Rights* (New York: Arno Press), 1976.

Jacobs, C. E.: *The Eleventh Amendment and Sovereign Immunity* (Westport. Conn.: Greenwood Press, Inc.), 1972.

Mathews, N.: *Municipal Charters: A Discussion of the Essentials of a City Charter* (College Park, Md.: McGrath Publishing Co.), 1969.

McGoldrick, J. D.: *Law and Practice of Municipal Home Rule, 1916–1930* (New York: AMS Press, Inc.), 1933.

Sheppard, P.: *Sovereignty and State Owned Entities* (New York: Twayne Publishers), 1965.

Sowle, C. R., Ed.: *Police Power and Individual Freedom* (Chicago, Ill.: Aldine Publishing Co.), 1962.

Wallace, S.: *State Administrative Supervision Over Cities in the United States* (New York: American Management Association), 1928.

CHAPTER 3

Legislative Authority and Executive Relationships in Public Recreational Service

Historically, municipal government has been exercised through a legislative body, usually referred to as a common council, whose members are elected for stated terms by the qualified voters of the city. In small towns all electors in the community may legislate through a town meeting. Daily operation of the community is vested with a board of selectmen, a town clerk, and a tax collector. Traditionally, however, the common council legislates and regulates all community affairs, with managerial or administrative duties assigned to a competent city manager and department heads.

As municipal responsibilities increased in number and complexity, a need for wider representation of the citizenry in public affairs arose. The plan of appointing commissions of laymen to preside over the affairs of the separate town functions evolved. In essence, these commissions were appendages of the common council. Their members, presumably well-informed citizens in their respective fields, were deemed competent to advise the common council, city manager and departmental executives and to provide effective communication between citizens and their government.

ESTABLISHMENT OF COMMISSIONS

In discussing the organization of recreational service within the structure of municipal government and the role of lay commissions, it is necessary to distinguish between government as an instrument for the preservation of society, and government as a means for the rendition of services desired by the citizenry. The view of government as an instrument for the provision of services is a comparatively recent one and has been dictated largely by necessity, stemming from the complexity of urban living. Many services presumably required by all citizens now, by common consent, are administered by local government.

Some functions of municipal government can be performed best by ministerial agents (city treasurer, city clerk, city auditor) without the aid of commissions. Law enforcement agencies (police, fire, zoning, building regulation, sanitary inspection) may be provided with commissions, not only to advise, but also to establish regulations according to legal authority and to hear appeals from decisions made by law enforcement agents. Their procedure must be formal and their finding recorded, because they are often put to the test of litigation. Commissions formed for the promotional fields (recreational service, library, arts, cultural affairs) are valued for their advisory functions, having little or no law enforcement duties in the customary sense, although some of their policy statements do regulate behavior at public recreational places. Such commissions rarely are required to hear appeals. Although their proceedings may be largely informal, the need to substantiate policy statements or other regulatory guides may arise, and for this reason, it is sound to record the work of the commission in minutes. Whether there shall be commissions, how they shall be appointed and organized, and what their responsibilities shall be will be set forth in the city charter. Their legislative duties are delegated by the common council; hence the council must confirm their actions, for example, in setting the charges for amenity services, or fixing of salary schedules. Their administrative prerogatives may be prescribed by the charter or delegated by the common council or the mayor (in cities of the so-called "strong" mayor type).

For convenience, commissions are often differentiated according to whether they are advisory or administrative (legislative). In fact, it is not an either/or situation; commissions may have limited or full administrative powers; in all cases their functions are advisory.

Students of government disagree as to whether a recreational service department should or should not have a lay commission. Administrators of recreational service departments heretofore have preferred commissions, but this preference appears to be waning. Commissions often are thought to be the most effective means for local government to learn of the needs of its constituent public, but in many instances this is no longer true. When citizens are appointed to commissions because of political affiliation, they may hinder efficient operations; when commission members have a high degree of interest and enthusiasm for public recreational service they may perform beneficially.

Until 1940, more than three fourths of American urban departments of recreational service were governed by commissions of laymen. Over the past 25 years the trend slowly has been reversed, although commissions still are in the majority. Executive directors, managers, or superintendents are being made responsible to city managers or city councils rather than to recreational service commissions.

Appointment and Tenure of Commission Members

Recreational service commissions are appointed by the governing body of the community and are generally nominated for such appointment by the presiding executive. Commissions may have any number of members, but five to seven have been found to be the most feasible number. They customarily serve without compensation, however, the city charter or local ordinance may provide a per diem for each meeting. Commissioners may be appointed for indefinite terms, for terms coinciding with that of the appointing power, or for set terms. In the latter case, appointments are staggered so that only half the terms expire each year so that several experienced commissioners remain on the board, thus providing continuity in policies. Under such a plan, commissioners need not resign with a change in municipal administration.

When a citizen is appointed to a recreational commission he is afforded many opportunities for unselfish service beneficial to the department executive, the recreational service system, and the city. Unless dedicated citizens with the ability to comprehend the function of recreational service and to exercise sound judgment in the public interest are appointed there is no advantage in having a commission.

Appointments to non-salaried commissions are not sought after as a rule. There are no emoluments of service to be had, but there is honor and satisfaction to be gained in rendering civic service. Usually, leading citizens respond generously when invited to serve on a recreational service commission because of their general interest in child welfare, education, city beautification, or because of a specific interest in an activity, such as amateur athletics, music, drama, or the arts.

Women no less than men have served with distinction on recreational service commissions and most commissions are composed of both men and women. The nature of the work of the recreational service commission is such that men and women together may make distinctive contributions to it.

Commissions usually elect their own presiding officer—a president or chairman. A secretary is required to keep minutes and other records of the commission and to certify its acts. Usually the secretary is an employee (the clerk of the commission) who may perform other duties. It is not unusual for one of the commissioners to act as secretary. The department executive rarely is burdened with this duty. The superintendent (executive) should meet with the commission and be free to participate in discussions, but he should not be accorded a vote. A treasurer is not necessary, because the disbursement of public funds is made by the city treasurer or other finance officer of the city. If the commission is empowered in any manner to disburse private funds, another arrangement must be improvised.

Meetings are held as often as necessary (usually monthly) and sometimes, by legal requirement, in a public place, preferably the city hall. The time and place of meetings should be published, and meetings should be open to the public so that it may be heard on all pending matters. If an internal matter arises during any public meeting, the commission is empowered to enter into executive session where the public is excluded so that unbiased solutions may be found.

Functions of Commissions

The principal functions of a commission are to formulate and promulgate policies governing the system. Commissions are responsible for the policies they adopt, but commissions may avail themselves of advice from the superintendent and suggestions from the citizenry in formulating policies. The commission also endeavors to conform to the policies of the general municipal administration as expressed by the mayor, the city manager, or the city council.

The recreational service commission typically performs the following functions:

1. Approves the acts of the department. As the governing board responsible for the results of the work of the department, the commission receives work reports through the superintendent and records its approval of them.
2. Acts as a court of final appeal. Any disagreement arising among employees or between the public and employees, if not satisfactorily resolved by the superintendent, may be considered by the commission, whose decisions are final.
3. Advises the superintendent on problems of administration. All superintendents need advice in the performance of their managerial duties and in carrying out the policies set by the commission. The advice of the commission should be sought by the superintendent but should not be interpreted as instructions or regulations unless given such force by action of the commission as a whole.
4. Interprets the department and the general operation of the system to the public. The commission fulfills this responsibility by published actions, by public discussion and address, and by planned use of available means of public communication. The members of

3

the commission often symbolize the aims and objectives of the department, for the character of the department is reflected in the members who are appointed commissioners no less than by the employees.

5. Represents the general public. Commissioners should conduct meetings that are open to the public and should permit individuals or delegations to address them on pertinent subjects. Most frequently the matter brought before a commission in this way is such that an immediate answer is not always possible or expedient. Often the petitioner is not in agreement with the commission. It should be remembered that the prerogative of the petitioner is only to state his views and not to participate in the action. The responsibility for the action, if any is taken, rests with the commission which, after giving a respectful hearing to the petitioner, makes its own decision based on the facts involved. The decision need not be made at the time the matter is brought before the commission; the subject may be taken under advisement and a decision announced in due course.

6. Represents the department at official occasions. Commissioners often act as spokesmen for the department at public ceremonies, public hearings on problems concerning the department, and conferences on recreational programs, policies, or other relevant issues.

7. Negotiates advantages for the department. Because of their individual and collective prestige, commissioners are often in a better position than the superintendent or others to negotiate advantages for the department with the local governing authority, other public officials, and the general public. Among these advantages might be an adequate budget for departmental operations. The layman who does not derive pecuniary gain from the appropriation for the department is usually more effective than a salaried employee in such negotiations.

8. Appoints standing and ad hoc committees. When the work of the department becomes extensive, the commission may appoint a special committee, usually consisting of only one person. A standing committee makes it convenient to assign to a commissioner, for further investigation and consideration, any matter on which the commission may not be ready to act. Committees will not have administrative powers in the matters referred to them. No committee or individual member has any authority except by referral to and through the entire body.

9. Separates managerial from policy-making activities. Execution of policy is delegated to the superintendent and the employed staff. Although there is no lack of interest in all phases of departmental operations by commission members, creation of an administrative

department to handle such matters provides for a sharp delineation between formulation and administration of policy.

Relationship between the Commission and the Executive

The relationship between the commission and the superintendent is a reciprocal one; they perform different functions, but are mutually dependent on each other. The commissioners must understand the functions and responsibilities of the superintendent and not trespass on them. The execution of the policies established by the commission, for example, is clearly a function of the superintendent. This clear-cut distinction is recognized as fundamentally important by all municipal authorities and should be strictly adhered to. Encroachment by the commission on the prerogatives of the superintendent destroys good management and tends to break down the system of responsible administration.

The superintendent also must respect the prerogatives of the commission. There must be a feeling of mutual trust and confidence between the commission and the superintendent if they are to function together efficiently. Since the superintendent is selected by the commission, this confidence is present at the beginning of the superintendent's service and should be cultivated and preserved continually.

The close association of commissioners and executive in the work which mutually engages them often results in personal friendships, but regardless of these personal relationships, the superintendent must be careful to treat all commissioners alike in his professional relations with them and certainly should not presume on his friendship with any member or members.

There are many occasions when commissioners and superintendent do not agree on the matters before them. The superintendent must reconcile himself to the decisions of the commission and must carry out its policies even when his own judgment is contrary. As in all group discussion and action there must be a certain amount of give and take in arriving at conclusions. In the interests of harmony, minor differences should not always be asserted. However, on major matters material differences should be expressed and asserted until the decision is reached. Such differences will be recorded when a vote on a motion is taken. The report of the superintendent should also be recorded whether his recommendation is adopted or not.

Matters may be brought before the commission by any member, by the superintendent, by other city officials, or by citizens. In the interest of proper recording, referral of matters to the commission should be by written communication or report, but strict adherence to this rule is not always possible nor convenient. Before a problem is fully discussed by the commission, the superintendent should be requested to give his report on it, thus encouraging his independent expression unswayed by consideration of the views of any commissioner. The contrary practice results in the cultivation of a "yes man" attitude on the part of the superintendent. Such an effect nullifies his special experiences and skills. Having received the report of the executive, the commission is empowered to approve, disapprove, or modify his recommendations. The executive's duty is to execute such decisions as have been made.

Selection of all employees should be made by the superintendent subject to the established municipal procedure affecting all departments. Only when the superintendent has the power of appointment can he be held responsible for the performance of the employees.

Any official dealings with employees by commissioners as individuals or as a body should be through the superintendent. Some employees may seek the ear of commissioners for one purpose or another, but they should be directed to bring the matter to the attention of the superintendent who will report on it to the commission if necessary. Most frequently such matters involve detail or questions of executive management which do not directly concern or fall within the purview of the commission.

Proper performance of the duties of a recreational service commissioner requires a sound understanding and acquaintance with the recreational problems of the city and a knowledge of the work being conducted by the department. A commissioner finds that more time is necessary to gain this background than is taken in official meetings. Visits to recreational centers, attendance at recreational activities, inspections, and participation in conferences with professional and lay leaders are very helpful. Systematic planning of such occasions is advisable. Opportunities for conference are afforded by the local, state, and national associations of workers and laymen.

One of the responsibilities of the superintendent is to aid commissioners in learning about the department, the work it performs, the manner in which it functions, and its traditions. Newly appointed commissioners especially are in need of assistance in these matters in order that they may assume their places in the deliberations of the commission. The superintendent renders this aid through conferences, correspondence, inspections of the work under varying conditions, and by furnishing reports and pertinent published material. The official meeting of the commission provides a good occasion to bring up matters for discussion. Participation of employees with the superintendent in discussion before the commission is sometimes helpful to the commissioners and stimulating to the employees.

Personality factors will always enter into any relationship between the commission and its executive. As long as the function and role of each are clearly defined, there should be little cause for friction. If the executive brings professional objectivity and empathy to his presentation, harmony and effectiveness must be the outcome in recreational service operations throughout the system.

Commission Procedure

The work of commissions is expedited and facilitated by proper physical arrangements. The meeting room of the commission should be prepared for the transaction of business; it should be well-ventilated and -illuminated, equipped with a suitable table, comfortable chairs, equipment to display maps, charts, or photographs, and facilities for the convenience of visitors. The commission should have a regular order of business and an agenda for each meeting should be prepared by the secretary or the superintendent. It is not unusual for the chairman of the commission to prepare the agenda.

Some commissions adopt plans of procedure and some prepare and adopt bylaws to govern their operations. The following is a typical plan of procedure for handling correspondence, reports, and recommendations that come before the commission:

1. The recommendation of the superintendent relative to any matter presented by him to the commission shall be written as a separate recommendation referring only to that matter and shall be attached to the complete file (if such a file exists) of papers referring to the same project.

2. Any recommendation made by the superintendent, or any subject presented by him to the commission, shall be automatically referred to the proper committee of the commission and action shall be postponed for one week unless immediate action is requested in the recommendation, or unless the committee to whom the matter would normally be referred is ready to move appropriate action. In submitting the recommendations to the commission, the superintendent may indicate the committee to which he thinks the matter should be referred. The secretary shall read the name of such committee, or any other committees to which he believes the matter may be referred, and the file shall be referred to the committee indicated or to a committee designated by the chairman unless otherwise decided by the commission.

3. All matters in the hands of committees shall be listed by the secretary and reports on the same shall be called for by the chairman at each meeting until finally disposed of.

4. When a file is referred to a committee, it shall be kept by the secretary, available for reference by the committee in whose hands the matter may be, and, if the committee so desires, the secretary shall provide extra copies, for their use, of the recommendation referred to them, together with other supporting data.

5. All communications on which a recommendation from the superintendent is desired or required shall be referred to him when read at a commission meeting, it being understood that if the letter is received sufficiently in advance of the meeting, the superintendent may attach his recommendation thereto, so that it may be available for the commission when the letter is first presented to them. To expedite business, correspondence that requires a statement from the superintendent should be routed through his office so that he may prepare his report and have it available when the correspondence first comes before the commission. (Much correspondence is only informative and routine and is merely filed without other action.)

6. Recommendations of committees shall be attached to their respective files when they are presented to the commission; recommendations may be written on an appropriate form to be provided, or verbal. If verbal, the secretary shall record such recommendations on the form when made.

Responsibilities of the Superintendent (Executive) to the Commission

The superintendent of recreational service should bring matters to the attention of the commission in written reports. Writing his opinions and recommendations serves to record them and assists him in organizing his thoughts. They may be:

1. Reports of information on matters that are of concern to the commission, including the condition of the department and the progress of its work.

2. Reports requesting instructions or expressions of policy.

3. Reports setting forth problems and recommending action to be taken in relation thereto.

The superintendent should adopt a standard report form. It should be typed clearly, with enough copies to furnish one to each commissioner and the secretary. It should be dated and numbered. The recommendation should appear in a summary sentence at the head of the dated report. The body of the report should state the origin of the problem, any other information essential to understanding the problem, and recommend a solution for the problem.

To insure proper functioning and to avoid excesses in the assumption of authority, it has been found expedient to spell out the duties of management in the city charter. Thus it is sometimes provided that the chief executive of each department has the duty to expend the funds of the department, subject to approval of the commission (if the commission is not limited to advisory functions only), to develop an annual budget and allocate subsequent appropriation, to appoint, suspend, discharge, assign, transfer, direct, and discipline employees (subject to the provisions of the civil service, if any), and to administer the work of the department.

Commission versus Single Executive Responsibility

Three traditional forms of organization are utilized in the structure of municipal government in the United States: mayor and council, council-manager, and commission. Where a municipality retains its mayor-and-council type of government, the city charter provides for a strong mayor and a unicameral council. The mayor is the chief executive of the community, with power to appoint heads of departments; therefore, he is responsible for the administration of the various municipal programs and for the fiscal position of the city.

The council-manager form has been rapidly accepted as the most effective type of municipal government because of the need for professionalization of public service. Under this plan, a unicameral council is elected by the voters and the council selects and employs a municipal manager. The council also elects a mayor from among its own membership, usually the individual who received the greatest number of votes. The city manager serves at the pleasure of the city council, but this specialized field of management has developed such ethical codes applicable to appointments and dismissal that members are fairly well protected from political pressure and personal enmity.

The commission form of government has steadily lost its place of eminence in recent years. Its basic defects include a lack of centralized responsibility for administrative assignment and, in some cases, incompetency of commissioners to assume the functions of departments regardless of their qualifications.

Clearly, the type of municipal organization plays a significant part in deciding on the structure of departments within the municipal family. The question almost always asked when establishing a new agency is whether it is to be headed by a single executive reporting to the managing authority of the community or by an appointed commission. In recreational service, there is support both for a single executive and for the commission type of organization.

Why are lay commissions established? The underlying reason most frequently given to support the establishment of an independent commission is that such a body is less subject to political pressure groups. There is also a quasi-judicial aspect of the commission and hearings before it are considered to be more impartial than appearances before an individual who might be biased. Unfortunately, the essential reason for establishing independent commissions is largely traditional rather than factual. Commissions have not succeeded in keeping political pressures out of the management of departmental affairs and such bodies have tended to be influenced by vociferous groups who may have an interest in specific social, cultural, economic, or related functions of the department.

The single executive directly responsible to the chief executive (or city manager) is the form generally favored by secure administrators and by students of government who seek improvement of departmental efficiency. Advocates of this type of organization have generally presented two arguments: first, such an arrangement conforms to the premise of efficient administration; second, this plan establishes clear lines of authority and responsibility for success or failure in the administration of departmental efforts. It is thereby assumed, with some logical basis, that all administrative work should be performed by professionally prepared individuals capable of producing quality services within an organizational plan leading up to and in direct contact with the executive managing authority of the community.

It would appear that a combination of the best features of the single executive and lay commission forms be applied to the municipal recreational service function. In effect, then, the commission would function in an advisory capacity only, bringing to the departmental executive the sense of the community which laymen are able to represent. Commissioners would still be drawn and appointed on the basis of their interest and knowledge of the recreational service problems that confront the community, but their responsibilities would be limited to the area of advice and recommendation to the professional in charge of the department. Thus the best of two organizational forms would be placed most effectively at the service of the community. The commission would serve as the chief public relations medium between the department and the public while continuing to offer advice or suggestions to the recreationist executive from a laymen's point of view. In this way, the department could function more efficiently, a sharply defined line of responsibility would be established, and the executive would benefit from the opinion and advice that the commissioners would offer. The commission would become an excellent sounding board for departmental policies and could serve as a buffer between disaffected citizens and the department. The commission would be in the best position to perpetuate the image of the department and develop goodwill between its personnel and the community. Offering a citizen's opinion of program or facility placement might prove highly beneficial to the community and future activities and the provision of systematized recreational services.

ADMINISTRATIVE PROBLEMS AND POLICIES

Problems of organization exist in several areas of the public administration of recreational service. Often it is difficult to separate administrative responsibility for the management of the agency from the prerogatives of the commission. It is sometimes uncertain just where policy making ends and administration starts. The line between executive authority for the execution of policy and the responsibility for guiding or shaping policy when there is a lay commission seldom is specifically defined. Furthermore, administrative functions have multiplied with such rapidity that division of work according to specialization and coordination of service often becomes confused.

The chief executive of the department should be a professional career person with primary responsibility to the governing authority of the community. The administrator should have sufficient authority to perform the tasks for which he is responsible. He should have the power to determine the operational organization of the respective sections and particularly to evaluate departmental policies and programs. He should have full discretion over the financial proposals insofar as the budget relates to the operational aspects of work performance.

The executive must also deal with the sensitive problem of public relations, which has become an acutely important function during the past decade. This is not only the area for the development of goodwill between the department and its clients but the major educational instrument that the department maintains for the enlightenment of the public concerning programming, plans, and services. Areas of friction may result when special groups demand the executive's time. Such groups, special interest, minority, ethnic, political, or whatever, are quite capable of creating discord and suspicion of departmental activities. For these reasons it is essential that the work of public relations be carried on daily throughout the operation of the system. The dual function of education and goodwill may not be lightly taken.

Personnel management, including all phases of employment, promotion, suspension, or discharge, must be assigned to the administrator. Recruitment of competent personnel, in-service development of staff, utilization of consistent measures to determine the efficiency of workers, position classification, and maintenance of appropriate working conditions are all part of the administrator's staff responsibilities and constitute important points for executive control. Nepotism and political appointments should be scrupulously avoided. Where personnel are employed on any but a professionally competitive basis, incompetency may develop so that there is bound to be dissatisfaction on the part of the public. Under such circumstances, when the executive is the appointing power, he can be held accountable for deteriorating departmental performance.

As the community grows in size and population, more services are required. Future contingencies must be planned for, and a schedule for the continued acquisition, development, and maintenance of land and facilities of all types must be prepared. Research is necessary to determine population trends, city growth and economic status, population densities, and land and facility needs as a basis for capital financing. The formulation of a master plan for the future development of the community and its people is an additional function of administrative research. The problems of an increasing proportion of aged citizens, young people under thirty, soaring birth rates, delinquency, vandalism, water pollution, resource spoliation, and constant competition for open space by public and private agencies must be considered by the administrator. The resolution of some of these problems is within the scope of recreationist responsibility, but the major problems that cities of all sizes and the nation face today must be attacked on a systematic basis and solved through concerted response.

Vandalism—A Case In Point

Vandalism may be described as any destructive activity usually associated with defacing of surfaces, wrecking of facilities, structures, or equipment, or the deliberate and wanton damage inflicted on objects, animals, or plants with malicious intent to spoil or harm. Why perpetrators of vandalism do what they do is still unclear. Some analysts have stated that contemporary vandalism stems from social alienation and is thought to be an attempt at vengeance against an uncaring or hostile society. Others believe that some forms of vandalism are spawned from racial, religious, or ethnic antagonisms and are manifestations of crude and ignorant outpourings of hate. Some apologists for types of vandalism are convinced that this anti-social behavior is a form of self-expression and may also be considered a modern art form. Whatever the causes of this socio-pathic behavior which is termed vandalism, it costs public recreational service authorities throughout the country hundreds of thousands of dollars—money that could and should be spent for the benefit of people rather than to clean up, repair, or replace facilities and fixtures that have been misused, abused, or destroyed.

Aside from the expense incurred in the aftermath of vandalism there are other, non-monetary, but equally serious consequences involved. The rendering of a facility useless by those who want to participate, as a result of vandalism, is not only discomforting to the potential participant, but is absolutely frustrating and discouraging to the recreationists who may have made tremendous efforts to program the facility. Preventing other people from utilizing a facility or recreational area because of a few warped individuals causes irritation, anxiety, and creates an atmosphere of mistrust. When people are discouraged from attending recreational places or are frightened for their personal security they react by seeking scapegoats. Generally, the public recreational service department is thrust into the role of miscreant because it does not move rapidly enough to secure its areas from vandals or because it simply does not have the fiscal resources to maintain its areas in terms of replacement parts or the personnel to deploy for these purposes. The public, apparently, does not understand these facts and, while deploring the consequences of vandalism, places the department in a disadvantageous light by blaming it for inadequate effort. The net result is an erosion of public confidence in the department with eventual decline in public support.

Remedial Possibilities

Administrative policy which develops in response to vandalism may take a variety of combative means. One of the ways in which vandalism may be countered is through the use of innovative design in the construction of new areas and facilities. Although there is really no such object as a vandal-proof facility or piece of equipment, structural materials that can withstand tremendous abuse without obvious damage are increasingly used. Smooth surface walls are being eliminated in favor of textured surfaces which either lose their attractiveness for graffiti writers or are resistant to the paint and other daubing and scrawling liquids or solids that are used by vandals.

Recessed and protected lighting has been found to be effective in maintaining illumination of areas that might otherwise provide darkened hunting grounds for muggers or other criminal elements. Lights have typically been the targets of opportunity of vandals, but with better installation practices, recessed receptacles, "unbreakable" plastic coverings, and speedy replacement of broken bulbs, vandals have sometimes been foiled.

A large expanse of glass for lighting effect has often offered inviting targets to vandals. New designs limit the use of ordinary window glass and substitute instead more exotic materials. Glass brick, glass substitutes, case hardened, or reinforced glass, and other defensive measures have been found useful in dissuading vandalistic breakage. In some instances recessed windows, sloped up and back, provide added protection against stone throwers.

Of course, vandalism may be reduced through increased watchfulness. The employment of uniformed guards, stepped-up police patrols, and security forces made up of neighborhood volunteers have a deterrent effect upon would-be vandals. Night lighting structures and hiring civilian watchers, whose payment consists of a free trailer permanently parked on the grounds, have been helpful.

The traditional method, and one that has not been disproved, is to provide attractive and varied activities at recreational areas. By offering needed recreational experiences, based upon neighborhood advisory committee recommendations, there appears to be an excellent chance to build local support from among those who find these opportunities worthwhile. By gaining local community support it is possible to discourage those who might vandalize the facility from doing so because they will then be the recipients of hostile and aggressive retaliation from the deprived community. Whenever recreationists can involve local people in the planning and determination of what kinds of activities will be available and the type of facility that could be constructed there is some reason to believe that the neighborhood population will come to think of the program and the facility as belonging to them.

Finally, recreationists should be provided with in-service education of a kind that will prepare them for working within inner-city situations, or any environment for that matter, where the potential for vandalism exists. Special sessions dealing with group dynamics, interpersonal behavior, and community organization may do much to off set incipient anti-social activities on the part of those who gain gratification and status from causing damage. Primarily, the concerned administrator will establish ways and means for implementing action to quell negative forces arrayed against departmental operations.

The soundest principles of administration are those which have been repeatedly applied successfully. These guiding rules to action operate in all phases of departmental function. The functions for which the executive is responsible are, or may be, delegated to staff subordinates. But although authority for executing these functions may be delegated, responsibility remains with the superintendent. Furthermore, certain areas of control devolve on the administrator and these can be neither waived nor given away.

Current practice in recreational service confirms the trend toward single executive control of departments and away from assumption of duties which would normally belong to other municipal agencies, e.g., police work and fire fighting. The levying of fees for certain activities to aid in financing recreational operations has become a general practice. Concessions granted for reasonable rent or other consideration (a percentage of gross receipts) are also resorted to as a means for financial support. Contributions or gifts of real property or funds for the operation of recreational services have been encouraged. The question of fees and charges still remains questionable. The ethics of levying fees when citizens already pay taxes to support the public agency requires considerable explanation.

Administrators obtain performance in accord with their policies and directions through the use of techniques common to all fields in which management and supervision are required. The organizational objectives may be achieved through coercion or through leadership. The two are mutually exclusive. Individuals may be driven to produce by implied or actual threats of wage cuts or dismissal, or they may be led to appreciate and share in the department's objective and thereby derive satisfaction in its achievement. Leadership largely determines whether personnel and personal relationships succeed or fail. It is essential to promote coordination, cooperative effort, and esprit de corps within the system and to avoid discord and friction. Without proper leadership, people work in an atmosphere of confusion and fear rather than one of order and confidence. Where there is suspicion, poor morale and disloyalty may result. In any organization, effective leadership develops only when an idea is present, when objectives are set and are understood by all, when acceptance of the objective is generalized, and when action is taken for the attainment of the predetermined objectives.

Selected References

Albanese, R.: *Management: Toward Accountability for Performance* (Homewood, Ill.: Richard D. Irwin, Inc.), 1975.

Batten, Thomas R. and M. Batten: *Human Factor in Community Work* (Fairlawn, N.J.: Oxford University Press), 1976.

Blau, Peter: *The Dynamics of Bureaucracy: A Study of Interpersonal Relationships in Two Government Agencies,* 2d rev. ed. (Chicago: University of Chicago Press), 1973.

Cooper, C. L., Ed.: *Developing Social Skills in Managers: Advances in Group Training* (New York: Halstead Press), 1976.

DuBrin, A. J.: *Managerial Deviance: How to Deal with Problem People in Key Jobs* (New York: Masan/Charter), 1975.

Feinberg, M. R.: *Effective Psychology for Managers* (Englewood Cliffs, N.J.: Prentice-Hall, Inc.), 1976.

Fox, J. F.: *Executive Qualities* (Reading, Mass.: Addison-Wesley Publishing Co., Inc.), 1976.

Likert, R. and J. G. Likert: *New Ways of Managing Conflict* (New York: McGraw-Hill Book Company, Inc.), 1976.

Parris, C.: *Mastering Executive Arts and Skills* (Englewood Cliffs, N.J.: Prentice-Hall, Inc.), 1969.

Singer, G. and M. Wallace: *The Administrative Waltz or Ten Commandments for the Administrator* (Elmsford, N.Y.: Pergamon Press, Inc.), 1976.

Smith, D. R. and L. K. Williamson: *Interpersonal Communication: Roles, Rules, Strategies and Games* (Dubuque, Iowa: W. C. Brown Company), 1977.

Turner, A. N. and G. F. Lombardi: *Interpersonal Behavior and Administration* (Riverside, N.J.: Free Press), 1969.

CHAPTER **4**

Administrative Policy Making

Policy is the result of decision making. It is a statement, usually formalized in writing, which implements substantive action within any agency. It is the end product of a process of information gathering, analysis, and proposed solutions to anticipated or previous problems. Policy formulation concerns administrative decisions taken in consequence of the operations in the recreational service department. The decision making process is intimately bound together with the primary mission of the department, methods for achieving objectives so that the mission can be accomplished, and inevitably focuses the use of critical resources on situations which appear advantageous to agency success. Policy making is an on-going conceivable activity in which the agency engages, it tends to have great significance for agency organization, management, and direction. Moreover, policy usually affects operations over a relatively extended period, and inevitably focuses the use of critical resources on situations which appear advantageous to agency success. Policy making is an on-going process based upon intelligent appraisal of human interaction within the organization as well as an assessment of environmental intrusions and the modifications which are necessary as opportunities occur.

If policies are defined as general guides for employee behavior in the achievement of objectives as well as lines of action necessary to control or promote certain activities, then it is necessary to recognize that several policies may be required in order to fulfill an objective. Each policy may need support and linkage to other policies if a specific mandate is to be carried out. How and why policies are formed is the subject of this chapter.

POLICY DETERMINATION

The development of the major elements of policy for any recreational service department will undoubtedly have implication for the following: (1) some designated component of the agency, the environment of which the agency is a part, or one or more operations carried on by the agency will be affected; (2) a desirable sequence of events will be implemented so that specific behaviors will occur; (3) a particular alternative will be chosen from among several possible courses of action so that a desired result is obtained; and (4) the intent of the decision maker or makers will be clearly perceived through the publication of some statement which notifies all who are affected. Some policies offer tangible benefits to those who make up the constituency of the department. Other policies prevent, control, or direct behaviors that have been deemed hazardous, destructive, or deleterious.

As has been aptly stated by Lindblom:

> One is tempted to think that policy is made through a sequence of steps (or a set of interlocked moves), such as: (a) preliminary appraisal of or inquiry into the problem; (b) identification of goals or objectives; (c) canvassing of possible policies to achieve the goals; and (d) choice or decision. This way of looking at policy making is useful for some purposes, but it tends to view policy making as though it were the product of one governing mind, which is clearly not the case. It fails to evoke or suggest the distinctively political aspects of policy making, its apparent disorder, and the consequent strikingly different ways in which policies emerge.[1]

The infringing forces of the political environment, containing as it does, various ideological viewpoints, special interests, particular aspirations, the political possibles of constituent demands, or the economic realities of fiscal resources, all lead to certain compromises. Sometimes the resultant policy is a creation which has little or nothing to do with the problem it was supposed to solve. On occasion policies are instituted to seize the advantage of opportunities rather than resolve problems. In some instances, conditions occur and *ipso facto* are policy because of importunate planning or the lack of foresight and no planning. Policy making is a complicated political process whose parameters are dimly seen and frequently unobserved. The mix of interacting forces necessitated by differentiated demands and requirements produces results which are described as policies. How this happens and how reasonable procedures can be introduced into this sometimes chaotic process are subject to analysis and, perhaps, comprehension. Still other policies are generated to encourage personnel performance so that waste of valuable resources is either eliminated or restricted and the delivery of primary services is made more effective.

---

[1] C. E. Lindblom, *The Policy-Making Process.* (Englewood Cliffs, N.J.: Prentice-Hall, Inc., 1968), p. 4.

The environment of the recreational service system incorporates the social, cultural, and economic impacts that prompt the policy decisions which administrators make and also the force of their decisions upon the policy quarry. Resources which affect and influence policy are both human and instrumentalities. Human resources are those which are translated into constituent demands, desires, or claims for specific services; or personnel skills, knowledge, and ability to perform required duties and responsibilities in carrying out the mission of the department. Instrumentalities are financial support, program development, materials, supplies, and equipment which indicate whether the department has the means to carry out its mandate.

Policy makers assimilate information derived from the available resources and develop policies based upon them. The results of policies usually become program services which either satisfy the recreational needs of those who participate or are rejected by participants and non-participants alike. In the latter instance new policy must be developed to counteract whatever dissatisfaction arises from inadequate program or other services. Included within the process of policy making are also the conflicting values, behavioral variations, jurisdictional infringements, insufficient resources, or non-compliance with procedures which cause friction and other injurious confrontation.

For the purposes of this text, it has been thought useful to differentiate between legislative policy and administrative policy. Legislative policies have typically been articulated by boards, commissions, or other designated executive bodies, i.e., city council, board of supervisors, etc., and are usually broadly stated. Administrative policies, on the other hand, are typically specific in nature and almost always limited to a particular subject, problem, or issue. Thus, a legislative policy that "the department will attempt to support area suppliers whenever possible" may become interpreted at the administrative level into a procedure that "when two suppliers of materials or goods bid for contracts and one is not from the community, the local supplier, not necessarily the lowest bidder, will be selected."

It should be emphasized that the chief executive of the department will probably influence legislative policy making because of the expertise that the administrator brings to the position. The professional invariably has more pertinent information about the operational needs of the agency than does anyone else at the decision-making level. It behooves him to supply information to policy makers so that they have the ability to make rational decisions. Where the chief executive answers to a legislative body, it is possible that said body will delegate the translation of legislative principles into policy statement. Furthermore, the administrator may also initiate policy in terms of general principles.

Policies at the executive or legislative level are determined from among the alternatives offered in terms of resources available or other controlling conditions. At the administrative level, however, the policies enunciated by the executive become the principles which guide the decision making process at lower levels. For example, at the legislative level, the executive may decide that, for promotion to supervisory rank, professional education and breadth of experience will count for more than seniority in the department. In coming to this decision, the administrator will have considered the variables of personal merit, education, ability, and seniority. At the administrative level, when several individuals are being examined for supervisory candidacy, the decision criteria employed in selection will be based upon professional education first and then length of service with the department.

Policies are injected into operational workings of an organization in several ways. From a legislative orientation they are the object of the decision making process. From an administrative orientation they become the basis for problem solving when implemented. The presumption here is that policies are developed upon rational models, although this is not always true.

POLICY VARIATIONS

To appreciate the operation of any organization, especially large ones, the pattern of personal relationships within the agency needs to be understood. Such patterns tend to be displayed in the habitual policies which are adopted by the agency in its operation. Assessment of a department usually discloses the various kinds of policy in effect and the methods by which such policies are instituted.

The Policy of Convention

Conventional policy is determined by custom, precedent, and usage. In its extreme form, such policy is restrictive, inflexible, and demands conformity. It is reduced to a formula which is its own end and is not conducive to logical intervention. There are agencies which do things in certain ways, not because there is any rational basis for the action, but simply because things have *always* been done this way and nobody challenges the object or method. Conventional policy may once have had some rational basis for its inception, but times change and so do conditions. Unless the organization is able to move with the times, it stands in the unforgiving position of becoming stagnant. Conventional policy produces static and finally stagnant conditions. Such policy is too rigid to be able to cope with rapidly changing situations.

Essentially, the policy of convention relies more upon historical precedent than it does upon rational decision making. This policy variety discourages questioning and demands conformity to long practice without explanation. Historical practice is habituated as a natural order of things.

Those who support such policy do so without any thought of change. In fact, it is considered irrelevant to offer rational suggestions for the modification of conventional policy. Conventional policy may be discovered in almost any organization. Each agency apparently establishes fundamental rules that are generally accepted even though those who accept them would be severely pressed to offer any reason for them. In a contemporary organization it may start with a legislative decision that establishes a precedent which then endures long after the cause for the decision has been forgotten and the condition that demanded it no longer exists. When such policy is only part of the organizational culture and affects performance in trifling ways, it has little consequence on agency efficiency. However, when it leads to static rigidity in an environment requiring the ability to adapt to rapid change, then serious problems can be expected.

"But we've always done it that way around here" may be the agonized cry of the traditionalist, but it is not a rational answer to situations which require change. Organizational policies that were based on sound reasoning and proved effective when they were initially introduced sometimes persist long after the reasons for their development have passed from the scene. Their only value is that of tradition. Policies which are produced under emergency conditions or from random decisions by administrators may breed standards that are accepted through force of habit. Such policies are largely inferred and, therefore, are not thoroughly analyzed or assessed.

The Policy of Dictum

Like any autocratic pronouncement, the policy of dictum is the willful issuance of guiding statements by one person. Such policy is exemplified by the abrogation of power by an individual and the capricious development of policy for the daily operation of the organization. Policy of this type is fast fading from the scene because it implies an entrepreneurial or charismatic personality that is not widely known in an era of technocratic managers. Edict policy, when observed in agencies, has the effect of requiring subordinates to maintain constant contact with the boss so that clarification of what is really wanted is understood. Since the boss is under no obligation to keep policy from moment to moment, subordinates generally have problems in determining how they are supposed to behave at any given time; hence, they have little discretion to act without first consulting the promoter.

Usually, policy by dictum is undesirable because it produces frustration among subordinates. There are instances when such policy procedure may be effective. That occurs when the situation is uncertain and rapidly moving events demand something close to instantaneous modification. Not hampered by precedent or logical processes in the development of policy, the arbitrary administrator utilizes his knowledge of the agency's resources and his own "instincts" to guide the organization.

Policy by dictum provides tremendous leverage and discretion to the individual who is the source of such policy, but dampens the enthusiasm of subordinates who are thwarted in their desire to perform and who remain in limbo as they try to anticipate what is expected of them. Such policy is diametrically opposed to group decision making. The only time that arbitrary policy is worthwhile is when subordinates gain satisfaction through a high level of interpersonal relationships as well as the expectation of great rewards from slavish devotion to the boss. Contemporary conditions are not conducive to such policy or relationships.

The Policy of Logic

Policy created from need and based upon accurate and pertinent information permits enlightened administration and frees organizational employees from the willful acts of a single head. The concept of policy as defined by a legislative body, rather than by one person, is well known in the literature. However, much policy is, and should be, made by individuals. In any modern organization, rational policy is usually expressed in terms of principles which guide behavior and set the operational tone of the agency. Generally policy of this type is supplemented by procedures, standards of performance, and monitoring techniques. Usually, these procedures are understood to be administrative policies designed to explain how legislative principles will be executed.

The rational model provides guidelines for handling recurrent situations or activities, or for avoiding behavior which is undesirable. Policy should propose intended behavior concomitant with agency goals. Policy based upon logical input produces consistent and coordinated action. Individuals within the department are able to guide their own actions and anticipate the actions of others because the policy is stable and not subject to whim. With rational policy, each member employed by the system has a common set of guidelines to follow. Logical policy development contains both the reasons why behavioral guides are necessary and the particular restrictions which control behavior. These two components, the rationale and the specifications, incorporate the fundamental factors of the soundly designed policy. For example:

Rationale: The department resolves that its professional staff will be recognized on the basis of merit and ability. It is determined that this is the most effective means to attract and retain qualified, competent, and highly motivated individuals. The department concludes that this is the most equitable method of compensation. Specification: Systematic evaluation of departmental personnel performance will be conducted on a routine basis and regular review of individual compensation will be conducted in terms of position requirements and performance.

Rationale: The safety of agency patrons is an essential responsibility of the department and all personnel associated with it. Scrupulous care must be taken to avoid placing patrons in jeopardy through error, lack of information, or negligence. To this end a safety education program will be devised, employees will inspect physical properties for damage or hazards, and patrons will be warned against dangerous practices or prevented from engaging in behavior which might lead to injury. Specification: Warning signs will be posted at all appropriate places, to prevent behavior inimical to the health or safety of patrons.

Whether in the form of a legislative statement, as in the first policy above, or in that of a definitive rule limiting action, as in the second administrative statement, these policies offer the reasons justifying the actions. When conditions change, if ever, so that the rationale becomes invalid, the policy could be changed. It is unlikely that a safety program will ever be unneeded. The vagaries of human nature being what they are, people will wittingly or unwittingly place themselves in danger in recreational situations because they do not believe that any danger exists in the "safe" environment of a park, playground, or other recreational area. When, however, justification for a policy can no longer be found, the policy should be changed or abolished. The real danger is that policies take on the trappings of tradition, become fixed, and are no longer derived from rational needs. When the reasons for policy are clearly understood, the danger of policy by precedent and rigid adherence without question can be radically reduced.

Clarification of the rationale for policy statements is useful in another connection. When personnel in a system understand the logic that justifies a constraint, they are more likely to accept it as a reasonable guide to their own behavior. While there are certain personality types, oriented to authoritarian attitudes, who tend to accept constraints with little or no question, others, who are more democratically oriented, require the reasoning behind the rules before acceptance is given. Administrators who explain their policies instead of attempting to enforce prescribed rules of conduct through edict are usually confirmed by the more willing acceptance on the part of subordinates.

Rational policy making requires both explanation and specificity. However, if the policy is to be considered worthwhile and capable of implementation, other elements will need to be included within the parameters of the policy. Policy should be the outcome of the values of the decision-makers. Once policy is determined it must be capable of acceptance by those who are affected by it. Despite logical basis and excellent design, policy can be circumvented or subverted by disaffected subordinates. This stipulation infers that subordinates should be participating in the decision-making process which formulates policy wherever feasible. Policy should be elastic to accommodate itself for discrepancies which are derived by extenuating circumstances. Policies which permit exceptions need not invalidate the policy. There are conditions or situations where exceptions can be made, but all exceptions require justification.

Policies provide stable rules that are in effect until they are modified; for this reason decisions arrived at, at various times, will be consistent. Legislative policies are meant to govern the entire system, not only distinct parts. Since the same policy is constant throughout the organization, decisions which are made are probably going to be more consistent at any time than in circumstances where policies are arbitrarily arrived at or non-existent. Policies based upon logic and factual input permit flexibility. Because they are designed rationally, with the reasons for their existence explicitly stated, they can be evaluated and changed as conditions mandate change. This is in direct contrast to those policies which are dynastic in type or created by executive caprice and are, therefore, much more difficult to assess or modify.

Scope of Policy

Whatever inputs there are to recreational service departments, it is probably safe to say that most departments are motivated by the beliefs of the decision makers that the primary function of the department is to supply recreational opportunities to all community residents. The perception of the administrator is that recreational services should be offered in such a manner that every person, regardless of ethnicity, disability, youth, age, or socio-economic status will receive whatever is required for personal satisfaction. The specific objectives, then, are the promotion of recreational experiences which can meet individual needs, take place in areas that are easily accessible insofar as having the kind of activities demanded, have sufficient personnel to take care of instructional and supervisory functions, and have availability of a diversified range of areas on which recreational activities may be experienced. All of these conditions are nominally offered because there is an adequate supply of money to produce the delivery of services.

However, the administrator is also aware of the fact that fiscal support for the comprehensive delivery of recreational service is less than what is required in all respects. Still the mission of the agency remains to be fulfilled. There are diverse lines of action which may be attempted. There can be an appeal to the governing authorities of the community for more funds to meet the needs; there may be a public relations campaign promoted which seeks direct support from the people of the community; it may be determined that only selected populations will receive well-publicized delivery of programs; maintenance items or other capital budget features may be delayed or neglected so that money can be diverted to program opportunities; or some combination of all of the above. Whatever option is selected, it will be transmitted to the rank and file of the agency through written materials as well as verbal communication by line supervisors who will have the real responsibility for executing the policy. However, the process does not stop with policy implementation. Every policy probably generates some reaction. The more people who are touched by the policy and the greater the significance to them, the surer will there be repercussions. Subtle or overt changes may have to be made as the full impact of policy begins to be felt by those concerned.

Any number of questions can be raised about policy as it affects the public and the operation of the agency. "Is the policy worthwhile?" "Does the policy do what it was intended to do?" "Was there a miscalculation with concomitant adverse effects?" All of these questions must be examined, but before any definitive answers can be obtained there is the necessity for investigating policy economics, service delivery, and impact.

Economics. Almost all policies which are enacted by the recreational service department will involve costs in one way or another. Except for purely symbolic statements designed to mollify or uplift the morale of particular social groupings, the expenditure of public money is to be one expected outcome of policy implementation. In times of economic retrenchment the question of budgetary allocations to recreational service departments becomes an explosive issue. There are many city services competing for the same tax dollar. To most citizens recreational service is a frill, hardly to be compared to the more significant functions of health, police, fire, sanitation, and the much maligned educational system. To discuss public recreational service under such circumstances is a risk. Few administrators want their budget allocations cut. Public recreational service departments may be able to justify financial requests, but whether such requests will be honored by the governing body is another issue. During times of financial stress, public recreational service agencies are nearly always cut back in terms of manpower through attrition, furlough, or discharge. Moreover, maintenance support is curtailed. Materials to operate activities are kept to a bare minimum. Any change in operations that is likely to cost money will be rejected. When citizens are hard pressed financially, then tax burdens are among the most critical and sensitive issues which can be raised. Each substantive policy becomes a money spending decision. Governing authorities focus their attention on budgetary problems and costs are generally seen as a fundamental component insofar as the production of services are concerned. While spending alone will not satisfy the demands for service, it does permit the purchase of those items which will produce the service. By judicious manipulation of line items and the creation of policy that requires high profile action for the most vociferous groups, the recreationist administrator can obtain financial support for the continuation of public recreational service. Until the economy begins to strengthen and the community once again begins to appreciate the value of public recreational service, the administrator may have to formulate policy which curtails comprehensiveness in favor of exclusivity.

Service Delivery. Policies may be judged in terms of the level of output obtained. Incorporated in this area are such questions as per capita expenditure; what program is actually purchased by such spending; and what combination of capital outlay, personnel expenditure, and activities are generated. Although the level of spending may indicate the degree of service attained, allocation of funds does not necessarily provide the quantity or quality of service which is required. There is little question that money is extremely important to the provision of recreational service delivery, but there is no guarantee that sufficient budgetary allocation will produce a corresponding level of service.[2] The real performance levels in public recreational programs are undoubtedly influenced by factors beyond the capability of the department to control. Depending upon the needs of the recipients, extra-departmental pressures, severity of deficiencies to be overcome, and other impinging stresses, the recreational service department may have little or no ability to influence such environmental conditions.

Impact. Recreational policy effects are disposed differentially within the community. Certain policies will affect every person living in the community, while others have greater significance for particular populations. For example, a safety policy enacted to prevent accidents and injuries from occurring may only affect those who utilize or participate in certain activities or areas. Nevertheless, the policy has been implemented with the idea of its affecting all citizens equally. On the other hand, some policies are enacted which influence only certain socio-economic classes or particular neighborhoods within the community. Policy may be enacted which discriminates against ethnic or economic groups. Some groups may receive more services in terms of facilities, leadership, or activities. That there is variability in service cannot be denied. To the extent that persons who reside in one neighborhood as opposed to another because of racial, religious, ethnic, social, or economic differences may enjoy more or less service of a particular type reflects their need or the administrator's perception of the need.[3]

Policy does not necessarily attain the objectives set out for it. Although the delivery of services may be offered by the department, they may not have their intended outcomes. The thrust of service may be effective or not. Impacts of delivery are the outcomes that services have upon the intended recipient population as well as on other aspects of the environment. Certain impacts will be deliberate or planned, others will be accidental, coincidental, or unanticipated effects. Non-intentional impacts

[2] I. Sharkansky, *The Politics of Taxing and Spending* (N.Y.: Bobbs-Merrill, 1969).
[3] C. S. Benson and P. B. Lund, *Neighborhood Distribution of Local Public Services* (Berkeley, Cal.: University of California, Institute of Governmental Studies, 1969).

occur because of the nature of urban life and the paucity of information about the potential influences that policy implementation can have.

One example of unanticipated results may provide clarification of the concept of impact. The summer vacation may produce tensions and increased hostility among out of work youth in the inner city. The department, in order to diminish free time establishes a series of "rock" music concerts which brings an influx of youth into the central city. The decision to alleviate pressure may encourage the very outbreaks which the department hoped to prevent. The expected outcome, instead of providing a few hours of respite from alienation, was not realized and in fact became a main contributor to riotous conditions. This situation can occur when administrators are not sensitive to problems which traumatize some elements of the potential patrons of the service. Whenever there is insufficient information about conditions and the consequences which might accrue as a product of specific policy, the actuality of unintentional negative effects is always present. An external aspiration of adroit administrators is to formulate policies whose chief outcomes are planned and whose unanticipated ripple effects are either innocuous or minuscule.

DECISION-MAKING AND POLICY

The amount of information which comes to the administrator complicates his responsibility for decision-making. However, it is only by accumulating information about the issues that rational judgments can be made so that policies will be best designed to satisfy constituent needs. The sheer volume of inputs needed to reach a decision which will enable sound policy to be formulated can be demoralizing. Unless knowledge of the environment is encyclopedic, spillover damage from policy can exacerbate the very problems the policy was supposed to resolve. Nevertheless, there are procedures which can be utilized to obtain the kinds of information necessary to reach a logical decision concerning policy design.

The Decision-Making Process

Logic should be the basis on which decisions are made. Emotionalism should be omitted from any process in which rational outcomes are expected. In analyzing the logical procedure it must be recognized that no agency has sufficient resources available to reach decisions that completely reduce unforeseen consequences to a bare minimum. The most logical procedure would include (1) identification of the problem; (2) listing of all resources available; (3) setting forth the obejctives of the agency in order to fulfill the mission; (4) determination of priority of objectives; (5) determination of the costs of each line of attack and the sequence of events that might flow as a consequence of adoption; (6) choice of the objectives that appear most amenable to fulfillment in association with the greatest benefits and accommodations; (7) formulation of the policy which incorporates the actions necessary to accomplish the task.

Administrators who follow this procedure require information about all of the potential opportunities and all possible outcomes developed from each opportunity. This need for information, unless retrieved or generated through electronic data processing, constitutes a huge responsibility. Furthermore, although cities have begun to use computers and EDP on a vastly expanded level than has ever been attempted previously, few recreational service departments either are equipped with terminals or, for that matter, have the skilled personnel assigned to program and operate computers. The need for collected intelligence is vital. Unless the administrator is prepared to gather information in some other way, his time will be almost completely absorbed in analyzing such data. Moreover, even when the information is collected and analyzed, the administrator cannot be biased for or against any alternative. Decisions have to be made on the basis of systematically collected information—thus, several objections come immediately to mind in developing policies based upon a logical decision-making process: (1) too much time will be spent in the collection and examination of information. There is not enough time to pursue all of the projected consequences of each possible alternative; (2) the price of gathering and analyzing pertinent information might be prohibitive; (3) the amalgamation of sometimes discrepant objectives that are simultaneously followed within the system; (4) organizational practices that thwart intelligent and cooperative actions; and (5) the restrictions of what is practical within the political climate.

Constraints on Logical Decision-Making

Time Limits. Almost all of the problems which public recreational service departments face have been developing for decades. There are no easy solutions to these problems nor will they disappear quickly. Despite this fact, administrators are constantly urged to develop policy that will lead to the instantaneous solution to these problems. Politicians work within reduced time frames and are therefore compelled to press their appointed officials for action on problematic conditions which abound throughout the community. Administrators are harried beyond their means to produce policies which will be effective. But the formulation of policy takes time. The collection and analysis of information on which to base substantive policy take time. Time is the commodity in shortest supply and it is one of the major reasons why policies cannot be developed in logical fashion. The pressure of having to make decisions without the necessary study of pertinent information or the accumulation of information about the consequences of various alternatives abrogates conformity to logical procedure. In short, there is insufficient time to work out all of the ramifications involved.

Cost Limits. Another decisive factor which prohibits logical decision-making is the financial involvement required for collecting information. Of all of the kinds of information needed none is more important than accumulating data which show the needs of people. Specialized information, which indicates methods for obtaining objectives, also requires considerable effort, cost, and time to obtain. Even after the information is gathered, there still remains the necessity for analysis and application. Administrators have only a limited amount of time to devote to decision-making. They can reflect upon few items simultaneously and can assimilate a restricted amount of data dealing with any one problem. Because capacities for collecting information are curtailed by existing resources, when does the administrator end his search for information and stop examining what he has obtained? Ideally, the reply is never. Reality, however, demands that at some pronounced point in the process of policy formulation there will have to be some decision. When this occurs, a value judgment will have been made and some policy will emerge. Too often, administrators cease their investigations when they perceive a method of work that contributes to the least radical change in their on-going operation. They do not seek out all of the likely alternatives until they discover the most appropriate one. Rather, they act pragmatically and investigate until they establish a technique that works, something that will offer a modicum of relief from recognized difficulties without jeopardizing the bureaucratic status quo or causing instability among the various pressure groups who are the agency's constituents. Thus, the search for information continues until the administrator feels that he must act. The costs are far too great and the pressures for policy commitments are too profound to continue a search until the single best mixture of objectives, data, and policy design has been found.

Discrepancy Limitations. Recreational service departments operate under disparate policy statements. Some of these, unless the administrator has been extremely careful, may be in diametric opposition. Such an obvious concept cannot be unexpected when it is recognized that a public recreational service department serves numerous interests and diverse constituencies. The department must, therefore, respond to many demands of which there are bound to be conflicts. How the department resolves the variety of inconsistencies which can occur does not contribute to the logical development of policy. It is not unusual to find departments advocating two policies which are completely antagonistic. One example is racial integration. Many urban departments are faced with *de facto* segregation due to neighborhood residences. The promotion of decentralized administration with concomitant dispersion of facilities does little to enhance racial integration or an avowed interest of the department. It is clear that a department's policies may sometimes fail to support its goals and may actually hinder or frustrate compliance.

Discrepancies are not only noted in terms of incompatibility. Policies may be in conflict insofar as cost benefits are concerned. There is inadequate information concerning departmental objectives and ineffective measuring devices to appraise their relative worth. Administrators have little idea of whether additional dollars allocated to certain recreational activities will produce greater benefits to the same population as would money devoted to maintenance operations of facilities. Even the primary objective of recreational service provision cannot be clearly measured in terms of which policy will more nearly meet the recreational needs of the public to be served. There is no substantial evidence that any one policy for supplying recreational services will be more effective than would any other policy.

Organizational Limits. If logical decisions require the ability to organize practices which are commensurate with the selection of objectives that are designed to satisfy the basic mission of the agency, then the organizational procedures of urban departments are not capable of optimum functioning. Rather, there are innumerable ways by which organizational structure frustrates the agency's mission. In fact, it is not unusual for several departments, with overlapping responsibilities, to have identical objectives and pursue different policies in attempting to achieve these objectives. Duplication of service or fragmentation of jurisdiction can lead to the formation of vastly different policies concerning the same or diverse goals, without any attempt at coordination.

One glaring example may be the divided responsibility for public recreational service by three or more departments. When the school system, recreational agency, park department, and housing authority all have impact on the provision of public recreational service, there is bound to be duplication, gaps in service, competition for the same clientele, inefficiency, ineffectiveness, and waste of time, money, and effort. All of these agencies may have recreational service as their stated objective, but the policies developed in pursuit of that idea may be responsible for the frustration of coherent and coordinated activities.

Political Limits. There are many services which the recreational agency can provide, but does not because of political interference by elected officials. The political climate may not permit the introduction of new activities, the construction of new facilities, or the employment of qualified workers because of infringement by politicians on the hiring practices of the department—in the case of patronage. Political feasibility also has reference to the social environment in which the department is situated. A variety of special interest groups may attempt or actually have political influence with the governing authorities to compel the recreational service department to satisfy their particular needs despite any resort to the logical input of factual information. Attitudes toward taxation, social philosophy, perceived need, or emotional issues tend to cloud factual representations. Elected officials, for the most part, are simply unwilling to mortgage their political futures by doing what is logical when, in effect, they can display themselves as listening to the demands of people and pass themselves off as popular heroes. There has seldom been a case of logically developed policies subordinating the self-interest of various pressure groups who require symbolic or actual gestures to appease their needs and to obtain their votes. Under such conditions political feasibility really means that parks, playgrounds, centers, or other necessary facilities will not be sited and constructed where logic dictates, but where special interests want them placed. In the final analysis, the judgment of what can be done about a specific question is decided not by what is logical, but by what potential voters will buy and what "wheeler-dealers" will accept.

Adjustment and Concession

The inability of decision-makers to adhere to the exacting directions of logical procedure does not mean that their choices are disordered, random, or determined without recourse to rationality. According to the strict prescription of logical behavior there is little that can be done by recreationists except to compromise. While concessions have to be made to the impediments which develop from practical policies, special pleading, and other constraints, there are techniques for contending with complexities that sanction judgments to be made without the complete analysis required by the logical pattern. Among such resource conserving practices are confidence in the equilibrium between routine activities and unmet needs to attract attention to the requirement of policy change; avoidance of confrontations; the utilization of standard operating procedure to simplify perplexing conditions, and the inclination to make adaptations to demands, instead of implementing decision-making procedures that pursue definitive objectives or policy. Not one of these techniques conforms to the stringency of logic, but they are all applied by administrators seeking bases for reaching decisions in the push-pull environment of time, money, and informational constraints. Underlying each of these factors is the dislike of administrators to deviate substantially from usual activities. Administrators prefer order and stability. Any attempt to hasten decision-making procedures is done to assist durability in an environment with increasing disposition toward inconstancy.

Complaints, for example, are looked upon by administrators as warnings of dissatisfaction with current services. An increase in complaints, falling attendance, increased vandalism, or other signals may lead to the design of new policies on manpower assignment, budget allocations, activity proposals, or advisory group establishment. Complaints can become the chief yardstick by which administrators determine when unsatisfied needs are so rigorous that modification or new policy is necessary. Administrators who depend upon complaints to signal the need for change do not develop policy logically, but simply wait for demands to become strong enough before action is taken. Some administrators delay decisions continually, seeking to assess who has the balance of power. If there is equilibrium, decisions will be put off until there is a clear cut dominance exhibited by one side or the other.

Standard operating procedures are employed by all administrators to avoid the stringent requirements of the logical model. Standard operating procedures designate which of the various criteria that might be pertinent are really to be examined in reaching a particular decision. Routinized practices simplify inputs, thereby making decisions less difficult. Administrators use certain methods in formulating policy. One is the inclination to believe whatever information is presented by subordinates, rather than to discover new sources of information by themselves. For example, in dealing with union representatives, the administrator may permit subordinates, who first approach him, to supply him with their opinions, rather than facts, and base his subsequent decisions on their biases. Able administrators will seek out their own sources, try to determine the facts, and make decisions for policy with as much knowledge of the situation as is possible to obtain.[4]

POLICY RATIONALE

All policy should be based upon well known standards of practice which are widely accepted within the field of recreational service. To the extent that an administrator can apply such standards of practice to the facts generated by systematic research concerning local conditions within which his department functions, policies will be developed which more nearly correspond to a logical model. Anticipatory policy making is of greater benefit to the department and the population being served than is defensive or "after-the-fact" policy. In the former instance, policy is derived from knowledge and facts regarding the operation of the department. In the latter instance, policy is developed because of some incident or problem which prompted the policy statement. Almost always, defensive policies result from poor planning, damage to things, or injuries and even death to people. Post implementation of policy invariably indicates lack of recognition of tension, unawareness of hazardous areas, facilities, or environments, inadequate supervision of personnel or patrons, incompetence, negligence, or any one, some, or all of these negative attributes. Policies that ensue because something went wrong is akin to locking the barn door after the horse has been stolen. The policy will not alter the facts, although there is the assumption that future deleterious conduct,

[4] Interview with Joseph Curtis, Commissioner of Recreational Service, New Rochelle, New York, November 18, 1975.

dangerous practices, or unsafe conditions will be avoided. Anticipatory policies, on the other hand, indicate positive qualities and concern on the part of the knowledgeable administrator. While few practitioners can claim to be seers, capable administrators try to foresee difficulties and act to prevent them.

There are certain pieces of routine information that should be placed at the administrator's disposal automatically. They should assist him in keeping alert to the daily operations of the system. Other managerial techniques can be employed to signal the administrator of potential problems before they escalate into full blown crises. Every skilled administrator realizes that certain personnel, safety, facility, record keeping, public relations, and activity policies have to be developed to forestall anticipated exigencies. It is not good to have to muddle through thorny issues regarding clientele, riotous priorities concerning patron use of facilities, concessions, or chain of command procedures. Far better to have instituted clear policy statements so that all concerned have the benefit of written guides when nettlesome situations arise or sensitive issues present themselves for response.

The following reasonable facsimiles of urban recreational service department policy statements are examples of the range and detail necessary for the extensive coverage and clarification for policy implementation.[5] Policies concerning administrative manuals, correspondence, park inspections, and public information are offered. Each policy statement is defined, described, and elaborated so that there is no mistake about to whom the policy applies or how it will be executed. Although these policies were originally developed for big city departments, they are applicable to any department with appropriate modification required to satisfy local needs.

SUBJECT: *ADMINISTRATIVE DIRECTIVE HANDBOOK POLICY*

PURPOSE:

To facilitate the communication of policies and procedures affecting the operations of the Department of Recreational Service, and to keep this information in a manner for easy reference, as needed, an Administrative Directive Handbook will be kept in the following prescribed manner at each of the designated administrative locations.

The Administrative Directives will generally contain information relating to the purpose of the Directive, the procedure by which it is to be implemented and, if appropriate, reference to the authority for the directive will be indicated.

---

[5] Developed by Joseph Halper, Chief Deputy Director, Department of Recreational Service, Los Angeles County, California, 1978.

IMPLEMENTATION

1. *Subject Index*

To provide a convenient reference system the various areas of administration will be divided and assigned series numbers by subject as follows:

INDEX

100   Administration
200   Personnel
300   Public Information
400   Program
500   Public Regulations
600   Finance and Accounting
700   Equipment and Supplies
800   Maintenance

APPENDIX

2. *Filing Instructions*

Additions, changes and/or replacements or amplifications of Directives will be designated as Directive Amendments and will be assigned the same series number with an added decimal. For example:
Administrative Directive #101, Administrative Directive Handbook.
Administrative Directive #101.1, Administrative Directive Handbook as amended.

Each time an amendment is added to the Handbook, a notation is to be placed in the left hand margin next to the appropriate subsection as per the following example:
Delete or Add to SS-4, refer to Adm. Dir. #101.1.

When a directive deviates from the facts to a degree where it becomes advisable to reissue the information, the existing directive on that subject will be listed as superseded and removed from the book. The new Directive will be assigned the number of the former Directive. Directives of this nature will be designated as Superseding Directives.

All directive amendments and new directives are to be listed in the Administrative Directive Handbook Index in the appropriate category. It will be the responsibility of the office to which the Handbook is assigned to update the index until such time as an updated Index is issued.

In situations where Departmental forms are referred to in Directives, such forms will be placed in the Appendix section of the Handbook. These forms will be identified in the Directive by the name to which they are commonly referred, and will also carry an identifying number for easy reference.

3. *Distribution of Administrative Directives*

Each appropriate administrative location will be supplied with a numbered ring binder with ten labelled dividers. This binder will be kept in the administrative office where it can easily be referred to by all staff members needing or desiring the information contained therein.

The following administrative locations will maintain and keep updated an Administrative Directive Handbook:
    Office of the Superintendent
    Office of the Deputy Superintendent
    Office of the Director of Park Facilities and Planning
    Office of the Director of Programs and Services
    Office of the Director of Administrative Services
    Office of Public Information

Field Offices—Parks, Pools and Golf Courses

Supervisors of Recreational Programs

Art Workshop
Athletics
Camping
Special Recreational Services
Performing Arts
Community Services

Extra copies of the Handbook will be available at the Administrative Office for specific desks, as required, and for replacements as needed.

Extra copies of Administrative Directives will be supplied to each administrative location, so that they may be distributed to key staff members within the organization, when appropriate, for their information. In this manner, the staff of the Department would be kept informed of the policies and procedures as they are developed. When appropriate, copies of the Administrative Directive should be posted on a bulletin board for a two week period.

4. *Effective Period of Directives*

All instructions contained in a Directive are to be carried out as specified until such time as a written Directive is issued which supersedes or countermands the instructions given. If a staff member or supervisor takes exception to any of the regulations or procedures set forth in a Directive, or if a Directive needs clarification, this information should be submitted through the normal chain of responsibility with appropriate comments at each level. The fact that exception has been taken to information in a Directive, or that a Directive is in the process of revision, does not in any way alleviate the responsibility of the staff members to follow the Directive until such time as it is changed.

Superintendent

SUBJECT: *CORRESPONDENCE POLICY*

PURPOSE:

To establish a uniform procedure for the handling of correspondence by members of the Department of Recreational Service. To identify issues in the Department, coordinate responses and monitor the time element in resolving issues. To keep personnel in key administrative positions advised of the issues and their major content.

1. *Stationery*

   Stationery for all divisions and facilities of the Department of Recreational Service shall be uniform. The official letterheads will be used by all those individuals whose major correspondence consists of individually typed letters, and will carry their name, title, and telephone number on the right side, the name of the mayor on the left.

   In order to obtain properly imprinted stationery, the section head should contact the Recreational Service Office of Public Information and request an amount necessary for one year's correspondence. Reorders on stationery will be handled in the same manner.

   When the department sends out a mailing for applications and/or checks to be returned for permits, camp registration, programs, etc., the return envelope should be marked or color coded so that it will go to the appropriate unit.

2. *Incoming Correspondence*

   All mail received by the Department of Recreational Service is considered to be departmental and will be processed by the Central Mail System, with the exception of:
   a. mail marked personal or confidential
   b. permit requests
   c. program registrations
   d. camp registrations
   e. athletic registrations
   f. newspapers and periodicals
   g. bills
   h. requests for department literature

   Material or information of particular interest to the Superintendent will be routed to him with a slip indicating "Reply Requested" or "No Reply Requested." Correspondence to the Superintendent concerning programs will be routed to the Director of Programs and Services for handling; on facilities to the Director of Operations; on Nature Study to the Naturalist, on photo requests or brochures to the Office of Public Information, etc.

   All correspondence must be answered by the person handling the matter within 72 hours. If there will be a delay involved in gathering information on which to base a reply, an acknowledgment must be sent within 72 hours advising that the matter is under investigation and a reply will be sent as quickly as possible. A carbon

4

copy of the reply must be returned to the Central Mail System so the issue may be closed out.

Correspondence from the mayor, Legislators, or elected officials to the Superintendent must be handled by the unit head within 24 hours. A copy of the correspondence and a draft of the reply prepared for the Superintendent's signature must be forwarded to the Superintendent within the time allotted. If this cannot be done for any reason, the Superintendent must be advised.

On drafts of letters prepared for the Superintendent's signature, the correspondence must be on the Superintendent's letterhead, and the Superintendent's initials, the drafter's initials, and the transcriber's initials must be on the carbon copies of the correspondence. For example, if the Deputy is replying for the Superintendent, the initials on the carbon would be GH/MLN/RS.

Outgoing Correspondence

A carbon copy of all important mail going out of each section should be sent to the Superintendent in order to keep him informed of the issues and problems. When a unit head sends an incoming piece of correspondence to the Field for action, a carbon of the reply plus the original letter must be returned to the Central Mail System.

The originator of the correspondence should send a carbon copy to those individuals in the organization who need to be apprised of that particular issue.

4. *Advisement*

To keep the Superintendent and Deputy Superintendent advised, a copy of the Correspondence Log pages for the week must be sent to each on Friday afternoon.

Superintendent

SUBJECT: *PUBLIC INFORMATION POLICY*

PURPOSE:

To establish a procedure for the handling of public information and press contacts by members of the City Department of Recreational Service.

1. *Initiation of Public Information Requests*

All publicity on Recreational Service programs, functions, and facilities must emanate from the Public Information Officer, and any contacts with media people (press, radio, TV) must be cleared through the Public Information Officer before any action may be taken.

Requests for public information support on recreational programs and facility operations must be submitted in writing to the Public Information Officer with as much information as possible provided to make a comprehensive release. The information may be typed, handwritten, or be contained in a flyer or informational letter to participating agencies. This must be supplied a minimum of 2 weeks prior to the event.

In the case of the opening or closing of a seasonal facility, a telephone call to the Public Information Office 1 week ahead will suffice.

2. *Changes in Program*

If any changes in the program schedule or plans which affect public information requirements, this information is to be reported by telephone to the Public Information Officer at the earliest possible time.

3. *Press Contacts*

Requests for information from the various media sources (i.e., magazines and newspapers, radio and television) are to be referred to the Public Information Officer. Recreational and field personnel of his organization are not authorized to give statements to the press regarding the department's policies or activities without prior consultation with the Public Information Officer.

However, inquiries concerning activity schedules or information regarding program content *already made public in releases* or by flyers or posters should be shared with the press on request.

All personnel who are contacted for radio interviews or programs, or for other speaking engagements, may accept the invitations, but must notify the Public Information Officer of the details of these invitations at the earliest possible time prior to the presentation date to allow for necessary coordination.

4. *Emergency Incidents*

In the event that an incident occurs in any facility or program which comes to the attention of the press where there are implications which might have an effect on the department, the staff member involved will call the unit head. In the event that this individual is not reachable, the next person in the chain of command is to be advised. It will be the responsibility of the unit head to make the determination as to the need of advising the department's Public Information Officer.

The Public Information Officer will be responsible for giving the necessary guidance to the individual as to what statements may be made to the press.

In any emergency event where members of the press corps are present, the Public Information Officer is to be notified immediately of the circumstances of the occurrence and, if possible, what press representatives were present. The office telephone number of the Public Information Officer is _____ and the home telephone _____.

5. *Results of Events*

Athletic scores, as well as the name of champions of various events, may be called in to the appropriate news media by participating personnel of this organization, providing the event in question has received the appropriate approval for public information support outlined in 1, and the event itself has been previously announced by the Public Information Office.

6. *Booklets, Signs, Posters and Flyers*

Arrangements for all booklets, signs, posters and flyers to be reproduced will be made by the Public Information Office.

All such requests shall contain—date required, number of copies required, and the distribution plan for the printed materials.

Superintendent

SUBJECT: *PARK INSPECTIONS POLICY*

PURPOSE

To effect a uniform inspection system to bring about the highest standards of park operation through continual upgrading by evaluation.

IMPLEMENTATION

1. *RESPONSIBILITY FOR INSPECTIONS*

   It is the responsibility of all levels of administration to conduct regular inspections to ascertain the level of efficiency of this organization, and its ability to perform its assigned mission. The Regional Supervisor, Technical Service Supervisor, Park Director, facility manager, leader-in-charge, or foreman will conduct regular field inspections as part of the routine supervisory responsibilities and will make corrections as required. All those making inspections who are not personnel indigenous to a park administration will be accompanied by the Park Director or his designee, whenever possible. The Regional Supervisor will be responsible for the organization of formal inspections and for overseeing the establishment of routine inspection procedures.

   Follow-up inspections are to be made by the Regional Supervisor approximately 20 days after the formal inspection to determine the progress made by the particular park administration in correcting discrepancies noted in the formal report.

   Informal inspections may be made by any supervisory level in either the Recreational or Parks Section without notice. When inspections of this nature are being conducted, the inspecting official should report to the Park Director's office and inform him of his presence and be accompanied on the tour of inspection by the Park Director or an appropriate designee, if practical.

   At the conclusion of informal inspections, a memorandum should be forwarded to the Park Director concerned, with copies to the Superintendent of Recreational Service and the Superintendent of Parks, listing any discrepancies or exemplary items noted. It is important that suggestions be given, through constructive criticism, as to how any noted discrepancies should be corrected.

The Superintendent's copy of this memorandum will be circulated, by the Superintendent, to his staff members within the respective Section on a need-to-know basis.

2. *QUARTERLY INSPECTIONS*

A formal inspection will be conducted at each active recreational area and special facility within the city parks system at least once each quarter. The Regional Supervisor will be responsible for setting up the schedule of this inspection. Prior notification is to be given to the Park Director, in writing, at least ten days in advance of the inspection. Each quarterly inspection will place special emphasis on a particular phase of a park's operation. Primary stress will be given to special selected areas to be designated by the Superintendent of Recreational Service at the beginning of the inspection quarter. These may include:

Compliance with specified Administrative Directives
Park maintenance and cleanliness
Recreational programming
Cash flow and security
Accountability and maintenance of equipment, supplies, etc.

An inspection team will be assembled by the responsible Regional Supervisor. This team should include representatives of the recreational, maintenance, and administrative units. The Regional Supervisor shall act as the inspection team leader and is responsible for assembling the team, team briefings, team de-briefings, and developing the necessary reports.

3. *INSPECTION PROCEDURES*

If at all possible and without interfering with the public service, parks should be inspected during the peak days and hours of operation. The inspector, or inspection team, will be accompanied by the Park Director, or his assistant, in case of his absence, during the course of the inspection.

Formal park inspections will be based on the General Park Inspection Guide. Under each sub-heading of the Inspection Guide an idea of the items to be checked under that heading has been provided. However, this should not be considered all inclusive.

During the course of the inspection, the inspector should note his comments, referring to the item on the checklist. When noting discrepancies, areas should be identified by name (such as athletic fields, tennis courts), light poles by number, first aid kits by location; vehicles by park serial number, etc.

The "Not Applicable" column in the Inspection Checklist is used when a facility or activity is not in operation because of the season, although this facility may be inspected for proper security, cleanliness, and storage of equipment.

4. *INSPECTION DE-BRIEFING*

A de-briefing session will be held immediately following the inspection at which time the Park Director and key members of his staff will meet with the inspection team. At that time the Park Director will submit copies of any work orders which have been processed prior to the date of the inspection which would indicate that appropriate action was taken by that level in regard to any unsatisfactory items that appear on the report. With this accomplished, the rating will then be adjusted to indicate that the unsatisfactory rating is not a reflection on the administration of the particular park.

5. *QUARTERLY INSPECTION REPORT*

A formal written report of the inspection is to be forwarded to the Park Director no later than one week after the inspection informing the Park Director of corrective action to be taken.

The report will consist of a memorandum stating the inspector's comments on any specific checklist items. In the case of a violation of an administrative directive, the memorandum should also include the directive number and sub-section. The cover memorandum is to be attached to the completed Inspection Guide Report.

If a discrepancy is a repeat from a previous quarterly inspection within the same calendar year, it is to be noted "Unsatisfactory", and indicated in the inspection report that it is a repeat deficiency.

Comments may be made on any checklist item regardless of the rating but "Unsatisfactory" and "Superior" ratings must be explained in the memorandum on the inspection report.

The following is the recommended standard format for the inspection report memorandum:

Third Quarter Inspection
Dink Park
August 3, 1978

Overall Rating   *Satisfactory*

I.   Entrance Area   *Superior*

    1. Entrance signs are well placed, legible, and facilitate the smooth flow of pedestrian and automobile traffic.

II. Safety and Emergency

    1. First Aid Equipment   *Unsatisfactory*
Band-Aids were not contained in the first-aid kit located at the field-house (*Repeat:* First Quarter Inspection, 2/16/78)

III. Equipment and Vehicles

    1. Storage Area   *Satisfactory*
The door to the storage area in the Administration Building was off its hinges and the bottom louvre was damaged. Athletic equipment is neatly arranged and maintained.

6. *PARK INSPECTION COMPLIANCE*

Replies to Park Inspection Reports must be returned to the Regional Supervisor no later than 7 days after the receipt of the inspection report, explaining corrective action taken. Responses to inspection discrepancies are to indicate what action was taken and the date completed. If completed action is not possible within the time period set forth by this directive, an estimated completion date is to be provided and the Regional Supervisor is to be promptly advised when the corrective action has been completed.

Submission of work orders, requisitions, and correspondence requesting action from another agency or section may be considered corrective action. The dates, work order numbers, etc. of these documents are to be indicated on the inspection reply. Verbal or written instructions to subordinate staff members in the park organization are not to be considered substantiating or corrective action. Completion of the tasks which are within the capabilities of the indigenous park staff will be the required remedy.

If the Park Director is in disagreement with an inspection discrepancy, a justification is to be submitted by memorandum, attached to the Inspection Report when returned. The subject of this memorandum is to be: "Request for Exception to Inspection Criteria." The specific item, or items, to which exception is being taken and the reason for the exception should be noted.

7. *"PARK OF THE QUARTER" AWARD*

Upon completion of all park inspections for a quarter, an Inspection Review Board will be convened by the Assistant Superintendent of Recreational Services. Members of this review board will consist of the Assistant to the Superintendent of Recreational Service for Program Development, the Section Administrative Officer, and appropriate supervisory personnel responsible for park maintenance of the Parks Maintenance Section as designated by the Superintendent of Parks.

All inspection reports and park replies will be reviewed to determine the "Park of the Quarter." This meeting is to be held prior to the last Friday of March, June, September, and December. The recommendation of the review board will be submitted to the Superintendent of Recreational Service for his action.

The determination of this award will be based on the following factors:

1. The ability of the park organization to perform its assigned mission.
2. The factors of size and complexity of facility will be considered.
3. The number of items inspected which met the standards of the Division of Recreational Service and Parks.
4. The efforts made by the indigenous park staff to correct the discrepancies prior to inspection.
5. The promptness and vigor with which the discrepancies pointed out, upon inspection, were corrected.

6. The general morale of the staff—by absentee records or other criteria.
7. The level of preparation of the staff in relationship to their assigned tasks.
8. The knowledge of the general park and recreational operations.
9. The public image presented by both the personnel and the facilities.
10. The efficiency of the administrative organization in maintaining report deadlines and records.
11. The efficiency in the utilization of manpower assigned.

If deemed desirable, more than one park may be nominated. Majority and minority reports may be filed. An appropriate banner will be awarded to the Park Director of the park facility receiving the commendation. This banner is to be flown on the flagstaff during the quarter following the inspection for which the award was made.

At the next Superintendent's Staff Meeting following the Inspection Review Board, the Superintendent will review all "Unsatisfactory" and "Superior" ratings with the entire staff and relate general areas of weakness and strength of the park operation. The "Park of the Quarter" award will be presented at this meeting.

Superintendent

Selected References

Anderson, J.: *Public Policy-Making* (New York: Praeger Pubs.), 1975.
Awerback, S. and W. A. Wallace: *Policy Evaluation for Community Development: Decision Tools for Local Government* (New York: Praeger Pubs.), 1976.
Baker, R. F., and others: *Public Policy Development: Linking the Technical and Political Processes* (New York: John Wiley & Sons, Inc.), 1975.
Frederickson, G. and C. Wise, Eds.: *Public Administration and Public Policy* (Lexington, Mass.: Lexington Books), 1977.
Houston, S. R., Ed.: *Judgement Analysis: Tools for Decision Makers* (New York: MSS information Corp.), 1975.
Schellenberger, R. E. and G. Boseman: *Policy Formulation and Strategy Management* (New York: John Wiley & Sons, Inc.), 1977.
Simmons, R. H. and E. P. Dvorin: *Public Administration: Values, Policy and Change* (Port Washington, N.Y.: Alfred Publishing Co., Inc.), 1977.
Tropman, J. E., and others: *Strategic Perspectives on Social Policy* (New York: Pergamon Press), 1976.
Woll, P.: *Public Policy* (Englewood Cliffs, N.J.: Winthrop Publishing Co.), 1974.

PART II

EXTERNAL INFLUENCES ON ADMINISTRATION

CHAPTER 5

Recreational Service and the Public Schools

Technology has provided an amazing increase in leisure, which in turn has profoundly influenced many social institutions, primarily the public schools. With the rapid expansion of leisure, the public schools have found it necessary to provide recreational activities, which are now recognized as a basic human need, and to adapt pedagogy, curriculum, and facilities to accommodate this new function.

Although private schools had initiated some aspects of recreational activity as early as 1821, no trend toward public facilities was discernible until 1885. By 1900, municipal recreational authorities were being established. But school systems showed the way in 1901 when the Boston School Committee was authorized to administer and operate the playgrounds of that city. In 1903, Chicago opened the most elaborate municipal park of the day. In the same year, the first Public School Athletic League was founded in New York City under the direction of Luther Halsey Gulick. In 1907, Rochester, New York, was the first community to use a school building for a community center. In 1908, the local government of Gary, Indiana, made legal provision for the public utilization of school buildings for recreational purposes. Significantly, the National Education Association approved the use of school buildings and grounds for recreational functions in 1911. In 1918, the NEA created its famous Commission on Reorganization of Secondary Education which proclaimed the now classic Seven Cardinal Principles of Secondary Education. These principles were directly concerned with the personal and social competencies of life in general. Among the principles was the worthy use of leisure. This one principle had vastly greater implication for the expanding field of recreational service than did the others, and its general acceptance tended to give status to school-centered recreational services. In part, the report stated:

> Education should equip the individual to secure from his leisure the re-creation of body, mind, and spirit, and the enrichment and enlargement of his personality. This objective calls for the ability to utilize the common means of enjoyment, such as music, art, literature, drama, and social intercourse, together with the fostering in each individual of one or more special avocational interests. Heretofore the high school has given little conscious attention to this objective. It has so exclusively sought intellectual discipline that it has seldom treated literature, art, and music so as to evoke right emotional response and produce positive enjoyment. Its presentation of science should aim, in part, to arouse a genuine appreciation of nature.

> The school has failed also to organize and direct the social activities of young people as it should. One of the surest ways in which to prepare pupils worthily to utilize leisure in adult life is by guiding and directing their use of leisure in youth. The school should, therefore, see that adequate recreation is provided both within the school and by proper agencies in the community.[1]

ROLE OF THE SCHOOL

What is the role of the school in our present society? What should the public schools attempt to accomplish? What assignments are not properly delegated to the school? What is the position of the school in relation to the provision of recreational service?

Because the school is concerned with preparing students for all aspects of modern living, there are few areas of community living in which the school has not been active or in which it has denied requested assistance. The school is no longer a triangular arrangement of teacher, pupil, and curriculum. The proliferation of school-centered activities ranges far beyond this simple concept. Schools have assumed responsibilities in civil defense, fire prevention, traffic control, driver safety education, and fund raising. Social modification has caused an ever-increasing acceptance by the schools of community welfare activities. Whether the schools should attempt to meet these diverse community needs or restrict themselves, as some critics suggest, to the intellectual development of their pupils can no longer be resolved in a simplistic manner. Since the schools have accepted some responsibility for community recreational service in the guise of adult education, school camping, extracurricular, and intra- and extra-mural sports programs, it would mean a major overhaul of the public school function in many communities. In

---

[1] "Cardinal Principles of Secondary Education," *Report of the Commission on the Reorganization of Secondary Education of the National Education Association* (Washington, D.C.: Department of the Interior, Bureau of Education Bulletin No. 35, 1918), p. 15.

a few instances, the public school's provision of services of a recreational nature may be the only public offering of this type. To remove the one agency sponsoring such activity would really mean a downgrading of normal living within a community.

Social institutions other than the school also make valuable contributions to the educational function. The assignment of a particular task to the school or to another agency should rest on the educational effectiveness that such an experience would have for the recipient.

Account must be made of many factors operating interdependently which concern the pupil's ability to learn; but the school is in no position to carry the burden of public welfare. The school should undertake only those responsibilities of non-educational character directly related to the satisfaction of the basic educational requirements. If other social instrumentalities are established to fulfill these functions, the school has no reason to arrogate such tasks to itself. On the other hand, when the performance of its prime assignment is not impaired, the school should do all in its power to assist other social institutions in adequately fulfilling their respective community responsibilities.

When the schools undertake the community recreational service function as the single public agency responsible for offering such services, they are not under the jurisdiction of local municipal authorities but perform, as in all other school functions, under the legal authority of the school board, and the local school system is a creature of the state, not subject to municipal governance.

Recognition of Recreational Experience as Educational

The awareness that extracurricular activity is an effective educational force is indicative of a change that has come about in the basic philosophy of educational practice. Interest and voluntary participation are now recognized as fundamental concomitants of learning. Broadly interpreted, education may be viewed as encompassing recreational pursuits. Changes in educational concepts and in school practice in relation to leisure needs indicate an increasing trend for the school to accept some responsibility for recreational service. The educational philosopher, Philip Phenix, views recreational experience and education as inseparable and indicates some of the reasons the school should be more receptive to educating students for leisure. Phenix asserts that:

> . . . since recreation is a major preoccupation of the great majority of people, the nature of leisure-time activities profoundly affects the whole tone of cultural life.

> Every person needs to be prepared not only for an occupation and for assuming the responsibilities of participation in civic life, but also for using his leisure time well. Hence, recreation is a proper educational con-

cern, and the nurture of recreational capacities is a part of the teaching task.[2]

Additionally, Richard Kraus reinforces this concept of the relationship between recreational experience and education by taking the position that:

> . . . both recreation and education are concerned with many of the same kinds of experiences and subject areas, and seek to accomplish similar outcomes. If one accepts that it is the task of education to develop the essential competencies needed for effective citizenship, economic independence, and family adjustment, then one must recognize the values of group living and the inculcation of desirable values and ways of behaving that come from constructive, satisfying recreation experiences.[3]

INFLUENCE OF LEISURE ON CURRICULA

The suggestion that recreational service in some of its manifestations is part of education has justified the modification of public school curricula to include many new subjects of instruction.[4] It has also brought about a change in emphasis in subjects that traditionally had been taught either because of their supposed cultural and disciplinary values or as preparation for a vocation. The modern public school curriculum provides opportunities for appreciation, participation, and creative experience in music, art, dance, drama, and crafts. Special interest clubs dealing with science, mathematics, language arts, and other so-called hard-core subjects also are included in this category because of their recreational implications.

It is no longer rare to find a rocket club developing from work in physics or chemistry, mock political conventions growing out of study in civics and the social sciences, the fascinating hobby of grinding optical glass for the fabrication of a telescope from studying astronomy in general science, or the study of foreign customs and habits generated by the student's introduction to a foreign language. In every curricular subject there exists the possibility of students becoming interested and engrossed in avocational and purely recreational experiences which are carried on during leisure. Because of intense personal desire and interest, the student may reap greater benefit from participating in a school-implemented hobby or recreational activity than he ever could have in the formalized setting of the classroom.

[2] Philip H. Phenix, *Education and the Common Good: A Moral Philosophy of the Curriculum* (New York: Harper & Row, Publishers, Inc., 1961), pp. 108–109.
[3] Richard G. Kraus, *Recreation and the Schools* (New York: The Macmillan Company, 1964), p. 62.
[4] Richard G. Kraus, *Recreation Today Program Planning and Leadership*, 2nd ed. (Santa Monica, Calif.: Goodyear Publishing Company, Inc., 1977), p. 9.

Not many years ago extracurricular activities were ignored in the schools. Later they were condoned, but the school accepted no responsibility for their guidance and direction. Today the schools organize extracurricular activities in nearly every area of the curriculum, particularly in areas of recreational interest and motivation, and they assume direct responsibility for leadership in these activities. School administrators take pride in having all or almost all pupils included in these experiences.

COMMUNITY RECREATIONAL USE OF SCHOOL PLANTS

Since Colonial days schools constructed at public expense have been considered as convenient and proper places to hold public gatherings for the discussion of public affairs. In New England the schools were places for religious worship, town meetings, social activities, and intellectual stimulation of various kinds. As other facilities for public meetings became available (churches, lodge halls, city halls), the dependence on the school as a center of community life waned; but in the late years of the past century and the early decades of the twentieth century, a growing interest in recreational experience and education once more turned the attention of the public toward the school as an obvious, possible neighborhood center.

The first state law providing for community use of school buildings was passed in Indiana in 1859, but the movement for wider use of schools received its first great impetus in 1907, when the Rochester Board of Education appropriated approximately 5 thousand dollars to open several schools as civic centers. The attention of other large cities was attracted to this innovation. Legislation followed in a number of states which, in effect, declared that the school was a civic center and which authorized, but rarely required, boards of education to permit the use of school buildings for community gatherings for civic, political, educational, recreational, and sometimes religious purposes. Almost all states now have laws recognizing the principle that schools should be available for wider community use.

Most of the legislation providing for wider use of schools goes only so far as to permit agencies other than the school board itself to make use of schools. In a few states, notably California, Massachusetts, Minnesota, Missouri, Illinois, New York, New Jersey, Ohio, Oklahoma, Utah, Wisconsin, and the District of Columbia, the law authorizes school boards to conduct school community centers and to charge the cost to the school funds. A number of school districts render extensive service. However, most laws treat recreational activity as an auxiliary function, as is implied in the requirement that the recreational use must not interfere with "regular school purposes." It is as if to say that education cannot comprehend the values that participation in recreational pursuits offers to the individual. Every intelligent assumption cries out that recreational experiences are as educational, if not more so, in developing individual skills, capacities, knowledge, and interests as are the formally constituted class sessions.

Nevertheless, examples of legislative inability to understand the mutuality of recreational experience and education may be understood better in terms of a state law passed by Minnesota which provided that "The facilities of any school district, operating a recreational program under provisions of this act, shall be used primarily for the purposes of conducting the regular school curriculum and related activities, and the use of the school facilities for recreational purposes authorized by this act shall be secondary."[5] It is plain that it was not the aim of the legislature to interpret recreational service as an integral part of education, but merely to "permit the use of school facilities."

The same distinction between recreational experience and education is contained in the California Civic Center Act of 1917. This Act provides that every school shall be a civic center where citizens of the school district "may engage in supervised recreational activities . . . provided, that such occupancy of said public school-house and grounds for said meetings shall in no wise interfere with such use and occupancy of said public school-house and grounds as is now or hereafter may be required for purposes of said public schools of the State of California."[6] General participation of the citizenry in supervised recreational activities was not intended as one of the purposes of the public schools but as an appendage, as it were, to regular work. But the participation of the regularly enrolled pupils within the school in supervised recreational activities continued to be within the purposes of the school.

In 1958, however, the State Superintendent of Public Instruction in California declared: "The schools of California stand ready to assume their responsibilities for recreation. . . . We have a responsibility to the citizens of this state and to our future citizens for developing recreational programs and facilities which will serve our growing society."[7] In 1960, acting in concerted effort with ". . . hundred of leaders from many fields and levels of responsibility . . .,"[6] The California Association for Health, Physical Education, and Recreation and the California State Department of Education issued an important document concerning the need for schools to undertake a more active part in administering recreational services for all people. This is perhaps the most significant statement of the aims and objectives of the school in meeting the growing leisure needs of people and of the belief that school recreational service is an integral part of education. This declaration calls for the institution of recreational service as a direct assignment of schools in fulfilling their

---

[5] Minnesota *Statutes* (1937), No. 672, Ch. 23.
[6] California *School Code* (1917), Nos. 16551–16565, Ch. V.
[7] Roy E. Simpson, "California Schools Look At the Problem of Leisure," *California Schools,* XXIX, January, 1958.

educational commitment. Here is displayed the understanding that recreational experience serves the purposes of education and should thus be a primary, rather than a secondary, consideration of the schools.

The Wisconsin Enabling Act relating to the use of school buildings and grounds for civic purposes, although of a more liberal construction than most acts of a similar nature, gives evidence of the same concept of the special nature of recreational activity when conducted under school auspices. This Act provides that:

> Boards of School districts in cities of the first, second, and third class may on their own initiation and shall, upon petition as provided in subsection (2), establish and maintain for children and adult persons, in the school building and on the school grounds under the custody and management of such boards, evening schools, vacation schools, reading rooms, library stations, debating clubs, gymnasiums, public playgrounds, public baths, and similar activities and accommodations to be determined by such boards. . . ."[8]

A special tax levy to carry out the purposes set forth after their approval by the electorate is provided for elsewhere. In other words, recreational service is an appendage of the educational program to be authorized and financed separately. Under such considerations a major question arises: Why has the school system undertaken any provision for recreational service to the community at all? Since authorization for such services requires extra financial support and legislation, it would seem more appropriate for a municipal department to carry out the recreational service function. A majority of recreationists hold to this latter point of view. However, it seems feasible to point out that the municipal department simply cannot cope with increasing populations and other environmental problems alone; other social institutions may be rallied to assist in a total community effort. If for no other reason, the school system should be considered as an intrinsic supplier of basic recreational service and as an augmenting force in the effort to mobilize the resources of the community in offering recreational services. There may be valid reasons for desiring a municipal recreational service department operating a system designed to deliver optimum recreational opportunities, but the schools should be integral to such a system, particularly since the school curriculum promotes the skills and knowledge necessary for life-long participation in all recreational pursuits.

ARGUMENTS FOR SCHOOL-OPERATED RECREATIONAL SERVICES

People advocating expansion of the function of public schools to include a large portion of the public responsibility for recreational service present many cogent reasons:

[8] Wisconsin, *Revised Statutes* (1959), c. 43, sec. 43–50.

1. The schools have many of the physical facilities required for recreational activities, such as playgrounds, athletic fields, auditoriums, gymnasiums, meeting rooms, shops, and music and art rooms. These facilities are usually idle during the times when a community recreational program would need them. With few exceptions, notably those in which schools are used for night and adult education programs or for vacation schools, the school buildings and grounds are unused more than one third of the year. On days when school is in session, they are utilized less than nine hours per day. It is difficult to think of any greater economic waste in the face of demonstrated community need. Ways must be devised to free the school facilities for full use.

2. Schools are distributed according to the same plan that would apply in locating community recreational centers. Every neighborhood has an elementary school, just as every neighborhood should have its recreational center. Every district has its middle or junior high school, just as every district should have a central recreational building. Every community (three or more districts) has its secondary or high school, just as every community should have a large regional recreational complex. The same considerations influencing the location of rural schools would apply in situating centers for recreational service for the rural population. School plants are typically situated to serve areas of dense population within the community and are set to provide easy accessibility with the least amount of hazard to those who utilize their premises.

3. The public schools have more regular contact with all children and with more of the total population than does any other public institution. Schools are organized to provide essential services to all children. There is an ever-widening area of service needed for other age groups which the school attempts to fulfill. If recreational service as a public function has any justification, it is as a universal opportunity for all. This goal can be achieved best by the total involvement of the public system of education in the community recreational service.

4. The aims, purposes, and techniques of public education are becoming indistinguishable from those of public recreational service. Educators have long realized that instruction cannot be divorced from practice nor from life. Similarly, recreational departments have increasingly coupled instruction, often incidentally and informally, with voluntary participation in recreational experiences.

5. The schools appear to have the potential leadership required in a recreational program. The many public school teachers and administrators (over 1,800,000) could become a tremendous leadership force for leisure as their programs are integrated with the recreational life of communities in which they work. The additional personnel required in a community recreational program would be less if it were attached to the present educational staff than if it were organized as an indepen-

dent system. Since recreational service must depend on the leadership of volunteers, students should be prepared to assume such leadership not only while in school, but also after completion of their schooling.

6. The tendency of public schools to enter the community recreational service field is perhaps of significance to rural districts. The incorporated city is a governmental device invented specifically for the purpose of organizing the local services of government. The rural areas still lack such a device except in the field of education, which is administered through a system of local school districts and school boards. These boards are often the only agency of government immediately in contact with local community needs. They also control, to a large extent, the publicly owned facilities that could be utilized in a rural recreational service program. Few agencies thus far have been created for local rural recreational service. It appears that as far as community recreational activities under public sponsorship are concerned, the district school offers the one instant hope for rural people.

The assumption of some responsibility for recreational service by public schools has not and never will be to the exclusion of other agencies. No single organization will ever be able to administer to all the people the varied recreational demands that can be placed upon it. The strategic position of the schools applies almost entirely to neighborhood and local district recreational activities. Regional, and to some extent, district services must continue to be rendered by other agencies.

ARGUMENTS AGAINST SCHOOL-OPERATED RECREATIONAL SERVICES

There are numerous questions about public recreational service being administered by a local school system. Several arguments carry considerable weight.

1. Education should cling to its own special task which is intellectual preparation. It should not be diverted from this assignment by being made responsible for conducting various activities of indirect intellectual value. The activity basis of curriculum organization is held by fundamentalists to be illogical and against the intended reason for establishing public schools. This orientation was characterized by R. M. Hutchins in the late 1930s and carried on in the latter half of the twentieth century by Arthur Bestor and the Council for Basic Education. This group stands by the "classics," by which is understood to mean the accumulated best thought and experience of the race through the ages as the basis of public school teaching. Any other emphasis, in which activities are utilized to enhance instruction, is wrong. Although this point of view has long been derided by contemporary educationists, it created no small controversy among educators. Fortunately, the early retardation of the trend toward broadening of the scope of public school

activities and taking on additional functions has been overcome, although not without opposition.

2. The public schools already have more to do than they can do well, and the addition of further responsibilities handicaps the schools in the performance of their work. Many schools still are conducted for short terms wholly inadequate for the needs of children. They are poorly housed, and teachers in many parts of the country are insufficiently compensated. These deficiencies should be remedied before additional burdens are placed on the system.

3. The adoption of the community recreational service function by the schools will give the recreational program the wrong emphasis. Recreational activities will be patterned after educational projects, classroom techniques will be used, and freedom of choice will be denied. The essential democracy of recreational activity will not be preserved, with the inevitable tendency toward regimentation of people in recreational pursuits. Recreational service will fare better if a special agency is established for its service that is unhampered by age-long educational traditions.

4. The use of schoolrooms, auditoriums, gymnasiums, and buildings for community recreational purposes during hours in which the schools are not ordinarily in session will render them less efficient for the regular teaching of school pupils. Equipment may be damaged and supplies will certainly be consumed, especially art and craft supplies, materials, and equipment, and shops. The use of the same equipment and supplies by different staffs in different programs is inefficient. Moreover, any extensive program will require alterations in school buildings causing major changes in school planning. It is questioned whether other structures cannot be more economically provided for the recreational program and whether they might not then be better adapted to the recreational function.

5. Coupling community recreational service with education in one agency will make it more difficult to secure funds for both programs. Both programs being admittedly inadequate, their problems are primarily problems of finance. Two agencies, each conducting its own program, can ordinarily obtain more finance than one agency performing two functions. Community recreational service, a function even at this time much weaker in public support than public education, will fare better if it is promoted by those whose singleness of purpose will make them more effective in establishing their status than if recreational service is grafted onto an established agency as a subordinate function. As an important social need, recreational service should be maintained as an identifiable function and not be a secondary mission of education.

6. School-operated community recreational service would tend to favor children and youth rather than the total population of the com-

munity. Recreational service is required at all hours of the day and evening. The schools could not serve the comprehensive needs of the community because they would be closed to recreational activity during the time school was in session.

7. Although many teachers are available for leadership within the recreational program, they are not specifically prepared for recreational service, which is an identifiable field of social service. Most teachers have not been oriented in the recreational philosophy and view programming as a series of formal instructional sessions. Teachers may not wish to be employed as recreational personnel after they have already completed their respective workdays. It is only during the summer months, or because of inadequate remuneration, that teachers "moonlight" in recreational programs.

8. Even if the schools assumed complete responsibility for purely local or neighborhood services, park administration and recreational facilities properly situated in parks (e.g., golf courses, picnic grounds, swimming pools, large athletic areas, incidental children's playgrounds, public beaches, camps, botanical or zoological gardens, or exhibits) would continue to be the function of agencies separate from the schools. The question is not, therefore, whether all recreational service should or may be administered by the public schools, but rather whether *some* recreational experiences, namely those centered in a neighborhood, should be so administered. Should the functions of public schools be extended, there would still be ample need for other public recreational agencies. In most cities public recreational service departments will continue to be needed to meet local playground and other neighborhood demands for many years to come.

CURRENT STATUS OF SCHOOL-CENTERED RECREATIONAL SERVICE

Notwithstanding pro and con arguments for public schools to assume responsibility for recreational service in the community, the problem of community recreational service is challenging the schools and the schools are meeting this challenge more and more. The extent to which they are doing so cannot be covered by any general statement relating to all schools, for the attention given to the matter varies from complete divorcement of schools from community recreational service in some districts to assumption of complete responsibility for providing facilities, organizing and promoting programs, and giving leadership to people in recreational activities in others.

Of the more than 3,600 public agencies that have been made responsible for the administration of community recreational service in America in 1978, less than 300 were boards of education or other school authorities, or approximately 10 percent. Although many of these agencies shared responsibility in given cities with other municipal agencies, the number cannot be interpreted as indicative of an increasing trend in the direction of school-centered community recreational service. Over the past 30 years, the proportion of school-operated community recreational service programs has declined in the number of publicly organized recreational programs. To be sure, the school-operated recreational service does not show signs of becoming the major administrative organization in this country. However, it is one arrangement whereby a large number of recreational programs are offered to people, and this is true in several major metropolitan areas of the nation.

Excluding classroom instruction in the leisure arts, extracurricular activities, and night school classes, what recreational services are schools rendering? An examination of school practice throughout the country shows that most schools render no additional recreational service, but an increasing number of schools are taking at least part of the responsibility. Among the instances where schools conduct recreational programs or permit utilization of their facilities for other non-school agency operations are:

1. Summer playgrounds on school areas wholly under the administration of the schools.
2. Summer playgrounds on school areas under the administration of other agencies.
3. Year-round recreational service by the school system under school board auspices.
4. Year-round recreational service in schools, but joint school and municipal administration or under non-school auspices.

Summer Playgrounds

Many school departments or boards of education open school grounds for summer recreational activity and employ personnel to supervise the recreational activities. Participation usually is not limited to regular pupils of a given school during the year, but is open to all. The supervisors are typically regular teachers employed at special rates of compensation for the summer period. In some cases the school may employ personnel who are not regularly employed by the board of education, such as college students or others with special skills in recreational activities. The general supervision and organization of programs are often assigned to members of the school system's department of physical education staff.

The summer program mainly consists of physical education activities with some simple forms of handicraft, music, and dramatics. Some attempt is made to involve adults and older children in the program, but activities chiefly cater to the needs of younger children. The facilities used are almost exclusively the outdoor play areas and, in many cases, access to buildings is not permitted or is restricted.

Numerous examples could be cited of individual schools that now permit the school grounds to be used throughout the summer for community recreational purposes and employ personnel to supervise the activities. Nevertheless, it should not be inferred that school grounds and buildings across the country are generally used for community recreational services or that the most efficient use is made of those that are operated during the summer. Thousands of schools do not attempt to answer their community's need for recreational facilities, and the schools remain closed, have no equipment or devices for recreational activities, lack adequate conveniences for the public's utilization of them, and, indeed, forbid such public use during the summer months when schools are not in session.

Summer Playgrounds under Non-School Agencies. It is not uncommon for recreational service departments to have the use of school grounds in the summer provided the school system itself does not operate its own program of recreational activities on the playgrounds. The cost of supplies and the payroll of summer employees are usually met from municipal appropriations. Some of the recreational service commissions and departments in American cities do not control facilities or areas of their own but depend on schools and public park departments. Most of these recreational agencies conduct all or most of their activities during the summer months. In a number of smaller communities the school playgrounds are operated by quasi-public bodies supported by the United Givers Fund or by private philanthropy with or without some public support. Often a project initiated under such sponsorship eventually leads to the establishment of a public department or to sponsorship by the schools. Quasi-public operation of community recreational service is almost a thing of the past, although some sections of the country may still rely on such agencies.

Full-Time Recreational Service by the School System

Although many school systems have made a significant start in the direction of providing their communities with recreational service, the number conducting year-round community recreational programs serving adults as well as children and offering an extensive and varied program is exceedingly small. Notable among these are New York, Los Angeles, Milwaukee, Newark, Albany, and Flint, Michigan, whose achievements are worthy of special study.

Milwaukee is known as the "City of the Lighted School Houses." Under its Extension Division, which is headed by the Assistant Superintendent of Schools (an executive of extensive and varied school and recreational service experience), the school department operates a system of year-round and summer playgrounds and indoor recreational centers in school buildings and on school grounds. The program is financed by a special district tax on the assessed valuation of real property, pursuant to the Wisconsin School Recreation Enabling Act which also stipulates that the school board may cooperate with any other municipal agency whose facilities may be utilized for recreational activity.

The activities in the "lighted school houses" include classes in applied arts, athletics, literary activities, music, dancing, dramatics, and a varied assortment of civic, patriotic, and social events. The indoor centers are open to school-age children after school hours to 6:30 p.m. and to others during the evening hours. Boy Scout troops and similar groups are accommodated during the evening hours by special permits from the principal. The activities on the outdoor playgrounds, both during the day and in the evening, include highly organized sports for youth and adults and special activities for older adults.

A distinctive feature of the Milwaukee program is that it is integrated closely with the regular school work and many of the directors of the evening program are also employed by the school during the day. Night school centers are under the general supervision of the day school principal or vice-principal, thus creating another tie with the general school program which minimizes administrative conflicts between the two programs.

Madison, Wisconsin, is another example of where a board of education controls the municipal recreational program. The program is administered through the Division of Recreation and is headed by the Director of Physical Education who also serves as the director of the community recreational program. Although Madison has the facilities for adequate operational service, these were not fully utilized to meet the needs of this growing community. Many of the school buildings and grounds had never been made available to the public during the times when most people have leisure. An almost strict adherence to the academic calendar prevented the use of the schools by the public during weekends, holidays, and other vacation periods. However, Madison, through its School Community Recreational Department, has improved its image and program opportunities.[9]

The Newark, New Jersey, system, similar to that of Milwaukee, is administered by a recreational department under the superintendent of schools and the board of education. It is not financed by a special tax, but its expense is incorporated in the regular school budget.

The board employs recreational workers who are given the title of teachers. They begin work at 3:15 p.m. when the schools close for the

[9] "Madison's Community-School Concept," *Parks and Recreation*, Vol. VI, No. 4 (April 1971), p. 49.

day. The schools literally are transformed into recreational centers where numerous recreational activities are conducted. During the summer months the school yards and playgrounds and the municipality's parks are also used by the same staff for recreational purposes. Each school is designated as a neighborhood recreational center and is so utilized. The persons who direct this program are selected from applicants whose professional preparation is comparable to that of school teachers and administrators. They are granted professional status, salary, and tenure accordingly.

Flint, Michigan, is another example of a community that utilizes its schools for recreational purposes under the auspices of the school board. Working in conjunction with the Mott Foundation and other agencies, each school becomes the center of recreational activity in the neighborhood.[10] Here the availability of supplementary private funds has been a great stimulus. The Mott Foundation has been the chief benefactor of Flint for many years, donating many millions of dollars.

By making fuller use of its public buildings, particularly school structures, many communities are being afforded the benefit of centrally situated centers and grounds which bring wider opportunity to the public for recreational experiences. Duplication of capital investment in buildings is avoided as are the more expensive acquisitions of land and specialized centers.

Los Angeles pioneered in providing school-offered community recreational services. In 1914, the school system of Los Angeles opened 20 playgrounds for use by elementary school children. Since then the schools have effectively coordinated their programs with the city and county recreational service systems through the Youth Services Section. This division provides a wide-ranging series of recreational opportunities for all people in more than 500 defined neighborhoods throughout Los Angeles. It is probably the most extensively based school-operated recreational system in the United States and has been responsible for some remarkable innovations in recreational program ideas and facilities.

Full-Time Recreational Service by a Non-School Agency

Where there is a well-established, separately financed, year-round local recreational service department, the question inevitably arises as to whether such a department shall be permitted to use the school grounds and buildings for its program. In some cities, the municipal department conducts year-round centers in the school buildings and on the school grounds, or the schools themselves have assumed the responsibility for the operation of year-round recreational centers. However,

---

[10] Frank Manley, "The Community-School Program in Flint, Michigan," in *Education for Leisure Conference Report,* 1957 (Washington, D.C.: American Association for Health, Physical Education, and Recreation, 1957), pp. 12–19.

school buildings that remain completely idle after school hours would, if utilized, be more than enough to provide every community in the United States with a well-placed center for recreational activities.

There are several splendid examples of municipal recreational centers in school buildings. For at least the past 30 years the Detroit Department of Recreational Service has been granted an annual permit to conduct community centers in over 80 school buildings. The Board of Education charges the city recreational agency for custodial and maintenance expenses, including breakage. The permits authorize the use of school playgrounds and athletic fields. The activities include athletics, gymnastics, music, art, handicraft, dance, concerts, motion pictures, lectures, literary clubs, nature study, and gardening. They are open to all on a free basis, but evening activities are primarily for adults or for those no longer enrolled in day schools. The program is conducted informally with self-direction and volunteer leadership.

The Detroit plan has much to commend it. Nevertheless, when a strong municipal recreational service department operates on school property it is only natural for the local board of education to refrain from offering direct recreational services to the public other than through classroom instruction and extracurricular activities for regularly enrolled pupils. The result is that the community recreational service is not regarded as an integral part of education, but as an appendage. It cannot be reiterated too often that education is not just preparation for life, it is an intrinsic part of life itself—a part of daily living. The two processes have much in common and should supplement one another with each being accepted as inherent in the other.

In New York City no single agency is wholly responsible for public recreational service. In a city of more than 7 million people, hundreds of public, quasi-public, and private agencies are involved in the provision of recreational opportunities. However, two major public agencies that have accepted the recreational service assignment are the Board of Education and the Recreational and Cultural Affairs Administration. These agencies have agreed to work in close cooperation. The Recreational and Cultural Affairs Administration, through the Park Department, develops and maintains new school playgrounds. The agreement provides that schools may use and control these playgrounds during school hours and the Recreational and Cultural Affairs Administration may use them for community recreational activities after school hours.

Portland, Oregon, also has achieved an excellent working agreement between the Board of Education and the Bureau of Recreational Service (a division of the Park Department). Each agency contributes to the overall provision of community recreational service with no duplication of effort. Skokie, Illinois, is another example of practical coordination and cooperation between municipal agencies and the schools. In this community, playgrounds are developed adjacent to schools by the municipal Recreational Service Department and the Board of Education plans the buildings in consultation with the Park District. Each system thus contributes efficiently and comprehensively to the work of the other.

When public recreational service departments use school facilities, they necessarily must be regarded as tenants and as such do not have the freedom in the control and use of facilities that make for efficient administration, particularly since the facilities they use also are used daily by the schools themselves. Experience has shown that the conflicts affecting innumerable details are almost intolerable to both agencies, and, as a result, operational freedom is handicapped and arrangements for use of the facilities are precarious to say the least. Much of this difficulty passes away when the schools themselves assume responsibility for the recreational program on their own properties.

Still another implication of possible far-reaching consequences is that this plan lays the burden of financial support wholly on the local district or city. Schools generally derive about half their support from state tax sources. If community recreational service, insofar as it may be a part of the school program, can share in such state support without detriment to other educational functions, recreational service may benefit greatly. This point of view deserves considerable attention, because state governments generally have arrogated to themselves many of the means of raising public revenues and left the cities with inadequate and impaired means of taxation.

Strategic Position of Schools in Rural Areas

Numerous rural schools, through the extraordinary vision and initiative of a principal, teacher, or district board, are making a contribution to the recreational life of their communities. The realization of possibilities inherent in the organization of rural recreational service around and through district schools, with the aid of the county department of education, was effectively demonstrated by St. Louis County, Minnesota, during the late 1930s. Under the direction of the Leisure Education Department of the County Board of Education, the most comprehensive rural leisure activities program in America was developed. The standards established by that program were a splendid pattern for the organization of rural recreational service, which might well be emulated by other rural counties. An outline of that program is given below. St. Louis County is situated in the northeastern part of Minnesota. The total population in 1937 was 205,000, but its population, exclusive of the cities in which there are independent school districts, was estimated to be 60,000. At that time, there were 28 rural school districts with 76 elementary schools. Today, there are 220,693 people residing in the county.

GENERAL OUTLINE[11]

LEISURE EDUCATION PROGRAM
ST. LOUIS COUNTY RURAL SCHOOLS

I. General Purposes

    The St. Louis County Idea—

        1. Putting knowledge into action through a "Work-Study-Play" educational plan of procedure.

        2. Self-help, self-teaching, self-motivating, self-support, and self-government as sound principles of a democratic rural leisure program which will stimulate the development of the rural individual and socially—for the general welfare of all.

II. General Outline of the Program

    The Leisure Education Program

      A. Social Center Work

          1. Adult Education

          2. Social Center Recreational Activities

          3. Special Feature Events

          4. Organization and Promotion Work

      B. Community and Countywide Rural Recreational Program

          1. Athletics

          2. Dramatics

          3. Music

          4. Arts and Crafts

          5. Social and Recreational Activities

      C. Special Feature Events

          1. Athletic Tournaments

          2. Winter Sports Meets and Frolics

          3. Picnics and Celebrations

          4. Holiday Programs and Celebrations

          5. Special Social Center Events

          6. Dramatic Programs

          7. Music Programs

          8. Arts and Crafts Demonstrations and Exhibits

          9. Garden Club Activities

        10. Civic Events

        11. Community Parties and Dances

        12. Novelty Events

      D. Organization and Promotion Work

          1. In-service Preparation of Workers and Volunteer Leaders

          2. Service Bureau Programs

          3. Organization and Promotion Services

          4. Groups Organized on a Countywide Basis

---

[11] Quoted by permission.

III. The Health and Physical Education Program of the Schools
   A. Grade School Physical Recreational Education
   B. High School Physical Recreational Education
   C. High School Intramural Athletics
   D. Interscholastic Athletics
   E. Grade and High School Special Feature Events

Unfortunately, the St. Louis County recreational service program has not completely withstood time and change. The present program of Recreational Services, provided by the Board of Education, St. Louis County Schools, has been focused on Adult Education rather than recreational services for all. The Community School Plan of Adult Education and Recreational Service is indicative of the direction in which this program is moving. There are organized classes in typing, farm shop, mathematics, home economics, survival preparedness, first aid, driver training, and other related subjects in most school buildings. These classes are held as evening sessions during the school year. The recreational activities are also evening sessions on a scheduled plan, with local volunteer leaders in charge of separate activities. The present program is based at the School-Community level, with the school principal and his teaching staff providing the necessary leadership, and the county staff of supervisors in the role of guidance and resource personnel. The program has been encouraged whenever a community, along with the school, showed an interest and a need for these activities.

Another rural county school district operating a program of recreational services for the people within its jurisdiction is that of Box Elder County School District in Utah.

1. The school district is a county unit whose boundaries are coterminus with Box Elder County, comprising an area of some 5,500 square miles.
2. The school district has a population of about 28,129 people and a student enrollment of about 8,000. The recreational program offers swimming, park activities, athletics, and organized games, camp-fire experiences, and crafts.
3. Four full-time recreational workers qualified to handle the above activities are employed during the summer months. These workers are employed as physical education teachers and athletic coaches during the school term.
4. Playgrounds and athletic fields provided by the school district and two swimming pools located in junior high schools are utilized within the recreational program.
5. Although an estimate of expenditures for maintenance and the operation of facilities cannot be approximated here, $6,000 for salaries is expended each summer.
6. The program has been in continuous operation since 1952 and works cooperatively with municipal recreational agencies.

Paul Woodring defined the thrust of contemporary education when he wrote:

> In a society of free men, the proper aim of education is to prepare the individual to make wise decisions. The educated man is one who can choose between good and bad, between truth and falsehood, between the beautiful and the ugly, between the worthwhile and the trivial. His education will enable him to make ethical decisions, decisions within the home and on the job. It will enable him to choose . . ."[12]

At a time when increasing leisure for all is being recorded, it is incumbent on the public system of education to undertake some responsibility for the preparation of the wise use of free time. Recreational activity must come to be considered an integral part of education. Although many schools have made a significant start in the direction of serving their communities in recreational service the number that can be said to conduct year-round community recreational programs serving adults as well as children and offering an extensive and varied program is exceedingly small. In the changes that have taken place in educational philosophy as well as in school practice in relation to leisure needs, there is noted a suggestion that public recreational service in some of its manifestations is a part of education and that the schools of the future may become one of the agencies through which a delivery system of community recreational services may be administered.

Selected References

Berridge, R. I.: *The Community Education Handbook* (Midland, Mi.: Pendell Publishing Co.), 1974.

Byrne, R. and E. Powell: *Strengthening School-Community Relations* (Reston, Va.: National Association of Secondary School Principals), 1976.

Kindred, L. W., and others: *The School and Community Relations* (Englewood Cliffs, N.J.: Prentice-Hall, Inc.), 1976.

Ringers, J. Jr.: *Community Schools and Interagency Programs* (Midland, Mi.: Pendell Publishing Company), 1976.

[12] From *A Fourth of a Nation* by Paul Woodring, p. 111. Copyright © 1957 by McGraw-Hill Book Company. Used with permission of McGraw-Hill Book Company.

CHAPTER **6**

Rural Structure and Organized Recreational Services

Generally speaking, the terms urban and rural are construed as opposites. Urban envisions apartment buildings, dense populations, traffic congestion, incessant noise, busy ports, railroad terminals, airports, and smog-filled skies. Rural, on the other hand, connotes open spaces, pastoral views, rich brown earth, woods, fields, streams, quiet, and few people. These ideas applied to rural-urban contrasts when striking differences actually existed between city and country. Realistically, however, these portraits are throwbacks to another era. There is no longer the sharp distinction between city streets and the pristine fastness of the country. Instead, urban areas often blend gradually into rural areas; no line of demarcation delineates these areas. Today, with wide-spread mobility, owing to the prevalence of private automobiles and excellent interstate and intrastate highway networks, as well as the incidence of privately owned means of communication such as television, radio, telephone, and other devices, rural populations enjoy the same amenities, material goods, and services that formerly characterized the city dweller.

In many sections of the United States there are many exurbanites. These individuals do not depend upon farming for their livelihood. They have cut their ties to the city and now reside in the exurban fringe around, but outside of, the city, or even further into the hinterlands. They are city expatriates who were never agriculturally employed but desired an atmosphere that was distinct from the city. Yet, these people brought city ways, needs, and material expectations with them when they moved into the rural environment. Some of these persons live in towns too small to be categorized as urban. Many others reside in single houses widely scattered over the countryside. Their requirements have profoundly affected the rural way of life so that it is no longer obviously different from city life.

RURAL-URBAN CONTRAST

Megalopolis is modifying the topographic and artificially created characteristics that have traditionally separated country and city since the inception of community life. A valid distinction exists between rural and urban life in some parts of the United States even today, particularly in the West, northern New England, the rural South, and in the region known as "Appalachia" where city and country continue to be separated in space, time, and characteristics. People in these regions work and participate in leisure experiences within a segregated area far removed from metropolitan centers which continue to attract more immigrants, traffic, congestion, and environmental dislocation. But the rural regions of the country are no longer a reflection of the mainstream of American life and they will slowly disappear in the metropolitan growth of the future. Except for recreational use during a specific portion of the year, the rural areas are little more than fixtures in people's imagination.

The rural fastness of the northeast is kept alive as a winter sports mecca for the ski enthusiast, the snowmobiler, or the transient tourist who follows the color changes of leaves in autumn. Parts of the Rockies and High Sierras also permit such use, particularly Aspen and Steamboat Springs, Colorado, and Squaw Valley, California. The same may be said of other rural areas in the spring, summer, or fall. Depending on their climate, geographic location, topography, natural resources, or other phenomena that serve as attractions to vacationers, tourists, naturalists, hikers, and campers, they serve for a few months during any given year. In fact, this is what keeps them viable. Were it not for their recreational usefulness, they would soon wither into the decay that characterizes old Western mining towns, far northern lumber towns, or old New England mill towns.

The trend toward residence in the metropolitan region, if not precisely in the center city, has been coupled with a high rate of internal migration. This is especially true of the westward movement, a great increase of white-collar positions, a decrease in trade or blue-collar workers, and leading the migration to cities are agricultural workers of all kinds. The great flood of population has been to metropolitan centers with the overflow moving into the urban fringe and suburbia. Most people reside in urban centers today. The Bureau of the Census is responsible for counting and classifying the United States population. Its bases for distinguishing urban from rural areas are of exceeding interest. The distinctions made by the Bureau have to be applied periodically because decennial reports must be made in terms of the number of urban, as opposed to rural, residents in various parts of the country. According to the Census Bureau's 1970 definition, the urban population comprises all persons living in:

1. places of 2,500 inhabitants or more incorporated as cities, boroughs, villages, and towns (except towns in New England, New York, and Wisconsin).
2. the densely settled urban fringe, whether incorporated or unincorporated, of urbanized areas.
3. towns in New England and townships in New Jersey and Pennsylvania that contain no incorporated municipalities as subdivisions and have either 25,000 inhabitants or more, or a population of 2,500 to 25,000 and a density of 1,500 persons or more per square mile.
4. counties in states other than the New England states, New Jersey, and Pennsylvania that have no incorporated municipalities within their borders and have a density of 1,500 persons per square mile.
5. unincorporated places of 2,500 inhabitants or more.

According to the Bureau of the Census the 1970 urban population consisted of: (1) the 100,000,000 inhabitants of the 4,000 incorporated places of 2,500 population or more; (2) the 5,000,000 inhabitants of the 600 unincorporated places of 2,500 population or more; (3) the 3,000,000 inhabitants of the 125 urban towns and townships and one urban county; and (4) the 10,000,000 persons living in urban-fringe areas outside urban centers.

The Census Bureau identifies urban and rural regions by densities and numbers of people. However, the definition relies on the location of places and areas which indicates urbanization or rurality. Thus it may be seen that the ancient contrasts between rural and urban places, rural and urban life styles, are being reduced or eliminated to a negligible number. The central and strip city continues to be the residence of the future. Some planners actually envision total population beyond the year 2,000 to reside in megalopolitan strips along all coasts and beside the great river systems of the country.[1] Should this concept become reality there will be no rural America in years to come.

The major characteristic of rural areas is that they are beyond the city. In rural areas the style of life progresses at a slower pace, communication is more difficult, occupational interests are based on the locale and family, the rate of interaction is less, and legal restrictions are decreased. These conditions are instrumental for particularism, emotional responsiveness (romantic, rather than logical ideas), provincialism, parochialism, and conformity to custom to be normal behavioral patterns. The ecological makeup under which rural people live conduces to produce differences in caliber between metropolitan and rural dwellers.

[1] Edmund K. Faltermayer, *Redoing America* (New York: Harper & Row, Publishers, Inc., 1968), pp. 147–151.

However, rural society has been altered in the past few decades. Such alteration is cumulative and has been a result of modern technology, communications, mobility, transportation, and education. This technological impact on rural life has caused population movement from rural to urban areas, dislocated some of the traditional views held by rural people, and required a distinct change in organizational patterns in the rural life style. Alterations in rural society may be observed from:

1. Increased capability of production that has caused a decrease in the number of farmers needed to work on farms.
2. A rise in connection of the rural and non-rural sectors in American life.
3. Increased specialization with accompanying heavy capital investment requires fewer farmers.
4. Mass communications and mobility are reducing value differences between rural and urban people.
5. An increasing cosmopolitanism is noticed as a result of increasingly sophisticated education, communication, transportation, and re-orientation of topical groups.
6. A centristic tendency in public affairs in the rural sector that has heretofore resisted governmental decision making.
7. An apparent withering of primary relationships for secondary linkage in terms of interest groups, government, recreational groups, and commercial enterprises.

All these features have a significant influence on the philosophy and realignment of value judgments, outlooks, and traditional ways of doing things which have effectively characterized rural people. With these modifications in life style has appeared a better understanding of the need for recreational experiences, and, in fact, a reliance on publicly provided recreational services.

RURAL RECREATIONAL ORGANIZATION AND SERVICE

Until a short time ago, the public recreational service movement had manifested itself primarily in urban areas. Now, however, a great deal of recreational service is offered by public agencies in rural areas of this country. The recreational service problems of rural populations have been quite different from the problems of urban dwellers. The growing sparsity of rural population has created conditions that do not lend themselves readily to the organization of public recreational services. Nevertheless, people who remain in rural areas are not without leisure, and their needs for, and the values which accrue from, recreational experience are no less vital than those of people residing in cities.

The recreational needs of rural people hitherto have been partly met through the services of agencies primarily organized for other purposes.

Such agencies have sometimes utilized recreational activity to accomplish their main purposes; but, recognizing the great need for recreational experiences, some have reoriented their operations mainly to satisfy that need. The Grange, a great voluntary organization for the improvement of the economic, political, and social conditions of farmers, has been valuable for the organization of social activities for farm families. The YMCA has initiated and conducted an extensive program of recreational activities. The 4-H Clubs of the Agricultural Extension Division of the United States Department of Agriculture and the Future Farmers of America have been helpful agencies in this field, too.

Agencies and Groups Offering Recreational Organization

Public schools, federal agencies, farm organizations, business groups, fraternities, churches, private agencies, and special-interest groups of a permanent or temporary type are some of the organizations that have taken leadership positions in the development of rural recreational service. In these groups are both professional and laymen who have the interest, enthusiasm, skill, or need to obtain citizen action on problems that concern leisure use and recreational activities.

Community, consolidated, and smaller local district school systems typically are concerned with the general welfare of their pupils. This means educational betterment, but it also affords a basis for support of extracurricular and noncurricular activities which tend to promote the health and welfare of all children and the community in general. Efforts to enhance opportunities for the child usually lead this group into many associated experiences. The school, by its very centrality in the rural community, may be the only governmental agency that can offer leadership and guidance for organized recreational activities, through adult education, club organizations, interest groups, supervised sports, games, and social activities oriented toward the provision of public recreational service in the rural area.

Rural community development for recreational activity has been sponsored by the cooperative extension service of land grant colleges and universities, public libraries, and various state departments. Among the latter are state departments of agriculture, parks, forests, fish and game commissions, developmental and/or industrial commissions, and, in the last few years, commissions dealing with youth, the aging, and human rights.

Cooperative Extension Service. The cooperative extension service has been primarily responsible for assisting rural people. When it was initiated, much of the service was on an individual farm basis. Over the years, however, the service has been equitably distributed throughout the rural community. It has undertaken the responsibility for providing leadership preparation to young people within the rural area. Regional camps, fairs, festivals, homemaking courses, conservation, nature clubs, and an array of activities and social experiences considered recreational have been part of this undertaking.

State Colleges and Universities. Many tax-supported colleges and universities are situated in rural areas. Although institutions of higher education generally like to think of the entire state as being their campus, the immediate rural area in which the institution is situated typically becomes the recipient of consultations, services, and technical assistance. The specialized skills of professional and technical personnel employed at colleges and universities are geared, not only toward teaching and research, but to community service. Although the institutions of higher education provide a variety of special services to all people in the state, there is a much greater impact when their vast resources are brought to bear on local community problems. In many instances the physical plant of the institution may be utilized for a variety of planned activities ranging from art shows, musical concerts, theater presentations, sports events, sports instruction, library use, to dances, socials, instructional workshops, symposiums, and other group or individual meetings that may be termed recreational. Because the community is coincidentally situated in close proximity to the college or university, its people are in the best possible position to make use of whatever personal services are available. While this aspect of university responsibility has not really been developed, there is a growing awareness on the part of such institutions for these kinds of services to be provided. Through an organized general extension division, the university or college may offer a broad range of recreational and community services to many regions of the state that could be classified as rural.

Libraries. Public libraries can materially assist the recreational development of rural communities by supplying needed literary information. The library performs a most valuable service by obtaining books, pamphlets, and journals that can supply information on how recreational services may be initiated, organized, and managed for rural residents. Well-established libraries also have human resources, people with the knowledge to guide and counsel effectively on problems that could effect potential recreational service.

Public libraries also transmit the cultural heritage of the area to the people. Libraries often organize discussion or lecture series dealing with books, stories, and literary achievements for all age groups. Local librarians frequently act the role of story-teller to a fascinated group of young children or advise an adult book club on the latest acquisitions or selections. Through the liberal use of a bookmobile, the library can be brought to those who cannot come to the library. This one feature, of all of the resource, consulting, and guidance functions performed by the library, can have profound impact on the community and its population. Reading is an intensely recreational activity, opening up new worlds for the reader, and it should be a significant feature in any recreational operation.

Farm Organizations. The major organizations with the greatest influence on rural farming populations are the National Grange, the American Farm Bureau, and the Farmers' Union. Each of these agencies is interested in stimulating community action through education, improving community life for youth and adults, and planning responsibility for the production of certain programs that can assist in the development of worthwhile and satisfying activities. Typically, such organizations are influential in gaining effective legislation directly affecting the farmer. In general, however, local units of these three agencies have been instrumental in offering a wide variety of recreational activities including socials, dances, crafts, art, historic displays, conservation practices, day camping, fairs, festivals, and other experiences that provide the rural population with direct participation.

Business and Fraternal Groups. The "animal" societies (Elks, Moose, Lions, Eagles) and other business, professional, civic, or social organizations voluntarily join together for recreational, social, business, and community benefit. These groups typically play an important role in assisting the general development of the community and in solving problems. The voluntary nature of these groups, which is in itself recreational, makes it possible for these organizations to stress worthwhile projects such as the acquisition of land for the development of baseball, football, soccer, or other play fields and grounds. It is not uncommon for such organizations to be involved with the establishment of youth sports and athletic leagues and tournaments. They may sponsor a variety of recreational activities throughout the year ranging from Christmas parties and lighting contests, to an annual band day or memorial observance. Such organizations may take the opportunity to cooperate with and even sponsor a series of activities that could be organized and promoted by the public recreational service department, if one exists, in the rural region, permitting these groups to direct their time, talents, and economic resources to a united effort of immense value to the community.

Church Groups. Except when strictly constructional or absolutely fundamentalist, the church can be one of the most important influences in the life of rural populations. The church and its affiliate organizations may become the center of community actions and development which permeates every facet of the community's way of doing things. Church socials, dances, dramatics, sports events, holidays, commemorations, and a host of other recreational activities are traditional in many rural areas, particularly where there is a homogeneous population or where one religious group predominates. In recent years churches have taken active positions in the development of community-wide recreational programs and have often sponsored or effectively coordinated their work and efforts with other socially oriented agencies within the area. The effort of churches is of great value in the complete growth of the community. The cooperation and coordination of the churches' action with other community-based agencies should be encouraged.

Special-Interest Groups. Many times the initial request for action at the community level does not come from governmental or long-lived privately organized agencies. It springs, instead, from ad hoc or special-interest groups which may come to life to solve a particular problem or advance a specific cause. These temporary and informal groupings may eventuate in highly organized and formal agencies, but more often they are geared for short-term efforts. Essentially such groups are formed as a direct result of some discontent affecting one segment of the community, one neighborhood, or may be the consequence of a widespread dissatisfaction with current affairs that normally constituted agencies do not seem able to handle. In such cases, the ad hoc committee will probably be broadly representative of the general community, attack the problem by bringing it to the attention of the citizens, create a local issue, get petitions signed, seek legislative surcease, or promote the establishment of a local governmental agency to deal effectively with the situation.

The twin roles of acting, either as stimulator to existing agencies or as organizer of temporary groups for action on a given problem, have been influential enough in obtaining the desired results to give such recognition as one means for generating action. From such groups, recreational agencies have established aquatic facilities and other recreational spaces, structures and areas have been acquired or developed, a wide variety of recreational activities have been started, and many existing agencies at the local rural level have been stimulated to afford coordinated services where none existed before.

Rural-Urban Organization

Urbanization is a fertile soil for the growth of leisure activities, probably because the city dweller may have more free time than his counterpart in the country. The greater success of public recreational service agencies in cities than in rural communities may be attributed largely to the traditional reluctance of rural people to accept government-sponsored functions. In recent years, however, this reluctance is being overcome. Many public or governmental functions that formerly may have been eschewed are readily accepted by rural dwellers. Until the age of mass media, particularly television, historical prejudice persisted against many leisure activities regarded as unworthy and even frivolous. That bias, however, did not extend to hunting and fishing. These activities, once needed for survival, have carried over and are considered honorable recreational activities to be pursued without guilt. Hunting and fishing, except in unusual situations, do not lend themselves to high organization but are subject everywhere to state control in the interest of conservation.

The continuing migration of farm families to cities or other urban centers accelerates the growth of the urban movement in the United States—today, only 7.5 percent of all Americans live in rural areas. Coincidentally, there has been a movement from the central cities, especially from the core, to the suburbs. The growth of suburbia has been phenomenal in the last decade softening the distinction between rural and urban life.

There is now a decided interest in the public provision of recreational services in rural areas. The development of such services is somewhat retarded by the sparsity of population and the inferior tax base typical of rural areas. In some states lack of enabling legislation has forced rural areas to rely on established agencies of public education for recreational services. In other states legislative restriction has sometimes prevented small communities from joining together to form consolidated public recreational services departments that could serve two or more rural communities on a proportional representative basis. In certain rural sections, consolidated schools have provided improved recreational opportunities to the population, children and adults.

The basic problem is, as it is in cities, essentially one of organizing local physical resources and human resources. Although private, quasi-public, and commercial agencies can do much to explore and exploit the field, and to experiment in the techniques of organization, there can be no program of opportunities for all rural people without public cooperation. The pattern of rural organizations that would most nearly fulfill requirements of rural life is the county or special district recreational service system. It is necessary, therefore, if this idea is to be better understood, to inquire into the nature of the county and its functions.

NATURE OF COUNTIES

The county form of local government was developed in England and exported to the American Colonies. For purposes of local government, the several Anglo-Saxon kingdoms, which were united in the ninth century to become the united kingdom of England, were each divided into shires or counties. These in turn were divided into "hundreds," each of which was a collection of townships. In the Colonies, the essential form of English governance was adopted, but with some variation between Colonies. The influence of other European governments was also present, notably in the Dutch settlements of New York and Pennsylvania. The Louisiana parishes, analogous to counties, are a geopolitical reflection of Spanish control. Louisiana also retains other governmental traditions that stem from the French. As new states were organized after 1789, they largely took on the forms of the original states. The township as a subdivision of a county became of less and less importance and now persists only in a few eastern, particularly New England, and the north-central states. Counties are merely portions into which a state is divided for the state's administrative convenience (see Chapter 2, pp. 28–29).

Counties are created by state legislatures in conformity to the limitations set forth in state constitutions. All states do not require the approval of the voters in creating a new county. In characterizing the legal nature of counties, courts have frequently declared that they are quasi-corporations created chiefly to carry out state purposes and, therefore, possess relatively fewer corporate powers to meet local needs. However, being a creature of the state, the county derives its power from the state, subject to provisions of the state constitution. Since counties are created primarily to serve the state's interests, they function in a *respondeat superior* relationship and are therefore protected under the immunities of the state against legal action based on tort liability. As in other questions of immunity, liberalized court decisions provide exceptions to this rule.

To the separate municipal corporations, state legislatures have granted wide latitude in the government of local affairs, facilitating the adaptation of local government to new conditions, which has been no small factor in the establishment of local agencies in the incorporated city for community recreational services. The rural districts have no such convenient local agency with almost unlimited powers and must depend on the county government with its limited powers, on the school district, or on special district governments with specific and distinctly limited powers.

Counties are merely certain portions of the territory of the state into which the state is divided to conveniently exercise the powers of the state government. All portions of a state are within some county, and the county is created expressly by the state to administer the policy of the state at large. All cities are likewise within some county.

The distinction between counties and municipal corporations, somewhat exemplified in Chapter 2, was well defined by the Supreme Court of Ohio in 1857. The court stated that:

> . . . counties are local subdivisions of a state, created by the sovereign power of the state, of its own sovereign will, without the particular solicitation, consent, or concurrent action of the people who inhabit them. The former organization is asked for, or at least assented to, by the people it embraces; the latter is superimposed by a sovereign and paramount authority. A municipal corporation proper is created mainly for the interest, advantage, and convenience of the locality and its people; a county organization is created almost exclusively with a view to the policy of the state at large, for purposes of finance, of education, of provision for the poor, of military organization, of the means of travel and transport,

and especially for the general administration of justice. With scarcely an exception, all powers and functions of the county organization have a direct and exclusive reference to the general policy of the state, and are, in fact, but a branch of the general administration of that policy.[2]

People residing in an incorporated city generally have two local governments: (1) the county, organized to administer locally the government of the state and (2) the municipal corporation, to administer such functions as the local body politic determines to be to its best interests. It is the latter that has been utilized to exercise the powers of organizing systems of public recreational service. Thus, people residing in rural districts outside the limits of separate municipal corporations do not have a local government well adapted to their local needs as do the city dwellers, except as the county governments may be adapted thereto.

In 1976 the United States had 3,006 counties. Delaware had the smallest number of counties, three, while Texas had 253. Counties varied in size from 22 square miles in New York County to 20,175 square miles in San Bernardino County, California. The average size of counties was 975 square miles. Although they are much larger in average land area than other local units, most counties are too small to meet current needs. The great majority of counties are distinctly rural in character; over 60 percent have less than 25,000 residents. Boundary lines, originally drawn more than 100 years ago to accommodate the then prevalent mode of travel (horseback), no longer meet modern requirements. Many state constitutions place a minimum on the size of counties, varying from 275 square miles in Tennessee to 900 square miles in Texas. Some constitutions prescribe minimum populations ranging from 700 in Tennessee to 20,000 in Pennsylvania. However, population ranges far beyond those drawn in some state constitutions. For example, Alpine County, California, contains approximately 300 people, while Cook County, Illinois, contains 4,000,000 inhabitants.

County Functions

Although counties have been considered as creatures of the state, they serve local governmental purposes as well. Although counties are administrative subdivisions for carrying out the intent of the state legislature, county officials are elected at the local level and are therefore responsible to the local electorate. County government was established at a period when decentralization of state government was a major consideration. However, counties really have little choice in the functions they are required to perform. Little latitude is granted to them for undertaking functions not normally required by the state. Yet local election does

[2] *Commissioners of Hamilton County v. Mighels.* 7 Ohio St. 109 (1857).

provide a means for selecting certain functions at the county's discretion, if there is enough local pressure applied to officials.

Traditional county functions include law enforcement through a sheriff's office, maintenance of jails or other correctional institutions, welfare services, health services, maintenance of roads, recording and maintenance of official population and vital statistics and other legal documents, and other functions which, through promulgation by enabling legislation, the county may undertake. These are permissive functions rather than required. During the past few years counties have been able to broaden their functions to include responsibility for providing proprietary services usually performed by municipalities. To a great extent the additional responsibilities have developed in response to the demands of rural populations in unincorporated communities lying within the urban fringe.[3]

Among the newer functions and responsibilities undertaken by counties are those dealing with the organization and administration of airports, hospitals, libraries, public housing, parks, and recreational facilities. More highly urbanized counties have also added the functions of fire protection, sewage and garbage disposal, water supply, and other public utilities. Some counties have undertaken to supply zoning, planning, subdivisional control, and building regulations. Within recent years, several states have offered increased discretionary powers to counties by which a county may almost attain the functional status of a municipal corporation. The duties thus included have to do with the satisfaction of local needs rather than with the administration of state policy. Unfortunately, few rural counties have taken advantage of these powers.

Most counties, however, have been hindered from assuming many significant new functions because they have insufficient legal authorization to do so. County home rule is a relatively recent development affecting few counties. It rests on the theory that county governments, like municipal corporations, should have the power to serve the needs and interests of their people directly, and be organized structurally for local use. There has been general unwillingness to provide counties with broader discretionary power, perhaps because they are really obsolete governmental forms. Approximately 100 counties have a chief executive, few have personnel merit systems, most are too poorly staffed to undertake new functions, and, for the most part, counties are really incompetent to carry out their constitutionally mandated functions.

Despite the failure of archaic county structures to provide effective local governmental needs for rural populations, some counties, notably the most highly urbanized, have performed magnificently. To a lesser extent rural counties have been able to offer the kinds and degrees of

[3] Raymond E. Murphy, *The American City: An Urban Geography* (New York: McGraw-Hill Book Company, Inc., 1966), pp. 42–49.

service that make them valuable as governmental structures and to provide a variety of facilities and programs that contribute to the recreational benefit of their constituencies. The first county park in America is reported to have been established by Essex County, New Jersey. Almost all states have now enacted laws specifically empowering counties to acquire, improve, and maintain parks and in several additional states the power is contained in general laws relating to other powers. Most of the specific laws relating to county parks vest powers of administration in a county board of supervisors, but several states provide for the appointment of a separate board of park commissioners. An enabling act passed by the Legislature of California in 1939, for example, specifically gave counties the power to promote, organize, and conduct recreational activities. The Pennsylvania act makes more specific mention of community recreational facilities than do other acts, which refer primarily to parks. The Pennsylvania act empowers counties to:

> designate and set apart for use as playgrounds, play fields, gymnasiums, public baths, swimming pools, or indoor recreation centers, any land or building owned by the county and not dedicated or devoted to other public use.[4]

In 1949, Wisconsin took an important step when its Legislature passed an act reading in part as follows:

> To aid in the development of rural and urban life conditions the county board may raise, by tax levies or otherwise, monies for the employment of a county recreation director . . . The duties of the recreation director shall be to promote, organize, and supervise recreation activities.[5]

DEVELOPMENT OF COUNTY PARKS AND RECREATIONAL SERVICE

The number of county parks has increased over the years. In 1937, the United States National Park Service reported that 77 counties in America had established parks; by 1940 the number had risen to 152. In 1950, although only 130 counties reported that they had established parks, park land acquisitions had increased over the previous ten-year period by 16,000 acres. The number of parks in 1960 was 290. In 1971 the number climbed to 2,811 containing over 35,000 acres. Among counties with notable park development and highly proclaimed recreational services are Cook County, Illinois; Union County, New Jersey; Westchester County, New York; Los Angeles County, California; Wayne County, Michigan; Milwaukee County, Wisconsin; and Cuyahoga County,

---

[4] Pennsylvania, *Complete Statutes* (1920), Sec. 15822–15823.
[5] Wisconsin, *Statutes* (1949), Ch. 187, Sec. 59.87 (3a).

Ohio. These counties, without exception, are in highly developed and densely populated metropolitan areas.

Union County, New Jersey, is an interesting case in that there is no unincorporated area in the county. The Union County Park Commission has responsibility for the provision of public recreational service rendered through the park system. Established by a New Jersey act of 1885, the permanent Union County Park Commission was initially appointed November 19, 1921, with five members appointed by the Assignment Judge of the Superior Court presiding in the district. The commissioners' appointments are non-political, unpaid, and are for five-year terms, one term expiring each year. The essential purpose of the Union County parks is to provide more facilities and a greater range of activities than can usually be provided in small municipal park and recreational systems. The county's parks are most often developed where their facilities can serve the people of more than one municipality. The Union County Park System maintains 27 units totaling 5,209 acres. Developmental funds are obtained by referendum vote or approval of requests submitted by the Union County Board of Chosen Freeholders. Maintenance funds are derived by means of an annual budget submitted to the Board of Freeholders with allowable limits of not less than one quarter nor more than three fifths of a mill per dollar of the value of the taxable property in Union County. In a report which commemorated the first 50 years of the County Park System it was reported that:

> Union County has a population of 564,255. The Union County Park Commission has areas and facilities in most of the cities and towns of the County. The Park Commission's jurisdiction comprises the County Parks. Cities and towns have either commissions or committees with facilities operating under local jurisdiction. City or town facilities, areas, and programs are primarily for local use. In contrast, the County park areas serve two or more towns, a district, or the County.

> The County Park System has a wide variety of revenue-producing facilities which are not found in the local units, such as golf courses, riding stables, swimming pools, rifle and pistol ranges, trap and skeet fields, boating, an artificial ice skating rink, etc. The County also operates and conducts the Nature and Science Center, which is the only facililty of its kind within the area. Cultural activities are included through community programs, dramas, concerts, art shows, flower shows, and other stage presentations. The parks also contain flower displays and arboretums, which are not found in the communities to any extent.

> The Union County Park System works in close cooperation with the local departments in the County. The city and town agencies depend, to a great extent, on the County parks for facilities in which to conduct their programs, particularly athletic events. In some instances, the County provides playground facilities and maintenance and local departments furnish personnel and equipment. In order to prevent duplication, generally, the local departments operate local athletic leagues and tournaments while

the County System conducts district and county-wide competitions. Inasmuch as the towns have practically no picnic facilities, the public and local agencies utilize the County facilities for this type of activity.

There is good coordination between the County and local jurisdictions, with each level of government respecting the other's sphere of influence and operation. The County fulfills a much needed service, support, and supplementary function by conducting professional preparatory institutes cooperatively with local departments. Local units and organizations look to the County for information concerning facilities, programs, and leadership. The County System employs approximately 170 full-time workers and an additional 200 seasonal employees.[6]

Although several county park commissions and departments conduct recreational activities on the regional park areas, the Westchester County Department of Parks, Recreation, and Conservation affords an excellent example of a county agency concerned primarily with the organization of a county-wide recreational activity program and the coordination of numerous community recreational agencies in the county.

Westchester County is a highly developed suburban area adjacent to, and north of, the Borough of the Bronx in New York City. Within the county are four cities ranging in population from 50,000 to 200,000 and about 60 smaller cities and villages. Total population is 894,406. Two thirds of the cities and villages have organized recreational service commissions or departments. The County Department maintains a field service through which it counsels the several local agencies, conducts institutes for the professional development of recreational service personnel and volunteers, makes surveys of local situations, conducts conferences for lay and professional leaders, and generally promotes public planning and interest in recreational opportunities. The County Department conducts a county-wide program of events and activities in which local groups, which have sprung from the city and village programs, participate. These activities include music, arts, crafts, drama, and athletics. A large public auditorium, known as the County Center, is spoken of as "the focal point of community life in Westchester." Many activities that originated as local activities in villages and cities throughout the county have become county-wide occasions centered in the County Center. The department operates over 160 miles of traffic parkways throughout the county, nine great inland reservations, and five waterfront parks on more than 14,000 acres. The improved recreational facilities include five swimming pools, five golf courses, numerous athletic fields, picnic grounds, boating facilities on lakes, bathing beaches, new bicycle paths, an interpretive farm, a bird and nature sanctuary, and a most elaborate amusement park, Playland. Completed in 1929, it set a new high standard for such parks. In

[6] John T. Cunningham, "To Benefit the Whole Population . . . The Union County Park Commission, 1921–1971," (Elizabeth, N.J.: The Commission, 1972), 45 pp.

recent years, however, Playland has been permitted to deteriorate. The County Department also conducts a large summer camp which provides outings for hundreds of boys and girls.[7]

The public schools of Westchester County are administered by many separate school district boards. Among the schools are some outstanding examples of extension of the school program into the recreational life of the community. The County Department works cooperatively with the school districts, but has no official or legal connection with them.

Types of County Recreational Areas

The areas acquired and improved by counties for park and recreational purposes may be considered as of six more or less distinct types:

Parkways. Several metropolitan counties have acquired sufficient land on both sides of heavily traveled highways to control roadside development. Where the highways pass through wooded regions the natural landscape is preserved or restored for a distance of 100 to 500 feet on either side of the highways. Driving these parkways, one has the impression of passing through a vast park. Interesting features, such as rock formations, lakes, streams, and long vistas, are exposed. At certain spots picnic facilities are provided. The Westchester County Park, Recreation, and Conservation Department in New York State has a network of over 160 miles of traffic parkways throughout the county. Other examples of county parkway systems are to be found in New Jersey, Michigan, and Wisconsin.

Beaches. A number of counties on the Atlantic, Pacific, and Gulf coasts have acquired beaches and have protected and developed them for public recreational purposes. Beaches are facilities that attract visitors from afar and consequently are considered a proper object for planning by governmental subdivisions larger than the city. Because beaches within city limits are usually occupied by commercial, industrial, and navigational enterprises, city dwellers usually must go beyond the city limits for beach recreational activities.

Local Parks. A number of counties have established parks within the boundaries of cities or immediately beyond municipal boundaries, which correspond in their development and service to the municipal district park and playground. Counties usually have come into possession of such areas by gift or bequest, or by transfer from other public uses. The areas vary in size from 10 to 50 acres. Sometimes they are equipped with an athletic field, children's playground, picnic area, swimming pool, and amusement devices of various kinds; occasionally they surround some spot of historic, scientific, or unusual scenic interest.

[7] "Parks, Recreation, and Conservation," (White Plains, N.Y.: Westchester County, 1977), 32 pp.

Regional Parks. Near large metropolitan areas are several examples of county parks that might be termed regional recreational areas. They are usually beyond the city boundaries and frequently characterized by wooded areas, lakes, streams, winter sports areas, picnic spots, and golf courses.

Reservations. A number of counties have acquired large reservations of wooded lands—in the Southwest, desert lands—to preserve the natural flora and fauna. Recreational activities such as winter sports, camping, hiking, fishing, and boating are permitted and encouraged. Notable examples of such reservations are the Denver City and County Mountain Park, the Cook County Forest Preserves in Illinois, and the Poundridge and Blue Mountain Reservations of Westchester County in New York.

Miscellaneous Small Parks. Counties come into possession, in one way or another, of small parcels of land which are designated as County Parks. Most frequently they are along the roadsides or at some historic or scenic spot. Sometimes they occupy land that has been improved for camping or picnicking. As a rule, they do not have an important place in the county scheme of recreational areas.

Regional Function of County Property

It is apparent from the foregoing discussion that the essential function of county parks and other properties is to provide a regional service. That counties should endeavor to meet the need for regional recreational facilities is logical. With improved highways and transport facilities, people are able to travel further afield than the confines of their neighborhoods, districts, and municipal boundaries for much of their recreational experiences. The regional recreational place, with its wooded and natural environment, its spaciousness, its extensive facilities capable of accommodating large numbers of people, occupies an indispensable place in the whole recreational plan.

The provision of neighborhood and district facilities for recreational service has already been well established as a legitimate service for cities to perform. All cities, except the largest, could hardly do more than properly take care of this need. The allocation of the regional areas to counties, to the states, and to the federal government is a reasonable division of the responsibility. Moreover, if counties are to expend, for recreational services, funds raised from general county taxes, to which the city property owners contribute a large share, it is proper that the object of expenditure be such that the city people might share in the benefits. The locations that lend themselves to the development of regional recreational facilities best are more likely to be outside the incorporated limits of cities and removed from city congestion than within such limits. It is better for the county to improve and administer them for the benefit of all the people in the county than for the cities to go beyond their limits to undertake the task. The county must complement the works and efforts of local political jurisdictions, not compete with or supplant them. The county's responsibility is, therefore, regional and falls into the following categories:

1. Regional facilities, serving in many different cities and communities, that no city is normally prepared to establish and maintain because of cost, uniqueness, size, or inter-city use.
2. Regional services, which help through instruction and in other ways to better serve the general public's leisure needs. The county is not directly involved with local programs, but rather with the improvement of such programs in one or more indirect ways; e.g., by providing instruction to volunteers and/or paid workers, through consultation or advice, and by preparation and distribution of instructional materials.
3. Regional programs furnishing all or part of the planning, equipment, supervision, and leadership, conducted on or off county facilities. Participants may represent several communities involved in projects jointly planned by the county and various municipal public recreational agencies, such as inter-city orchestras, athletic leagues, choral festivals, and traveling exhibits.[8]

The role of counties in providing recreational services is one of offering day-use facilities for participants, space to meet recreational requirements, and adequate finances to support competent services. As Bollens and Yerbry reported:

> . . . counties are moving toward a more significant commitment in outdoor recreation services as a county function . . ., although resistance is evident in some counties. In these counties, political opposition will have a long-time effect on recreational program.[9]

Counties have been provided with the legislative means to perform recreational services on a broad basis. California, by passing the County Service Area Law, provided one means by which recreational service might be offered through park development and other recreational facilities. It stated, in effect, that a service area may be instituted by the county board of supervisors on its own initiative, or it may be implemented when two members of the board, or 10 percent of the registered voters residing within the county, file a petition or request to this effect. The parks, recreational facilities, or other areas created under this Act must be primarily for the benefit and use of the area's residents.[10]

[8] Letter from Norman S. Johnson, Emeritus Director, Department of Parks and Recreation, Los Angeles County, California.
[9] John C. Bollens and Richard D. Yerbry, "Outdoor Recreation in Southern California," BGR *Observer* (Los Angeles: Bureau of Governmental Research, University of California, February, 1962), 4 pps.
[10] California, *Government Code* Sec. 25210.10 *et seq.*

OTHER LOCAL UNITS OFFERING RURAL RECREATIONAL SERVICE

Other local units function mainly as agents of state governments, they perform many functions provided in other places by different units. Typical of such a governmental unit is the New England town.

New England Towns. Of the 1,400 unincorporated towns of New England most expended half of their budgets in the provision of public education, usually a responsibility of independent school districts in other parts of the county. Towns also performed many, if not all, of the functions generally offered by municipalities. Additionally, towns provided road maintenance and public welfare operations which are typically reserved to county forms of government. New England towns have historically operated through town meetings. Qualified voters are entitled to participate personally in enacting the town's business at public meetings in which the pros and cons of any issue are raised, questioned, and settled by majority vote. In such situations the day-to-day operation of the town is placed in the hands of a board of selectmen. At an annual budget hearing, voting citizens of the town may consider new taxes, budget requests of the various commissions carrying out town functions, and all other problems or issues arising at that time. Whereas this form of government theoretically permits a voice to every individual residing in the town, thereby offering the greatest democratic government possible, in fact the structure is archaic and sometimes totally unworkable, particularly when the town's population and problems increase as modern-day operations impinge on formerly purely farm communities.

Anticipating needed reform, some New England towns have taken remedial steps through public referenda, to modify their existing charters and to restructure their government. In most instances the towns have adopted a manager-council form of government, abolishing operating commissions, and, instead, have installed operating departments headed by professional personnel dealing directly with the professionally employed town manager.

Townships. There are approximately 15,700 recognized township governments in the United States, but only in New York, New Jersey, Pennsylvania, and Michigan do such governmental units perform significantly. Their functions consist of efforts to maintain highways and such municipal functions as police and fire protection, sewage and garbage disposal, and the operation of public utilities. Rural townships have generally been superseded in their functions by counties. While these structural forms are maintained they are virtually powerless and anachronistic.

Special Districts. Of all forms of local government, special districts have proliferated most during the past decade. Such districts have proved to be extremely beneficial to rural populations residing in regions where other governmental units either cannot or do not perform or provide certain necessary services, such as recreational opportunities. However, where special districts have been created in metropolitan areas residents are often forced to live under layers of local governmental units and support each of them through tax levies. These independent and autonomous local governmental units provide specific and unique functions to the resident. Nevertheless, these functions should be consolidated. It is not unusual for metropolitan districts to provide individual functions. Thus, a citizen may obtain water from one, have garbage removed by another, receive fire protection from another, pest control from another, health services from another, and recreational services through park and other facilities from another. All these districts require taxes for their support. More than 18,000 special districts are currently operating in the United States.

Almost all special districts are established to provide some urban service in unincorporated areas. Some were created to resolve problems that extended over several jurisdictions; others have been established coterminously with existing units where the latter, by legal restriction, could not provide the specific function that was demanded. In too many cases there is overlapping of jurisdiction, noncongruent boundaries that add to confusion, and finally, the fact that special districts may perform their function extremely well, but, in so doing, actually contribute to the rise of additional problems which beset the area in which they function.

Rural School Districts. Most independent rural school districts are managed by boards of education. The boards are policy-making bodies which set the rules and regulations for school operation as imposed by state law. The 25,000 independent school districts have no coterminous boundaries with other existing local governmental units, set and raise their own taxes, issue bonds, and now account for nearly 80 percent of public school enrollments. More than 3,000 independent school districts have no school-age children residing in their district and therefore maintain no schools. About 50 percent of all independent school districts have less than 50 pupils enrolled. Most independent school districts are too small to offer effective educational opportunities, much less to provide additional services of a recreational nature.

SPECIAL GOVERNMENTAL DISTRICTS

The problem of providing local recreational areas and programs, as distinguished from regional services, in unincorporated county territory and in rural areas still must be solved effectively. There are several alternatives, none of which has really proved to be adequate in the face of mounting taxation, inflation, and widespread overlapping of jurisdictions, duplication of functions, and narrow orientations which tend to disturb the environment. In some instances it has been suggested that the function of public schools be expanded to include some services in providing recreational activities. Another method is to permit the organization of special recreational districts within counties with powers to establish recreational service systems and to tax property within the district presumed to benefit thereby.

As rural and urban life become more complex, many problems peculiar to certain sections, but not to the whole county, arise. This condition has given rise to the creation of special districts for the alleviation of these problems. The districts are created by state legislatures or by county boards of supervisors under authority granted by state legislatures. The initiative for the formation of the districts is taken by the landowners or voters and is evinced by petition addressed to the county board of supervisors. Districts are variously governed by boards appointed by state authority or by elected boards. In some cases the board of supervisors acts as the district board. Districts have the right to sue, be sued, acquire and dispose of property, and make contracts. Certain problems are of specific concern to a city and the adjacent unincorporated area; others to unincorporated areas alone. There are, for example, metropolitan utility districts, sanitation, flood control, park, and recreational districts. There are also many rural special districts as well for highways, drainage, fire protection, irrigation, public health, special schools, and soil conservation, to name but a few. The creation of such districts to handle certain problems peculiar to large metropolitan areas has removed one of the most urgent reasons for consolidating cities in metropolitan areas, has negated much of the promise that such services could bring to people living within the established district by inflicting other more serious problems or compounding existing problems, and has offered one method for administering special services vital to the area. The contradiction between benefits derived and malpractices compounded has tended to make the continual use of special districts questionable (see Chapter 1, pp. 10–12).

Nevertheless, the special district renders its services within the confines of the district and raises its revenues from direct assessment on the real property or by ad valorem tax, and by fees and charges for special services. Taxes are usually assessed and collected by the county.

Functions of Special Districts

The functions of special districts are complex and of such great number that is it difficult to group them. However, they may be categorized as health, housing, transportation, natural resources, education, parks, and recreational services. Not all districts perform to the limit of their enumerated powers, but the following functions are essentially those of special districts.

Special districts for health provide hospitals, sanitary facilities, water and air pollution controls, pest extermination, food and drug inspection, sewage and garbage disposal, and other health protection activities.

District housing authorities develop, build, and operate low-rent public housing projects, provide recreational activities and facilities for the residents of these projects, and engage in urban renewal or redevelopment projects.

Special districts furnish transportation facilities, construct and maintain streets, tunnels, bridges, parking facilities, street lighting, parkways, and roadside parks; develop, construct and operate airports, seaports, and harbors; and improve waterways and navigation routes.

In districts specializing in natural resources, provision is made for flood control, water and soil conservation, reclamation, pest control, reforestation, and wilderness preservation.

In education, special districts offer instruction in many educational services from kindergarten to college. They build, operate, and maintain libraries, provide transportation to and from schools, furnish lunches (sometimes free for school children), and perform the functions related to recreational opportunities.

The functions of park and recreational service districts include the acquisition and management of regional and local parks, playgrounds, reservations, beaches, camps, auditoriums, stadiums, and other community recreational facilities and spaces. A district may act to protect fish and wildlife, prevent erosion of soil or beaches, construct recreational buildings, and employ personnel for the conduct and supervision of activities of a recreational nature.

Special Districts Offering Recreational Services

Metropolitan Districts. Special districts whose territories coincide with or overlap a substantial portion of a metropolitan area are termed metropolitan districts. Few metropolitan districts are congruent with metropolitan areas, and many are smaller than the entire metropolitan area. Conversely, some metropolitan districts are larger than metropolitan areas and may include rural spaces. Usually, a district is termed metropolitan only if it performs an urban function and includes at least one central city within its territory.

Metropolitan areas that overlap municipal and sometimes county boundaries, in a few instances, have created metropolitan park districts, usually with independent taxing powers. If they are located in more than one county, they collect taxes through the tax collection agencies of the counties in which they are situated. The best-known metropolitan park districts are in and around Boston, Massachusetts, the Cleveland Metropolitan Park District, The Huron-Clinton Metropolitan Authority of Detroit, and the Chicago Park District.

The Cleveland Metropolitan Park District operates in almost 480 square miles holding a total population of approximately two million people. The district controls nearly 14,000 acres of land. Its basic program has been to preserve, restore, or develop scenic areas. It also provides a wide range of recreational opportunities through such facilities as trailways, bathing beaches, golf courses, ice-skating rinks, bicycle trails, camping centers, swimming pools, softball and baseball diamonds, picnic grounds, and other recreational areas.

The Huron-Clinton Metropolitan Authority was authorized to provide parks, connecting drives, and limited access highways within and without its territorial area. It was created to meet more satisfactorily the need for recreational places and services resulting from the rapid increase in population in and around Detroit during the first part of the twentieth century. Today, the Authority operates within a five-county, populated district. It has constructed a beach site, numerous parks and recreational facilities in two river valleys, and owns more than 6,300 acres.[11]

The Chicago Park District was created in 1935 when 22 separate park authorities were consolidated as one metropolitan park agency. A recreational bureau is in charge of all recreational activities under the jurisdiction of the district. The Chicago Park District has functioned as a separate governmental unit under powers granted to it by the consolidation act. It is coextensive with Chicago and operates 165 parks totaling more than 6,000 acres and over 200 miles of parkways. The District levies a general tax on all property in Chicago, collects fees, licenses, and other levies. It issues bonds for acquisition and development of park lands, with the approval of the electorate.

Rural Districts. Irrigation, flood control, and soil conservation districts are three rural non-school districts of extreme importance to the populations they serve. Their primary functions are to supply irrigation water to cultivated lands, to provide drainage, flood control, water for domestic use, and, in some cases, electric power. Soil and water conservation, tree planting, woodland management, and education in intelligent land use practices are among the services of these districts.

Secondary, but nonetheless important, functions provided by these districts are improved land utilization and the development of spaces that can be used for recreational purposes. Through efforts at land reclamation and water conservation, swampy areas, formerly of no economic use, are turned to productive and recreational uses within a preserved ecosystem.

School Districts. Independent school districts are autonomous governmental units having direct taxing powers and providing educational services. The place of the public schools in the whole recreational service

[11] American Public Works Association, *The Huron-Clinton Metropolitan Authority* (Chicago: The Association, 1948), p. 9.

plan was discussed in Chapter 5. It was pointed out that the schools are becoming increasingly related to the recreational problem, both in the provision of instruction in the leisure arts and in the promotion and formulation of recreational programs for the entire local community. This tendency has been less pronounced in rural schools than in city schools. If it is accepted that community recreational service, in some of its manifestations at least, may properly become part of the educational functions, then the rural school districts constitute an existing form of local government through which rural recreational service may be administered.

Elementary and secondary education is administered through a system of local school districts of which there are many in almost every county. With some notable exceptions, i.e., Maryland, North Carolina, Rhode Island, Virginia, and in remote and sparsely settled portions of some states, it may be accepted that wherever there are children (in sufficient number) there is a school district and a school building located with a view to the convenience of travel of the children of the district. The district is governed, under definite limitations of county and state educational authorities, by a local board elected by the people of the district. The district is financed partly by local taxes and partly by county and state appropriations. With improved transportation facilities there has been a movement toward consolidation of school districts to promote economy and efficiency.[12] In some places, townships and counties have taken over the functions of the local district boards of education. Nevertheless, it is evident that the whole structure of local organization of education is identical with what might be considered an ideal form of organization for local recreational services.

Certainly no more economical method of organizing rural America for local recreational service, excluding regional services, could be conceived than to adapt existing agencies and programs to the need. The cost would be relatively small. In the smallest districts no additional personnel would be required. The program in the rural districts would not call for daily activities except for pupils enrolled in the school, for whom the program would be only an enrichment of the curricular and extracurricular activities already a part of the educational program. For the community at large there would be only the occasional community gatherings, largely self-managed. The larger the school and the population of the district, the more frequently such events might be held. In the community large enough to have a complete graded school, the program could be continuous, as is that in the city neighborhood school or recreational center, with evening as well as daytime recreational

---

[12] Committee for Economic Development, *Modernizing Local Government,* A Statement by the Research and Policy Committee (New York: Committee for Economic Development, 1966), p. 27.

activities. Recreationists could be shared by several districts and general supervision and promotion and organization of volunteer leadership could be provided by the county education authority.

Recreational Districts. The organization of special districts for local community recreational service in rural areas has been developed within recent years. These districts have been established in rural sections as such populations recognize their own recreational needs. This device has been utilized to overcome what appears to be the principal difficulty confronting county provision of rural recreational service, namely, the inequality inherent in using county funds, raised in large part through taxes assessed against city property, to benefit non-city people.

A recreational district could be composed of all the unincorporated areas in the county, or portions of all such areas of one or more counties with sparsely populated regions. The district would be coextensive with an economic area or a natural geographic region, rather than with political boundaries. Thus, in rural areas where populations are sparse and the economic ability of citizens is limited, it would be feasible to assign the recreational function to a district recreational service department.

In small municipalities, such as incorporated towns, boroughs, villages, and townships that are too small to justify separate boards, commissions, or public departments to render recreational services, the district could contract through the individual local units to provide such services. The local corporations would pay the district for services from which they receive direct benefit. Thus, a small corps of recreationists operating out of a district headquarters could offer recreational services to a large region covering any center of rural population through the use of public buildings and grounds or the development of centralized recreational facilities that could be shared by several communities.

Special recreational districts have been established in only three states, California, Colorado, and Oregon. Typical of these districts are the Rocky Mountain Metropolitan Recreational District and District No. 50 Metropolitan Recreational District. The Rocky Mountain Metropolitan Recreational District, an area of 350 square miles, was formally approved April 9, 1955, the first of such districts to be formed in Colorado. By law, communities in Colorado were enabled to provide recreational services that could not otherwise be offered by local governing bodies.

The District is supported by a 4-mill tax on property within its jurisdiction. Other sources of revenue come from facilities that the District operates: golf course, swimming pool, and Lake Estes. The summer and winter programs of recreational activities vary greatly owing to seasonal changes in population, ranging from 2,500 during the winter to 45,000 summer visitors. The District constructed and operates an 18-hole golf course, Olympic-size swimming pool, recreational center, playgrounds, and a marina for boating and fishing. The District leases lakes Estes and

Mary from the Bureau of Reclamation, as well as East Portal of Adams Tunnel and Stanley Park. Recreational activities include camping, hiking, picnicking, aquatics, boating, fishing, organized athletics, and other experiences which would normally be directed by a public recreational agency. In winter the District conducts a ski school for the children, sponsors tap dance and ballet classes, the Fine Arts Guild (a group interested in producing plays), and square and round-dance activities.

District No. 50 Metropolitan Recreational District was created in 1958, and has jurisdiction over a 15-square-mile area, coextensive with one county. Its headquarters are located in Westminster, Colorado. Operating revenues are received from a 3.25-mill levy. All recreational programming is planned and directed under the supervision of the District. The parks and other recreational areas are also under the direct control of the District.

ORGANIZATION OF RURAL RECREATIONAL AGENCIES

The recreational service problem in the rural community primarily resolves itself into one of organizing the resources already available in the community for recreational opportunities, and mobilizing the voluntary unpaid leadership which is always present but which, without organization and stimulation, remains inert and unused. The techniques of organizing these factors have been performed by several agencies: e.g., school systems, counties, and state and federal sources.

Federally Sponsored Recreational Service

The program of the Works Progress Administration (WPA) was the most widespread demonstration of organization of rural communities for recreational service of its day. This agency had workers in thousands of villages and hamlets across the country. The assumption of responsibility for finance, personnel, and a large measure of general direction by the WPA was one of the most significant federally organized programs for rural areas. Although the WPA was a temporary agency existing chiefly to afford job opportunities, it required sponsorship through local public agencies, including the boards of supervisors of counties, temporary commissions and committees appointed by such boards, town trustees and officials, district boards of education, county park and forestry departments, and various state agencies.

The federal government, through its Departments of Agriculture, Interior, Defense, Health, Education and Welfare, Housing and Urban Development, and administrative agencies such as the Tennessee Valley Authority (TVA) and the Bureau of Outdoor Recreation, has done much to further the satisfaction of recreational needs of rural people. The United States Department of Agriculture (USDA), through its extension services, particularly 4-H programs, makes an outstanding contribution to the recreational opportunities for people in rural regions. Through the United States Forest Service and the National Park Service, the federal government has recognized the recreational value of natural resources and has organized programs taking place in the parks and forests. All these federally created agencies have provided recreational service to a vast public. Such federal initiative is for all the people, but since these natural resources are usually situated in predominantly rural areas it seems obvious that rural populations can benefit most by their proximity.

State-Sponsored Recreational Service

Since the construction of highways through counties is rapidly becoming a state function, the parkway has become a feature of the state highway and park systems. New York State has made available well-planned parkway areas enhanced by the development of beaches and other recreational facilities operated by the state. State parks and the programs conducted by state personnel also contribute to the recreational picture for nearby rural residents. State extension services from institutions of higher learning have also done much to stimulate recreational activities in local rural communities. Where a state college or university is situated in the hinterlands, its specialized faculty has provided technical assistance to the local community. In these instances, technical assistance, advice, and counseling have led to the development and operation of town or county public recreational service operations. Various state agencies, e.g., the Farm Bureau, developmental commissions, fish and game commissions, water resources board, state health department, state department of education, state park and forestry commission, and others, play a great part in conducting institutes where instruction on conservation of natural resources, land acquisition for the development of recreational places, construction of recreational facilities, and leadership of specific recreational activity forms are given. Through these state-sponsored programs, rural community workers are provided with a better understanding of the recreational needs of people and are afforded sufficient material to enable them to undertake the establishment of recreational programs within their respective communities.

Recently, states have also shown an interest in coordinating natural resource and recreational programs. Connecticut enacted an enabling law in 1961 granting local rural communities or towns the power to establish conservation commissions. In 1963, Connecticut passed a law granting towns funds for the acquisition of open space land for conservation and recreational purposes. The state would pay up to 50 percent of the non-federal share of the cost of such acquisition. In part, the act states:

Recreational and conservation purposes means use of lands for agriculture, parks, natural areas, forests, camping, fishing, wetland preservation, wild life habitat, reservoirs, hunting, golfing, boating, historic and scenic preservation and other purposes . . .[13]

In 1963, Illinois passed legislation providing for:

. . . the creation of conservation districts that can acquire, preserve, and maintain wildland, other open land, scenic roadways and pathways, or rights thereto, hold them with or without public access for the education, pleasure, and recreation of the public or for other open-space values, and use them in such manner and with such restrictions as will leave them unimpaired for the benefit of future generations.[14]

The principal advantages of these legislative devices are that they permit local governmental units, particularly those in rural areas, to gain both state and federal monies for the acquisition and development of recreational spaces. Thus local rural units of government are being stimulated to organize and operate various commissions whose intent is to establish operational recreational resources for the citizens residing within their jurisdiction. Such legislative acts have been aimed specifically at reluctant rural communities whose tax base is not broad enough to instigate property acquisition nor to plan comprehensive programs for their populations.

County-Sponsored Recreational Service

Until the last decade counties, with a few notable exceptions, had undertaken a minor role in the provision of public recreational service, particularly for rural people. Since the middle 1960s county officials have recognized the obvious deficits in recreational service which their rural residents wanted and needed. In 1964, the National Association of Counties adopted a resolution calling for nation-wide activation of recreational services as they concerned facilities and program. The policy statement suggested that:

. . . the special role of the county is to acquire, develop, and maintain parks and to administer public recreation programs that will serve the needs of communities broader than the local neighborhood or municipality, but less than state-wide or national in scope.[15]

County-wide, professionally staffed, recreational operations have been the stated responsibility of few county governments. Now, however,

[13] Connecticut, *Public Acts* (1963), No. 649.
[14] Illinois, *Revised Statutes* (1963), Ch. 57½, secs. 101–117.
[15] National Association of Counties, *County Parks and Recreation: A Basis for Action* (Washington, D.C.: The Association, 1964).

there seems to be a growing recognition on the part of such authorities for the need of comprehensive recreational services. Several counties have always offered outstanding leadership and programming to meet the varied demands of their constituency, but these have essentially been metropolitan, rather than rurally based, counties. Among the rural county units that provide inspired leadership is Jefferson County, Kentucky.

County programs vary in range and comprehension from the handling of relatively few special or seasonal events to the daily organization, maintenance, and operation of full-time recreational services under professionally qualified staffs.

Selected References

Bacon, E.: *Design of Cities, rev. ed.* (New York: Penguin Books, Inc.), 1976.

Bollens, J. C.: *Special District Governments in the United States* (Berkeley, Calif.: University of California Press), 1957.

Branch, M. C., Ed.: *Urban Planning Theory* (New York: Dowden, Hutchinson and Ross, Inc.), 1975.

Brinkman, G. L., Ed.: *Development of Rural America* (Lawrence, Kansas: Regents Press of Kansas), 1974.

Cameron, G. and L. Wingo: *Cities, Regions and Public Policy* (New York: Longmans, Inc.), 1973.

Curie, L.: *Taming the Megalopolis: A Design for Urban Growth* (Elmsford, N.Y.: Pergamon Press, Inc.), 1976.

Doxiades, K.: *Ekistics: An Introduction to the Science of Human Settlements* (New York: Oxford University Press), 1968.

Doxiades, K. and J. G. Papaionnou: *Ecumenopolis: The Inevitable City of the Future* (New York: W. W. Norton, Inc.), 1976.

Finlayson, J., Ed.: *Guide to County Organization and Management* (Washington, D.C.: National Association of Counties), 1968.

Gillingwater, D.: *Regional Planning and Social Change* (Lexington, Mass.: Lexington Books), 1976.

Haar, C. M.: *Land Use Planning: A Casebook on the Use, Misuse, and Re-Use of Urban Land,* 3d ed. (Waltham, Mass.: Little, Brown & Co.), 1976.

Healy, R. G.: *Land Use and the States* (Baltimore, Md.: Johns Hopkins University Press), 1976.

Hunter, G. and others, Eds.: *Policy and Practice in Rural Development* (New York: Universe Books, Inc.), 1976.

Lynch, K. A.: *Managing the Sense of a Region* (Boston, Mass.: Massachusetts Institute of Technology Press), 1976.

CHAPTER 7

The Total Recreational Service System

Specifically what constitutes a total recreational service system in today's city? In this chapter the total system with its components and elements will be detailed and the parts supplied by the school system and by the municipal recreational service system will be discussed. County and regional contributions to the whole will be considered incidentally.

At the outset it must be recognized that the recreational role of school districts must be regarded as ancillary and subordinate to the traditional role of public schools in America. It is true that the traditional role has changed greatly in the past half century in many ways. Notable is the emphasis in the curriculum on the culture of leisure and the teaching of recreational knowledge and skills in the arts of recreational activities. Additionally, the schools have entered recreational service, partly filling the need for organized and informal recreational experiences of the people, through the conduct of extracurricular activities for pupils and in providing direction to the non-enrolled public in the use of school resources for community recreational service.

The role of recreational service in cities is not ancillary and subordinate to any other municipal responsibility or function. It is on a parity with them. It is, however, a permissive role, subject to the discretion of cities' governing bodies and to their fiscal limitations and the provisions of their charters.

Development of the Park Function

Parks have been established in cities through the centuries to serve several purposes, including those arising unpredictably as population proliferates and social problems (which must be solved) emerge in our society. Among these purposes has been the need to provide places for organized and unorganized active recreational pursuits, and to give guidance and direction for them. This modern function of parks derives from the expanding role of leisure and the recognition of the importance of recreational service in modern society.

Historically, parks have been used as places for public assembly, public markets, and refuges in times of disaster. They have served as mobilization centers for common defense against an aggressor. As cities have become dense in population, parks have tended to relieve the effects of congestion. Always, they are favored as places of beauty and repose and as sites for civic and recreational buildings. Today their use as places of active recreational experience, passive reflection, and appreciation, and for children's play and the competitive sports of youth is widely recognized.

A modern park system contains neighborhood parks—comparatively small areas supplementing neighborhood schools; community parks—larger areas providing special facilities for all age groups; regional parks, frequently within or near large metropolitan complexes; reservations and wilderness areas, wherever nature has placed them; special areas of extraordinary beauty; and places for active recreational pursuits, such as large sports areas, lakes, trails, golf courses, conservatories, arboretums, zoological gardens, museums, and so forth. These large areas and highly specialized facilities are within the category or component of regional parks. The larger a city becomes in area and population, the greater its need and inclination to provide regional recreational places. Regional recreational places otherwise are accepted as a responsibility of counties, states, and the federal government.

The Park-School Concept

"Park-school" is a term applied to a situation in which a school and a park are in juxtaposition. It should not be confused with a more recently used term "school-park," which is used to describe a complex of school units (elementary, secondary, and others) and certain special social service facilities in a park-like development. The positioning is sometimes planned deliberately to afford the school more outdoor space than would otherwise be practicable and at the same time to provide a park. On the other hand, it is sometimes a fortuitous situation resulting from land being available for acquisition which is suitable for either purpose but which is too large to be afforded by either agency alone. The park is then used by the school for its program of outdoor education and for more recreational activities than would otherwise be possible. If the park is provided with facilities used in a park-administered program that are not found in a standard schoolground development, the combined facilities permit a broader and larger program. The park-school may become a single operable unit adding amenities and opportunities for recreational experiences that could not be attained by other means.

The park-school concept has gained great favor especially in planning new communities. It is difficult to apply to the redevelopment of communities where the schools are surrounded by other development rendering the acquisition cost of additional land prohibitive. In the long view, the principle may be well applied, but not to the exclusion of other properties removed from schools where the need for a park might transcend the need to add park improvements to a school property.

Under the park-school plan it becomes incumbent on the two independent administrations, municipal recreational service or parks and schools, to effect harmonious cooperation and coordination of day-to-day operations. The school system is not set up to administer park services, nor can the city recreational service administration assume the functions of the school. The ideal is that programs emanating from the two independent agencies appear, for practical purposes, to be programs of a single agency.

Roles of County and Region

The role of counties in respect to parks and recreational needs is primarily a regional role and secondarily a local role, because counties are subdivisions of a state created to administer state governmental services, enforce state laws, and collect taxes, whereas cities are municipal corporations permitted and authorized by the legislature to attend to local problems. Public education is a function of state government and school districts are a convenient subdivision of a state, all parts of a state being within a school district, whereas cities are found only where resident population has seen fit to exercise its prerogative to incorporate as a city. Populated unincorporated areas generally have no instrument for performing purely local services, such as recreational service, other than the schools or by the establishment of special districts, which are municipal corporations for the performance of a stated and particular service. Sometimes special districts include portions of cities, usually, however, smaller cities.

Suburban-type cities with limited areas and populations (less than 100,000) as a rule do not provide regional parks or other regional components. This responsibility devolves on the counties, the states, and the federal government. Consequently, criteria or standards applicable to cities, especially cities that are a part of a large metropolitan complex (a region), need contain no reference to regional park areas or facilities. When a regional park lies wholly or partly within the boundaries of a city, and residential development adjoins the area, it may contain local areas and facilities intended for the use of the population of the neighborhood or community. In some situations control of the area so improved is assigned to the local recreational service department for operational purposes in order to incorporate its operation in the uniform plan of administration of local services.

PHYSICAL COMPONENTS OF A LOCAL PUBLIC SYSTEM

The two most important components of a local recreational service system are neighborhood recreational centers and community recreational centers. A neighborhood is the area served by an elementary school, a residential area approximately ½ mile in diameter, or an area in which local service facilities are accessible within walking distance for use on a day-to-day basis. Neighborhood recreational centers may be at a school, in a public park, or in a combined park-school complex, equipped primarily for the recreational needs of children and, within limits, for others in the neighborhood.

A community is a natural grouping of districts containing many neighborhoods with a common civic life and historic identity. Community recreational centers are larger than neighborhood centers and contain facilities that are required by teen-agers, adults, and family groups. Their facilities require more space (preferably 10 or more acres in already developed communities and in communities being planned in totality) than that found in neighborhood centers, and their location is often determined by fortuitous circumstances, such as availability of land for park use, rather than by precise planning according to general standards.

One neighborhood site per 2,000 population and one community site per 20,000 are generally considered as minimal requirements; hence, the ratio of neighborhood to community sites should be roughly ten to one. The neighborhood category includes schools serving as neighborhood playgrounds and recreational centers, complemented by local parks also serving as neighborhood recreational centers, either in conjunction with the school under the park-school plan or in neighborhoods that cannot be served by an existing school.

An accepted principle guiding the selection of facilities to be placed on neighborhood and community recreational sites is that the facilities permit a satisfactory program of day-to-day and seasonal activities suited to the needs and demands of people generally and arranged for the most efficient and economical use of the available land and buildings. A degree of standardization is possible. Standards proposed in Chapter 22 are consonant with the proposals of professional park and recreational planners and national professional societies.

Facilities for a Neighborhood Recreational Center

The activities in a neighborhood recreational center require both indoor and outdoor facilities. The minimal facilities are:

Indoor Facilities

1. Large all-purpose room for meetings, entertainments, square and social dancing, table games, parties, and limited fitness activities. Limited food service facilities and storage space for chairs, game tables, and other gear should be provided.
2. Craft room for elementary crafts requiring works tables and hand tools.
3. Clubroom for small club or group meetings.

Outdoor Facilities

1. Softball or junior baseball diamond adaptable to the official rules of Little League baseball. Junior diamonds are small replicas of official diamonds and should be of turf. Paved surfaces are most frequently found in elementary school yards because the foot traffic is too heavy to permit the maintenance of turf.
2. Children's playground apparatus for vigorous play on school grounds or in parks. The variety of apparatus selected should be installed with a view to safe use with soft landing surfaces (sand, tanbark, synthetic rubber, or composite material) under them.
3. Outdoor gymnasium equipped with apparatus offering graduated challenges to teen-agers with equipment at hand for "pick-up" games and lights for use at night. It should be placed close to the outdoor gymnasium to allow better safety-surface installation, better supervision, and economy in lighting during the evening hours.
4. Game courts such as mentioned under "outdoor gymnasium." Dimensions of courts should be adjusted to the maturity of the users.

Facilities for a Community Recreational Center

The community recreational center requires all of the elements proposed for the neighborhood center plus elements to accommodate persons of all age groups who come to the center from several districts in larger numbers than those attending a district or neighborhood center and who participate in a larger variety of activities. The additional facility elements should include:

Indoor Facilities

1. Gymnasium large enough for a standard basketball court. The ceiling should have no beam or other obstruction lower than 20 feet from the floor. Spectator accommodations are desirable.

Dressing rooms and showers are necessary. It may be used for sports other than basketball.

2. Auditorium, separate and apart from a gymnasium, designed for lectures, dramatic presentations, exhibits, and musical concerts and having a stage.

3. Swimming pools to be used for instruction and recreational purposes. Junior and senior high schools often have indoor pools to meet the requirements of a compulsory physical education program. Park pools are almost always outdoor pools. Whether indoor or outdoor, pools are not yet accepted as standard equipment for neighborhood parks nor for neighborhood elementary schools; hence they are specified among the essential facilities for community parks.

4. Tennis courts for teen-agers and adults in community parks, where space permits more than one court. A battery of four or more courts permits organization of tournament play and class instruction.

Auxiliary Parks or Centers

Auxiliary parks and centers are not required in all neighborhoods or in all communities of a city. They may be desired in some neighborhoods or in one or more communities or in a location apart from other parks. The auxiliary parks may be park triangles, park circles, park strips, sitting areas, tot lots, and parklets or "vest-pocket parks."

Park Triangles and Circles. When cities and subdivisions were laid out a century ago, it was considered good practice to provide park circles about 50 feet in diameter at the intersection of two major streets. These areas were intended to be planted to provide an interesting landscape as they were approached from any direction, a sitting area and a place for statues or fountains or unusual planting. The traffic circled the area to the right; persons on foot could cross the streets at any point comparatively safely and linger on the circle. This plan does not fit the conditions of today, for traffic moves too fast to make access safe, traffic semaphore signals often are installed, view is obstructed, and traffic is delayed. The circles usually remain, but are no longer planned in new developments.

Park triangles at intersections were improvised when two streets did not intersect each other at right angles, sometimes when a new development joined an older one. They were intended to perform the same function as the circles. Both are difficult to maintain in a manner satisfactory to the owners of nearby property. Maintenance of the property houseward from the curb, including the sidewalk, belongs to the property owner; maintenance of circles and triangles is the responsibility of the city. Uniform maintenance is difficult to achieve.

6

Park Strips. When a wide street was planned, a strip of land in the center of the street extending for any distance was provided. They were planted in a manner equal to the circles and triangles. Often they were intended as rights-of-way for streetcar lines and interurban transportation. Sometimes the strips were owned or held as easements by the transportation company, especially if the lines preceded the adjoining area in development. When the rights-of-way were abandoned or taken over by the city, with or without compensation, the strips became parks or were used to widen the street on either side. In congested areas like Manhattan and Brooklyn in New York City, they are a much appreciated amenity and perform a very useful park purpose. In replanning business areas, decorative malls have been laid out in the center strip of the street, the traffic has been bypassed to other streets, and the whole area has been improved to provide an attractive locale for shopping. Sidewalks and building fronts have been dressed up. Parking has been accommodated at the rear of commercial buildings.

Sitting Areas. In places of impacted population, as in the downtown areas of older cities, places to sit and pass the time of day or to rest become very important. It is good planning, appreciated by the business interests, the shoppers, and the people residing in the area, to take advantage of any odd properties to provide sitting areas with attractive landscaping.

Vest-Pocket Parks. The origin of this term is not known but it came into common use in New York City and Philadelphia in the 1950s. It was first used to denote a vacant piece of property, privately or publicly owned, on which a playground was improvised for the children or youth, in the absence of any other play areas serving the block or neighborhood. Frequently they were inadequately improved and had nondurable apparatus, and they tended to fall into disuse or were deliberately misused and vandalized. Municipal park departments were loath to take them over because of poor planning, the necessity of replanning and reconstruction, and funds were not budgeted to do the necessary work nor to provide the supervision that was deemed necessary for the protection of the neighbors for the obtaining of proper behavior for constructive recreational activity. However, some have proved themselves. Above all they have demonstrated the need for auxiliary park facilities in areas of great need.

Tot Lots. The term "tot lot" has long been used to denote a small area within the residential block for children of pre-school or early school age. It is an equipped area within a residential block available to mothers and small children residing in the block, without street exposure, fronting on a street or, perhaps, at a corner, thus being available to the mothers and children of several blocks. It must be regarded as an auxiliary park planned for neighborhoods where there is a special need and not as one to be provided throughout the city. There are two conditions that indicate the need for tot lots. One is the percentage of women (particularly mothers) in the labor market, and the other is the average family income of the neighborhood. A third condition might well be the density of population of the neighborhood. These conditions can be determined from the findings of the United States Census Bureau.

Teen-age Recreational Centers. Modern experience in the conduct of recreational activities for the youth makes it very plain that the conventional programs conducted by most agencies leave a void insofar as participation of some of the youths are concerned. Many of the youths from age 15 to 19 are dropouts from the established programs. They appear to be waiting for some opportunity to socialize with their peers and to pursue a variety of opportunities for recreational experience. The teen-age recreational center should be an integral unit, preferably part of a community park, which can be described best as a "drop-in" center at which there are a variety of incentives and inducements to freely participate in many activities known to be attractive to older teen-agers. The center is presided over by specially prepared and dedicated youth leaders who cultivate the involvement of the youth in self-directed and self-managed activities. Preferably it should be an outdoor and indoor facility, operated the year-round, day and evening. In short, it should be a place that the teen-agers regard as their own. It must still be regarded as an optional facility in the public recreational service system and should be introduced where experience and investigation reveal an unmet need. A large community park, if otherwise well located, is the appropriate place for the center.

Senior Citizens' Recreational Center. This facility is accepted and recognized as more of a necessity than the teen-age recreational center, owing to the rapid growth of "retirement" in an increasingly large segment of the population. Special indoor and outdoor facilities, somewhat removed from the areas used by children in a public park, have been in great demand. Organized programs, conducted in large measure by the seniors themselves, are indicated, with some professional oversight.

Optional Elements. The facilities listed as essential elements in several categories are minimal in respect to the number of each and to the inclusion of other elements. Every recreational service system should seek to have at least one outstanding park development to give the city distinction and recognition. The locale of the city, such as beside an ocean, or with a lake or other geographic, geological, climatic, or historic advantage, frequently causes a city to exploit its uniqueness by an addition to its inventory of park facilities and advantages. Such unique facilities cannot be considered as standard components to be found in every neighborhood, district, or community.

Public Conveniences in the Park and Recreational System

Not mentioned in the catalogue of elements for a recreational service system are sanitary conveniences for men and women and boys and girls. Often it is desirable to have separate conveniences for children and adults, and for persons participating in indoor activities and those using the outdoor facilities. They may be in the same building with a wall dividing them, for when admission is charged for indoor activities or when a group must be supervised, such as a teen-age dance, exit through the lavatories to the out-of-doors is not desirable.

Early plans for neighborhood and community parks included no space or arrangements for parking the automobiles of clientele. Parking areas are now considered to be an essential facility in community parks and sometimes in neighborhood parks as well. Even in school areas, parking spaces should be provided for the staff if not for the neighborhood adult and older teen-age clientele. In well-organized cities of considerable size, building and construction regulations applicable to building permits require certain numbers of parking spaces related to the attendance capacities of the facilities.

To add utility to a neighborhood and community park, night lighting of play areas is very important. Except for children, there is more recreational activity for people in the evening hours than at any other time. The recreational service system must be developed to provide for activities during the evening hours. Portions of large parks through which people must pass to reach the activity areas require illumination also. These observations apply to neighborhood school yards when they are improved for the use of those older than elementary school age.

Landscaping

Landscaping of parks, playgrounds, and recreational centers might well have been mentioned as an absolute imperative in the development of a park and recreational system. Traditionally, this was the initial improvement to be made of an area acquired and developed for park purposes. Parks were places for the enjoyment of the beauties of the landscape. Recreational facilities gradually intruded on the landscape, and park planners sometimes opposed this seeming intrusion. Some believed that the two functions—parks and recreational service—were mutually exclusive. Gradually, the view has come to be accepted that a park, especially in local neighborhoods and communities, should be a place of beauty with an equitable share of the area devoted to landscape developments, and that a playground or recreational center should be efficiently and functionally developed for active recreational experiences with ample attention to landscape. The two functions are not incompatible even in small areas. Grassed areas for certain play places should be provided, because certain activities require softer and safer surfaces than asphalt or "black top."

Comparison of School and Park Recreational Centers

The thesis has been advanced in this text that the public school is and must inevitably be the prime place for the recreational activities of the public in the cities of America. If it is apparent that there must eventually be a recreational center in every neighborhood, and more sophisticated centers in districts and communities, there can be no other answer, except in very affluent communities. Schools are provided wherever there are children, and they are usually distributed so that children can walk to them. It is inconceivable that there could be as many public recreational centers in parks as there are in schools. If this supposition is to be sustained, it becomes of interest to examine the schools and their facilities and to ponder what further development is necessary to have the schools adequately perform the services that society might require of them, and to provide some guidelines for park development to complement the school facilities.

Inventory of a System

Any system composed of finite entities requires an inventory of its parts in order to measure and appraise it. A well-organized recreational service system should have inventories of real estate and of permanent structures and equipment to assist in providing equitable allocation or distribution of the properties among the neighborhoods, districts, and communities. Inventories of movable equipment and supplies are used for several purposes including accountability for its care and replacement. Compiling an inventory in a form that makes its data available for study can become an involved procedure; to relate its data to other available data, such as demographic studies obtained from the decennial United States Census, complicates the procedure. Fortunately, technology has provided computers to expedite the process and permit countless comparative displays, summaries, and rankings.

Until recent years, the technological instruments to deal profitably with sophisticated detail were lacking, and inventories were inadequate. Inventories became more significant as the basic items in categories to be measured became easier to classify. Earlier in this chapter the components and elements considered essential to the organization of a competent program were described. To array an inventory of the recreational areas and facilities most often found in a typical American city, let us utilize a community of approximately 50,000 population. Table 7-1 (p. 154) illustrates the data. The inventory is of an actual city reputed to have a competent system. There are eight elementary schools, with customary equipment, and one junior and one senior high school, both equipped to carry out activities having a place in the physical education program of the schools.

The park system of the city includes one fully developed park of 90 acres, approximately in the center of the city, a quite well-equipped neighborhood park of less than an acre, and three tot lots. In the subsequent sections of this chapter, following a discussion of standards of components of a complete system, the inventory of both the schools and the city for appraisal of their adequacy according to proposed standards or criteria will be presented.

STANDARDS FOR SPACES AND FACILITIES

The systematization of public recreational service administration specifically applies to the numerous physical properties. Systems analysis can be employed for this aspect of administration and planning, as it is used for program analysis, personnel selection, compensation, assignment to duties, finances, and the like. For systems analysis, the physical properties and the planning of them require their organization and arrangement according to a generic classification based on accepted definitions. Hypothetical criteria of adequacy should be agreed on in order to compare the components with population aggregates. The criteria must be empirical, i.e., based on proved experience, which is now sufficient in the recreational service to permit consensus. The criteria may be called "standards."

Determining Standards

There are two main approaches to establishing recreational space and facility standards: (1) criteria expressed in terms of ratio of population to space (acres) and to essential facilities; and (2) criteria based on the habits, dispositions, and characteristics of the public (users or consumers). The former is a logistic computation to determine comparative supply or adequacy. The latter is a strategic determination based on value judgments of the activities deemed to serve the objectives of the responsible administrative agency and to meet the public's demand.

These judgments take into account demographic facts, the variable and changing recreational culture, prevailing fads and fashions, the time the public has available, the disposition of the people involved in publicly sponsored programs, mobility, and transportation to recreational places, and the like.

Standards for Land Spaces

Standards for land space should begin with a consideration of the open areas required for environmental beautification and conservation, the space required to relieve the effects of congestion and proliferation of population in the urban setting, and the space needed for the installation of facilities and the organization of activities for the public. Standards should apply also to the minimal essential facilities described in the previous section which comprise the recreational service system.

The quest for authoritative standards has been a preoccupation of recreationist administrators and planners from the beginning of the recreational service movement. At the National Recreation Congress in 1923, a proposal was advanced for outdoor space at the public schools. In the late 1920s, with considerable agreement among the several professional associations, it was proposed that a reasonable provision of space for outdoor recreational activities in cities should be 1 acre of land for each 100 persons (10 acres per 1,000 persons) of present and future population. In an inquiry in 1942, the American Institute of Park Executives found that all authorities agreed that 10 acres of park should be provided for each 1,000 population (100 persons per 1 acre). Because it was reasonable and simply stated, the figure was widely accepted and is still the most generally accepted standard. It is typically defined as including recreational and park areas lying within or immediately adjacent to the city; areas desired for neighborhood and community use as well as areas serving regional park and conservation purposes.

A Committee on Park and Recreational Standards of the American Society of Planning Officials in 1943 expressed the opinion that 1 acre per 100 persons was not practical of attainment in larger cities and more densely populated areas, and a standard of 1 acre per 200 population in cities was suggested.

The most thorough analysis of the outdoor recreational space requirements of New York City was made by the Committee on the Regional Plan of New York and Environs, whose report was published in five volumes in 1928. The Committee stated:

> Those who study recreational problems hesitate to state minimum space requirements for the various types of open areas because of the wide variation in local conditions, and also because such minimum standards might be mistaken as implying entirely adequate provision. . . .
>
> There can be no excessive provision for recreational experience, subject to the limits of economic considerations.
>
> All that can be done is to make the best of a bad situation, and to add to the neighborhood parks and playgrounds of the city wherever opportunity affords.[1]

Analysis of space and facility requirements for park and recreational purposes was made by the California Committee for Recreation, Park

[1] Russell Sage Foundation, *Public Recreation, A Study of Parks, Playgrounds and Other Outdoor Recreation Facilities, Regional Plan of New York and Environs* (New York: Russell Sage Foundation, 1928), pp. 130 and 133.

Areas and Facilities in 1956.[2] The Committee recommended that "each recreational agency or school district should establish its own standards, in accordance with what the people consider adequate and are willing to pay for."[3]

However, the National Recreation and Park Association has continued to examine its position on area and facility standards and has attempted to formulate criteria based upon appropriate research which might be utilized as guides.[4]

A minimum of 2 acres per 1,000 persons has the widest acceptance for neighborhood recreational experiences supplied on school areas (excluding building areas) and within parks, and a minimum of 2 acres per 1,000 persons for community parks. Together the two amount to 4 acres per 1,000, or 1 acre per 250 people. One neighborhood recreational site per 2,000 persons and one community park per 20,000 also have acceptance as a minimal standard. Acceptance and application are quite different. In many instances, there is little correlation between the two. Despite praiseworthy efforts to devise standards based upon population density, land availability, particular facilities, and financial capability, great disparity exists between the creation of reliable standards and current research being undertaken to determine user patterns, resources, and recreational needs of potential participants.[5]

Agreement on the amount of space required and desirable for regional parks has not yet been stated. Incorporating large spaces in the public domain for conservation of open spaces, wildlife conservation, and regionally oriented recreational activity is a still-to-be-realized goal. Large areas suited to regional purposes have not been evenly distributed by nature. Notwithstanding, the Bureau of Outdoor Recreation of the federal government has formulated some guidelines for the retention of many federally owned and state-owned lands, and for the acquisition of other privately owned lands recommended to be incorporated in the public domain.

Facility Standards

The number and kinds of facilities that should be constructed or supplied on school and park areas within the city are related to the amount of space available, the physical conformation of the areas (topography), and the pattern of their distribution throughout the city.

[2] California Committee on Planning for Recreation, Park Areas and Facilities, *Guide for Planning Recreation Parks in California* (Sacramento: Documents Section, Printing Division, State of California, 1956), p. 50.

[3] *Ibid.*, p. 34.

[4] R. D. Beechner, ed., *National Park, Recreation, and Open-Space Standards* (Washington, D.C.: National Recreation and Park Association, 1971), p. 7.

[5] National Academy of Sciences, *A Program for Outdoor Recreation Research* (Washington, D.C.: The Academy, 1969), p. 5.

The kinds of spaces (neighborhood and community) that should be distributed through the city and the facilities that should be installed on them are set forth in the previous section. Table 7-1 presents minimal standards for city recreational areas, the facilities that should be placed on them, and the actual number of each component found in a typical city of 50,000 population. The percent of adequacy compared with the standard is also shown.

Some desirable facilities are not found uniformly in all neighborhood, district, and community parks or in the school system. They have not been included in the table or in the evaluation of adequacy.

Summary of Adequacies and Comparative Supply, City and Schools

Table 7-1 lists 21 elements capable of quantitative measurement. Because the average percent of adequacy for all components in the "typical city" amounts to only 57 percent, it might be assumed that the standard is too high to be applied to an average city, and this may be so even though the standard is recommended by the professional and service associations footnoted at the bottom of the table. Repeating the observation of one study, each city should determine its own standard, the important consideration being that criteria for the kinds and quantities of elements are established.

The array of facilities provided by the schools on the one hand and by the city on the other provides a basis for comparison of the contribution of each toward the total equipment required. In summary, some comparisons and general observations may be made:

1. The total acreage supplied by both agencies falls short of the standard of 4 acres per 1,000 population, or 1 acre per 250 people, being only 65 percent of standard.
2. The city provides the greater amount of acreage, two and one-half times that provided by the schools.
3. The schools provide more sites for local recreational activity, twice as many as are provided by the city.
4. The average space for school centers is only 3.7 acres, whereas at parks it is 18 acres; however, the city has consolidated most of its acreage in one 90-acre park. The school grounds are much smaller than the standards recommended by school planners.
5. The categories with a reasonably adequate supply (over 75 percent) are all-purpose rooms, craft rooms, auditoriums, regulation baseball diamonds, and game courts.
6. The categories with shortest supply (less than 50 percent) are clubrooms, tennis courts, swimming pools, outdoor gymnasiums, and special centers (community recreational centers, teen-age recreational centers, and senior citizens' recreational centers).

TABLE 7-1   MINIMAL STANDARDS AND COMPARATIVE INVENTORIES OF SCHOOL AND CITY AREAS AND FACILITIES FOR 50,000 POPULATION

	MINIMAL STANDARD	SCHOOLS	CITY	TOTAL	ADEQUACY (%)
Acreage for Neighborhood and Community Recreational Places[1]	4/1,000	37	92	129	65
Recreational Sites or Centers	1/2,000	10	5	15	60
Indoor Facilities[2]					
All-purpose room	1/3,000	10	2	12	77
Craft room	1/3,000	10	2	12	77
Clubroom	1/3,000	3	1	4	24
Gymnasium	1/10,000	2	1	3	60
Auditorium	1/10,000	4	1	5	100
Outdoor Facilities[2,3]					
Baseball diamond, official	1/6,000	0	5	5	83
Softball or junior diamond	1/2,000	10	3	13	52
Tennis courts	1/2,000	4	6	10	40
Swimming pools	1/15,000	0	1	1	33
Children's apparatus	1/2,000	9	5	14	56
Outdoor gymnasium	1/6,000	1	2	3	24
Game courts	1/3,000	10	2	12	77
Special Centers[2,4]					
Community recreational centers	1/20,000	0	1	1	40
Teen-age recreational centers	1/20,000	0	1	1	40
Senior citizens' recreational center	1/20,000	0	1	1	40
Conveniences and Amenities					
Grassed areas	1/center	1	5	6	40
Outdoor lighting	1/center	1	2	3	20
Sanitary facilities	1/center	10	2	12	80
Protective fencing	1/center	10	5	15	100
		Total average percent of adequacy			57

[1] National Recreation Association, *Outdoor Recreation Space Standards* (New York: National Recreation Association, 1965), p. 20.
[2] National Recreation Association, *Standards: Playgrounds, Recreation Buildings, Indoor Facilities* (New York: National Recreation Association, 1965), pp. 7–9.
[3] U.S. Department of the Interior, Bureau of Outdoor Recreation, *Outdoor Recreation Standards* (Washington, D.C.: U.S. Government Printing Office, April, 1967), pp. 1–57.
[4] National Recreation Association, *Standards for Municipal Recreation Areas,* rev. ed. (New York: National Recreation Association, 1962), pp. 21–22.

7. The public conveniences in short supply are grassed areas on the school playgrounds and lighting installations on school grounds.

Application of Minimal Standards in Planning

A table of minimal standards may be used for comparing the adequacy of recreational space and facilities in one community with that of another within the same city, or between two or more cities. Utilization of the device requires four steps: (1) identification of United States Census tracts within the several community boundaries and computation of the total population of each; (2) inventory of the physical resources for recreational purposes according to the categories in the table of standards; (3) computation of the percent of adequacy within each category; and (4) summation of the separate percentages for each community and determination of the average adequacy for each.

The use of this measuring device is, of course, less than perfect. Its validity depends on the degree of standardization of specifications of the facilities and the accuracy of the inventory. Another inaccuracy in the use of the device derives from the fact that all elements are not of equal importance. Moreover, totaling of averages is not a precise statistical technique. Nevertheless, the device can be beneficially applied to indicate guidelines for achieving parity in spaces and facilities among communities in the same city. It will forcefully reveal the errors in planning in the past, and it provides a basis for determining priorities for future allocation of funds.

Selected References

Benjamin, J.: *Grounds for Play* (New York: International Publications Service), 1975.

Cutler, L. S. and S. S. Cutler: *Recycling Cities for People* (Boston, Mass.: Cahners Books International, Inc.), 1976.

Dattner, R.: *Design for Play* (Boston, Mass.: Massachusetts Institute of Technology Press), 1974.

Flynn, R. B.: "Forces on Community Recreational Facilities," *JOPER* (Nov.–Dec., 1977), pp. 33–46.

Gertler, L.: *Making Man's Environment: Urban Issues* (Cincinnati, Ohio: Van Nostrand Reinhold Co.), 1976.

Gugenheimer, E. C.: *Planning for Parks and Recreation Needs* (New York: Twayne Publishers, Inc.), 1967.

Heckscher, A.: *Open Spaces* (New York: Harper & Row), 1977.

Hogan, P.: *Playgrounds for Free: The Utilization of Used and Surplus Materials in Playground Construction* (Boston, Mass.: Massachusetts Institute of Technology Press), 1974.

Hurtwood, Lady Allen: *Planning for Play* (Boston, Mass.: Massachusetts Institute of Technology Press), 1974.

Ledermann, A. and A. Traschel: *Creative Playgrounds and Recreation Centers, rev. ed.* (New York: Praeger Publishers), 1968.

Merhabian. A.: *Public Places and Private Spaces: The Psychology of Work, Play and Living Environments* (New York: Basic Books), 1976.

Shivers, J. S. and G. Hjelte: *Planning Recreational Places* (Cranbury, N.J.: Associated University Presses, Inc.), 1971.

Williams, W. R.: *Recreation Places* (New York: Reinhold Publishing Corporation), 1958.

CHAPTER 8

Liability and Public Administration of Recreational Services

The incidence of litigation against public recreational service departments, in all parts of the country, is rising. A more liberalized view of the accountability owed to patrons of public recreational places by the courts has, in part, been one factor. Legislative enactments which permit a broadened basis for bringing tort claims against public jurisdictions have also assisted in the public's desire to sue and recover for damages or injuries incurred in publicly sponsored/operated places. Of course, the plaintiff must still prove that the defendant was negligent in the administration of the area, facility, equipment, or degree of supervision available.

Several variables inevitably intrude upon any understanding of liability and the court actions which may be undertaken by private citizens against public entities. This chapter supplies information concerning the various aspects of tort claims, offers defenses against alleged claims of negligence, and provides one case study which exemplifies how legislation has changed a basic concept for defending against charges of negligence. This has been done by providing the background, exposition, and denouement of a recently held jury trial with a defendant public agency. The case shows how imperative it is that the administrators of public agencies have a protective plan of action to insure the safe operation of all recreational areas under their control. More to the point, however, this incident illustrates that complacency and casual toleration of potentially dangerous situations can only lead to the waste of tax monies. It really means that public recreational service departments are laying themselves open to litigation against which they have no defense. When there are neither comprehensive patron and employee safety policies, logical plans for the imple-

156

mentation of safety practices, and operational routines which will insure that all reasonable and prudent actions have been taken to avoid placing patrons in jeopardy, successful suits follow. In effect, then, public recreational service departments must recognize that they are responsible for the health, safety, and welfare of their patrons. Minimization of this responsibility is tantamount to being culpably negligent and irresponsible.

This by no means suggests that public recreational service departments should eliminate activities which are risky.[1] Rather, it demands that public agencies refrain from acting in ways that are calculated to bring about property damage or personal injury. There is little doubt that almost all recreational activities have some element of risk for the participant. Perhaps this is one of the reasons that individuals become involved with such recreational activities. If these experiences were abolished or curtailed, people would certainly find ways to accomplish the same objectives in less safe environments. The public recreational agency has a three-fold task: (1) it must offer stimulating and, perhaps, adventurous activities; (2) it must supervise those activities in such a manner that the consequences are neither perilous to the individual nor catastrophic to the department; and (3) it must protect the individual from committing foolish acts or behaving in a reckless manner. All of the foregoing requires consummate ability, vigilance, and a knowledge of what constitutes the appropriate conduct of a recreational service system.

It would appear to be stating the obvious that a recreationist, despite being a professional in his/her chosen field, is really a layman in the field of law. For this reason recreationists should be given the same consideration usually offered to laymen to whom knowledge of the civil law is not attributed. However, the experienced recreationist administrator knows that, frequently, a requirement to understand the civil law attaches forcibly, almost destructively, to all of those who attempt to provide recreational services to the public. The recreationist must, therefore, be cognizant of the laws of the locale in which he is employed. Lack of such knowledge could adversely affect the department, the community at large, as well as the professional himself; thus, ignorance is no excuse.

Not having the benefit of formal legal education, what can the recreationist do to reduce the potential for litigation? There are no simple answers to this question. The only practical response, at best partial and subject to real limitations, is for the practitioner to become conversant, insofar as is possible, with legal problems which have ensnared other members of his profession. Such knowledge will enable the recreationist to try to avoid repeating the errors committed by others through deficiency of understanding of technical facets of the law.

[1] Janna Rankin, "Legal Risks and Bold Programming," *Parks & Recreation* (July, 1977), pp. 47–48, 67–69.

One of the objectives of this chapter is to make all those engaged in the provision of public recreational service more deeply conscious of the law, and to make them appreciate certain potential difficulties so that they may recognize danger in sufficient time to obtain legal advice. It is not intended that recreationists will act as their own attorneys nor is it possible to cover every contingency that might arise.

The laws of each state assume great importance when they concern the rights of citizens, the health, safety, protection, and general welfare of people, and the protection of property. The whole concept of civil and human rights has become of paramount importance in terms of recent congressional legislation and the decisions of the United States Supreme Court. The Civil Rights Act of 1964 and subsequent court decisions have had a great impact on the provision of recreational service to all citizens of the United States. Discrimination against any person, whether for reasons of color, sex, age, religion, or other artificial social barriers, has been discredited. This is only right under a social system where all are equal before the law.

Administrators must be increasingly knowledgeable about questions of equity and the standards of protection prescribed by law. Two factors are involved in any question of equity: (1) the implicit language of the law and (2) the judicial interpretation of the law. Who or what was damaged? Who is responsible? Can negligence be shown? Did the individual who suffered injuries to person or damage to property act in such a way as to bring the injuries on himself? Was the injured individual or the one who committed the damaging act a minor?

Questions of legal responsibility and of immunity from litigation brought for damage against the municipal corporation are vital to those who seek redress. These same questions are no less vital to authorities whose responsibility it is to provide and operate public recreational services. Public recreational service system administrators must know how to avoid legal liability should an accident causing personal injury or property damage occur.

Fear and ignorance of the legalities involved in public recreational service either can frustrate and limit an otherwise excellent recreational program or can invite the possibility of great financial loss to the city. If damages are awarded in suits against the municipality, tax funds allocated to support the operations of the recreational service system may have to be diverted to make payment. Thus, the entire recreational service program and the municipality may suffer owing to negligence.

All employees of public recreational service systems must accept the risk of personal damage suits instigated against them if an individual is injured while under their supervision and if negligence is proved against them. This risk is related to the doctrine that all persons are responsible for their own acts. Injuries may occur anywhere at any time, on playgrounds, athletic fields, swimming pools, locker rooms, craft or shop rooms, and in recreational structures of all types. It is only human to seek a cause of accident other than one's own negligence; hence negligence of another is frequently alleged. Often a suit against the city will name an employee as co-defendant. He is usually defended by the counsel for the city. Only in a few cases have judgments been found against employees. Personal liability insurance is available at the employee's cost. The municipality also may carry insurance protection against litigation. Actually, the only adequate protection is prudent and correct action on the part of the recreationist under all circumstances. Laxity, at any point, invites disaster.

Governmental and Proprietary Functions and Immunity

When a new municipal function is established, local officials become apprehensive about the community's financial posture in liability cases in which injuries to persons or damage to property is sustained. The functions that government performs are either governmental or proprietary in character. Governmental functions are those functions performed by the state acting in its sovereign capacity, or by a subdivision acting for the state, that are essential for the protection of the state and for the general welfare. Proprietary functions, on the other hand, are defined as those that municipal corporations perform in their separate corporate capacities. They are not performed for the people of the state generally but optionally for the corporation itself and its people. Liability accrues with proprietary functions, but immunity is attached to governmental functions.[2]

The theory by which municipalities are held to be free of tort liability when operating in a governmental capacity is that liability would place a deterrent on their performance of an essential governmental duty. Taxes are assessed and raised for definite governmental objectives and to channel them to the payment of damage claims arising out of necessary governmental duties would tend to restrain municipalities in the performance of those duties.[3]

Although there is no firm definition, it has been generally agreed that public education, indigent care, law enforcement, fire protection, and public health regulation are governmental functions. The construction and maintenance of streets, bridges, and sewers, the collection of refuse, and the operation of water, gas, electric, and other public utilities are generally held to be proprietary functions. The distinction between the two functions originated in the courts, yet, in its application to particular cases, there is wide divergence of judicial opinion. Whether

---

[2] *City of Trenton v. State of New Jersey,* 262 U.S. 182 (1923).
[3] *O'Connell v. Merchants and Police District Telephone Company* (Ky.), 180 S.W. 845, L.B.A. (1915), p. 508.

recreational service is a governmental or proprietary function is a moot point. There have been many decisions on both sides by courts of nearly all states. Those leaning toward the proprietary interpretation take the general view that in the particular case the municipality was not acting for the state or the people at large but, on the contrary, was acting in an optional manner for its own benefit. Decisions interpreting the service as governmental have generally pointed out that the benefits of recreational service have value far beyond the corporate boundaries of the municipality and as such are not restricted to the inhabitants of the city in question. Furthermore, public recreational services have not been regarded traditionally as efforts of private enterprise.

Almost all the decisions have been based on two specific factors: the purpose of and the source of authority for the function in question. Five primary purposes are cited: public welfare, health, education, specific benefit, and monetary considerations. Authority for the performance of a function derives from expressed or implied power of either a mandatory or a permissive nature.

Fees and Charges and Public Liability

The effect of charging fees for recreational services has had some influence on court decisions concerning liability. If the fees were of an incidental nature and were not established for the purpose of conducting the activity at a profit to the municipality, the function retained its governmental character. But if charges consistently produced a profit, the function usually has been deemed proprietary.

The nature of the municipalities' responsibility for performance of public recreational service devolves on whether such services are mandatory for the general welfare of the people. If they are, the doctrine of governmental function applies. But the mere fact of permissiveness does not preclude immunity; there are jurisdictions where permissive right is immune to liability. Whether the function is expressed in the charter or granted in state legislation is held to be immaterial.

The wide divergence of legal opinion in regard to this subject makes generalization almost impossible. Because the law is not static, but reflects both the growing knowledge of the jurist and the shifting of public opinion, court interpretations, regardless of decisions, can and do change. The operation of parks and other recreational places may very well be considered a governmental function, but a particular activity may be interpreted as a proprietary function. For example, a department may operate an amusement park, a swimming pool, or other facilities that consistently produce a profit, and that could be shown to be not wholly limited to public agencies, but also typical of private endeavor. Courts have held that cities conducting profit-making activities were of a governmental character.

The Supreme Court of New Jersey affirmed a decision that the city of Newark was liable for injuries resulting from negligence at a municipal swimming pool. After paying 10 cents admission to the city pool, the plaintiff suffered a brain concussion when he fell on the "wet, filmy, and slippery" washroom floor. There was no permanent injury, however. By a vote of 6-0, the court upheld a judgment awarded by a county district court to the plaintiff. The judge found negligence on Newark's part, but the city appealed on grounds that it was immune from liability under a state law which stated that "no municipality or county shall be liable for injury to the person from the use of any public grounds, buildings, or structure." The judge was upheld by the Superior Court Appellate Division. The jurist ruled that the statute did not apply in this case because operation of a pool is a "proprietary function."[4] The court found that a hazardous floor condition had existed "for some time." The Supreme Court relied on the Appellate Division's opinion, which said the law in question holds a municipality liable for negligence "in the maintenance of a building devoted to the performance of a function voluntarily assumed under its general powers, or by permissive legislation, or where it performs a service which could be provided as well (and often is) by a private corporation . . . rather than for the purpose of carrying out the public functions of the state without special advantage to the city."[5] In the above case, the state of New Jersey appears to consider recreational service as a proprietary function under certain circumstances.

Illinois, on the other hand, considers recreational services performed by municipal and other governmental agencies to be a governmental function. The Illinois courts had uniformly held that park districts and municipal corporations were immune from tort liability when acting in a governmental capacity. Yet, in 1959, the Supreme Court of the State of Illinois filed an opinion holding that a municipal corporation is now fully liable for negligence in personal injury and property damage cases. Although this opinion was limited strictly to school districts, it could apply in the future to all municipal departments, including park districts and recreational service departments. This abrupt reversal, particularly aimed at a social institution clearly and traditionally held to be a creature of the state and operating in a governmental capacity, might pave the way for a series of suits against other legal subdivisions hitherto thought to be immune.[6]

The traditional separation of governmental and proprietary functions was dealt another blow when the Supreme Court of Wisconsin apparently

[4] *Weeks v. City of Newark,* 34 N.J. 250 168 At 12d 11 (1969).
[5] Letter from Hon. Charles S. Barret, Jr., Judge, Essex County Court, New Jersey, January 16, 1962.
[6] *Molitor v. Kaneland Community Unit School District,* (1959).

deleted governmental immunity from court claims in the state. The case involved a three-year-old child who had been injured while playing on a recreational area in Milwaukee. The decision of the court was to remove immunity because the courts, not the state legislature, had initially fixed the doctrine.[7]

What has brought about this change? Years ago, the courts recognized the fact that certain hazards accrue from recreational activities, but they felt that if reasonable care was exercised the benefits derived from such experiences would greatly outweigh the possible results of injury. But the immunity doctrine is being carefully considered as a matter of equity in terms of what is in the best interest of the public welfare. Negligence and hazards that occur because of stupidity no longer are questions of morality; they have assumed the aspect of legal responsibility. Accidents ensuing because of the negligence of those individuals responsible for such recreational activities have caused a change in the attitude of the courts. The courts are now returning decisions that uphold the plaintiff when negligence can be proved. Conservatives who maintain that payment for injury and damage constitutes a misapplication of public funds seem to be fighting a rearguard and losing battle. More and more, liberal court interpretations hold that no individual should bear the cost of personal injury or damage to property when negligence can be shown. Equity and justice will be served only when the cost of injury and/or damage to individuals and property is shared by all. No person should have to bear the burden of personal injury or property damage when the proximate cause has been negligence.

The contributory negligence concept prevents a plaintiff from recouping any part of his/her loss despite the triviality of plaintiff's negligence with regard to the cause of the accident. Although the plaintiff's negligence may have been relatively small in comparison to the defendant's, the contributory doctrine has permitted the defendant to be free of all liability. To compensate for the burdens placed upon one person, where two parties are responsible, some progressive states have abolished contributory negligence and substituted a doctrine of comparative negligence. Wisconsin[8] has been one of these pioneering states as has been Illinois, Connecticut, Massachusetts, Rhode Island, Maine, New Hampshire, Vermont, Texas, and a few others, in adopting a doctrine of comparative negligence. Now, plaintiffs have a more equitable opportunity to attempt to recover for losses received.

In view of the current situation and the continued liberal opinion of the courts, it is imperative that recreationists maintain close contact with legislative enactments and those court decisions which are pertinent to

[7] "Municipality Immunity from Tort Claims Abolished," *The Municipality,* League of Wisconsin Municipalities, Madison, Wisconsin, July, 1962.
[8] Wisconsin Statute Annals, 895,045

the provision of public recreational service. Regardless of whether recreational service is viewed as a governmental or proprietary function, the recreationist should understand what his position is as a public agent of the state or of one of its local legal subdivisions. It is likely that the trend of liberal interpretation of the doctrine of immunity will continue and enlarge. For this reason, the recreationist should become familiar with the legal concepts that now determine the consequences of most litigation for tortious acts and the legal terminology in these cases.

Legal Terminology and Concepts of Liability

In recent years, questions concerning legal liability increasingly have confronted recreationists in public recreational service. There appears to be a mounting public recognition of liability and an increasing propensity for individuals to seek litigation whenever injury or damage occurs. The number of claim settlements awarded by the various courts over the past few years tends to be in favor of the plaintiff. The laws that deal with liability have always been based on common law, or generalized principles of equity, rather than on statute law. It is likely, therefore, that legal interpretation depends on a given jury, subject to appeal. It seems relevant that the recreationist should be informed about the doctrines on which liability and various defenses rest.

Liability. Liability is that condition for which an individual or corporation is answerable and out of which arises a responsibility to perform in specific ways, which obligation is enforceable by court action; hence, a legal responsibility. When an individual is injured or property is damaged through proved negligence on the part of an agent of a recreational service system, that agent and/or the department may be sued in order to obtain redress. Even though ordinarily protected from liability by reason of the nature of the function performed, the municipality, its agents, and its employees can be held liable in the event of negligence. Courts have consistently held that reasonable diligence by members of governing boards or commissions in assigning duties is sufficient to absolve them of personal liability. Commission members act in a corporate capacity and not for themselves. They cannot be held personally liable for the acts of their agents or the doctrine of *respondeat superior* (let the master answer). With respect to existence of an attractive nuisance, it must be shown that they had prior notice of the condition before liability could be imputed to members of governing commissions for the existence and continuance of the attractive nuisance.

Tort. Tort is a civil rather than a criminal wrong, not involving a breach of contract, which infringes on the rights of another and entitles the injured party to sue for redress. A *tortious act* is construed as a legal wrong resulting in some form of injury to another individual or damage to property. Thus, torts may accrue as a result of malfeasance, misfeasance, or nonfeasance.

Malfeasance. Malfeasance is an act of commission, without legal justification, with malicious intent to hurt, cause harm, or otherwise injure another party or his property through misconduct or abuse of the power of position. One in an administrative position might be found guilty of malfeasance if he was involved in the handling of certain public construction and accepted bribe money to award a contract for such construction.

Misfeasance. Misfeasance is an act of commission with legal justification but performed in such a bungling manner as to engender harm or injury to another party or his property. Thus, misfeasance is the improper or incompetent execution of a lawful act without malicious intent. For example, the Police Athletic League of a municipality sets aside certain streets as playgrounds for children, prohibiting traffic from using those streets. If the traffic signs were placed improperly or not at all, so that a car came through by error and a child was injured, then the person responsible for placing the signs might be held guilty of misfeasance.

Nonfeasance. Nonfeasance is the omission of a lawful act or failure to perform a legal duty, without malicious intent, which causes damage or injury to persons and/or property. If a child sustains a serious injury on a playground, it is the responsibility of the recreationist in charge to apply whatever first aid measures are necessary. Failure to perform the required first aid procedures may be construed as nonfeasance.

In Loco Parentis. In loco parentis means acting in the place of a parent, i.e., assuming a guardian's responsibility for a minor. When a child is injured in a recreational situation through some aspect of negligence, it is assumed that the degree of care owed to the child by the individual acting the guardian's role was not maintained in a reasonable manner. In such a situation, the guardian has a recognized obligation to use a high degree of care to prevent exposing the minor to risk.

Negligence. Negligence is the failure to exercise reasonable and prudent care in relation to a situation. The duties and obligations that are imposed on the managing authority of any public facility concern the exercise of reasonable or ordinary care in its operation. The degree of care necessary in the operation of a public facility is sometimes referred to as "highest degree of care," such as is associated with the handling of high tension lines, and "ordinary care," such as is concerned with the usual and customary activities of daily living. Ordinary and reasonable care is the degree of care that would be exercised by a reasonably prudent person under similar circumstances. The question of whether such care has been exercised must be determined by a jury.

Negligence is the fundamental factor to be proved before liability is assessed for injury or damage. In negligence, the law attaches great significance to the foreseeability of hazard. *Foreseeability* is a term applied to an event or action that could or should have been anticipated and prevented by reasonable and prudent action. It is a significant factor in liability cases because it relates whether or not a defendant, as a reasonably skilled and prudent person, should have been able to foresee and thus avoid the possibility of the plaintiff's injury. Negligence, in terms of foreseeability, must be based on factual evidence. Recreationists should specifically strive to anticipate all possible risks in any given situation and make every effort to alleviate or curtail them.

An example of the foreseeability concept in determining negligence and liability is contained in the following situation: At a swimming meet to which the public was invited, seats were arranged around the swimming pool. Loudspeaker equipment was placed at strategic points, several speakers were located on the roof of the locker room building. During the meet, a sudden gust of wind knocked one of the loudspeakers from the roof of the locker room building onto the head of a spectator, producing a slight concussion that later affected his vision. The operator of the swimming facility was charged with negligence arising from his failure to foresee the possibility of such injuries in consequence of the conditions that prevailed. He did not exercise that degree of care necessary for the arrangement of the event and he was liable for redress to the injured party for all damages that directly and proximately resulted from his failure to exercise the reasonable and prudent care required of him.

In another instance, a child was visiting a relative in a city away from her home. She visited a public playground where two boys were throwing a ball between them. One of the boys threw a wild pitch that struck the child. The court held that the city was not negligent. It was the court's opinion that ". . . The mere failure of the city to prevent a single dangerous act of some child or children on the playgrounds . . . does not make the city liable when there is nothing to show that the city had reason to suppose that the act would be committed. To hold the city liable under the circumstances disclosed by this record, because the superintendent in charge of his playground did not instantly stop these boys from playing an innocent game of catch, but permitted it to continue for a few minutes, is, to my mind, imposing upon the municipality an unreasonable burden. I do not think that this unfortunate occurrence is anything which the city, or its employees, could have foreseen in the exercise of reasonable care."[9]

Last Clear Chance. Last clear chance is the final opportunity to prevent injury to another, who, because of contributory negligence, has placed himself in a hazardous condition.

[9] *Peterson v. City of New York*, N.Y. 204 (1935).

Proximate Cause. Proximate cause is a specific act, directly producing events or a set of circumstances leading to some injury.

Res Ipse Loquitur. Res ipse loquitur means the facts speak for themselves. A self-evident condition or situation in which the factor of negligence is obvious.

Attractive Nuisance. Attractive nuisance is any dangerous device, instrument, equipment, contrivance, structure, or condition of land that is naturally dangerous and where the hazard is a continuing one. The attractive nuisance doctrine applies to situations involving children whose immaturity prevents them from exercising ordinary common sense. It is based on the theory that the condition, which is naturally and usually attractive to children at play but which may result in injury, is an attractive nuisance—being attractive and a nuisance at the same time. Liability, in such cases, is based on the proposition that any person of reasonable prudence would foresee that a child would be attracted to such a condition and that injuries or death might ensue from the child's attraction. The courts take the position that the doctrine of attractive nuisance does not hold for a child ten years of age.

Comparative Negligence. The doctrine of comparative negligence insures that contributory negligence will not prevent restitution in an action to obtain compensation for negligence resulting in personal injury, death, or damage to property, if such negligence is equal to the negligence of the person or agency against whom recovery is sought. Comparative negligence permits a plaintiff to recover for damages sustained in an accident if the degree of negligence is less than or equal to the negligence of the defendant.[10]

Defenses to Negligence Action

One method for dealing with the risk of liability is by eliminating or reducing the factors or conditions that may cause injury or damage. The recreationist who acts in a competent manner, thereby fulfilling his functions in a reasonable and prudent manner, can expect to escape the burdens of litigation for tortious acts. There are defenses, however, that may be utilized in cases in which the defendant has acted reasonably, the incident could not have been prevented by any known means, or the plaintiff brought the injury on himself.

Vis Major. Vis major is an uncontrollable act of nature (act of God) causing injury. It is an accidental occurrence caused by some superior and unforeseeable force beyond human control and one that could not have been prevented even with reasonable and prudent care.

Assumption of Risk. Assumption of risk is an individual's voluntary involvement in a situation with full and complete knowledge of the

---

[10] *Public Law 1973*, c. 146; N.J.S.A. 2A:15–5.1, *et seq.*

possibility of hazard to be encountered through participation in that particular situation. Thus, an individual who participates in body contact sports knowingly assumes a certain risk of injury.

The plaintiff played softball on a public playground that had concrete benches and curbing near the playing fields. The plaintiff was aware of the risks and fully assumed the hazards. Having done so, the plaintiff must suffer the consequences; his voluntary and knowing exposure of himself to risk precluded recovery from the defendant.[11]

Contributory Negligence. Contributory negligence is an action taken by an individual who, because of failure to perform properly, sustains personal injury or property damage. People who foolishly expose themselves to danger are subject to contributory negligence. However, primary consideration is accorded to the age of the individual involved and the action in which he was engaged at the time of the injury. Contributory negligence ensues when an individual performs on a lower level or standard of behavior than is required for the activity. When the person fails to offer protection to himself, the courts ordinarily do not allow recovery for damages sustained. If, however, the recreationist in charge does not take advantage of a "last clear chance" to prevent the injury or damage, he may be held liable despite any contributory negligence on the plaintiff's part.

Negligence Is not Proximate Cause of Damage. When a minor was struck on the head by a baseball thrown on a playground by another minor to a third player who ducked the pitch, proximate cause of injury was unforeseen action of the child who threw the ball. The absence of the recreationist, who was handing out craft supplies from a nearby supply room, was not the proximate cause of the injury so as to impose liability for damage on the recreational service department.

Denial of Negligence. A denial of negligence on the part of the defendant would require a court proceeding thereby presenting a factual situation on which the court or the jury must decide. The defendant would have to prove that he acted in accordance with standard operating procedures universally accepted or known, that his actions were those of a reasonable and prudent person under similar circumstances, or other evidence that would absolve him from liability.

Trespasser. A trespasser is one who is in a given location without invitation or right to be present in a given situation. Trespass is a clear violation of the right of protection from infringement on one's person or property through unauthorized presence.

An exception to the rule of non-liability to the trespasser is the attractive nuisance doctrine and generally applies to children. Swimming facilities, for example, should be enclosed by high fences and the entrance

[11] *Scala v. City of New York* 102 N.Y.S., 2nd—709.

guarded by gates kept locked during the off-season or whenever the facility is closed. Children are likely to visit unfenced and unguarded pools and injury or even death could be the consequence. This could raise the question of contributory negligence as well as trespassing. A very young child who has not yet reached the age of discretion cannot be guilty of contributory negligence; however, he can be a trespasser regardless of age.

In the case of a young child who enters a pool area by climbing a fence or crawling under a gate and then falls into the pool and drowns, two points may be made. First, negligence on the part of the swimming facility authority for not constructing a better fence, and, second, trespassing by the child on the ground that the facility authority has no obligation other than to refrain from willfully injuring the child. Recent court decisions, however, indicate that public authorities owe more to the trespassing child than mere refrainment from willful injury. The authority must use reasonable care to prevent exposing the child to unreasonable risk or injury.

COMPARATIVE NEGLIGENCE AND PUBLIC AGENCY LIABILITY —1977

In the case of Dambro vs. Union County Park Commission, et al.,[12] a review of the facts would, superficially, indicate that the plaintiff acted in such a manner as to bring about his own injury through contributory negligence. However, the State of New Jersey has enacted a comparative negligence statute which vastly changes the possibilities of the plaintiff to recover damages for injuries suffered. The facts appear as follows:

> Vincent Dambro, Jr., a 23-year-old man, was injured on or about May 28, 1973, at approximately 4:15 p.m., when he, while in the company of three friends, dove into a certain pond; which is known as Lower Seeley's Pond located within the Watchung Reservation operated by the Union County Park Commission. Vincent struck his head on an underground obstruction, rock, or other debris existing in the bed of the pond. He had never visited this place before and, of course, has not been there since.

> On the day in question, the water level was high and Vincent, after seeing one of his companions dive into the water and stand in neck high water, dove into the same general vicinity. He came to the surface semiconscious, was rushed to the hospital where a fracture of the neck was diagnosed along with other injuries. At the present time, Vincent is a quadriplegic with no hope of recovery of the use of his upper and lower extremities.

Further investigation disclosed the following information. Such information was garnered from documents existing in the public record as well

[12] 130 New Jersey *Superior Court Reports*, p. 540, October 11, 1974.

as through depositions taken from employees of the Union County Park Commission. It was revealed that a now destroyed stone dam abuts Lower Seeley's Pond and it was from this general area that the Plaintiff dove into the water. The Union County Park Commission is the owner of property which extends to the center of the stream. Ownership of the balance of the stream is uncertain because of property seizure in lieu of tax payments by former owners. Depositions disclosed that in 1968 the dam was secure and functioning and further, that in that year, as a result of a violent storm the dam was breached resulting in the river bed being strewn with debris.

Investigation also indicates that as a result of and through the persistence of the State Water Policy Commission, the Union County Park Commission undertook a program in 1970 which was intended to remove the debris from the breached dam from this stream. The program was under the direction of an employee of the Union County Park Commission. The employee was not a licensed engineer. The Park Commission hired and rented equipment and retained operators to run the equipment under the direction of their employee and his immediate supervisor in an effort to clean the stream of debris.

Furthermore, the Union County Park Commission has made improvement and maintains waterways within its boundaries upstream of the locus of the accident and throughout the entire Watchung Reservation recreational facility. Recreational activities are permitted within the park system. However, an ordinance was enacted in 1938 specifically prohibiting swimming except in permitted areas. The ordinance is posted at all entrances to the park.

The area in question is acknowledged to have been a "swimming hole" for a number of years. Mr. R. S. indicated that during his tenure as Superintendent for the past 10 years, he has been given reports of individuals swimming in and about the area of the accident. Mr. J. G., Tax Assessor, Borough of Watchung, likewise acknowledged that Lower Seeley's Pond has been used for swimming purposes for at least 40 years. Nevertheless, the Union County Park Commission has not embarked, to his knowledge, on any affirmative action program intended to implement the prohibition. There is not presently, and has not in the past been, a policy of posting the property. There is not presently, and has not in the past been, a policy of screening or fencing the property. It would appear that the Union County Park Commission, although having knowledge of circumstances and uses being made of its waterways, has taken absolutely no steps to implement the prohibitions against these uses.

On the day in question, evidence and investigation has disclosed that in addition to the party which included Vincent Dambro, Jr., the waterways were also being used for wading by other individuals. The people with Vincent on the date of the accident had indicated that on prior occasions they and numerous friends had made use of the swimming hole without interference. It appears as though this waterway has been used with the actual knowledge, or certainly with the implied knowledge, of the owners for an extensive period of time and that no attempt has been made by them to take any active steps to discourage its use.

Vincent Dambro, Jr., in an attempt to recover damages for the injuries he received, employed legal counsel to represent him in any legal proceedings that might ensue.[13] Subsequently, plaintiff's attorney employed a qualified expert witness to provide substantive material which could be utilized in any court action. The following information was generated by the expert witness based upon site inspection and discovery of the facts previously indicated:

1. Insofar as the facilities of the Watchung Reservation are concerned the following commonly accepted planning and safety promotional principles in the field of recreational service apply: Improvident behavior on the part of participants has required those employed within the field of recreational service to establish certain safety standards to guard people against their own foibles and less than circumspect activity. For these reasons, it is generally considered standard practice to post those areas which are either unsafe or which are to be prohibited from use.

2. Most people consider park and recreational facilities or areas under public jurisdiction to be safe. The public assumes that operating authorities have acted in ways which omit any hazardous areas or spaces within the confines of a park or other recreational place. The public also presumes that warnings about dangerous or prohibited areas, by well and frequently displayed notices, will be posted for protection purposes. This practice has become a widespread standard within the field of recreational service. The posting of clearly readable signs of warning at frequent intervals at specific sites from which potential users are to be prohibited or restricted has been a standard practice to insure the safety of patrons.

3. The operational authorities of Watchung Reservation, the Union County Park Commission, have continuously administered the facilities which people in the vicinity use for recreational purposes. Among the natural areas is Green Brook which lets into a section known as Lower Seeley's Pond. According to local custom and at least two highly placed and authoritative employees, one of the Union County Park Commission the other of the Borough of Watchung, Lower Seeley's Pond has been used for more than 40 years as a swimming place. Mr. R. G., Superintendent of Field Operations and Chief, Engineering Department of the Union County Park Commission, stated this in his deposition and Mr. J. G., Tax Assessor, Borough of Watchung, also acknowledged that Lower Seeley's Pond has been used for swimming for many years.

4. The Park authorities have known about this area and the practices of people to habitually use Lower Seeley's Pond for swimming and wading purposes.

5. Although there are Park regulations restricting swimming to other swimming places within the Park and despite the fact that Park employ-

[13] Letter from Joseph J. Triarsi, Attorney at Law, August 18, 1975.

ees have on various occasions directed persons who have been swimming to leave Lower Seeley's Pond, indications are that Park authorities have known about the use which nearby residents and others make of this area. Additionally, "no swimming" signs were posted, but this practice has been discontinued. The fact that Watchung Reservation has numerous entry ways, and not only special entrances, requires that the Union County Park Commission operators take cognizance of the reservation's accessibility by the public. This means that dangerous or prohibited areas of the reservation must be properly posted to protect against use or entry by an unwarned public who may not gain access at specified reservation entries. The Union County Park Commission had a higher responsibility than merely posting notices at entryways. In order to maximize safety of reservation users the Union County Park Commission should have posted any and all areas which the authorities wanted to restrict from public use.

6. New Providence Road abutting the "Falls Area" has numerous turnouts which would appear to invite potential patrons for rest-stops, viewing, and picnicking. It is well within reason for the Union County Park Commission to have stencilled restrictive warnings at regular intervals on the steel divider between the highway and Green Brook. The failure to replace other signs which alleged vandals had stolen or damaged does not preclude the Union County Park Commission from responsibility for posting such areas if, indeed, the Union County Park Commission wanted to prohibit the use which custom has made prevalent, i.e., as a swimming place.

7. The Union County Park Commission was enjoined by the Division of Water Policy and Supply of the DEP, a state agency, to clean-up, dredge out, or otherwise rid the stream bed of debris and any other obstructions. The Union County Park Commission failed to perform this function adequately. Consequently, obstructions continued to exist in the stream bed at Seeley's Pond. By neglecting to post the area, failing to warn off potential users, failing to conform to state agency directions, the Union County Park Commission did not act in a reasonable and prudent manner in its operation and administration of an area within a recreational facility under its jurisdiction.

8. By omitting the posting of signs, notifications, or restriction of use at various points along Green Brook and particularly at Lower Seeley's Pond, the Union County Park Commission failed to act responsibly and in accordance with well-established field practices for the protection of the safety of its patrons.

9. Union County Park Commission continuously maintained all of the waterways, including Green Brook, for a number of years and were fully aware of the consequences from the breached dam at Lower Seeley's Pond by the State DEP. The Union County Park Commission not only acknowledged the necessity for removing residual debris from the ruptured dam site but did, in fact, lease equipment and assign one of the Union County Park Commission employees to supervise the work. Mr. K., not a licensed engineer, apparently acted in an incompetent or negligent manner because Lower Seeley's Pond was not cleansed nor made free of rubble and debris. It is probable that by placing an inexperienced and unknowledgeable person in direct charge of this project, the Union County Park Commission deviated substantially from good practices currently prevalent in the field of recreational service. This poorly advised

action was undertaken without compliance with normally accepted standards of operational practices common to the field of recreational service.

    10. By failing to fulfill those safety obligations with which it was charged and operating in ways which deviated from recognized standards, the Union County Park Commission materially contributed to the conditions which resulted in the injuries to Vincent Dambro, Jr.

The Union County Park Commission carried liability insurance in the amount of $1,000,000. Acting as attorney for the defendant, the insurance company's legal representative employed its own expert witness, a licensed engineer. Herewith is a copy of the engineer's report to the lawyer who represented both the park commission and the insurance company:

VINCENT DAMBRO, JR. VS. UNION COUNTY PARK COMMISSION, ET AL.

REPORT

A. INTRODUCTION

    Four young people decided to go for a ride Saturday afternoon, May 26, 1973. They wound up at a natural scenic area surrounding a stream-fed pool. K.M. had visited this rock-carved "swimming hole" with other friends 10 or 12 times previous. While the two girls watched, both dungareed boys dove successfully from a rock perch into a downstream pool near a previously breached dam. First, K. dove out further, in a more shallow dive toward the pool (water) center after cautioning Vincent Dambro not to dive to the bottom because there were rocks there. As he came up, in the process of climbing onto a rock, he turned and saw Vincent floating to the surface of the water, his head bleeding, not far behind where he had previously surfaced. He dove back in, swam a few strokes with Vincent and pulled him from the water to shore. The girls had seen the deeper, shorter dive by Vincent, blood in the water, and rescue by K. from shallow water. They ran to the road to flag down a car and obtain assistance. Vincent Dambro was 21 years old at the time. He had been a fairly good swimmer and knew how to dive. He knew that if he hit his head against any rocks he could injure himself. If he swam too far underwater—across the rock pool—he would hit his head against rocks. He stated he didn't see any rocks on the bottom because the water was too muddy ("polluted") to see the bottom. He knew—as an adult in his majority—that diving into that pool of water was foreseeably risky. He went ahead, and did it anyway.

B. SUMMARY

    1. This accident occurred, unequivocally and completely, in SOMERSET COUNTY, Borough of Watchung: not in UNION COUNTY, Township of Scotch Plains.

2. Plaintiff and party of three parked their car in a sand and gravel area located in SOMERSET COUNTY over which Defendant UNION COUNTY PARK COMMISSION herein exercises no governmental control.

3. Plaintiff and party of three entered improperly into a natural un-improved public scenic area of imposing beauty and scenic quali-ties involving a bubbling stream and minor waterfall—the lovely nature of the area appealing to sensory perceptions of odor, feel, touch and sight—by climbing over a protective, substantial metallic guardrail, and trespassing therein for personal recreational pur-poses on public property.

4. Plaintiff exercised reckless, unwarranted, foreseeably dangerous, and totally negligent behavior in attempting to dive and swim in a natural pool carved in rock formations—highly visible.

5. Plaintiff's behavior was irresponsible, careless, and wanton, after being warned by the other boy in the party about "rocks on the bottom" and—"not to dive to the bottom."

6. Plaintiff's accident in striking the rock-pool bottom would have most likely occurred under identical circumstances in any back-yard or public swimming pool built to *nationally recognized de-sign standards* because improper nature of Plaintiff's dive, body kinematics, and actual impact location were the *fault, sole re-sponsibility* and absolute *personal control* of Plaintiff.

7. *Actual dive trajectory* underscores gross imprudence of Plaintiff's dive, his amateurism and ineptness and most importantly, specific physical location of the accident site to be clearly *WEST* of and beyond the property line of Defendant PARK COMMISSION.

C. BACKGROUND

This case involves a natural stream flowing through Watchung Res-ervation, in which course it passes through Surprise Lake where as Blue Brook it is dammed to form that lake. Downstream we find Upper Seeley's Pond, and further southward in the natural flow of the stream we find another dam exists at Lower Seeley's Pond where this accident is alleged to have happened. Blue Brook flows eventu-ally into Green Brook, but it is all the same natural water course, meandering as it approaches the accident area along the border line of Union and Somerset Counties.

In 1968, there was an exceptionally intense storm. Stone center por-tion of the dam at Lower Seeley's Pond, primarily in *County of Somerset*, was blown out.

In June 1968, R.G., Chief, Engineering Department of Union County Park Commission prepared an Inspection Report of Seeley's lower dam indicating "Typical (as-built)" section of quarry rock wall with concrete or bluestone top and one foot plain concrete backing. He indicated extent of breached channel and five conditions to be considered in any rebuilding program. In December of 1968, Mr. S. was "almost convinced" this dam should not be rebuilt. "The former pond behind it has filled in with silt. The natural rock waterfall would be prettier. The absence of a dam would not affect downstream flows because upper Seeley's and the Diamond Hill Road Bridge on Green Brook would still control."

Subsequently, in May 1969 it was determined that the condition of the Lower Seeley's Dam "......does not do any damage to any private property in its present state." Furthermore, at the urging of State of New Jersey, Department of Conservation and Economic Development, it was determined (in a series of memorandums based on inspections and confirming opinions) reconstruction of the dam would provide no effective stream-flow control advantage. Other than considerations of clearing the bed of the stream channel, *it would be best if this natural area reverted to natural flow conditions.* In August of 1969, as the natural flow and course of nature developed, this opinion crystalized when on August 7, 1969, Engineer R.S. stated in Memorandum *"In my opinion, Seeley's Lower Dam should not be rebuilt.* It affords a greater benefit to Scotch Plains in its present breached condition by starting wet period with an empty pond."

The Department of Conservation and Economic Development, Trenton, New Jersey, was notified formally of this decision on October 3, 1969. Mr. R., P.E., Director and Chief of that Department was advised of S.'s professional opinion for the dam not being rebuilt:

"1) the pond behind the dam had become filled with silt, thereby reducing any potential storage capacity it may have offered, and also diminishing its value in regards to recreation and ecology.
2) from a flood control standpoint, it would be better to begin the wet period with an empty pond; any sound remnants of the old dam could be left in place to control the release of flood waters into the downstream reach; the absence of the dam would not adversely change or affect downstream areas because the dam, prior to breaching, offered little or no flood control benefit."

Mr. R.L., P.E., Chief, Bureau of Water Control for the State of New Jersey, Department of Conservation and Economic Development, confirmed receipt of that letter and requested only "......it will be necessary to remove the remnants of the structure from the stream channel and the primary flood plain for the preservation of flood control capacity......".

As a result of these observations extending over one year, permitting observation during subsequent storms and flooding, a firming up of the decision that the dam *need not,* and *would not* be rebuilt occurred. The dam had very little, if any, relationship to flooding after the storms. It was also determined that flooding was a result of natural stream flow and many other factors of local nature and, in conclusion, it was recognized that the stream "will in time revert *to natural conditions* without the dam."

Effectively, therefore, since 1968, Lower Seeley's Pond and the former dammed area of Green Brook has been naturalized, brambling along —a country stream area, subject only to natural physical forces, and random whimsy of nature.

At time of the accident, therefore, alleged accident scene; both actual water pool and impact bottom location in Somerset County; and the generalized area in that vicinity, North and East, lying in Union County, was by design *unimproved public property.* The stream, most certainly, was in a natural condition. The entire locale, including several hundred foot reach *in either direction,* upstream and downstream, of formerly breached dam at Lower Seeley's Pond must by all account and record be considered unimproved, in a most natural condition.

This naturalized, unimproved waterway was protected by entrance from New Providence Road (Somerset County) in suitable manner by substantial guardrail. It is necessary to climb over this rail to obtain access to the accident-site, water-pool. Alleged "swimming" area is somewhat like a quarry, being approximately 8 feet in its deepest part—surrounded by trees; highly visible, irregularly protruding rocks of all sizes, and the falls area. On the day of the accident, the water was muddy, turbid and unclear from rain the night before. All four young adults could not, as they stated, see bottom. As an unimproved area of public property there were no signs, either invitational or warning, no fences at the stream or falls, and no indication that this was in any way a "swimming area." On day of the accident, when Plaintiff's party arrived, *there was nobody else swimming* at this location, *neither did anybody join* this party *after they arrived.*

It was into this beautfiul, unique and almost private country brook and rock pool setting on the last Saturday afternoon in May, that Plaintiff decided "to cool off; it was a hot day."

D. FINDINGS
From testimony of depositions (References 1, 2, 3, 4) of Plaintiff and three associates witness to the accident, it is possible to reconstruct

from their testimony, photographic exhibits, and more particularly, AREA SURVEY by H. O., Incorporated with S. and S. (Reference 5), the accident dynamics.

On Drawing 974-D1, herewith, we have reproduced SECTION B-B of reference Survey which very closely approximates the cross-section of the rock quarry into which the young men dove, as testified. For purposes of this analysis, if this section were canted as much as 10° in either direction, or offset approximately 3 feet north or south of the indicated section, the CROSS-SECTION would be substantially the same.

A PROJECTED IMPACT AREA occurs approximately 5 to 6 feet from the water (shore) line. The cervical fractures at C-5 and C-6 occurred when the top of Vincent's head impacted the rock bottom, being restrained at that point, with his vertebrae and neck musculature unable to resist vigorous dynamic forces of his body, resulting in his characteristic neck injury. Severity of the impact, as evidenced by visible surfacing blood at shallow water location, further substantiates Dambro's *improper diving technique, dramatically sharp downturn in the water* which was the proximate cause of impact.

Testimony that K.M.'s dive was shallow and further out, *toward* center of the pool, is in clear contrast to the shortfall, closer to shore, and much steeper surface entrance of the Plaintiff.

While clearly establishing Plaintiff's total negligence and personal accountability for his dive, *most important from Plaintiff's impact location,* surfacing, subsequent rescue and recovery: each and every action in this accident sequence starting with the dive take-off, occurred in Somerset County. Closest approach to Union County property line, as shown by Licensed Survey, could not be *nearer than 6 feet.*

Plaintiff and his associates at all times were trespassing the public property of Somerset County, including their entrance to this naturalized site, the dive location, impact location with bottom, post-impact surfacing, recovery, rescue, and injury assistance.

Union County Park Commission, the public entity in this action, *did not* own or control adjacent contiguous property which is public property and real estate owned and controlled by other public entities. Union County Park Commission *did not* have right to any easement, encroachments or legal use of that portion of the natural waterway designated "Green Brook" either upstream or downstream of alleged accident site in Somerset County. That watercourse has been maintained substantially in its natural condition, *as unimproved public property,* subject only to driving forces of natural condition from a period in time at, and preceding the questioned breach of Lower Seeley's Pond Dam in 1968. The participation of Union County Park Commission, and their public concern in removing loose rocks and debris on their side of the brook in 1970 was only for the purpose of maintaining *natural stream conditions* and preventing any further impediment to natural flow of Green Brook. This was a proper and reasonable public interest, safeguarding their property to the north and east of property line dividing interests with the adjacent County of Somerset.

While establishing the accident site to be in Somerset, a study of dive trajectories also indicates basic ineptitude and totally negligent behavior by Plaintiff. Had the water been crystal clear, the bottom sharply delineated, even painted white, Plaintiff's accident *could have very similarly occurred in any other "pool" of water.* The "deep end" of a residential swimming pool built to design standards of National Swimming Pool Institute (NSPI) would be as shown on Drawing 974-D1. Any backyard pool with deck-level diving board would be this deep, and yet from the violent fracture and head injury of the Plaintiff it can be postulated that similar accident *would have happened in a properly designed, specifically intended swimming pool!* Similar neck injuries are known to occur in properly designed, maintained and supervised swimming pools, *including conventional entering dives,* such as that purported by the Plaintiff into the shallow end of such swimming pools, for which contour geometry is also indicated on Reference Drawing. Plaintiff, therefore, must be recognized as being entirely, contributorily responsible for his dive which took him so violently to the rock bottom, very possibly into 6 feet, and more probably 4 feet of water. Similar tragic behavior is well documented in Swimming Pool litigation.

Inspection of the accident site (1976) and review of earlier photographs exhibited during discovery, confirm the continuing rustic, beautiful natural composition of the brook, falls and pond areas. Fractured rock of igneous granitic character predominates above and into the waterway.

That the Plaintiff struck his head on rock bottom must be attributed to several entirely negligent assumptions of risk on his part:

> i—*a first time dive* into turbid (polluted) and muddy waters not knowing absolute character of bottom in the highly visible presence of so many surface and protruding stream rocks must in itself stand for nakedly reckless, and truly foolhardy personal behavior.

7

ii—after being warned about "rocks" on the bottom, and not to dive to the bottom, and having witnessed a shallow dive to the center of the pool, to do other than a plain, flat "bellywhop," is unfortunate retrospect of this tragedy, must be classified as gravely irrational behavior and reckless abandon in view of such foreseeable hazard and danger.

That K.M. has testified of his previous preoccupation with unauthorized swimming at this location on "10 or 12 occasions" is moot testimony to the critical parameter, and major difference between a proper and improper dive by respective parties. It is very possible in view of stated physical limitations and previous handicap noted by the Plaintiff, that his courage and will to attempt a proper dive exceeded limitations imposed by his actions and ability to even control same. (1)—Witnessed trajectory, and (2)—impact information again tragically bespeak this vital criteria leading to Dambro's high velocity bottom impact. His *attempted dive,* under such circumstances can only be his negligent responsibility and painful shortcoming.

With the receipt of the engineer's report, the Plaintiff's Attorney requested his own expert witness to review the statement and advise him concerning its accuracy and appropriateness. The expert's evaluation of the report is contained below:

1. The accident occurred on property under the administrative jurisdiction of the Union County Park Commission which is solely responsible for all operations, activities, and functions carried out, on, or upon The Watchung Reservation. The Watchung Reservation is a recreational facility combining a variety of features, both man-made and natural, and designed to provide recreational opportunities to potential patrons or users. It is irrelevant whether the Watchung Reservation meanders into counties other than Union. The Union County Park Commission is the declared and legally constituted agency charged with the responsibility for the reservation. According to the fiftieth anniversary brochure entitled, "To Benefit the Whole Population" printed and published by the Union County Park Commission in 1971, the following excerpt belies the attempt to disassociate the Watchung Reservation from the jurisdiction of the Union County Park Commission: "But when the Commissioners permitted themselves even the slightest immodesty, they hoped they were judged for *the Watchung Reservation,* the crown jewel of the system."
2. Plaintiff and party of three parked their car in what appears, to the casual observer, to be a turnout for parking, particularly as there are no signs forbidding such activity.
3. There can be no doubt that the area in question was artificially contrived. The area known as Lower Seeley's Pond has been constructed upon through the intrusion of a man-made dam and an earlier mill which utilized the stream for water power. The remnants of the blown-out dam still partially obstruct the stream flow and the res-

idue of debris from the dam still lies at the bottom of the stream. To claim that this area is natural and unimproved is erroneous. It may be that the Union County Park Commission would like the facts to be altered so that this area would be considered a natural place, but, in fact, the stream and its immediate surroundings have been impacted by man-made objects, obstructions, and machinery. To state that the Dambro party entered the property improperly is a gross error. It is questionable as to whether an open public recreational facility can ever be trespassed upon unless there are time limits for use and these restrictions are both well known and obviously posted. This was not the case in the incident. Furthermore, unless there are significant barriers to prevent access everywhere throughout the reservation, with the exception of one or more designated entryways, the public's use cannot be restricted. Even then, a public and open recreational facility admits invitees by implication and direction. It is, after all, what public recreational facilities are established to do.

4. Plaintiff's attempt to swim in Lower Seeley's Pond was only one more action in a forty (40) year history of such pond use. The Union County Park Commission knew of this use directly, had posted signs forbidding such use, and then, unaccountably, discontinued the use of warning signs. The irresponsible discontinuance of warning signs in that heavily used area is a clear breach in standard recreational park and safety practices if the Union County Park Commission actually wanted to prevent Lower Seeley's Pond from being used for swimming, wading, and other assorted and associated aquatic uses.

5. It is highly unlikely that Vincent Dambro deliberately attempted to either reach or hit the bottom of the stream bed. On the contrary, after seeing K.M. dive in and re-surface, the more plausible idea was to assume that the pond was adequate for swimming and diving.

6. There is no precise way to determine Dambro's exact body position or dive trajectory. One would have to have specific measurements, exact location of take off and entry. It is a very difficult matter to perform a steep dive from a position either level with the water into which one is diving or from a height of a few feet above the water line. Much more likely is the presumption that Dambro launched himself in a relatively shallow or flat dive. In order to enter the water in the way the report describes, Dambro would have had to have jumped vertically before piking in mid-air to enter the water at such a steep angle. The engineer's statement can be dismissed as spurious. The statement concerning swimming pools constructed to N.S.P.I. standards is pure conjecture and in no way mitigates the fact that the Union County Park Commission was negligent in not having warning signs erected indicating the prohibition of the use of the water course for wading, swimming, diving, fishing, or other recreational purposes. The reservation is clearly a facility for recreational use and unless otherwise prohibited, potential patrons will continue to make use of the facility. The Union County Park Commission had absolute prior knowledge of the use of Lower Seeley's Pond and made relatively little or no administrative attempt to control access or prevent its use for aquatic purposes. The absence of any policy statement setting up preventative measures to eliminate the public's con-

tinued use of Lower Seeley's Pond is one of careless, reckless disregard for the safety of reservation patrons and deviates substantially from known and recognized recreational service field practices and standards.

7. Dambro cannot at the same time be cited as a fairly good swimmer with a knowledge of diving and scored for being inept. Either the first or the second statement is wrong. If the first statement is in error then the Union County Park Commission should have acted more responsibly to foresee the fact that inept persons might attempt to swim and dive into Lower Seeley's Pond with tragic consequences. They did not protect an innocent public and hence are negligent in carrying out basic safety procedures. If the second sentence is incorrect, then it invalidates the engineer's arguments as to entry dive. A knowledgeable person would have used a shallow dive and certainly not a relatively acrobatic entry as was indicated in the report. In either case, the engineer's report is of dubious value and still does not alleviate the Union County Park Commission's responsibility to act in a reasonable and prudent manner in operating Watchung Reservation.

The case went to trial before an empaneled jury in the New Jersey Superior Court of Judge F.C. Kentz, on June 13, 1977. After 2 days of hearings and before any of the expert or other witnesses could be called upon to testify, the Union County Park Commission's own attorney prevailed upon the insurance company's legal counsel to settle the case without further trial. Vincent Dambro, Jr., received a lump sum payment of $125,000 in cash and a lifetime annuity of $225,000. This annuity should be able to generate approximately $13,000 to $14,000 per year for the maintenance of Mr. Dambro during the rest of his life. Actuarial figures indicate that he should, with reasonable care, survive for at least another 44.6 years.

Recreationists are expected to guide, direct and operate the various activities under their immediate supervision in a safe, reasonable, and prudent manner. If precautions are not taken, they risk their employer and themselves to exposure to litigation for redress of tortious acts owing to negligence.

Recreational activities at playgrounds and other recreational places involve many unpremeditated hazardous situations. Elimination of all possible hazardous situations would be equivalent to the very denial of the right and opportunity to participate in recreational experiences. Recreational activity is so important to the growth and development of children that departments responsible for playgrounds and other recreational facilities should use all reasonable precautions, including adequate supervision at all times. Supervision should be exercised not only in reference to people, especially children, but to physical facilities and areas as well. Unsafe conditions must be removed or repaired with reasonable diligence. To perform incompetently or in a manner that indicates negligence in any way invites litigation and places a greater administrative burden on the department and the citizens of any community.

Selected References

Avenet, I.: *How to Prove Damages in Wrongful Personal Injury and Death Cases* (Englewood Cliffs, N.J.: Prentice-Hall, Inc.), 1973.

Beuscher, J. H., and others: *Cases and Materials on Land Use, 2d ed.* (St. Paul, Minn.: West Publishing Company), 1976.

Epstein, R. A.: *Defenses and Subsequent Pleas in a System of Strict Liability* (Chicago, Ill.: American Bar Foundation), 1974.

Heft, C. R. and C. J. Heft: *Comparative Negligence Manual* (Chicago, Ill.: Callaghan & Company), 1971.

Iavicoli, M. A.: *No Fault and Comparative Negligence in New Jersey* (Haddonfield, N.J.: Barrister Publishing Company), 1973.

Pirsig, M. E. and K. F. Kirwin: *Cases and Materials on Professional Responsibility, 3d ed.* (Stanford, Calif.: Stanford University Press), 1976.

Speiser, S. M.: *The Negligence Case: Res Ipse Loquitor, 2 vols.* (Rochester, N.Y.: Lawyers Cooperative Publishing Company), 1972.

CHAPTER 9

Public Relations Procedures in Administration

In any municipal recreational service department, public relations is one of the most important administrative functions. The attention of the public must be aroused, interest in agency-sponsored activities must be created and maintained, knowledge of agency problems must be disseminated, and support must be enlisted.

A recreational service department cannot render the fullest service of which it is capable without the support of favorable public opinion, which is based on understanding and goodwill. Private enterprises have long recognized that favorable public relations are vital to their success and that they may be consciously planned and created. For this purpose they give attention to every detail of their operations that brings them into contact with the public and often employ specialists as public relations counselors to organize a comprehensive program of public relations for the entire establishment. Public tax-supported agencies have formerly not been as aware of the necessity for planned public relations as have private enterprises. This day is fast passing. Public administrators now tend to adopt the public relations methods of private business—subject, however, to proper legal restrictions.

Among the legal restrictions is one prohibiting the use of tax funds by governmental agencies for purposes of advertising, unless specific authorization has been granted by the state legislature or by the city charter. Such authorization has been given in a number of instances, particularly for advertising and exploiting the advantages of the city, county, or state as a residential or industrial place, but no authorization has yet been granted to departments to advertise themselves or their services on the ground that it would constitute a use of public funds for the purpose of keeping the incumbent administration in office.

Notwithstanding this traditional prohibition, it has been generally recognized that public agencies and departments have an obligation to inform the public concerning the work done and the services and benefits available through their operations. Imparting public information has been considered to be incidental to the purposes for which the agencies have been established. The expenditure of a reasonable portion of the funds for disseminating information and for reporting has been construed as a proper use of public funds.

Although public departments do not advertise, they are employing the methods of publicity more and more. Advertising in the business world is for the purpose of directly promoting or creating sales. Publicity makes no sales but promotes goodwill and understanding. Advertising is a commodity for which a price is paid; publicity usually is associated with news and flows through free communications channels. The propriety of the use of publicity in public work has to be judged in relation to its purposes. Publicity, however, represents only one of many methods of public relations used by recreational service departments.

Education and Propaganda

Education is the basic instrument by which recreationists can cultivate a desire on the part of the public to conform to stated agency policies. It is, perhaps, the most tedious process and at the same time the most effective and durable. Once an individual has learned to appreciate the objectives of recreational service and to enjoy recreational experiences, he more willingly supports the department's program and contributes to its success.

Education for leisure, particularly as it concerns recreational service, implies that communities should have at least a minimum of personnel to give leadership to the community's leisure. It is vital if the public is to utilize safely and profitably the abundance of free time now generally available. Education influences the attitudes and behavior of individuals and groups toward whom it is directed and reduces administrative problems or areas of friction. Through enlightenment of potential participants voluntary interest and performance are garnered and monetary savings that can be translated into more effective programs for continued public betterment are made.

Admittedly, public recreational service has been somewhat lax in utilizing this greatest of all administrative devices for the implementation of public policy. The field and its individual agencies should employ a more complete educational program, through home visitations by recreationists, who can establish contact with potential clientele, provide information, create incentives, organize groups, and otherwise stimulate participation and support of recreational policies and programs. The recreationist should therefore be skilled in a wide variety of recreational experiences in which individuals may engage and be well versed in principles of public health, sanitation, law enforcement, education, community organization, and group dynamics.

In all public relations undertaken by public departments, there is a mutual interest on the part of both the public and the department: the improvement of the public service. The public desire to express their wishes, demands, and criticisms and to bring about adjustments. The department, on the other hand, desires to ascertain the public's interest and needs and to adapt itself to the changing interests and needs insofar as it is permitted to do so consistent with its powers. The department considers as part of its public relations program measures it may take to become informed concerning the public as well as the means it adopts to interpret itself to the public and to create public goodwill toward the department.

The public relations section of the department acts as a two-way funnel by directing and channeling information to the public, interpreting the facts about the agency, and serving as a sounding board for the programs initiated by the agency. It discovers what the community has to say about recreational activities and is therefore in a position to assist in the determination of policies and to recommend immediate changes in the program offerings as interest mounts or declines.

All the activities programs and other work of the department absolutely depend on public knowledge of them and public support based on understanding. The department must overcome inhibition and apathy. Some of its activities are on a revenue-producing basis, and their continuance depends on paid attendance. Because participation in the activities of the recreational service department is purely voluntary, the department must employ the methods of promotion to secure the maximum public response.

COMMUNITY ORGANIZATION AND PUBLIC RELATIONS

Good public relations are generated through activities conducted by the department and through contacts made with organizations and groups of many kinds that use department facilities on permit. The numerous volunteer leaders involved in all these group activities and the many participants become agents of goodwill for the department and its services, assuming, of course, that their experience is satisfactory and that the service given them by the department merits their approbation.

Agencies with which the department is officially affiliated also mirror the esteem with which the department is held and assist in cultivating a favorable public image. Among such organizations are councils of community social services, interagency recreational councils and coordinating councils.

Levels of Coordination

It is sometimes erroneously assumed that two or more agencies can be coordinated through efforts at the uppermost levels. It is not sufficient to have the executives of two or more policy-making bodies agree on a coordinated plan of operation. Coordination can be effected only through cooperation at various levels of administration. Unless the employees in each agency understand the need for such coordination and are willing to work harmoniously with their opposite numbers from other community agencies, there is little hope for actual joint effort.

Thus the factor of personality enters into the problem of coordination. In many instances efforts at coordination have been unsuccessful because of personality clashes between key members of the council or between personnel in contributing agencies. Harmonious official relations tend to be cultivated through personal contact and joint effort. A plan of coordination can be effective only if it cultivates goodwill between the representatives and disseminates information among them of what each is doing and can do toward the common objective.

If personality factors are allowed to intervene, the goal of total recreational service for the community is obscured. Professional personnel should rise above petty bickering, minor irritations, or supposed personal slights and point the way toward purposeful activities that accrue from objective relationships.

Mutual Assistance

Cooperative relations between agencies and their personnel at all levels are cultivated by mutual assistance rendered by one agency to another. For example, the municipal recreational service agency may supply a dance instructor or square dance caller to direct a Girl Scout jamboree; advise the school board on school playground equipment and placement; lend prepackaged picnic supplies and equipment to community groups; provide instructions and plans for social events; establish leadership workshops or other professional development programs for participation by any community agency; supply skilled volunteers for instructional or leadership purposes in the program of different agencies; provide necessary officials for athletic events and contests; hold classes for leaders in various activities (dance, arts and crafts, photography).

The department can serve the community by establishing interagency priorities for use of recreational facilities. Such use must not conflict with or supersede activities sponsored or controlled by the agency in possession of the facility. In this way all buildings, structures, and land or water areas available for recreational purposes are utilized to a maximum degree. This necessitates a high level of coordination and cooperation between all of the community agencies. Each agency indicates the type of facility or space that it operates and the times when these places may be used by others. Individuals or organizations could request specific facilities and confirm appointments for their use without concern about conflicting interests. Individual agencies may even establish fees for the use of their facilities. Such a plan would also be beneficial to neighborhoods without adequate facilities. Duplication of recreational structures and areas might thus be avoided and optimum use made of existing places.

Coordination may also be fostered by organizing a master schedule for facilities within the community, indicating when, where, and what activities are programmed. Naturally, such a schedule would have to be prepared at least one month in advance if it is to be useful. The master schedule serves as a central communications device so that unnecessary competition for the enlistment of the same participants is avoided. Such a plan reveals where there was a dearth of recreational activity in the community and which organizations should supply service. (It is presumed, of course, that the public agency program is supplemented by other agency activities.) Better relations between agencies might result, for each agency may plan its activities for a specific group and know that it was contributing to the provision of overall community recreational service. A more harmonious climate is engendered and coordinated action for total recreational development encouraged.

Coordination by Conference and Agreement

Various other devices to effect coordination of recreational agencies have been adopted with beneficial results. The simplest is the frequent interchange of information through conference. Conferences are arranged between representatives of two agencies when problems of mutual concern arise. To facilitate such conferences, regular meetings are sometimes held. Occasionally a third agency or person, such as the Parent-Teacher Association, the Chamber of Commerce, or the mayor, calls representatives of both agencies together to initiate the process of coordination. Coordinate understanding and policies are sometimes set forth in informal agreements or memoranda.

A typical policy statement regarding cooperative practice instituted between two public agencies (the school system and the recreational department) might be issued in this manner:

The Board of Education and the Department of Recreational Service recognize that cooperative effort is essential in providing areas, facilities, and leadership which may be required to meet the recreational needs of the community. Such responsibility is herein accepted by the two departments.

1. Buildings and grounds owned by the Board of Education will be available for recreational purposes by citizens of the community with such reasonable limitations imposed on their use as determined by the type of school involved and prior commitments of educational activities, or because of financial or other conditions.
2. School areas and facilities are not sufficient in themselves, even when maximum recreational use is made of them, to meet the recreational needs of the community. The construction, maintenance, operation, and supervision of additional facilities and spaces by the Department of Recreational Service are therefore necessary and consistent if such requirements are to be met.
3. The recreational agency will acquire no sites adjoining or close to existing or contemplated school sites if said areas are capable of meeting the recreational needs of the neighborhood which it may later serve as a center. However, it may be necessary to establish recreational facilities adjoining existing school grounds where such areas are inadequate to meet recreational needs or where the location of special facilities enables certain school grounds to serve the neighborhood or district more comprehensively.
4. The Department of Recreational Service will establish programs and staff facilities located near schools or adjoining such schools. The School Board will refrain from operating such playgrounds during after-school hours providing the public department can render such recreational service as may be required by the neighborhood concerned.
5. The desirable forms of cooperation that may be mutually engaged in by the respective departments concern the utilization of certain facilities or instruction in certain skills sponsored by either department. Among facilities placed at the disposal of either department are school gymnasiums, auditoriums, and athletic facilities, or public parks, playgrounds, camps, museums, and nature trails. Instruction may be afforded in any major activities, swimming, life-saving, nature study, sports.
6. All necessary action that the administrative officers of the School Board and the Department of Recreational Service must take to establish cooperative development of uniform administration of public recreational service should be taken. Each department, therefore, expresses its willingness to undertake cooperative action in order to render the most effective recreational service possible to the citizens of the community.

Joint Employment of a Coordinator

Another plan suggests itself whereby a coordinator free of all managerial duties and primarily concerned with coordination is jointly employed by school department and municipality. He would be accountable respectively to the two superintendents. As an employee of the school department (which would pay half his salary), he would have access to the entire school personnel, records, and facilities; as an employee of the city recreational service department (which would pay the other half of his salary), he would have the same advantage there. Being in effect an assistant superintendent in both departments, he would have enough authority to carry out his various functions, which may be summarized as follows:

1. to interpret to the staff of the recreational services department the best educational philosophy and techniques and their application to community recreational services.
2. to interpret to the school department staff the best recreational philosophy and techniques.
3. to investigate and make recommendations concerning neighborhood problems for which the school department and the recreational department should make some contribution to their solution.
4. to confer with representatives of community agencies, such as the Parent-Teacher Association, the Council of Social Agencies, civic service groups, and other organizations, on community recreational problems affecting the school department and the recreational department.
5. to assist in forwarding certain cooperative undertakings, such as:
   a. priority use of municipal playgrounds and swimming pools by organized school groups.
   b. priority use of school buildings and grounds by municipal department groups.
   c. "carryover" activities growing out of school experience fostered by the recreational department.
6. to aid in the coordination of school and municipal playground programs and to develop uniform rules of activities, seasons, hours of service, and general policies, so that a joint coordinated program might be presented to the public.
7. to coordinate any and all public agency programs on any governmental level connected with school and municipal recreational services.

This plan recognizes that coordination affects not only policies but also details of operation in the field. In every large city there is plenty of work for such a coordinator. If the coordinator were both educator and recreationist and a person of tact and imagination, his efforts would undoubtedly produce many worthwhile joint projects.

The Neighborhood Recreational Council or Committee

Neighborhood recreational councils, which may receive their impetus from the public department of recreational service or through the enthusiastic support of laymen within the community, exemplify the democratic process in the field of social work. They are at once a laboratory, a school of instruction, and a device for the formulation of public opinion. These councils can facilitate neighborhood recreational planning and cooperative enterprise. Such unofficial groups usually gain prestige from their early support of urgently needed recreational facilities, areas, or personnel. The members may be drawn from any agencies or groups located in the neighborhood. When such councils are organized by the department of recreational service, they are strictly advisory, although their functions may include raising funds for the improvement of neighborhood facilities, interpreting the department's recreational operations to the public, circulating recreational information throughout the neighborhood, assisting in neighborhood surveys that may lead to better recreational facilities or activities, sponsoring certain recreational activities, and implementing public inspections of local recreational centers.

The basic goals of these councils are to promote public interest in the services the public department offers, to support the department's budgetary request, and to assist in the planning of recreational activities in the neighborhood in conjunction with the community-wide program. The enlistment of neighborhood residents in councils of this nature may result in a widespread demand by citizens that various public agencies pool their resources or coordinate their activities in order to effect a larger community recreational service.

Extra-official affiliation with such organizations as the Parent-Teacher Association, the Chamber of Commerce, the Junior Chamber of Commerce, organized labor, service clubs, and community improvement clubs creates avenues for promotion of public relations. Membership dues in these organizations may not qualify as a legally reimbursable expense, but insofar as these may be afforded by an executive as a personal expense membership may be desirable. Each executive must decide this for himself.

Physical Facilities and Public Relations

Many persons gain their impressions of the department from its facilities and their physical condition. If the office has a neat and business-like appearance, if the grounds are well laid out and carefully maintained, if the buildings are in good repair and kept in a clean and orderly manner, the esteem in which the department is held by the public grows. City fathers tend to quarter the department away from the city hall, with facilities incomparably worse than those enjoyed by other departments. A standard of maintenance far below that acceptable for fire stations, police stations, and other longer established departments is sometimes tolerated. Recreational service departments themselves are partly to blame for this condition, because they are so imbued with interest in the activity program and its educational implications that they are sometimes inclined to accept improvisations unacceptable to other departments. Recreational service departments must insist that the standard of physical appointments be equal to that applied to other departments.

Employee Contacts

Every employee in the department is a public relations agent. A larger percentage of the employees of a recreational service department comes in contact with the public than in any other municipal department. Maintenance of favorable public relations is their duty and obligation as well as their privilege. A slovenly caretaker at a neighborhood center, a disgruntled recreational director, or a discourteous office clerk can do more damage to the public relations of a department than reams of published material can correct. Also important are telephone contacts, not only in the office but at the several centers, the courteous conduct of correspondence, and the strategic position of the information clerk or receptionist in the central office.

Some recreational service department employees do not appreciate their importance. Those who, by temperament or incapacity, are unable to contact the public advantageously should be assigned to duties where they have little contact with the public.

Newspapers

The metropolitan newspapers in the largest cities and the leading dailies in other cities are undoubtedly the most important printed media of publicity. The attitude of the department toward newspapers should be friendly, cooperative, and at the same time persistent. The employee in charge of department publicity should regard himself as a reporter for all newspapers and attempt to give them the kind of material suitable for their particular purpose. Different newspapers have different policies and different ways of presenting the news. The publicity person must know what these are so that he may supply their needs. Frequent contacts with news executives are of vital importance in improving the relationship of the department to the newspapers. It is not sufficient simply to write news releases, mail them out, and hope some of them will be used. By going to the editors in person, reasons for the use or the rejection of stories may be ascertained and put to good advantage in the future.

The utmost impartiality in dealing with the papers, if there are more than one, is vitally necessary. The greatest frankness must be observed in writing news releases and real news should not be withheld. Through a long period of contacts with editors, their confidence is cultivated and an atmosphere conducive to the growth of cooperation is created.

Regular News.   This news includes such stories as those dealing with action of the recreational service commission or department, announcements of new policies, dedications of new playgrounds, adoption of budgets, summary of attendance figures, and similar items.

Features.   Features offer the best opportunities for securing space in metropolitan newspapers, since they belong to the class that is known as "human interest" stories. The opportunities for developing this type of publicity are almost unlimited: boys make a new type of kite, foreign children get together and organize a band, life guards get new equipment. The metropolitan newspapers are very willing to cooperate in working up these features. A regular news event may be arranged so as to bring much greater publicity by treating it from the feature angle.

Continuous Publicity.   Under this heading comes publicity intended to popularize municipal camps, swimming pools, golf courses, boathouses, and similar facilities. It is the most difficult kind of publicity to get across because it is necessary to go over and over the same ground, to hammer away with news stories and pictures on these subjects without necessarily having any real news on which to hang the story. This work requires ingenuity in discovering new things to be said about these facilities. Special programs and events at playgrounds or swimming pools help in securing publicity, because they furnish an excuse for writing about them. When there are no special events, it is up to the person in charge of publicity to "make" news about them. One way of making news about a municipal camp is to arrange what is known as a "tie-up" with an automobile concern, or its advertising agents: the automobile concern sends one of its cars to the camp and uses the camp as a means of publicity for its car. In this way it is possible to secure "motorlogs" in automobile sections of newspapers, which are read by numerous persons planning vacation trips. The municipal swimming pools are always good places where feature publicity may be worked up whether or not an occasion has arisen to provide an excuse. Special stunts may always be developed there and prove satisfactory for use as swimming pool publicity.

Use of Special Departments.   When a playground is built, the real estate section may yield some desirable publicity. The automobile section may be used as outlined above. The sports section, of course, is always useful in chronicling tournaments and sports of all kinds. The Sunday feature section is valuable for the publication of some special items. The picture and rotogravure sections are fertile fields for the placing of recreational publicity.

Cooperation with Promotion Departments.   When it is desirable to get continuous publicity for some special activity, the promotion department of a newspaper may be willing to cooperate. The promotion department works to increase the circulation and advertising volume and any event or activity that will enlist the interest of any additional readers is carefully considered by this department. Model airplane tournaments, backyard playground contests, and swimming carnivals are events that have been backed by newspaper promotion departments in many cities. One paper, by publishing a series of twelve Christmas carols on the twelve days preceding Christmas, gave effective aid to a recreational service department program of carol singing on the streets.

Newspapers sometimes conduct athletic and other contests of their own as part of their promotion program. In doing so they solicit the assistance of the recreational service department to conduct or officiate at these events. If these contests are free and open to all and are not tied in with subscription campaigns, departments often render assistance. Occasionally the events are held at playgrounds. When the department lends its collaboration, excellent publicity can be obtained for as long as the events receive notice in the papers. For their own events papers devote a quantity of space far in excess of the space they would allot them if conducted under the auspices of others. The Soap Box Derby and the Roller Skates Derby held in all large cities, with final national contests, are events that many newspapers throughout the country have conducted. Recreational service departments assist in conducting these contests and in return receive much favorable mention in the papers.

When a tie-up with one newspaper is made, other papers, as a matter of fixed policy, withhold cooperation. When a department evidences willingness to associate itself with one paper, it must, to preserve goodwill, be equally willing to join with other papers under substantially the same conditions. Nothing is more destructive of newspaper cooperation than partiality in dealing with several papers or media.

Annual Editions. Newspapers put out annual editions summarizing various activities for the year. Editors are willing to use recreational articles of the summarizing type.

Editorials. When frequent mention of recreational articles is made in metropolitan newspapers, editorials come without being sought, as an outgrowth of the goodwill of the newspaper and its interest in the subject. However, another method of securing editorials is by sending material to editorial writers, packed with food for thought, for example, the annual report of the department, statement of attendance for the year, or similar analytical material.

Printed Circulars and Reports

The annual report, which all recreational service departments prepare and submit to the mayor and city council and which most departments

publish and distribute in considerable quantity, provides information
helpful to the citizens in interpreting the value of the work. It is a comprehensive and consolidated statement of the purposes and accomplishments of the department during the year. Its format should be attractive
and the contents readable and interesting. Even before publication portions may be extracted and released to the newspapers and other media.
The citizen particularly needs information as to where the facilities of
the department are located, what services are offered there, and how he
and his family may avail themselves of them. The annual report is too
voluminous to serve this purpose well or to be published in sufficient
quantity. Accordingly, departments frequently publish brief circulars
containing this information. These are available throughout the year at
the central office and are passed out at meetings, exhibitions, and demonstrations. Separate inexpensive circulars may be published in quantity
for different types of services, such as camping, picnicking, swimming,
playgrounds for children, and adult hobbies.

Printed Publicity

Under this heading may be listed folders, posters, window cards, and
other printed material calculated to carry the message of the department
to the public. It is well to make these as attractive as possible with
photographs, art work, and the like.

The recreational service department has splendid opportunities to distribute printed material. It may be posted and handed out at the neighborhood recreational places. Children attending the recreational center
may be asked to take the material to their parents. Since it concerns the
public business and is not commercial matter, the heads of large industries and business houses are generally willing to distribute the material
to their employees.

Weekly and Neighborhood Papers

The issuance of a regular news bulletin to these papers produces much
publicity. This bulletin should contain stories of general interest that are
not too lengthy so that they may be used in any space a newspaper or
magazine has available. When special information affecting a particular
district is available, such as the dedication of a new playground, it is
well to send a special story to the newspaper covering that neighborhood.
Because neighborhood newspapers cannot afford the use of many cuts
in their news columns, they always welcome the receipt of matrices from
which they may cast lead cuts. Recreational service departments may
use the matrices to illustrate municipal facilities and activities that they
are endeavoring to popularize. These materials cost little and are highly
effective.

Magazines

In every community there are numerous publications of both general and special interest in which it is possible to place articles on recreational work, including parent-teacher bulletins, teachers' journals, magazines of special interest to women, chamber of commerce publications, and others. Before writing articles for these publications it is always best to consult the editor and secure his version of what the magazine needs and wants.

Motion Pictures, Wire Services, and Syndicates

Included in this group are the various motion picture newsreel companies, the picture syndicates, and press services. They are valuable in securing national publicity for a recreational service department. This kind of publicity often returns to its source and results in local publicity as well. These organizations generally are interested in publicity of the feature variety rather than news of purely local significance. They will use human interest material that is truly unusual. Only the best portion of the features suitable for local use is of any value to these agencies. It is well, therefore, to call on them only when there is a feature that people all over the country might view with interest.

Motion Pictures

A number of the largest departments have developed motion pictures illustrating department activities and dealing with public recreational service problems. Some also have portable projectors which are used to present programs at civic meetings and other occasions. It is advisable, if a good impression is to be made, that films be up-to-date and, if possible, in color with sound accompaniment. With the tremendous rise of amateur motion picture photography, the voluntary aid of competent persons can be enlisted to produce these pictures if professional assistance is prohibitive in cost. Volunteer assistance in dramatization is readily available everywhere.

Radio and Television

Television is probably the most important medium for publicizing the activities of the department. The radio too may be used as a significant means of mass communications. Television and radio stations are required by the Federal Communications Commission to devote a certain percentage of their time to affairs of civic interest. Recreational activities conducted under public auspices fall in this category. Station managers often welcome opportunities to present good programs emanating from the public recreational service.

There is much competition for television and radio time so programs need to be carefully planned to meet the exacting requirements of the stations. The address is the simplest form of presentation but it is also of least value. Amateur dramatic programs are acceptable to many stations if well presented, but stations are usually more receptive to amateur musical programs than to amateur drama. Interviews and novelty programs, such as contests and presentation of awards, are effective. For projects that serve obvious public purpose, such as programs for May Day, Christmas, patriotic occasions, and the like, stations frequently make a series of spot announcements or telecasts in intervals between programs or for later release on video tape. If an event is of sufficient public interest, radio stations consider the practicability of installing remote control equipment on the site for broadcasting or telecasting the event.

Program Demonstrations

The recreational service department has the best opportunity of all municipal departments to cultivate good public relations. The total of its individual contacts with citizens is greater than that of other departments, the contacts are of a somewhat intimate nature, and they take place on occasions which the citizen enjoys. The mood of the citizen when he makes his contact with the work of the department is almost always a happy, expectant, and appreciative one, which is conducive to the formation of a fine impression. If the experience of the citizen is a happy one he will publicize it widely by word of mouth. The effects of work conducted on an efficient and high plane and in a manner meriting the approbation of the citizenry are far-reaching in any public relations program.

Exhibits

Exhibits are worth the effort required to put them on only when large numbers of people get to see them and when they present material of general public interest. Consequently, exhibits that are carefully arranged with a view toward presenting a real message, and that are seen by an adequate number of visitors are of considerable value. Recreational service departments, when invited to participate in general exhibitions, fairs, and shows, should give serious consideration to participation and its possible benefits. If an exhibit is entered, it should be truly representative of the department's work.

The most effective exhibits are live demonstrations. Practical demonstrations of skill in archery, badminton, fly casting, sketching, horseshoe pitching, handicrafts, or any of a thousand activities are immeasurably more effective than posters or printed matter referring to them. Any recreational service department can easily find many persons among its large clientele who delight in exhibiting personal skills in activities.

Window Displays

Window displays may be placed in the windows of banks, department stores, large drugstores, food markets, and similar business organizations. These should be attractive and representative of departmental activities.

Tie-ups

In addition to tie-ups with newspapers and their special departments, tie-ups with other civic agencies in a joint program are also of great value. One department had a most effective tie-up with the local fire department in a fire-prevention educational program. Another department had a tie-up with the Parent-Teacher Association and the department of education in a "Planned Vacation Program for Every Child," including a backyard playground contest. These associated projects resulted in favorable mention of the recreational service department in all publicity relative to these events. If a newspaper can be associated in the project, it is most generous with its space. The recreational service department must take care that standards of competition and recreational values are left to their determination in such joint projects. It must be assured that participants will not be exploited for private or commercial advantage.

Public Addresses

Public speaking affords another excellent avenue through which public relations may be cultivated. The recreational service department has many interesting stories to tell about its general services, events, and activities, the philosophy of its work, and related subjects. Its representatives are welcome speakers at many community occasions. Members of the recreational service board, the superintendent, and the several executives in charge of features of the work may fill engagements. Efforts should be made to solicit opportunities of this kind and the staff should be prepared by practice and encouraged to cultivate the ability to act as spokesmen for the department at public meetings.

Organization of Public Relations

Small departments of recreational service cannot afford to employ a specialist to organize and dispense publicity, but this should not deter them from considerable effort in obtaining a good hearing. Board members and superintendents should devote much time to public relations work, more in the recreational service department than in other municipal departments because recreational activities are so closely related to the public interest. Other members of the staff can be drawn into the program as well. Each department should have a carefully worked out program in which responsibility for the publicity devices outlined above is divided among the department employees. This division of responsibility should recognize the particular abilities of each person involved.

At present, no less than a score of park and recreational service departments in large cities assign the major duties and the general management of public relations to a specialist. The specialist is a staff employee and should have access to all phases of the work of the department. He should be associated with the superintendent and should work closely with him and with the board, if there is one, so that he may be aware of policies and plans of the department. The employment of a special publicity person should not absolve other employees from public relations responsibilities, but any special publicity undertaken by other employees should be cleared through the specialist.

Development of Public Support

Determining the needs of the community in relation to recreational needs and financial capacity is difficult because there are few, if any, standards to guide the recreationist. Other functions of government are not faced with this difficulty. Educators begin with an accepted standard that graded instruction shall be provided in an approved curriculum for all children for a given number of days. A government agency, the school board, is given the mandatory function to provide the services and the power to assess the necessary taxes to perform it. The whole matter lends itself to mathematical computation.

The same is true of nearly all municipal functions. Water supply required by homes, business, and industry can be computed; streets and pavements are of standard design; police and fire services may be objectively planned. Recreational service, including the areas and facilities or improvements required for it and the personal leadership involved, is still unstandardized. It is still an amenity, something added when the essential things have been taken care of.

Does appraising the park and recreational needs of the community begin with public demand? This is a high-minded concept: all public service depends on public demand. How is public demand appraised? Is it judged by petitions? Petitions are uncertain and inconclusive. Diligent solicitors can get any number of names signed to any petition, especially if the signer does not thereby commit himself immediately and directly to pay for something.

Appraising Public Demand

Is public demand appraised by attendance at a promotional meeting or public hearing? This is a method of public expression, but only a small percentage of the interested and affected citizenry attends such meetings, and every public officer knows that a meeting can be systematically packed with proponents or opponents, as the case may be. Is public demand appraised by letters to the editors of newspapers or by newspaper editorials? These are important indicators of public opinion but not altogether reliable or representative. But all these, together with correspondence, telephone contacts, visits, casual expressions of citizens, and actions by civic organizations, are indices of public demand.

Role of Leadership in Formulating Public Demand

Public demand, however, is not always enough. Sometimes the public does not have the basic information for the intelligent expression of its demand. Sometimes leadership must promote public demand in accordance with prudent judgment. Those officially and unofficially endowed with responsibility for exercising judgment must apprehend needs, guide community opinion, and formulate expressions which come to be recognized as embodying public demand. This is one of the prime responsibilities of the park and recreational service executive.

In the earlier stages of the modern urban park and recreational service movement, the role of leadership in planning and promoting service was simple. The public had little or no comprehension of its need for parks and recreational services and was ready to accept the opinions of those pioneers in the field who had more definite ideas. Consequently, whatever was provided was small and experimental, reflecting itself meagerly in public budgets. Few gave thought to the logical consequences in terms of financial cost of the extension of the service to all citizenry. Whatever was provided here and there was avidly accepted, but only a small part of the total need was served.

Recreationist executives and lay members of committees and commissions were missionaries, going forth into the neighborhoods to exhort the people to demand something of which they had no experience and the form of which they had not seen. The same personnel pleaded with officials, especially those in charge of budgets, to provide funds. Had the holders of the purse strings been able to project the eventual demand for more and more funds, they would doubtless have been less prompt in the beginning to give financial encouragement.

Now, however, the situation is quite different, especially in communities that are well established in the recreational service function. The public has caught up. Recreational service is no longer a way of getting the children off the streets. It no longer means only frivolous time-killing or purposeless freedom from toil. The citizen knows how important recreational experience is for people of all ages, and how inconclusive it is of all things done in our abundant leisure which make for happy living. He realizes that public provision of space and recreational facilities is necessary and he is willing that public tax funds be spent for it.

Recreationists used to have to persuade citizens of these things; now they are on the receiving end of the persuasion.

Slow progress is made because cities are burdened with so many new functions and the squeeze on the municipal tax dollar is getting greater and greater. The problem of financing essential public services of many kinds is so complicated and involved that the great mass of the citizenry finds it beyond comprehension. They are further confused by the existence of multiple jurisdictions—cities, counties, school and special districts, and the state. Hence it devolves on the members of legislative bodies, local and otherwise, to determine the financing of all functions.

Mobilizing Fragmented Public Opinion

There is strong public demand for recreational services but there are few means for implementing this demand. The difficulty is that public opinion is expressed in support of a multitude of little things. It is easy to mobilize public opinion toward effective legislative action in favor of a main highway, an airport, more schools, and the like because everybody can visualize the results. The mobilization of sectional opinions favoring a multiplicity of recreational interests, each having no communication with the others, is more difficult but it must be done. Public action must be made responsive to public opinion in the field of recreational service.

Community support can be enlisted in support of simple concepts capable of comprehension by everyone. The public demand for separate recreational entities must be related to a whole concept—for example, the concept of parks, playgrounds, or beaches. Campaigns in behalf of tennis courts, bowling greens, a golf course, an art workshop, a bandstand, a launching ramp, or any of a multitude of things avail little unless they can be consolidated in terms of public demand for parks or some other large recreational concept which embodies them all.

This problem is akin to that inherent in marketing recreational commodities. No other market is as fragmented as the recreational commodities market even though it represents only a fraction of the national income. A writer in *Fortune Magazine*, commenting on the situation, remarked hopefully that the recreational market "some day will simply take off." It is hoped that community recreational needs, fragmented as they are, will simply "take off" and become vocal and effective.

Financial Support through Public Relations

Financial planning with the whole community necessarily includes planning with the separate communities making up the whole. This matter must be considered not from the standpoint of the small village, which is a single community in itself, but from the view of the larger city, which is a collection of communities. Planning there must proceed both on the local and the city-wide levels. There are important civic organizations and influential individuals who are effective on both levels. Recreationists must work with both. Recently, the phenomenon of urban sprawl has effected a shift in the municipal political power structure from the center of a city to the satellite communities.

Effective planning of recreational services and finance begins at the local level. Professional staff, buttressed by lay personnel, are the usual means of energizing both planning and action at this level. The participants in the local recreational service center—the playground and park—become the nucleus. They enlist members of purely local business organizations, lodges, activity clubs, civic organizations, churches, synagogues, and local chapters of federated organizations like the PTA and the American Legion. "Ground roots" leadership so formed can become very intelligent and vocal concerning local needs, and concerning the needs of the whole community through consolidated affiliation with similar groups from other communities of the same city. Effective means of influencing city action are discovered through this channel of representation. The neighborhood weekly newspaper, usually distributed free, is another potential force on this level.

Duplicate organization in planning and securing financial support is necessary on the city-wide level. There are many organizations representing city-wide opinion, which is expressed independently of the local neighborhood and community opinion. These are, among others, the chamber of commerce, service clubs, women's clubs, union labor, metropolitan newspapers, and central federated boards of such organizations as the PTA, and city-wide activity organizations not identified with neighborhood of residence. Their membership comes from all parts of the city and their organization or society is identified with the whole city. Sometimes *ad hoc* representative committees are created to prepare a financial plan for the development of the recreational services.

Recreational service systems throughout the country are just beginning to appreciate the importance of public relations and the attendant responsibilities for analysis and interpretation. With effective public relations, most public recreational service departments will succeed in presenting well-rounded and suitable programs that can stimulate and sustain the enthusiasm of the public; without effective public relations, few systems can succeed—and most fail.

Selected References

Bronzan, R. T.: *Public Relations, Promotions, and Fund-Raising for Athletics and Physical Education Programs* (New York: John Wiley & Sons, Inc.), 1977.

International City Management Association: *Public Relations in Local Government* (Washington, D.C.: International City Management), 1975.

Kadon, J. and A. Kadon: *Successful Public Relations Techniques* (Scottsdale, Ariz.: Modern Schools), 1976.

Lewis, G. A.: *Public Relations for Local Government* (Boston, Mass.: Cahners Books International, Inc.), 1973.

Marshall, S. H.: *Public Relations Basics for Community Organizations* (Sacramento, Calif.: Creative Books Co.), 1975.

Moor, H. F. and B. K. Canfield: *Public Relations: Principles, Cases, and Problems*, 7th Ed. (Homewood, Ill.: Richard D. Irwin, Inc.), 1977.

Newsom, D. and A. Scott: *This is PR: The Realities of Public Relations* (Belmont, Calif.: Wadsworth Publishing Co., Inc.), 1976.

Walker, J. E.: *Public Relations: A Team Effort* (Midland, Mi.: Pendell Publishing Co.), 1976.

PART III

ORGANIZATIONAL FUNCTIONS

CHAPTER 10

Organization of Public Recreational Service

Organization is a highly regarded development whereby the effort of any group may be functionally designated. The basic premise is that some action must occur to perform a given purpose; secondly, several individuals are concerned with the effectuation of a specific task. In a relatively elementary situation, organization may be irregular and even latent or it may rely upon custom or habit. As the work becomes more complex and the objectives become increasingly dependent upon diverse forces, with consequent augmentation of the personnel force, organization develops specificity. Any explanation of organization also involves aspects of structure. Traditionally, structural definitions have taken on a non-human or impersonalized format.[1] However, in attempting to define recreational service organization, there is an explicit need to understand that organizational structure is developed around interpersonal relationships and not around things. Organization has meaning only as the expectations and performance of humans give it value. Organizational structures, therefore, reflect a recognized pattern uniting components of an organization to the aims of the organization as a whole. Any such model comprises some combination of roles for parts and agents and associations created among them by responsibility and ethics. These relationships, roles, and standards of behavior may either be formal or informal. The basic difference between them is that formal organization is more likely to be arranged by those who hold positions of authority.

In analyzing any organization there is a tendency to be concerned with positions or roles rather than with the individuals in them. It often appears that functions, prestige, and authority are identified with the role

[1] Robert Presthus, *Public Administration, Sixth Edition* (New York: The Ronald Press Company, 1975), p. 8.

205

rather than the incumbent at any given time. This characteristic gives the organization continuity and lessens, to some extent, its need for any particular individual. Coincidently, it is important to understand that any role is affected to some extent by the incumbent.[2]

ELEMENTS OF RECREATIONAL SERVICE ORGANIZATION

Sound practical principles of organization are guiding rules for action and not mandatory requirements. Principles serve as the rationale for structure and vary in the particulars of application as the needs of the agency vary.

Purpose. Basic to the establishment of a recreational service department is a precise definition of the purposes to be accomplished. Such a statement clarifies agency philosophy and policy, facilitates development of plans, and focuses attention and enterprise to achieve the purposes. The objectives of the department are the major premises on which the agency has been founded; all other aims are minor and secondary.

Research. All aspects of the recreational service system should be thoroughly analyzed so that each unit of the organization can be apprised of its specific function and the separate units brought into a related whole. The prime object of organizational research is to classify each factor having a bearing on the provision of service and assign specific activities or functions to particular components of the agency for more inclusive and effective operation.

Adaptation. Activities of departments are always changing as new needs arise and as the concepts of their functions change. When the first municipal playground departments were organized, the suggestion that schools open their yards and supervise the play of children after school hours and during vacations was regarded as radical. The same suggestion is now accepted in most places, although not in all. Legal, financial, and administrative difficulties have been ameliorated through legislation, contractual agreement, voluntary cooperation, mandated coordination and response to public pressure.

In many cities, a division of recreational service between municipal departments, the schools, and the recreational service department—if one exists—appears to be working in the public interest. The services of all agencies need to avoid duplication and promote coordinated action.

Necessity. Every activity necessary for adequately and effectively providing recreational service in the community should be instituted. Activities merely incidental to such service should be in subordinate positions or eliminated. Thus, the operation of lunch counters or soda

[2] Ibid., pp. 9–11, 186.

fountains by the department may be a convenience to the public but not essential for recreational service and may actually hinder effective service. Should the amenity interfere with routine recreational activities, it should be discontinued. If the department personnel believe that such accessory functions are necessary, the department may lease, rent, or sell the space to a concessionaire and simply control the concession against excesses or abuse of the privilege. When the department personnel wish to operate an amenity service in order to augment the operational budget, the ancillary service should not interfere with the primary purpose of the department.

Functionalism. The agency is concerned only with the achievement of the purpose for which it was created. Therefore, the department must be organized in relation to activities that aid in the attainment of that objective, not around specialized activities and personnel that serve limited, ulterior, or ancillary purposes.

When departments are based on main functions, the program offerings and other opportunities are likely to be comprehensive and balanced, and should afford wide experiences for general participation. When an agency is built around an individual or group of individuals, the program becomes merely an extension of their skills, talents, or abilities. In too many instances, public departments of recreational service have employed directors whose only competence lay within the field of sports and games; thus the program tended to become overloaded with athletic competition and participation to the exclusion of almost all other recreational activities.

Unity. The agency and its subdivisions and their respective functions should be precisely defined and fixed. This in no way implies that the executive should perform all the duties within the department; however, it does mean that he should delegate appropriate duties, authority, and responsibilities to his staff and subordinates. Each person within the department thereby knows his function, to whom and for whom he is responsible, and the chain of command for the alleviation of problems that he cannot solve on his level.

At any level within the department, authority should be centralized. The individual who is charged with the operation of any division or unit of the department must also be given the requisite authority to execute that responsibility. The failure or the achievement of that unit then rests with the individual in whom authority and responsibility are vested. Such an employee has a chance to develop ideas, whereas one who is constantly supervised lacks the opportunity to initiate action.

Centralized executive control with delegated authority and responsibility essentially calls for the establishment of a definite line organization with direct triangular communication branching from the chief executive at the apex down through administrative, supervisory, and program levels. Such a structure allows for a sound foundation of control and coordinated activity.

NATURE OF THE RECREATIONAL SERVICE FUNCTION

The basic function of the recreational service system is to provide daily, year-round recreational opportunities to all citizens of the community. It entails the utilization of both indoor and outdoor areas, spaces, facilities, and programmed or spontaneous activities. The proper performance of this function involves the organization or mobilization of the total environment and its resources; thus both personal (individual) and physical (natural and artificial) resources have to be discovered, listed, classified, and integrated into the total organizational pattern. Eventually, it may mean the development of a recreational needs profile on every citizen residing within the community and the offering of a variety of possible recreational activities or ideas that could bring recreational satisfaction.

Physical resources include natural, inanimate, and artificial objects, items, entities, and phenomena such as land, water, structures, aesthetic vistas, geologic formations, and other material assets. Personal resources include the individual skills, talents, aptitudes, leadership ability, interests, knowledge, organizational ability, and willingness to voluntarily serve others. In addition, the resources of the community are comprised of its history, traditions, cultural patterns, groupings of people to be found within the community, commitment in favor of recreational services, financial position to support a comprehensive and balanced planned program of public recreational services, and any fortuitous arrangement of temperature, weather, or climate that tends to promote recreational activity.

The problem of organizing the community for recreational service may be viewed as the organization of people, including professional and volunteer workers, and the establishment of recreational places incorporating the operation, maintenance, and administration of materials, funds, and activities. Material resources are of value only when they contribute to the satisfaction of human needs and the realization of human aspirations. Providing recreational opportunities, rather than engaging in directed recreational activities, is the prime function of the public recreational service agency.

The real nature of the recreational service function can be made clearer by drawing an analogy between the work of recreational service systems and that of school systems. The paramount function of the school system is not to build schools and to maintain grounds and buildings, but to provide activities that will contribute to children's growth and development. Similarly, the effectiveness of a recreational service system is to be judged not so much from the standpoint of the material facilities it provides (playgrounds, swimming pools, tennis courts, baseball diamonds, auditoriums, stadiums, and the like) and the manner in which the properties are maintained, but from the activities and other opportunities it carries on, sponsors, or coordinates and their contribution to individual satisfaction, enjoyment, personal growth, social objectives, and whatever distinct values may be derived by the individual.

The establishment of separate departments of recreational service in many cities has probably speeded the development of the function of municipal recreational service. Departments charged with a special, clearly differentiated function usually give this development more consideration than departments with other functions to perform and which are likely to view the function as secondary. Moreover, the special departments are freer to undertake experiments, are less bound to traditional practice, and are more militant and aggressive in the defense of their function during times of stress and retrenchment.

ORGANIZATION AND MOBILIZATION OF RESOURCES

Organization is defined simply as a systematic combination of people involved with the achievement of definite goals. Organization is concerned with internal structure, and is created for the purpose of assigning and defining duties, establishing lines of responsibility and communication, and effecting economy in the use of employee time and funds. Organization may be thought of as combining various and disparate components, resources, and functions and arranging them to produce a smoothly coordinated operational entity. Thus, organization is essentially concerned with the logical connection of parts into effective correlation and cooperation. At the community level, the various elements that must be brought into correlation and cooperation by effective organization are:

Physical Resources
  Land and Water Areas
  1. Intended primarily for recreational activity:
     a. Playgrounds, fields, reservations
     b. Lakes
     c. Beaches
     d. Rivers and streams
     e. Park lands
  2. Intended secondarily for recreational activity:
     a. School lands
     b. Forest lands
     c. Harbor areas

8

d. Reservoir and watershed areas and adjacent lands
e. River basins, deltas, and adjacent lands

Buildings and Structures
1. Intended primarily for recreational activities:
   a. Recreational centers, field houses, courts
   b. Community centers or club houses
   c. Gymnasiums
   d. Stadiums
   e. Bath houses, boat houses, locker facilities (ancillary)
   f. Swimming pools and aquatic facilities
   g. Camp structures and facilities
   h. Band shells, marinas, outdoor theaters
   i. Commercial properties—bowling centers, dance halls, billiard parlors, movie houses, legitimate theaters
2. Intended secondarily for recreational activities:
   a. School buildings and facilities
   b. Museums, aquariums, planetariums, and observatories
   c. Zoological, botanical, and horticultural gardens, arboretums
   d. Libraries and other public buildings and facilities
   e. Commercial properties—shopping center parking lots
   f. Private facilities—youth-serving agency facilities

Personal Resources
   People of the community according to:
   a. Neighborhood
   b. Age
   c. Sex
   d. Interests, skills, talent, knowledge
   e. Previous experiences
   f. Traditions, mores, customs
   g. Ethnic groupings and/or religious affiliations or traditions
   h. Economic status, social status, community recognition
   i. Educational preparation
   j. Leisure available
   k. Artificial groupings (social, political, economic, professional, ethnic, racial, religious organizations)

Program Resources
   Activities, according to their nature:
   a. Art
   b. Crafts
   c. Dance
   d. Drama
   e. Education

f. Environmental and/or nature-oriented activities
g. Hobbies
h. Motor activities (individual, dual, group, team)
i. Music
j. Service (volunteer)
k. Social
l. Special projects or events

Activities, according to environment or equipment required:
a. Playground activities
b. Park activities
c. School activities (extracurricula)
d. Aquatic activities (beach, pool, pond, or waterfront)
e. Camping and outdoor educational activities
f. Water-borne activities (boating, sailing, surfing, scuba diving)
g. Stadium activities
h. Field activities
i. Special area activities—golf, archery range, rifle range
j. Workshop, studio, kitchen, laboratory activities

Activities, differentiated according to degree of expertness required:
a. Instructional and developmental
b. Opportunity for continued practice
c. Variety after attainment of high degree of skill

Professional Skills
1. Planning
2. Organization
3. Leadership
4. Supervision
5. Management
6. Design
7. Maintenance, construction
8. Public education, public relations

The problem of organizing recreational service administration in a community is extremely complicated. If all things that serve a common purpose are to be grouped together in the municipal organization, then a single department—responsible for all services suggested in the outline—would be in order. Such an assumption is impractical, since many of the resources are under the control of agencies serving purposes other than recreational experiences.

That large cities sometimes have more than one department contributing to the public recreational service function is not in itself invalid. The recreational service process in the modern community is many-sided and several departments may be involved in its administration. Insofar as the services rendered by the several departments are dissimilar, their existence violates no fundamental principle of efficient governmental organization. It is only when such departments embark on innovations that interfere and conflict with the activities of others that efficiency requires either re-assignment of activities, consolidation, or a definite plan of coordination. Consolidation of similar departments has been effective in providing better recreational service to the people of the community, e.g., when park and recreational service departments have been combined.

The primary advantage in operating along purposive lines is the enthusiasm and coordination achieved throughout the hierarchical levels as a result of each person's knowledge of the agency's basic function and his own understanding of cooperation toward that goal. Thus administrative control is obtained not only through chain-of-command relationships and structure, but also through unanimous focus on the general objective. The ideal condition within any organizational structure is maximum efficiency in the pursuit of a common goal. Personal rapport plays a most significant part in such efficiency, for, as always, people are more important than flow charts.

A second advantage of purpose orientation, as opposed to process or function orientation, is that generalists, rather than functional specialists, may be employed in managerial posts. Thus administrators with administerial skills rather than specialized program recreationists may be employed in the topmost positions. This does not mean that recreationists should not be employed in top management positions; on the contrary, since professional preparatory and graduate recreational service education programs are training students for administrative positions, more and more such persons will become available. These individuals will be specialists in recreational service, but they will be generalists in administration.

RECREATIONAL SERVICE AS A DELIVERY SYSTEM

The necessity for coordination of the community effort to provide recreational services to all constituents when and where they desire such opportunities is a mandate that no existing department is capable of fulfilling. Increasing population, sophistication of demands on the public system, the increasing complexity of community organization, and the variety of public, quasi-public, and private sector agencies require correlation for the satisfaction of public recreational needs. The work of public recreational service agencies sometimes duplicates or impinges on that of municipal school, community-supported private agencies, and privately operated organizations to the detriment of public service and welfare. Such duplication and competition for the same clientele often may leave gaps in community service. Some populations are the direct concern and focus of several different agencies, whereas other populations receive little or no service at all. Often the line of demarcation between the functions and prerogatives of each group is not clear. Therefore, the areas of service must be defined and differentiated to effect coordination and to integrate the activities of all groups that have direct or indirect responsibility for the provision of recreational services to people within a given community.

Coordinating Local Agencies

Sometimes several departments and agencies contribute to the attainment of a common objective, for example, crime prevention, public health, public housing, and public safety. A school department organizes and supervises extracurricular activities; a municipal recreational service department conducts a parallel program in the neighborhoods. Community, but not tax-supported, agencies conduct programs of recreational activities for public participation which utilize the parks and other public facilities while the public agency operating the facilities directs a similar program, which proves wasteful of human and physical resources unless the overlapping of service or duplication of effort is overcome.

A more or less standard pattern of organization in the coordination of social planning is the Council of Social Welfare Agencies (sometimes called the Community Welfare Planning Council). The social welfare concerns and enterprises, private and public, are so numerous in large cities that it is necessary to organize them into divisions. The recreational service agencies, once called group work and youth-serving agencies, constitute one of these divisions.

Many cities have undertaken to coordinate recreational services by organizing an advisory body with representation from the several public, quasi-public, and private social agencies. This group may be a division of the welfare planning board or some other overhead coordinating body. The council provides an effective process for dividing responsibilities and services among the agencies. It coordinates activities and arranges for reciprocity in the use of facilities and occasionally personnel. It mobilizes all resources of leisure-oriented service agencies for recreational problems of community-wide importance.

The functions of the public recreational service department, the school system, and other agencies conducting community recreational programs (such as the YMCA, YWCA, Boy and Girl Scouts, CYO, Jewish Community Center, YMHA, Camp Fire Girls, Boys' Clubs, and Social Settlements) are closely related. The principal concern of the public departments is to provide recreational facilities and to organize mass recreational activities for all citizens under the person-to-person leadership of individuals and groups. Private agencies specialize in reaching certain segments of the population through mass, individual, and group activities, each with its own program and its own conception of the ultimate objective. Private agencies are accorded extensive use of public facilities. This is as it should be. However, unless there is close cooperation there is also great likelihood of ineffectual programming and waste of time, money, and effort.

The public recreational service department should be actively related to all such attempts at coordination within the community. In fact, the public department may provide the impetus for coordination with and between various social agencies of the community. The value of such a council in this coordinating relationship is limited only by its capacity for leadership. It functions chiefly to coordinate the recreational programs that are administered by different municipal agencies. Additionally, it may serve as a consultative body, may render advice, and may provide assistance to private and quasi-public organizations concerned with recreational service. The purpose of such activities is to obtain the greatest possible benefit from existing resources by the administration of a comprehensive, long-term plan.

If a community service agency council has been established without the participation of the public recreational service department, the department should take steps to gain representation. Many conflicts of interest will be avoided and recreational services may be improved when all, or almost all, of the social agencies within a given community direct their attention to a single goal.

Coordination and Systematization

If public recreational service is viewed as a delivery system instead of an agency that provides specific recreational activities with concomitant attempts to enlist the aid and cooperation of other organizations operating within the three sectors of the community, there is likely to be better comprehension of what recreational service departments should be doing. Although the public recreational service department is charged with the responsibility for the provision of recreational activities and analogous services to all citizens in the community during their respective leisure, the plain truth is that no one agency can be truly effective in carrying out this impossible mission. The realization of such a task is quite inconceivable because too many hindrances stand between mandated responsibility and effective execution. No department, regardless of its size, adroitness, facilities, or innovational ideas, will ever be able to accommodate all the people with agency-sponsored activities. No agency has the necessary resources for the operational execution of such an assignment. Too many other municipal departments simultaneously vie for personnel, fiscal support, and equipment for local government to provide what is absolutely essential to recreational service departments to achieve their responsibilities.

All or most agencies from the three sectors of society are needed to assist in the promulgation and fulfillment of human recreational needs in the community. All agencies are invited, even welcomed, to join in the provision of whatever personnel, facilities, and program of a recreational nature they may be able to organize and/or sponsor. Beyond the cooperative aspect, private agencies have the legal or constitutional right to provide whatever recreational services they desire, as long as such activities do not conflict with constitutional or other legally enacted provisions of the law. In a free society, private enterprise may provide any service for which people will pay; assuming that such provision does not cater to the prurient, is not degrading, or does not involve willful misconduct with malicious intent to destroy property or injure individuals.

Recreational service in the public sector, indeed, may be formulated on the structure of an operational department, but the range and scope of the functions of such a department must be looked on in a far different manner than recreational service agencies operate under today. If public recreational service is seen as a delivery system instead of as an agency of particular performance, a method by which the primary responsibility for which the department was established could be effected. At this time, no operating agency is capable of carrying out its mandate; there are too many gaps in service. Overlapping and duplication of functions can be expected as various organizations compete for the same clientele at the same time. To reduce monetary, personnel, and material wastage, a delivery system concept appears to be in order.

The Meaning of System

Webster's Dictionary offers several definitions for the word system. However, the first statement identifies system as "an aggregation or assemblage of objects united by some form of regular interaction or interdependence; a group of divers units so combined by nature or art as to form an integral whole, and to function, operate, or move in unison and, often, in obedience to some form of control; an organic or organized whole."[1]

The essence of system suggests an interaction between objectives and methods. It is to be anticipated, therefore, that in typical operation, goals are viewed as formative insofar as the model is concerned and, naturally, the system for which it stands. Goals affect the system's time and spatial perimeters, the factors considered or omitted, and how its coordination with congruent and abutting environments is managed.

If a system is, as Buckley states, "a whole which functions as a whole by virtue of the interdependency of its parts,"[2] then it may be defined as

[1] Webster's *New International Dictionary*, 2nd Ed. Unabridged.
[2] Walter Buckley, ed., Foreword to *Modern Systems Research for the Behavioral Scientist* (Chicago: Aldine, 1968), p. xv.

Figure 10-1.   An elementary system.

an open-ended[3] organization designed to effect some specific function by utilizing certain information or material, converting that input into usable components, transmitting the products of the conversion so that they can be utilized practically, discarding impertinent or unusable material (information), receiving additional information or material as a direct result of transmitting earlier applicable forms, reconditioning or refining the material for practical use, and repeatedly transmitting material (in the form of usable products, ideas, activities, or services) to a consumer or other entity. Systems are usually represented by diagrams and flow charts. An elementary system is shown schematically in Figure 10-1.

As a recreational service system, the functional department could be ordered and organized so as to permit collection of data dealing with individual recreational needs from all persons residing within a community. This profile would serve as the basis for preparing possible alternative recreational solutions to the problems such differentiated needs would require. A realistic presumption is that where such a system was implemented a centralized computer bank would be needed into which statistics and individual profiles (detailing whatever physical, social, psychological, attitudinal, experiential, economic, educational, religious, ethnic, or other needs and traits characterizing the individual) could be fed. From this mass of data an individual program based on relevant facts could be processed to meet the unique and specific recreational requirements of each person in the community. Such a proposal may sound fantastic in the contemporary world where many governmental processes are still geared to nineteenth century operations, but it is not beyond the realm of feasibility or reality. In fact, it is probable that within the next few decades all public recreational services will flourish along such systematic lines, initially necessitating an enormous amount of financial support, expert technical personnel, and a matchless (in terms of current affairs) innovational series of planned activities and ideas. However, there is every expectation that through computer hook-ups, particularly in the field of cybernetics, this idealized system will eventuate.

As a delivery system, the paramount function of the recreational service department would be to coordinate the disparate agencies, resources, and available financial support at the community level so that the recreational needs of individuals, groups, and masses could be accom-

---

[3] Talcott Parsons, "Systems Analysis: Social Systems" *International Encyclopedia of the Social Sciences,* Vol. 15, 1968, p. 44.

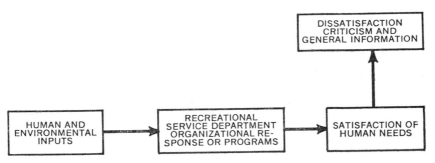

Figure 10-2.   A simplified recreational service system.

modated, obviating the need for the specialist personnel now employed by recreational service departments. Instead, generalists whose function would be dictated by the total mobilization of all pertinent resources of the community or perhaps of the region in which the municipality was situated would be required. Thus, the function of the agency might be to enumerate possible activities in which the individual could engage given his prior skills, experiences, knowledge, physical, and mental capabilities. Furthermore, it would call for the extensive coordination of all agencies with primary, secondary, or tertiary recreational interest to lend their resources to afford community-wide services to all citizens. The public system would be the central clearinghouse where specialist personnel could be brought together for the benefit of the consuming public.

Under such a system social, political, economic, and environmental resources can be organized into highly complex programs having great social value for those who participate. Such a system is shown in Figure 10-2.

The basic parts of the system are inputs, process, and outputs. Inputs are understood in their relation to the operation of the system. Inputs may be classified as information, material, energy, or any combination thereof. In a recreational service system, humans are the material that enters the system and on which some operation is performed or behavior or attitude modified. Thus, people constitute the raw material on which the recreational service system acts in order for some desired end or output to occur. Environmental inputs may be natural or artificial. The latter will be understood best as customs, traditions, or law which tends to restrict or otherwise affect the operation of the public system. Personnel attrition within the system requires replacement; such added personnel become part of the input.

The process aspect of the system requires that inputs be acted on in proper sequence, at the appropriate time and place so that the objective of the system will be achieved. Since the inputs are participants within the recreational program, this material will be acted on by recreationists, environmental factors, and other people who participate or observe. The process of participation will effect some change in the individual, either giving satisfaction and concomitant benefits or not. If the process concludes with the individual's personal satisfaction, then the system may be said to have fulfilled the function for which it was established. When the system does not achieve the desired end result, the process must be reconstituted and modified so that the final outcome is the stated objective.

The third phase of the system is output. In evaluating the product or accomplishment of the system, two requirements are essential: First, the performance of the system must be stable, i.e., have continuity of productivity. Second, the operation must be reliable in relation to the personnel who make up its components. In this case, recreationists would be required to function in the most professionally competent manner, thereby reducing the error rates typically found in human encounters. When the system is supplied with inputs of such diverse nature that it cannot adjust, the final result is negatively affected. When the system cannot adjust to various inputs, the outputs are inversely affected. The system is designed to produce solutions (activities or programs) satisfying to the user. Optimum results occur when program activities that produce the greatest satisfaction to those who actively participate or receive value from vicarious experience are selected.

Organizational Modification

The recreational service department must be susceptible to all environmental changes so that their impact on the organization is analyzed correctly. The organization must select the best solutions for advancing its goals, thereby reacting effectively to environmental influences. If the department is to attain its stated aims, it will have to compensate for changes in political (legal) or natural environment and in the human factors that demand adjustment. These are the conditions that sustain the department, and, unless there is a symbiotic relationship between the department and its environment, the existence of the department will be threatened if not destroyed.

Changing environments afford intimations of future occurrences which should be perceived and interpreted by the department. Appropriate responses to such changing external conditions result in the greatest possible value to the agency and the public. Correct responses lead to maximized worth, and in this manner the department is judged by its constituent clientele. The more often the department satisfies the public the more likely it is that the organization will receive and retain increased financial and moral support from the public.

Therefore, if the department effectively responds to its environment, not only its own welfare will be sustained, but the value it purports to offer to the general public also will be enhanced. Whenever an organization reacts to environmental change (public opinion or need) in either inappropriate or insensitive ways, or if it fails to take a realistic stance in determining its functions, there is little likelihood that it will be successful. Much more probable is imminent failure and nullification.

Programs of organizational behavior are established to achieve certain objectives (within the limitations imposed by environment), and these programs are successful when these aims are attained. Recreational service tends to repeat successful programs until they become the habitual pattern of agency response. The pragmatic administrator is heard to say, "Why fight success?" The organization's greatest danger lies in that cliché. Instead of realizing that the needs and wants of people change as better education opens wider vistas or inculcates greater degrees of sophistication, the habitual response is given despite environmental cues. Thus the department gradually becomes unresponsive; it may not be capable of rapid adjustment, or, even worse, it may be incapable of recognizing the need for change. When this occurs, there is a lessened benefit to the public and in a few instances a completely negative response from the constituency. Problems in personnel competencies, supplies, materials, use of designated spaces, maintenance, behavioral problems, and organizational dissatisfaction arise daily. If the system is to perform well, all aspects of its operation should be coordinated, solutions must be effective, and continuity of program is required.

The Managerial Process

The problems that beset the recreational service system of an environmental or organizational type must be resolved for the good of the agency and its constituency. The actual resolution of problems may not always be handled with all personnel comprising a general assembly in which each and every problem is placed under the scrutiny of all personnel. Such deliberate attempt to involve the entire work force in a democratically contrived process places the system in jeopardy because personnel would spend all of their time problem solving and no time would be given to the work of the department, not only proving inefficient, but permitting the system to grind to a halt.

It is by division of labor that the analysis and continuous resolution of environmental and internal problems of the system are to be solved. The department has clearly designated certain specialists (administrators), who focus their attention on unravelling problems and become highly skilled at it, to deal with problems as they arise. When an individual has shown that he is adept in dealing with the manifold pressures generated by the problems that the system confronts, he is generally assigned to a management position where decisions are made for the solution of problems.

Administration therefore may be looked on as a fundamental regulating mechanism of the organization, and, in this connection, the functions of management and regulation are identical. Management is that part of the organization which attempts to regulate the system in such a manner that a highly effective output is maintained. Management serves as a pacemaker for the organization insofar as it enables the system to cope with changing environmental stimuli. It is the adjustive component charged with arranging the resources of the system to meet changing environmental situations as they arise. The managerial or control factor is a homeostatic device that permits continual operation of the system while modifying its output (program satisfaction) until the output equals a predetermined goal or standard of excellence. Thus an evaluating procedure that compares the actual output of a system with a selected standard of excellence must be coupled to the basic system. If the actual output is lower than the standard expectation, the management process requires the operational system to change. Such modification of the program continues until program satisfaction equals intended or standard objectives.

The managerial process as a regulating mechanism is diagramed in Figure 10-3. The department answers to specific modifications in environmental conditions and provides a particular response for its clientele measured in terms of satisfaction. For any given situation, expectations are based on previous experiences and successful programs. Program output is evaluated in comparison with some predetermined standard. If the actual program satisfaction is below the expected standard, imbalance is created in the form of a problem. Management determines what must be done to effect a solution and injects the corrected material into the organizational response pattern. The corrected material should successfully resolve the problem and produce program satisfaction at a level commensurate with the standard or expected satisfaction. Thus the system is perpetuated by automatically compensating for errors or below standard results and modifying departmental responses to meet changing environmental conditions.

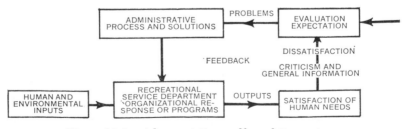

Figure 10-3.   A homeostatic or self-regulating system.

The managerial or regulatory process provides the organization with a mechanism for coping with different environmental stimuli through adaptation. As the organization is stimulated by changing human needs or situations, it becomes capable of devising innovative activities in response to inputs. Under this system, problems continuously flow into the managerial segment until the correct solution is found.

Integration of Operations

Every division of the recreational service system is a specialized function and all must be coordinated so that the departmental responses are satisfying to all who wish to participate. No division may remain isolated from other components of the department. The essential function of the recreational service system is to produce or sponsor opportunities that every citizen of the community may utilize. This necessitates the integration of all departmental specialities so that each contributes to a final net worth or satisfaction without waste. When problems arise, the managerial process devises correct solutions, which are inserted into the system for use. Administration produces solutions in the form of appropriate departmental activity. Solutions, which may be called policy, standards, regulations, or instructions for the guidance of personnel, may be utilized according to prevailing conditions. Thus at any specified time a selection of solutions (or instructions) will be available. Given a particular problem, the recreationist will be expected to adopt the correct solution from this roster. If all the responses recommended by management are feasible and suitable, the function of the administrator is to augment or devise a register of appropriate responses that are reiterated in the organization's internal and external environments. From that point on, the functional worker's task is to use these solutions in an acceptable manner.

Administrative resolutions (programs) may be catalogued by use. Some programs are regular, routine activities; some are intermittent, irregular and recurring; others are infrequently or rarely used. For example, administration may provide for an annual pyrotechnical display or Christmas festival. Some activities take place each day on a routine instructional basis. Other conditions might occur for which no managerial program was prepared. These latter situations still require some action. Either new solutions have to be worked out, or, if no alteration of procedure is necessary, program functionaries will be directed by operational procedures and policies.

Systems are artificially contrived to produce some ultimate goal that is satisfying to man; they are designed, intended, and logically conceived for serving human purposes. The administrative process as a part of the system is useful in rendering decisions dealing with problems that arise during the operation of the organization. Organization is a system of cooperation and coordination among individuals intent on the achievement of some predetermined objective, generally of a satisfying nature that could not be attained without cooperation. Solutions to problems are generated as the organization reacts to environmental stimuli and are handled best by specialists whose primary function is to work out appropriate answers, thereby maximizing the value received or human satisfaction. Essentially, problems occur because resource allocation requires guidance, because planned satisfaction from program does not meet estimated or expected standards, and because there is the continual need to respond to changes in internal and external environments. These problems require solutions. Solutions are viewed in terms of the adjusted or correct program response which management devises.

Administration as a process is coordinated with all other phases of the organization by effecting a catalogue of appropriate solutions that functional workers can draw from at any given time during the operation of the department. When particular situations or relatively similar conditions arise, the recreationist has a schedule of solutions available. His responsibility is to select the correct response called forth by the event. In Chapter 13, Systems Management and Analysis, is a more thorough and detailed account of systems and their utility within the recreational service field. The introduction of systems into recreational service is slow, but several departments are already using system devices to make them more capable of answering the public's needs. Recreational service as a public system will occur when it is finally realized that the field and its agencies cannot meet nor satisfy human needs unless it acts as a catalytic and coordinating mechanism. Systematization is the device that will permit total useful allocation of all resources within the environment for optimum production of recreational satisfaction.

Selected References

Eddy, W. B., and others, Eds.: *Behavioral Science and the Manager's Role* (San Diego, Calif.: University Associates), 1976.

Hersey, P. and K. Blanchard: *Management of Organizational Behavior: Utilizing Human Resources, 3d ed.* (Englewood Cliffs, N.J.: Prentice-Hall, Inc.), 1977.

Gibson, J. L., and others: *Readings in Organization: Behavior, Structure, Processes, rev. ed.* (Homewood, Ill.: Business Publications), 1976.

Herzberg, F.: *The Managerial Choice: To Be Effective and To Be Human* (Homewood, Ill.: Dow-Jones-Irwin, Inc.), 1976.

Sanford, E. and H. Adelman: *Management Decisions* (Englewood Cliffs, N.J.: Winthrop Publishing Co.), 1977.

CHAPTER 11

Housing the Public Recreational Service System

The form of a public recreational service system largely is determined by the social setting in which it is conceived and by the particular orientation of its founders. If the recreational service system is conceived in terms of children's playgrounds, one form of initial structure will be favored; if in terms of municipal beach, golf, swimming pool activities, organized sports, and adult hobbies, another form will be indicated.

Cities have experimented and are experimenting with different types of organization. However, the organization of community recreational services and the establishment of some branch of municipal government responsible for such provision have given rise to much confusion. The question is not simply: Where in the municipal structure the recreational service function shall lodge? The questions to be answered are: Which governmental agency shall be responsible for recreational services in the community? Which agency is best able to supply the manifold activities of municipal recreational service? Which agency has the personnel with the most acceptable orientation for providing community services of a recreational nature? Which agency performs services most closely related to community recreational service? What additional personnel and administrative structure are required for the most effective and efficient performance of this function?

Park departments, welfare departments, school boards, quasi-public agencies, and private recreational agencies are all interested in the community's expanding need for adequate recreational service and often are planning and organizing their facilities, personnel, and budgets to meet this need. Shall an independent tax-supported recreational service department be created that will have control of all municipal recreational services? Can such a system adequately satisfy the recreational needs of all the people in the community?

DEPARTMENTAL ORGANIZATION

Recreationists are still discussing whether recreational services are best administered under a special agency, park department, board of education, or some plan joining two or more agencies. All plans have their advantages and disadvantages. Moreover, what is best for one community may not be valuable in another. Essentially, the organizational plan depends on local conditions. Although each specific plan has something to commend it, some forms of organization are decidedly more advantageous than others regardless of size, condition, or economic ability of the community. At least one type of organization will serve the community best.

During the past few years there has been an unmistakable trend toward more effective organization and integration of the several functions of municipal government, owing to a number of factors. The universal expansion of municipal functions since the beginning of the twentieth century has resulted in the establishment of so many new departments and bureaus that consolidation of some for efficient administration became inevitable. The economic depression of the 1930s and the insistent demand for reduction of property taxes dictated a necessity for more economical operation and elimination of duplicated services. The growth of certain agencies, notably those concerned with education, library, park, and recreational programming, has been such that a certain amount of overlapping was created, pointing up the need for greater coordination of these services and more effective organization. The spiraling costs of inflation, an unprecedented boom economy, negligible unemployment, and a proliferation of taxes have done nothing to still the cry for less taxation. The municipality is caught between rising population, demand for more and better services, and insistence on lower taxes. The 1980s should see an even greater effort to coordinate and consolidate services. Because of the continuing money squeeze, standardized organizational structures have been defined.

The Human Services Movement

The decline in urban fiscal resources has caused widespread panic among elected and appointed political officials. They seek ways and means of cutting down on their overhead. For the most part this has meant a diminution of human services to citizens. It has also been manifested by layoffs or reduction in forces from departments serving a variety of clients within the city. By reducing the number of employees it was thought that tremendous savings could be gained. Little savings

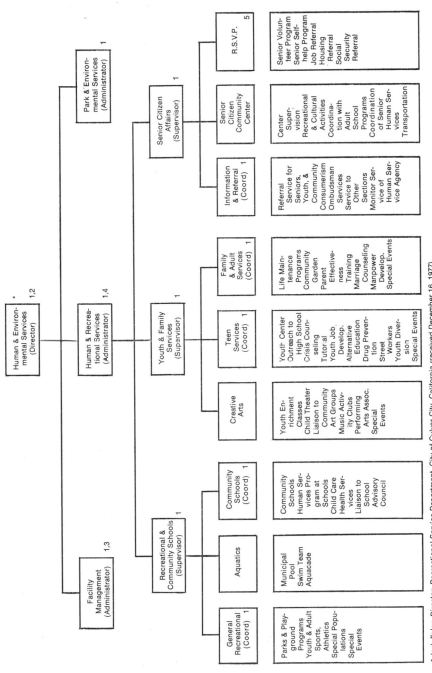

* Jack Foley, Director, Recreational Service Department, City of Culver City, California (received December 16, 1977).
Proposed Department of Human and Environmental Services, Human and Recreational Services Division

have resulted, but the city's welfare costs have risen and service deficiencies have grown in proportion to the number of persons cut from payrolls.

Officials have begun to realize that simply cutting the work force neither saves a great deal of money nor enhances the productivity of those who remain on the job. Rather, there seems to be a decline in morale and the service normally rendered by those who retain their employment. Other innovative methods must be sought to gain effective services to citizens who pay their taxes and have a right to expect services in return. The current movement toward consolidation of urban departments is most clearly observed in the development of a super-agency—the human services department. This organization combines the personnel and functions of formerly independent line agencies (see chart p. 225).

For good or ill, public recreational service departments have come to be seen as the repository of these combined departments. Thus, all human resource agencies within the community may be placed within the organizational structure of an existing recreational service department or an overhead agency may be established to administer the functions of several departments under the aegis of one chief executive. Instead of having five or six commissioners, superintendents, or directors there is only one. The heads of these former departments are down-graded to assistant administrator positions. Either they accept the new title or they may resign. The current trend is to look to one of the administrators of a line agency and select him/her as the new chief executive. Rarely is an individual not employed by the city in some administrative capacity chosen to head up the newly created department.

The single criterion associated with the super-agency executive is that the selected person be capable of administering many disparate line agencies, provide continuity of service and functions, and coordinate all operations so that there is no over-lapping or duplication. It is, to say the least, an Herculean job. Interestingly enough, many of the overhead administrators being chosen come from recreational service departments. Why this should be is no mystery. For the most part, these recreationist administrators have proved themselves capable of operating a complex department whose organization is broadly based within the community. There are no particular clientele to be served, the entire population of the city is the constituency of the department. Moreover, the very nature of public recreational service requires the ability to deal with diverse personnel and their problems. Recreationist administrators learn to accommodate technicians, professionals, ancillary, and volunteer personnel. They deal with planning, maintenance, record keeping, personnel policy, public behavior, programming, physical plant administration, and a host of other activities necessary for the efficient and effective operation of the agency. Therefore, it is suggested, recreationists should be able to handle other kinds of human service agencies because they are typically concerned with coordination within the community framework.

It may be valid to state that recreationists can be effective human services administrators simply because the field of recreational service is one of the great humanitarian organizations and administrators of such agencies have had long practice in coping with the manifold problems which beset any complex urban department. However, there are numerous functions being thrust upon recreationists for which they are ill-prepared to play a role. It seems little likely that recreationists will either want or have dealt with welfare, health care, job placement, drug control, personal counseling, family relations, etc., which are part of the human services package. Nevertheless, it behooves recreationist administrators to undertake these additional chores and perform to the best of their respective abilities because the alternative is to have other administrators, not oriented to recreational service, placed in the chief executive's position. While the administrator of a super-agency must be equitable in his dealings with subordinates and see that each agency receives a budgetary allocation which would enable it to carry out its mandate, there are non-recreationists who might slight recreational service in favor of those departments which provide direct health, education, or welfare care to recipients. The entire question of making a conglomerate of the recreational service department and saddling its administration with the heavy burdens of other human service functions is one that requires much study and evaluation. It is an area that may come to haunt the field of recreational service in the next few years.

The Independent Recreational Service Department

The plan illustrated in Figure 11-1 is used in several cities. Recreational service is a function separate and distinct from any other public service with centralized control of areas specifically intended for recreational activity and recreational programming in a recreational service department. This department has no organic connection with the park department or with the school board. Nevertheless, all three agencies are expected to cooperate.

This plan is advantageous because it places community recreational service under the control of a special agency. By concentrating on one task, such a department is usually successful in securing greater attention to recreational service from city government and from the citizenry and a more adequate budget. Its staff is likely to be selected with more specific attention to professional qualifications in recreational service. By having control of its own facilities, it is able to organize its program more comprehensively and efficiently than if it depended on other agencies

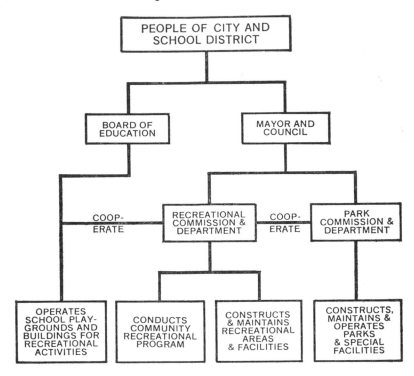

Figure 11-1.   The independent recreational service department.

for the use of land and buildings. The plan commends itself to large cities where the park department is likely to be engrossed in regional park problems. Smaller cities, however, may not be able to afford the degree of differentiation between school, park, and recreational services on which the plan is predicated.

The principal disadvantage is that coordination of related recreational services is difficult to effect between schools, parks, and public recreational service departments. Frequently the three departments misunderstand each other and fail to cooperate, so that lack of coordination, duplication of functions, less than full use of available physical facilities, and general ineffectiveness of service result.

Another disadvantage arises from the public's confusion as to which agency is responsible for any of the several parts of the total service, especially when both school system and recreational service department conduct playgrounds and when the park department operates picnic grounds, golf courses, swimming facilities, and other special recreational places. Similar services rendered by the three agencies impede comprehensive planning of recreational service for the entire city.

Possible overlap of the school system and the recreational service department increases under this plan when the board of education undertakes to operate schools as recreational centers. Under such plans, in all except the largest cities, the schools do but little work insofar as the recreational function is concerned, being content to leave this function to the municipal department. But the possession of facilities that might be put to good use for public recreational activities tends to force the schools to permit their use for community recreational purposes. The question of whether such services should be delegated to the public department through contractual or policy agreement or should be rendered directly by the schools arises. In the former case, coordination of the recreational function with the curricular and extracurricular school activities is difficult but not insurmountable. In the latter instance, coordination of the school recreational program with the municipal program requires adjustments in administration, personalities, and policy.

The Subordinate Recreational Service Division

The plan illustrated in Figure 11-2 shows recreational service as the responsibility of a municipal park department. The plan facilitates the

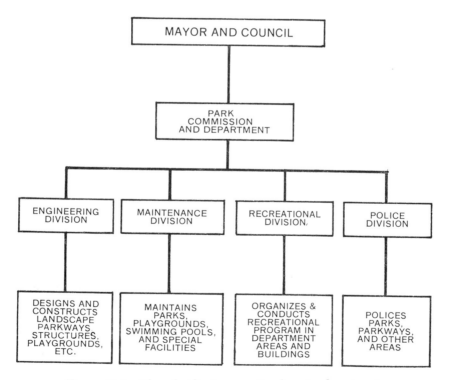

Figure 11-2.   The subordinate recreational service department.

use of all park areas and buildings for recreational purposes. It is an economical and sometimes a highly effective form of organization which is in effect in many large and small cities.

The park commission might have authority ranging from advisory power only to full administrative power, depending on the form of organization generally found within the city.

When recreational services are placed as mere appendages to the primary functions of the park department, the plan falls short of meeting the need. Usually such a condition occurs when the park department annexes or absorbs an existing recreational service department or when a long-established park department simply adopts recreational programming as a new function and becomes the administrative housing for recreational services.

This plan recognizes no official responsibility for recreational service on the part of the school system. Where this plan is in effect, school-directed recreational service develops independently of municipal services. Close integration with the school program remains a problem not inherently solved by this form of organization.

Although traditional park departments fulfill some recreational needs—provide spaces and attractive settings—they are primarily absorbed in problems of maintenance, city beautification, and landscape arrangement rather than with recreational services. Assumption of the recreational service function by departments of welfare, public works, or housing is likely to be even more ineffective. Recreational service bears little relation to the relief of unemployed persons; to the construction and maintenance of sewers, streets, or water supply; or to the construction and management of housing developments and the adjustment of tenant problems. Under such conditions, recreational operations are curtailed and the community denies itself an adequate agency's specialized service.

Perhaps the greatest disadvantage that accrues to the subordinated recreational service function is that it always loses out to the primary interest of the overhead department. This means less financial support for programming, specialized personnel, and all necessary material, supplies, and equipment required to provide comprehensive recreational service to the citizens of the community. In short, no agency with its main interests centered on another function will provide the wherewithal so that recreational services may be performed effectively throughout the community. In addition, in times of retrenchment, the newly acquired function or secondary functions are typically the first to be discontinued.

The Coordinated Recreational Service Agency

Without Control of Properties. A public recreational service department that is solely concerned with the development and administration of recreational activities without the responsibility for acquiring, improving, and

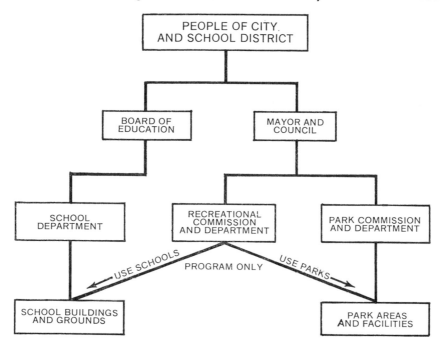

Figure 11-3.   The coordinated recreational service agency.

maintaining land and structures is shown in Figure 11-3. It uses the facilities of the city that are under the direct control of the park department and the facilities of the public schools.

The plan suggests that recreational service is a function distinct from education and park operation, yet it requires the use of existing facilities of schools and parks. The plan is obviously adopted as an expediency when neither the school system nor the park department is willing or able to encompass recreational service in their plans and operations.

This plan divorces the process of education from that of recreational service, whereas education should include preparation for leisure through recreational and other learning experiences. Such a plan disassociates the parks from the recreational service and encourages park authorities to hold a restrictive view of the function of parks. What appears to be an elevation of the status of a recreational service department is, in reality, a degradation, because it denies to the department the control of the facilities it must use. Such a plan might enable the department to secure larger appropriations more readily than if recreational services were assigned as ancillary functions in park, school, or other municipal departments. But since the department is not charged with the cost of acquiring, improving, and maintaining the facilities it uses, its funds may appear to purchase more recreational opportunities than they actually do, particularly when a portion of the recreational budget must be allocated to paying fees for using school, park, or other public agency facilities. The appearance of financial support, in such cases, is extremely deceptive. After negotiating with a school board for the right to utilize school buildings and grounds, the charges may be such that almost one third of the recreational budget is taken by such items as payment to custodians or other school personnel, pro rata charges for heat, light, and power in buildings, and breakage, damage, or replacement fees.

From the operating standpoint, this plan has the serious defect of making the recreational service department wholly dependent on the goodwill of two other agencies for the use of urgently required facilities. Either of these agencies, by withholding cooperation, can strangle the recreational service department or render its work ineffective. Facilities for recreational service provided by one department for activities under control of another are almost uniformly inferior to similar facilities under the direct jurisdiction of the operational agency. In some instances, the recreational service department is permitted only to utilize facilities on sufferance because it does not have to pay anything for the facilities it uses.

Even if a wholehearted desire to cooperate exists on the part of the policy-making boards and the chief executives of the school system and the park department, it is too much to expect that the first-line employees who maintain the separate facilities will serve with equal zeal the agency that uses the facilities they maintain. Employees first serve the agency employing them, and this is as it should be, but the genuine desire to cooperate should extend downward throughout the entire school system or park department. There have been many occasions when the recreational activities operated in a school building either failed or could not get started, as a direct result of a school custodian's disinclination to cooperate.

Under this plan, park departments often retain, under their own jurisdiction, certain of the larger recreational facilities and services, such as golf courses, swimming pools, beaches, picnic grounds, and stadiums, which leads to even greater confusion.

The Shared Executive Plan

The plan shown in Figure 11-4 recognizes that the problem of public recreational service concerns both the educational system and the general city government; that each may be expected to contribute to public recreational services, but that close coordination of effort is vital. This coordination is brought about by an agreement between the school board and the recreational service commission (or local governmental authority) to employ the same executive to supervise school recreational activity and physical education and to act as chief executive of a combined park and recreational service department. Theoretically, he devotes half his time to each task; half of his salary is paid by the school system and half by the city government. In his school capacity he reports through the superintendent of schools to the board of education, and in his municipal capacity he reports to the city managing authority, i.e., the council, mayor, manager, or other designated executive.

Under this plan the schools do not delegate any responsibility for the recreational services provided on school premises. Their recreational program is developed as an integral part of the educational program and is often closely integrated with physical education. The staff re-

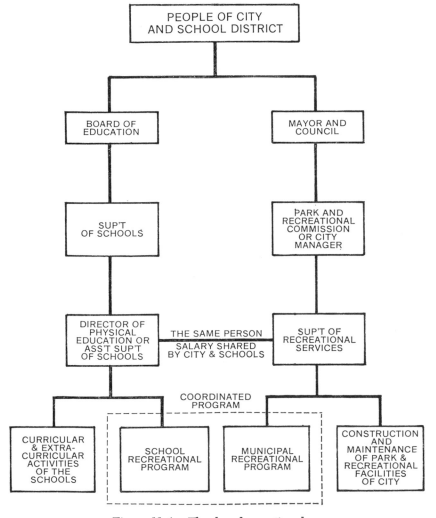

Figure 11-4.   The shared executive plan.

quired to supervise the school facilities and program is employed by the school system, thereby constituting one of the strongest elements in the plan, for it cultivates an increasing sense of responsibility for recreational services by the whole school system. Other plans, under which the schools lend their facilities to another agency, lack this important feature. No city can hope to have a comprehensive system of public recreational service unless it can fully utilize all physical plants and equipment and unless the program is closely integrated with the teaching program. This does not mean that the schools should occupy the field to the exclusion of the municipal agencies, but rather that both systems should share the task under a coordinated plan.

Complete coordination of school and municipal recreational service is brought about under this plan since one executive directs both programs. Another advantage is that the plan enables the smaller community to secure the services of a competent recreationist as executive. The combined executive position requires a high degree of skill and varied experience; but since the executive's compensation is paid from two separate funds, one for each of two full-time positions, in neither organization does the salary seem out of proportion with other salaries.

The plan is not without drawbacks and difficulties. There are few executives whose experience and preparation are so varied and responsible as to enable them to understand and provide leadership in all phases of the several responsibilities—school-centered recreational activity, municipal recreational service, and park administration (unless the latter is a separate department). Few administrators can work happily and successfully in the municipal administrative organization and, at the same time, in the school system. The administrative connections this executive must maintain—legal, policy-making, budgetary, personnel, public relations, professional relations—are extremely diversified. It is therefore difficult to secure someone competent to fill the position.

Another objection is that the plan has no legal security. It is created by informal agreement between two agencies and can be dissolved as readily. A further difficulty is that, since the executive employed in this capacity is usually highly specialized in education, park, or recreational service administration, programs unrelated to his speciality may suffer because of his lack of preparation. In communities that employ a coordinating executive, complete development of recreational services may be impeded because school officials and/or municipal officials (to whom the coordinator is subordinate) do not have an adequate conception of community recreational service and do not permit full utilization of school or municipal property for recreational purposes. In such instances, the use of schools tends to conform to the school week, i.e., the schools are shut on weekends and holidays and during the evening hours when they should be operating for the full benefit of the public who are at leisure during such times. The grounds and indoor facilities therefore are rarely brought into the city-wide recreational program to their greatest capacity.

This plan subordinates the park and recreational function to the school function and relegates it to an inferior position in the municipal structure. It divides authority and vitiates agency responsibility. It complicates and doubles the executive's burden. Although it commends itself to small towns, it does not offer an acceptable solution to the problem of recreational organization in medium-size or large cities.

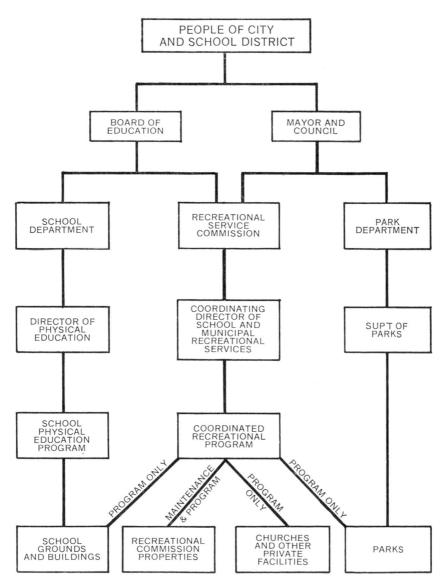

Figure 11-5.   The representative commission or board.

The Representative Commission or Board

Figure 11-5 shows a plan with special commission or board composed of representatives of the city and school governments and the citizens at large. Both schools and city, in effect, delegate full jurisdiction over public recreational services to the body, regardless of where the services are conducted. The program is jointly financed, sometimes in part by a special tax allocation. Only a small amount of its revenue is expended on maintenance, construction, and land acquisition, because the commission uses school and park facilities. Coordination between school and municipal recreational services is implemented by the creation of the position of coordinator and director of school and municipal recreational services.

One advantage of this plan over that illustrated in Figure 11-7 (p. 242) is that the recreational service commission occupies a more independent and important position as the central overhead policy-making and planning body for the utilization of all public resources for community recreational service.

A disadvantage of this plan is that the school system largely is relieved of responsibility for direct recreational services. The schools and park department lend their facilities, but their assistance may be less energetic than if the function were their own.

This plan includes practically all of the disadvantages already enumerated for the shared executive plan shown in Figure 11-4 (p. 233). Also, it assigns responsibility without commensurate authority. Cooperation with the separate school system and park department must be voluntary. The effectiveness of recreational service offerings is crippled if either schools or park department withholds full collaboration or fails to commit all of its facilities and areas to recreational service. This plan does not suit the needs of cities with over 100,000 population.

The Consolidated Recreational Service and Park Department

The plan shown in Figure 11-6 is similar to the one illustrated in Figure 11-2 (p. 229), except that the entire department is oriented to a single, but comprehensive, purpose—rendering recreational services. Parks are not separated from other recreational facilities. All facilities under the control of the department are interrelated to implement recreational services. This implies a modern, broadened concept of parks by viewing parks as areas for both active and passive participation and enjoyment without denying the importance of aesthetic landscaping.

This plan is actually a refinement of the Independent or Autonomous Recreational Service Department and has long been in practice in cities in which recreational services were initially assumed by established park departments or commissions. When recreational services originated as an appendage to park functions, the two merged. Park services came to

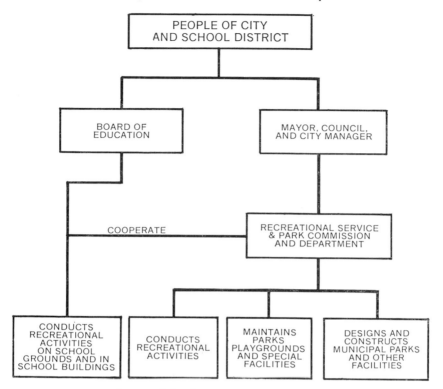

Figure 11-6.　The consolidated recreational service and park department.

include recreational services. The use of the two terms is, in fact, an incongruity and in time may give way to the use of the functional term *recreational services* as inclusive of both, particularly since parks are places where recreational experience, in the broad and narrow sense, is achieved.

The major advantage of this plan is that it consolidates all municipal recreational service under one department and avoids the controversy that may arise between separate authorities responsible for parks and recreational services. Thus it offers an opportunity for developing a more comprehensive and diversified program. It encourages and adds aesthetic quality to activity programs in landscaped and buffered areas that otherwise would serve only limited purposes. It encourages economical administration and improves the quality of recreational opportunities available to the citizenry.

The plan illustrated in Figure 11-2 (p. 229) raised the question of whether recreational service might not be seriously subordinated to park functions. So it may be asked whether this plan might not similarly subordinate park development to the functions of recreational service. The likelihood here is less probable, however, because the park function is more deeply rooted in municipal tradition than is recreational service. Then, too, the enlarged, enlightened concept of recreational service would normally encompass parks as essential for recreational programming.

The consolidated plan, because of its advantages, is commended to large or small communities. It is feasible even in the largest urban centers, where extensive systems of parkways and reservations, beaches, and other regional developments require extensive organization of material and personnel. Although these areas have little in common with the conduct of conventional recreational activities, they may serve as effective sites to produce major special events, which are an intrinsic part of the comprehensive recreational program.

In the largest urban centers, separate agencies may handle the development and construction of beaches, parkways, and reservations, but they should consult park and recreational planners. Some large park systems have their own police force, however, this is not a function of recreational service. Regardless of the size of the park system, the municipal, county, or state police force should be the agency of law enforcement. When uniformed personnel are necessary, they should be employed as attendants, custodians, or grounds keepers, not as police.

This plan offers no organic connection with the school system. The municipality may conduct activities on school grounds and in school buildings on a contractual or other agreed-upon basis. Questions of jurisdictional control of school facilities may arise if some written agreement is not made providing for use of school facilities by the public department. Without contractual obligation the schools are free to develop their own programs and facilities with or without the assistance of the public recreational service department, which can lead to duplication of service and competition for the same clientele. However, if close coordination and cooperation are maintained between the two systems, a more comprehensive service may be performed for the community at large. In some cities the school system either does not open its facilities at all for recreational activity or operates them wholly under school control. The importance of the schools to the provision of community-wide recreational services has already been examined in greater detail in Chapter 5, pages 92–98 and 107–110.

There are numerous other plans in use in small cities and rural communities and in cities just beginning to organize themselves for recreational service. In most of these communities recreational service is a municipal concern only during the summer months; during the rest of the year there is little community recreational service except that provided by the schools through their adult education and/or extracurricular activities. Such cities usually employ some personnel to direct the summer school playground and adult activities program each year. Often the appointee is an elementary school teacher, a physical education teacher, or a school athletic team coach. Typically, such programs center around sports and games and little else. These programs frequently serve as experiments; when successful, they grow into more permanent organization and, with the passage of time, they become institutionalized as one of the organizational forms previously discussed for year-round community recreational service.

INTERNAL STRUCTURE OF A PUBLIC RECREATIONAL SERVICE DEPARTMENT

The relation of recreational service departments to other functions of government and to the whole structure of governmental organization has been discussed. We are concerned now with the internal organization of a public recreational service department. Such a department should be large and should comprehend all community recreational services rendered by it. Thus all relationships will be well illustrated in terms of areas, facilities, finances, and personnel.

Principles of Internal Organization

Although it is valid to say that organizational principles may be applied to any structural situation, some principles of administrative organization more specifically are directed toward the public recreational service department by virtue of the content and terminology under consideration.

Delegation of Responsibility and Authority. The organization of a department should be such that all employees have a clear understanding of their duties and to whom they are responsible or accountable. Written instructions and charts indicating lines of responsibility are useful for this purpose. Employees should know how their work is related to the accomplishment of the objectives of the department. Delegation of responsibility should be plain and as challenging to the employee as possible. With the assignment of responsibility should go the authority to carry it out.

Chain of Command. Lines of administrative responsibility should be direct. Supervisory responsibility descends from the top of the organization "through channels" to the employees who perform the unit of work for which the department is organized. The employee who performs any unit of work reports to and is responsible to his immediate superior. No employee should be accountable to or direct the work of another employee of equal rank.

Delegation of Executive Control. In all organizations, executive functions tend to be overcentralized, possibly owing to the human frailty of enjoying the exercise of control. Executives should delegate control and pass the responsibility for making decisions as far down the line of organization as may be consistent with getting the work done, because it reduces executive overhead, encourages growth and the sense of responsibility, is conducive to wider experimentation, allows adaption to local conditions, and saves time. The tendency to overcentralize executive functions inclines to establishment of an unnecessarily large central executive staff. The effort of the executive staff should be to get as many of the employees on the program level as possible consistent with the efficient executive control of the work. The relation between the number of executive and office employees and the employees at the places where the basic work is done should be reexamined from time to time. Often employees are brought to the central office for special work and their re-assignment to the field is unduly delayed. A reappraisal of the work performed in the central office often reveals that some of it is no longer necessary and can well be dispensed with.

Balance in the Executive Staff. In filling executive positions, care should be taken that the members complement each other in the qualities and abilities they bring to the organization. All executives should not be of the same temperament. There is the need for the promoter with his imagination and enthusiasm, for the person with broad social sympathy and zeal for the improvement of social conditions, for the conservative business-minded executive with a good sense of economic values, for the patient, painstaking, approachable, and empathetic executive who can counsel employees well. No executive can be all of these things and yet all executives together may constitute a balanced staff. In selecting the staff, consideration should be given to the contacts to be made with different elements of the population—religious, ethnic, and cultural groups, and various civic, service, social, and governmental agencies. The department is fortunate if it has persons fitted for cultivating all of these contacts and relationships on its executive staff. Executive positions in recreational service should be open to both sexes.

Designation of Duties. Division of functions and duties within a department should be based on a clear-cut differentiation of the activities to be performed by the employees involved. Duties that are similar in respect to the skills and education required in their performance should be grouped together. Duties that are dissimilar in respect to the skills and preparation required ordinarily should not be assigned to the same person. Unfortunately, many recreational centers have only a small staff and this principle is often necessarily violated.

Coordination of Production. Administrative responsibility at any recreational facility with more than one employee should be delegated to a single employee. Because numerous activities that require coordination in accord with departmental policy are performed, such coordination must be effected at the place where the duties are performed. Someone at the place of work must have the authority to make decisions. Assigning administrative responsibility to one person facilitates various transactions between the central headquarters of the department and the staff of the facility and tends to minimize conflict between employees at a given place. This practice is, in fact, a partial decentralization of the executive function, which is advisable in a system whose work is carried on at many diverse places.

Division of Responsibility. When an employee is responsible for performing two or more distinguishable duties, he properly may be required to report to two or more superiors. For example, the director in charge of a recreational facility has, under his supervision, employees who perform instructional and directorial duties and other employees who perform maintenance functions. With respect to the former, he may report to the executive in charge of recreational activities, and, with respect to the latter, to the executive in charge of plant maintenance.

Definition of Line Positions. Any employee directly responsible for the execution of program functions, i.e., who is involved in direct lines of responsibility for the provision of specific activities of a recreational nature in which the public participates, is a *line employee.*

Definition of Staff Positions. Any employee not directly responsible for program functions of a recreational nature but who, by his specialized knowledge, provides technical advice and guidance to line personnel so they will be more productive, efficient, and increasingly competent in accomplishing the agency's objectives, is a *staff employee.*

Ancillary Staff Positions. All employees not involved in line or staff capacities but who are utilized in non-technical positions necessary for the continued operation of the department, are *auxiliary* or *ancillary staff employees.* Such personnel typically are: stenographers, clerks, telephone operators, receptionists, custodians, and the like.

Organizational Flexibility. The organization of a department must be sufficiently flexible to enable the system to make the fullest possible use of personnel. Fundamentally, the functions a department must perform determine its structure. Employees who can competently perform the required duties should be hired. In practice, the organizational form, more in the lower echelons than in the higher, should be capable of adapting to the peculiar skills and abilities of available personnel. When changes in personnel occur, redistribution of duties often is necessary. Sometimes an employee is outstanding in certain activities and deficient in others, which occasionally calls for a change in organization.

Table of Organization

Organization of a hypothetical recreational service department, including both park and recreational programming functions, is illustrated in Figure 11-7. This chart exemplifies the general principles of depart-

9

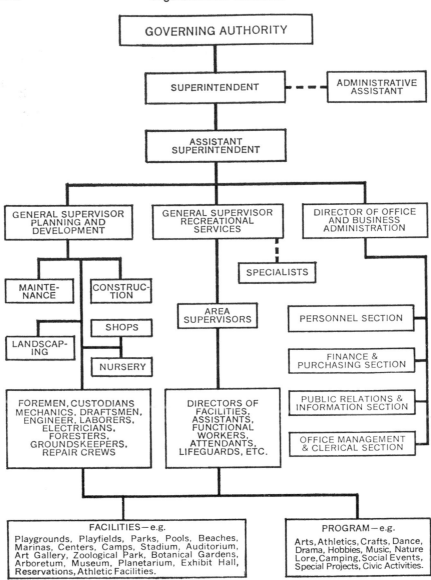

Figure 11-7. Organizational chart for a hypothetical recreational service department.

mental organization but should not be regarded as an ideal plan. The organization must be adapted to the general organization of the municipal government which is usually dictated by local traditions, procedures, and expediency.

The same principles of organization apply to smaller departments, but, in many cases, duties and responsibilities are consolidated and assigned to fewer persons than in the large department. Recording and filing may be combined with accounting and auditing; supervision of several generic recreational activities may be consolidated; direction and management of beaches and swimming pools or other aquatic facilities may be combined.

Line responsibilities and relationships are indicated by ascending and descending lines, and staff responsibilities are indicated by horizontal lines. Several departments in the country are large enough to require the subdivisions of organization shown here. The degree of ramification in organization and specialization in particular administrative and executive duties increases with the size of the department.

If a department does its own construction work, elaboration of this function will be necessary. Sometimes construction is consolidated with maintenance and planning. Special establishments (museums, art galleries, zoological parks, and botanical gardens) are shown for the sake of completeness. In special instances, highly specialized facilities may have their own governing bodies and be completely separated from the recreational service department. Under each group of areas or facilities there may be a number of unit facilities and each of these will be under the supervision of a director. Some of the unit facilities require two services—maintenance and operation of the program. These functions are coordinated by the director.

Policy-making Functions

The chart shows a governing body as a policy-making (legislative) and administrative authority. This group formulates policy; i.e., it states positions or rules governing departmental decisions. Policies are determined by previous experience, the purpose for which the department was established, and the legalities involved. Legality, in this instance, may be either an explicitly stated law or the political climate and influence of the community. Policies may be either stated or implied in custom. They are not immutable and do not have the force of law unless they are incorporated in municipal ordinances. If a city dispenses with a board or commission, then the city council or other managing authority will have to perform the functions ordinarily undertaken by the commission.

Line Functions and Organization

The superintendent is responsible for the general management of the department and for the efficient maintenance and operation of all facilities and programs. If there are enough units, intermediary executives who will be accountable for the performance of employees assigned to the facilities and programs in their charge may be employed. For example, there may be sufficient playgrounds to call for a supervisor of playgrounds who will be in general charge of the personnel employed at all playgrounds. He may be provided with the assistance of certain workers assigned to no particular area or facility but related to the promotion and conduct of programs at all centers.

Supervisors of all distinguishable facilities, such as playgrounds, beaches, camps, and parks, may report directly to the superintendent, but if the department is large enough there may be two intermediate executives—one in general charge of all plant maintenance and the other in charge of all activities. In some large departments the former is called director or supervisor of maintenance and the latter director or supervisor of recreational activities. If the title *superintendent* is given to them, then the department head is called general superintendent, commissioner, or general manager.

The following line functions are typically found in large recreational service departments:

1. Supervision of the public in the use of areas and facilities;
2. Instruction of individuals and groups in certain recreational activities;
3. Organization and promotion of activities adapted to available facilities;
4. Organization, promotion, and management of special programs;
5. Safeguarding the lives of the public in the use of aquatic facilities;
6. Safeguarding the health, welfare, and morals of the public in the conduct of any recreational activity at any publicly sponsored program.

Staff Functions and Organization

Certain staff duties are related to the entire plan of operation and maintenance. These are illustrated by the functions depicted under the offices of supervisor of planning and development and director of office and business administration respectively. Both positions are directly related to the entire organization and provide technical information, assistance, and other supportive services throughout the system. The services of the technical staff are centralized in the general office where they are accessible to all who need them. The services of the field staff are decentralized for ready availability wherever they are required. The staff functions are:

1. Planning and development of new areas and facilities;
2. Maintenance of all areas and facilities to enhance recreational service and other functions related thereto;
3. Public relations and information;

4. Personnel management;
5. Finance administration;
6. Office management and clerical work.

The planning and development of recreational places and physical facilities are necessary in order that the most adequate materials, design, and construction are utilized in the development of suitable physical properties where recreational opportunities may be enjoyed.

Efficient maintenance of all recreational property is necessary for maximum operation, safe use of facilities and equipment, and enhancement of the attractiveness of all structures and areas. Cleaning services, landscape maintenance, and prompt repairing and other related functions are essential to optimum participation in recreational activities. Convenient and orderly arrangement, attractive setting, and adequate equipment and space are important to the improvement of satisfaction in activities and the enjoyment of participation and observation.

Public relations and public information are concerned with the development of goodwill between the public and the system and with the dissemination of information concerning policies, program, and the function of the department. This is distinctly a staff function and related to all the facilities and services of the system. The person in charge of this responsibility should be close enough to the superintendent to know the regulations and policies of the system and to be aware of any modifications.

Personnel management has far-reaching consequences in the recreational service system. All records and reports of employed personnel must be kept current and available for study for promotion, transfer, or discharge. All aspects of personnel relations have important effects on the system's service capability. Professional salary structure, commendation, supervision, in-service staff development, and professional growth and dedication to the discipline and the system are integral parts of personnel administration.

Financial administration includes custodianship of public funds, control of such funds, and records of purchases, receipts, and other fiscal transactions for the guidance of the executive. Every department has a certain amount of accounting to perform and, in some instances, will audit its accounts to ensure their correctness.

Office management and clerical work refer to recording, filing, clerical, and stenographic work, custodianship of supplies, and the maintenance of inventory. These services are incidental, though necessary, to the efficiency of the system's work. Modern office practice favors consolidation or centralization of these duties as far as is practicable. Maintenance of supply depots or a storehouse and a current inventory of supplies and equipment, indicating quantities and location throughout the system, are essential to the discharge of accounting responsibilities and for buying purposes.

Internal Coordination

In a large organization in which functions are departmentalized, there is always the danger that coordination between divisions may be lacking. The fact that the work of the system is conducted at widely separated facilities contributes to this tendency. Joint projects in which all parts of the department must cooperate, such as city-wide events, intermural competitions, pageants, parades, or special projects requiring cooperative endeavors, assist in correlating the several parts. Divisional and departmental meetings, supervisory conferences, regular bulletins or a departmental newspaper dealing with every aspect of the recreational system and its affairs, sound personnel practices, and social occasions for employees are also useful devices to promote mutual understanding and coordination.

Selected References

Eddy, W. B., and others, Eds.: *Behavioral Science and the Manager's Role* (San Diego, Calif.: University Associates), 1976.

Hersey, P. and K. Blanchard: *Management of Organizational Behavior: Utilizing Human Resources, 3rd ed.* (Englewood Cliffs, N.J.: Prentice-Hall, Inc.), 1977.

Herzberg, F.: *The Managerial Choice: To be Efficient and To Be Human* (Homewood, Ill.: Dow-Jones-Irwin, Inc.), 1976.

Gibson, J. L., and others: *Readings in Organization: Behavior, Structure, Processes, rev. ed.* (Homewood, Ill.: Business Publications), 1976.

Sanford, E. and H. Adelman: *Management Decisions* (Englewood Cliffs, N.J.: Prentice-Hall, Inc.), 1977.

CHAPTER 12

Computer Applications in Public Recreational Service Administration

The computer is gaining importance in the field of recreational service, particularly in the public sector, because it processes information quickly, precisely, and economically. Naturally, this suggests that there is information which needs to be processed. The generation and dissemination of knowledge about things, people, and resources have assumed a proportion and rate that is significant to the well-being of society as a whole, and, by inference, to the public sector of recreational service.

Each passing year records an increasing amount of time, money, and effort in producing, processing, translating, recording, and eventually retrieving information, and concurrently we invest relatively less in dealing with the material products of our technological society. This surely holds true for service based fields of endeavor. Although recreationists have traditionally provided services that required no physical product, other than the supplies necessary for the participant in an activity, the need for informational services from which direct leadership services can be programmed has grown at a faster pace than ever before. Recreationists are now beginning to understand that the way they perform their jobs may hinge less upon their direct expertise in the activities program than upon the way a variety of resources—either physical, personal, environmental, time, or fiscal—can be brought together, transformed, examined, reduced, and translated into the kinds of recreational services necessary for the satisfaction of people's needs.

It has been stated that the most vexing problem confronting society is learning to appreciate and adjust to complexity. In many fields this perception is almost axiomatic. Computers are one means whereby people can rapidly cope with complex and interacting situations such as will increasingly face the field of recreational service in the near future. Under these circumstances, electronic data processing and the machines which perform the computations should become more prominent in assisting the decision makers to do their human jobs more rapidly, accurately, and effectively.

Acquiring and assessing data are basic aspects of the administrative process; in fact, such procurement and appraisal are the objectives toward which the entire process of administration moves. Electronic-digital computers are having such a phenomenal effect on the collection and processing of data that administrators should have some insight into what computers are capable of doing and what is concerned in their utilization.

The rapid growth of computer terminals within the United States has, at last, placed this electronic marvel within the grasp of every public recreational service agency which contemplates rapid data processing. Many public and private organizations have their own computers, although some public agencies have associated themselves with computer systems serving a network of clients. It is almost inconceivable to imagine an urban based recreational service department without computer facilities and just as hard to contemplate an administrative situation in which the department could not profitably benefit from one of the diverse computer applications now in use.

Today, technology concerning data processing is approaching a point where public agencies of government find it economically necessary to introduce it as a tool for the rapid solution of the manifold problems of public administration. Factors which should be considered in determining the potential of electronic data processing machines are the volume of repetitive tasks, present clerical costs, costs of machine installation, and the availability of previously unobtainable management control information. The determination of how computers may be put to best use in the solution of local administrative problems must be analyzed in terms of costs incurred by such operations, as compared to operations currently carried on without machines.

Successful electronic data processing (EDP) application has been found advantageous in each of the various fields of government. Used in many ways for record keeping, the planning of material requirements in a system, the controlling of materials or inventories on hand, land use planning, storage and retrieval of information, or programmed to handle detailed bits of data from which city planning studies may be made and conclusions drawn about public needs can really be performed only by computers.

THE ELECTRONIC DATA PROCESSING CHALLENGE

The extent to which automation and electronic application has spread among public agencies throughout the country indicates a growing recognition on the part of governmental functionaries of the requirement for fast, accurate, and reliable information on which substantive decisions may be made. Wherever there is voluminous clerical work to be performed, and surely large metropolitan recreational service systems employ many clerks, it may be safely assumed that there is a need for some kind of machine adaptation by punched card or computer means. The potentialities of electronic data processing make possible, through their application to vital functions, a greater public service at less cost and with minimum error than any other currently available work force. By using EDP in planning, research and decision-making, governmental jurisdictions, particularly those systems which are concerned with the general welfare, education, or health of people, can alleviate many of the difficult choices which are open to policy makers or executives. Computers must be used to delineate purposes, make acute value judgments, refine plans, make more appropriate allocations of economic, material, and natural resources, clarify the proper roles of the public, quasi-public, and private sectors of society, and perform those functions which can revitalize local government and public administration.

The impact of computers on public recreational service administration is almost revolutionary. There are specific universal questions which must be solved stemming directly from the paramount issues of our day, the present state of technology, and the character of cybernetics. These factors work on all administrators. Mastery of the techniques dealing with advanced data processing methods can result is a highly efficient operation at lower costs and the sharpening of the decision making process whereby the science of management can be improved.

Continued production of knowledge can no longer be handled by the archaic methods of the past. New concepts, the future development of materials, and systems for the control of products will continue only through the application of technological innovation. The rapid obsolescence of information makes impractical any public planning without the use of EDP and other scientific devices. There are now so many alternatives from which to choose that it is beyond the powers of administrators to cope with the volume of information and the complexities which modern life produces. The fundamental assignment of all administrators is to select the best possible alternative from a complex mass, make such a decision swiftly and accurately, and be correct. Such a task appears to require powers far above those of human ability. There is a need, therefore, for the production of planning, organizing, and decision making systems that can tackle the complexities of contemporary affairs with optimum effectiveness. Public administration in alliance with knowledge gained from the behavioral sciences and cybernetics offers the technical assistance necessary.

Cybernetics and Systems Theory

Fragmentation of knowledge through specialization has provoked a reaction against compartmentalization in recognition of the fact that esoteric knowledge is merely a component of general knowledge. This has been made more apparent through systems analysis, wherein various units and subunits are interdependent, correlated, and, indeed, where an understanding of the whole is absolutely dependent upon information, theory, and abilities culled from other segments. This understanding has unquestionably been refined by the developing comprehension that knowledge is so involved that a method must be devised to determine any meaning that may prevail.

At least two prevalent conditions have necessitated the current appreciation of the interdependency of all knowledge, despite specialization, and have been characteristic of the speculations embodied by the scientific movement: the first has been a growing public recognition, through vastly publicized means, of the deteriorating environment and cybernetics. The first concept, that of ecology, while well known to biologists and other natural scientists for many years, has only during the past decade received widespread mass media attention and is even yet little understood by the public. Ecology, or the study of life forms in relation to their environment, is a biological science manifested by absolute interdependency. There is a complete chain of phenomena for existence of all living things and any imbalance within the links, for whatever reasons, is subsequently felt by all life forms. Such reactions to modifications within the environment may take relatively short or long periods of time, but the ultimate effect directly influences the state of being of living things. Ecology has also been adopted by the social sciences as human ecology with reference to the relationship between the distribution of people in connection with material resources and the consequent social and cultural patterns. In this context, various social forces and systems are interrelated and reciprocally dependent.

In cybernetics, the model for which was obtained from the physiologic process known as homeostasis, there is a basic premise that self-regulation for the production of certain outputs may be built into machines so that one part regulates the operation of the other. The fundamental assumption is that the energy source is detached from the instructional source.[1] The chief characteristic of a self-regulating system is the existence of a control loop which activates or modifies the behavior of the

[1] G. T. Guilbaud, *What is Cybernetics* (New York: Grove Press, 1960), p. 11.

system. Information, constituting system regulators, is fed into the machine (or man) dealing with performance and the comparison of present performance standards. Information received thereby controls the output of the system. A closed loop control may be understood in terms of the thermostat for household heat. In this example, controls built into the machine regulate temperature changes. When a certain temperature is reached, the thermostat shuts off the furnace. If the temperature falls below specified level, the furnace is activated. In open loop feedback, outside forces influence the system. Information from an infinite variety of environmental sources, i.e., political, economic, demographic, social, etc., which are outside of the system boundary, flows into the system and influences or modifies system outputs. This is more nearly analogous to the public recreational service system whose activities are directed in terms of the needs of people. In the latter instance, information (or feedback) is transmitted to the department by various means. The data received are compared to the goals, purposes, and philosophy as criteria under which the system operates. The executive or decision maker, after comparison has been made, determines any changes that are required to meet demands and requests or orders personnel within the department to carry out changes that are necessary.

Control for the self-regulating system involves communication or feedback which is basically concerned with data that are transmitted to the seat of decision making, influences the attitudes, actions, or behavior of the recipient, and an alteration of effort or enterprise if the information warrants such a conclusion. As Pfiffner and Presthus explain:

> Organization theory has always embraced the concept of feedback but under such designations as "control" or "management by exception." The difference today is that electronic data processing has made it possible to collect and store a much wider spectrum and volume of information, which can be tapped readily and provide messages about events almost as they occur.[2]

In its refined use, communications and control theory has become a chief component in contemporary technology and is fundamental to the concept of the new revolution known as cybernetics. Cybernetics should completely change the life style of people in advanced technological countries. With automation, process and production are controlled by machines. Human operators simply monitor. Eventually, machines will program, monitor, and maintain themselves in an heuristic system.

Although the term cybernetics is no longer an acceptable term used by technologists working in the area of self-regulating systems, there are

---

[2]John M. Pfiffner and Robert Presthus, *Public Administration,* 5th ed. (New York: The Ronald Press Company, 1967), p. 242.

those who consider cybernetics in its broadest possible context. Thus, cybernetics is viewed less as limited to bionics, engineering, and control system engineering, and given a meaning that considers it as the science of control over complex systems, information, and communications. It is entirely appropriate, therefore, that this discussion should continue the utilization of cybernetics insofar as the term can be understood for its social implications. The term "cybernetics" used here connotes a broader meaning. It is valued that this should be so because of the general political and social implication of the term governance, but also because of the role undertaken by the social and behavioral sciences in the extension and development of social and decision-making models.

The Computer

The computer of the day is a machine designed to use information. By information is meant any symbol, whether it is numerical, alphabetical, or punctuation. In this way a computer can use any data that translate into written language. Using, in this connotation, means the collection, storage, manipulation, and production of information. Of course, computers can also process many types of information that is not technically language. Symbols, for example, are encoded and reproduced as pictures in both two dimensional and three dimensional format.

The material parts of the computer are typically thought of as hardware. It is the hardware that receives, stores, manipulates, and produces information. The receiving unit or input device feeds information into the computer. These devices may be punched cards, the keyboard terminal, optical scanner, optical-reader, or card reader.

The storage capacity of the computer consists of miniaturized magnetic cores, each of which is magnetized in two directions. It is typical to think of the binary digits 0 and 1 with the two directions in which a core can be magnetized. Usually, computers employ a code of six or more binary digits (bits) in length for the storage of a character of information. Thus, if a computer employed a six bit code for its internal storage of characters, the word "recreational" would employ 72 bits of storage. The size of a computer's storage capacity or memory is an indication of the size of the computer. Small computers may have storage capacities of approximately 15,000 characters of information whereas large computers may be able to store several million characters.

Because the cost of primary computer memory is high and a computer's memory is quite small insofar as the quantity of information that should be stored for processing, it is necessary that auxiliary devices be available. The most common of these secondary devices are magnetic tape and disc pack.

When the information has been received by the computer and processed in whichever way the programmer has previously decided upon, there is the necessity for the results to be transformed so that humans can understand the output. The interpretation of processed information into useful and comprehensible material is the function of a device called the conversion or output unit. Computer output mechanisms differ in terms of speeds and costs. Perhaps the line printer is typical of the output devices where, at extremely high speeds, up to 1,000 lines per minute and line lengths of more than 130 characters, books of 300,000 words could be produced within five minutes. Additional output instruments are the keyboard terminal, which has a dual role in that it is both input and output appliance, and punch card or microfilm devices. The latter is capable of operating at speeds of up to 20 times the rate of a line printer and is, therefore, a more economical means of output.

The essence of the computer is the central processing element. This is an automatic calculator and monitor. The calculator handles characters, e.g., add, subtract, multiply, divide, compare for sameness, sequence, and so forth. The monitor automatically obeys a prepared schedule of commands that have been encoded for that particular computer and retained in its storage units or memory. These step-by-step directions or program permits the computer to manipulate the input and process information that is both useful and comprehensible by human operators.

The Use of Computers

The utility of the computer depends upon its program. Computer programs are distinctly separated into software and applications. Software is defined as those programs specifically intended to enable people to use a computer system. There are devices which can be employed to feed the computer's memory, e.g., a loader. Compilers, on the other hand, are designed to translate programs written in one computer language into that which can be read and digested by the specific machine being used. Thus, learning such computer programming language as Basic, Fortran, or Cobol, relatively simple program languages, will not be wasted because a particular computer is not produced to handle one of these languages. The compiler does the job for each individual machine—insofar as the computer is designed to accept a specific language. Software is a vital feature of a computer system.

Programming languages have become the chief means by which an individual with a problem and the digital computer used to solve it can communicate. Unless there existed programming language it would be unfeasible to solve most problems if the computer had to be programmed in machine language. Because most machines operate in binary, it is clear that humans would find it most difficult to communicate; therefore, the major method for communication between the computer user and the computer is the programming language. There have been many programming languages developed since 1956, but many of them are either no longer used, are obsolete, or so specialized that they do not have wide application. It is not the intention of this section to describe computer operations or language in detail or even to instruct in programming. Rather, the inclusion of this section is to inform the reader of the development of certain programming languages which can be applicable for the resolution of problems arising in the field of recreational service. To this end, Basic, Fortran, and Cobol are exemplified as programming languages which are relatively easy to learn and which can be used by nonprogrammers, i.e., recreationists, in processing information so that it appears as a useful tool in the administrative function of decision-making.

It might be useful, at this time, to define and discuss some of the programming languages which enable information to be utilized in a computer's memory.

Basic (Beginner's All-Purpose Symbolic Instruction Code)

Basic was developed, as were other higher level programming languages, so that programmers would not have to write their programs directly in machine language. Thus, Basic has a standard set of options for entering data into a computer and obtaining data as well. Moreover, it also contains a set of sub-routines, small specialized programs, which can be reiterated at different points in a large program so that the computation of common mathematical operations and functions can be performed. The Basic language was designed to be conversational, i.e., the user's terminal is placed in a direct interactive mode with the computer. This means that the original program statements can be entered directly in the computer's memory from the user's terminal. With some Basic interpreters, a statement that violates the grammatical rules for applying such language is rejected as the operator attempts to enter it and a diagnostic error is displayed. Further, the language is set in order in such a way that the user's terminal is maintained in a completely interactive mode with the computer, while the user's program is running. Under these circumstances, the programmer can enter various numbers from the keyboard for use within the program while the program is running. In like manner, the programmer can request the computer to print different parts of a solution on the terminal as they are computed, and actually stop the computer from running the program at any point without having to wait for the computer to reach the normal end statement.

The single greatest advantage of Basic is that the programmer can run small pieces of a large program in which print statements can be either injected or deleted to permit monitoring questionable elements of the program. In this way it can be immediately determined whether or not the program is actually calculating the quantities which are desired.

Additionally, the basic instruction set is so similar to high school arithmetic and algebra that it can be learned easily.

Finally, it should be emphasized that Basic is so exactly a subset of Fortran that it enables an experienced programmer to write a Fortran program that will translate a general Basic program into Fortran and compile the result. This makes possible tremendous time reduction in very long programs on mini-computers. By writing and correcting the program in conversational Basic, a routine Fortran program may then be used to compile the result. This saves both time and money.

Fortran (Formula Translation)

Fortran is a generally utilized program language for scientific and numeric computational processing. The language focuses on efficiency of execution and its structure is simple. Fortran can be applied on almost any computer so that execution is efficient. Fortran was the first high-level programming language to be widely accepted and used. The language has developed through several versions of which the most important were Fortran II and Fortran IV.

A Fortran program is comprised of a main program and a set of subprograms, each of which is collected independently of the others, with the interpreted programs linked during loading. Each subprogram is compiled into an exactly stationary allotted area including the compiled ready-to-be-effected machine code and programmer- and system-defined data areas. Common data areas may also be determined. Subprograms communicate by coming into contact with shared data areas, passing parameters, and passing control through *nonrecursive* subprogram calls. A subunit is recursive if it can be employed or referenced from itself. *Recursive* is a term applied only to those subunits for which there are parameters involved.

Originally the Fortran language was intended to be capable of delivering any problems containing large sets of formulas and variables with the variables having up to three independent subscripts. Fortran is procedure oriented, problem oriented and problem solving. It was developed to assist the nonprogrammer to program his or her own problems without the intermediary of a professional programmer. More importantly, as the Fortran language has developed more things are capable of being stated in the language and there is greater flexibility as well.

Cobol (Common Business Oriented Language)

Cobol is a language which has had wide acceptance for use in business applications. However, Cobol is not a concise language. Its objective was to make use of the regular business data-processing vocabulary to the maximum extent possible. Its logic is similar to that used in non-computer data-processing situations. Cobol was designed with the purpose of creating a language as close to the *English* currently used in business practice as was possible. Thus, programming was made comprehensible to individuals familiar with business conditions much more rapidly than if machine language programming was required.

The users of Cobol are typically inexperienced programmers for whom the English-like qualities of the language would be advantageous and any other person who had not written the program initially. The readability of the Cobol programs would provide documentation to any who might want to examine the program.

Cobol's advantages are its convertibility from one machine to another and its facilitation of communication and documentation. There are a number of steps which must be taken when a Cobol program is compiled and executed. It is understood that the computer has a card reader and that program and data are fed in through this device.

Initially, a program must be developed. This necessitates a careful analysis of the situation to be programmed and its contraction to solution by use of Cobol logic. This means that the logic of solution is rigidly restricted to that of the language. Once the proper logic for resolving the situation is performed, it is encoded in Cobol. The outcome of such coding is the source program which will instruct the computer in terms of the actions it is to perform.

After the Cobol program is written, it is translated into a form readable by the machine. This is the interface between man-comprehensible language and machine-sensible commands and is termed the object program. During the translation cycle the computer monitors the source program for errors. If there are any errors, the machine lists them and displays them for the user. Translation may then continue, depending upon the magnitude of the discovered errors. There is no way that the computer can determine the accuracy of the programmer's logic because it has no way of knowing the programmer's intentions. Although the computer can detect errors of a clerical nature, it cannot ascertain errors in logic or strategy. Once the source program is translated into machine language, it may be executed directly or written out for later use.

When the translation phase is completed, the computer is ready for any assignment. If the object program is to be executed immediately, it is read back into the computer's memory. Once the process of reading in the object program is complete, computer control is given over to this program and the execution begins. The object program may also be stored for later use if desired without having to retranslate it.

The computer uses both information and characterization of processes which reflect the sequences of 0's and 1's. The arithmetic unit and index registers have particular arithmetic qualities, but basically the machine only uses 0's and 1's links. More to the point the machine only performs absolute binary instructions. With programming language machines can be made to use a language for which the hardware of the machine was not originally designed to receive. If the computer has the appropriate software, it can understand and use a variety of programming languages.

The second division of computer programs deals with applications. Applications may be written specifically for a unique set of data with highly limited or one-time-only usage or it may be generalized and applied repeatedly to frequently used operations on disparate kinds of data. Generalized programs are packaged and are employed to execute most of the standard statistical processes in data analysis. In order to use such a program there is only the requirement that the recreationist learn relatively easy rules about the manner in which the data should be arrayed for input. Fortunately, every major computer center has a bank of applications programs that have been devised and tested and are therefore available to solve the standard types of problems that occur most often.

The confrontation of society with computer technology is important for recreationists everywhere. Surely western culture is entering an era in which absolute automation and cybernation will finally free all men from work. Of course, a radical change in economy, education, and social organization is to be expected, but the result may well prove beneficial beyond the wildest dreams of those who look to the future. Most laymen look upon the computer as a common tool to assist in processing the simple routine jobs of payroll checks, inventory control, personnel records, and the like. Certainly the computer can do these functions, but they are wasted if this is the only task to which they will be put. There is a better understanding of the use of computers for a wide variety of functions. Computers are being introduced into operations and the shaping of human decisions which was once thought to be the sole province of technician and executive.

A computer is a device which is able to ingest and retain information of whatever kind is supplied, perform whatever is required in terms of comparing, offering alternatives, selecting best choices, etc., on the information which is necessary in problem solving, and produces solutions. Information for the machine is simply encoded as symbols, a series of digits arranged on a magnetic spool which when activated becomes meaningful to the human user. The machine does not understand, that is, has no knowledge of what any symbol means. There is only the logic of mathematical consistency of the data inputs with which the machine works. Humans program or organize the machines to accept and store certain marked materials so that at some later time they may be utilized in terms of instructions which the machine is programmed to receive and act upon.

As to performing specific manipulations or operating upon the information, these are both mathematical and logical efforts. Mathematical manipulations comprise all those functions which deal with addition, subtraction, algebra, or any other mathematical operation or expression similar to numbers. Logical manipulation, on the other hand, is performed in terms of comparisons, selections, dispersing, matching, combining, or merging, and so forth. These are outputs which may be effected either on numbers, symbols, expressions, or letters. By artfully combining these operations in several ways, intricate outputs may be derived. A significant logical operation which the computer performs, for example, is to determine which of a variety of instructions it receives is to be performed in sequence. The computer decides because it has been programmed to apply a previously encoded rule to a predetermined result which is available in storage only when that time in the sequence of operations arrives.

The computer is not concerned with the meaning of the information with which it begins operations, nor is it concerned with the truth of the initiating information. However, the computer can determine the consequences which the starting data contain. Thus, the computer saves a great deal of time in calculating by not having to be concerned with objective meanings or truth. To this extent, then, the computer can only provide results consistent with the quality of which it is supplied. Gibberish supplied to the computer will beget gibberish.

Computers are, of course, of basic significance to cybernetics, primarily because they compose so much communications and guidance technique, and also because they require a differentiation from dimly perceived or vaguely outlined concepts from sharply defined ideas and associations if they are to be operationally manipulated by machine. Ultimately, when facts, ideas, and relationships are identified and made clear, the machine accomplishes the swift and accurate calculations of a logical nature that are beyond human endurance or capability. In many instances computers permit an acuteness in making choices or accuracy of control previously unimaginable. Until recently it was inconceivable to compare extensive possibilities in order to resolve a problem or find the most beneficial alternative. Now, through the utilization of aids such as linear and dynamic programming, critical path analysis, factor analysis, network analysis, and simulation; decision making with precision and rationality is currently attainable.

Computer Graphics

The utilization of computers for the presentation of films, animated drawing, and other graphic displays can be a tool of immense value to planners and administrators. Animation of static drawings, whereby individual images, with small, controlled differences in their outlines or position, are photographed frame by frame in order to provide the appearance of movement can be used to instruct personnel in the proper handling of unfamiliar equipment. This technique might also be employed to simulate landscape features and the development of recreational areas and facilities within a given planning period. Such information could be useful in determining which areas should be developed, should be maintained in present form, or modified in some way. Moreover, the computer could offer alternative plans based upon potential user capacity, carrying capacity of the property, cost/benefit ratios and other variables.

Both animated and motion pictures, particularly insofar as time-lapse photography is concerned, would be capable of informing the general public about future recreational developments within the community as a sound public relations device. When people are shown how certain plans will affect their environment as well as provide for their own recreational opportunities they may react with greater support for the department and the planning program. Visual stimuli seem to have a greater impact upon the viewer than does an oral presentation. If the laymen can see the animated or photographed project developing before his/her eyes, rather than being subjected to maps, drawings, and models, there may be a better understanding of what the planner is attempting.

One of the advantages of computer graphics is that the display can show modifications, different views or perspectives, and probable benefits both to the potential user and the environment before any attempt is made to turn the first shovelful of earth. There is little doubt that computer animation is perfectly suited to scientific planning, and that its application could be justified in terms of scientific research alone. However, there are other ways in which computer techniques can be used. These are in the areas of public relations, personnel instruction, and the most economical and efficient methods for determining recreational sites, constructing centers and other facilities, or assisting in the development of safety procedures necessary to insure the health and welfare of patrons of recreational service systems. Animated pictures coupled to computers may offer information about faulty equipment, unrestricted access to areas, potentially dangerous facilities, and the means for preventing or forestalling such dangers.

With the availability of miniaturized computers capable of operating more economically than ever before, more artists and planners will gain access to them. This expansion of electronic cinematography might do much to provide the correct answers upon which decisions can be made for the greatest possible recreational service at the least cost in time, money and personnel effort.

PERT (Program Evaluation Review Techniques)

Of the many applications to which computers may be put is PERT or as it is sometimes known the Critical Path Method (CPM). The initial action in PERT is to carefully analyze whatever process, activity, or project is involved in the provision of recreational service to the community and then to chart the sequences which must be executed if the system is to carry out its function. The PERT chart is typically drawn as a complex diagram. Circles and arrows represent time periods and processes respectively. Each circle has arrows running to it or from it. These depict the various processes which either depend upon it or which must be performed before it can be initiated.

For the development of a particular recreational program involving physical resources, e.g., facilities, equipment, supplies, materials, personnel, transportation, public relations, and so forth, the graph will contain many circles and arrows. Actually, as with a flowchart, there is no single final level of detail, only levels of detail that support different purposes. It is possible, therefore, to expand one PERT chart into sub-PERT charts illustrating greater detail. For example, the construction of a beach facility which contains a pavillion to house administrative personnel, eating places, and a central life guard station can become a chart showing the development of the pavillion in the process of constructing the beach.

Once the PERT chart is graphed it is then necessary to obtain accurate estimates of the time required to carry out each process that is depicted on the graph. A PERT chart contains numbered circles and time estimates for each process that appears on the graph. With these data programmed for the computer, together with the desired completion data, i.e., the last circle on the graph, the computer can scan the entire procedure from the last circle to those immediately preceding and from the time estimates of the associated processes determine and assign the date at which each of these earlier activities has to be finished. These earlier activities can be scanned back to their preceding circles. When two or more process lines emanate from the same circle, a not infrequent occurrence, then the process having the earliest time is used to assign the time at which this circle must be attained if the entire program is to be completed at the desired date. In this manner, the time to be linked with any circle can be determined, especially when all those processes which depend upon it have their respective times assigned, by selecting the earliest date necessary. By utilizing this method, the graph is arranged with the times each circle (or completed process) must be reached if the entire program is to be carried through successfully and on time.

Additionally, the limiting path or paths are designated. This critical path is the one needing the most time to travel. If any process on this path is lengthened, then the total program will require more time. The critical path provides the administrator with information dealing with the entire program and indicates which segments must be carefully followed up while checking the whole program. The administrator needs to monitor the procedure to make sure that each process on the critical path is on schedule. Other processes, not on the critical path, are not delayed.

Often, the consequences of having administrators check the critical path is that processes on the path are accelerated while other parts become slower. At routine intervals, those processes which are completed are listed and old parts of the chart are filed. Also, due to early preparation for some of the processes on the critical path, and sometimes others, the time estimates for the different processes may be extended or reduced more than originally calculated. Therefore, the critical path will have to be recomputed. The new critical path will center the administrator's attention on what to look for. This interaction between reshuffled charts and the administration's focus maintains emphasis approximately on where it is most required. The entire program moves more rapidly than it would otherwise, and the terminal date for program operation gradually moves up. This simple decision instrument, the determination of the critical path by computer with regular search procedures for the critical path whenever there are revised data or new time estimates, is an extremely valuable managerial device. Of course, PERTs can be done by hand, but this is time consuming and may not be as reliable as computerized PERTs.

An example of a PERT chart and table is presented in Figure 12-1. In developing a PERT chart certain information must be obtained. The number of activities necessary to complete a given project, the length of time required for each activity completion, and the sequence of activities to be performed:

1.   Activities A and B begin the project. Both activities are independent and may be concomitant. A requires 4 time units and B requires 3.

2.   C requires 6 time units and D requires 4. D cannot begin until A is completed.

3.   E requires 5 time units and cannot begin until B is completed.

4.   F requires 2 time units and cannot begin until A and B are completed.

5.   C requires 1 time unit and cannot begin until D and F are completed.

6.   H requires 2 time units and cannot begin until E is completed.

7.   I requires 7 time units and cannot begin until A is completed.

8.   J requires 5 time units and cannot begin until C and G are completed.

9. K requires 1 time unit and cannot begin until C, G, and H are completed.

10. L is terminal and requires 4 time units and cannot begin until I, J, and K are completed.

Activity	Event	Duration	Least Time	Maximum Time
A	1–2	4	20	20
B	1–3	3	15	15
	2–6	0	12	
C	2–4	6	16	16
D	2–5	4	15	
I	2–11	11		
E	3–8	12		
F	6–7	2	12	
G	5–7	1	11	
H	8–10	2	7	
J	9–10	5	10	10
K	10–11	1	5	
L	11–12	4	4	4

Obviously, the shortest possible time which can elapse between all of the activities and events starting at point one (1) and finishing at point (12) is determined by that sequence of activities which takes the longest time and is therefore known as the critical path.

Computer Applications in Public Administration

How may computers best be utilized for the development of a better human social order? Essentially, the application of EDP to complex social relationships must be studied. All social relationships are analogous to systems. Systems may be defined as organized assemblies of ordered interdependent components identified by a common restriction and operational cohesion. The idea of system stresses the actuality of intricate relational intersections and allows the investigation of reciprocal causal processes concerning masses of interacting units. Each system by its own definition ordains specific limitations to the organized interrelationships. These boundaries can void the common principles of a good system and work to its detriment. Although attitudinal, ideological, and symbolic systems have a prominent part in human affairs, social systems are described, for purposes of explanation, as extant compound entities in constant self-controlled interaction with their environment.

PERT Diagram (Initial)

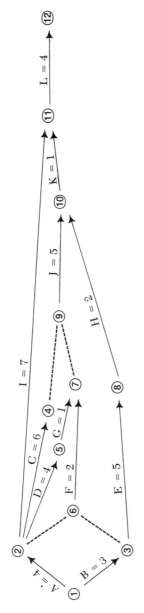

PERT Diagram (Consolidated)

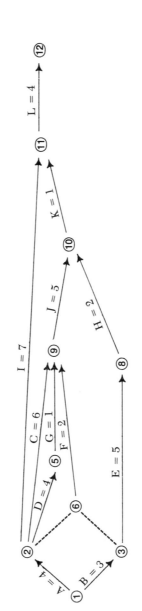

Critical Path

This determining sequence is critical to the performance of the program.

Figure 12-1.   PERT Diagram and Time Chart with Critical Path Sequence

263

Social systems involve every stage of elaboration from the basic group or family through the infinitely complex dynamics of cities, states, nation, and ultimately of the entire human community. Basic groups and all other groups are composed of self-regulating individuals who react and adjust to environmental changes—environment meaning social, physical, emotional, internal, and external. The larger the group, the more necessary it is to have arrangements wherein subgroups or subsystems are formulated along specialized lines. Thus, large social groups or systems typically comprise functional groups as their constituent subsystems. The coordinated efforts of large social systems are the effect of competent interior networks of communication as well as the cooperativeness on the part of leaders within their subgroups and the responsiveness on the part of all individuals involved to react in a forecastable and predetermined manner to a specified array of sensory stimuli. Essentially, a representation of self-regulation demands an operational definition between awareness, decision making, and execution or performance. This is usually obtained by an organic difference between receiving, decision making, and performance units within the system. As social systems increase in magnitude and complexity, these separate roles and their interrelated data exchange activities have a propensity for becoming centralized in constituent social subsystems.

Application of these fundamental concepts to social organization, particularly those agencies of government that have immediacy for the provision of recreational services, should provide a better understanding of EDP and systems theory. Every individual brings with him to any situation all of the previous experiences, relationships, and behaviors which characterize him as a person. Whatever has been part of our existence or experience, whether inanimate object, living organism, or social confrontation, exists temporally and correlates with others in time. In the social order the future cannot be foreseen and processed as a component piece of data ingested by the system and utilized to chart some substantive action. However, the future, projected as possibilities, may offer an estimated data source. Thus, it may be stated that the present condition of a system is decided by its previous conditions. Therefore, the future condition of a system is actually based upon predictable events or probabilities relying upon the potential condition of its environment. For self-regulating systems future conditions may, in fact, be dependent upon current or present actions. To the extent that self-regulating systems recognize not only contemporary conditions or states, but can probably prognosticate and project alternate courses of action for the future, estimations of the future may be used in the process of decision making.

Although it is recognized that attempts to prognosticate the condition of critical variables over which there is no certain control, social planning is basically concerned with alternative projections as direct outcomes of current actions, indirect consequences of efforts undertaken by the system on its environment, and selecting the optimum alternative which will probably result in a future condition that appears to be most valuable. It seems quite logical to assume that current actions taken to bring about some desired future state do occur. If carried to its ultimate conclusion it is apparent that insofar as the course of human events are concerned, means and ends are inseparable. Means are ends in view.

Social systems not only act to cope with present problems, but are capable of looking ahead and visualizing possible future problems as well. Planning is the method by which social systems attempt to resolve future problems or to modify them to such an extent that their impact is greatly lessened if disadvantageous to the social order. Naturally, the responsiveness of society to the future is influenced by the concept of the future state that seems most beneficial to contemporary decision makers. The extent of possible reaction to an existing problem is usually rather restricted, while the scope of independent response becomes increasingly greater as longer time-spans are considered. As specific future objectives are more clearly determined, actually defined, social behavior may more nearly resemble that of an heuristic system whereby counsel is replaced by management by the degree of error at which the matter stands at a particular time in relation to a relatively well-defined goal. Substantive action may then be undertaken for routine technical management.

There must now be understood the man-machine relationship which is essentially the use to which machines may be put for human value. The machine is nothing more or less than an extension of human capability subjected to human control. The computing machine is already affecting man's social existence, methods of education, political control, relationship to social and physical environment, and may eventually radically reorder all existence.

With the utilization of computer technology, administrators now have at their disposal data which are composed of extremely reliable facts. High quality data in quantity permit decision making that must be more efficacious than that which is based upon attitude, prejudice, or supposed knowledge. It is at the point of decision that the administrator ultimately confronts the results and interactions of his managerial, political, and behavioral activities. The administrator's effort is best made in terms of specialized knowledge or expertness and high quality data. Under such circumstances, the system that relies upon EDP will probably be more efficient, effective, rational, and capable of correct responses to the variable needs of the constituency.

The recreationist, in an executive position, has the opportunity to begin to increase the utilization of computer technology for the benefit of the public recreational service system and the people which it serves. It may be as an outgrowth of local city management use of automation for fiscal matters, personnel matters, or land usage. However the computer is introduced within the local jurisdiction for whom the recreationist works, there is currently available technology which can advance the services that the department can perform. Computerized budget-making, payroll processing, statistical data collection for all divisions within the system, the development of recreational activities for literally every individual within a community, planning new recreational places, selection of types of facilities, apparatus, design of areas, equipment as well as inventory control are all well within the most simplified use of the computer. While there is as yet no completely automated administrative system in American cities, centralized data banks are being established. The data bank is designed to provide administrative information in a centralized location.[3] The retrieval of these data is hastened by simple methods which include tabulations of specific units having common characteristics. The recovery of this information is based upon the parameters which are indicated as required. Additionally, data banks also include storage files, and record maintenance for updating and modifying information.

The extreme pace of urbanization in the United States has actually overburdened the historic governmental functions and placed increased pressure on the political decision-makers to such an extent that the public business is almost always performed expediently rather than logically. Metropolitan growth literally swamped political jurisdictions. Under the impact of population growth, inflation, recession, war, political upheaval, power shortages, and demands of many minorities the ability of planners, administrators, and elected officials to define the destinies of their own communities was sharply reduced. As the extension of the perimeters of old central cities failed to maintain pace with the expanding urban region, it became increasingly clear that the scope and scale of real planning problems have moved beyond the capacity and range of urban departments staffed with planners.

That such urbanization is swiftly magnifying the complexity of problems facing public administrators cannot be denied. The physical and mental capacity of humans to cope with this veritable flood of emergencies, and the results of conurbation, is constantly frustrated. The only apparent hope is for the rapid establishment of automated systems to permit the administrator to keep up with quickly changing urban conditions. As Cambell and LeBlanc indicate: "The question of metropolitan administration is not, . . . , whether or not an information sys-

[3]K. C. Laudon, *Computers and Bureaucratic Reform* (New York: John Wiley & Sons, 1974), pp. 8–14.

tem should be adopted, but rather how soon it should be instituted and what should be the magnitude of the effort."[4] Public administration EDP is required if local governments are ever to react rationally to envisioned problems.

The power of computers is of such immensity, and the capability of programming a computer is so broad in scope, that in almost every field where a mass of data is to be processed, computers are now being applied. How may the computer be of specific assistance to the recreationist administrator? The following samples are just a few specific applications of computers and data processors to the field of public service administration:

Departmental Finance Factors

1. Forecasting revenues from whatever fees and charges are levied.
2. Forecasting expenditures for all operations including personnel, maintenance, construction, program, office management, and other services.
3. Budget formulation, either line-item, program, or project.
4. Budgetary and appropriation accounting.
5. General ledger and fund accounting where required.
6. Supplies, material, and equipment inventory.
7. Property inventory.
8. Motor vehicle equipment retrieval list.
10. Fixed asset accounting.
11. Purchase order writing and control.
12. Audit of all fiscal records.

Personnel Administration

1. Personnel inventory in terms of speaking, writing, activity performance skills.
2. Actuarial statistics.
3. Personnel services budget requests.
4. Established position control.
5. Effective employee-public ratio for service.
6. Payroll.
7. Payroll distribution accounting.
8. Psychological test scoring.
9. Eligible applicants roster listing.
10. Personnel evaluating and rating records.
11. Time and leave records.

[4]Robert D. Cambell and Hugh LeBlanc, *An Information System for Urban Planning* (Washington, D.C.: Urban Renewal Administration, HHFA, 1965), p. 96.

Construction of Recreational Facilities and Places

1. Construction cost accounting.
2. Bid rating.
3. Contract progress estimates and payments.
4. Work order distribution.
5. Force account accounting.
6. Traffic survey for traffic pattern evaluation.
7. Origin and destination programs.
8. Right-of-way taking line computation.
9. Terrain handling data.
10. Earth work computation.
11. Functional space analysis, carrying capacity.

Planning for Recreational Spaces, Areas, and Facility Placement

1. Land use data and analysis.
2. Site situation and geographical indexing.
3. Area and percent vacant land analysis.
4. Land use by area and number of units.
5. Land use by geographical location.
6. Transportation needs and studies.

Population Information

1. Population movement and trends, both internal and external.
2. Population distributions by age, sex, race, religion, ethnic background, education, social, and economic status.
3. Population densities.
4. Population distribution in terms of where employed for transit projections.
5. Recreational area and facility placement and projections in terms of population movements.
6. Types of activities and/or programs which might be arranged in terms of popularity or expectation.

Program Possibilities

1. Listing of all possible areas, facilities. or spaces where potential planned recreational activities might occur.
2. Listing of all possible recreational activities in which people may participate on an organized or spontaneous basis.
3. Scheduling all available spaces in terms of activity demand.
4. Providing information as to the maximum size of instructional activities for most effective performance and participation.

5. Matching participant skill, talent, or knowledge with available activities.
6. Offering various alternative choices to participants in terms of available leisure, skills, interests.

Of course, computers are no more infallible than the data fed into them by human programmers. However, once the electronic data processing is initiated, it performs a job in seconds no single or even many humans could possibly do. Automatically matching people to activities, places, free spaces and free time, or calculating cost-benefit ratios, personnel on the job at any given time and an almost infinite variety of information variables makes the computer an invaluable device for providing better recreational services to the community. With EDP, it is more likely that individuals are going to obtain greater satisfaction from the recreational program because each person's individual needs may be more completely met. With EDP it is possible to develop activities and programs that are designed to suit individual needs and preferences.

Computer Impact on Recreational Service Administration

The chief modification to be observed from the technological confrontation between men and machines, particularly as it applies to the field of public recreational service, is that a generalist breed of professionals must be developed to administer the various functions of the system. Automation may certainly replace the clerical work force which is now of importance to current departmental operation. However, increasingly sophisticated machines may one day make these ancillary positions obsolete. It is also probable that many of the so-called middle management positions will be relegated to the dust heap as well. The age of cybernation should require individuals who are both technically and professionally prepared to perform decision making functions so as to meet the increasing complexities of modern life. As society becomes more bureaucratic, technology oriented individuals will be required who can interface with machines and use the information being rapidly produced. It may well mean that those recreationists who desire to achieve administrative responsibility will have to combine both the professional preparation of the humanist, people oriented education (including those experiences designed to effect optimum program experiences), with a scientific and technological education.

It is understood, however, that recreationists, at the management level, should probably be generalists for they will need the leadership qualities that are pertinent to public officials in areas where influence by emulation is a key factor. The need for recreationists who can program computers is undeniable. For the best possible mix, insofar as understanding the nature of computer technology, systems analysis, and operational research are concerned it is probable that recreationists will have some knowledge of management science as well as the professional preparation now offered. It is certain that as technology becomes increasingly esoteric and intricate it will be necessary for more administrative functionaries to have sound technical education. The generalist will always be a part of the recreational service by virtue of the nature of the field. It is a people oriented field and cannot be divorced from that concept. Much more to the point is that the recreationist will have to think more in terms of an automated environment which necessitates an understanding of the EDP concepts. To be successful as an administrator, the recreationist must begin to lend himself to a rational mixture of philosophy and science. Despite the seeming dichotomy involved in the development of such personnel, it now appears that logic and reason decree the necessity for discovering individuals who have the blend of humanism and technology to perform the complex function of public administration. It seems obvious that continued progress with computer technology and the imminent onset of cybernation demands a combination of talent, personality, and knowledge that will permit the achievement of administrative effectiveness.

Selected References

Birkle, J. and R. Yearsley, Eds.: *Computer Applications in Management* (New York: Halstead Press), 1976.

Dorf, R. C.: *Computers and Man*, 2nd ed. (San Francisco, Calif.: Boyd and Fraser Publishing Company), 1978.

Fuchs, J. R.: *Computerized Financial Controls* (Englewood Cliffs, N.J.: Prentice-Hall, Inc.), 1977.

Holoien, M. O.: *Computers and Their Social Impact* (New York: John Wiley & Sons), 1977.

Hoyt, D. B.: *Computer Handbook for Senior Management* (New York: Macmillan Information), 1977.

Jancura, E.: *Computers*, 2nd ed. (New York: Petrocelli Books), 1977.

Kolence, K. W. and R. A. James: *EDP Job Costs and Charges* (Palo Alto, Calif.: Institute for Software Engineering), 1976.

Leavitt, R., Ed.: *Artist and Computer* (New York: Harmony), 1976.

Lynch, R. E. and J. R. Rice: *Computers: Their Impact and Use Structured Programming in Fortran* (New York: Holt, Rinehart and Winston), 1977.

Matick, R.: *Computer Storage Systems and Technology* (New York: John Wiley & Sons), 1977.

Sanders, D.: *Computers in Society* (New York: McGraw-Hill Book Company), 1977.

Tucker, A. B., Jr.: *Programming Languages* (New York: McGraw-Hill Book Company), 1977.

CHAPTER **13**

Systems Management and Analysis for Use in Recreational Service Administration

The fundamental idea of a system is that it is a complete entity. Ellis and Ludwig define a system as:

> . . . a device, procedure, or scheme which behaves according to some description, its function being to operate on information and/or energy and/or matter in a time reference to yield information and/or energy and/or matter.[1]

The word *system* connotes a total on-going operation rather than an aggregate of fragments or components. Systems are usually represented by drawings and the simplest system may be conceived as:

The essential parts of any system are the input, the process or manipulative cycle, and the output or product. Input refers to information from outside of the system transferred into the system for processing. Processing consists of obtaining information about a predetermined condition or situation, applying reasonable manipulative procedures to the information, and supplying the results of these procedures. Output is information that has been processed or worked on within a system and is transferred from the system for whatever use is demanded. The concept of system applies to any operational processes, physical or biologic means initiating operational processes, and mathematical models in which some alterna-

[1] David O. Ellis and Fred J. Ludwig, *Systems Philosophy: An Introduction* © 1962, p. 3. Reprinted by permission of Prentice-Hall, Inc., Englewood Cliffs, New Jersey.

tives are offered and others subjected to examination. In self-regulating systems an additional factor is the control or regulating mechanism. Control is activated by feedback.

The return of a fraction of the output of a system to the input, to which the fraction is added or subtracted, is termed feedback. Feedback may be positive or negative. Negative feedback is that fraction of the output returned to the input from which the fraction is subtracted. If the result of such feedback produces an increase in output reflecting a decrease in input, there is control. Positive feedback, on the other hand, is associated with both increased input and output, resulting in a further increase of input. This increase indicates no control or a system gone wild. For most systems, therefore, control is a self-regulating mechanism for restricting variables to specified limits within the system's environment. The fundamental purpose of control is to maintain output, which necessitates an ability to modify means as conditions vary; the control instrument thus adjusts the operating components of the system. When control mechanisms are added to the system, the representation may be schematically shown as:

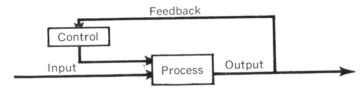

The control aspects of a system deal with the measurement of output, some device that can evaluate the output and return a fraction of it (feedback) to a point of control. The control unit compares the output with predetermined objectives (criteria). If the comparison shows the actual output to be too deviant from the standard or expected output, a regulatory unit modifies the operation. The self-regulating mechanism continues to function until the actual output meets the expectations of the preset criteria. Thus, in a recreational service system, administration is the essential controlling element. The department or system should reflect changing environmental situations (community needs, problems, resources) and act accordingly. Such a system may be represented as:

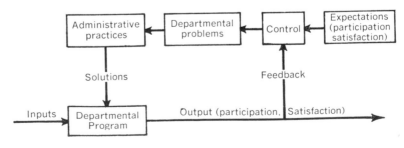

The recreational service system responds to particular environmental conditions (inputs) and attempts to produce activities designed to enhance the satisfaction, enjoyment, and life of its constituents (output). For given situations and responses, the criteria on which expectations are based are previous departmental experiences that attempted to meet the needs of the public. The actual participation (output) is compared at the point of control with expected levels, and, if the quality or quantity of program is lower than expected, a departmental problem exists and must be processed through administrative practices. Administrative responses produce possible solutions which are then transmitted to the system as inputs. These solutions become part of the departmental responses to the situations that evoked them. If the solution is correct (meets the public's need), the actual program and its attendant satisfactions will be equivalent to the criteria or expected public response. The administrative process has the capability to control the entire system.

Administrative procedures for the determination of solutions to departmental problems provide the system with the flexibility or adjustment mechanism with which valid responses can be found to environmental changes.[2] Administration is the system's self-regulating instrument, and it is supposed that departmental problems are given to administration for resolution. The ultimate aim of all administrative procedures is to find satisfactory solutions which then become program experiences for public consumption through participation. For effective solutions to problems confronting a recreational service system, some process that inculcates all factors of the department's performance, the devisement of a general system for handling operational matters, system-wide simulation or model construction, and the assembly of information directly related to the department's ability to perform must be formulated. The final step is the utilization or application of specific data that can produce optimum levels of effectiveness.

Recreational service departments may be looked on as systems with meaningful direction whereby the cooperative efforts of many persons are required if the aims of the system are to be realized. The aims of every public recreational service department are a varied and comprehensive series of individual, dual, group, and mass recreational activities and experiences that directly lead to human satisfaction, enjoyment, and enhancement of life.

SYSTEMS ANALYSIS

Systems analysis is a method that reduces a total system into increasingly smaller components until the smallest unit making up the entire system is defined. Systems analysis attempts to determine the most ap-

[2] Stanley Young, *Management: A Systems Analysis* (Glenview, Ill.: Scott, Foresman and Company, 1966), p. 24.

10

propriate, practical, and effective means for performing a particular purpose. For best results it is well to produce a working model of the system to be analyzed. Simulation is a working analogy. It involves the construction of an operational model giving similarity of conditions and relationships with the system under investigation. In this way a system may be operated for laboratory examination without actually slowing or stopping it. Additionally, the characteristics that make up its totality may be analyzed for optimum productivity. Simulation studies require models that are as precisely aligned to the living system as is possible. Thus, a specific model represents the system in such a manner that it is possible ". . . to state exactly what will happen to every possible input at every stage of its passage through the system, or to describe every response which it will evoke in the system."[3] To understand the functions of a complete system, the system must be subdivided into its components in order to determine the behavior of the system.

In examining a system it is well to recall the basic diagram depicting input, process, and output. This system may be ramified into subsystems. Initially, all factors pertinent to the development of the model must be collected, including a description of the system under study and its performance and history. The model is tested with actual information to obtain reasonably accurate data. From such testing, modifications in the model are made until tests indicate that the simulation is really representative of the actual system. The approximation of the simulated model to reality is generally restricted by such factors as time, cost, knowledge of the system, and analysis experience. However, because simulation permits the critical examination of a system prior to actual operation, it is a tremendously effective tool to use to discover the possible impacts of decisions, conditions, and use of resources in varying situations.

The department has a responsibility to deliver certain kinds of activities or to provide particular settings wherein satisfying recreational experiences may occur. The department's environment is made up of the needs of the public that the department serves and the varied economic, personnel, facility, and program resources. This environment serves as input for the system. Given this input, the department (system) attempts to devise reasonable recreational experiences which may satisfy the public. The procedure by which departmental personnel become involved in discovering the best mixture of activities constitutes the process of the system. The solution or output is the actual program content that the department develops for meeting people's needs in relation to the department's financial ability, available personnel, places, facilities, and material. This procedure may be compartmentalized. Any decisions that have to

[3] Harry H. Goode and Robert E. Machol, *System Engineering* (New York: McGraw-Hill Book Company, Inc., 1957), p. 305.

be made in order to produce a comprehensive and varied program of recreational experiences require a series of concomitant decisions based on particular organizational sectors to be administered, such as personnel, plant maintenance, finance, materials, and other variables. Schematically, the representation appears as:

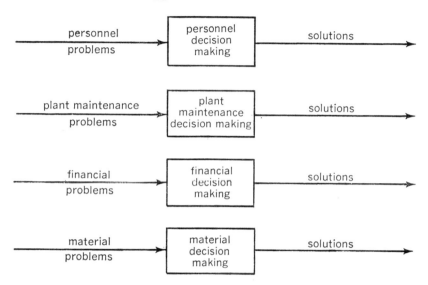

The decision-making function may be divided to a greater degree, in terms of specialization, depending on the number of individuals who are engaged in rendering judgments or opinions that can influence alternative choices in making a decision. Personnel within the lower levels of the administrative process are developing positions that are passed up the line to the level where the final choices are made.

The decision-making process may be analyzed serially, meaning that the initial problem is partially resolved as a component of the final solution. The partial resolution or output becomes the input for the next stage of the process. The subprocesses of the decision-making process may be examined infinitesimally until an ultimate set of actions is determined. Decision making is subdivided into a series of consecutively collected processes represented as:

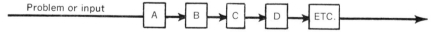

Each of these series may be broken down further until a final set of actions becomes available. Block A may be examined sequentially as:

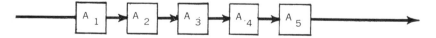

This ramification continues as long as there are actions that can be divided. Each block denotes an array of directions (to an individual) that indicates how a particular function is to be carried out, given a known input and an expected output from each practice. The single objective for such scrupulous attention to detail is the development of a set of orders or charges that will result in optimum, or at least improved, solutions.

In an administrative system, discretionary programmed directions should be offered to the analyst. However, the problem solver may select the appropriate techniques to use. The range and depth of analysis rely on the character of the output obtained by the deviser. Thus, if an administrative system is expected to deliver solutions that will achieve a particular average value, and if such output is not attained, greater ramified programming is necessary.

Developing a model schematically indicating all components of the system provides the designer with the means to analyze the complete system without losing even the smallest subparts and still maintain the relationship of the components to the total system. Once the process is subjected to analysis, the designer recombines or synthesizes the system. Such synthesis may be diagrammed as:

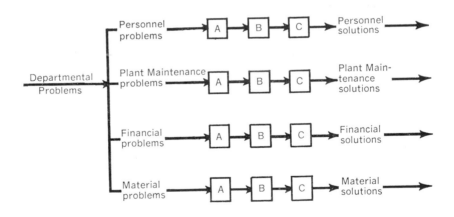

Several types of analysis may be defined by the objectives to be achieved. These types are needs, facility, and practicability analyses. Each analysis attempts to answer specific questions about the system's ability to perform certain tasks. Needs analysis is concerned with determining whether the system has the capacity to initiate a particular assignment or to satisfy an established norm. Facility analysis has to do with what assignments the system has the capacity to initiate and what expectations it can meet. Practicability analysis deals with whether the system can initiate a particular assignment or actually satisfy a particular norm.

Needs Analysis

Needs analysis is concerned not only with particular problems but is the foundation of long-range planning. In order to plan logically for performance in the public sector or for carrying out the mandated responsibility of the department, tendencies and conditions must be extrapolated so that a conclusion may be reached about the kinds of systems that will be required in the future. Typically, the exactness of necessary detail declines rapidly as the length of extrapolation increases.

Facility Analysis

Facility analysis functions in generalized and specific levels. One basic need of those engaged in the work of systems is to remain current in the techniques and/or machines influencing that aspect of the system. It really means perpetual facility analysis of whatever developments occur in the specialized areas either in improved methods or in machine innovations.

Practicability Analysis

Practicability analysis is almost always directed toward detailed work or some specific problem. This analysis is analogous to hypothesis testing in the scientific method. Practicability analysis also may be looked on as a synthesizing of needs and facility techniques for the purpose of reappraisal.

Systems analysis is performed so that the most efficient and effective administrative system can be designed. Systems are developed to maximize results that are considered valuable to the community and to the department responsible for performance. The entire concept of systems study is to provide valuable data, suitable to the time and pertinent to current conditions. Techniques developed to report mismanagement of paper work, to handle repetitive activities, and to minimize the amount of human judgment required to perform these tasks can be utilized to increase administrative efficiency. This procedure should lower costs and reduce operating time by eliminating a number of procedural steps within the system, thereby making the process more effective.

A comprehensive study of an administrative data system must consider all the probable methods available for implementing and transmitting information. A significant characteristic of system design is the precise selection of pertinent and useful information necessary to the decision-making process from the mass of available data. Once the requisite information has been obtained through systems analysis, the design and development of an effective administrative system can be proposed.

Administrative systems may be thought of as an informational flow process producing organizational solutions. Thus, all organizational problems flow through a preselected course, with the proper person engaged in problem-solving tasks appropriate for him. This idea by no means indicates that all problems are treated in precisely the same way; certain problems may require individualized study and handling. Neither does it mean that there is only one procedure for dealing with a problem. The department may devise several alternative procedures to resolve a problem. A predetermined plan of action is absolutely necessary, however, so that, when a decision is made as to how a problem is to be treated, that course of action will be followed explicitly.

SYSTEM DESIGN

In order to design an administrative system, there must be a sound basis for making decisions and resolving the problems confronting the department. A detailed procedure for assigning responsibility and incorporating all aspects into a single operating system must be performed. Thus, the total system is viewed in terms of the relationships among its component processes. An administrative system can be thought of as a task process producing solutions to the problems that arise during the operation of the department. All such problems are handled by channeling them through a devised program whereby the administrator is concerned only with those decision-making procedures that would normally be assigned to him.

To demonstrate the system's operation, each component or subprocess will be described. The entire administrative system is concerned with problem designation, analysis, alternative procedures, testing, agreement, permission, initiation, instruction, and evaluation.

Problem Designation

Problems are the raw material on which the system feeds, the input to activate the system. Problems are raised, expressed, or confirmed from external and internal sources. They may be designated, discovered, or stressed by employees of the department, the clientele of the department, or the institution (political, social, educational) under whose aegis it operates. The department has an almost limitless supply of problems concerning literally every conceivable factor of its basic intent—a comprehensive recreational program.

The department has to develop a screening unit to collect, classify, and arrange the information streaming into it from internal or external sources. The data are compared to criteria defined by the philosophy and organizational aims of the department. If the department is actually meeting the public's needs, as conceived by predetermined standards, then no problem exists and other procedures are set in motion. If, on the other hand, the information generated indicates that substandard practices are operational, then there is a problem and the problem-solving process is implemented.

The screening unit is chiefly concerned with information about the department's environment. It gathers information about political, economic, social, educational, ethnic, racial, religious, departmental organization, employee competence, program performance, physical plant capacity, maintenance, materials, specific activities, attendance, in short, everything that might impinge on the ability of the department to perform its task successfully. Significant variables are defined, and the constituent public is surveyed. A schedule indicating how often the unit collects pertinent information from specialized samples of the public, other agencies and institutions, or internally is devised. Some information is generated without the need to elicit it. The public, public officials, employees, and others continually supply data for department action. Complaints against department activities, facility maintenance, employment practices, and other personal or physical problems can always be expected.

The screening unit may be either centralized or decentralized, depending on the size of the department, the specialized data to be handled,

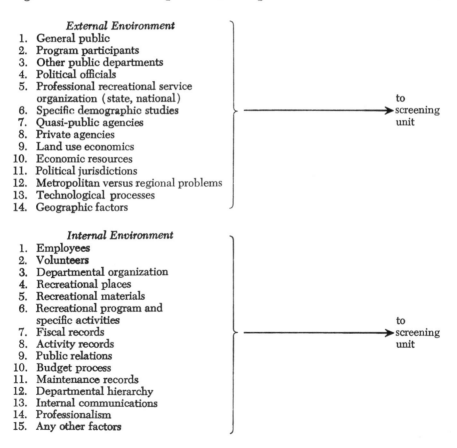

External Environment
1. General public
2. Program participants
3. Other public departments
4. Political officials
5. Professional recreational service organization (state, national)
6. Specific demographic studies
7. Quasi-public agencies
8. Private agencies
9. Land use economics
10. Economic resources
11. Political jurisdictions
12. Metropolitan versus regional problems
13. Technological processes
14. Geographic factors

to screening unit

Internal Environment
1. Employees
2. Volunteers
3. Departmental organization
4. Recreational places
5. Recreational materials
6. Recreational program and specific activities
7. Fiscal records
8. Activity records
9. Public relations
10. Budget process
11. Maintenance records
12. Departmental hierarchy
13. Internal communications
14. Professionalism
15. Any other factors

to screening unit

and the pertinent information that each operating facility of the department needs to perform its functions most effectively. Or a combined screening unit might be established which would accommodate only specific information at a central office, all other data being decentralized.

To illustrate how the problem-designation process works, the schematic on page 279 represents the flow of information to the screening unit.

To facilitate the problem-resolution procedure, a variety of record and report forms must be designed. The actual design and handling of paper work will be discussed more fully in Chapter 14. Nevertheless, the design of a problem-designating form is offered here. Note that the problem is defined, the person who brought the potential problem to the attention of the department is identified, the conditions causing the problem are presented in factual occurrences (if any), the reasons evoking initial concern are presented, and possible satisfaction is offered by providing appropriate space for recording the desired solutions. The form should be distributed throughout the department and utilized whenever any individual believes a problem exists.

Within the screening unit there must be some point of control. The control is a subunit with the responsibility for appraising each problem as it arises and determining whether there is a legitimate problem need-

---

```
 _____
|                                                           |
|      Departmental Problem                                 |
|                                     Administration        |
|                                 Date Received:_____  |
|                                                           |
|                                 Problem                    |
|  1.  Problem situation:         Allocation:_____    |
|      (This may be a complaint,                            |
|      recommendation, suggestion,                          |
|      recognition of a problem, or                         |
|      general information concerning   Item #:_____    |
|      the department)                                      |
|                                                           |
|                                 Treatment                  |
|  2.  Problem facts:             of Problem:_____     |
|      (Provide facts dealing with                          |
|      names, dates, incidents,                             |
|      etc.)                      _____    |
|                                                           |
|                                 _____    |
|  3.  Problem resolution:                                  |
|      (What should be done?)                               |
|                                 _____    |
|                                                           |
|  Name_____ |
|                                                           |
|  Section (unit, office, center, etc.)_____  |
|                                                           |
|  Position_____ |
|_____|
```

Figure 13-1.   A problem-designating form.

ing further investigation, or whether the supposed problem is, in fact, a fantasy, unrelated to the department, already resolved, or simply harassment. The subunit attempts to coordinate the problem-solving process by screening out non-problems, assigning problems to competent authorities, determining what facts are pertinent to the designated problem, scheduling the length of time required for processing a problem, and providing other assistance as necessary.

All designated legitimate problems are processed in a precise manner so that complete control of the situation is maintained. Non-legitimate problems are screened out, and a form letter is sent to the originator indicating the action being taken or why no action is being taken. If a problem is legitimate, the control unit records in a ledger the date of receipt, source, and to whom the problem was allocated for solution. A record is thereby maintained for future reference so that a final solution to any problem is available should the same problem arise at another time or from a different source. The record certifies that no problem is overlooked and no overlapping is permitted. Problem taxonomy is a requirement once the initial screening activity is completed. Problems are logged in terms of existing solutions, existing solutions that are not being applied, existing solutions that are not productive, and duplication of effort. If there are no programmed solutions, the problem is assigned on the basis of its departmental location. If the problem relates to more than one division of the organization, it is analyzed to determine the functional factors and then assigned on the basis of operating unit designation.

When no solution exists, the control unit has to determine whether or not the problem requires resolution or additional information, or whether it should be returned to the sender as being unsuitable for action (it is trivial). When a solution has been prepared but is ineffective, a new problem arises and constitutes a condition that requires production. Finally, the control unit considers the importance and immediacy of the problem and assigns some order to it. Thus, extremely significant problems receive top priority and are allocated to top management for resolution. Problems are assigned priority rating in descending order and are routed to the personnel capable of dealing with them. If a backlog develops, the problems are held until appropriate personnel are mustered to work on them.

All problems are routed through a decision-making process. Whatever a given problem requires for solution is determined by the control unit, which indicates the procedures to be taken. Problems are continuously flowing through the system, some partially completed and others that are particularly difficult to solve. As with all problems, the control unit routes and schedules them for processing throughout the entire system, with recall to the unit for additional work, or for partial routing through the system. The control unit routes the problem through the procedural steps and assigns certain employees to work on it. By scheduling the work of problem solvers, the control unit can plan the resolution of the problem. It knows how many people are at work on a given problem, is aware of how much time should be spent (unless there is some unforeseen hindrance) on a typical problem, and understands the benefit gained by the department when the solution of a given problem can be applied to other problems. With experience, the control unit becomes increasingly capable of estimating problem significance, priority, and allocation of time for resolution. It should maintain the flexibility necessary to revise processing schedules so that adjustments may be made during ongoing operations.

By maintaining a master calendar, the control unit is able to follow the problem-solving process throughout every phase of the route at a glance. Each procedure, which may be assigned a certain time sequence, is reviewed to see that it is on schedule. If a bottleneck occurs or other situations arise that throw the process out of sequence, the control unit determines the cause of the difficulty and adjusts the schedule accordingly. If the problem solver needs additional assistance or instruction, the control unit provides it. Of course, the individual who is assigned problem-solving responsibilities is assumed to be competent to undertake the work. Each person given a problem to solve is required to accept all such assignments as a basic part of his job.

Problem Analysis

Problems arise for a variety of reasons. When the screening unit transmits problem information to the problem solver, analysis of the problem is begun. Among the possible causes for problems are:

1. Conditions have produced a situation for which no solution has been worked out;
2. A previous solution to the problem has not been applied;
3. A supposed solution to the problem was ineffective when applied;
4. A supposed solution to the problem is false;
5. No solution to the problem has been offered;
6. An existing solution was ineffectually administered;
7. The condition or conditions creating the problem have changed so that current solutions are no longer applicable; or
8. The problem's resolution is within the system and is only partially completed.

The manager has to examine the causal factors and determine the reason or reasons for the problem so that remedial practices can be programmed. The examination of any problem might require several routine actions. Since solutions are cataloged, the examiner refers to the operating

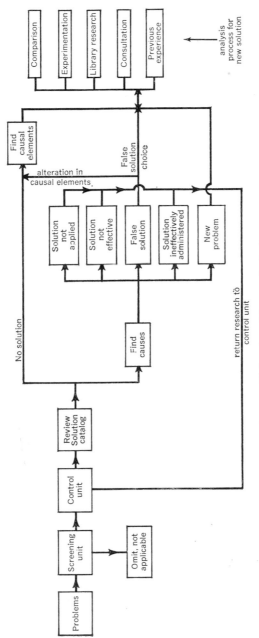

Figure 13-2. A problem-analysis chart.

directory in order to establish whether a solution to the problem exists. The examiner may request more information from the problem originator. When a solution applies to the situation the operation is investigated to determine whether the solution is being followed, is correctly applied, is ineffectual, or is not a solution at all. Freedom of inquiry is absolutely essential throughout the examination process. All components of the department are to render complete cooperation. There is no such thing as confidential information within a public department. All data, unless the information might prove injurious to a private individual if disclosed, are considered and what is pertinent to the resolution should be forthcoming. A data retrieval system is likely to prove of great assistance and all technological improvement, particularly EDP, should be operational for obvious reasons.

When the examiner determines the cause of the problem, he reports his conclusions to the control subunit. Whatever actions are necessary are then taken by control. Thus, existing solutions are implemented, ineffective solutions modified, abolished, or corrected, appropriate divisions notified to act or discontinue action, or the problem-solving process is activated in the event that a solution has not been devised. The discovery of a problem gives rise to related problems. If the initial problem cannot be solved until another problem is resolved, the former is delayed until the latter is resolved. The problem-solving process is continuous. As problems are discovered, analyzed, and resolved, or fed back into the system for additional work, constant attention should be given to the loci of the problems. Some procedure, practice, or unit may produce a bottleneck, be inefficient, or function in a way that creates problems. The control subunit should be able to identify and isolate the problem-causing practice and devise methods by which deficiencies can be avoided in the future. Figure 13-2 illustrates a problem-analysis chart.

Alternative Procedures

The next logical step in the decision-making process is the selection of the best possible solution based on appropriate research and investigation of the cause of the problem. This step requires an in-service education program so that competent personnel have the technical knowledge at their disposal in devising suitable answers to problems as they arise. Based on previous experience in handling similar problems, maintaining pertinent information about standard practices in the field, being able to utilize consultants, having access to resources that should afford bases for formulating solutions, and having the professional qualifications to arrive at solutions or innovate solutions, the examiner should be capable of creating new solutions and resolving problems. Figure 13-3 shows this procedure schematically.

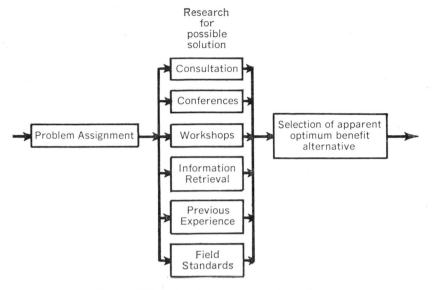

Figure 13-3.   An alternative-procedures chart.

Testing

The assigned examiner is expected to evaluate potential solutions and determine the one he considers to be the best possible solution under existing conditions. The examiner attempts to select a solution that maximizes results, provides the most efficient, effective service possible, and considers the economic impact that such a solution will have on the present and future budgets of the department. It may be that the problem and potential solution are calculated on a cost-benefit ratio. On whatever premise he bases his judgment, he is also expected to propose when, how, and by whom the solution is to be activated, administered, and reviewed. He must note whatever fiscal changes are required and include them in his recommendation.

Agreement

The subsequent procedural step in decision making is gaining the consent of the personnel in those units or divisions of the department that will be affected by the proposed solution. It is undertaken to determine the effect that a proposed solution will have on the operational outcomes of the units involved. The control subunit receives all information directly related to the original problem and the potential solution selected by the examiner. The control unit then determines which sections of the department will be directly or indirectly influenced by such proposals and calls for deliberate examination of the proposal.

There are a variety of ways in which a proposed solution can affect an operating unit of the department. A unit may be required to modify its performance, discontinue certain practices, or initiate other policies or procedures. Other components of the department may be influenced by the substantive changes that a proposed solution requires. It is possible for a change in performance by one division to obviate the establishment of another unit, to require a change of practice in a second unit, or to demand the creation of another unit. Any or all of these outcomes could be suggested or requested by particular changes in a given operation.

Once the control unit has determined the components that will be affected, it chooses the divisional or section personnel with whom the proposition should be settled, arranges their time logically, and fixes a date when their deliberations should be returned to the subunit. Control utilizes its master calendar for retaining direction over the clearance sequence, that is, who receives the proposal, how the proposal is processed, when it is returned to control, how, and by whom it is to be initiated, any serious objections to the proposal by operating units affected by it, review proceedings for modifications, and then transmits it to the executive for permission to activate the solution.

Permission

In any decision-making process, delegation of authority should coincide with responsibility for job performance. In departmental organization problems require solution to maintain efficient and effective operation. When problems arise and solutions are proposed, the agreement procedure is activated so that common accord may be reached. Should any unit supervisor disagree with the solution, he must be prepared to substantiate his criticism on factual grounds. Even when logical grounds for disagreement are supportable in one unit, the benefit to the entire organization may far outweigh the need to consider a single unit. The unit supervisor should be convinced of the rightness of the solution as it affects the department. When consensus is reached the proposal should then be reviewed by the executive for final approval to act. Typically, authorization may be granted at lower levels within the organization if routine problems having small expenditures are delegated to subunits. However, when complex problems having potentially high expenditures are generated it is probable that the executive will reserve the right of final review and authorization.

The decision to grant permission to proceed with implementing the solution generally lies with the chief executive of the system. He has the necessary time to review the proposed solution as well as the capability to determine whether other solutions might not be more optimizing to the department. The executive generally spends his time reviewing and/ or approving the propositions forwarded to him by the control unit for authorization to initiate action. Permission to commit the organization to

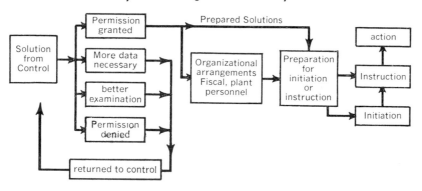

Figure 13-4.   A permission procedure.

a specific course of action involves monetary and other departmental resources (supplies, material, personnel, and facilities). Such commitment means that the control unit will have to transmit the solution to the proper fiscal unit for whatever financial support is necessary to execute the solution. Other manpower, plant use, and stores required for the operation must be prepared and coordinated by the control unit. A chart depicting the permission procedure is shown in Figure 13-4.

Initiation

Initiation of the procedure occurs after permission to implement the solution has been given. The various units of the system are provided with a set of directions or instructions indicating the effective date for activating the solution. Schedules are developed by the control unit so that the necessary preparations may be made in sequence or coincidentally. If the solution requires additional personnel or necessitates additional financial support, supplies, or facilities, the control unit originates a calendar that permits enough time for the preparation of competent personnel to execute the plan and for the deployment of all the organizational resources needed to support the solution. When these preparations have been adequately developed, control transmits directions for enactment to the several departmental units affected, informing them of their part in the solution. The instructions they receive are then made a part of their manual of procedures, together with the date of operational initiation.

Instruction

Although some solutions will have been developed to cover particular exigency situations, not all programmed solutions are applicable. When solutions are available they should be activated as has been explained. This process permits a high degree of coordination among the various units of the organization and makes the entire planning procedure feasible. When an organization has developed a system that can react to certain internal or external conditions, that is, can adjust or compensate for changing situations, the unit concerned with receiving and transmitting information about conditions is able to signal the components of the system that are or will be affected by those conditions that certain procedures should be activated. Thus, preprogrammed solutions are set in motion as conditions arise to which they are applicable. A precise analysis must indicate the situations for which any solution may be put into practice. It is possible for an organization to have solutions ready for all conceivable conditions, in which case the organization would be capable of adjusting to meet whatever condition prevailed. Every operating unit should have a manual of solutions that can be applied as needed. New solutions might be forthcoming on occasion, or old solutions modified, but under such circumstances new solutions should simply be acted on as standard operating procedure.

Supervisory responsibility for operational units consists of keeping the unit's ability to initiate programmed solutions intact. Whatever problems arise in the course of operating the department, appropriate solutions are available to resolve them. However, solutions merely offer instruction for resolving such problems. Responsibility for operational effectiveness devolves on the supervisor. For example, all fiscal aspects of the department are directed by the chief fiscal officer, program factors are directed by the person in charge of the program division, and plant maintenance, design, or construction is directed by the appropriate supervisor.

If the supervisor has a thorough understanding of the operating manual (the solutions catalog), he maintains the required employee practices as set forth in the manual. If performance does not follow the operating manual, the supervisor makes whatever adaptations are required. If situations occur for which there are no solutions at hand, the supervisor issues a problem-originating form to the control unit. It is at the instructional level that solutions are changed from statement to performance. A major responsibility of the supervisor is to act as the intermediary between written instructions and employee behavior. Constant validation of employee practice as compared with operations procedures ensures that appropriate, prepared solutions are activated for organizational benefit.

Evaluation

Evaluation is a feedback procedure designed to examine current programs (or whatever the recreational service system produces for its clientele) to determine whether organizational output is as effective as had been expected. There are several techniques for determining the usefulness of a solution. A comparison can be made to discover whether the expected benefit and the actual benefit are at par or if a negligible difference exists. When excessive deviations are observed, the solution is deemed ineffective and a problem originates for the control unit. Another technique is actual observation of performance through visitation or inspection. Inspection is a non-scheduled, on-site appearance in order to determine whether something that is expected is really being performed. Visitation, on the other hand, is a regular on-site appearance for appraisal of performance. Problems may also originate because internal intelligence is operational, meaning that one unit complains that another unit is not performing in an expected or acceptable manner thereby compromising performance.

All activities are expected to eventuate in a specific output. For a recreational service department, the product is recreational services and programs designed to satisfy actual and potential clientele. When an organizational solution is expected to produce a particular attendance at a given activity, the actual attendance is compared to the estimated figure to determine the solution's capability.

Basically, the instrument of evaluation is selected on the basis of what is to be calculated or measured. If an appropriate measuring device cannot be found, the validity of the solution's effectiveness is suspect. Thus, the decision maker must provide the mechanism for actual measurement of outcomes. New instruments may have to be invented or old devices adapted so that accurate measurement can be established. One significant result of devising such a measuring procedure is that it stimulates the decision maker to specify his inputs and outputs accurately. If a solution's benefit cannot be calculated precisely, questions may be raised about whether its variables were exactly formulated during the investigation of the problem.

Information for determining the consequences of a solution generally is located in an organization's operating figures. When the organization utilizes electronic data processing machines, the EDP center can formulate procedures for identifying and sorting out the required data. With a competent internal cost system, it is feasible to define the input of any organizational solution. When such solutions can be measured or at least quantified as monetary needs, this is readily fixed. Thus, with combined input and output data, benefits can be measured. When working with people, some solutions cannot be quantified. Therefore another evaluative method must be found. In recreational service, only that phase of a solution amenable to calculation may have to be investigated. Individual performance evaluated by field visitation or inspection may be the required method. Retention of employees or rate of employee turnover may be the unit by which intangibles such as loyalty, morale, or individual dedication to the department may be measured.

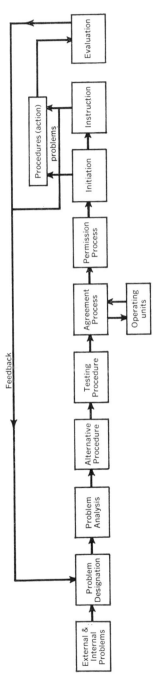

Figure 13-5. The management system.

All these procedural steps must have a connecting link. The control unit is the factor that assures coordination and sequential input from output and input. Thus, the complete system operates along integrated lines. The total system is illustrated in Figure 13-5.

CONVERSION TO AUTOMATED ADMINISTRATIVE SYSTEMS

Administrators continuously experiment with improved technology to increase efficiency, effectiveness, and economy. With the rapid advances made in computer technology and an array of management information systems from which to choose, it is not difficult to understand why more progressive departments, municipalities, and other governmental jurisdictions have decided to organize for automation. Within a relatively short period machines will be capable of performing many of the decision-making tasks that currently occupy the time of many middle- and upper-echelon administrators. Herbert Simon has indicated that such technological innovation as is operational may shortly relieve managers from the routine or programmed decision-making activities and offer them time to work out solutions to problems for which no program has been conceived.

> The area of programmed decision making is being rapidly extended as we find ways to apply the tools of operations research to types of decisions that have up to now been regarded as judgmental . . .[4]

Additionally, Simon states:

> With operations research and electronic data processing we have acquired the technical capacity to automate programmed decision making and to bring into the programmed area some important classes of decisions that were formerly unprogrammed . . .[5]

From these statements it would appear that the administrative position within the next several years should undergo considerable modification through adaptation of tools that can eliminate costly errors in personnel assignment, fiscal decisions, resource allocation, paperwork management, and other work of the department. Recreationist administrators should look forward to conversion to automated data processing systems within the management process, because such conversion can be of great benefit to them, the department, and ultimately the public.

Electronic Data Processing Conversion

The basic reason for introducing automated informational programs into any management situation is to improve the decision-making proc-

---

[4] Herbert A. Simon, *The New Science of Management Decision* (New York: Harper & Row Publishers, Inc., 1960), p. 20.
[5] *Ibid.*, p. 35.

ess. Essentially, electronic data processing may be useful in focusing attention on how and where to allocate scarce community resources among various means to achieve goals.

In order for successful conversion from traditional administrative decision-making procedures to electronic data processing, objectives must be defined, programs established to effect such objectives, demonstrable outputs and criteria available to indicate whether expectations have been satisfied, and objectives and programs perpetually analyzed and evaluated.

For optimum efficiency, evaluation of performance is necessary. This evaluation includes relative productivity, costs, and responsibility and should have a sharply remedial effect leading to a carefully screened and detailed budget system. Program evaluation supplies information interface, offers alternatives computed on a cost-benefit ratio, and encourages program ideas.

The structure of a program dealing with recreational services within a community may be analyzed by aims and standards, subprograms, and those components involved in existing performance. The aim of the basic program in recreational service is the provision of a comprehensive series of recreational opportunities for community residents. Standards are devised from available recreational services. The subprogram is geared to specific age groups or deals with particular program content such as art, crafts, special events, drama, music, social activities, and the like. The objective of the subprogram is to examine current and anticipated recreational needs within the community; to establish and initiate procedures for modifying such activities or devising and supplying additional recreational opportunities; and to maintain, promote, and operate current effective recreational activities and places. Thus, standards for the subprogram are the existence, dispersion, availability, and participation in a comprehensive and balanced program of recreational activities and such additional services as are required.

Allocation of Resources

The program evaluation methods utilized in reaching a decision for resource expenditures are determination of a problem and identification of the fundamental objective, describing and appraising alternatives in terms of economic expenditure, and, finally, devising a plan to solve the problem.

Problem determination develops as problems arise within the community or the organization. Once a problem is raised, the sequential process of solution begins. First, the salient features of the problem are described and identified. Thus, causes are defined, demographic studies are incorporated, if necessary, and the extent of the problem is determined. Objectives are set up and programs are formulated for resolving the problem. Determination is made as to what services are currently operated relative to the problem. Other community resources are examined for possible use in resolving the problem. Investigation discloses whether there are any paramount issues which might restrict problem solution with the currently available resources. Possible alternatives are studied for use in satisfying the problem. Identification of a problem merely indicates the issues involved and calls attention to data that are required prior to any attempt at solution.

Following determination of a problem, cost effectiveness must be examined. Measures of effectiveness, which permit calculation of progress compared to basic objectives, are chosen and should include qualifiable as well as quantifiable data. Identification and specification of the major characteristics of the alternative means of solving the problem are made. Assessments of the total cost (present and future) of each alternative are provided. The total effects (present and future) of each alternative are assessed. A sharply defined explanation of benefits to be received from among the alternatives, with reference to the costs and results as assessed previously, is obtained. Ascertainment of the chief doubts and the extent of these doubts, where possible, should be included. Recognition of the principal assumptions made in the investigation with a representation of the range to which program selections may be susceptible to these assumptions should be made. Justification and verification of the investigation, by appropriate research techniques so as to permit other people to appreciate what was performed in the analysis, should be presented. All cost-effectiveness studies should use methods that fit the need. Thus, operations research, economic analysis, mathematical concepts, and other pertinent investigatory techniques may be drawn upon for proper presentation. The cost-effectiveness investigation deals with the problems raised through internal or external means. After thorough analysis, the findings from a cost-effectiveness study should be compiled for use in the most suitable program structure.

Thus, a formalized system for assuring valid and reliable information necessary for making intelligent decisions becomes reality. Once analytic studies have been made, activities are grouped according to broad common objectives. The broad objective of a public recreational service system is the provision of recreational opportunities for all community residents. Then a public recreational service department will have several principal program classifications, each focused on a specific objective such as: recreational opportunities for certain age groups, maintenance of facilities, acquisition of land for recreational purposes, counseling or instruction in leisure arts and skills, and so forth. Each major category may have subprograms. Each program coordinates all components concerned with its fundamental objective. The program is studied to determine how effectively it satisfies the goals. The results of the program (output) are related to the costs of the program (input). If an economic valuation can be placed on the output (and this is sometimes impossible when dealing with personal satisfaction or enjoyment), the cost-benefit analysis is made.

Program plans are interpreted as monetary needs for the annual appropriation and accounting process. When all of the above-described procedures are operable, the system may be established. Conversion to electronic data processing and cost-benefit analysis is not an attempt to eliminate the human judgment and the intangible aspects from the decision-making process. Rather it is a means for effectuating better public services so that logical decisions may be made in allocating scarce resources, for substituting intelligent solutions for decisions based on emotion, and for resolving problems before they become emergencies.

From a variety of choices, an administrative system that can offer optimum benefits to the department and the community must be selected. How the selection is made will probably depend on the measurability of performance and the program currently produced by the organization. Performance is capable of appraisal and the outcome of the process of the system, recreational services, may be compared by expectations and actuality. Through a selection procedure that permits examination of personnel practice (behavior) and evaluation of product (program), an administrative system can be chosen that should represent practicality, certainty, constancy, computability, and optimum results.

Organization for Conversion

When a particular management system has been selected, it must be insinuated into the organization for operational effect. Absolutely vital to the success of any conversion process are the professional staff's acceptance of the new system and its conformity to the requirements that the system will impose on decision makers and problem solvers. Equally significant, but necessitating a lesser priority, are the cost factors and the amount or kind of derangement that installation of the new system may have on current operations.

To motivate employees so that they will accept the system and perform their tasks effectively to achieve success, a basic educational and accurate informational program should be implemented. The maintenance of employee morale may be the single most important factor determining the installation and operation of any new administrative system. The executive must do everything he can to remove the potential hostility from misinformation, anxiety, and a sense of futility which can be generated when a new management system is introduced.

Staff members at every level must be notified when the initial suggestions or recommendations for a new management system are being considered. Implicit in the educational program is the involvement of any and all potentially affected employees to participate in the design of the new system. Identification with the new system does much to enhance ego-satisfaction and reduces the shapeless fear of something that is unfamiliar or unknown. By seeking employee participation in the devisement of a new management system, most employees will probably realize the benefits. Personal involvement with the new plan invariably produces satisfaction in having participated in the preparation and development of personal ideas. Thus, employees will look upon the system as being "their" plan.

Organizational problems are always encountered whenever a new system is introduced to employees. However, if the new system can be shown to produce benefits that employees value, if the results of the system can be shown to enhance departmental service for increased community support, if a sound educational program is implemented, and if potentially affected employees are sought out for their opinions, suggestions, and efforts in the development of the new system, ready acceptance of the process can be accomplished.

Establishment of the System

Once the new process has been clarified, the most logical procedure is its establishment and employment. It is most effective to install the system on a sequential basis rather than in toto. The former method permits proper acquaintance with the new system, allows time for the adjustments necessary when employees are attempting to learn about new performance requirements, and enables this learning to occur faster.

Another basis for examining a sequential introduction is that the system's various components can be tried out, improved, or changed when and where necessary prior to the establishment of the next unit. Despite the purity of design and model, establishment and operation may indicate some needed corrections or modifications. Even in a sequential establishment, some minor disruptions may occur as the old system is phased out.

With the establishment of the system, departmental supervisors will have personal responsibility for the operational success of the system. The executive should reserve the permissions process as one monitoring aspect of the system. Supervisory participation is necessary because staff personnel will always require some assistance in determining solutions.

Faculty of the System

A significant feature of operating the system is the requirement of coping with the daily load of problems or input. System faculty is concerned with the endowment or power of a system to adjust to modifications in the quantity and nature of problems that it must resolve. Should the system prove of insufficient capacity, a bottleneck will develop as problems remain unresolved. Therefore, decision-making methods will have to be refined or altered to compensate for variations in problem input.

To a certain extent, the faculty of a system rests with the time that is required to perform the sequential steps in decision making. In a system that necessitates several procedures for devising a particular solution, the time factor of each of these steps will probably differ. In a specific situation the agreement component may require as much time as do all other operations combined. Under this condition, the only method of expediting solutions is by shortening the time taken for reaching agreements. Unless this is done, a backlog of problems piles up. The agreements procedure must be carefully analyzed and, perhaps, changed or streamlined so that problem input can be accommodated more swiftly.

Several techniques are effective in adjusting the system to problem variances. A repository for problems may be devised so that they can be processed in chronological order. The slowest operation may be modified so that it takes less time to process problems than it took formerly. Ultimately, it may be necessary to provide more alternative pathways at the point of stricture or to enlarge the system's capacity to perform.

Equalizing the time between steps remains a constant factor. Optimally, the capability of each suboperation, or number of pathways, should approximate each other so that the time allotted for each step would be equal. Whichever suboperation utilizes the most time requires that many additional personnel to speed the process. It will be better for the system if a mobile work force is available so that work assignments can be altered as need dictates. Thus, supervisory personnel may be reassigned to different phases of the department operation as conditions require. Overload is a problem in all systems, and, unless some harmony is sustained between suboperations, there is likelihood of breakdown or at least a high inventory of unresolved current problems.

Furnishing sufficient endowment for system operation indicates flexibility to assure movement of personnel where and when needed in terms of fluctuations in the character of problems. During any operational year, for example, the programming division's number of problems concerning public relations may increase whereas those dealing with action research may decrease. The control unit can plan its maximum allotment faculty, but a point will be reached where only additional personnel can create a balance. Thus, requests for additional personnel are channeled to the executive for action. The executive should be constantly alerted to the condition of the decision-making system by the control unit and should assign personnel to maintain equilibrium between problem input and solution output.

Systems analysis and management begin to reflect significance when a total system is developed and the subunits or components are seen in the context of a total system. Because components of the system can be readily identifiable, observed, and measured, a more logical approach to providing quality solutions to problems that are created within the department's environment is possible. There is an increasing dissatisfaction with the traditional principles for organizing the work of administrators. With an augmented intricacy of operations, with the need for problem solvers, and with the emergence of computers for quality information as well as quantifying data, an awareness is developing that the usual techniques for assigning the work of administrators may be obsolete. It is to this end that systems analysis is dedicated.

Selected References

Coyle, R. G.: *Management System Dynamics* (New York: John Wiley & Sons), 1977.

Davis, G. B. and G. Everest: *Readings in Management Information Systems* (New York: McGraw-Hill Book Company), 1976.

Enger, N. L.: *Management Standards for Developing Information Systems* (New York: American Management Association, Inc.), 1977.

Gross, P. and R. D. Smith: *Systems Analysis and Design for Management* (New York: Donnelley, Dunn Publishing Company), 1976.

Joslin, E. and R. Bassler: *Managing Data Processing* (Alexandria, Va.: College Readings, Inc.), 1976.

Kanter, J.: *Management Oriented Management Information Systems, 2d ed.* (Englewood Cliffs, N.J.: Prentice-Hall, Inc.), 1977.

Lawler, E. E. and J. G. Rhode: *Information and Control in Organizations* (Salt Lake City, Utah: Goodyear Publishing Co.), 1976.

Miller, D. W. and M. K. Starr: *Executive Decisions and Operations Research, 2d ed.* (Englewood Cliffs, N.J.: Prentice Hall, Inc.), 1969.

Schoderbek, P. B., and others: *Management System: Conceptual Considerations* (Homewood, Ill.: Business Publications), 1975.

Starr, M. K.: *Systems Management of Operations, rev. ed.* (Englewood Cliffs, N.J.: Prentice-Hall, Inc.), 1971.

CHAPTER 14

Office Management, Control, and Procedures in Public Recreational Service

A public recreational service system must routinely plan to satisfy present and future needs by recognizing what is to be done, when certain steps must be undertaken, where such action should be performed, and by arranging priorities for the completion of the work. Planning is essential if future outcomes are to be anticipated, thereby avoiding difficulties. It includes the identification of techniques necessary for efficient performance and an understanding of the logical steps that will produce optimized results for the department. The necessity for establishing an operating structure where the department may be coordinated and made to serve the community requires development of a central office to facilitate the work of the system.

A central office permits the establishment of a base of operations so that specific assignments can be apportioned among the various units and divisions of the system. It is in the central office that primary decisions typically affecting the total system are made. All office work is a service or facilitating function—the main medium through which the widespread efforts of the public recreational system are coordinated. All administrative functions depend on the convenience-producing assets of the office. A tremendous volume of factual data is required for intelligently planning and coordinating recreational service program, personnel, physical plant and equipment, and financial resources. Such information involves report writing, record keeping, and filing procedures for retrieval purposes which in turn necessitate office work. Whether a department is large or small, the need for a central office to channel requests, disseminate information, and maintain the records so vital in terms of public accountability remains.

Additionally, management requires appraisal and evaluation practices so that a determination may be made as to how closely predetermined objectives have been approximated. Furthermore, the technical function of each division within the department is implemented, integrated, and kept informed by communication processes necessitating office work.

OFFICE MANAGEMENT AND CONTROL

Office work facilitates the operation of the system, and it is performed chiefly to promote the efforts of the divisions of the system. It is a staff function because it assists the personnel of other units to carry out their jobs more effectively, economically, and efficiently by removing many of the routine and time-consuming tasks normally associated with recording, filing, making reports, transcribing statistics, and by supplying whatever information is required to various divisions for their use. Office work is essentially handling and managing paper work. Although it constitutes a large portion of the work performed in public agencies, by reason of legal requirements, the work of the office is not directly concerned with the line function of the department, rather it contributes indirectly to the over-all success of the operation by servicing the components with records, statistics, files, and internal communication.

Office work should be judged by the consequences of the tasks it carries out. It is not an end in itself but is a medium by which the recreational services, generated by the system, may be expedited and offered to the public. Office work may be analyzed and appraised readily. It may be divided into several segments for easier examination and determination as to whether it is accomplishing the purposes that it was originally intended to perform. The whole concept of management—organizing, coordinating, controlling, planning, and directing—thus may be imposed on the work of the office.

The functions of office management may be outlined best as:

1. Establishment of a useful office organization
    a. Functions determined and proper personnel deployed
    b. Specified lines of hierarchical relationships
    c. Delegation of authority and responsibility for execution of work
    d. Definite assignment of responsibility among workers
2. Maintenance of physical facilities and design of office
    a. Physical layout and arrangement of space, supplies, equipment, and furniture
    b. Environmental planning: heating, light, ventilation, control of noise, and appropriate interior decoration
3. Identification of needed furnishings, material, supplies, and equipment
4. Purchase of specified office equipment, material, and furnishings

5. Development and maintenance of appropriate information services
   a. Report writing, record keeping, and filing
   b. Stenographic and other correspondence work
   c. Reception or information functions
   d. Public relations center
6. Management of office personnel
   a. Position analysis and job description
   b. Selection, orientation, and assignment
   c. In-service education and development, supervision, and promotion
   d. Discipline
   e. Salary and/or wage administration
   f. Safety practices
7. Technical improvement of office practices
   a. Work simplification
   b. Criteria for performance
   c. Analysis of time and motion studies for better efficiency
8. Control of office output
   a. Planning, organizing, and scheduling of assignments
   b. Development of standardized work procedures and manuals of practice
   c. Analysis of costs, control of expenditures, and budget making

Not all of these office management functions are carried out in every recreational service system. The ramifications of office work and its management depend on the size of the department: how extensive the area and work of the system, the number of personnel employed in the system, and the need for coordinating diverse and far-flung units of the department. In one-man departments the chief executive considers himself fortunate if he can obtain the service of a full-time secretary. He must usually content himself with a part-time "girl Friday." Therefore, the administrator must spend a considerable portion of his time handling routine paper work that a clerk would be able to perform better. Small departments often have insufficient money to employ specialists who can perform the tasks that are typically concerned in office management. The executive must be prepared to function accordingly. As a result, necessary office management functions typically are curtailed or, at the very least, they are not used in the most efficient manner. In larger departments, the employment of a director of central office may be necessary if an entire cycle of office activity is carried out by a variety of office personnel whose work is essential to the successful accomplishment of the system's purpose. In the largest departments, there is a tendency to appoint a specialist who is responsible for the management of all office work. He may combine a variety of functions including that of controller, business director, or personnel manager, but he has the responsibility for managing the work of the central office.

Office Organization

The organization of an office can be understood most easily by its relation to the system as a whole. The office provides a facilitating or staff service to the entire system. For this reason it is vital that the functions of the recreational service be kept uppermost in mind to understand how office activities lend themselves most realistically and effectively. Since office work is done in almost every unit of the department, it follows that the responsibility for such activity should be associated with the individual who is in executive control of the department. In this manner, the total benefits to be derived from office work permeate the entire system. Therefore, whoever manages the office should report directly to the chief executive of the department. The office manager is one of the major staff personnel who can give precise counsel and make recommendations to the superintendent concerning more facilitating services throughout the department.

Office work may be performed at a centralized or decentralized location. It is possible to have such work done at the various units of the system or to have a centralized office where all of the functions of paper work and communication within the department are executed. Centralization means concentration of diverse activities into a single group with a clearly identifiable person responsible for performance. For all, if not almost all, public recreational service departments, whether they operate far-flung properties and employ hundreds or even thousands of personnel, or only a few people within a small department, the utilization of a centralized office is probably of greater advantage than decentralization.

Since the question of centralization or decentralization is often proposed in the development of offices, it is best to point out the obvious advantages of each form. In centralization the following advantages are obvious:

1. Specialists may be employed to perform particular functions at which they become particularly adept. They are continuously employed to work to maximum extent.
2. Adaptability to changing needs is facilitated. Peak loads of work can be handled more easily and office machinery may be used more efficiently, thereby bringing down per unit costs of operation.
3. Wage and salary schedules may be apportioned more equitably, since equal pay for equal work is easily determined. The measurement of office production is encouraged.

4. On-the-job staff development is expedited and made more efficient. Additional employees may be added to the office force without retarding the work of employees. The preparation of employees for new positions is accomplished more easily in centralized offices.
5. Office procedure and practice may be applied more evenly and swiftly. Common standards of work and operations that affect the entire system may be implemented with little delay. Modifications and improvements in work practices may be accomplished more rapidly without undue friction or wasted effort.
6. Monetary expenditures for office equipment, supervisory staff, materials, supplies, floor space, and maintenance are reduced.

The advantages of decentralization are:

1. Confidentiality is protected because what needs to be maintained or handled separately, for reasons of trust or personal security, can be performed by the unit responsible.
2. Separately maintained files are utilized by the unit that must have access to information and whose personnel are most familiar with the necessary details. Corrections of whatever nature may be made immediately.
3. Work is performed on a priority basis and delays are minimized. The operating efficiency of each division is thereby kept at an optimum level.
4. A significant amount of time may be saved by not having to transmit important information from one office or division to another. Routing of paper work is time consuming, which may be negated when material and personnel dealing with it remain within the area of the division.
5. The development of "generalist" personnel capable of handling diverse problems may be the consequence of decentralization. Individuals who have broadened capacities to perform are probably necessary in every department.

A combination of the two types is realistically a matter of practicality. In a combined form, almost all of the advantages listed for each type would be in effect. Confidentiality can be maintained where necessary. Important materials can be kept close at hand, thereby reducing delays. The best filing procedure can be applied to the centralized components. The operation of a main office influences the practices utilized. Thus, filing, computer use, mail, and correspondence are typically handled on a partly centralized basis. Where divisions of the system are widely distributed throughout a metropolitan area, it may be necessary to maintain individual office layouts with all of the factors involved in the design of the office. In this instance combinations of types are more applicable.

It is likely that the director of the central office will prove invaluable in setting up and/or arranging for the organization of office work on these far-flung units. Valuable staff assistance and guidance may be furnished by the office manager about the portions of office work that must be decentralized.

Office Divisions

For purposes of clarification, it is necessary to indicate the major units that make up the activities of the central office. As previously indicated, the individual responsible for the central office is the administrative head of one of the divisions of the department or system. For this discussion, a large recreational service department will be depicted in order to illustrate the functions and activities that comprise the division. Of the three major divisions of the department—planning and its ramifications, programming and its ramifications, and administration with its component features—a chart shows relationship and organization more easily. Figure 14-1 indicates the major divisions into which the department is divided. Figure 14-2 shows the ramifications of the office and business administration division. This division is composed of an administrator or director and three sections composing the division: office management and clerical section, public relations and information section, and the financial section. Subsections are composed of personnel services, main office, and district office. The latter indicates the influence of decentralized practices within the system. The subsection of the finance and purchasing indicates the nature of activities conducted by this component.

It is not the function of this text to enumerate and detail the complete workings of office management procedures and practices but simply to indicate that there is an important division within the organizational structure of a public recreational service system. Generally, all public departments, whether large or small, require some office practice. If such practices are not undertaken, only confusion and misadventure result. As systems grow larger and are more widely distributed within a metropolitan region, the necessity for implementing good office management

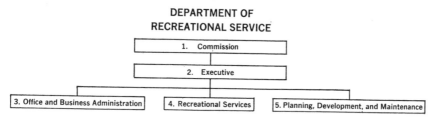

Figure 14–1.   Major divisions of a recreational service department.

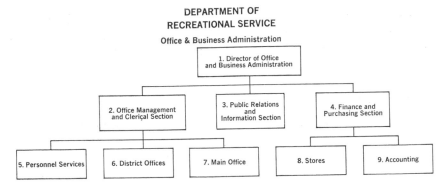

Figure 14–2. Sections and subsections of office and business administration division
of a recreational service department.

and control activities is even more striking. Often overlooked in the
establishment of the office management division is, perhaps, the essential reason for its existence—control. Control is the method by which the
work of the office is expedited and, in fact, is the influence that sees to
the actual performance of the functions of the office.

The effective output of any office is regulated by the methods and
procedures developed for the operating efficiency of the division and the
system as a whole. It is the central office administrator, for example,
working in coordination with other divisional administrators, who develops the standardized forms on which records and reports of the
system are maintained. The central office is responsible for the working
up of whatever manuals are required for the most effective personnel performance throughout the system. Additionally, standard operating procedures are researched and implemented to accomplish office-related
work. The management of paper work, the sequential steps or stops that
any routine or extraordinary record, report, or correspondence must pass
prior to taking action, is reviewed for time-saving and work-saving simplification. Whatever intermediate steps can be omitted, consolidated,
or improved are acted upon.

Constant thought and consideration must be focused on departmental
organization so that the most effective structure can be designed to accomplish the purpose of the system. Although the organization of
central offices does not conform to any preconceived model because of
the different needs of local departments, there are universally recognized principles which may be applied. In general, office management
and business administration rely on certain principles that, when followed,
tend to produce effective, efficient, and economical operations. Good
office management practices are basic to a logically developed organiza-

tion. Depending on local conditions and requirements, effective office organization assists in the maximized achievement of goals determined to be fundamental to the existence of the recreational service system.

OFFICE SITUATION

Physical facilities and placement of the office are significant considerations in accomplishing the work to be done. Office situation and the development of sound physical factors to accommodate the volume and exigencies of the work must be given attention.

Office Location

Most public recreational service system offices are located without any regard to the essential needs of the system and usually by expediency only. Recreational service departments typically have been "Johnnie-come-latelies" to the municipal or county function in the jurisdictions where they operate. For this reason, if for no other, space was allotted from what was available, rather than on the basis of logical office management considerations. It is not surprising to find the central recreational service department office in the basement or under the eaves of a town hall or other municipal building. It even may be possible to determine the prestige that the recreational service system has within the local governmental family by its office assignment. The less well-thought-of department in governmental circles is more likely to be relegated to some boiler room, attic storage space, or forgotten supply room. When the public department of recreational service is accommodated in a physical environment equal to that of other members of the governmental family, it may be said to have arrived. When careful plans have been made for the development of a centralized office, it is not unusual to find that the department has its own office building, or at least is situated in quarters that prove eminently satisfactory to the production of the work it must carry out.

A number of factors should account for the selection of office location and whether a suite of rooms or a separate building is required. Among the most important considerations are:

1. Physical space and property available
2. Accessibility of the proposed office area to citizens, other governmental agencies, and personnel
3. Capital expenditures for acquiring the property, constructing an appropriate facility, or renovating an already existing structure or office so that it can accommodate the needs of the recreational service department.

11

4. Environmental factors: heat, lighting, ventilation, distracting noise, freedom from disturbing conditions including dust, dirt, or continuous in and out traffic

5. General appearance of the proposed facility and adaptability of the space available.

All these factors impinge on whether or not a building can or should be constructed to house the central administration of the recreational service system. In large metropolitan centers it is likely that the diverse needs and size of the department will cause a demand for a separate office facility whereby the far-flung activities of the system may be coordinated and effectuated best. Medium-sized departments may also have their own building (usually office space in a centrally situated recreational facility such as a boathouse, field house, auditorium, or recreational center). In other instances the department will be housed in a central municipal building in which all other components of city government are also found. In the latter case a suite of offices or one or more floors of the building may be given over to the needs of the system. Space needs vary depending on the work to be performed by a central office and overhead administration. Small departments or one-man departments are seldom housed in any but a few rooms in a city or town hall. In extremely fortuitous circumstances a small department may acquire a facility that can be renovated to suit its needs as a central office, doubling as a meeting place and conference facility where commission hearings may be held. A great deal depends on the status the department enjoys within the community it serves as well as the financial support it may call upon for the acquisition and development of suitable office space.

Office Equipment

To perform the diverse function of the central office, suitable furniture, equipment, and machines in proper working condition must be made available so that operations may be carried out at optimum efficiency. The central office should not be called on to attain its fullest potential output unless employees are provided with the appropriate supplies, materials, and equipment to accomplish their responsibilities. Equipping an office is not merely a question of physical means for achieving administrative tasks, it is also a psychologically motivating factor, because the atmosphere produced by supplying the correct means for carrying out responsibilities stimulates cooperative behaviors and induces the necessary employee attitudes for efficient work.

The utilization of technologically advanced machinery and equipment has contributed in no little magnitude to the increased capacity of the central office of public recreational systems to fulfill their responsibilities.

Adequate consideration must therefore be given to the types of equipment available, their respective costs, the maintenance costs, and the actual work processes that will profit most by being adapted to automatic, or at least machine, attachment. The decision to use a piece of equipment should be based on the individual requirements necessitating its adoption. Not all office functions require mechanization. Only when there is constant repetitive work will such obvious necessity make partial or complete automation desirable. The question as to whether a certain type, size, or unit of machine should be purchased must be evaluated on the basis of need, number required, speed of production, accuracy obtainable, cost, and other factors.

The adaptation of machine technology to office work serves several important conditions. The chief consideration is the work to be done and the method by which it must be accomplished. Careful analysis of the work situation, space needs, environmental conditions, initial costs, maintenance costs, and production achieved plays a part in deciding what routine or special work assignments can or should be mechanized. Time and motion studies also aid in the purchase of non-mechanized furniture or equipment. Desks, tables, chairs, and cabinets should be selected for their comfort, convenience, cost, dependability, and appropriateness. A final consideration is the effect that office machinery, equipment, and furniture, as well as office layout and decor, have on the personnel and their requirements. In some cases, the installation of new furnishings, equipment, and physical arrangement may modify the requirements for the number of personnel and their respective skill levels. Wherever machines can be employed to replace time-consuming, repetitive, and monotonous work they should be. A work force that does not have to perform boring assignments is more productive in the tasks for which they have responsibility and some discretion.

Types of Machines, Equipment, Furniture, and Supplies. Among the kinds and types of office furnishings are basic and universally recognized items: desks, chairs, tables, files, office machines, carpeting, typewriters, air-conditioning systems, communication machines, and the like. All these items may be found in any reasonably well-run office. In recent years more technical equipment has been introduced, such as copiers, computers, and dictation and other machines. In designating furnishings and equipment for the modern office, types of machines and the uses to which they will be put should be analyzed. Various types of chairs and the features associated with each should be studied so that suitable seating may be provided for both office personnel and visitors. Office desks, the work place of many office employees, should be of a type and size that most adequately care for the needs of personnel and their work. Desks should be designed so that their dimensions, height, appearance, and arrangement of parts meet individual requirements.

Filing equipment comes in a variety of shapes, sizes, and costs. Depending on use, file equipment of the common vertical cabinet type for manual use or motorized equipment that accommodates thousands of individual entries on cards, punched in code, that provide essential information with the flick of a switch are available. Visible reference equipment may be indexed strips, folders that are hung and turned on a cylinder, rotary filing, or other forms that may or may not be mechanized. Punch card machines, tabulating machines, accounting machines, adding machines, calculators, reproducing machines, typewriters of various kinds, addressing machines, and, of course, computers all fall into the category of office equipment that has a considerable influence on the amount, accuracy, and cost of providing information, storing data, transmitting questions, or supplying answers in the modern office.

Physical Office and Working Conditions

Surely office furnishings, equipment, and materials are of great importance to the efficiency of the operation but also of great significance is the physical arrangement or layout of the office and the level or quality of working conditions therein.

The provision and maintenance of suitable and sufficient physical work space and situation are of considerable influence in the operation of a successful office. The physical environment should be pleasing, comfortable, and psychologically appropriate to office staff and visitors to maximize output in relation to the expense of producing a positive climate for work performance. The most frequently considered factors of the physical working environment with respect to work are the effects of light, color scheme, ventilation, noise, upkeep against dirt, and distracting influences.

Lighting seems to be one of the most important physical elements to be considered in office facilities. Depending on the type of work to be performed, whether it be close as in transcribing shorthand notes, discrimination of fine detail as in art work or illustrating, bookkeeping, accounting, drafting, and tabulation, or in the ordinary tasks of walking in halls or stairwells and the like, an adequate quantity of light is required so that the performance of work is unhindered and therefore most efficient. Lighting engineers are best able to offer advice and guidance on the kinds and types of illumination required for the variety of office practices. Fixtures, contrasts, sources, and arrangement of the lighting system necessitate the consultation of an electrical engineer or illuminating engineer who can recommend the best artificial lighting systems in consideration of all factors concerned with the office.[1]

---

[1] Illuminating Engineering Society, *IES Lighting Handbook* (New York: The Society, 1947), pp. 10,50–10,60.

Color schemes also have a direct effect on the work force. No one wants to work in a drab office. Harmonious colors selected for their appropriate effect on people should be chosen. Colors can have a stimulating, restraining, cheerful, or depressing effect on those who are subjected to them.[2] The selection of colors should be reflected in the kind of work performed and the area in which it is done. Also included in any selection should be the factor of exposure to natural light which varies in intensity and tone. Depending on the work area, appropriate colors should be chosen.[3]

Temperature control, air circulation, moisture content, and cleanliness are basic conditions regulating atmospheric conditions within the office. Aside from health and comfort, controlled temperature or air conditioning, including proper ventilation, has surprising economic advantages. Office workers are much more likely to produce a greater volume of work and a more reliable body of material when they are comfortable on the job. It is almost impossible for office workers to concentrate on their work at hand when they feel uncomfortable.

Noise or discordant sound produces effects that are not well calculated to maintain an efficient office. It is distracting, unpleasant, and destructive of work effectiveness, therefore it is costly to maintain. It is therefore economical to install sound conditioning elements in the office, which may include baffles in ceilings or walls, acoustic materials in walls, floors, or ceilings to dampen the effects of noise. Noise-producing machinery should be segregated. Furniture and the physical office should be arranged to deaden discordant sound. The effects of noise on the performance of employees is explained in the following statement:

> Office noises, according to physicians and psychiatrists, may cause many physical disorders such as increased pulse rate and irregular rhythm of the heart, transient changes in blood and brain pressure, and, most common of all, disturbances of digestion. It is a grave error to speak of "getting used to noise." While one may not momentarily be aware of its effect, the result is evidenced by the fact that individuals whose work, as such, is not laborious, are completely tired out at the end of eight hours. It is the biological reaction to the tenseness they are under to do their job with any kind of application.[4]

Space requirements and utilization of available space are two of the chief conditioning factors in the physical development of an office. The

[2] Robert C. Daly, "The Power of Color," *Buildings* (Cedar Rapids, Iowa: Stamats Publishing Co., 1951), p. 28.

[3] Faber Birren, *Functional Color* (New York: Crimson Press, 1937), pp. 36–55, 87–108.

[4] George H. Sherwood, "The Noise Factor in Office Fatigue," *The Journal of Accountancy* (New York: The American Institute of Accountants, September, 1946), p. 252.

amount of space desired or needed and the arrangement of the interior so that maximized functional usage is obtained can be considered as critical items.[5] Essentially, the layout of the office deals with available space and the practical placement of furnishings and equipment. Layout involves such diverse conditions as traffic patterns into and out of the office, work flow, and functional use of space without waste.[6] Generally the physical arrangement of any office may be designed on the basis of:

1. A chart or blueprint of the office area
2. An understanding of the kinds of work to be performed in the office
3. Analysis of work flow
4. Identification of traffic patterns in relation to entrances, exits, waiting rooms and the like
5. Identification of the different work groups using the office
6. Determination of the number, size, and type of physical units to be placed
7. Formulation of functional design on the basis of scale models or the use of templates with identifying types clearly marked
8. Arrangement of the office through model manipulation until the most effective and functional use of space is reached
9. Ascertaining that traffic patterns conform to appropriate areas so that visitors do not conflict with the continual movements of office employees. Conversely, employee traffic should not restrict visitor movement
10. Re-evaluation of the entire design to ascertain whether or not all office functions and traffic flow are suitably taken care of by the physical arrangement.

Careful treatment should be given to space requirements for the types of furnishings, equipment, and office space necessary for the comfort, convenience, and functional utility of the work force within reasonable cost. The need for segregated office space for executive and administrative personnel should also be accounted for in the layout. General office workers may have access to the largest space available in one room or in partitioned spaces. The layout of the office must reflect a design that will assist in gaining the greatest output from the office staff thereby minimizing per capita costs. Features such as window space, power outlets, entrances and exits, support columns, railings, or individual offices must be considered in the physical development of the central office of the system.

[5] Jay S. Shivers and George Hjelte, *Planning Recreational Places* (Cranbury, N.J.: Associated University Presses, Inc., 1971), p. 85.
[6] Shivers and Hjelte, *op. cit.*, pp. 86–93.

OFFICE PROCEDURES

To achieve effective operation of the public recreational service department, superintendents and their subordinates must have factual records to serve as a basis for planning future work, to appraise current performance, and to evaluate the system as a whole. Efficient management of the system is founded on written accounts of situations and occurrences. Valid information must be obtained, examined, disseminated, and deposited for reference when necessary. When records and reports are not faithfully compiled and correctly filed for retrieval, they may not be conveniently available for their many uses. The filing procedure, proper record and report forms, written data, and available pertinent information are essential for the orderly and effective management and administration of a department and the system that it represents.

Records are the factual bases on which an accounting of the work done is made to higher authority and to the public. They are invaluable as reference material for administrators and office employees to use in performing their respective duties, in fact, they are the basis of administrative action. The recorded information is used as reference material in planning facilities and programs and in evaluating personnel performance.

Although the form of some records is regulated by law or by higher authority, the form of most reports and records of the recreational service system is left to the discretion of the department itself. It is impossible to set forth the form of all written material kept by recreational service departments because of the wide variation in plans of organization and in the size and function of the departments. However, a sampling of the kinds of forms that may be utilized is provided as well as the information that should be logged on any given record.

Records have several significant purposes for the administration and general program of recreational activities:

1. *To provide valid evidence.* Proper records deal with the actual happenings and outcomes that occur in the daily operation of the department. Mere opinion or approximation need not be relied on for records present the facts.
2. *To indicate the status of the department.* Records make it possible to understand why the department was established, what authority it has, what its structure is, what position it holds within the municipal organization (or other governmental auspice), whether it is developing, maintaining *status quo,* or is inadequate. Levels of achievement may be ascertained and indications of various aspects of the operation may be evaluated or determined.
3. *To detect inefficiency, duplication of other agency services, and errors.* Records assist in the determination of efficient and effec-

tive service. They provide the tools whereby measurement may be made between standard and substandard performance. They help to evaluate the department in terms of goals set and actual attainment.

4. *To afford a basis for compliance with legal regulations.* Records are valid evidence of the current operation of the department. They provide the required written information pertaining to custodianship of and accounting for public funds and property. They may be utilized in litigation cases in which accidents, fraud, or misfeasance, malfeasance, or nonfeasance may be a central issue. They may be the instruments whereby tax assessments are made, insurance benefits paid, and gifts, bequests, or awards donated.

5. *To effect comparisons.* The consequences of operating the department and providing a program of recreational activities may be appreciated and evaluated more readily by comparison with other departments. Certain standards have been established as a basis for such measurement. The service performed by the recreational system can be evaluated by comparing these criteria with what has actually been produced and noting any deviation from good practice. In this way, too, contemporary practices in comprehensive and balanced programming can be appraised. Both the quality and the quantity of opportunities may thus be brought under scrutiny.

6. *To provide a basis for policy formulation and orientation.* Examination of the records by recreationists offers a better understanding of why certain activities succeed and others fail. Analysis tends to reveal the strengths and weaknesses of the program and the current operation of the system. From this analysis comes the origin for many policy decisions, modifications in programs, and better service to the public.

The essential records and reports for a recreational service system are determined by the size of the department. In large metropolitan departments and in those having complete control of their funds and operations, records ordinarily kept by the city treasurer, controller, engineer, or other city officials may have to be kept by the department of recreational service. The records discussed below might conceivably be utilized under any form of organization. Records related to legal governing commissions are also given. Records are described in relation to the superintendent, finance, supplies, property, legal matters, personnel, and program.

Commission Records

Commission Minutes. The minutes of commission meetings constitute official authority for the work which the department performs. In the minutes are contained the enunciations of policy, the instructions to administrators, the approval of administrators' reports, and decisions of a particular nature regarding many details which have come before the board for consideration.

The minutes should state where and at what time each meeting took place, what members were present, when each arrived and departed, and whether any member or members did not remain for the entire meeting. They should contain a clear and concise statement of each action taken with a record of the vote of each member on every motion. They should mention briefly reports and correspondence received and their contents. Each report and communication should be given a reference number so that it can be readily produced from the files and its full contents examined.

When the minutes have been approved, they become the official record of the meeting and may not be changed. They are of such importance that they should be carefully indexed and bound. The loose-leaf form is usually preferred and then is accurately paged and permanently bound at the end of the year. The minutes should be kept only in the official office of the commission and should not be removed therefrom except on order of the commission and should be kept under lock.

Board Correspondence. The correspondence of the commission often relates to matters on which some statement of policy or some decision is required. All letters, reports, memoranda, or other papers that refer to a single problem are assembled, fastened together, and constitute a file on the given subject. It is usually advisable to keep the board files separate from the general operating files of the department, both because of their great importance as official original records and because they frequently need to be reproduced on short notice. These files are sometimes referred to by the superintendent, secretary, or other person as they work on the problems involved. It is advisable to keep a record of their assignment and to check them periodically.

Agreements and Contracts. A special file should be kept for copies of all legal contracts and agreements or other obligations or commitments of the board. These have dates of expiration or rental due dates or dates when notice is to be given. A calendar of such dates should be kept by the secretary.

Reports to the Commission. The commission receives official reports from the superintendent and from others, usually through the superintendent. It also prepares or causes to be prepared reports for transmittal to other commissions or officials. Both types of reports should be indexed and become a part of the commission records. Important portions of them, if not their entire contents, should be recorded in the minutes.

Policies and Legal Opinions. Various individual actions taken by the commission are expressions of official policy, as are legal opinions of the city attorney or other duly constituted legal advisers. They should be assembled in a cumulative file so that there may be a complete compendium of legal opinions and policies.

Superintendent's Records

All records of the department are in a general sense the records of the superintendent even though they may refer to matters regularly delegated to others. The superintendent keeps for his own reference a record of instructions given him by the commission, reports to the commission, and instructions issued to personnel. The instructions to personnel are often compiled in an instruction manual which should be kept up to date and in such form as to permit convenient reference and frequent additions or amendments.

Financial Records

Budget. A record of the current budget and of previous budgets, broken down according to various segregations, is essential. A monthly memorandum showing encumbrances against each segregation and unencumbered balances should be made part of this record.

Register of Encumbrances. The register of encumbrances is an original record of all authorized encumbrances. Each encumbrance is charged against its proper budget segregation and corrected as its actual amount is found to differ from the original estimate. A working balance of unencumbered funds is also kept and is the record from which the monthly memorandum report (see above) is compiled. Operating policies are often affected by comparisons of such data.

Register of Cash Receipts or Income. Although all cash received must usually be deposited daily with the city treasurer, an original register or ledger should be kept in which the individual items of income are recorded as received. From this register, weekly or monthly memorandum reports should be prepared in which the amount of cash received under each type of operation is compared with the estimated revenues.

Duplicates of Original Receipts. All cash received by the recreational service department is recorded in duplicate on numbered receipt forms or by cash register, turnstile, meter, or other mechanical device. Carbon copies of the numbered receipts or original certified records of the mechanical devices—such as cash register tapes—should be kept.

Cash Transmittal Forms. Income deposited with the city treasurer is recorded on a transmittal form showing the amount and source. The treasurer either returns an acknowledged copy of this form or issues a receipt based on it. These are kept as the official department record.

Payroll. The payroll is a prescribed form showing the names of all employees to whom payments of salaries and wages are to be made by the treasurer at the rate indicated thereon, and the hours worked. It must be certified as correct by the superintendent. Payrolls are submitted weekly, bi-monthly, or monthly in accordance with general practice. It is usually the practice to transmit payrolls to the auditor who checks them against available funds. A copy is sent to the civil service department, if there is one, which checks each name against legal employment records. The total payroll is also broken down into charges against each of the several budget segregations. Duplicate copies of payrolls are kept by the department.

Record of Financial Operations.   The original record of financial operations, showing receipts and disbursements in various segregations, is kept by the auditor. This record is sufficient for the recreational service department; copies of it showing monthly and yearly operations are kept by the department for reference. The registers of receipts and encumbrances will correspond roughly if not exactly with the operation statements. The official operating statement requires some time to compile and decisions that result in the expenditure of funds or receipt of income often have to be made on the basis of the information contained in the registers of receipts and encumbrances.

Capital Account Records.   These records show the investment made by the government in land, buildings, other structures and equipment of a permanent nature used by the department. They are kept by the auditor, but copies are sent to each department annually.

Insurance Policies.   Property of the several departments of a city is often insured by order of the city council. Policy concerning insurance is usually determined for the entire city government by the city council. Each department, however, should keep a record of its insurance policies, including the expiration dates, coverage, premiums, and the like.

Supply Records

Inventory of Stores.   Most recreational service departments maintain a central store of supplies from which the various centers may draw. Records of consignments received by the store, disbursements or deliveries made from stock, and a periodic inventory must be kept. These records are necessary to determine the cost of supplying each center, to enable needs to be anticipated, and to discourage waste.

Delivery Records.   Many items of supply or equipment are delivered directly to recreational centers without being cleared through the central storeroom. It is necessary to have a record in the central office of these deliveries in order to be able to certify that goods purchased have been received in good order and that they are according to specifications. The center concerned usually receives a copy of the purchase order which certifies delivery, and returns it to the central office. Similar records of deliveries to the central storeroom are transmitted to the office by the person in charge of stores.

Specifications for Standard Supplies. Many items of supply are standard. Detailed specifications for these should be compiled and kept available for use when new requisitions and purchase orders are issued. These specifications may be altered from time to time as the supplies are tested in use.

Property and Equipment Records

Land Records. Land used by a recreational service department is owned not by the department but by the municipal corporation. Original deeds, easements, or grants in trust are kept by the city clerk, but copies or digests of all such documents should be kept by the department.

The department should also have on file sketches—or preferably plane table surveys—of all lands under its jurisdiction, showing dimensions, elevations or contours, and locations to scale of all excavations, fills, buildings, structures, pipelines, sewers, and drains. These records should be kept strictly up to date so that decisions may be made in the office concerning various problems without necessitating a trip to the area. It is particularly important to record the location of underground installations when they are made, otherwise great expense in locating and tracing them in order to make repairs may have to be incurred later.

The history of the acquisition of parcels of land is another important record. It should show the manner in which the land was acquired, the date, cost, financing, and any other pertinent data.

Records of Buildings and Structures. The recreational service department should keep a record of all buildings, structures, landscaping, improvements to grounds and equipment, and ground layout in the form of blue prints, working drawings, and typed specifications properly dated and certified. The cost of construction should be broken down into cost of materials, labor, and the like, and an account of when and how the buildings and other improvements were constructed should be part of the record. The record should also show what separate recreational facilities exist at each center.

Equipment, Furniture, and Fixture Inventory. Whatever equipment, furniture, and fixtures are provided at each center should be recorded in a property inventory. Removable articles of equipment, such as desks, tables, and file cases, should be numbered and a tag or plate with the number and name of the department should be affixed to them. Tools and removable fixtures may have the department name or initials stamped or painted on them.

Legal Records

The legal records of a recreational service department should include copies of state laws affecting recreational service departments, the city charter, the city ordinances, court orders (if any of direct application to the department), legal opinions rendered by authorized advisers (usually city attorneys), and instructions issued by legal advisers on legal procedures.

Personnel Records

Personal Information about Employees. There should be on file a card for each employee in the department giving age, sex, address, and other personal information, professional preparation (if any), previous experience, official status in the department, and date of employment. The employee's cumulative department record, including vacations, leaves of absence, absences due to illness, accidents, additional education, assignments, disciplinary measures, and special achievements or commendations should be recorded on this card or in another convenient form.

Schedule of Assignments. The assignment of every employee should be recorded in convenient form and should show where and during what hours the employee is scheduled to work. This record should be classified according to places of employment and cross indexed on the individual personnel record cards.

Time Records. Original time sheets or cards are required in most departments for each employee. These records show the exact time that the employee has worked and are certified by the employee's immediate superior. Various payroll computations based on the time worked and the rate of compensation become part of the record.

Applications for Employment. Most applications for employment are of no record value, but those of persons whose services might some day be required should be kept classified for ready reference.

Fidelity Bonds. Certain employees who handle funds should be under bond. The bonds are usually prescribed by the city council or the auditor but record of them, as to amount, what they cover, name of the underwriters, date of expirations and cost, should be on file in the department. The cost of securing bonds is usually borne by the department.

Transportation. Some employees travel in department automobiles from place to place in the line of duty. Frequently they travel in their own automobiles, in which case they are reimbursed for their expense on a mileage basis. In either case records of their destinations and original odometer records are necessary. Odometer records are as important for mileage reimbursement as are time records for payroll purposes.

Program and Attendance Records

Program Instructions and Policies. A recreational service department is continually issuing instructions, announcing policies, and making suggestions concerning what activities may be conducted and in what manner. These instructions should be combined in convenient form and classified according to the activities to which they refer. They form the basis for an activity manual. These manuals are sometimes published so that the instructions may be conveniently available at the several recreational centers. In some departments the activity manual and the administrative manual are combined, but this is often unwise because the activity program is constantly changing. Moreover, the volume of suggestive program material is so great that it tends to encumber the manual.

Master Calendar of Events. Certain events and occasions are prescribed by the department for general observance and determine the programs of each center. They constitute a master calendar or program and should be published for the information of all concerned.

Weekly or Seasonal Forecasts. Just as the superintendent and supervisors set up a yearly program for the entire department, so the staff at each center prepares a weekly or seasonal forecast of events. They should be filed with the office, not only to provide information of what and when events are expected to take place but also to encourage systematic planning by the staff.

Weekly Reports from Recreational Centers. Each center is usually required to file a weekly record. These records are compiled into consolidated reports of the entire department and enable executives to keep in close touch with what is happening at each center. They should be on standard forms drawn up in such manner as to enable essential information to be recorded plainly and with a minimum of effort. No information should be on the record which is not likely to be put to important use afterward. The specific information that a supervisor or superintendent requires from each center weekly is:

1. Name of each employee and record of his hours at work at the center. This may or may not represent the total time worked. If some of his work was performed at another place, that will appear elsewhere in the record. Occasions arise when it is necessary to find out who was on duty at a given center. The original record on the weekly report is of value for this purpose. It also enables other information on the form to be interpreted in terms of who was on duty at a given time.

2. Scheduled activities which took place, who was in charge of each, the time they occurred, and attendance of participants and spectators. This information enables the actual program to be checked against the planned program. Special events should be similarly recorded but elaborated under "Remarks." The routine or free play activities should not be recorded except as they are revealed in the total attendance, since they can be assumed to have taken place

and will be largely of the same nature each week. If new and novel routine activities are introduced they should be commented on under "Remarks."

3. Scheduled events planned by outside agencies but conducted at the center. If the permit has been issued by the central office, the number of the permit should be given.
4. Total estimated attendance at all activities (morning, afternoon, and evening) by participants and spectators. Methods of estimating this attendance have to be prescribed to suit each separate type of center. For some the record might be very exact (e.g., at swimming pools where fees are charged), but for others the attendance is at best a careful estimate.
5. Visits of staff supervisors or other important visitors and time of visits.
6. Important community contacts and their outcome.

Cumulative Program Records. From the data submitted by the staff at various centers and by supervisors of special programs which do not necessarily take place at departmental centers, a cumulative program and attendance record may be compiled. This record becomes the basis for consolidated weekly, monthly, and annual reports.

Records of Accidents. It is important in public work to record, at the time they occur, any accidents that are serious from the standpoint of injury sustained, disposition, or possible liability, or as an indication of faulty accident prevention procedures. Departments usually require a separate form to be filled out by the recreationist in charge of the center where the accident occurred, showing:

1. Name, address, age, and sex of the injured person
2. Exact time, place, and circumstances concerning the accident
3. Description of the injury
4. Disposition of the case
5. Names and addresses of witnesses
6. Comments as to cause and prevention of similar accidents; also significant information of value in the event of damage suits. In the case of serious accidents, statements of the injured person and of material witnesses made at the time should be recorded.

Permits for Use of Facilities. Self-organized and self-managed groups may use recreational service department facilities on permit from the central office. Such permits are granted for large picnics, use of gymnasiums, use of auditoriums, and use of athletic fields. The original permit is given to the permittee. A carbon copy of such permits should be kept at the central office. A third copy should be sent to the center.

The original is presented by the permittee to the staff at the center who record on it a report on the activity. The copy is then returned to the office.

Reports and Their Purposes

A report is a synthesis of many records on the same subject which have been summarized for cogent analysis. Reports are vital to administration. The somewhat specialized and therefore decentralized functions necessary in the daily operation of a recreational service department make it increasingly necessary for the superintendent and other managerial staff to receive concise data so that they may keep in touch with all phases of the agency. Coordination, direction, and management are significantly aided by the use of reports. Reports supply the required factual data from which policy decisions are rendered, program and departmental planning is accomplished, and public information is disseminated.

Reports are expository and present concisely the facts about a specific subject. The main purpose of the report is to define the object under consideration and specify the problems—if any—which were encountered, the method of collecting the information, the conclusions drawn on the basis of known facts, and any recommendations if further action is necessary.

Routine Administrative Reports. It is good administrative practice for the head of a department to require periodic reports from the chief administrative employee of each division of the department whether the division is concerned with the administration of a group of separate facilities or places of recreational service or with the administration of programs of special activities. Division heads usually require periodic reports from the directors of separate recreational places. These reports, which may be daily, weekly, or monthly, enable a cumulative record of the work to be assembled and summarized and assist the administrators in keeping abreast of the progress and trends of the work. Those required to render reports are encouraged to think in terms of factual material related to their work and to analyze measured accomplishment in relation to expended effort. The contents of such reports vary according to the nature of the work.

Annual Department Reports. Heads of governmental departments are usually required, by the city charter or other legal enactment, to render an official annual report of the work of their departments. These reports must be submitted to the mayor, the city council, or the city manager. The reports of all departments are then synthesized, consolidated, and published for the information of the general public. The department reports are sometimes published separately by the departments and sent to interested persons and to public and institutional libraries. They are always available at the central office on request of any interested citizen.

Most voting and tax-paying citizens are conspicuously disinterested in the reams of published government statistics and accounts and are inept at analyzing and understanding them. This has not been wholly the fault of citizens, for the material has been published in a form not easily comprehensible. In fact, it has frequently been charged that some public officials publish their reports in highly complex and technical form for the specific purpose of confounding the inquiring citizen. In recent years there has been a distinct effort on the part of progressive public officials to encourage public interest by publishing reports in more attractive and understandable form. Some have carried this to such an extreme that it is difficult to distinguish the official report from advertising matter. The printing of attractive and comprehensible circulars and other material to cultivate public interest and to inform the citizen has an important place in the work of public relations of any department, but it should not replace the annual report, which is a comprehensive outline of the state of the department and its accomplishments. The annual report can be improved by art work, charts, photographs, and popular narrative form, but the essential information that distinguishes it as a report should not be omitted.

Contents of the Annual Report. The report should contain such material as will enable the reader to obtain a better understanding of the work of the department, to appraise the accomplishments of the department for the period to which the report refers, and to learn about the department's plans for the future or the important needs of the city with respect to the matters for which the department is responsible. It should be as brief as is consistent with its purpose and should not be an encyclopedic compendium of information about recreational services or about the department. It should include the following information:

1. *Functions.* A clear statement of the functions of the department and the legal authority by which they are undertaken will assist in interpreting the rest of the material. The division of these functions into subfunctions, upon the basis of which the department is organized, may also be included.
2. *Organization.* A description of the manner in which the department is organized, internal relationships, and relationships to other agencies. A chart is often valuable in making these relationships clear. Any changes in organization should be reported.
3. *Properties.* The number of properties on which the department operates and the improved facilities located thereon indicate to a degree the extent of the department services. Since one of the most important problems of the city is to obtain a sufficient number of areas, buildings, and other structures to enable its services to cover the entire city, tabulation of such additions year by year is an

important index to growth. Noteworthy new acquisitions and alterations should be mentioned and stressed according to their relative importance.

4. *Program.* Although the program of activities is perhaps the most important item in the report, it is not necessary to describe each event in detail. It should rather be the object to summarize the program to indicate the underlying purposes in conducting certain types of activity and the extent to which such purposes were accomplished.

Yearly summaries of attendance of participants, non-participants, or spectators, classified according to types of places (i.e., playgrounds, swimming pools, indoor recreational centers, or golf courses) are almost inevitably quoted. These are often unduly emphasized. In connection with some activities they are at best inaccurate estimates, albeit the only quantitative measure of public response. Their imperfections should be acknowledged and interpretations, perhaps, provided. The familiar bar, pie, and curve charts are valuable for interpretive purposes.

Special problems for which specific programs have been devised should be discussed briefly. For example, if evening activities have been stressed to attract older youth from unwholesome pursuits, or if the department has inaugurated winter sports for the first time, these features might be discussed. Such incidents create opportunities to emphasize qualitative considerations that cannot be treated statistically.

5. *Personnel.* The organization of personnel, number of employees, seasons employed, changes in staff, and similar information might well be included. Measures taken to select competent employees and to provide in-service education might be used to emphasize qualitative aspects. The names of all employees need not be included, but it is customary to publish the names of members of the commission and secretary, if any, and the chief executive and divisional heads.

6. *Finance.* A report is not complete without certain financial statements. An essential one is the report of financial operations giving sources of revenue (taxes, fees, gifts, or other) and details of expenditures classified by principal objects for which made. Both revenues and expenditures should be further classified according to the functions to which they apply (e.g., playgrounds, indoor community centers, swimming pools, golf courses). Unit costs of rendering various services may also be included, but with interpretations, for they can be easily misunderstood.

A capital statement, showing the book value of lands, buildings, and equipment, and any important additions or losses during the year, is often valuable in an annual report. If the department controls its own funds entirely, it is advisable to include a balance sheet with classified assets and liabilities (including bonds unredeemed).

7. *Needs.* The needs of the city in regard to public recreational service as viewed by the department are an important part of the annual report. If these needs can be based on valid surveys rather than on opinion, they are all the more valuable. It is, of course, the duty of the department not only to operate the facilities it has as efficiently as possible but also to inform the general city officials and the public concerning problems unsolved and needs unprovided for. The annual report is a proper instrument through which to emphasize such points.

8. *Recommendations.* A list of specific recommendations may logically follow the factual record.

Files and Filing Procedures

The file is a repository for current as well as long-term operational documents related to the management and control of the public recreational service department. It is merely a physical container for public records and reports which by law must be maintained in proper form for a given period of time. The file also serves as a convenient receptacle for a variety of written material, both current and historic, that is continuously utilized for reference purposes.

Filing has a very important place in the control of personnel, program, and finances. Sooner or later most of the paper work that flows through the department finds its way to some part of the filing system of the agency. It is through this procedure that intradepartmental communication is made. A competent filing system facilitates the smooth coordination of department operations. Filing does not merely indicate placement and retention of documents, it also concerns the selection of specific materials at any time for the pertinent information they contain.

Historic references related to agency establishment, purpose, and function are contained in departmental files. Information about what has occurred in agency operation; past work performance of personnel; type, nature, and number of facilities; program outlines; and previous policy statements may all be located in the file for immediate reference. With such information, new policy and decisions on present and future activity can be formulated intelligently.

Filing serves one other important purpose: it provides the necessary repository wherein physical evidence of a legal nature may be kept until disposal or exposure is required. The law states that certain papers be maintained for definite periods of time. Thus tax records, insurance policies, land and property records, and other legal instruments are safeguarded until such time as they are needed for examination.

Filing of records, reports, and miscellaneous information in a manner that admits of convenient reference presents a problem in all public executive offices. Few departments, however, encounter greater difficulty than the recreational service department. The recreational service department is not concerned with a single activity but with many diversified activities. The recreational service office must have available not only the official records of business transactions, but also a great quantity of reference material concerning these countless activities. Such material is of great assistance to the staff as a source of information in planning programs and in answering the public's questions about all sorts of recreational activities. Moreover, the department program is not static or routine but constantly changing and developing.

The filing of material according to subject and the logical relation of the subject matter to the organization of the department's functions is the most efficient method in recreational service departments. This procedure results in the accumulation of material of similar nature in one location. It also renders indexing and cross indexing unnecessary and helps those who consult the files, since they must continually think in terms of organization and interrelation of the several functions of the department rather than in terms only of a particular subject.

A filing system appropriate for a recreational service executive office is outlined below. This outline assigns all materials to three separate files: one having to do with administration of business transactions, facilities, and programs; another with miscellaneous information concerning activities; a third with information concerning the field of work, or the community. It does not deal with filing devices and mechanisms, such as the coding of file folders to facilitate their return to the proper places, memoranda to be left when material is withdrawn, cross references, choice of tabs and folders, and disposition of matter referring to more than one subject.

The outline is adaptable to either the centralized plan of filing, in which all material from all parts of the executive office is assembled in a central place, or the decentralized plan, which permits each executive supervisor or director to keep such files in his office as relate to his particular duties.

Filing is more of a problem for the larger departments, but the principles of efficient filing apply to small departments as well. The subdivision of subjects to the extent indicated in the outline below will hardly be necessary in the smaller departments.

The *administrative file* contains official records, memoranda, correspondence, and reports kept as a permanent record of transactions for ready reference. Most of this material may be conveniently filed in vertical lettersize drawer files. It should be filed according to subject. Subjects should be indicated by tabs or indicators and classified according to a functional separation of duties. Arrangement of the file will largely conform to the staff organization. (See outline.)

Some of this material is referred to so frequently that it is more convenient to keep it in special desk filing devices of various kinds. Board minutes, for example, may be typed and kept in loose-leaf folders. At the end of the year, these minutes should be bound and indexed. A cumulative register of encumbrances against the budget may be kept in a vertical card file or in a loose-leaf ledger. Duplicate receipts of income from various sources may be kept in bound receipt books. A register of cash receipts should be posted in a cash book from duplicate receipts. An up-to-date storeroom inventory, showing quantities withdrawn on requisition, should be kept in a vertical card file.

Employees' time records filled out by them may be filed in loose-leaf binders or in vertical files. The weekly attendance reports submitted by the directors, may be filed in loose-leaf binders. A master calendar of important events may be kept on the desk, in a drawer, or on the wall.

The *activity file* contains information having to do with activities of many kinds. It consists of rules, descriptions, plans, and suggestions on organization, leadership, and the like. It is mimeographed or printed matter in the form of circulars, bulletins, articles, books, and memoranda of every sort. Material too bulky to file or bound material may be kept in bookcases. The material should not be included in the administration file. The activity file should be arranged according to some well-understood classification of activities.

The activity file contains purely suggestive information, not records. For example, the program of a pageant prepared and presented by the playgrounds of the department belongs in the administration file as a record of the activity. But sample programs of pageants presented in other cities may be collected in the activity file to serve as a source of ideas for future pageants. Baseball rules, for instance, belong in the activity file, but any special rules of eligibility for a local league belong in the administration file.

The *survey file* contains information concerning the community and its recreational resources. The recreational service department is continuously conducting research on the community, the people who make up the community, the groups into which they are organized, and the facilities that exist for their recreational service. This information should be assembled under appropriate titles in a vertical lettersize drawer file.

Outline for Administration File

Department history
The Charter
The governing body

Legislation
The Commission or Board
   Composition, appointment, terms of office
   Duties and powers
   Minutes
   Reports
   Procedures and bylaws
   Instructions
Department administration
   Organization
   Acquisition and development of properties
   Development of service
   Finance
     The current budget
     The past year's budget
     Purchasing
     Accounting reports
       Capital
       Operating
       Auditor's reports
       Treasurer's reports
   The staff
     Staff organization
     Qualifications
     Applications
     Selection
     Recommendations received
     Recommendations given
     Recruiting
     Promotion
     Discharge
     Compensation
     Payroll
     Interrelationships
     In-service education
     Grading of employees
     Discipline
     Staff activities
     Voluntary leadership
   Publicity and promotion
     Instructions and policy concerning publicity
     Articles
     News releases
     Photographs

Mailing lists
Addresses (speeches)
Relations with other agencies
  The national movement
    Conferences
    Reports
    Yearbook statistics
  City departments
    School department or system
    Park department, if not consolidated
    City planning department
    Welfare department
    Engineering department
    Legal department
    Library department
    Public works department
    Police department
    Juvenile court authority
    Housing department
    Urban renewal or redevelopment department
    Health department
  Quasi-public agencies
    University or college unions, Police Athletic League, Red Cross
  Private agencies
    Boy Scouts, Girl Scouts, YMCA, YWCA, Boys' Clubs, Camp Fire
      Girls, YMHA, YWHA, CYO, and the like
    Clubs and leagues
    Homes
    Churches
    Fraternal orders
    Industries
Construction and maintenance
  Construction, general
  Maintenance, general
  Equipment, general
  Supplies, general
  Office
    Supplies
    Staff
    Equipment
  Playgrounds
    General (applying to all playgrounds)
    Specific (for each playground)
      Staff

Plans and layout
Equipment
Repairs
Supplies
Utilities
Inventory
Swimming pools
General (applying to all pools)
Specific (for each swimming pool)
Staff
Plans and layout
Equipment
Repairs
Supplies
Utilities
Inventory
Beaches
Camps
Golf courses
Others
Administration of program by places
Playgrounds (one tab for each with further subdivision by
activities if necessary)
Athletics
Music
Art
Craft
Drama
Outdoor education and camping
Special events
Others
Swimming pools (one tab for each with further subdivision
by activities if necessary)
Beaches
Camps
Others
Administration of programs by activity
Athletics
General program by activities (one tab for each with further
subdivision if necessary)
Basketball
General correspondence
Officials
Rules

       Municipal leagues
          Eligibility
          Protests
          Schedules
          Awards
          Officials
        Baseball
        Others
     Drama
       Program
       One tab for each project (subdivided further if necessary)
     Music
       Program
       One tab for each project (subdivided further if necessary)
     Outdoor education and camping
       Program
       One tab for each project (subdivided further if necessary)
     Handicraft
       Program
       One tab for each project (subdivided further if necessary)

Outline for Activity File

Athletics
   Football
   Soccer
   Basketball
   Volleyball
   Track and field
   Swimming
   Others
Outdoor education and camping
   Hiking
   Astronomy
   Horticulture
   Nature study
   Camping
   Bird watching
Handicrafts
Fine arts
Drama
Music
   Program in general
   Band
   Orchestral

Chamber
Choral
Other instrumental
  Harmonica
  Ukulele
  Banjo
  Guitar
  Others
Community singing
Dancing
  Folk
  Social
  Interpretive
Literary Activities
Science
Unclassified activities
  Playground activities, informal
  Home play
  Social activities
  Others

Outline for Survey File

The City and Community
  Geographic and topographic data
  Population (distribution by districts, age groups, neighborhoods,
    nationality, and the like)
  Physical resources
    Public school areas and facilities
      Playgrounds
      Athletic fields
      Others
    Parochial school areas and facilities
    Other public facilities
      Parks
      Libraries
      Housing projects
    Privately owned facilities
      Churches
      Lodge halls
      Theaters
      Bowling centers
      Golf clubs
      Tennis clubs
      Skating rinks

Parochial schools
Library
Churches
Commercial agencies
Boy Scouts
Girl Scouts
YWCA
YMCA
Others
Fraternal organizations and activities
Foreign and ethnic groups
Athletic leagues and clubs
Social clubs
Dramatic clubs
Civic clubs
Welfare organizations

TYPES OF RECORD AND REPORT FORMS

Below are some of the forms that public recreational service departments utilize in officially recording and collecting pertinent information concerning agency operations.

REPORT OF SUPERINTENDENT

No...

Date...

To the Recreation Commission

Honorable Members:

Subject:

Recommendation:

....

Superintendent.

Approved ☐   Disapproved ☐   Further Report ☐   Committee ☐

Detailed Report:

COMMUNITY CONTACTS DURING WEEK   Talks given, conferences with local people, newspapers, etc.

Nature of Contact	Made by Whom	Purpose

SAFETY REPORT

Number Accidents—Minor (Not Reported)   Major (Reported)

I hereby certify that I have personally inspected all equipment under my jurisdiction, and found same to be safe for use, with the following exceptions:

....

....

....

I have put out of use the equipment listed above. I further certify that the information given in this report is correct to the best of my knowledge.

Signed...
                                                   Chief Director.

REMARKS: Suggestions for improvement of program, administrative conferences desired, mention of activities especially successful, equipment lost, stolen or wilfully damaged, serious disciplinary problems, attendance fluctuation causes, scheduled events which have special publicity value.

ACCIDENT FACTORS (Causes)

Unsafe Acts

Operating without authority, failure to secure or warn

Operating or working at unsafe speed

Making safety devices inoperative

Using unsafe equipment, hands instead of equipment, or equipment unsafely

Unsafe loading, placing, mixing, combining, handling, etc.

Taking unsafe position or posture

Working on moving or dangerous equipment

Distracting, teasing, abusing, startling, horseplay

Failure to use personal protective devices, or the using of unsafe attire

Unsafe Conditions

Improperly guarded

Defects of tools, equipment, or substance

Hazardous arrangement, procedure, etc., in, on, or around work place

Improper illumination

Improper ventilation, or uncontrolled hazardous substance

Unsafe dress or apparel

Personal Factors
(Subcauses of Unsafe Acts)

Physical condition of employee

Lack of knowledge or skill

Failure to understand instructions

Improper attitude

Circumstances make safe action difficult

Unsafe act of other person

CORRECTION (Control of Factors)

Medical treatment

Provide safety devices and proper tools

Correct job placement

Job training, instruction

Proper job briefing

Repair defective equipment, maintain in good condition

Discipline and enforcement of standards, closer supervision

Engineering revision, including job planning and standardization

MEDICAL SERVICE ORDER

Workmen's Compensation Division

Date_____

Dr. _____ Address _____

Please examine Mr., Mrs., Miss_____

and thereafter follow established procedures based upon instructions of the City Attorney.

(by) _____

REPORT OF PERSONAL INJURY TO CITY EMPLOYEE File No._____

DEPARTMENT		BUREAU OR DIVISION					UNIT OR SECTION			

EMPLOYEE

	LAST NAME	FIRST	MIDDLE	OCCUPATION		SALARY	AGE	SEX

LENGTH OF EMPLOYMENT IN CITY	PRES. CLASS	HOURS OF EMPLOYMENT FROM	TO	ADDRESS OF PLACE OF EMPLOYMENT AND/OR PHONE

INJURY

	DATE	HOUR	FIRST AID GIVEN? YES ☐ NO ☐	BY WHOM

PLACE OF ACCIDENT	FUNCTION

INJURY FIRST REPORTED	DATE	HOUR	TO WHOM

SENT TO DOCTOR (NAME)	DATE	HOUR	BY WHOM

DESCRIPTION OF INJURY	WITNESSES

SIGNATURE OF INJURED	HOME ADDRESS AND PHONE

SUPERVISOR'S ANALYSIS OF THE ACCIDENT

ACCIDENT DESCRIBE: WHAT WAS EMPLOYEE DOING?—INCLUDE MACHINE, OBJECT OR SUBSTANCE INVOLVED—USE OTHER SIDE IF NECESSARY.

CAUSE WHY DID THIS ACCIDENT HAPPEN? (SEE OTHER SIDE FOR COMMON CAUSES)

HAD EMPLOYEE BEEN INSTRUCTED IN SAFE PERFORMANCE OF OPERATION? YES ☐ NO ☐ WAS THIS PART OF EMPLOYEE'S JOB? YES ☐ NO ☐

CORRECTION WHAT ACTION HAS OR WILL BE TAKEN TO PREVENT A SIMILAR ACCIDENT? (SEE OTHER SIDE FOR SUGGESTIONS)

SUPERVISOR'S SIGNATURE AND TITLE	DATE OF REPORT	REVIEWED BY

Distribution: (Fill out completely in quadruplicate) **WHITE**—City Atty's. Off. (lower portion removed) **PINK**—Safety Engineer **BLUE**—Immediate Superior **CANARY**—Bur. of Acctg. of your dept. or your dept. head

Accident Report
Department of Recreational Service

Note: This report must be sent to the office within 24 hours after the accident.

Name of Injured Person................................Address................................

Age................Sex................................Phone................................

Date of Accident................................Hour................................

State Exact Nature of Injury................................

State in Detail How Accident Occurred................................

Give Name and Address of Physician or Hospital Used................................

What Was Done with Injured Person and by Whose Orders?................................

Did a Director Witness Accident?................If Not, Where were Directors when Accident Occurred?................................

Give Names and Addresses of Three Witnesses of Accident:

Give your opinion as to cause of accident, whether carelessness of injured, carelessness of another, defective apparatus, violating safety rules, etc.

Was this Activity on Permit?................If so, give Number of the Permit................Was the injured a spectator or player?

Signed................................

Playground ....   Title ....

DEPARTMENT OF RECREATIONAL SERVICE

RECREATION SUPPLIES REQUISITION

Playground_____For the Month of_____

Re-quested	On Hand		Re-quested	On Hand		Re-quested	On Hand	
		ATHLETIC SUPPLIES			**Bases**			Only, Inflators
		Arm Bands	___	___	Sets (3), Baseball			Only, Inflators, with Gauge
___	___	Doz., Attendant	___	___	Sets (3), Playground	___	___	50-ft. Jump Ropes, No. 10 Sash Cord
___	___	Doz., Director			**Bats**	___	___	Only, Laces, Rawhide
___	___	Doz., Leader	___	___	Only, Baseball, Regulation	___	___	½ Pints, Neatsfoot Oil
___	___	Doz., Patrol	___	___	Only, Baseball, Fungo	___	___	Only, Needles, Lacing
		Awards	___	___	Only, Playground	___	___	Only, Needles, Mattress (for Leather)
___	___	Only, Commendation Certificates			**Bladders**	___	___	Only, Punching Bags
___	___	Only, Ribbons, First	___	___	Only, Basketball	___	___	Only, Rubber Patch Outfits
___	___	Only, Ribbons, Second	___	___	Only, Football	___	___	Only, Thread, Linen, for Repairs
___	___	Only, Ribbons, Third	___	___	Only, Punching Bag			**Game Supplies**
___	___	Only, Honorable Mention	___	___	Only, Soccer Ball	___	___	Only, Bean Bags
		Balls	___	___	Only, Volley Ball	___	___	Only, Bean Bag Boards
___	___	Only, Baseballs			**Nets**	___	___	Sets, Chess Men
___	___	Only, Basketballs, Inseam	___	___	Only, Badminton	___	___	Only, Checker Boards
___	___	Only, Basketballs, Outseam	___	___	Only, Basketball	___	___	Sets, Checker Men
___	___	Only, Croquet Balls	___	___	Only, Paddle Tennis	___	___	Only, Crokinole Boards
___	___	Only, Footballs	___	___	Only, Ping Pong	___	___	Only, Crokinole Cues
___	___	Only, Handballs	___	___	Only, Volley Ball, White, Outdoor	___	___	Sets, Crokinole Discs
___	___	Only, Inflated Balls, 5-in.	___	___	Only, Volley Ball, Black, Indoor	___	___	Only, Croquet Mallets
___	___	Only, Paddle Tennis Balls			**Miscellaneous**	___	___	Sets, Friends (Tags)
___	___	Only, Ping Pong Balls	___	___	Only, Bamboo Bars	___	___	Sets, Horseshoes (4 in Set)
___	___	Only, Playground Balls, 12-in.	___	___	Only, Baseball Catcher's Glove	___	___	Sets, Horseshoe Stakes (2 in Set)
___	___	Only, Playground Balls, 14-in.	___	___	Only, Baseball Catcher's Mask	___	___	Doz., Jacks (Dozen)
___	___	Only, Put Shot Balls, 5-lb.	___	___	Only, Baseball Catcher's Protector	___	___	Only, Paddles, Paddle Tennis
___	___	Only, Rubber Sponge Balls, 1½ in.				___	___	Only, Paddles, Ping Pong
___	___	Only, Soccer Balls				___	___	Only, Sprinkling Cans (Sand Box)
___	___	Only, Volley Balls						

Playground_____For the Month of_____

Re-quested	On Hand		Re-quested	On Hand		Re-quested	On Hand	
___	___	Only, Trowels (Sand Shovels)			**OFFICE SUPPLIES**	___	___	Sheets, Carbon, Typewriter, 8½x13 in.
		Stamp Supplies	___	___	Pad, Accident Reports, Employees	___	___	Box, Paper Fasteners
___	___	Pkg. Stamps, Cancelled	___	___	Pad, Accident Reports, Patron	___	___	Only, Pencils, No. 2
___	___	Pkg., Stamp Hinges	___	___	Only, Blotters, Desk Size	___	___	Only, Pencil Sharpeners
___	___	Inch, Stamp Sheets, Ruled	___	___	Only, Blotters, Hand Size	___	___	Only, Pencil Sharpener Blades
___	___	Only, Stamp Tongs	___	___	100 Cards, Ruled, 3x5 in.	___	___	Only, Pen Holders
		FIRST AID SUPPLIES	___	___	25 Cards, Index, for 3x5 in.	___	___	Doz., Pen Points
___	___	Roll, Adhesive Tape, 2-in.	___	___	Only, Cards, Invitation	___	___	Pads, Requisitions, Caretaker
___	___	Bot., Ammonia, Aromatic Spirits	___	___	Only, Cards, Membership	___	___	Pads, " Handicraft
___	___	Box, Antiseptic	___	___	Only, Trays, Oak, for 3x5 in. Cards	___	___	Pads, " Mechanical
___	___	Box, Anti-Pyrol, 1 oz.	___	___	Box, Clips, Paper	___	___	Pads, " Miscellaneous
___	___	Roll, Bandage, 1-in.	___	___	Doz., Envelopes, Stamped	___	___	Pads, " Recreation
___	___	Roll, Bandage, 2-in.	___	___	Only, Erasers, Blackboard	___	___	Box, Rubber Bands
___	___	Roll, Bandage, 3-in.	___	___	Only, Erasers, Ruby Rubber			*Scratch Pads*
___	___	Can, Boric Acid, Cans	___	___	Only, Expense Sheets	___	___	Only, Small
___	___	Roll, Cotton, 4 oz.	___	___	Only, Files, Letter	___	___	Only, Medium
___	___	Bot., Hexylresorcinal, 1 oz. bottle	___	___	Only, Files, No. 591, for Folders	___	___	Only, Large
___	___	Bot., Iodine, 1 oz. bottle	___	___	Only, Folders, Manila	___	___	Pads, Time Sheets, Blue
___	___	Bot., Mercurochrome, 1 oz. bot.	___	___	Only, Grip Binders, Letter, No. 400-S	___	___	Pads, Time Sheets, Pink
___	___	Pr., Scissors, Surgical	___	___	Bot., Ink, Black, Desk Size	___	___	Box, Thumb Tacks
___	___	Only, Tweezers	___	___	Bot., Ink, Red, Desk Size	___	___	Only, Visors, Directors
		MECHANICAL HANDICRAFT	___	___	Sheets, Letter Heads	___	___	Only, Waste Baskets, Volcot
		Brads	___	___	Only, Letter Trays, Wire	___	___	Only, Waste Baskets, Wire
___	___	Lbs., No. 16, ¾, 1 in.	___	___	Pads, Office Memorandums	___	___	Only, Weekly Reports
___	___	Lbs., No. 18, ½, ¾ in.	___	___	Sheets, Paper, 8½x11 in., White Bond	___	___	Only, Weekly Reports, Half Sheets.
___	___	Lbs., No. 20, ½, ¾ in.	___	___	Sheets, Paper, 8½x13 in., White Bond			
		Wire Nails	___	___	Sheets, Carbon, Pencil 9x12 in.			*Director.*
___	___	Lbs., No. 16, ¾, 1 in.						Use "Miscellaneous Requisition" form for
___	___	Lbs., No. 18, ¾, 1 in.						items not listed.
___	___	Lbs., No. 20, ¾, 1 in.						No requisition honored unless "ON
___	___	Doz., Coping Saw Blades						HAND" shown.
___	___	Pints, Glue						

WEEKLY MILEAGE
STATEMENT
FOR PRIVATELY OWNED MACHINES

Recreational Service: Department

FOR WEEK OR PERIOD ENDING
_____, 19 _____

Name_____ Position_____ Group_____ Class_____

Home Garage_____ Headquarters_____ Round Trip Distance_____ Miles

Auto Make_____ Model_____ License No._____

	REGULAR MILEAGE To Be Filled In By All Employees					HOME MILEAGE ALLOWANCES To Be Filled In By Dispatcher				
		ODOMETER READING								
DATE	Start at Garage	Job or Headquarters Start / Finish		Finish at Garage	Regular Mileage	DATE	JOB LOCATION	Job Zone	Home Zone	Allow-ance

Total Regular Mileage_____

Regular Mileage_____

Home Mileage Allowance_____

Total Mileage_____

Total Home Mileage Allowance_____

Approved_____, 19 _____

Head of Division._____

Calculations, Terminal Points, etc. Checked
_____

DETAILED TRIP STATEMENT

To Be Filled In By All Employees

DATE	TERMINAL POINTS	NATURE OF WORK	DATE	TERMINAL POINTS	NATURE OF WORK

INSTRUCTIONS:—Each owner of a motor vehicle using same for City Business and authorized to receive payment for such service, must make out one of these reports in full each week or period and send same to the Accounting Division. Use both sides. All blanks must be filled in accurately by the employee except "Home Mileage Allowance" which will be filled in by Dispatcher. "Regular Mileage" is obtained by subtracting odometer reading shown under "Start at Job or H.Q." from "Finish of Job or H.Q." In the "Detailed Trip Statement," specify the exact location visited. Under "Nature of Work" state the class of work performed at that terminal point, giving Job No., Order No. or Permit No., if any.

NOTE: The term "Dispatcher" refers to employee who is charged with the duty of computing mileage allowances.

FORM OF PERMIT

FOR USE OF BUILDINGS BY SELF-MANAGED GROUPS

DEPARTMENT OF RECREATIONAL SERVICE

Permit   Date_____, 19 __

Permission is hereby granted to_____
                                                  (Name of organization)

to use_____at the_____
                                                  (Specific facilities)

Recreation Center on the date of_____, 19 __, from_____to_____

o'clock for the purpose of conducting a_____
                                                  (Type of activity)

     This permit is issued with the understanding that_____
                                       (Name of responsible party requesting permit)

of_____, _____, will be responsible for adherence
               (Address)   (Phone)

to "Regulations For the Use of Community Building" enclosed herewith and information printed on the back of this permit. Your organization is classified as a_____group, and will therefore be charged $_____ for the use of facilities for the hours requested in accord with statement on back of permit. Please forward check or money order made payable to the Department of Recreational Service, or hand to Director with this permit, which must be relinquished at time of meeting herein authorized.

                                         JOHN DOE, Superintendent.

                                         By_____

         Read information on other side of permit carefully.   Permits not transferable.

(PRINTED ON REVERSE SIDE OF PERMIT)

READ CAREFULLY

1. Unless specifically stated on this permit it is understood that the gathering to be held is not a benefit affair, that no admission is to be charged, that no tickets will be sold, and that any collections taken up will be to defray expense of the affair only.
2. If dining room and kitchen equipment is used a deposit must be posted with the Director to cover possible loss or breakage, such deposit to be returned if no such loss or breakage should occur.
3. Charges for use of facilities will be made as follows:
     (a) Program groups—no charge.
     (b) Charter groups—no charge.
     (c) Outside groups—If at hours when center is not normally open, $3.00 for first two hours, and $1.00 for each hour or fraction thereafter.
     (d) Private or closed—$3.00 for first two hours and $1.00 for each hour or fraction thereafter.
4. Permits are not issued for later than midnight.
5. The Department of Recreational Service is not responsible for accident, injury or loss of property.
6. For cause, permits are subject to cancellation by this Department.
7. At all gatherings of young people two or more adults must always be present throughout the affair.
8. In case of disagreement regarding interpretation of regulations governing use of facilities of the Department, patrons are requested to conform to the statements of Recreational Director in charge and submit written report to the main office of the Department.

Recreational Director must sign and return permits to Department Office on Monday morning of each week.

Time group left Building_____ | Remarks:_____

Receipt No._____ | _____

Amount_____ | _____

Participants_____ | _____

Spectators_____

                                             Recreational Director in Charge

From-to	
Total	
From-to	
Total	
From-to	
Total	
From-to	
Total	
From-to	
Total	
From-to	
Total	
From-to	
Total	
	Total Pay Roll

POOL GUARD RESCUE AND ACCIDENT REPORT

Date_____Time_____Guard_____Victim_____Remarks_____

Date_____Time_____Guard_____Victim_____Remarks_____

Date_____Time_____Guard_____Victim_____Remarks_____

Date_____Time_____Guard_____Victim_____Remarks_____

Date_____Time_____Guard_____Victim_____Remarks_____

Date_____Time_____Guard_____Victim_____Remarks_____

SAFETY REPORT

I have made a daily report of the condition of clearness of the water, and put all dangerous equipment out of service.

(Signed)_____

FORM OF PERMIT

FOR THE USE OF ATHLETIC FACILITIES

PERMIT			Receipt No._____
No.		DEPARTMENT OF RECREATIONAL SERVICE	Amt._____

Place_____Date_____, 19____

Sport_____Time_____

Teams_____vs._____

Issued to:_____of_____

Address_____Phone_____

1. Postponement or cancellation of game must be immediately reported to Sports Office and Playground.
2. All permits and schedules are subject to cancellation by the Department of Recreational Service and are not transferable.
3. The Playground Director is in charge of the ground and will interpret all rules and regulations of the Department pertaining thereto.
4. Failure of team to appear will result in forfeiture of forfeit fee.
5. Manager of team will be held responsible for conduct of players.

JOHN DOE, Superintendent,

By_____

Paid _____	Part _____
Collect _____	Spec. _____

Permit must be handed to Director in Charge.

WEEKLY SWIMMING POOL REPORT
DEPARTMENT OF RECREATIONAL SERVICE

Pool_____ For Week Ending Sat._____, 19____

	Attendance	Sun.	Mon.	Tues.	Wed.	Thur.	Fri.	Sat.	Total	Number in Organized Activities	Sun.	Mon.	Tues.	Wed.	Thur.	Fri.	Sat.	Total
Boys	A.M. to Noon									Boys' Lessons								
	P.M.									Men's Lessons								
	If Night 5:00 on									Girls' Lessons								
Men	A.M. to Noon									Women's Lessons								
	P.M.									Mixed Group Lessons								
	If Night 5:00 on									Diving Lessons								
Girls	A.M. to Noon									No. of Swimming Tests								
	P.M.									Life Saving Instructions								
	If Night 5:00 on									Other Org. Act.								
Women	A.M. to Noon																	
	P.M.																	
	If Night 5:00 on																	
Total Paid Attend.																		
Total Spectators																		
Gross Attendance																		
No. Towels Sent																		
No. Suits Sent										Total in Org. Act.								

(PRINTED ON REVERSE SIDE OF SWIMMING POOL REPORT)

Remarks:

_____
_____
_____
_____
_____
_____
_____
_____
_____

Time Record of all Employees for Week Ending Sat._____, 19_____

Employees (Last Name First)	Classification	Total Hours Worked Per Week							Total Hours	Rate Per Hour	Total Estimated
		Sun.	Mon.	Tues.	Wed.	Thur.	Fri.	Sat.			
	From-to										
	Total										
	From-to										
	Total										
	From-to										
	Total										
	From-to										
	Total										
	From-to										
	Total										

DAILY JOURNAL

Day	Activity	In Charge	Hour	Accom-panist	Par.	Spec.	Day	Activity	In Charge	Hour	Accom-panist	Par.	Spec.
								Carried over from Column 1					
	TOTAL, COLUMN 1								GRAND TOTAL				

Report of Special Programmed Events: Under this heading list events which have taken place during past week, also those planned for coming week, such as Exhibitions, Meets, Pageants, Life Saving Contests, Polo Games, Parties, etc.

Date	Hour	Event	Organization, Remarks	No. Participating	Spectators

Remarks: Record here such items as visits from Superintendent, Supervisor, Maintenance Division, equipment out of repair, causes of attendance fluctuations, complaints, etc.

Suggestions for publicity, pictures, human interest stories, etc.

DEPARTMENT OF RECREATIONAL SERVICE
PLAYGROUND AND COMMUNITY CENTER WEEKLY REPORT

Record for week ending_____, 19____

Name of Center_____

Entries in the daily journal will be made by director conducting the activity. Chief Directors will verify total report.

Daily Attendance	Sunday		Monday		Tuesday		Wednesday		Thursday		Friday		Saturday		Total Weekly Attendance	
	Par.	Spec.	Par.	Spec.	Par.	Spec.	Par.	Spec.	Par.	Spec.	Par.	Spec.	Par.	Spec.	Par.	Spec.
Morning																
Afternoon																
Evening																
Total																

The above attendance count is the sum total of all persons for the period, including free play, organized activities, and building, sports and playground permit groups. For purposes of determining attendance, one or more visits by one person within a time period, shall be counted as a unit attendance.

Staff Record	On	Off	On	Off	On	Off	On	Off	On	Off	On	Off	On	Off	Staff Visits (Record day and hour)

(PRINTED ON REVERSE SIDE OF REPORT)

CENTER

WEEKLY PLAYGROUND REPORT

FOR WEEK ENDING

_____19____

EXTRA SERVICE REQUIRED

(Should be requested well in advance)

Type of Service	Approved by	Worker Desired	Date	From	To	Reason

SCHEDULE CHANGE REPORT

Type of Activity and Group	New Group Will Begin		Group Now Meeting On		Will Meet		Will Discontinue	Approved
	Day of Week	Hour	Day of Week	Hour	Day of Week	Hour	Date	By

SPECIAL EVENTS FOR NEXT WEEK

Activity	Date	Hour	Activity	Date	Hour

Form of Application Blank

PERSONNEL RECORD

Name_____ Date_____

Street Address_____ City_____ Phone_____

Date of Birth_____ Wt._____ Ht._____ U. S. Citizen?_____ How long in'city?_____

What dependents have you?_____ Do you own a car?_____

State all physical or health defects_____

Ancestry_____ Foreign languages spoken_____

High School attended_____ City_____ When graduated_____

College attended_____ City_____ Number years_____ When graduated_____

Major courses in college_____

Number of courses in Physical Education or Recreation_____ Total hours_____

Other school work_____

EXPERIENCE—List all recreation positions held for which you have received a salary and any other positions which would help to qualify you for recreation work.

NAME OF EMPLOYER	ADDRESS OF EMPLOYER	WHAT DID YOU DO?	When Employed From	To	SALARY

(Printed on Reverse Side of Blank)

ACTIVITIES CHECK LIST

On the following list, check once any activities you have taken part in regularly, and check twice those in which you have actually organized and directed others. Add any recreational activities not listed.

AQUATICS
____Life Saving
____Boating
____Swimming

ATHLETICS
____Baseball
____Basketball
____Hockey
____Football
____Soccer
____Track
____Volleyball
____Playground Ball

CHARACTER BUILDING GROUPS
____Boy Scouts
____Y. M. C. A. - Y. W. C. A.
____Girl Scouts
____Campfire Girls
____Sunday School
____Church Societies
____Other Groups

CHILDREN'S ACTIVITIES
____Circle Games
____Relay Games
____Tag Games
____Singing Games

DANCING
____Social
____Folk
____Square
____Clog
____Tap

DRAMATIC ACTIVITIES
____Dramatics
____Pageantry
____Story Telling

GYMNASIUM ACTIVITIES
____Tumbling
____Pyramids
____Gymnastics
____Apparatus
____Calisthenics

MANUAL AND ART ACTIVITIES
____Model Building
____Wood Work
____Crepe Paper Work
____Paper and Cardboard Work
____Painting
____Modeling
____Sketching

MUSIC
____Band
____Orchestra
____Community Singing
____Part Singing
____Harmonica
____Ukulele
____Accompanist

OUTDOOR ACTIVITIES
____Hiking
____Camping
____Picnics
____Nature Study

SPORTS
____Boxing
____Golf
____Horseshoes
____Tennis
____Handball
____Wrestling
____Archery
____Bowling
____Pool
____Billiards

MISCELLANEOUS
____Minstrel
____Vaudeville
____School Journalism
____Debating
____ _____
____ _____
____ _____
____ _____
____ _____
____ _____

ATTACH
RECENT
PHOTO
—
SMALL
KODAK PICTURE
IS
SUFFICIENT

Selected References

Bassett, E. D., and others: *Business Filing and Records Control, 4th ed.* (Cincinnati, Ohio: South-Western Publishing Co.), 1974.

Fetridge, C. and R. Minor: *Office Administration Handbook* (Chicago, Ill.: Dartnell Corp.), 1975.

Kahn, G., and others: *Progressive Filing and Records Management, 2d ed.* (New York: McGraw-Hill Book Company), 1971.

Maedke, W. D., and others: *Information and Records Management* (Riverside, N.J.: Glencoe Press), 1974.

Terry, G. R.: *Office Management and Control, 7th ed.* (Homewood, Ill.: Richard D. Irwin, Inc.), 1975.

Wally, B. H.: *Office Administration Handbook* (New York: Beekman Pubs., Inc.), 1975.

PART IV

PERSONNEL ADMINISTRATION

CHAPTER 15

Personnel Management in Public Recreational Service

Current organizational theory and practice recognizes the requirement for both interpersonal relationships and the structure of administration. Rather than presupposing that people are made for organizations, this enlightened concept negotiates between the extremes of organizational necessity and individualization. This management orientation is clearly observed from efforts to develop a personnel-organizational contract as a coordinating process, in which neither aspect can be truly intelligible apart from the other. This chapter concerns the human factor in management and the principles and practices that have been utilized for dealing with personnel working in an enterprise governed by public policy.

Personnel employed by a public recreational service department perform duties related to three more or less distinct functions: (1) organization, promotion, supervision, and leadership of the recreational program; (2) planning, construction, and maintenance of recreational facilities and places; and (3) business administration, clerical duties, and other office work. Employees in the last two categories are recruited from the general labor pool of mechanics, laborers, office workers, and other functionaries available to all agencies. Their titles are generally similar to those of their corresponding numbers in other businesses and governmental agencies. Their preparation is not necessarily slanted toward recreational service. The adaptation of their skills to the requirements of the recreational service department is a problem of in-service education and staff development. Of course, there are employees who have been prepared in the planning and development specialization for employment in recreational service agencies. These individuals may have studied park planning and design or architectural design with major emphasis on recreational places and structures. Such personnel may have been indoctrinated with concepts of recreational resources. These people would not be recruited from the general labor market but would be selected from institutions of higher education where such specialized programs exist.

Employees engaged to perform duties and undertake responsibilities directly concerned with recreational service operations are either generalists or specialists who may be presumed to have had professional educational preparation. The uniqueness of the recreationist lies in his general orientation to recreational service and in his special knowledge, appreciation, and skill in specific recreational activities. The abilities necessary for the organization and administration of recreational service for the public contribute to his stature as a specialist and as a member of a discipline aspiring to professionalism.

Administration of any organization depends on the persons employed in it. The success or failure of departmental activity is based on the soundness of personnel administration. Human factors must be considered as the vital source for analysis, research, and scientific formulation of policies and principles. In the over-all picture of public service administration, the management of personnel is the most important function.

FUNCTIONS OF PERSONNEL MANAGEMENT

Although the basic activities depicted by the term *personnel management* vary with the locale, they comprise a body of responsibilities or functions that must be carried out by one or more individuals in almost every organization. The major services generally performed are:

1. Position analysis, classification, and specification: a rendering of the nature of the work to be performed in any given position so as to establish requirements for recruitment practices.
2. Recruitment, screening, induction, orientation, and placement: the procedure by which individuals are identified in terms of skills, interests, talents, and knowledge coincidental with position requirements.
3. Appraisal, assignment, and promotion: the methods utilized to recognize and reward achievement so that individuals may be placed to the greatest advantage for the organization and themselves.
4. Remuneration: compensatory plans by which monetary scales, increments, and schedules are equitably distributed for the type of work performed.
5. In-service education, development, supervision, and conditions of

work: the process by which competency, efficiency, effectiveness, high morale, and organizational devotion are stimulated.

6. Disciplinary activities: the techniques utilized to discourage incompetency, disaffection, misfeasance, malfeasance, nonfeasance, or any negative behavior by an individual.

7. Evaluation: the process by which employee efforts are compared with previously set goals to determine approximation.

8. Records, reports, and research: the maintenance of all records concerned with the employee's hiring, work productivity, appraisals, evaluations, compensation, leaves, and any psychological testing performed to match the individual with his position.

These activities and the fundamental beliefs characterizing them have

developed over a considerable period of time. The assumptions are undergoing continual scrutiny and are subject to modification as changing situations and conditions are brought to light by research into the processes and practices of organizational behavior. The staff activity of personnel management is generally concerned with the recruitment, selection, induction, in-service education, staff development, promotion, motivation, and disciplinary practices of all employees for the most effective coordination of work performance. Personnel management carries out general policies established by the community in question, and, more specifically, the policies adopted by the particular recreational service agency. In accordance with the needs of the system, personnel management initiates basic rules governing requirements in education and experience, examinations pertinent to the several specializations, recruiting for available positions, reference of eligible applicants for selection and ultimate placement, and the keeping of official personnel records.

The personnel function also includes the classification of positions by direct analysis, typically performed by the central employing agency of the city with guidance from the department, the application of the position classification process to individual job descriptions which were formulated after proper analysis, and the establishment of compensatory rates by legislative enactment. The position classification process is, perhaps, the primary responsibility of personnel management, but other functions include provisions for the health, safety, and welfare of employees; salary schedules; hours of work; leaves; vacations; overtime; salary increments; disciplinary actions; personnel ratings; personnel research; and final separation from the department.

Management Aids

Four basic procedures facilitate the selection, education, rating, and direction of personnel: (1) formally adopted rules and regulations that guide personnel in agency operation, purpose, and jurisdiction; (2) a handbook of personnel procedures listing in detail the steps to be followed in fulfilling the duties and responsibilities of different positions, conduct required of incumbents, rules and regulations for employees, and technical information required by employees to execute their respective assignments effectively; (3) forms specifically designed to record all pertinent information relating to the employee's personal, educational, professional, technical, medical, and/or health qualifications; and (4) personnel folders containing personnel data sheets and records of relevant information about each employee.

A Merit System

The decision to employ any individual in a municipal or governmentally operated department of recreational service should be based on that person's competence to render the indicated service and to hold a position. A system based on individual merit does much to offset nepotism or nefarious political patronage. A logical merit system should encompass the following factors: (1) a firm and enlightened policy established for all municipal employment; (2) a personnel section adequate to handle the details of classification procedure; (3) position classification concerning duties, responsibilities, requirements, and relationships; (4) a uniform grading and salary schedule; (5) open competitive examinations; (6) promotional examinations; (7) a probationary period following appointment; (8) merit ratings used in counseling and promotions or transfers; (9) uniform regulations for leave, retirement, hours of work, vacations, disciplinary actions, and separations; (10) arrangements for pooling personnel for seasonal or emergency conditions; and (11) group medical, hospital, life insurance, or general health plans.

PERSONNEL POLICY

Supplementary to the development of processes to speed certain essential practices, personnel management necessitates devising conditions under which these processes will operate. Policies are the chief structural variables in the administration of personnel practices and, in great degree, fix the level or caliber of personnel direction in the agency. Personnel policies are statements of intent with relation to the utilization of all employees within the organization. Policies may be either general or specific; almost every department requires a mixture of both.

Procedures, on the other hand, are methods for executing policy or reaching some predetermined objective. Rules or regulations are even more specific and are concerned with behavior of employees. Procedures and rules are deliberate representations of broad policy, whether suggested or explained.

Personnel policies develop because they perform several useful functions. Policies reduce the need for reiteration in decision making. After reaching a logical decision dealing with personnel relationships within the organization, particularly after the decision is recorded, the need for repetitive activity is obviated. Personnel policies are the instruments by which employees may determine that the treatment they receive is of a quality that should enhance their devotion to the organization, thereby achieving the purposes for which the department was established. Personnel policies are important in promoting employee morale and in stimulating successful performance. They are significant to the consistency and stability of human relationships between employees and the department. To the extent that all parties are aware of the consequences of specific behaviors, a high degree of predictability is established; thus, every employee knows precisely where he stands on any given problem. Job security is thereby engendered because there are no inconsistent revelations. Finally, personnel policies give an employee a feeling of fair play and equality in treatment. The way individuals are treated in relation to others becomes extremely important as far as job security, morale, and motivation are concerned.[1]

Kinds of Policy Statements

Examination of the personnel practices of many municipal recreational service departments reveals the following kinds of policies to be prevalent:

General Statements.   Statements dealing with the ethical concepts of social equity are general statements. For example, "All participants will be treated respectfully and will be given whatever assistance or guidance is required for their benefit and satisfaction." They deal with compensation, conditions of work, disciplinary procedures, and rewards for service.

Specific Statements.   Specific policy statements are ramifications of general policy statements giving detailed explanations of the broad statement. For example, the general policy statement dealing with social equity becomes more specific by issuing such statements as, "No person will be discriminated against because of race, religion, place of origin, educational level, social status, or economic status. As public servants, recreationists have a mandatory responsibility to render professional services to all people with whom they come in contact and to perform whatever functions are required to the best of their individual abilities on a wholly objective basis." Policy statements of this kind are generally found in most agencies and cover a wide range of matters: hiring practices, performance appraisal, compensation, working conditions, leaves,

---

[1] Abraham K. Korman, *Industrial and Organizational Psychology*. (Englewood Cliffs, N.J.: Prentice-Hall, Inc., 1971), pp. 160–162, 321–322.

and the like. Copies are typically distributed to all employees in a staff manual or handbook that contains all rules, regulations, and procedures for organizational matters.

Inferred Policy. Unwritten policies may be deduced from the current practices utilized in the organization. Certain departments may have permitted some practices that are at odds with written statements. This occurs, particularly in hiring, when discriminatory practices are permitted to invade policy insidiously, because subordinates in critical positions simply assume that superiors really feel one way about current practice even though written statements indicate the opposite or do not cover the subject. Thus, an analysis of practice should indicate distinctly what inferred policies are actually being utilized within the agency and remedial measures taken when such are indicated.

Specialization in Recreational Service

Within each organization is an intricate series of events through which the work of the system is performed. These complex tasks are divided into components for effective management. This division of labor into specialized spheres determines position analysis and classification. Administration, in part, organizes and groups duties and responsibilities so that the work of the agency may proceed unhampered, and this aspect of personnel management requires examination.

Generally, division of labor or specialization consists of sequential activities beginning with the original purposes for establishing the system and the primary objectives of the organization; organizational planning based on position and methods utilized in attaining the agency's goals; development of job descriptions and position analysis for tasks to be performed; position specifications comprising education and experience; development of performance criteria for appraisal and evaluation of each position and establishment of general and specific policies, rules, and regulations governing the work to be performed and the method by which it is to be performed. Although each of these segments emanates from the one directly preceding it, there is considerable interdependency and reciprocity in the process. Thus, the process of job specialization is based on organizational goals, organizational planning, position descriptions leading in turn to job analysis and specification, performance criteria, personnel policies, and regulations governing performance. Specialization may therefore be divided into organizational goals, position delineation, position analysis, and specifications.

Organizational Goals

Identification of organizational goals stems from administrative oversight and precedes all other organizational aspects. The aim of identifying organizational goals is necessary if the work of the agency is to satisfy community needs. Essentially, all recreational service agencies have one basic goal—to provide experiences that can meet the recreational needs of all residents of the community during their respective leisure. Private and quasi-public agencies have similar goals, but they are concerned less broadly. These organizations must plan to meet the recreational needs of their members or potential clients. The public recreational service system has the comprehensive task of fulfilling recreational needs for all of the people in the community in which the department is situated. Therefore, its aim is not only focused on present residents but also on transients and future citizens of the community. Additionally, there are subgoals which every recreational service department desires to achieve. These subgoals deal with the development of the most efficient and effective personnel possible through the enhancement of individual talents, skills, and capacities of professional and technical employees; the development of an established and dedicated work force; and the creation of a community climate of goodwill, which can foster better service through increased public support of the system.

Organizational Planning and Position Delineation

When organizational goals have been clearly defined, the structure of the system can be planned. The aim of organizational planning is to separate the components of the task to be performed into feasible and practical segments and to provide for their effective correlation. Through this process, the entire system is broken down into manageable units, such as individual positions, sections, and divisions within the department or system. Not only is there a subsection of effort throughout the system, with various tasks being undertaken by specialists (linear subdivision), but there is a longitudinal subdivision of work that forms an organizational hierarchy. Thus, at each succeeding level within the organization there is greater responsibility for the supervision of more employees, the coordination of a larger proportion of the work being performed, and more intricate and comprehensive planning. The use of improved technological processes (systems analysis, computer technology, and the like) is a basic part of organizational planning. In a modern recreational service department, the reliance on systems technology, particularly as it concerns informational displays, work simplification, retrieval, and recording, must be considered as a constituent part of organizational planning if the resultant structure is not to create conflict in effectuating the work to be performed.

Organizational planning and position delineation, originating from the basic goals of the system, affect the desired levels of performance in a variety of positions created to carry out the goal-dictated tasks. Furthermore, this expectation identifies position specifications, the educational preparation and in-service staff development required, the complete compensation schedule, and the motivation of employees. Organizational planning and position delineation cause the need for some form of classification procedure.

THE POSITION CLASSIFICATION SYSTEM

The development of position classification is a consequence of the increasingly technical and specialized duties that employees perform in public recreational service and the need to fit personnel with specific skills and abilities to specified jobs. Position classification is more than the process of arranging functions into groups for facilitation of administration, it is part of a process whereby the whole task of recreational service is rendered more susceptible to effective management.

A *position* is a specific employment or job calling for performance. The duties, responsibilities, and relationships it requires are set forth in a job description. The employee is appointed to the job described and is presumed to perform no other job. Positions may be short- or long-term, full- or part-time, occupied or vacant. Employees may come and go, but once created, the position continues until abolished.

A *class* is a group of positions whose duties and responsibilities are similar enough to require personnel to have comparable education, experience, skill, and knowledge, and whose responsibility and difficulty are sufficiently alike to justify similar or identical remuneration, promotional practices, orientation, and in-service education for personnel filling the positions.

A *vertical* or *longitudinal classification* or *series* includes all positions that are related to a specific technological or professional group, but which differ in degree of difficulty and responsibility. Hence the work involved, the kind and degree of supervision or authority emanating from the position and the kind and degree of supervision governing it, the responsibilities, qualifications, prerequisites, and capacities necessary for employment in that position indicate the level that has been attained within a service series.

A *horizontal* or *linear classification* or *grade* groups positions according to levels of similar requirements in responsibility, supervision given and received, and difficulty of the work. Grades cut across vertical series. Routine positions requiring little responsibility or technical skill are classified at the lowest level or grade. Positions are graded correspondingly higher as the work becomes more difficult and the responsibility greater. Wages and salaries usually are assigned by a graded schedule.

The *classification plan* is a system of classes of positions, series, and grade definitions and descriptions, and a procedure by which job descriptions may be kept up to date. Each position is carefully analyzed and all tasks necessary to accomplish agency goals involved with the creation of that position are thoroughly detailed. The requirements of the position, in terms of education and experience, as well as the duties and responsibilities, are recorded. Illustrative examples of the work to be performed are also provided.

The value of the plan is its impersonal objectivity and ease of administration in dealing with personnel problems, conflicts, or questions. The plan provides a sound basis for formulating equitable salary schedules and assists in the recruitment, selection, induction, and orientation of personnel; encourages the use of common terminology or position nomenclature; facilitates appraisal and evaluative techniques for performance, promotions, demotions, transfers, or separations; aids in the identification of specific duties and responsibilities; and tends to avoid inconsistencies by clarifying personnel practices.

Once such information is collected, each position is placed in a series. Series are then broken down into classes which then may be described by title, functions, responsibilities, illustrations of the work, and required qualifications. The allocation of individual positions within the classification series is the final step in the plan.

REQUIREMENTS FOR AND DUTIES OF RECREATIONIST POSITIONS

Although organizational goals and planning identify and determine almost exclusively the duties, range, and status of individual positions within the system, jobs are also delineated through the development of descriptions, specifications, performance criteria, and policies, rules, and regulations. Not only do these instrumentalities tend to qualify the essence of such positions, but they clarify the behavior and special features required. These instrumentalities are not only significant facets of the specialization process but units of other personnel procedures as well.

Position Descriptions

Position descriptions are summaries of fundamental tasks, assigned to one employee, performed on a given job. The description has a title or label. The basis for a position description varies from some mental picture the prospective employer has to a comprehensive investigation of the actual position. This procedure, called *analysis,* is typically the basis for the title and description. Position descriptions have several useful functions: (1) for the development of job specifications, i.e., qualifications required to perform the work; (2) for recruiting a staff; (3) for orientation once the position is filled; (4) in developing performance criteria, i.e., quantitative and qualitative performance to be achieved within a specific time period; and (5) for evaluation procedures to determine the proximity of performance to stated objectives.

It is necessary to differentiate between requirements for and the duties of various types of professional positions in departments of recreational service. Obviously, the duties of a superintendent of a department employing only two or three recreationists are different from those of a superintendent of a department employing a staff of a hundred or more. In the small department the superintendent performs duties of all descriptions. In the larger department the superintendent's duties are more specifically managerial and executive. Although the latter requires preparation and aptitude of a specialized nature, the superintendent must be well grounded in the basic operations of the department.

Standardization of titles and duties of personnel in the public recreational service movement has only now begun to take hold. An examination of the titles used by numerous cities carrying on this work reveals substantial, although not unanimous, agreement as to titles of employment and duties assigned. A description of the titles generally used and the duties, responsibilities, and qualifications usually assigned to each type of position within the classification of recreationist follows.

1. *Superintendent of Recreational Service.* The superintendent is the chief executive officer in charge of a system, department, or division and its personnel; usually responsible to a board or commission; increasingly responsible to a city manager, city council, city commissioner, or mayor. When the public recreational service function is administered as a division of some other department, the superintendent is typically responsible to the chief executive of the over-all line department.

   Requirements. Education equivalent to graduation from a university or college of recognized standing with major specialization in recreational service education, and graduate study in the same field with some emphasis on public administration, sociology, and related fields; at least five years' experience in recreational service, not less than one year of which shall have been in an agency of public administration; successful experience in formulating recreational programs, directing and supervising recreational programs and staff, planning and managing recreational areas and facilities, and conducting public relations; broad knowledge of the recreational service movement and its philosophy; knowledge of the principles of financial management and personnel work as applied to recreational service administration.

   Duties. To be in executive charge of the system, department, division, or bureau of recreational service; to supervise the staff of recreationists, technical, and ancillary workers; to prepare and administer programs of operation including budgets for same; generally to plan recreational areas and facilities; to study the needs of the community and to formulate plans for future development to meet the needs; to prepare reports for submission to higher authority for their consideration and action; to carry on cooperative relations with other agencies of similar purpose and with other municipal departments; to organize and administer a public relations program.

2. *General Supervisor.*   The general supervisor is an executive officer responsible to the superintendent and in charge of a group of recreational facilities of similar kind and their personnel or of some special function such as planning and maintenance or business administration. Generally applicable to all facilities, e.g., Supervisor of Playgrounds, Supervisor of Community Centers, Supervisor of Planning and Maintenance.

Requirements.   Education equivalent to graduation from a university or college of recognized standing with major work in recreational service education; at least three years' responsible experience in recreational and community center activities, one year of which shall have been in a supervisory capacity; knowledge of modern methods followed in playground and community center activities; supervisory ability; and good judgment.

Duties.   Under executive supervision, to be responsible for and in charge of the recreational and community center activities of the department; to supervise the work of all recreationists in directorial positions; to visit recreational centers and to observe their administration; to make special research studies and reports for the superintendent of the department concerning district or community needs for recreational service; to make recommendations on proposed playground sites and layouts of buildings and grounds; to represent the department at conferences and public meetings where playground and community center matters are involved; to plan for exhibits and programs in which the department is represented; to supervise the conduct of playgrounds and the assignment of personnel; to study and solve personnel problems within his jurisdiction; to appraise and evaluate the performance of employees; to administer budget control affecting playground and community center operations; generally to make studies, perform pertinent research, initiate investigations of operations, submit reports, and give advice, counsel, or recommendations where and when required.

The requirements for a *general supervisor of planning and maintenance* for an entire department will have certain similarities to the above-mentioned position, but because of the specialized nature of the work performed, other qualifying educational and responsibility experiences will be necessary.

> *Requirements.* Education equivalent to graduation from a university or college of recognized standing with a master's degree or equivalent in experience in civil, structural, or architectural engineering; at least three years' responsible experience in the design and construction of buildings and other structures, one year of which shall have been in a supervisory capacity, preferably in connection with parks and recreational service; a thorough knowledge of surveying, structural materials used in construction, an understanding of design and materials necessary for adequate recreational areas, facilities, and structures; supervisory ability; and good judgment.
>
> *Duties.* Under executive direction, to be in responsible charge of planning and development in the recreational service system or department; to supervise the planning, designing, construction, and maintenance of recreational areas, buildings, apparatus, equipment, swimming pools, filtration and sterilization or purification systems, and the like; to prepare complete specifications for the construction of buildings and other structures contemplated for recreational purposes; to make land surveys as needed; and to perform related work as required.

3. *Director of Facilities.* Directors are executive officers charged with administering the facilities, staff, and program of a recreational center such as a playground, community center, swimming pool, golf course, or camp. These officers are usually responsible to a general supervisor (if there are sufficient centers to warrant the employment of a supervisor) or to the superintendent or his designated assistant. The title of *manager*, rather than director, is often applied to the person in charge of a golf course, bathing beach, or swimming pool; however, such designations vary widely in practice.

> *Requirements.* Education equivalent to graduation from a university or college of recognized standing with major work in recreational service education; at least two years' experience as a paid employee in recreational service with public, quasi-public, or private agencies; a general knowledge of organized recreational activities with a thorough knowledge and creative ability in at least five phases of recreational activity (low organization games, social recreational activities, aquatics, music, camping, handicraft, art,

rhythmic activities, dramatics, outdoor education, sports skills, and special projects); knowledge of the philosophy and objectives of the public recreational service movement; ability to meet and deal with the public; pleasing personality; leadership ability; enthusiasm; dedication; firmness; and tact.

Duties. Under general supervision, to be in responsible charge of a playground, recreational center, camp, swimming pool, auditorium, or other recreational area or facility (or a combination of such areas and facilities); to formulate, organize, and supervise a well-rounded program of recreational activities designed to meet the recreational needs of people of all ages and stations of life frequenting or having potential access to such areas or facilities; to develop staff members to carry out such programs; to give immediate direction to employees required in the conduct of such activities and in the care of the areas and facilities used; and to perform related work as required.

4. *Supervisor of Special Activities.* Supervisors of special activities are specialists charged with particular phases of program development. The responsibilities of these employees vary greatly. Supervisor of Municipal Athletics, Supervisor of Music, Supervisor of Drama and Pageants, Supervisor of Girls and Women's Activities, Supervisor of Dance, Supervisor of Arts and Crafts, Supervisor of Nature Activities, and supervisors of such other activities as the local program requires. These workers usually are responsible to the superintendent or general supervisors and have staff rather than line responsibilities. Examples of the requirements and duties for different supervisory specialists are offered below.

A. *Supervisor of Municipal Athletics. Requirements.* Education equivalent to graduation from a university or college of recognized standing with major work in physical education or recreational service education or wide experience in the promotion of industrial athletics and recreational service; at least three years' responsible experience in the conduct of athletic games, tournaments, leagues, and contests, one year of which shall have been in a supervisory capacity; a thorough knowledge of and familiarity with the recreational facilities of industrial organizations, churches, schools, and athletic clubs; supervisory and leadership ability; and good judgment.

Duties. Under executive direction, to be in responsible charge of the organized athletic program of the recreational service department; to organize, develop, supervise, and direct a program of participation in all branches of organized sport (archery, baseball, softball, tennis, badminton, bowling, basketball, volleyball, track and field, horseshoe pitching, soccer, football, swimming, fencing, gymnastics, lacrosse, skiing, skating) for teams, groups, or individuals; to develop leagues for the various branches of athletics; to supervise the selection and purchase of awards for sports programs; to pass on permits for use of various athletic facilities; to make studies, investigations, reports, and recommendations pertaining to municipal athletics; and to perform related work as required.

B. *Supervisor of Music. Requirements.* Education equivalent to graduation from a school or college of music of recognized standing; at least three years' responsible experience in organizing and directing musical activities (music clubs, classes, orchestras, bands, glee clubs, or community singing); familiarity with the philosophy of recreational service and its relationship to musical activities; supervisory and leadership ability; and good judgment in musical matters.

Duties. Under executive direction, to be in responsible charge of the musical activities of the recreational service department; to supervise playground and community musical activities; to organize new activities and projects; to represent the department at meetings and conferences of local music societies; to prepare volunteer leaders; to advise individuals and groups on matters pertaining to music; to supervise the work of music directors; and to perform related work as required.

C. *Supervisor of Dramatics and Pageantry. Requirements.* Education equivalent to graduation from a university or college of recognized standing with major work in theater, speech, or related fields; at least three years' responsible experience, preferably in recreational service (storytelling, dramatization of stories, and the presentation of simple dramas and pageants), one year of which shall have been in a supervisory capacity; a thorough knowledge of pageantry and simple dramatics especially adapted to the interests and abilities of children and amateur theatrical groups and of inexpensive methods for producing color effects and for designing and making costumes, scenery, lighting, make-up, production, and direction, and of storytelling technique; supervisory and leadership ability; and good judgment.

Duties. Under executive direction, to be in responsible charge of the dramatics and pageantry activities of the recreational service department; to organize plays, festivals, and pageants throughout the year at the various playgrounds or other recreational facilities, and to organize community pageants; to supervise the department costume facility (if one exists); to plan weekly matinees during summer vacation periods; to select, adapt, and write suitable plays and pageants; to arrange special dramatics classes for recreational directors; to arrange schedules for storytellers and the like; to supervise extemporaneous rehearsals and programs; to assist in the formation of amateur theatrical groups and their programs; and to perform related work as required.

D. *Supervisor of Beaches and Swimming Pools. Requirements.* Education equivalent to graduation from a college or university of recognized standing with special training in aquatics; at least three years' responsible experience in connection with recreational swimming and water sports, one year of which shall have been in a supervisory capacity; a thorough knowledge of the philosophy of recreational service, of resuscitation, of first aid, of lifesaving and water safety techniques, of the use, maintenance, and repair of lifelines, towers, boats, and other beach equipment, of the maintenance and operation of swimming pools, including knowledge of modern filtration systems and methods, of the municipal ordinances and state laws governing administration of public beaches and swimming pools; good physical condition; administrative ability; and good judgment.

Duties. To direct the activities of the beaches and swimming pools; to organize a program of recreational swimming, water sports, beach activities, junior and senior lifesaving classes, and give swimming instruction; to enforce rules, regulations, and ordinances governing the conduct of persons on public beaches and in swimming pools; to supervise and instruct subordinates in the operation and maintenance of pools and beaches.

5. *Program Workers.* These workers are employees who, under the close direction of directors or assistant directors, exercise general supervision over the recreational activities of children and adults on a playground or in a community center, lead groups in organized activities, or assist with special projects. They may be employed part-time, full-time, or seasonally. Frequently they are students preparing for professional careers in recreational service.

Requirements. Education equivalent to graduation from an accredited two-year or community college or, rarely, from a university or college of recognized standing with a major in recreational service education or in related fields; a general knowledge of low organized games and free play activities and general skill in at least three phases of recreational activity (e.g., social recreational activities, aquatics, music, drama, camp craft, art, handicraft, sports, nature study and outdoor education, dance and rhythm, pageantry, storytelling); a knowledge of the philosophy and objectives of the public recreational service movement; ability to meet and deal with the public; pleasing personality; leadership ability; enthusiasm; dedication; firmness; and tact.

Duties. As qualified, to conduct, under direction or supervision, recreational activities at playgrounds and at recreational centers where only limited programs are possible, or to conduct a portion of the program at larger recreational centers (such as sports and games, singing, parties, social activities, aquatics, music, nature study, hiking, art, handicraft, folk dancing, storytelling, dramatics, or other forms of recreational activity); to administer activities and care for facilities as assigned; and to perform related work as required.

6. *Specialists.* Employees who serve as instructors in a special activity, usually at more than one center or on a part-time basis, are specialists. Their duties are largely restricted to organizing and teaching groups in a particular activity (golf, tennis, swimming, tap dancing, puppetry, gymnastics, archery, or a special type of craft project). They differ from supervisors of special activities in that they usually do not have responsibility for promoting or supervising a phase of the program on a community-wide basis.

Other types of employment may be inferred from the following list of titles used by a large, well-established department of recreational service:

Accompanist	Comptometer operator
Automobile machinist	Electrician
Automobile machinist's helper	Equipment repairman
Bathhouse attendant	Filter mechanic
Beach Guard captain	House painter
Blacksmith	Junior accountant
Bookkeeper	Junior stenographer
Building repairman	Laborer
Caretaker (custodian)	Labor foreman
Clerk	Locker-room attendant
Carpenter	Secretary
Cook	Senior stenographer
Cement finisher	Telephone operator

It is unnecessary to describe the duties of special craftsmen in the various trades, such as painters, carpenters, plumbers, and electricians who may be employed in the construction and maintenance work of a recreational service department; these duties are well known and are the same everywhere. The position of general supervisor of planning and development has already been presented. Several positions within the division of planning and development or construction and maintenance are peculiar to recreational service departments. Additionally, there are positions within other divisions of the department, such as the public relations sections of the central office division, whose requirements and duties should be explained. A suggested schedule of requirements and duties for these positions is given below.

1. *Director of Public Relations and Recreational Promotion. Requirements.* Education equivalent to graduation from a university or college of recognized standing with major work in journalism or mass communications; experience in preparation of publicity material for metropolitan newspapers and other publications, in the preparation of material suitable for presentation over radio and television, in the preparation of printed and advertising materials (folders, leaflets, window cards, and posters), in the planning and organization of exhibits; knowledge of methods of contacting groups and organizations for disseminating information about recreational services; knowledge of the preparation of printed annual reports; understanding the requirements of newspapers and magazines as applied to news photos; experience in the planning of 16-mm. motion pictures showing the work of the department, the preparation of appropriate continuity for the guidance of cameramen in making the pictures, and the preparation of the proper vocal descriptions to accompany these films when sound is added; understanding the methods of dealing with established agencies (newspapers, radio stations, television stations, publications, news- and picture-gathering agencies) for the dissemination of information; knowledge of the organization, operation, and functions of the recreational service department.

Duties. To have responsible direction of the publicity and public relations work of the department; to organize educational campaigns for special features of the department's work (camps, swimming pools, and city-wide events), to present a continuing program of public relations and publicity to keep the public informed of the department's work and of available recreational opportunities that tend to increase attendance and participation, foster better understanding, correct misapprehensions, and promote development of public recreational service for the benefit of the citizens of the community; to employ, in a proper manner and in their correct relationships, the various media of public relations work (newspapers and periodicals), and arrange for their publication; to give assignments to photographers and projectionists and supervise their work; to arrange showings of the department's motion pictures; to secure time for radio and television programs about the department and arrange programs for such presentation; to plan and prepare printed materials required by the department (folders, leaflets, posters, circulars, and annual reports); to supervise the distribution of printed and advertising materials to groups and organizations; to supervise the securing of space and the installation of exhibits; to plan 16-mm. motion pictures of the department's work, prepare continuity, direct cameramen or other technicians, and properly prepare vocal descriptions for sound; and to perform related work as required.

2. *Repairman. Requirements.* Education equivalent to completion of twelfth grade in a public school; experience and skill in the use of mechanics' tools; mechanical aptitude; and ingenuity.

Duties. Under supervision, to make minor repairs to buildings, plumbing fixtures, electrical fixtures, playground and gymnasium apparatus, leaky roofs; replace broken window glass; repair and adjust locks and door stops; clean and repair sewers and pipelines; repair fences, electric lighting fixtures, switches, rings, horizontal bars, basketball equipment, swings, and other playground and gymnasium apparatus; to paint woodwork; and to perform related work as required.

3. *Custodian (Caretaker). Requirements.* Education equivalent to completion of twelfth grade in a public school, preferably some specialized schooling in horticulture, agriculture, vocational, or technical trades; at least one year's experience in caring for gardens, nurseries, cemeteries, parks, playgrounds, or in farm work; a thorough knowledge of janitorial work; good physical condition; reliability; trustworthiness; and good moral reputation.

Duties. Under immediate supervision of director of facility, to keep playground premises and buildings clean and in order; to perform routine janitorial work; to assist in making minor repairs to grounds, equipment, and buildings; to care for equipment commonly used on playgrounds and in recreational buildings; to set up equipment used in games on playgrounds; to mark play areas for baseball, volleyball, basketball, and other sports; to maintain order in a recreational area during the absence of the recreationist (should it ever occur); to cultivate, fertilize, water, prune, spray, and trim flowers, trees, shrubs, and lawns; and to perform related work as required.

Analysis of Facility Director's Duties

The duties of persons employed by recreational service systems vary because of the great differences in size of the agencies, in the facilities they operate, and in the programs they conduct. Furthermore, the variance occurs because the work of recreational service is comparatively new and relatively unstandardized. The recreationist's job still tends to conform to the individual employee, unlike jobs in industry in which the individual must conform to the job, because the number of recreational activities is literally infinite, and no recreationist can be expected to be skilled in all activities. Moreover, a recreational center's program is determined partly by the preferences of those who attend it and partly by the interests and skills of the recreationists. Recreational service also calls for a marked degree of independent thinking, talent, enthusiasm, ingenuity, and imagination, which does not readily lend itself to conformity or standardization.

Duties Performed	Percentage of Time Devoted to Each Group
Management	23
Management of the staff, the public, supplies, equipment, finance; preparation of reports; keeping records; ordering supplies	
Maintenance	2
Preparation of facilities; cleaning; repairing; and the like	
Public Relations	9
Promotion and publicity; contacts with parents, organizations, and agencies; acting as department representative	
Organization	23
Organizing staff and volunteer personnel, activity groups, clubs, classes; arranging materials and facilities; planning activities and special events; conducting surveys; analyzing needs	
Supervision	33
Exercising general oversight of the use of facilities and the participation of the public in various activities; being present at meetings, dances, plays, and contests in a general supervisory capacity	
Teaching	10
Class teaching and direction; individual instruction; coaching; counseling	
	100

WAGE AND SALARY ADMINISTRATION

Salaries in public recreational service, as in all governmental services, are established by legislative act and are basically a matter of legal review. Local governmental policies dealing with the salaries of public employees are subject to the normal circumstances of administration. Administrators may recommend salary schedules, but they must be fixed by enactment of law. Several factors usually influence administrative practices:

1. *Salaries of comparable positions in other public service jurisdictions and in private organizations.* Competitive salaries of comparable positions have a marked influence on any public service agency in its efforts to attract and retain competent personnel. Dedication to public service and the advantage of a governmental position (such as security, earned vacations, compensatory pay, leave, medical allowances, or other fringe benefits) are not enough to attract and hold individuals with the necessary talent and preparation for the job. Salaries constitute roughly three fourths of local governmental operation budgets and are carefully adapted to the services to be performed. Although monetary compensation is not the primary reason for entering public recreational service, so many positions are available to the qualified worker that competitive salaries must be maintained if recreational service positions are to be filled effectively.

2. *Legal limits for professional positions in the jurisdiction.* The fixed ceiling for salaries in municipal positions will often affect the amount that can be awarded to anyone employed by the municipality. For example, if the chief executive officer of the city receives a salary of $40,000 per year, all other positions within the city government usually are scaled in a descending series below that sum.

3. *Financial ability of the municipality.* If a city cannot afford adequate salaries, the amount and quality of municipal services necessarily must be restricted. The ability to compensate adequately is largely based on the willingness of the citizenry to be taxed or bonded for the essential governmental services for their health, protection, and welfare; the economic capacity of the community; and the financial aid available from county, state, and federal sources.

4. *Advancement.* The lack of opportunity for continual advancement occasionally forces some personnel to resign in favor of more lucrative or prestigious positions. When a position does not allow the employee to progress beyond a certain rank, incentive or longevity pay may be provided as a device for retaining qualified personnel. Such salary increments may result in a higher rate than would otherwise have been provided.

5. *Fringe benefits for public service.* In fixing local government

salaries, the value of the additional benefits accruing to the incumbent should always be appraised in addition to the real money compensation. These benefits include retirement and disability programs, prepaid hospital, medical, and group life insurance, liberal vacations with pay, and allowances for room, board, transportation, equipment, and clothing. These benefits also should be taken into account by employees in comparing governmental compensation with that available in quasi-public or private enterprises.

6. *Duties and responsibilities.* The type of position, degree of difficulty, relative responsibility, necessary qualifications, and other factors weigh heavily in salary determination. The entire salary schedule or plan of compensation rests more on an effective analysis of positions and on a sound position classification plan than on evaluation of the individual employee's merit, which tends to be more important when promotion is being considered.

The Salary Schedule and Plan

In the establishment of a salary plan, a financial value must be placed on performance or personal services so that comparable positions have equitable compensation.

When the position classification plan has been implemented, the salary schedule may be initiated, which usually involves: (1) identification of positions according to classes, comparison of present salaries with salaries of similar positions in the public jurisdiction and in private enterprise, and adjustments required in recruitment to fill vacancies; (2) an examination of the community's ability to satisfy requirements of a compensation plan; and (3) establishment of minimum and maximum salary limits for each class.

Entrance salaries for special professional positions for which there may be no comparable data must sometimes be determined on the basis of competition for such services, the preparation and experience required, and the need of the system.

Salary Range

The maximum and minimum salaries of any given class of positions are known as the *salary range*, consisting of an entrance salary (usually at the minimum point) and two or more annual grade increments toward the maximum rate. The basic objective of a salary range is to provide incentive and remunerative reward for efficient performance. Advancement within classes by increments is usually automatic but subject to a satisfactory performance rating. Acceleration of advancements by increments is sometimes granted as a reward for additional education or superior performance.

The complexities of modern life and the professional requirements in recreational service have deepened the need for individuals of extraordinary education, talent, skill, and intelligence. To attract and retain such individuals, salaries should be equal to those of other professionals in the public service. Realistically, salaries of public service personnel are paid in relation to the esteem in which the service is held by the public. Only recently has recreational service had any impact on the general public. During the past decade a noteworthy trend toward higher salaries for recreationists has been observed. This rise, in part, may be due to a cost-of-living increment in an inflationary economy. However, there is good reason to believe that recreational service is entering a new period of recognition and value. The services that recreationists provide to the general public may be making more people aware of their need for this service. In consequence, compensation for recreational service personnel has almost doubled within the decade 1960 to 1970. Although there are executive positions that now call for salaries at $55,000 and there are many salaries being paid between $15,000 and $25,000, in many communities compensation for the recreationist is still not comparable to salaries in allied fields, i.e., education, social work, and public health.

In the large cities, chief executives of the recreational service system should be remunerated at a level closely approximating that of the superintendent of schools. Subordinate employees of the system should receive salaries at least equal to that of their hierarchical counterparts within the school system. Equitable compensation for recreationist positions should compare favorably with that of school personnel everywhere. In instances in which degree of difficulty and job responsibility are of greater intensity, the salary should reflect the added burden of educational and experiential requirements. There is little question that recreationist's salaries at all levels will rise dramatically over the next few years as public demand for recreational services becomes more intense.

The larger and longer-established systems generally compensate their workers at higher rates than do newer and smaller departments. Compensation is generally higher in far-Western and southwestern states than in southeastern and northern New England states. The midwestern and mid-Atlantic states rank somewhere between the two extremes. Several states prove exceptions to the regional rule. California, New York, Pennsylvania, Michigan, Texas, Minnesota, Massachusetts, Colorado, and Washington have often been the leaders in higher salaries for recreationists. But recreationists usually are paid less than public school teachers and executives, and public systems as a rule pay less than some private agencies.

The suggested salaries in Table 15-1 have their realistic counterparts in actual compensation earned by recreationists in localities throughout the United States.

TABLE 15-1 SUGGESTED SALARIES

Position	Population of City		
	Over 500,000	100,000 to 500,000	Under 100,000
Superintendent	$35,000 to $55,000	$20,500 to $32,500	$12,800 to $22,500
Assistant Superintendent	$28,000 to $44,000	$18,800 to $25,800	$10,900 to $17,500
General Supervisor	$25,400 to $33,500	$15,800 to $20,500	$ 9,800 to $13,500
Director of Facility	$14,600 to $19,000	$13,400 to $15,000	$ 9,200 to $12,500
Assistant Director of Facility	$12,200 to $15,500	$11,200 to $13,500	$ 8,800 to $11,000
Program or Functional Worker	$ 9,500 to $18,200	$ 8,200 to $12,800	$ 8,200 to $10,500
Specialists	$ 8,200 to $13,400	$ 8,200 to $ 9,800	$ 8,200 to $ 9,400

The salary range recommended in Table 15-1 is not ideal since it does not reflect the variations in responsibility assigned to a specific title in many localities. A "director" may be responsible for one small playground within a neighborhood or direct a recreational complex designed to serve the needs of an entire city district. Then, too, there are differences in standards of compensation in particular regions of the country. Recreational service is important to people everywhere, regardless of the size of local jurisdictions, but some communities have a more profound recognition of its value and offer higher salaries than do cities of comparable size, because they wish to secure and retain effective professionals.

The incidence of higher salaries, although gratifying, is still not sufficient to attract and retain outstanding individuals. The highest salaries paid may be encountered in one or two of the giant metropolitan areas in the country. In too many instances, recreationists are grossly underpaid for the position, degree of difficulty, required educational preparation, and experience that they must have to perform competently.

PROFESSIONAL CONDUCT

In recreational service, the conduct of employees on and off the job is a matter of official concern. Appropriate behavior during and after working hours reflects not only on the employee, but also on the public system that employs him. Exemplary conduct is expected of personnel in this field of public service quite as much as in public education. Recreationists, as do other public employees with professional interests, affiliate with local, state, and national organizations for mutual benefit. In recent years, some attempt has been made to establish one master professional society by which the discipline might gain unity and status.

The continuing expansion of the field and the increased demand for qualified, competent, and professional practitioners have given rise to the adoption of certain principles of professional conduct by state professional societies or associations of recreationists, to raise the standards of practice and maintain the ethics of professionalism.

STATE CERTIFICATION OF RECREATIONISTS

States have generally established programs of state sanction or certification for specific professional employment, in order to promote the acceptance of high standards of professional preparation and to discourage, and in some cases to prohibit, the employment of incompetent persons. Such state programs are well known in connection with the certification of physicians, dentists, nurses, teachers, lawyers, architects, engineers, and accountants. Recreationists have long believed that similar registration of qualified recreational service personnel would enhance the standing of the field and promote better practices. However, opinion is still widely divergent as to whether such workers should be registered under the programs of teacher certification, social work certification, or the recreational service system alone. Certainly state certification and national board examination, certification, and reciprocal arrangements among states will be established one day. At that time, recreational service will have passed an important milestone toward its recognition as a profession.

Selected References

Braun, C. F.: *Management and Leadership* (Alhambra, Calif.: C. F. Braun & Co.), 1976.

Burack, E. H. and R. D. Smith: *Personnel Management: A Human Resource Systems Approach* (St. Paul, Minn.: West Publishing Co.), 1977.

Cayer, N. J.: *Public Personnel Administration in the United States* (New York: St. Martin's Press, Inc.), 1975.

Chruden, H. J. and A. W. Sherman, Jr.: *Personnel Management, 5th ed.* (Cincinnati, Ohio: South-Western Publishing Co.), 1976.

Donovan, J. J., Ed.: *Recruitment and Selection in the Public Service* (Chicago: Public Personnel Association), 1968.

French, W. L.: *Personnel Management Process, 4th ed.*: (New York: Houghton Mifflin Co.), 1977.

Jucius, M.: *Personnel Management, 8th ed.*: (Homewood, Ill.: Richard D. Irwin), 1975.

Pigors, P. and C. A. Meyers: *Personnel Administration: A Point of View and Method, 8th ed.* (New York: McGraw-Hill Book Company), 1977.

Robbins, S. P.: *Personnel: The Management of Human Resources* (Englewood Cliffs, N.J.: Prentice-Hall, Inc.), 1978.

CHAPTER 16

Staffing, Employee Relations, and Employee Organizations

The staffing process comprises all sequential and reciprocal procedures related to filling all positions within the hierarchy of the recreational service system. Staffing is concerned with developing positions, authorization for employment, identifying source of labor, recruitment, induction, orientation, in-service education, retention, and separations. Therefore, staffing deals with people moving into, within, and out of the system. These activities may occur independently, interdependently, separately, simultaneously, or coincidentally.

Several methods and procedures have been developed to facilitate the staffing process. Arrangements to deter friction, dissatisfaction, or poor morale include devices for the selection, retention, evaluation, and promotion of capable employees. Conversely, other methods have been devised to assist in the decision to separate an employee for cause from the system. These instrumentalities are time and motion studies to determine the need for positions, the development of application forms, psychological examinations (rarely used even at this late date), interviews, reference recommendations, physical examinations or medical records (in negligible use), and performance appraisal and evaluation.

THE STAFFING PROCESS

There is a definite tendency to raise recreational service to the level or status of a profession, especially as far as prerequisite educational preparation is concerned. A broad cultural background is the first requirement for employment related to the leadership of people within recreational service. Regardless of what other qualifications may be required, recreational service agencies lay great emphasis on general educational background. Graduation from an institution of higher education is preferred, but increasingly a minimum of two years of community or two-year college work in an accredited curriculum of recreational service education is being permitted for functional or program level workers. Two years of college or university work beyond the high school level are acceptable for some specialist positions. High school graduation is often accepted as the minimum qualification for summer or seasonal work in non-professional and technical positions.

Personal skills in the activities constituting the recreational program are also required. A limited number of recreationists are employed in specialized fields of activity; most program workers are employed to direct a varied activity program. Although the recreationist need not be highly skilled or expert in all activities, he should at least be able to recognize good performance when he sees it and to demonstrate good form in a given activity for beginners and those with moderate skill. Such skills are the product of a rich recreational life through the years. Although much can be obtained from high school and college courses designed to improve and teach certain skills, if the individual has not lived an active recreational life he is at best poorly equipped for recreational service as a career.

Knowledge of human nature—or, as one writer stated it, "wisdom with people"—is another requirement. It is necessary in order that the needs, capacities, and interests of those for whom the program was organized may be understood. Experience in community living contributes much, but there can be no substitute for study of the biological, social, and physical sciences and of the humanities. Courses in the philosophy and methodology of recreational service and related disciplines are also important. Through such courses the individual acquires an understanding of the objectives of recreational service and the methods employed to achieve them. Closely linked with this instruction are courses dealing with the history of the recreational service movement, the structural organization of various recreational service agencies and systems, and the social and political environment in which such services are performed.

Although technical preparation is of great importance, it will avail the potential recreationist little unless he also possesses the personal attributes that distinguish a leader. These characteristics justify the confidence placed in him for services so definitely designed to improve human behavior. Foremost among such personal qualities is the trait of sociability, extroversion, the ability to make friends, to inspire confidence, and to be acceptable among all types of people. High moral and ethical standards, awareness of social situations that generate problems of behavior, tolerance, and zeal for the great humanitarian work of recreational service are essential. Lack of any of these qualities may be the difference between success and failure. No amount of academic preparation or specific skills in activities will compensate for the absence of good personal qualities.

Professionally equipped persons are continuously needed for public recreational service employment, not only to replace retiring workers or separated individuals, but also to fill positions newly created by the establishment of departments and the expansion of operational departments. Despite the efforts of some administrators to employ part-time staff at the program level, in order to avoid fringe benefit payments, unionization of employees, and other expenditures typically associated with full-time workers, particularly during periods of economic retrenchment, the need for greater numbers of professional personnel in recreational service will probably continue unabated for years to come. In all likelihood, with the growth of leisure in American society there may never be a sufficient number of recreationists to staff contemplated or established positions.

Recruitment

Recruitment is the enlisting of qualified personnel. To ensure against a dearth of workers in any segment of the recreational service operation, lists of qualified applicants are established by examinations. Schedules of examinations inform interested individuals of the positions open and the dates when examinations for the positions will be given. Announcements are circulated through mass communications media and by direct correspondence with interested groups, especially the departments of colleges and universities with professional preparatory courses or curricula in natural resources and recreational service education.

When the usual forms of recruitment do not appear to satisfy the need for qualified applicants, more direct means of attracting capable persons may be utilized, e.g., visits to institutions of higher education for determining potential candidates and personal interviews with prospective applicants.

Since a large number of the workers employed by local recreational service departments are either part-time or seasonal workers, they constitute a valuable source from which the permanent full-time staff may be recruited. Seasonal positions are not usually considered permanent; reappointment must be made each season or periodically. Many people who perform seasonal or part-time work are preparing for full-time career employment. In-service education and on-the-job development are often provided for such workers.

Obtaining candidates and applications is merely the first step in the staffing process. The next stage is examination and selection.

Examination and Selection of Potential Recreationists

Examination is a device that attempts to confirm whether or not an apparent good quality, skill, or pertinent knowledge is actually present in the applicant. Tests of several types may be utilized to differentiate the qualifications of applicants and to classify them in order of merit. They are also a means of eliminating from consideration those applicants who do not meet the required minimum standards. Examinations explore and measure the applicant's skill and knowledge about the duties of a specific position. They may be written, oral, practical, or any combination of these. Tests of general aptitude, intelligence, achievement, and health may be included also.

Written tests covering, as far as it is practicable, the whole range of knowledge related to the position are typically given. Oral tests are generally conducted by a panel of three or more examiners who rate the personal qualifications of the applicant after a personal interview and through information of the applicant's performance in previously held positions. Practical tests (scored by a panel or by one expert) rate the ability of the applicant to perform in situations calling for actual leadership and direction of individuals and groups in various activities. They also test and rate the applicant's familiarity with the materials and resources used in the program as well as his capacity to put them to skilled and effective use.

Employment

Employees selected to fill positions in the public recreational service should be appointed wholly on merit. Although many cities and other jurisdictions have no legally established systems of civil service, there is usually a sincere effort to select persons properly fitted for the work. Difficulty arises less from a lack of desire to appoint competent persons than from inadequate information as to what constitutes competence in this field. Where there are systems of civil service, the employment of recreational service personnel falls within the purview of the system and is subject to established examinations and certification procedures.

Many recreational service departments in non-civil service jurisdictions establish their own examination procedures to guide them in the selection of potential employees from lists of applicants. The effectiveness of the examination program depends on the validity of the tests used and the diligence to which they are adhered. An examination gives the appointing authority an objective basis by which to grade candidates, and it may be used to good advantage in resisting pressure tactics favoring the employment of inadequately prepared or otherwise unqualified applicants. Lacking objective information, the appointing official must depend solely on his subjective judgment. This arrangement is not always accepted by others and may lead to gross errors and serious conflict of interest.

Probational Appointment

The organized civil service exists not only for systematizing the selection of employees for public service, but also to grant employees security from unwarranted discharge. The probationary period may be considered as part of the employee's examination, albeit a post-examination. Under civil service rules an employee is usually on probation for periods varying from three to twelve months; rarely is probationary status prolonged beyond that time. During this period the competent supervisor studies the appointee's work, attitude toward the department, personality, and all-round fitness for the position. During the probationary period an employee may be discharged without formal charges being preferred against him by the appointing official. If such separation is determined to be necessary, the employee is notified of the action and arrangements made for an informal hearing at the employee's request. Typically, however, such informal hearings tend to leave the probationer with the same status he held prior to the hearing, i.e., he will be separated from employment. Following the probationary period, formal charges citing valid and documented reasons must be filed against the offending employee. Under such circumstances, the employee being charged may request a formal hearing during which he may attempt to refute the charges and defend his position. Unless there is absolute certainty that documented charges may be laid against the employee, hearings are not convened by the appointing official.

During the probationary period, orientation, a method by which the newly inducted employee is assimilated into the system, is initiated. It assists the employee in adjusting to the organization by acquainting him with agency philosophy, policies, rules, regulations, requirements, and practices. It includes introduction of new colleagues, orientation to the position, staff meetings, tours of the system's facilities and components (particularly when a group of newly inducted employees are processed simultaneously), and other personnel practices that are designed to make the transition into the system a pleasant and confidence-building experience.

Transfers

Transfer is appointment from one position to another within the organization, at the same grade and pay and without loss of any work time. Transfer is usually resorted to at the instigation of the department or at the request of the employee with the approval of the department. Transfers serve a number of objectives: (1) When there is personality maladjustment of an employee at one area of the system, he may be transferred to another section or division of the system or given different working hours; thus, he is given a second opportunity to adjust himself to new conditions of employment. (2) An employee may be transferred to another location where his talents are needed more urgently. (3) Employees may be moved to vacated positions or fill positions that have greater significance for the system's organizational goals.

Promotion

Promotion is the advancement of an employee from a given position to a position of higher grade by his assumption of different duties and responsibilities, usually of a more difficult nature, accompanied by a change of title and generally by an increase in salary. Eligibility for promotion requires the satisfaction of certain requirements established by the department: length of service in a given grade, education, experience, past performance, extraordinary skill, talent, or knowledge, and sometimes the ability to pass a competitive promotional examination.

The basic intent of promotion is to fill higher positions with the best qualified personnel while maintaining morale throughout the system. Promotion enables the department to make greater utilization of more highly competent and qualified workers, reduces the risk of bringing in a relatively unknown person, who may not be as easily evaluated, and lessens the rate of employee turnover. In some instances, opening higher positions to persons outside of the system may be absolutely necessary, but such practice must be determined by the conditions involved. Incentive usually evolves from a well-conducted promotion plan. Employees regard the program as a way to win greater prestige, remuneration, security, and as an enhancement to ego. They thereby strive to perform to the best of their capabilities and tend to cultivate loyalty to the department.

Disciplinary Action

All administrative measures to correct malfeasance, misfeasance, or nonfeasance of employees on the job are disciplinary actions. Discipline may be oral, written, or substantive in form. Listed below are measures that administrators may utilize for disciplinary activities.

1. *Verbal reprimand* is an admonishment given for minor infractions of personnel policies or rules that are not serious enough to warrant further action. Usually an oral admonition is all that is required for correction.
2. *Written reprimand* is a written statement placed in the employee's service record resulting from infractions of personnel policies or regulations that are not serious enough to warrant further action. The employee, of course, is informed of this action. The written

statement may be withdrawn from the service record after the incumbent has maintained himself in a satisfactory manner for a period of time, usually six months.

3. *Involuntary transfer* is moving an employee from one position to another within the department, owing to personal friction with co-workers or other reasons, when it is deemed advisable to reassign an effective worker rather than to separate him from the agency.

4. *Demotion* is a transfer involving a reduction in pay, status, privilege, or opportunity. Demotions occur from an employee's inability to perform adequately in a particular position, which may have resulted from an initial error in placement.

5. *Suspension* is enforced relinquishment of duties for a specified period of time without compensation. The loss of time involved depends on the nature of the incident. It is the most serious form of disciplinary action for causes sufficient to warrant immediate investigation and possible filing of criminal charges or other necessary actions. Pending investigation of the incumbent's activities, his pay is usually withheld. Ultimate termination of employment may ensue, the filing of criminal charges may result, or the findings may vindicate the innocence of the employee. In the latter instance the employee is reinstated with reimbursement of pay retroactive to the time of his initial suspension.

6. *Discharge* is termination of employment with prejudice. Permanent separation from the agency for just cause usually occurs following suspension, and after investigation proves the allegations of guilt valid. In some cases, the employee's conduct may be so completely reprehensible that summary action is not only justified but required.

Causes of Disciplinary Action.   Among the offenses an employee may commit in relation to his position are those resulting from inattention to job responsibilities. Such infractions as tardiness, laziness, carelessness, breakage, damage, or loss of property are minor acts which, through repetition, show an undeniable immaturity and misconduct. These continuous breaches of good conduct and professional practice indicate poor job orientation or lack of fitness for a position. Inattention to the rules governing these matters sometimes leads to friction among personnel, lowers morale within the system, and impairs public relations.

Other offenses are inefficiency owing to insufficient preparation, incompetency, insubordination, intoxication, immorality, lack of integrity (violation of public ethics, failure to meet financial obligations, accepting bribes, extortion, embezzlement, theft of property, failure to enforce a specific department policy, absence without authorization, gross negligence, conduct unbecoming an employee of the public recreational service system, brutality, and the like). Any of these breaches of conduct may, and probably should, result in disciplinary action, the form of action to be determined by the seriousness of the offense.

Working Conditions

Recreational service is conducted when people have leisure to spend. Many recreationists therefore are employed during evening hours, Saturdays, Sundays, and holidays, as well as during weekdays throughout the year. This is a necessary, but somewhat disagreeable, condition of the work. Recreationist executives endeavor to limit the amount of work assigned during such times by rotating evening, Saturday, Sunday, and holiday assignments among all recreational service system personnel and by placing a definite time limit on the amount of such work any employee may be required to perform. Some recreationists are employed with the understanding that they will have working hours only during late afternoons and evenings; others are employed specifically for days; still others work weekends and holidays. The total number of hours worked per week, compensatory pay for overtime, compensatory time off in lieu of overtime pay, and other fringe benefits (Workmen's Compensation, group medical and health insurance plans, sabbaticals, vacations, leaves, and disability and retirement privileges) conform to local practices for public service employees and tend to conform to good practice in well-established private employment.

Uniforms. Although recreational service personnel should present a clean and neat appearance and directors of facilities should be recognized as such when at work, there is no unanimity of opinion as to how these objectives may be accomplished best. A few departments have adopted uniforms for playground workers. Sometimes the employees are required to purchase such uniforms at their own expense. In most cases the department simply issues whatever uniform is required by policy. Uniforms more frequently have been specified for beach and pool lifeguards, custodians, groundkeepers, and maintenance personnel. For those who organize, conduct, and instruct in varied recreational activities, departments are content to prescribe that the attire shall be neat, clean, and suitable to the activity being directed. Sometimes a sweater or shirt with a distinctive emblem is prescribed for use in athletic or playground activities. Arm bands, sun visors, caps, jackets, pullovers, and badges are also used as insignia indicating official connection with the department.

Leave of Absence

Leave is permission to be absent from assigned duties granted by the employing authority according to legally established regulations uniformly to all employees.

Annual or vacation leave is earned by continuous permanent employment within the department and is granted for a fixed length of time, usually two weeks after one full year of employment and more after ten or more years of employment. With satisfactory service, the recreationist may expect to receive an annual leave of two to four weeks. In many localities accumulated leave may be carried forward for use in succeeding years; however, there is usually a fixed maximum beyond which the employee may not be able to accumulate additional leave.[1]

Judicial leave is granted when a recreationist must attend court as a governmental witness, for jury duty, or is summoned for other than personal reasons. Before such leave is granted the employee must submit a true copy of the subpoena or other court order prior to the beginning date of the summons.

Full-time employees are usually excused from work on official legal holidays without loss of pay or, if required to work, are excused from duty on another day. When a religious observance is to be made during a working day, the absence of the employee may be charged to annual leave, if the employee has leave to his credit; otherwise, the employee gets leave without pay. It is usual, however, for employees to be given consideration to attend religious exercises.

Sick leave is customarily granted an employee for personal illness, injury, pregnancy, medical or dental examination, or following exposure to some contagious disease. Some departments, in coordination with the municipal or county public health department, provide time off so that employees may receive immunization vaccinations. Generally, one day per month, or a fraction of a day, is granted and sick leave may be accumulated to a maximum of 14 days each year, increasing progressively to a total accumulation of 90 days with seniority in service.

Extended leave without pay is usually granted for therapeutic purposes after a year or more of satisfactory service. Extended leave without pay also may be granted for study that will benefit the department or for essential personal reasons.

In certain departments it may be the policy to authorize specific absences if the employee wishes to vote, to donate blood, to visit a dying relative, to be present at a relative's funeral, to take a promotional examination or other departmentally connected test, to attend a professional institute, conference, or workshop, or for medical reasons. These excused absences are granted for short periods, ranging from one hour to five days.

Unauthorized leave is absence without official authorization and without notification of the reason for absence. In this case an employee is carried on a pay or non-pay status until the cause of the absence has

[1] Richard G. Kraus and Joseph E. Curtis, *Creative Administration in Recreation and Parks,* 2d ed. (St. Louis, Mo.: The C. V. Mosby Company, 1977) pp. 88–89.

been determined; if the absence is not justified, appropriate disciplinary action is taken.

Efficiency Ratings

Evaluation and appraisal of employees are necessary to provide incentive for improvement, to reward meritorious service, and to determine the efficiency and effectiveness of personnel in approximating the goals set by the system. They are also an effective aid in counseling and supervisory efforts. The ratings are obtained by (1) supervisory observation and visitation, (2) performance reporting, (3) comparison scales, (4) periodic examinations, (5) supervisory interviews, and (6) personal appraisal. Efficiency ratings evaluate an employee's actual accomplishment against the duties prescribed for his position. A composite rating, such as "Outstanding or Superior," "Satisfactory," or "Unsatisfactory," is recorded and filed for future reference. The employee is apprised of this rating and the reasons for it. The rating is consulted for an employee's reassignment, promotion, demotion, need for additional development or education, and separation from the agency.

Separation

Separation is the termination of employee services with a given organization. Separations occur for varied reasons originating either with the employee or with the organization.

When the employee makes the decision to leave the agency, he may resign or, if eligible, retire. Whatever the cause of the resignation, it is a voluntary ending of services with the department. In some instances, however, resignation may be permitted in lieu of discharge to avoid a blight on the employee's personnel record or because the department wishes to avoid a drawn-out investigatory procedure and a formal hearing.

In the case of retirement, the employee terminates his active service with the department on reaching the minimum age permitted by the retirement plan (if there is one) or the age of compulsory retirement. Retirement for disability at partial compensation, increasing in proportion to years served, is a feature of most retirement plans.

Retirement Plans. Every modern public recreational service system should have a retirement program that provides earned benefits to employees who, because of advanced age, physical disability, or in-service tenure, are no longer effective in their positions. A sound personnel plan includes a retirement program, because such a procedure is advantageous both to the department and to its employees.

A retirement plan provides an equitable method for terminating employment of those who have become inefficient or ineffective because of age. It offers security, which attracts and retains competent individuals to the department. It tends to reduce the rate of employee turnover since benefits are earned only after continuous employment with the system over a prescribed number of years, and it serves as a morale-booster throughout the system. It also should be recognized that early retirement is sometimes used as a remedial device for correcting an initial staffing error. Voluntary early retirement also occurs occasionally.

Layoff or Furlough.   These terms signify an enforced separation without compensation for an indeterminate period of time for lack of work or to reduce expenses. During the aftermath of the depression, 1932 to 1939, when federally funded programs were first curtailed and then abolished, the importance of layoffs and/or furloughs had been insignificant in recreational service. However, beginning in the latter part of the 1960s reduction in personnel forces were noted in major urban centers in the United States. A steady attrition rate, without replacement, as well as layoffs curtailed the services of several city recreational service departments. The economic recession of 1974–1975 also produced a period of drastic reduction among professional personnel in urban departments. Many public recreational service agencies were required to function with less than 50 percent of their former work force. Such layoffs were common at the height of the recession, and at least one city completely abolished its public recreational service department in order to save money. It was only during late 1976 that economic recovery produced conditions favorable to the reinstatement of recreational service personnel and permitted the demand for more recreational services to be satisfied by opening recreational service positions in governmental agencies.

GRIEVANCES

Imagined and real employee grievances arise in all organizations and ways must be found to express them and to have them satisfied or adjusted. They are usually related to compensation, advancement, work load, physical environment, treatment by supervisors, and, sometimes, purely personal matters. It is important for employees to know that a mechanism for the expression of grievances exists and that all grievances will be heard with tolerance and understanding and without resentment or unjust recrimination. Imagined grievances often can be dispelled by frank discussion. Real grievances frequently may be adjusted by simple administrative action.

Arbitration of grievance involves logical employee–employer discussion of a complaint (generally filed by an employee) at successively higher levels in the system. The grievance may be ameliorated at any level, but, if not, the problem may be submitted to the chief executive or to an impartial third party for final mediation. The main purpose of all grievance procedures is to achieve equity for both parties to a complaint or problem without deterioration of service or personnel morale.

Secondarily, the grievance process is a communicative device reaching from the line workers to the highest administrative levels within the system. It is surely the simplest and most direct link between line and staff, between functional employees and top management. The entire grievance procedure provides a morale appraisal by the executive staff of the system, indicating where and what type of difficulties are present or potential.

Finally, the grievance procedure almost forces some concept of justice within the system through performance standards and compensatory practices. There must be uniform application of personnel policies and regulations when similar jobs are concerned. Within the recreational service system, particularly when there is no direct check by an organization representing employees, the administration of justice becomes extremely important. Supervisors and administrators must take a professional view of all employee grievances. Being sure to maintain absolute objectivity and mature deliberations in hearing about complaints and problems will produce an atmosphere more conducive to high morale, goodwill, and effective service to the community.

Day-to-day treatment of subordinates requires consistency of action over time. Systematic procedures for determining decisions about the allocation of rewards and discipline are of inestimable value in the administration of equity within any organization. Systematic planning, sympathetic understanding, and consistent application must be part of the established criteria of position and employee value. Scrupulous attention to standards must be maintained, with an equal opportunity for review. The quality of human judgment is an essential aspect in the grievance process. Systematic procedures assist in refining judgment.

EMPLOYEE ORGANIZATIONS AND MANAGEMENT RELATIONS

Until a few years ago, there was general resistence on the part of recreationists to join trade union organizations. This reluctance has now given way to a very real inclination, on the part of subordinate line and staff personnel, to become represented in collective bargaining units. During the past decade an upsurge in the number of public recreational service employees seeking affiliation with independent employee associations or labor organizations has been manifested. There are numerous reasons for this noticeable trend and an ostrich-like attitude on the part of administrators, who hope that this movement will vanish if they ignore it long enough, can only compound present problems. The desire on the part of employees to seek collective bargaining should not be viewed as a direct assault on the administrator or as a sign that subordinates are attacking the administrator personally. Rather, employee requests for bargaining units must be seen as a logical outcome of both legislation and court decisions regulating public employee relations. A majority of the states now have laws which require management and subordinates to meet, confer, negotiate, and otherwise bargain collectively. It is only natural that recreationists in the public sector should avail themselves of this condition of employment.

Changes in the law and directives issued by the attorney general have led to a revised labor-management environment. Whereas recreationists at all levels formerly identified themselves with management and resisted unionization, for the most part, several significant influences have contributed to increased recreational service personnel union activity just recently. First, are the profound frustrations which program recreationists felt, arising from a relatively authoritarian concept of superior-subordinate relationships pervading the system. This is reflected in the type of department where policy statements are issued from the administrator's office as fiat, without any input by those who must execute such policy. Secondly, there has been a disinclination on the part of local government to be responsive to the demands of departmental employees for wage improvement and other fringe benefits. Finally, there has been the feeling that public recreational service is merely a frill and therefore can be chopped with impunity. The question of job security for competent work performed was either ignored or thought to be unimportant. Little wonder then when line recreationists began to turn to those organizations which appeared to be able to offer relief from these circumstances.

Community taxpayers who reside within the city have a right to expect a variety of services, including health, education, and protection, as well as the opportunity for leisure activities provided in a clean and safe environment. All of these city services must be delivered at a price which is within the community's ability to pay without undue stress. In the same way, employees should be able to expect competitive salaries and fringe benefits. Unfortunately, equitability between the expectations of community residents and municipal employees frequently are denied when tax rates zoom or employee demands become too burdensome. The largest cities in the United States are faced with economic shortfalls and are limited financially or have actually approached bankruptcy.

In the public sector, the chief concern of elected officials is re-election, rather than economic self-sufficiency. One result of this political tunnel vision is to make elected officials susceptible to pressure tactics by members of labor organizations. Labor lobbyists continue their influence attempts by making politicians assume positions or promise financial commitments prior to any consideration of the effect that such assurances will have upon the provision of community services. For this reason, professional negotiators who deal in labor-management relations almost always advise elected officials to remain aloof from the collective bargaining procedure. The distance which elected officials maintain permits the necessary disinterest so that they may execute a policy-making status that is effective for the diverse aspects of local governmental performance.

In many instances, public employees seek better wages, working conditions, and hours. Sometimes employees become concerned about the kind of supervision imposed upon them, inappropriate job assignments, inequitable selection for advancement, poor in-service education, unsafe working situations, unfair disciplinary procedures, and cronyism—to list but a few of the reasons for which employees will become militant. The significance of and the corresponding reaction to such practices as they relate to employee satisfaction, stimulation, and output cannot be overlooked or emphasized too much in determining employer-employee relations. Perhaps the most important objectives of employee associations are the basic items of a fair wage and conditions of work. Additionally, recreationists want to be a part of the decision-making process within the agency. As professionals, they will want to share in the practices which critically affect them. On the other hand, administrators want to control the operation of the agency in all respects, particularly in terms of specified powers and responsibilities which have been delegated to them. Specifically, administrators desire unshared authority in the following areas:

1. To recruit, induct, assign, transfer, and promote employees;
2. To take appropriate disciplinary actions against employees for just cause, including: suspension, transfer, admonishment, demotion, or discharge;
3. To devise the procedures and practices for personnel management insofar as numbers, responsibilities, and supervision is concerned for the efficient operation of the agency;
4. To regulate the departmental budget;
5. To take whatever steps are required during crisis situations in order that the proper functioning of the department is maintained.

Collective Bargaining

Free collective bargaining is a process whereby organized employee associations and management negotiate the terms and conditions of employment which are then incorporated in a collective bargaining agreement. Although the collective bargaining process is conducted under adversary arrangements, there are certain common ends towards which both management and labor strive. These shared interests comprise the following:

1. Offering and maintaining high-quality services to the citizens of the community based upon financial considerations which will not place such services in a threatened position;

2. Promoting superior performance among employees while enhancing efficiency and economy;
3. Providing in-service education and maintaining professionalism among employees.
4. Maintaining the appropriate supplies, materials, and equipment as well as the places where recreational services are to be carried out so that personnel may perform their duties most effectively;
5. Retaining productive personnel through competitive remuneration and conditions of work;
6. Establishing and sustaining a labor-management relationship based upon mutual trust and respect;
7. Establishing and maintaining a positive and impartial *modus operendi* for the resolution of departmental problems.

Departmental executives should be familiar with the applicable legislation as well as the development of labor-management relations as they have matured in cities of similar size. In negotiating with employee associations they should request assistance from city staff experts, if the community operates its collective bargaining procedure on a departmental basis, or obtain professional assistance from professional consultants on a fee or contract basis. When the bargaining process is transacted professionally, there is greater likelihood that employee interests will be served while administrative authority will be preserved. Any concessions made will be appropriate to the situation and in areas that are assistive. Professional expertese brought to bear should enable the process to be conducted on a logical, problem-oriented basis rather than on subjective, personality-centered approaches.

Collective bargaining is an evolutionary process and, therefore, it should prevent management from simply meeting demands by offering everything for which it is asked. When this occurs, management is reduced to a rubber stamp because it often has nothing left with which to negotiate. Recreationist administrators have become cognizant of this fact. To forestall any poverty of position, some administrators are developing plans to more nearly equalize bargaining outcomes. The following statement deals with productivity measures resulting from negotiating with employee organizations:

> Historically, employee organizations have annually made demands on governmental agencies for increases in salaries, fringe benefits, and improved working conditions. Many times the demands have been linked to the reduction of management prerogatives. At this juncture in time, when we are considering how we will be able to deliver effective services to the public in a period of austerity, it is important that we give adequate attention to the development of counter demands which we can present to the employee organizations at the bargaining table. These management demands should focus on recapturing the various management preroga-

tives which were given away at previous negotiations or as a result of past practice which can help us increase the organization's productivity. Also, it would be valuable at the time of negotiations to present our new program directions and manning patterns which we would like to introduce to increase productivity and to cope with the attrition situation. It would be our objective to gain acceptance of these directions as part of the salary negotiation process.[2]

By developing negotiating positions before any actual bargaining occurs and making plans to present managerial demands, rather than assuming a defensive stance and reacting to employee demands, administrators can take a more successful posture. Where negotiating issues are worked out well in advance there is more latitude for the give and take of bargaining where each side's desires are worked out to the satisfaction of all parties concerned. The entire process of good faith negotiations should end in a mutually agreed upon contract containing all of the provisions which were discussed and ratified. Neither party to the process can be compelled to agree to any proposition. Moreover, neither party must concede its position by virtue of any proposal which is brought up. The process of collective bargaining proceeds through several stages from an initial point when the employees want to organize or gain representation for future collective bargaining through negotiation, and final contract administration. It is not the intent of this section to summarize the collective bargaining process.[3] However, there are some tactics from which administrators can profit.

Avoiding Past Errors

Learning from past mistakes is indicative of administrative precaution. Only a fool repeats mistakes and these inevitably prove costly for all concerned. By studying the history of previous collective bargaining sessions it is likely that excellent insight into how future negotiations should be conducted will be acquired. In planning negotiations, the following observations appear to be important:

1. How well did the previous negotiating team perform? Unless the agency's negotiators have the authority to reach definite decisions, nothing can really be accomplished. The best settlements are those which leave both parties satisfied.
2. It is important to come to the negotiating table with a well thought out position plan, including a logical comprehension as to what expectations the opposing side has for a contract settlement. The worst fault that administrators reveal is an embarrassing lack of information as to

[2] Letter from Joseph Halper, Acting Director, Recreational Service Department, Los Angeles County, September 21, 1976.
[3] Winston W. Crouch, Ed., *Local Government Personnel Administration* (Washington, D.C.: International City Management Association, 1976), pp. 218–223.

what the other side will give or expect because of supposed "inside information" which proves to be erroneous.

3. It is always dangerous for management to interfere in local employee association politics. Generally, it is beneficial for management to adopt a policy of avoidance of local union politics completely and prepare for negotiations despite any opposition.

4. The use of misleading or falsified information should be scrupulously avoided. Unless factual data are properly utilized the material will be ineffective to support issues which management wants to bring out. More importantly, future statistical representations will be greeted with scepticism and have little impact on negotiations.

5. The timing of proposals has an important influence upon negotiations. Modified demands presented too early or too late will obviously lose the intended impact. Proper timing is something which develops with accumulated experience.

6. In developing appropriate bargaining units, management should remember that its supervisory personnel need to be closely allied to managerial postures and represent management on a day-to-day basis. If members of the supervisory level are permitted to affiliate with the collective bargaining unit, the administration has lost a significant part of its ability to deal with personnel problems that arise in the course of daily operations. Far better for supervisors to have their own bargaining unit, if they feel that they too must organize, than to have middle-management personnel in association with those whom they normally have to direct. To the extent that the administration can successfully maintain its management personnel by requiring a separate bargaining unit, when one is required, they will have lessened the probability of uncontrolled service break-downs.

7. It is undesirable to present so many demands that they cannot possibly be worked out during the current negotiating session. One of the more useless tactics used by parties to a negotiation is to present too many demands and end up with few, if any, obtained. The adversary will probably discount many of the demands in advance and not seriously appreciate what the opposing party actually wants. It is far better to propose what is really wanted together with a few additional demands abhorrent to the employees' association to be used for trading purposes.

8. Negotiating subjectively or permitting one's emotions to become involved in the oftentimes delicate matters of contract agreements can lead to disappointment and dissatisfaction with the results. When emotions are allowed to hold sway, the several persons who are party to the negotiations may make statements in the heat of argument which come home to roost later. Every attempt should be made to cool tempers, offer dispassionate debate, and at the conclusion of negotiations to smooth out any hurt feelings that may have developed. Everyone will not be absolutely satisfied with the negotiated contract, but if negotiations have been conducted in the objective atmosphere of economic reality, rather than having dwelt upon personality factors or aroused emotional feelings, acceptance of the end product is usually assured.

Experienced professionals realize that at the negotiating sessions the members of the bargaining teams play out scenarios. The sessions permit each person to act out some latent fantasies. With the bargaining table as the stage there is an opportunity to make speeches, curse, debate, and take the limelight. All of this is part of the negotiating program. Some employers might object to large employee negotiating committees without realizing that there are both political and substantive reasons involved. A large committee provides the audience to play to; a larger group can more easily disseminate information to the rank and file; and, most importantly, a large committee comes under less suspicion from other employees.

Bargaining strategy requires patience and recognizes the need for permitting the other party to state the position and reveal whatever knowledge has been acquired about the issues. The climate in which negotiations are conducted should be relatively informal without rigid rules of procedure. However, certain minimum rules can help. It would be both unseemly and disorderly to have everybody shouting at once. Finally, it behooves management to clearly understand what has been determined upon before the signing of any contract. That is another excellent reason for having professional consultants or permanent staff personnel undertake the collective bargaining process. The language of the contract should be clear and the parties to the contract should be absolutely certain they understand all of the ideas which have been formulated. This can be the basis for saving the taxpayers' money.

Selected References

Chickering, A. L.: *Public Employee Unions: A Study in the Crisis in Public Sector Labor Relations* (Lexington, Mass.: Lexington Books), 1977.

Gallagher, J.: *Contract Administration in Public Sector Collective Bargaining* (Los Angeles, Cal.: University of California in Los Angeles Industrial Relations), 1976.

Gorman, R. A.: *Labor Law—Unionization and Collective Bargaining* (St. Paul, Minn.: West Publishing Company), 1976.

Jones, R. T.: *City Employee Unions: Labor and Politics in New York and Chicago* (Philadelphia, Pa.: Ballinger Publishing Co.), 1977.

Sloane, A. A. and F. Witney: *Labor Relations* (Englewood Cliffs, N.J.: Prentice-Hall, Inc.), 1977.

Stanley, D. T. and C. L. Cooper: *Managing Local Government Under Union Pressure* (Washington, D.C.: Brookings Institution), 1972.

CHAPTER 17

Management by Objectives

Any organization must develop a real team cooperative and unite individual effort into a coordinated enterprise. Each person employed by the agency contributes personal skills, knowledge, appreciations, and energy in varying degrees, but all persons necessarily contribute toward some commonly defined goal. The efforts of all those who are engaged in the provision of recreational service, whether they represent professionally educated backgrounds or are ancillary personnel should be committed to the successful operation of the agency. Their activities should be unified by some general purpose to which they must adhere and in which they believe. The work of each, as they tend to the daily routine of operations, must coincide to produce a unified front. They should be capable of performing without friction, gaps in service, duplication of effort, or other wasted motion.

Professional recreational service operation in the public sector requires that each task be guided by the goals of the entire organization. Specifically, each administrator's position must be concentrated upon the successful completion of the mission of the agency. The productivity expected of the administrator must be obtained from the accomplishments achieved by the agency. The performance of any manager can be evaluated in terms of his efforts in bringing success to the agency operation. The administrator must recognize and understand what the mission of the agency demands insofar as performance is concerned, and those to whom he is responsible must realize what work is necessary by the manager, expect it, and appraise on that basis. When these needs are not satisfied, administrators are negligent or worse. Their efforts are fruitless. Instead of the desired cooperation and coordination, there is hostility, failure, and confrontation.

MANAGEMENT BY OBJECTIVES

Management by objectives urgently needs intense action and particular methods. In any major occupation, specifically in the field of public service, administrators are not inexorably drawn toward some end in view. Far from it, public recreational service administration, by its very nature, comprises powerful forces for misapplication: in the specialized function of most administrators; in the hierarchical structure of the organization; and in the various perceptions of the mission of the agency and the consequent layering which occurs between what should be done and the distinct levels of management.

To be sure, there are a large number of administrators who are only concerned with highly specialized work. Thus we observe administrators who are only concerned with functional specialties without regard for the basic objective for which the recreational service agency was established. They become too parochial in their outlooks, striving to become better personnel managers, central business office managers, or public relations experts while forgetting the mission of the organization. As Drucker has written:

> The functional work becomes an end in itself. In far too many instances the functional manager no longer measures his performance by its contribution to the enterprise, but only by his own professional criteria of workmanship. He tends to appraise his subordinates by their craftsmanship, to reward and to promote them accordingly.[1]

Unless top administration develops coordinated perspective among all personnel employed by the agency, there will be a tendency to concentrate on the specialized workings of one division of the organization to the detriment of the whole. It is necessary, therefore, that managers view their functions as inputs into the greater enterprise and be able to understand how and where their efforts effect the organizational mission.

Implementation of the MBO Method

The management by objectives orientation to performance appraisal is based upon the premise that MBO is both philosophical as well as a managerial style. Several exploratory procedures must become operational if MBO is to be established as a significant process:

1. Formal approval and adoption of substantive plans for the employment of MBO must originate from the agency executive. Basic organizational objectives which offer direction to each departmental element, as well as individual objectives, that support and complement the organizational purpose should be established.

[1] Peter F. Drucker, *The Practice of Management* (New York: Harper & Row, Publishers, 1954), p. 123.

2. This approval and adoption plan must be widely disseminated throughout the organization and be reinforced by administrative action.
3. In-service staff education is vital to the success of MBO. Staff must have an understanding of the fundamental philosophy, processes, technical aspects, and reinforcement so that MBO can be implemented.
4. The process begins with the superior and subordinate administrators jointly defining the common objectives of the agency, defining each individual's function insofar as expectations are concerned, and utilizing the fulfillment of these responsibilities as determinants for operating the unit and appraising the contribution of each of its members.
5. MBO requires an on-going monitoring of work performance. This may involve the need for continuous guidance of subordinate personnel so that understanding and better effort may be forthcoming. Above all, all persons in the organization need to recognize the importance of their functions and the role which they play in achieving agency goals. Organizational commitment to MBO means complete involvement with the process for all employees of the department.

Essentially, MBO is a process where work planning, review, and performance appraisal is a natural outgrowth of the degree of involvement and participation of the subordinate and his superior in establishing the subordinate's objectives. Instead of examining the employee on personal characteristics, the concept is based upon the development of job-related criteria which are observable, measurable, or capable of verification. On the basis of such established criteria evaluation of performance can be made.

The underlying assumption of MBO is that any subordinate knowledge and understanding of his responsibilities will be greatly increased, communication between superior and subordinate will be improved, and achievement of the agency's goals will be accomplished. Through interaction and discussion with his superior, a subordinate can learn exactly what is expected of him, thereby reducing whatever ambiguities exist about job expectations. Frustration and anxiety should be diminished. By increasing the subordinates' involvement in the goal-setting process which increases the likelihood of ego-identification, a higher degree of personal motivation should accrue. Moreover, the process lends itself to the integration of organizational and individual objectives by giving the employee input into the development of organizational objectives to which he is expected to contribute.

Essentially, MBO should assist in clarifying objectives, contribute to the coincidence of organizational and personal objectives, improve communication between organizational hierarchies, and reduce or mitigate friction between the individual and the organization.[2]

[2] Heinz Weihrich, "MBO: Appraisal With Transactional Analysis," *Personnel Journal*, Vol. 55, No. 4 (April, 1976), pp. 173–175.
W. W. Couch, (Ed.), *Local Government Personnel Administration* (Washington, D.C.: International City Management Association, 1976), pp. 159–160.

Developing Measurable Objectives

A variety of managerial objectives may be catalogued for any recreational agency, but four general groupings should normally cover the range of possible objectives. There are, for example, several clusters which subsume all other conceivable problems:

1. Routine objectives, e.g., employment of personnel, budget-making, maintenance operations, record keeping, and report writing.

2. Problem-solving objectives, e.g., reducing ethnic tensions, coping with reduced budgets, handling employee grievance procedures, dealing with union representation, satisfying constituent demands.

3. Creative objectives, e.g., developing new activities for inclusion within the program, determining methods by which recreational activities can be made more attractive to potential participants.

Table 17-1. Graphic Rating Scale

Learning: Ability to learn new skills or functions

Slow to learn; requires constant instruction	Moderate ability to learn; requires detailed instructions for new functions	Reasonable speed in learning; requires average amount of instruction	Learns well with little instruction	Rapid learner; Superior ability to acquire new skills and functions

Realiability: Supervisor's confidence in subordinate's ability to accept responsibility

Cannot or will not accept responsibility; requires constant monitoring	Generally follows instructions; requires some monitoring	Assumes some responsibility; requires moderate monitoring	Willing and able to accept responsibility; requires little monitoring	Performs in a superior manner; is absolutely dependable

Functional Knowledge: Technical understanding of the position of related assignments

Limited knowledge; knows nothing of related work	Some knowledge of job; little knowledge of related work	Good knowledge of job; moderate knowledge of related work	Good command of job knowledge and related assignments; is well informed	Complete command of job and related assignments; is extremely well informed

Reporting: Accuracy in observing and making written reports

Is inaccurate; frequently makes mistakes; does unsatisfactory work	Reports are relatively accurate; some errors are noticed; does passable work	Reports are usually reliable; makes few errors; does better than average work	Reports are accurate and infrequently contain errors; does high quality work	Reports are error-free; highest accuracy

Industriousness: Quality of work performed

Slow worker; requires constant stimulation and oversight	Performs methodically and carries out prescribed assignments; needs some supervision	Performs in a satisfactory manner; Work performance is slightly above average	Finishes assignment and looks for more work to do; Performs well and exceeds standard	Completes assignments with exceptional speed; finds more work to do and does it with dispatch

4. Personal objectives, e.g., learning new skills in a specific area, such as PPBS, computer programming, public relations, or facility planning.

These examples are intended as indicators only. This is not a last word listing. It is offered simply as a guide for explanatory purposes. The MBO system must be utilized to develop the initiative and planning skills of administrative staff, not to find a more efficient means for prescribing central-office orders.

Some areas of endeavor are more easily measured than others. However, difficulties encountered in the development of methods of measurement probably reveal the need for rethinking an objective and the means for achieving it. In this way staff supervision will become more accurate, systematic, objective, and less subject to the vagaries of personality inclination or personal insecurity. Typical of the instruments used for measuring job performance is a graphic rating scale which is convenient to use, flexible, and objective in its scoring. An example of the GRS is offered in Table 17-1.

These factors do not reflect any value insofar as the scale is concerned in terms of their respective positions on the scale. The rater should check the point on each scale which corresponds to the appraisal. Several points should be kept uppermost concerning the rater's use of the instrument; (1) Only those qualities which can be observed should be rated; (2) Statements should reflect internal consistency; (3) Avoid generalized words such as *always, never, all,* or *every;* (4) Avoid ambiguities.

ADMINISTRATIVE STYLE FOR ACHIEVING GOALS

Administration is concerned with obtaining desired organizational goals by effectively coordinating the human and material resources of the agency in such a way that economic, efficient, and cooperative effort is achieved without waste. The administrator must define agency mission and then see that performance to accomplish that mission is carried out. His responsibility is to assure that cooperative effort is produced to achieve fundamental aims while coordinating such endeavors to facilitate the work of the entire agency. Additionally, the administrator must function as a catalyst, initiating innovative concepts and programs that will enhance the performance and improve the technical capacity of those subordinates with whom he works.

The Leadership Demands of Management

What is the administrator's leadership role? When policy is determined and decisions are made about any phase of agency operation, it is important that the decisions are communicated to those who will see to their execution.

The administrator obtains and analyzes the decisions which have been taken and makes other decisions which deal with implementation. These sequential acts become the job assignments for which employees are made responsible. These duties may either be issued directly or indirectly, verbally or in writing. No matter how they are issued, communication has begun; there is support and guidance where necessary; and there is appropriate supervision to assure that the task is accomplished in the manner which is most beneficial to all concerned.

The administrator has the responsibility of performing two different functions simultaneously. He must be a conceptualizer, analyst, and planner while he is also supposed to organize, administer, and supervise. This poses a dilemma. To be an effective leader, an administrator must understand the varied aspects of complex conditions and then reach a logical decision for achieving the objective which his agency has undertaken. Receiving the available information, analyzing it systematically, determining which alternative course will produce the most beneficial results, attempting to plan for future events, and implementing a reasonable procedure for accomplishment is an administrative task.

There is the necessity for planning in order to formulate the procedures and then activate them. The higher one ascends in the organizational hierarchy, the more knowledge is required for decision-making. The administrator must be able to work out the consequences of certain actions without actually having performed them. It is almost as if he were involved in the solution of some gigantic jig-saw puzzle where many possibilities exist, where almost any alternative selected could work, but where only one or a few will actually offer the most efficient, effective, and economical return. Because the administrative leader works with people as well as resources, he confronts the typical ambiguities which human nature develops. If it were only a matter of material resources the process would be mechanical. When, however, one deals with people—both personnel employed within the agency and clients to be served by the agency —the intangibles of personality, need, and motivation must also be taken into account. This latter aspect is one which really requires leadership.

As a logical thinker, the administrator must make decisions. In order to be most effective, however, he needs to weigh objective data received with his subjective knowledge or empathy which can also provide valuable insight for the people involved in the situation. To correctly appraise the situation so that a rational decision can be reached, one must have a sensitivity for the problem and for the individuals concerned. Specifically is this true when materially based information is inconclusive. To the extent that he deals with people and not things, the administrative leader needs to develop his empathetic tendencies so as to be able to perceive the viewpoint of those who will have to execute policy and those who are receiving the services from the agency. Empathy endows the leader with an understanding of how subordinate employees will probably react to some policy decision.

In any leadership position, unless the administrator is willing to support his own position the likelihood of achieving along the lines which were indicated by objective reasoning and pertinent experiences will fail. Once an administrator has reached a decision, and truly believes in its efficacy, he should see to its execution regardless of its popularity. If he has provided the kind of communication which is necessary, then the basis for his judgment will be well known, the conditions on which the decision was made will also be available, and his reputation for equity should suffice to obtain support. It may sometimes be required that decisions will be made that create negative feelings on the part of some employees. It is unfortunate that this should be so, but the administrator should have the courage of his convictions even when they alienate the opinion of others. The administrator is in a better position to envision the entire situation which subordinates or specialists cannot appreciate. Under such circumstances, the administrator utilizes the process of communication not only to transmit orders, but to educate. Even if he is not successful in persuading his peers of the rightness of his decision, he must still act. If one judges a situation and determines a course of action based upon knowledge, experience, and analysis, then the individual must proceed with that judgment.

Administrative Influence on Personnel Behavior

Administrators are always concerned with methods in which leadership is exerted so that the needs of subordinates may be satisfied while they make effective contributions to their immediate place of employment and to the entire system. The view of administration as a process of guiding the activities of people toward accomplishment of stated objectives elicits several functions from the leader. Thus, he must assist subordinates to achieve satisfaction in their work, reduce friction and conflicts between staff as well as within the work situation, communicate praise and admonishment, supervise, educate, encourage self-development of personnel, provide emotional support, define performance criteria, and stimulate achievement-seeking behavior. The administrative behavior inherent in such responsibilities is directly related to the willingness of personnel to cooperate in the accomplishment of organizational goals.

As Levinson has stated:

> The organizational task becomes one of first understanding the man's needs, and then, with him, assessing how well they can be met in this organization, doing what the organization needs to have done. Thus the highest point of self-motivation arises when there is a complementary conjunction of the man's needs and the organization's requirements. The requirements of both mesh, interrelate, and become synergistic. The energies of man and organization are pooled for mutual advantage.[3]

[3] Harry Levinson, "Management by Whose Objectives?", *Harvard Business Review* (July–August, 1970), p. 129.

The ability of the department to achieve success as it operates is closely connected to leadership style personalized at the administrative level. Personnel cooperation and concern for responsibility rely upon positive interpersonal behavior between administrators and subordinates. The type of behavior most likely to elicit voluntary efforts on the part of subordinate personnel to effect agency goals is one which heavily emphasizes satisfaction of individual needs and less upon the use of positional constraints, i.e., authority to gain desirable ends. However, this too will be shaped by administrator inclination and philosophy.

One of the basic needs of any effective leadership style is comprehension of the relationship between the satisfaction of human needs and personnel performance. Perhaps the essential problem of all administrators is not that their subordinate personnel lack motivation, but that some administrators are either disinclined or do not have the capacity to stimulate it. The normal course of the administrator's behavior sharply affects the performance of subordinates. Personnel are extremely perceptive when it comes to detecting how a superior actually feels about departmental intent and institutionalized procedures. How the administrator behaves, his deportment and activities, invariably convey certain significant signals to those under his immediate supervision. The extent to which the leader espouses the achievement of agency objectives; the actions which he undertakes to advance his own professional development; his tendency to retain functions which are solely within his province to perform; his effectiveness in handling departmental problems; and his earnestness and desire to provide support for his subordinates all are examples of administrative behavior that are observable by associates and subordinates and which serve to condition the behavioral repsonses of agency personnel.

The administrative process offers countless opportunities for leaders to exercise those behaviors which will motivate employees to achieve at higher levels of productivity and, in effect, volunteer their active cooperation in the service of the enterprise. The kinds of leadership behavior that influences subordinate cooperation and willingness to perform are observed when superior-subordinate relations are established on the foundation of reciprocity in terms of mutual trust and understanding. Individuals within the recreational service field and in specific agencies are involved in the cycle of employment. From recruitment and induction to the initial job placement and then throughout their respective careers, there is a continual need for appraisal and evaluation.

Employment Requirements

When the recreationist is first employed, there is an adjustment process usually during a probationary period. Here the individual experiences some of his immediate reactions to job responsibility, frictions, and self-growth. The newly inducted employee must understand the objectives, responsibilities, and relationships of his position. In the same respect, the careerist, just short of retirement, has different needs and interests. Because the viewpoints, capacities, and emotions of personnel are undergoing modification throughout their careers, the behavior of any superior should be appropriate in meeting the differing needs of each of the individuals for whom he has responsibility. The forms of assistance rendered, guidance, counseling, appraisal, promotion, discipline, and stimulation required will depend upon the individual who is the recipient; thus the administrative approach will be dictated by individual needs. The cohesiveness upon which any department depends for self-maintenance will be absent to the degree that relations between superiors and subordinates do not accommodate individual differences through the employment cycle and as the professional tasks for which they are responsible change.

It may be possible to transform professional work so that the recreationist's satisfaction on the job will meet his needs for self-development and self-actualization. This is the ideal toward which every administrative officer should strive as he improves his own behavior by providing staff support. The methods for improving professional work so that job satisfaction can occur will be by position augmentation and position variation. The administrator should attempt to vary the kinds of work an individual experiences within the recreational service organization. As new skills are learned, advanced educational preparation attained, and greater insights into the needs of clientele are perceived, the recreationist can be shifted to other centers, groups, or specialities. Position augmentation, on the other hand, requires an adjustment in the ways that personal skills are utilized so that contributions will be made to the entire organization as well as to the individual's self-growth and actualization. The recreationist's functions may be enlarged through a number of increasingly sophisticated assignments, within the decision-making process by which democratic organizations are guided, and through participation in those agency activities which will have a direct effect upon the work life of the individual. In this manner the line recreationist is given the opportunity to exercise whatever creativity and knowledge he has by cooperatively setting performance and agency goals and then working to accomplish the goals which he has helped to establish.

Because people are one of the essential components making up the resources of the organization, their behavior largely determines the effectiveness of the recreational service system. The responsibility of adjusting to and making the needs of the individual and the demands of the organization compatible is, perhaps, the chief function of the administrative leader. While it is true that the administrator has no influence over some of the pressure which impinges upon the agency and its personnel, insofar as satisfying human needs is concerned, there are areas in which leadership has a profound influence. Among the methods which the administrator can use to affect personnel satisfaction and performance, is the style of leadership which he employs and the development of rapport with all subordinates. Leadership style and interpersonal relationships will be dependent upon the process of communication and is reciprocal. The interdependency of superior-subordinate relations is well known, although there remain some unconvinced administrators of this fact of life. The success of the leader relies heavily on the performance of those personnel for whom he is responsible. To the degree that the administrator can gain cooperative effort he will be successful. The *quid pro quo* is to provide subordinate need satisfaction.

MANAGEMENT AND LEADERSHIP

The individual who wrote that, "Great leaders do not always leave strong organizations. Great managers do."[4] did not really understand the phenomenon of leadership. Valid leadership is not a process wherein one person stamps his personality forever upon a docile following and builds an enduring organization based upon the cult of his own personality; rather it is a mutually dependent relationship where influence is given and received on a voluntary basis. There is no cult of personality, nor is the real leader concerned for the perpetuation of himself at the expense of all others. Quite the contrary. The leader attempts to develop secondary leaders as he leads because he realizes that he may not be able to supply all the answers or handle all of the problems which arise in the course of departmental operation. Furthermore, he is aware that as situations change there may be a need for those who have other personal characteristics and competencies which may far surpass his own in enabling the group to continue to flourish in the face of adversity. The real leader has an abiding concern for the maintenance of his group and it is for this reason that he is prepared to raise up secondary leaders to take over when he can no longer fulfill those tasks and responsibilities which have thrust him into the leadership role. Of course, there are of necessity, ambiguous feelings about giving up the role of leadership for this has been a primary motivation for the individual. But, as the leader foresees the decline of his personal powers or the deterioration of his capacity to guide the group in the satisfaction of membership needs, he realizes that the group will be better served through another's leadership.

In the same sense, leadership growing out of the administrator's position can be the greatest combination for the success of any organization. Administrative techniques should ensure innovation and productivity while leadership capability will maximize employee satisfaction and willing

[4] David Ewing, *The Managerial Mind* (New York: The Free Press, 1964), p. 105.

effort to see that the agency performs the tasks assigned to it in ways that bring approbation and support from a grateful public.

Management Techniques

Those administrators who cannot combine the roles of leadership and manager will never be concerned with any matters beyond the purely mechanical considerations of economic and material resources. They will be content to perform the routinized activities which require little more than a cursory inspection to see that an adequate supply of things is maintained. This may be accomplished by any mediocrity. It takes no gift nor a sense of wonder at the vastness of and complexity of human organizations to take care of the mundane aspects of things. Leaders, on the other hand, are concerned with people and deal with the critical factors that personality insists upon injecting into what would be routine matters. Thus the imponderables, ambiguities, and vacillations of ordinary behavioral inputs creates enigmas out of the common activity which organizations process as they produce goods or services.

In the field of recreational service the executive will be judged on the basis of how well agency clientele are served. To attain this primary goal, leadership ability is essential and managerial finesse is significant. It requires no leadership skill or managerial adroitness to obtain average work from average people. The quantitative factors will continue to function whether there is management or not. Once inertia is overcome, the ordinary routine simply perpetuates itself. The great challenge to managerial leadership, then, is to administer the personal and material organizational resources in such a way that optimized results will be obtained. The manager must raise efficiency and personnel effectiveness by skillfully deploying his forces, expertly planning, organizing, directing, and supervising activities aimed at achieving objectives with maximum satisfaction and a minimum of wasted time, talent, energy, and other resources.

The administrator must be the great energizer of the agency. As a leader he knows where he is going, influences others to follow, and vigorously pursues his course of action with the single-minded intensity of one who is convinced that the end-in-view is worth the effort. If he is wise, his aims will have been developed in concert with the purposes of the agency, in conjunction with his professional staff, and the expressed needs of those whom the agency serves. The methods utilized to accomplish these goals should be flexible and take into account the situational realities which condition responses and expectations.

EMPLOYEE MOTIVATION

Just as any leader is stimulated to lead by his own anxieties and ambitions, the administrative leader should spark subordinate action through the use of anxiety-provoking mechanisms. This by no means advocates an authoritarian or coercive approach at all. A little anxiety induced as a motivational factor may become a powerful personal incentive which can drive individuals to perform at higher and higher levels of efficiency and effectiveness. Anxiety producing feelings should be intellectual which causes dissatisfaction rather than fear. The manager cannot productively utilize anxiety which makes the employee fearful, because that will prevent efficiency and induce apathy or excessive caution. In neither case will good work be produced. By cooperatively setting goals and communicating the idea of expectation, the consequences may be employee striving to achieve his own predetermined objectives. Where these objectives coincide with those of the manager and the agency, then maximum efficiency is the outcome. Goal striving reduces the likelihood of complacency, stimulates the worker to attempt innovative activities, encourages dissatisfaction with *status quo,* and elicits personal happiness as objectives are attained along with concomitant recognition and other rewards. The purpose of inducing intellectual anxiety is to motivate employees to enlarge their positions and to extend themselves. Maxwell Maltz has written of this phenomenon in this way:

> Man is by nature a goal-striving being. And because man is "built that way" he is not happy unless he is functioning as he was made to function —as a goal-striver. Thus true success and true happiness not only go together but each enhances the other.[5]

Delegation as Motivation

Delegation of authority and responsibility for carrying out agency functions is far more than a process which simply lightens the manager's burden. Delegation is the end product of a symbiotic process whose reciprocal relationships are deeply rooted in rapport. When the superior-subordinate relationship has developed to a point where mutual trust and confidence repose in each contributor then the concept of delegation can bring personal satisfaction and great incentive for the individual so designated. Fundamentally, delegation is a process of job enrichment. It should be challenging to the deputy and still be within his capacity to perform. He will have to stretch himself to accomplish the assignment, but in the performance he will have achieved at a higher level and will gain more confidence and knowledge than he had previously.

Delegation must be in terms of authority, although there is a consonent degree of responsibility involved. However, the manager cannot delegate his ultimate responsibility for what his subordinates do. Delegation is one of the displayed acts of confidence which provides a subordinate with the

---

[5] Maxwell Maltz, *Psycho-Cybernetics* (Hollywood, Calif.: Wiltshire Book Company, 1964), p. xvi. Reprinted by permission.

opportunity to earn a more significant place within the organizational hierarchy, permits him to express himself insofar as skills and knowledge are concerned, and offers valuable instruction for the next time. The subordinate realizes that he will be held accountable for the assigned task and that his contributions will be duly noted in terms of the authority which he has handled.

In order to delegate appropriate assignments, the administrator must know his subordinates well. He should understand their strengths and weaknesses and be able to recognize their attitudes toward the work to be performed. Of great import will be the subordinate's interest in advancement as well as his ability to act autonomously. Delegation should not be given in an off-handed manner. It should not consist of appointment by chance, fortuitous circumstance, or to relieve the manager of an onerous assignment. Rather, delegation should be a carefully planned procedure whose steps are incremental. This means that consideration of the current ability of the individual to deal with the task must be made. If the assignment is too much for the individual, then the result will be failure and dissatisfaction. Of course, there are always those individuals, who are underrated, who rise to the occasion and perform their functions superbly. But for the most part, the perceptive administrator will know the limitations of his subordinates and delegate accordingly. As subordinates develop competencies, skills, and knowledge, the assignments will become more exacting and complicated. In this situation the administrator is a teacher who must patiently instruct the learner without doing the job for him. Errors will be made, but this will also serve as part of the learning process.

When the administrator has delegated authority for some function, it is well to spell out the latitude which has been given. The parameters of delegation may range from complete autonomy to a very circumscribed basis wherein the subordinate must lay his plans before his superior, who will then decide and act on them. Close supervision means almost no delegation. However, at the outset, the wise administrator prudently suggests some points of contact so that progress and problems can be discussed. As the subordinate proves himself able, the superior diplomatically withdraws until the subordinate is autonomous. As the individual exhibits improvement there must be some appreciation expressed for work well done. This, too, serves to motivate. As Kappel indicates:

Leadership is stirring people so that they are moved from inside of themselves. It is stating goals that excite them and lift their sights, it is setting the personal example, putting enthusiasm into operation, communicating both ways (listening as well as talking). It is rewarding merit and penalizing demerit, honestly and fairly. It is the right combination of these so that people will do the work that makes a business successful *because they want to.*[6]

Focusing as it has on the leadership process, the idea of administration as the repository of all that is good is an inescapable outcome. This is hardly the truth. Administrators are not supermen. They have the same human failings as the rest of mankind. Nevertheless, the administrative leader attempts to overcome his biases and foibles by concentrating upon his skills, knowledge, and talent in carrying out his responsibilities. No administrator can be all things to all men. At best he will be one significant influence on the behavior of others. To the extent that he can assist in bringing their latent talents, abilities, and experiences to the fore, thereby gaining a better perspective of their own functions and performing at a high level of efficiency and effectiveness, the administrator will have done the job for which he is paid. He serves as a model for his subordinates. His style of leadership will directly affect subordinate attitudes and serve as a basis for his instruction of them.

The administrative function is now concerned with human matters, rather than the traditional measures of output in determining organizational performance. Such factors as degrees of confidence and trust, loyalty, motivation, ability to communicate, and the capacity to achieve sound decisions are the measures which more nearly coincide with administrative effectiveness. If subordinates feel that the administrator is supportive of them rather than threatening, there will be a better pattern of interaction. To the degree that administrators promote cohesiveness within their organization, so that each person feels himself to be a member of a close-knit and effective work group, there will be concomitant increments in the accomplishment of tasks assigned. As Likert has shown:

> The units achieving the best performance are much more likely than the poor performance units to have managers who deal with their subordinates in a supportive manner and build high group loyalty and teamwork.[7]

The chief executive of the organization has it within his power to shape and guide the policies, philosophy, and subordinate behaviors. His concepts of human relations and interpersonal development will become the pervasive influence within his agency. If he is democratic in outlook and practices organizational democracy, there will be a corresponding attitude operating throughout all levels of the hierarchy. It is the responsibiilty of the executive to develop and maintain the total human resource system within the department and to create an atmosphere that will stimulate

[6] F. R. Kappel, *Business Purpose and Performance* (New York: Duell, Sloan and Pearce, 1964), p. 194. By permission of Hawthorn Books, Inc.

[7] R. Likert, "Measuring Organizational Performance," in B. L. Hinton and H. J. Reitz (eds.), *Groups and Organizations: Integrated Readings in the Analysis of Social Behavior* (Belmont, Cal.: Wadsworth Publishing Company, Inc., 1971), p. 556.

this process to continue vigorously and imaginatively. The executive's work is made easier by a style of leadership which actually promotes collaboration in those phases of planning where consensus is essential. He recognizes individual and social needs as he works toward agency goals; he controls the intervention of purely functional aspects; and he encourages and rewards participation and effective contribution.

> The example set by all members of supervision in their daily activities is observed, evaluated, and in many instances imitated by people in lower levels of the organization. Employees, whether they are in research, production, or sales, are particularly influenced by the example set by their immediate supervisor. Every supervisor uses this method whether he realizes it or not. For instance, a supervisor who is open-minded in his dealings with those he supervises will influence them by his example to use similar approaches in their dealing with others. . . .[8]

One of the hallmarks of administrative leadership is flexibility of behavior. Different leadership behaviors are required in varying situations in order to gain effectiveness. It has been found that leaders do have the ability to modify their approach to problem solving when faced with changing conditions.

> Thus, the successful manager of men can be primarily characterized neither as a strong leader nor as a permissive one. Rather, he is one who maintains a high batting average in accurately assessing the forces that determine what his most appropriate behavior at any given time should be and in actually being able to behave accordingly.[9]

There seems to be some likelihood that managers who display leadership will probably be more capable of adapting their behaviors as conditions vary. As Hill indicates:

> . . . the type of problem confronting a manager does influence the leadership style which he employs to solve it. These data suggest that some managers are perceived to rely upon a fixed leadership style to handle certain types of problems but handle other problems with a variety of styles.[10]

Flexibility is a necessary behavioral form if the administrator is to survive the complex situational variables which typically confront any executive operating in the public domain. Administration requires an adaptable

[8] J. J. Famularo, (ed.), *Handbook of Modern Personnel Administration* (New York: McGraw-Hill Book Company, 1972), p. 22–10. Reprinted by permission.
[9] R. Tannenbaum and W. H. Schmidt, "How to Choose a Leadership Pattern" *Harvard Business Review*, Vol. 36 (1958), p. 301. Reprinted by permission.
[10] W. A. Hill, "Leadership Style Flexibility, Satisfaction and Performance," in E. A. Fleishman and J. G. Hunt, (eds.), Current Developments in the Study of Leadership (Carbondale, Ill.: Southern Illinois University Press, 1973), p. 80. Reprinted by permission.

person who has the capacity to cope with the mechanical aspects of tasks and the subjective judgments which must be made in dealing with subordinates and the unknown quantity of personality.

Essentially, the manager's role requires that he do the following:

1. He is a planner. As a conceptualizer of the organization, the one whose philosophy will probably permeate and give overall guidance to agency personnel, he must project ideas into the future so that agency employees will be better enabled to maximize their time, talent, and knowledge. In anticipation of the future, the manager comes to grips with possible problems that may arise under any given set of circumstances, selects feasible alternative solutions to the problems, and exploits potential opportunities which future planning offers to the careful analyst.

2. He is an organizer. He mobilizes all of the resources of his agency, whether human, material, economic, or technical and welds them into a smoothly integrated cohesive unit so that primary objectives can be reached with optimum efficiency, maximum effectiveness, and a minimum of friction, duplication, or inadequacy.

3. He is concerned with personnel. His staffing function is not merely one of expediency, i.e., to obtain a specialist for today's activity, but more significantly, to insure that the individual workers of the department have the capability for professional growth and development so that the accomplishment of recreational service provisions will be promoted along with worker satisfaction.

4. He is an allocator. He determines necessary functions to be executed, assigns personnel the authority and responsibility for carrying out particular tasks, formulates objectives by which work standards may be measured, and by exacting accountability for the consequences in agreement with the predetermined job criteria.

5. He is an evaluator. He directs the efforts of subordinates by maintaining a feedback system that provides him with sufficient early warning data so that corrective action may be implemented when warranted. Such data also provides the material for initiating incentive plans and assuring that meritorious work will be praised and appropriately regarded and rewarded. He neither plays politics nor permits favoritism to gain a foothold within the agency. As he evaluates the work performance of his subordinates and the accomplishments of the institution, he contributes to enhanced worker proficiency which tends to raise their value to the department.

6. He is a leader. He establishes open lines of communication throughout the organization so that information about working conditions, job satisfaction, and organizational objectives are harmonized. He is concerned about and for the development of interpersonal relationships among and between those who work for the agency. He attempts to develop rapport with his subordinates so that an atmosphere of cooperation and reciprocity of interests is created. Finally, he leads the personnel of the organization so that they willingly undertake their respective functions in a way that reflects professional esteem, zeal, and technical competency. In all of his behavior he must exemplify those characteristics which make others want to emulate him.

All of these attributes and functions are centered upon top-level administration. The chief executive is responsible for organizing and managing the provision of recreational service to clientele which is based in specialized facilities and other physical resources within the community, and is directly in charge of all personnel within the system.

Summary

The single most important element in the provision of recreational service is the quality of recreationists employed within the agency. The next most important element is the quality of administrative service provided throughout the system. It is through administrative services that facilitation of technical competencies of all other personnel levels is promoted. Furthermore, administration is initiated to assist all efforts on the part of agency employees in providing effective and competent services through the program. The success of the recreational service offering will be in direct proportion to the quality of line leadership available and the reinforcement of the line by managerial leaders. The manager makes the difference between superior and mediocre results. Whether at the middle or upper echelon of management, the manager must still maintain his professional competency and display those characteristics which enable him to sustain influence with others despite his position within the department. There seems to be an immediate and positive correlation between a manager's leadership ability and his effectiveness as a manager, for leadership is the foundation on which the requirements of the organization and the demands of the individual worker are balanced.

Selected References

Drucker, P. F.: *Management: Tasks, Responsibilities, Practices* (New York: Harper Trade Books), 1974.

Humble, J. W.: *How to Manage By Objectives* (New York: American Management Association, Inc.), 1973.

Jun, J. S.: *Management By Objectives in Government: Theory and Practice* (Beverly Hills, Calif.: Sage Publications, Inc.), 1976.

Morrisey, G. L.: *Management By Objectives and Results in the Public Sector* (Reading, Mass.: Addison-Wesley Publishing Co., Inc.), 1976.

CHAPTER **18**

Supervisory Functions of Management

Certain inherent problems confront managers of professional personnel because the duties and performance criteria of such employees in recreational service are not effectively established. The performance of recreationists is less easily measured, while the relative significance of a position does not readily lend itself to facile judgments. Finally, the basis for evaluation becomes progressively more difficult to develop than in other positions. These and similar complexities of professional-technical positions mean that personnel practices, processes, and policies generally utilized may not be completely appropriate to the management of recreationists.

Characteristics of Recreationists

Any discussion of the generalized personal characteristics of recreationists is bound to be criticized as either belaboring the obvious or not based on fully validated evidence. However, certain characteristics appear to be present among all recreationists. A recreationist is a professionally educated, ethically guided, and experientially competent individual in career-for-life recreational service. By implication, the concept of professionalism and the ideology of the professional person also must be understood. Thus, we must proceed from a point of humanitarian service and add personal ethics and probity, the intellectual honesty required for constant curiosity (questioning), stimulation of others, critical ability to evaluate ideas on their own merit without prejudgment, and a desire to learn.

It is probably safe to assume that all personnel of the recreational service department have the same basic social, physiological, and psychological needs. However, the differences between recreationists and non-professional personnel are in terms of motivation or drives and the degree of differences extant in particular areas. It is probable that the recreationist has a more comprehensive educational background with a coincidental ability to solve problems, although this is not true of all those classified as professionals. Typically, the recreationist has a college degree and far surpasses the educational achievement of most non-professional workers. This trend will become increasingly apparent as brighter students enter recreational service. There is evidence that the more intelligent young people are more committed to the various fields of social service than to more materially oriented areas. If this observation is correct there will be an increased incidence of more intelligent people entering recreational service.

Evidence is mounting that recreationists' personalities tend to diverge from the norm of the general population. Recreationists not only have high achievement drives but they are essentially extroverted with a preference for working with people rather than with things. They are socially precocious and tend to become more gregarious with maturity and experience.

Although it is probable that a recreationist's values do not conflict with organizational aims and objectives, his impatience with hierarchical structure and bureaucratic slowness may, at times, cause dissatisfaction and disenchantment with the system and its methods. The conflict between desire to perform in the most effective manner possible and an apparent indifference to the needs of both community and departmental personnel can lead to a breakdown in communication and ultimate rupture of relations between the professional and the system. Therefore, management must take special pains to cultivate an organizational atmosphere that is conducive to meeting the personal needs, drives, and goals of professional personnel. Recreational service can be practiced best by people having the competence to understand the needs of people and to carry out the functions that require, not only technical competence, but also ingenuity, initiative, and intelligence.

The education, personal values, personality, and intelligence of recreationists make them desire certain outcomes from being members of the field. The following objectives seem to be the attributes that a recreationist desires from his position within a recreational service system:

1. Freedom to participate in the decision-making processes affecting the department
2. Association with and intellectual stimulation from erudite colleagues
3. A professionally prepared management staff who are highly regarded by other professionals in the field
4. Treatment as an individual worthy of respect

5. Freedom to discuss problems, to question current practices, to receive attention without fear of supervisory retaliation or hindrance
6. Adequate supplies, materials, equipment, resources, and support
7. Opportunity for advancement in salary and/or prestige
8. Competitive salaries commensurate with educational preparation, experience, and job performance
9. Opportunity for personal development through continued formal education while employed
10. A certain amount of discretionary latitude in perceiving, implementing, and carrying out program ideas
11. Security on the job.

ADMINISTRATIVE PROCEDURES FOR MANAGERIAL POLICIES

The superintendent of a public recreational service department is vitally concerned with carrying out the objectives for which the department was created. The principal objective is the provision of recreational services, presumably through the planned program of activities, spontaneous experiences performed individually or in groups, and the full public utilization of the physical resources constituting the public recreational system. Once this objective is identified the administrator must recognize all of the managerial methods that can be used to attain it. Their selection is left to the discretion and ethics of the individual administrator. Some methods are severe but achieve results swiftly. Other techniques, although time-consuming and even tedious, may produce lasting effects with considerably less friction and greater satisfaction. So many variables are interposed between conformance and nonconformance with administrative policy that only the highly skilled executive will have the sensitivity to discriminate as to which methods may be most effective and appropriate.

The adept administrator may select one procedure or another to elicit positive results from an individual or group, depending on his own knowledge, the skill of his associates, the professionalism of subordinates, the necessity for compliance, and the result desired. Once the superintendent recognizes the basic objectives that are desired, he is in the best possible position to choose correct techniques to gain compliance to departmental policies and practices. However, certain restricting conditions are concurrently operational in gaining such compliance. The administrator's own beliefs, experiences, and concepts of organizational decision making; the expectations of employees as to their participation in decision making, employees' understanding of supervisory behavior, the individual needs of employees; and the environmental or working conditions having a direct influence on the philosophical climate of the system.[1]

Administrative Factors

Pressures or proclivities within the administrator color his view of departmental needs, his subordinate's competence in executing assignments, and how he conceives of delegation of authority. When an administrator believes that the department must be organized along democratic lines he will strive to promote a broadly based employee-centered process of decision making. He will offer all professionals within the system the opportunity to assist in planning courses of action so that all may feel a personal responsibility and self-expression within organizational politics. If, however, the administrator has little faith or respect for a subordinate's competency, knowledge, or talent, the administrator may feel strongly that only he should make decisions which all will then carry out. The administrator's own personality, experience, knowledge of the present situation, attitude, and biases will dominate his thinking about who should make decisions and whether or not they share in the decision-making process that affects the individuals of the department.

Employee Factors

Influences emanating from employees essentially reflect the level of participation that such employees, as professionals, expect to have in the decision-making processes of the system. They also refer to employees' understanding and expectation of supervisors' behaviors toward them. The personality characteristics of individual employees generate expressed needs or drives that can be satisfied within the organizational operation for security, mastery, self-expression, status, respect, affection, recognition, and other social, psychological, and/or physiological requirements, which employment within the system may or may not provide. Thus, employees have greater discretionary powers when they show and have a need for autonomy of action, a desire to assume responsibility, wide latitude for interpreting directives, keen interest in meeting the problems of the organization, a sound conception of the aims or objectives of the organization as well as the capability for identifying with them, the knowledge and skill required to effectively handle problems, professional expectations in assuming part of decision making. When these factors exist the administrator may broadly share the functions of decision making. The converse is also true.

[1] Robert Tannenbaum and Warren H. Schmidt, "How to Choose a Leadership Pattern." *Harvard Business Review*, XXXVI, No. 2 (March-April, 1958), pp. 95-101.

Environmental Factors

The history of the department, its traditions, methods of performing, expected behavior of administrators and employees, all conduce to influence the degree and type of management practices to be utilized. Other forces tending to influence behavior are the number of employees, the dispersement of departmental facilities, and the number of areas or centers operated by the department. Where there is vast decentralization, because of the size of population to be served, there are fewer centralized gatherings of employees. However, this should not preclude democratic proceedings wherever employees are. Thus, democratic administration is operational in widely dispersed recreational centers even if such employees do not play a direct role in system-wide decision making.

The time factor also plays an important part in terms of administrator-centered or employee-delegated responsibilities. If an objective must be implemented in a relatively short time, there seems greater likelihood that specific instructions and directives originate from the administrator for compliance. If time is relatively unimportant, employee responsibility may be encouraged.

All these factors work interdependently; each exerts its own conditioning pressures on a given situation. Thus, in the initiation of policy statements as well as in their execution and the desire for compliance with them, the administrator's selection of procedural methods must be meaningful for the situation. Perhaps the single most effective personnel instrumentality for developing democratic procedures within the system and concomitant staff assumption of responsibilities for compliance, as well as initiation of decision-making functions, is supervision in all of its ramifications.

SUPERVISION

Obtaining cooperation from groups or individuals and coordinating such activity toward established desirable objectives are the purpose of supervision. This aspect of leadership arises from the formulation of recreational policies, the planning and evaluating of the program, and the selection, orientation, and education of workers within a face-to-face frame of reference. Supervision focuses on the improvement of educative processes and the production of more effective and competent recreational service workers through the development of their abilities and potential.

Supervisor's Role in Administration

Although the vague statement that all levels of administration perform basically the same functions (planning, organizing, ordering, and managing) is valid, it has a restricted meaning for the supervisor who desires a better understanding of the organization he manages and the differentiation between his position and that of administration. All administration requires the supervisory function, but all supervision is not administratively oriented. Essentially, the line supervisor is considered to be within the management, rather than the worker, hierarchy. Such supervisors are on a face-to-face level of confrontation with subordinates and are directly responsible for the transmission of rules, regulations, policy, and philosophy of those who clearly are not of the functional force. The supervisor immediately directs the work of individual subordinates and, in fact, may perform some of the work himself. A great deal of his time is spent in interpreting, applying, and transmitting the policy statement and specific instructions of his superiors. He is responsible for attaining effective performance from subordinates in the area assigned to him. He must be largely concerned with the particulars and methods of achievement.

The supervisory position requires the incumbent to find the most effective ways to motivate others to carry out plans, policies, and objectives. That supervision is essentially a leadership process cannot be denied in the face of the supervisor's need to succeed through others. Supervision requires patient attention and the most sensitive form of guidance. The supervisor must always be in a learning situation; his work requires perpetual education because he deals with people and not materials.

Supervisory levels differ from those of higher administration by virtue of those they supervise. Management positions require supervision of other management workers, not face-to-face supervision of functional employees. More direct supervision of line employees is done by supervisors than by all other higher-management levels combined. Administrators typically have fewer subordinates reporting to them at each successively higher level of the organization. Generally, first-line supervisors are more highly specialized in skills and experiences whereas higher echelons of administration deal with more widely dissimilar functions. To that extent, administrators are considered to be generalists rather than specialists. Administrators are more concerned with establishing broad objectives and policies, developing strategies for their implementation, and coordinating various subordinate level positions than are supervisors. On the other hand, supervisors are expected to concentrate on performance; they must be constantly attuned to the execution of specialized tasks in the best possible manner given enough functional workers for that purpose.

Supervisory Functions

Supervision is characterized by the following functions in recreational service:

1. The interpretation of recreational and system objectives within the organization and to the community that the department serves
2. The study and improvement of the program of activities as well as the materials, instructional methods, demonstrations, and leadership techniques utilized within the departmental program
3. The determination of the individual worker's ability and proclivity toward learning new methods of program presentation
4. The assistance of program workers in their professional development
5. The in-service education of recreational service personnel and the improvement of their respective work habits
6. The field observation and visitation of staff personnel and program operation to aid in the improvement of worker techniques as well as for recommending desirable changes in the program in terms of the findings
7. The education and improvement of supervisory personnel and the evaluation of the techniques of supervision accompanied by recommendations for whatever improvement is necessary.

Effective supervision is based on consideration of changing conditions in the community and the system, and on the basic aims and policies of the department. It is built on information collected in the appraisal, evaluation, and execution of methods and techniques. The supervisor recognizes not only personality, mental, and physical differences among people but also educational and experiential differences affecting skills and the technical capabilities of personnel for effectively presenting pertinent material.

Rapport between individuals must be built and maintained so as to effect cooperation by leadership rather than subservience to official authority. Additionally, the supervisor must nurture the relationship between himself and subordinates by encouraging the growth of each worker to the fullest range of his capacities. When narrow-minded individuals are placed in supervisory positions they have a tendency to supervise their subordinates tightly, closely watching for any deviation from what they consider to be routine procedures and practices. They are disinclined to permit worker latitude or discretion, and they exhibit their own apprehension insofar as confidence in the worker's ability to perform well is concerned. Thus, they generally manage to make the worker feel that he is under close and constant surveillance. Such a situation neither produces good interpersonal relationships nor conduces to effective performance.

The supervisor always has a difficult function in any case. He must try to motivate the worker to perform most effectively. Yet, the supervisor is faced with an immediate negative factor that he must fight to overcome. All workers are initially fearful or suspicious of supervisors—a natural enough feeling, because it stems from the superior–subordinate relationship of the hierarchy. Such a relationship carries the overt or implied threat of punishment for non-compliance with directives, procedures, or supervisory "suggestions." Almost every worker faces a new supervisor with some hesitation. The supervisor has real power over the subordinate, or the worker *feels* that the supervisor has such power whether the authority exists or is simply a myth. Whatever the job situation, the worker approaches the supervisor with the idea, if not the knowledge, that the supervisor has the power to economically punish him if the worker does not subscribe to orders. There can be no real leadership under these conditions.

If supervision is a leadership process, as it truly must be, the supervisor must find ways of overcoming worker distrust. Leadership, in the most valid sense, is not a matter of techniques as much as it is of applied intelligence, good judgment, and the ability to empathize with others. These attributes, except intelligence, are derivatives of appropriate insights, attitudes toward people in general, and value judgments that are formed from logical bases.

All workers, or almost all workers, desire to be placed in situations where their immediate supervisors have confidence in themselves and in their subordinates' abilities to permit generalized oversight rather than under harassingly close direction. A supervisor, particularly when dealing with other professionals (as recreationists are supposed to be), should have the self-confidence and belief in the professional capacity of a subordinate to assume success in performance. He should not have to scrutinize every move, fearful of errors, indeed, forecasting disaster at every turn. Supervisor's expectations of the performance of others who consider themselves to be professionals should be high and realistic. Then supervision may proceed in a more generalized and tension-free atmosphere.

In too many instances, unfortunately, there is a tendency among supervisors to force workers to comply with specific instructions because of the supervisor's inability to interpret his functions properly. Such individuals activate the inherent fear, which all subordinate employees have, of supervisors because of the implied threat of dismissal or demotion. But this type of relationship can never lead to effective worker participation and probably results in worker discouragement and possible malingering. Even when professionally minded people are involved, the resentment accruing from harsh imposition of authority gives rise to inadequacies in performance. Tyranny of workers defeats its own purpose. The most high-minded recreationist eventually may lose his perspective in the face of continuing dictatorship and bullying tactics. Even if he wanted to perform well, the disaffection that builds up in a recreationist dissipates the resolve. Either the worker adopts an "I-don't-care" attitude performing only those tasks specifically assigned to him and nothing else, or he simply resigns from the system. In all such events, there is a compounded loss for recreational service in general, the department in particular, and the worker immediately.

Supervisory leadership should be such that it generates admiration and provides direction for the worker instead of imposing arbitrary and autocratic methods. A factor ordinarily related to enhancing worker–supervisor relations is the wider sharing of responsibilities and the concomitant authority for executing assignments. Perhaps in no other discipline is there such need to delegate responsibility and authority for the performance of functions as in recreational service. The discipline deals with people not things. People should not be handled routinely. For this reason, recreationists should be permitted a greater degree of discretion for instigating activities and solving problems than, say, a factory worker. A sharing of responsibility or commitment on the part of the worker to ensure the success of the enterprise, as well as an appropriate amount of authority to carry out the task, is vital. Supervision must shape the system and the community environment so as to encourage the creativity and productivity inherent within the workers.

Overcoming initial mistrust and establishing rapport, mutual trust, and confidence are the essential functions of the supervisor. He must provide a democratic climate in which the worker feels and knows that he may make suggestions, criticisms, and actually assist in shaping departmental policies. The supervisor must convince the worker of his peer status with the supervisor. Although the supervisor and the worker may be differentiated by hierarchical levels, they are still professionally coequals. Secondly, the supervisor must treat each worker with the respect to which any individual is entitled. A worker's questions, criticisms, suggestions, or recommendations should be heard and answered or acted on without the worker feeling threatened for having dared to make them. This can be developed only over a period of time when the supervisor actually creates the climate for such interaction to occur. It does not mean that the supervisor abdicates his own responsibilities; it simply reinforces the belief that professionals have something of value to offer to the department if they are encouraged to think and are given the chance to voice opinions, however harsh or unjustified, without fear of retaliation. It is in this vein that rapport develops.[2]

Open communications are the simplest and most effective method by which supervisors may effect worker productivity and motivation. Communication is a morale factor that cannot be overlooked. All workers in the system should be informed about the matters that concern or affect

[2] A. Q. Sartain and A. W. Baker, *The Supervisor And His Job* (New York: McGraw-Hill Book Co., 1965), pp. 222-224.

them. Such matters are as varied as are the individuals employed by the department. Information should be supplied about long-range plans that have been formulated by the department as well as the details dealing with such mundane matters as supply inventories. Communication and acquisition of knowledge do not come from disseminating data, helpful as these might be. They arise from a developmental process by which the worker is assisted in gaining information. This process means in-service education, not merely telling the employee certain facts. Therefore, maintaining communications may just require the highest degree of intelligence and ability on the part of supervisors.[3]

Supervision as a process is facilitated through the careful selection and assignment of recreationists, accomplished through adequate recruitment procedures, in-service educational methods, orientation of workers to the job, and continuous interpretation of departmental aims and methods. Supervision is made easier by the consistency and evenness in operation of departmental routine, the chain-of-command function of the line and staff management, and standard operating procedures understood by all personnel.

Among the techniques utilized to facilitate supervision is the process of improving work methods by modifying employee work habits, so that efficiency of performance is increased through job simplification or in concert with the employee to determine better ways of doing the work. Typically, supervisors have attempted to develop better work methods for their subordinates, but it has been found that workers who are deprived of making decisions in areas that directly concern them are apt to prove apathetic to work reform or may actively prevent such reform. For this reason, supervisors must involve workers who are directly affected by such modifications or reform in the process. This process ensures communication from the inception of the process. The employee never feels omitted from the important facets that will later affect his job, he may make significant contributions to any work simplification or job efficiency decided on, and he will more closely identify himself with the position and the department.

Work simplification develops in consequence of employee performance which tends to be bogged down in paper work, repetitious functions, or time spent in performing work that could be handled by less educated or less professionally competent individuals. It is not likely that the responsibilities of working with people can be simplified because people are so unpredictable. However, when mechanical or thing-oriented work has to be done on a reiterated basis, e.g., report writing or record keeping, such tasks may be modified so that greater production and less wasted time result.

[3] Danice M. Goodacre, "Stimulating Improved Man Management." *Personnel Psychology*. Vol. 16, no. 2 (Summer, 1962), pp. 133-143.

Supervisors should be concerned primarily with the human element in the organization. Work modification for productivity may not be so much a change in material arrangement, or even in terms of time and motion studies, as of worker recognition and reward. Perhaps the most frequently overlooked factor in effective work performance is non-recognition of employees for their efforts in attempting to improve the work situation of which they are a part perhaps by suggesting a superior technique in program planning, report writing, dissemination of public information, or any one of a thousand different procedures that develop greater creativity, effectiveness, and service to the public. Recognition, which may be a monetary reward, promotion, public praise, or a personal pat-on-the-back, does much to motivate an employee's desire to perform at even greater heights.

Irritating environmental factors, whether of a personal or material nature, should be removed in order that supervision may be more effective. Should friction between workers cause a breakdown in service to the public, measures must be taken to eliminate the causes of friction. It may necessitate supervisory counseling. Not infrequently, subordinate employees turn to the supervisor for personal advice, particularly when the supervisor has created an atmosphere conducive to the development of mutual trust and confidence between himself and subordinates. One of the advantages that accrues when the supervisor assumes the counseling responsibility is a better chance to know the individual on a more intimate basis, by discovering the behavioral patterns indicating not only how the individual acts but why he does what he does. Additionally, continuous contact is maintained with the employee and the outcomes of counseling over a period of time can be observed, proving to be especially helpful in dealing with problems that may arise during the course of the working relationship between the employee and the supervisor.

Professional attitudes toward the position and the entire field of recreational service, including such intangibles as loyalty, discretion, dependability, initiative, and dedication, must be stimulated in the program worker as well as in others employed by the department. Better employee–supervisor relations and employee incentive for higher creativity and productivity will result. When frictions arise between employees, counseling techniques should be applied. Sometimes transfers are arranged so that personality clashes or other friction-causing matters do not result in the loss of valued employees of the department. Transfers to different sections, changes in working hours, or other adroit maneuvers often eradicate such problems; in extreme cases, however, dismissal may be the only solution. Of course, such action tends to reflect on the employer who made the original mistake in judgment. If environmental situations such as poor working conditions, excessive noise, or other factors are creating strain or irritation, steps should be taken to alleviate these conditions.

Finally, the supervisor should encourage self-evaluation among professional and voluntary workers, since it is only when the individual actually wants to improve, because he sees and understands the necessity for so doing, that any improvement in performance occurs. Regardless of hints or threats, in the last analysis it is the individual worker who decides whether or not he will apply himself to better his techniques and his relationships with his co-workers.

Supervision takes place whenever any help is given through personal contact, such as by individual, group, and staff conferences, by the supervisor's reliability in keeping appointments and confidences, and by the supervisor's consistent, stable, and mature attitude as he offers objective attention to individual problems of either a professional or a personal nature. The supervisory process is typically facilitated when valid communication occurs between the supervised and the supervisor. In fact, communication may be the most effective device by which maximum efficiency and effectiveness are accomplished. Among the elements of communication that the supervisor must bear in mind are the dissemination of information, determination that understanding occurs (i.e., words have varied meanings to individuals so common values or at least common attitudes toward certain subjects should be present if real communication is to take place), and the ability to emphathize or demonstrate a genuine concern for the needs of others.

A variety of methods may be utilized in communicating with subordinates: interviews, staff meetings, letters, bulletin boards, a house organ (departmental newspaper or newsletter), and formal or informal conferences. Within the supervisory methodology there is, in addition to the above-mentioned methods, the face-to-face confrontations of observation, visitation, and in-service staff development or education. The supervisor's selection of tools must be meaningful for the situation. Each technique serves a particular purpose and has a specific effectiveness according to its use.

Field Observation and Visitation

Field observation is probably the most common method used by supervisors to determine whether agency policies are being executed and whether particular standards are being met and maintained. Field observation may be informal, casual, and unannounced, or it may be formal and by appointment. By actually inspecting the performance of employees, the nature of activities conducted, the condition of the facilities, the public response to program, and other pertinent factors, some evaluation can be made. In the unlikely event that recreationists are negligent in their duties, or that upkeep of facilities is unsatisfactory, or that any recreational structure or place has been permitted to deteriorate without proper steps attempted to resist or retard such deterioration, specific measures are undertaken to clear up these conditions. When field observation reveals instances of incompetence, inappropriate behavior, repeated tardiness, inefficiency, disregard of departmental regulations or policies, professional ineptitude, or any other substandard effort, definite personnel actions are the consequence. Depending on the severity or policy infraction, personnel action may range from mere admonition to termination of services with prejudice.

Inspection, a form of field observation, may be made to ensure that equipment is in safe condition, that correct safety precautions and practices are being carried out in all activities, and that facilities are routinely maintained in satisfactory condition. Patron conduct and compliance to departmental rules, regulations, and policy are also evaluated during field observation.

Visitation, or reconnaissance, unlike field observation, occurs as a consequence of the supervisor's desire to maintain liaison with program, employees, and the public. It is a simple procedure by which a storehouse of current information about any given subject may be obtained for further use. Visitations are usually made to various recreational centers, neighborhoods, or other sites, and to events within and without the public recreational service system. It is an effective means of becoming acquainted with the prospective clientele residing in the neighborhood served by an existing facility or to be served by a planned facility. It is helpful in appraising the temper of public opinion, to which departmental operation and program must be adjusted. Additionally, since it provides opportunities and occasions to interpret department policies, problems, needs, and objectives, visitation should be regarded as an important instrument of public relations.

Observation and visitation must never be equated with spying. From the day of employment, the recreationist in a public system must be made aware that he will be under constant scrutiny, not only by his immediate supervisors, but by the public he serves. The recreationist's work is conducted in the goldfish bowl of the public eye. Everything that he does is held up to public scrutiny for good or bad. The employee must fully understand that field observation and visitation are conducted, not as a means of "snooping," but to protect the public welfare and the department's reputation. As a public employee the recreationist must realize that as long as he is paid from tax funds he is a public figure who must submit to such scrutiny. It is part of his job responsibility. At any time and under all conditions, he should expect to be observed in the performance of his duties.

As long as field observation and visitation are clearly understood and accepted by the recreationist at the time of his employment, and sub-

sequently thereafter, he should have absolutely no trouble accommodating himself to on-the-job appraisals. The recreationist should be professional enough, endowed with the self-confidence that comes from his
own competence, and objective about realistically complying with departmental policy so that he will be unmindful of supervisory appearance
or any other visitation. Imbued with the professional's capacity for
high-quality performance, the recreationist need never be anxious about
supervisory observation. This point should be even more validly reinforced as a result of democratic practices and the climate produced by
the supervisor's understanding and acceptance of professional peer status
despite hierarchical differences caused by organizational structure. Supervisors may enjoy a higher ranking within the recreational service system,
but as professionals they are coequal with the most recently employed
recreationist. It is the concept of professionalism that does much to
sweep away any defensiveness or unwarranted feelings of imposition,
which some employees feel when faced with supervisory field observations. No such attitude as intrusion of privacy can be built up in the mind
of a public employee. A public employee does not enjoy the right of
privacy when he is performing a public function. As do all other citizens,
however, he enjoys the right of privacy off-the-job.

In-service Education and Staff Development

There has to be some duplication of methods to achieve intradepartmental adherence to policy. However, two basic devices that the supervisor may utilize have proved highly effective: in-service education and
development of morale.

Staff indoctrination and development are extremely beneficial in public
recreational service departments. Orientation of newly inducted workers
bridges the gap between the preprofessional academic preparation and
the practicalities of system demands and performance. In-service education is not a substitute for the professional preparation obtained in an
institution of higher education, but it serves to orient employees just
entering professional recreational service to the work for which they
have been engaged. In addition, it tends to transform the theoretically
prepared individual into one who knows and understands department
policy and objectives. He is therefore more competent to undertake the
duties and responsibilities of the recreationist position. Furthermore, in-
service education increases the technical competency of workers by
offering them opportunities to increase their technical skills. In-service
education attempts to stimulate continuing professionalization among
employees to ensure the optimum output of creativity, instructional
capacity, and service to the public.

The introductory period of the recreationist's assimilation into the
public system consists of being exposed to the basic policies that reflect

department objectives. The department's origins, declared purposes, acceptance by the community, performance, and relationship to other agencies are some of the focal points for employee orientation sessions. To these areas are added the specific policy statements that guide employees in their professional performance and off-the-job conduct. Departmental rules and regulations, promotional procedures as well as disciplinary measures, must be carefully emphasized.

All the administrative operations are presented in an initial orientation program, which may well last at least two weeks, so that the worker has a chance to learn the intricacies of line and staff organization, forms, reports, records, personnel policies, required professional conduct, and other facets of departmental expectation. It is a poor organizational procedure that immediately throws a newly employed person onto the line without giving him some special preparation as to what is expected of him. Agencies that do not have orientation periods for newly inducted employees typically find that such employees require longer periods of adjustment than oriented employees before they really begin to function effectively as part of the departmental team. The time taken to carefully orient new employees to the larger picture of the system is more than made up by the rapid comprehension of work details and skilled performance that generally accompanies this procedure.

> To learn method alone would be sterile, however, unless such learning was accompanied by efforts to understand the process of applying them. This is the professional heart of the matter. There can be no effective application without knowledge and learned and intuitive skill. The knowledge required to make methods effective is vast. Skill implies talent as well as understanding, and can only be perfected by practice and by a continual assessment of practice. Time alone dictates that in-service training can do no more than introduce these purely professional ingredients. The introduction may nevertheless be incisive enough to be immediately useful, enabling the trainee not only to function but to proceed from then on consciously to refine his skills and deepen his knowledge.[4]

The new employee is easily instilled with a high degree of inspiration that may set the tone of his work performance throughout his professional career. This is the time to plant *esprit de corps*. Continuous programs of staff development through in-service education are now considered to be essential to personnel administration in all areas of private and public endeavor. Such programs are especially necessary in public recreational service because of the relative newness of this type of public service. Many employees have been recruited with comparatively little or no previous special preparation directly related to their duties.

[4] Martha Moscrop, *In-Service Training for Social Agency Practice* (Toronto: University of Toronto Press; London: Oxford University Press, 1958), p. 10.

Although the total recruitment picture is brightening as far as attracting professionally prepared and highly competent workers into the field, to a great extent public recreational service systems still depend on individuals who have had little academic or theoretical background for this work. Nevertheless, many such employees bring to their jobs recreational skills that were developed in avocational or vocational experiences in other fields.

The type of in-service instruction that can be given under the auspices of any department is influenced to a certain extent by the assistance that can be obtained from institutions of higher learning. Because recreationists in administrative and supervisory capacities tend toward greater utilization of informal teaching methods, they need special assistance from recognized experts in the use of discussion methods, lectures, demonstrations, audiovisual materials, and the unit-of-interest method. A number of recreational service departments are located where their employees do not reside close to, or have no access to, colleges or universities offering professional courses for recreational service. For these workers, in-service education is more necessary than for those who have easy access to experts and reference materials.

In-service education is composed of six types of instructional procedures:

1. Physical and mental examination of employees for aptitude in various activities. Placement according to the individual's talent, skill, knowledge, and interest. Provision of basic orientation to the department in terms of its history, functions, objectives, and policies.
2. Staff meetings and personal conferences, held weekly, monthly, or as necessary, including discussion of policies, activities, and regulations; presentation of useful materials, interesting books and articles; demonstrations of new and proved techniques; utilization of audiovisual methods for worker instruction; and lectures by non-staff members on related knowledge.
3. Attendance at professional conferences of recreationists and similar groups on a state, regional, or national basis.
4. Visitation to other recreational places on an intrasystem or intersystem basis for observation of programs and methods employed by others, and for the infusion of new ideas for better service.
5. Stimulation of home study by calling attention to extension center courses, new literature, and study outlines; by obtaining correspondence study courses from leading universities and colleges; and by development of a department library with pertinent books, bulletins, bibliographies, journals, and audiovisual aids.
6. Short-term institutes or workshops conducted by staff supervisors with the aid of departmental specialists and other employed rec-

reationists who are particularly skilled in certain fields or activities. Sometimes non-agency or system experts are called in to augment the staff. The consultants who usually are recognized authorities in their respective fields present current practical information to those in attendance. These institutes or workshops normally include such subjects as the organization and administration of recreational programs, leadership, conduct of recreational activities including social, music, art, crafts, outdoor education (nature study, camping), dramatics, and a variety of other forms of activity. Additionally, they may be geared to the attempt to modify worker attitudes toward the people they serve as well as the inculcation of professional ethics, practices, and habits. Short-term institutes vary in a number of ways:

a. Intensive institutes requiring the full time of the enrollee for several consecutive days
b. Institutes consisting of one or more periods per week for a given season
c. Comprehensive institutes of either type mentioned above and covering a variety of subjects, often undertaken to give a superficial survey of the entire field of knowledge related to the work
d. Institutes or clinics specializing in a single activity or area of administration
e. Institutes limited to lectures, discussions, demonstrations
f. Institutes that include practice of recreational skills under instructional guidance.

There is little question that in-service education affects the quality of work, produces more capable leaders, provides the incentive to encourage increased participation in recreational activities, promotes the development of cultural fields, and provides unlimited opportunity for testing increasingly selected effective types and techniques of on-the-job education. Although in-service education can develop an employee to the point where he can maintain high standards of work in recreational service, it should not preempt, nor will it ever take the place of, professional education in accredited universities and colleges prior to entry into the field.

Evaluation and Appraisal

Among the supervisory practices that vitally concern every employee are appraisal and evaluation. These measures can be applied to program, use of facilities, managerial processes, professional leadership practices, and every aspect of recreational service. Appraisal of program and leadership is performed during the conduct of the activity or during some performance when the effects of leadership are made apparent.

Generally, appraisal is based on known standards applicable to a present situation or condition.

The appraisal of individual performance is considered essential to previously established aims or objectives. There is a continual process of selection that occurs as a result of past performance. Thus, the effectiveness of an individual is judged by what he has accomplished which gives some prognostication of what he may be able to accomplish. Eventually, guidelines are created to assist in the selection process. These guidelines or criteria permit the search for restricted or only certain types of data believed to be important in assessing values. There is a great variation in the ability to make value judgments among all people, probably because each person brings the sum of his previous experiences and knowledge to every situation that requires the making of judgments. Some individuals have greater objectivity, sensitivity, talent, or skill in making such judgments than do others. All people bring their biases to each judging situation. To the extent that an individual can control a bias more valid judgments are made on the basis of whatever evidence is present.

The very basic human experience of appraisal and consequent actions that occur as outcomes of such appraisal tends to train the behavior of individuals to conform to social patterns or the requirements of organizations. An organization typically has objectives that may or may not coincide with the aims of its employees. Restricted kinds of behavior are desired of employees for specific periods and are arranged so that the total performance of all employees, taken together, contributes to the attainment of organizational objectives. If the organization is to carry out the functions for which it was established, with specialized personnel in formally identified roles, then reliable information must be generated about the performances and capabilities of all personnel. The needs of individuals and their varying abilities, the requirements of the organization for valid information, the division of labor or specialization necessitate appraisal.

> The increasing attention paid by management to the systematic appraisal of an employee's performance by his supervisor, and the development of his capacity to perform more effectively on the job, has resulted largely from the findings of human relations research on the functioning of human beings in group or organizational settings. Research has shown that the quality of leadership displayed by the supervisor is a key factor in effective group functioning. Formal appraisal and development practices provide an opportunity for the use of effective leadership, as well as for meeting employee's needs in such areas as security in work relationships, aid in self-development, and recognition of achievements.[5]

[5] George E. Brown, Jr., and Allan F. Larson, "Current Trends in Appraisal and Development." Reprinted by permission of the publisher from *Personnel* © Jan./Feb., 1958 by the American Management Association, Inc.

Evaluation, on the other hand, is concerned with how nearly a specific activity or program approximates an accepted standard or a defined need. It attempts to indicate retrospectively the net and relative worth of an object, program, individual behavior, or procedure. Evaluation is utilized to make comparisons in relation to assumed or accepted criteria, i.e., value derived, public response achieved in terms of participation, increase or decrease in attendance, results of leadership employed, approbation or disapproval expressed, atmosphere created, economy achieved, and the like. Evaluation is a systematic process of determining the degree to which organizational goals are reached by employees. Thus, goals must be determined, identified, and subjected to some priority arrangement before evaluation is done. Without such an array, there can be no evaluation. Evaluation includes both qualitative and quantitative analyses of employee behavior (performance) and the value judgments dealing with the appropriateness of that conduct. The chief purpose of evaluation is to ascertain the degree to which organizational goals have been achieved.

Various methods are necessary if the evaluation process is to succeed. Broadly understood, the major purpose of the recreational service system is the provision of recreational opportunities for all of the people during their respective leisure. Evaluation therefore becomes part of the overall process for attaining that ideal. A variety of objectives must be met if the recreational needs of people are to be served. To the extent that every aspect of the public recreational service system may be evaluated, a determination may be made as to whether or not the purpose of the system is being fulfilled (see Chapter 25). In many instances, supervisory personnel identify and determine the methods to be used for evaluation and appraisal of employees and facets of the system. Among the devices and techniques most often devised for these procedures are employee merit-rating scales, critical incident ratings, performance records, field review methods, supervisory ratings, ranking techniques, self-ratings, and interviewing.

TYPES OF SUPERVISION

Supervision, as a leadership process, not only inspires workers to become receptive to the assistance that it can give, but also stimulates self-evaluation of personal efforts. Supervision, impartial, firmly grounded in scientific analysis, and democratically and creatively applied, spurs morale among personnel so that the department enjoys the fruit of cooperative and coordinated work. The success of supervision is measured by worker improvement and program effectiveness.

Supervision may be classified by four distinct characteristics or types: critical, custodial, instructional, and developmental. The supervisor who uses criticism is universally successful in uncovering factors for caustic comment. It is relatively easy to identify petty errors, or supposed errors, even in the best worker methods as these methods are utilized on the functional level. In some instances it is merely a matter of interpretation rather than a realistic appraisal of the methods used. In other situations the error lies with the supervisor's unwillingness to accept the fact that a functional worker may have more skill, knowledge, or talent than the supervisor has. In such cases the fault becomes one of malicious intent to harm the worker's reputation or of complete fantasy. Unfortunately, such supervisors are "snoopervisors" rather than leaders. The easiest thing in the world is to find fault, especially if no hint as to how the error may be overcome is offered. One who uses criticism in place of supervision engenders ill will and impairs on-the-job human relations through carping. There is a legitimate place for criticism, but it must be founded on fact and used with the best of intentions, i.e., for the development of the worker's technique and total performance. Criticism by itself means little and can actually poison the working atmosphere. Criticism based on fact with encouraging supervisory recommendations does much to lift morale and enhance worker confidence.

Custodial supervision is provided in anticipation of possible difficulties. This concept of so-called supervision is that "an ounce of prevention is worth a pound of cure." Thus it appears better to save the worker from getting into difficulty than to assist him after he has experienced trouble. A custodial supervisor reflects a state of "no confidence" in his subordinates. The supervisor, in effect, is so mistrustful of a subordinate's capability that he prefers to do all of the work himself. He rarely, if ever, permits his subordinates to perform in ways for which they have been employed, and, when he does permit subordinates to exercise judgment, he anxiously awaits a disaster, indicating that the worker does not have his supervisor's respect and showing that the supervisor neither knows nor cares about delegating responsibility and authority. This kind of supervision is only an expediency. When this method is used, the functional worker rarely receives the chance to confront or to resolve friction-causing problems.

Instructional supervision perceives weaknesses, aids the worker in recognizing and understanding the reasons for the weaknesses and constructively demonstrates how they may be remedied. It is the direct opposite of critical supervision. Logical advice in a cooperative vein characterizes this type of supervision. Again, however, instructional supervision is a telling and showing form rather than a coordinative effort between the subordinate and supervisor working together as co-equals. The subordinate–supervisor roles are maintained. Although there may be an attempt to initiate rapport, emphasis is on the hierarchical relationship rather than on developing a democratic framework in which each may operate.

Developmental supervision places emphasis on a worker's freedom to increase his individual effectiveness and productivity. The supervisor gives advice and assistance when needed but encourages the worker's cooperation and stimulates his self-evaluation by leadership rather than by position in the organization. This form of supervision creates a climate for building mutual trust and confidence. The worker is credited with a professional role; the supervisor treats the worker in a way that shows he has confidence in the worker's abilities and knowledge. There is no attempt to hover over the worker, maintaining a constant scrutiny as though the worker were about to promote the greatest calamity that could befall an organization. The worker's suggestions and recommendations are sought by the supervisor who becomes a resource person to whom the recreationist can apply if and when an event or problem arises that, in his experience or comprehension, he cannot handle. The development of a professional peer role between the supervised and the supervisor goes a long way toward the creation of mutually beneficial relations for all concerned.

The person responsible for the supervision of functional personnel involved in the activities program of a recreational service department should have a purposive and wide knowledge of recreational service and the attendant responsibilities of providing that service. He generally must be open to suggestions, but he should also have special education in various methods and techniques. He should be aware that not all workers can utilize the same procedures with the same degree of success, because there is more to being a recreationist than the mere use of standardized methods suggests. Unorthodox procedures may be the very ones that contribute the greatest success to the organization, but the local situation has a tendency to govern or condition methods for the meeting of certain needs. In today's rapidly changing society, the "tried-and-true" methods may not be so successful when they rest on past successes. The pragmatic approach to solving various problems, i.e., "It has worked in the past," may not be viable now. New thoughts, ideas, and practices that appear to be quite different from formula techniques applied in the past are coming to light. A non-conformist technique may achieve the purpose of the system, whereas a rigidly precribed series of do's and don'ts, based on widely held platitudes, results in gross failure. "The times they are a-changing," and the discipline and its agents must change with the times.

The supervisor must be impartial and exhibit integrity at all times. He must recognize superior methods and encourage workers to change their methods to the extent that they are capable. All employees of a recreational service system are human. To the extent that each has certain ego needs, they are no different one from the other. Supervisors also have a need to shine, to achieve mastery, status, and plaudits just as functional workers and administrators do. It is not enough to simply state an ideal about recreationists regardless of their positions in the hierarchy of any organization and hope for the best. Realistically, all employees are not imbued with the special skills, talents, insights, and knowledge that recreationists should have. Recognized also is the fact that not all employees act within the idealized roles of their professional capacities. Thus, personnel policies, rules, regulations, and disciplinary practices are needed. For good or bad, people make up the organizational structure of departments attempting to provide satisfaction for other people. As far as possible, supervision, as a leadership process, is undertaken to achieve the laudable goals of public recreational service. For this reason, the supervisor's education must be richer than that of the workers he is supervising, and his experiences should be wider and deeper in scope. Whenever this is possible, better supervision should be engendered. It must be kept in mind, however, that personality, intelligence, and good personal judgment remain the factors on which supervisory leadership develops. Good human relations tend to promote the highest morale and the greatest degree of productivity among workers.

Supervisors must be responsible for the achievement of the recreational program at their level of the total system. No supervisor, regardless of his personal excellence, can overcome administrative incompetence or political maladroitness. However, he can promote the best possible program given even the least tangible hint of administrative encouragement or support. Historically, the failure to reach departmental goals devolved on the functional workers, with such failure being registered to worker's inability, but it is the competent first-line supervisor who creates the climate of democracy whereby functional recreationists are enabled to perform more effectively. There is little question that the philosophy of the department emanates from the administrator, but the supervisor is still the communications link between the levels of the system, and he can do much to interpret both departmental goals and realistic worker requirements so that less energy is expended on futile tasks and greater effectiveness is the consequence. With a skilled supervisor to recommend criteria for the department as well as his stimulation of close cooperation and coordination among all individuals and groups working with him, the system should be able to accomplish the aims and objectives for which it was established. The supervisor's dedicated and professionalized leadership serves as a catalyst for encouraging concentrated effort and maximum output in reaching the recreational goals of the department in compliance with administrative policy.

Selected References

Boyd, B. B.: *Management-Minded Supervision* (New York: McGraw-Hill Book Company), 1976.

Dougherty, J. L.: *The Union Free Supervisor* (Houston, Texas: Gulf Publishing Co.), 1974.

Fickett, H. L., Jr.: *Peter's Principles, from I and II Peter* (Glendale, Calif: Regal Books), 1977.

Fulmer, R. M.: *Supervision: Principles of Management* (Riverside, N.J.: Glencoe Press), 1976.

Gellerman, S. W.: *Managers and Subordinates* (New York: Holt, Rinehart & Winston, Inc.), 1976.

George, C. S.: *Supervision in Action: The Art of Being Effective* (Englewood Cliffs, N.J.: Reston Publishing Company, Inc.), 1976.

Kadushin, A.: *Supervision in Social Work* (New York: Columbia University Press), 1976.

Le Tourneau, R.: *Management Plus: Getting Things Done Through People* (Grand Rapids, Mich.: Zonderman Publishing House), 1976.

Newport, M. G.: *Supervisory Management: Tools and Techniques* (St. Paul, Minn.: West Publishing Co.), 1976.

Van Dersal, W. R.: *Successful Supervisor: In Government and Business, 3d. ed.* (New York: Harper & Row, Publishers, Inc.), 1974.

White, J. R.: *Successful Supervision* (New York: McGraw-Hill Book Company), 1976.

PART V

FISCAL ADMINISTRATION

CHAPTER 19

Financial Management for Public Recreational Service

Alexander Hamilton stated, in No. 30 of *The Federalist,* that "Money is, with propriety, considered as the vital principle of the body politic; as that which sustains its life and motion, and enables it to perform its most essential functions." This statement simply means that government must have enough money, secured routinely, to maintain its operation. How funds are obtained, where they are allocated, controlled, and accounted for constitutes the formidable responsibility of fiscal management.

Financial management comprises three major facets. Fundamental to such management is fiscal policy definition, which deals with the political aspects of setting guidelines for public programs and appropriating money to execute the programs. Fiscal policy concerns taxation, revenue, and allocation of money. A second component is responsibility, that is, of certifying that the allocation of public money is spent in conformity with legal criteria and in the most efficient manner to give the greatest return to the public. The third aspect relates to the duties and responsibilities of fiscal structure and the budgetary process.

FINANCIAL POLICY

Members of public recreational service boards and/or commissions are responsible for advising on and supervising the expenditure of funds for recreational service, and to advise on and assist in the procurement of funds for recreational service in their jurisdictions. Fiscal policy is determined by political leaders and is the outcome of adjustment to diverse factors, including the condition of state and local economy, the availability of revenues for public programs, the monies expended on current programs, and the demand for additional programs. In relation to such elements are a complex of basically normative powers: the economic orientation of political leaders and their immediate advisers and their concept toward the function of government, and the vociferous requests of lobbies and the importance attached to these lobbies by legislators, executives, and administrators. The following discussion attempts to illustrate how fiscal decisions are reached and the kinds of factors that intrude on financing public recreational service systems.

FISCAL ADMINISTRATION

Fiscal administration is the management and control of all revenues received by the recreational service system from taxes, fees, private donations, or other sources that are utilized in the operation of the department. The custody of such finances is delegated to specific officers who are responsible to the public for protecting such monies from misuse, embezzlement, and fraudulent misappropriation and for expending them prudently.

The purposes of fiscal administration are to supply pertinent data about how public funds are acquired, safeguarded, allocated, and used; to determine whether the fiscal system is performing adequately; and to discover ways and means for reducing expenditures while receiving greater returns on facilities, equipment, and programs. Money is the basic tool of administration.

In public work a specific finance bureau or department is usually constituted by law and charged directly with the responsibility of compiling and recording the financial transactions of the department and of preparing essential statements interpreting the financial facts. Such bureaus are headed by an official known variously as auditor, controller, comptroller, or director of finance. Other fiscal officials of the city include the treasurer who invests, disburses, and safeguards the public funds; the tax collector, who collects all taxes levied; and the assessor, who places a value on all taxable property.

The several line departments of a city perform certain accounting and auditing duties to provide original information to the finance director and to avail themselves of more detailed and accessible records than those kept by the controller. The form of such records may be prescribed by the controller and the records are subject to verification. All original accounts, which require detailed verification, are inspected periodically and audited. The accounts of the auditor and, if necessary, of the several departments are subject to further validation, sometimes by state auditors or by private auditing firms engaged by the governing body of the city on contract.

Fiscal management within a recreational service system is assigned to the chief executive of the department, but responsibility is shared with other employees, including the assistant superintendent, accountants, auditors, clerks, and employees at facilities where fees are collected and transmitted. All are responsible to the chief executive of the system who in turn is responsible to the city manager, the mayor, or other governing body, and ultimately to the public.

Financing Operations

The development and operation of a municipal recreational service system may be financed from any funds accruing to a general fund or from an earmarked fund supported by a special tax levied on property and established by ordinances. After consideration of requests and recommendations from department executives and the chief administrative officer, the governing body adopts an ordinance fixing the budget for the ensuing fiscal year. The expenditures budget may not exceed the revenue budget, which is an estimate of the revenue from all sources classified according to the several sources. The proposed budget is published in legally approved newspapers for a stated number of days. Prior to final action the citizens and taxpayers have an opportunity to be heard. The foregoing practice is customary but there are minor deviations. Once a budget is adopted, the administrative officers are empowered to expend the funds accordingly throughout the year.

Revenue to support municipal government is obtained from many sources. The general property tax yields by far the greatest amount (see pp. 436–437). Revenue is also collected from commercial, industrial, and corporate enterprises. Federal, state, and county governments contribute grants for specific purposes: urban renewal, public health, civil defense, purchase of open space, and road building. Taxes on gasoline, cigarettes, sales, licenses, franchises, and fines, forfeits, fees, and donations are also revenue sources. Some cities assess income and payroll taxes.

FINANCING RECREATIONAL SERVICES

The financial ability of a city to sustain a recreational service system from ordinary tax and other sources depends on the share of the tax burden carried by commercial, industrial, and other corporate enterprises compared to the burden carried by individual property owners and residents. The ratio of population to assessed valuation of property subject to local taxes is a fair measure of the financial capacity of a city. This ratio varies from a medium on either side of approximately $1,000 per unit of population.

The dependence of city government on the general property tax for general revenue (including recreational services) is perhaps an important reason why community recreational service has not been funded better. Functions of the municipal government have greatly increased in number and the cost of traditional functions has also increased. This increasing cost has been charged against the general property tax. Thus the claims of public recreational service must be evaluated in comparison to the claims of numerous other municipal functions, and, because it is a relatively new function, the recreational service department is somewhat at a disadvantage. The longer-established functions are cared for first and then small appropriations are doled out to the newer departments and bureaus. Recreational service has just begun to achieve sufficient recognition to command insistent support. Many jurisdictions are finding to their alarm and dismay that public recreational service is coming to be considered as an essential requirement, especially among inner-city residents and concerned teen-age and adult populations in smaller towns and cities.[1]

Recreational service departments do endeavor to procure a fair share of the budgeted revenue of their city for the support of their departments. The amount is determined, however, not by any set formula as to what may constitute a fair share, but rather by a careful estimate of the needs of the city in respect to the many functions it must perform. Recreational services do well if they are allotted about 12 percent of the general fund revenue.

As a general rule states do not make grants to cities specifically for local recreational service purposes, although they do allocate funds from state tax revenues for general purposes. Specific grants are sometimes made for special purposes, such as street improvements, relief in times of disaster, and the like. Some cities have been granted funds, which usually had to be matched by local funds, to acquire regional parks, historical sites, and public beaches.

The federal government has established many programs to aid cities. Many of these programs were part of the now defunct "war on poverty." They often required matching funds and their implementation depended on appropriations by the Congress. The federal government has funded the acquisition of open spaces for conservation and regional parks by outright appropriations and by grants to states, but they have been *regional* and not local. Hopefully the federal government will extend generous aid to the cities to improve their local environments.

Taxes

General Property Tax. The general property tax is levied on real and personal property. Each year valuation is placed on all such property by the municipal assessor. The total assessed valuation of all taxable property is divided into the amount of required revenue in order to determine

---

[1] Richard Kraus, *Public Recreation and the Negro: A Study of Participation and Administrative Practices* (New York: The Center for Urban Education, 1968), pp. 5–20.

the exact tax rate. The rate is expressed in mills per dollar of assessed value or, for convenience, in cents per hundred dollars of assessed value. Thus a tax of 1 mill per 1 dollar is equivalent to a tax of 10 cents per 100 dollars.

The determination of true or cash value is difficult because there is no scientific manner of computing it. Values fluctuate, and the value of property is largely a matter of judgment. Theoretically, a true or cash value is considered by assessors to be the price that a property would bring in a sale by a solvent debtor to satisfy a debt. Except by actually selling the property, there is no exact way of confirming this estimate. Comparisons of assessed valuation of taxable property in different cities and of tax rates derived therefrom are of little significance unless the variable bases of valuation are taken into consideration. These vary from 20 percent to 100 percent of true or cash value. In many states, the basis is determined by state law.

The maximum tax rate is usually fixed by the governing body of the city. Cities with charters may set their own maximum tax rate, which, however, does not apply to any rate that must be fixed for payment of interest on municipal bonds.

A half century ago property taxes produced over 90 percent of the general fund revenue raised by cities for municipal functions and for support of the public schools; present property taxes scarcely produce more than 30 percent.

Recreational Millage Tax. Another way public recreational service is supported is by levying a special tax for it. This tax is sometimes referred to as a *millage tax,* i.e., a tax whose rate is in mills or tenths of a mill, and often it is expressed in terms of cents per hundred dollars of assessed valuation. Is the special levy advantageous for public recreational service? The answer is different for each city, since it depends on whether more adequate funds can be obtained by a fixed levy or by appealing annually to the governing body of the city, thus contending with all other departments for a portion of the general revenues. One objection to the special levy is that it tends to freeze appropriations at a given rate for a period of years since it can be changed only by amending the charter by vote of the electorate.

Capital Improvements by Bond Issues. Although there have been some improvements within the last 20 years, most cities are far behind modern standards in acquiring and improving recreational spaces, places, facilities, and structures. Capital improvements (purchase of land, construction of buildings and other structures, and general plant improvements) can be financed by the issuance of municipal bonds for general purposes or particular projects. Capital improvements for public recreational services are only meagerly financed from annual municipal operating funds.

Cities have frequently resorted to borrowing by issuance of bonds with 20, 30, and 40 years' maturity.

With few exceptions, bond issues must be submitted to the electors at a general or special election and usually require an approval by a two-thirds majority of the electorate. Since such bonds are a lien upon property, the two-thirds majority has become most difficult to achieve. The legality of the two-thirds rule is being challenged in various suits on the basis of the "one man, one vote" decision of the United States Supreme Court. Blocking a needed public improvement by a decision of one third or more of the electorate is held to be a denial of a constitutional right. It will probably take several years to resolve this question.

Once approved, the retirement of the bonds and the interest paid on them are a charge against the assessable real property of the taxpayers, although the tax rate is computed and listed separately on the individual tax bill. State laws regulate the amount of bonds that any city may issue for general governmental purposes, including recreational service, and this limit is typically about 3 percent of the assessed valuation of all taxable property. This limit does not apply to bonds for nongovernmental purposes (as for self-liquidating public utility enterprises which carry a considerably higher limit). The reasonable limits of bonding capacity, independent of statutory limitations, are also influenced by the rating computed by large bond-buying houses. If a city overextends itself, it may be difficult to sell the bonds and the city will have to pay a premium or offer prohibitive rates of interest.

When municipalities have wanted to finance large-scale capital construction above the immediate revenue capacity of the city, they have necessarily resorted to bonding. Bonds may be classified according to means of payment or according to form of obligation.

Sinking Fund Bonds and Serial Bonds. Sinking fund bonds and serial bonds are classified by the method of payment. Sinking fund bonds require complete payment with accrued interest at maturity. During the life of the bond, the municipality makes payments into what is called a *sinking fund.* These funds are then invested and the monies accruing from them are finally used to amortize the bond. This method has the advantage of flexibility. However, a major disadvantage is the difficulty of administration owing to the required computation of actuarial rates and the accounting and investment of city funds. On the other hand, serial bonds are amortized in annual installments, which eliminate the complexity of sinking fund operations and saves administrative charges.

General Obligation Bonds and Revenue Bonds. General obligation bonds are issued in amounts not in excess of constitutional or statutory restrictions. If city revenue proves insufficient, taxes may be increased to the statutory limit in order to meet payments on the interest and principal. General obligation bonds are those having the faith and credit of the community as support. Interest and risk are lessened with this type of bond.

A revenue bond, on the other hand, may be defined as an "obligation of a revenue-producing enterprise or property, payable solely from revenues of that enterprise or property."[2] When cities have approached the legal limit of their bonding capacity or when the enterprise is clearly profitable, the utilization of revenue bonds may be indicated. Although use of revenue bonds has not been a general practice of municipalities for the development of recreational structures and facilities, some communities have resorted to this type of bonding for marinas, auditoriums, stadiums, swimming facilities, or golf links.

Many people object to financing municipal improvements by borrowing and issuance of bonds. The cost of such improvements is increased because of interest payments and the burden of repayment falls on future generations. These objections are less applicable to bonds for recreational places and improvements because new values are created, and the investment, especially in land, is of permanent worth. The benefits continue to be enjoyed long after the bond issue has been paid off, and since future generations will enjoy the benefits, they may justifiably be called on to pay a portion of the cost. Perhaps the most distinct advantage of the bond plan is that it is the only plan under which a large comprehensive program of improvements and acquisitions can be undertaken and accomplished in a few years.

Pay-As-You-Go Plan. Some cities prefer the "pay-as-you-go" method of financing improvements, scheduling a series of desired improvements in several fields over a period of years according to a priority estimate of comparative need. In using this method a city may draw on its general fund or levy a special tax above the statutory limit for general purposes. Some states authorize special levies, the proceeds of which are then deposited in a special fund for the particular purpose.

The advantages of the pay-as-you-go method, under which additions and improvement are made yearly out of current funds, are obvious. Such a plan requires payments to be made out of the annual tax levy or through the utilization of a reserve fund which is built up through annual accumulations to meet anticipated expenditures. In the long run, this plan is less expensive than bonding, since it eliminates the need for an expensive debt service. All cities endeavor to employ this method to some extent, but in the area of recreational service it has generally been used only for comparatively inexpensive improvements.

In most instances, the city simply cannot afford to finance large capital construction on the basis of current revenue. If the pay-as-you-go method were the only means for providing improvements and acquisitions, the

[2] C. H. Chatters and A. M. Hillhouse, *Local Government Debt Administration* (Englewood Cliffs, N.J.: Prentice-Hall, Inc., 1939), p. 241.

major portion of such needed development and construction never would be accomplished.[3]

Special Assessments. The special assessment plan for financing the acquisition and improvement of lands for recreational purposes has been used in several cities. The cost of the project is assessed against the property in the district that presumably will benefit from the project. The assessment may be paid in cash or, if it exceeds a specific sum (25, 50, or 100 dollars), it may be permitted to go to bond; then its principal and interest would be paid in annual installments over a given period (usually 10 years). In principle, this is the same method as that used for many years to finance the opening, widening and paving of streets that are purely for local benefit.

The special assessment plan seems eminently fair at first glance because those who desire and are willing to pay for the improvements and services may have them. If, however, the plan is generally applied, the less well-to-do neighborhoods suffer and this is not compatible with the principles of democratic government. If community recreational service is a general governmental function, it must be provided for all and financed by the same means as other governmental functions are financed.

Other objections to the plan arise out of the difficulty of administering it. The determination of a district including only those properties that will benefit by the improvement is almost impossible to assess and must, in the last analysis, be arbitrary. Grading of assessments according to proximity, those residing close to the improvements paying more and those residing farther away paying less, presents another difficulty. Moreover, the plan is costly to administer, particularly in the computation and collection of each assessment. For a comparatively inexpensive local recreational improvement involving many small assessments, the total cost of the project often is exorbitant.

Other Financial Resources

Private monies channeled into the public treasury and earmarked for public recreational service purposes are a considerable resource for the support of these services at the municipal level. The resources are of three kinds: first, fees and charges paid by individuals as users of public facilities and services; second, gifts of funds or materials to support stated programs and events; and third, grants or bequests of real or personal property, improved and unimproved. Leaseback, rents, and concessions also bring money into the department.

Fees or Charges. It is common practice among public recreational service departments to charge individual and group fees for certain services, admittance to some public recreational places, use of areas and

---

[3] R. E. Brown, "Pay-As-You-Go for Local Government," *The Tax Review*, VIII (1947), pp. 28–32.

facilities, instruction, and administration of athletic competitions. The practice of charging fees arose primarily from a desire to augment the meager appropriations obtained from tax sources. The once frequently made objection that fees constituted double taxation has now been fully dissipated.

Not all recreational services should be self-supporting and public recreational service should never enter into profit-making schemes. If a service can be rendered commercially it is better left to private enterprise.

Policies Governing Fees. In general, authorities are agreed that recreational services should be rendered free provided sufficient funds can be obtained from other sources to make such a policy practicable. The question of policy, therefore, becomes one of economics.

If it is necessary to levy fees for recreational and related services, the following rules are suggested as to when fees should be charged:

1. When the particular service is relatively costly to render and few persons participate at one time, although the demand is great.
2. When the particular service is demanded by a comparatively few persons and the cost of providing the facility is relatively high.
3. When services are offered in competition with private business. Many believe that such services should not be rendered at all; however, if offered for some special reason, they should be offered at a fee. Dancing instruction is an example.
4. When the service is primarily for adults, since adults are better able to pay for special services than are children.
5. When participation in the activity is limited to an exclusive group, a charge for the utilization of a public facility is justified for the the special privilege accorded to closed groups.
6. When the service is enjoyed by a considerable number of non-residents. The justification for levying fees is based upon self-protection, either by making the visitor pay a share of the cost or by reserving the service to local people.
7. When collection is practical. Frequently a fee seems justifiable, but the cost of collection is greater than the revenue that would be collected, or the revenue does not exceed the cost sufficiently to make a system of levies practicable.
8. When levying fees does not create poor public relations. Any fee tends to arouse public opposition, especially when it is established after service has been rendered free. Probable revenue should be weighed against the public ill-will which might be created.
9. When the fee deprives persons of limited means from the benefits of necessary community recreational service it should *not* be established. *Activities that are universal in appeal and that serve a universal need should be free.*

Fees for Services or Privileges. The charging of fees for particular services or privileges has been justified on various grounds. Special services are enjoyed by comparatively few persons, thus those enjoying them should pay directly so that the costs of the services are not a burden on all the taxpayers. Without fees, some costly services could not be offered. Fees permit higher quality services than would be available otherwise. Some recreationists believe the practice of charging fees favorably affects the behavior of persons taking advantage of the service. However, it may be that those who can afford a fee may be more amenable to control.

Fees for Use of Recreational Areas and Facilities. Fees are sometimes collected for the use of areas and facilities.

1. Baseball, football, soccer, hockey fields, tracks, tennis courts, and basketball courts. Usually the use of these facilities is free; occasionally when the facilities are maintained in a manner desired by the most skilled teams a flat fee is levied. The fee is collected from the group to which a permit is issued for a given period.
2. Archery, golf driving, skeet, rifle, and pistol ranges; handball, horseshoes, roque, badminton, and volleyball courts. These facilities are used by individuals rather than by teams, consequently the problem of collecting fees is complicated. Usually the fees are on an hourly basis or per unit of equipment.
3. Golf courses. With few exceptions a fee is levied. The fee is collected from the individual when he reports for play or a season ticket is sold. When no fee is charged, the course is usually inadequate.
4. Bowling greens. Sometimes a fee is levied, usually a membership fee for a month or a year.
5. Ice-skating, skiing, tobogganing. The use of areas for winter sports is usually free, but equipment required by the individual often must be rented.
6. Bathing beaches. The use of public bathing beaches is usually free. A few cities with small beaches and great demand levy admission fees.
7. Swimming pools. About as many cities levy admission fees for the use of swimming pools as offer the service free. When a fee is high, it usually includes the use of locker, suit, towel, and soap.

Fees for Instruction. Fees are also levied for individual or group instruction in specific activities, especially when the undivided attention of the instructor is required.

1. Individual golf lessons
2. Individual and group swimming lessons

3. Individual and group scuba diving lessons
4. Sailing lessons
5. Individual and class tennis lessons
6. Individual and class instruction in arts and crafts
7. Dramatic classes
8. Class lessons in dancing, twirling, gymnastics, horseback riding, and the like.

Fees for Administration of Athletic Competition. There is an increasing tendency to levy fees for the administration of adult athletic competition. Fees are charged to cover drawing and publishing schedules; services of umpires, referees, and linemen; trophies; and incidental expenses. A forfeit fee to guarantee appearance of teams and a registration fee for individual athletes are also frequently charged. These fees are often collected and disbursed by extra-official agencies, such as municipal athletic associations, which operate on public facilities and are subject to varying degrees of control by the public recreational service departments. However, many departments now handle all details of administration of athletic league competition. This is most desirable when dealing with funds involved in athletics and in promotion of other activities.

Amounts of Fees or Charges. Fees should not be so high that persons with limited financial resources will be unable to avail themselves of the services. Public recreational service may be the last recourse that many inner-city dwellers have for participation in worthwhile recreational experiences, and, if such services are closed to them because of exorbitant fees, the entire public system should be called into question. To permit economic discrimination to interfere with the provision of recreational service undermines the essential principle that public recreational service must meet the needs of all the people regardless of their social or economic level.

The amount of fees for recreational services must be determined by local conditions.

1. The fee may be determined on the basis of the actual cost of rendering the service, including interest on and amortization of the investment.
2. The fee may be computed on the basis of direct operating expenditures, disregarding capital items.
3. The fee may be determined at the rate that would represent the cost of rendering the service over the normal cost of other services taken together.
4. The fee may be computed at the rate that will result in efficient use of a given area or improvement.

Gifts and Other Benefactions. Money and real property are sometimes received from a philanthropic agency, private organization, individual, or group for which the contributor expects no repayment or special service. Donations and bequests are not infrequent and often assist in expanding public recreational services. Outright gifts of cash or materials to public agencies are small in comparison to total revenue from fees. Such aid is frequently contributed for a special and limited program that appeals to the giver. Sometimes the contribution pays for prizes, or non-returnable costumes for which public funds may not be expended. It should be added that when the gifts for such "private" purposes are received, they should be accepted by non-official agents, for once deposited in the public treasury they may not be permitted to be expended for their intended purpose.

Grants or Bequests of Real and Personal Property. Park and recreational service systems often receive valuable properties from private donors, dedicated in perpetuity, usually by terms of the grant or will. It is a curious fact that no other function of cities is similarly benefitted, not even the public school system. Advantage should be taken of this disposition of citizens to convey to the city a gift of property for park and recreational purposes and perhaps systematic procedures should be employed to encourage this practice, but how to do it is difficult to state. Voluntary agencies have developed fund campaigns with conspicuous success, not so much in the donation of real and personal property as in the procurement of money for annual operating budgets and capital purposes. The promotions are organized on a personal solicitation basis. The impact of the need and relevance of an agency program on the consciousness of individuals and organizations often inspires them to make extraordinary gifts of cash, securities, and real property.

Leaseback. Leaseback is another method, rather infrequently used, to build facilities by contract with private corporations under the provision that the finished facility will be leased back to the city at an annual rent over a stated period of years. Plans are subject to the approval of the city. Under this plan the cumulative rent must be sufficient to compensate the private corporation for the investment, including interest and profit on the investment. It is a way of substituting private credit for public credit. However, since cities may borrow money at a lower interest rate than private corporations and since the public cost may not include an element of profit, the plan is necessarily a costly one.

Rents and Leases. Revenue is sometimes had from rents and leases of property that is not required for recreational purposes. Usually the property is pending sale or other disposal and the renting of it is a temporary expedient.

Concessions. Many recreational service departments and park agencies have adopted the practice of granting concessions to private operators to offer services and to sell commodities to patrons of parks and recreational centers. The most common service concessions are parking automobiles; renting boats, horses, and various kinds of equipment; conducting boating excursions; and operating amusement devices. Commodity concessions are refreshment stands, vending privileges on grounds and in grandstands, and stores for sale and repair of sport equipment.

When the problem of providing certain services and commodities first arises the question inevitably raised is whether or not the municipality should enter into merchandising in competition with private business. The current view is that public business should not be inaugurated unless private business is unable to render the required services. The justification for the public business is not primarily to make a profit but to render a needed service, and this point should always be kept foremost. If the needed service cannot be conveniently supplied by private business on its own premises adjacent to or outside the public area, then the services must be rendered directly by the municipal agency or through the granting of a concession.

The concession plan is open to serious objections: (1) It permits making private profit from public investment. (2) It encourages use of political influence to gain private advantage. (3) Concessionaires apply commercial standards to their operations and are not inclined to uphold the high standards of public recreational service, particularly when these conflict with profit making. Accordingly, public park and recreational service authorities have recently assumed more direct responsibility for this type of business. Full-time specialists may be employed by the department, not for their recreational service skills or knowledge, but for their merchandising effectiveness. In this way the department may set the standards for safety, equity, quality, and service while making the patron's experience more enjoyable.

Concession Contracts. If it seems necessary to grant a concession, it is advisable to enter into a formal contract with the concessionaire. The concessionaire should be selected on the basis of competitive bids. Advertisements for bids should be made in the customary manner and should state the detailed specifications that will govern the concession and become a part of the concession contract.

Specifications should provide for payment of a flat sum or a percentage of the gross receipts to the department. Flat sums are usually preferable, but they can be employed only when the nature of the business permits the prospective concessionaire to estimate with reasonable accuracy how much business he may do and what he can afford to offer for the privilege of doing it. If this cannot be done, a percentage is charged, preferably on the gross receipts of the concessionaire from all sources, rather than on his net income. Concessionaires operating on a percentage should be required to use cash registers, duplicate numbered receipts, or numbered tickets so that a record of every sale may be had. Printing of the receipts and tickets should be subject to audit and to inspection at any time. Payments should be made weekly or monthly, and if in a form of rent they should be paid in advance. Payment must be prompt lest delinquencies mount and a crisis eventually precipitates with the department appearing in the role of a major creditor, often leading to an involved legal procedure. The concession specifications should give the department control of approval of concession personnel and commodities. Specifications may regulate hours of business, signs and other advertising devices, and methods of vending.

Concessionaires should be required to post a cash or surety bond to guarantee faithful performance under the contract and should take out public liability policies naming the municipality as one of the insured.

Concession contracts should be limited to one, two, or three years to facilitate change of concessionaires should this be necessary. Short terms are not practicable, however, if the concessionaires are required to make relatively large investments for building and fixtures. Cities may construct buildings or designate the place of business in an existing building in which the enterprise is to be conducted. The city then installs and owns the necessary fixtures, making it easier to control the architecture, arrangement, and appearance of the place of business as well as facilitating the change of concessionaire if needed. A higher percentage or greater total guarantee may be obtained from the concessionaire if he is relieved of the capital investment.

ACCOUNTING AND AUDITING

Accounting concerns the computation and use of financial data. It has a real and specific function, broadly stated, control over finances and revenue. Control over personnel is a consequence of employees' responsibility for handling finances. Accounting involves the examination of operating effects and the resultant financial condition, as well as budgeting. The functions of accounting may be detailed as:

1. Capital:
   a. Determination
      (1) of the worth of each asset
      (2) of the amount of all liabilities
      (3) of net worth
   b. Protection
      (1) of all capital to prevent monetary corruption through the mishandling of funds, misappropriation, or improper use of funds
      (2) by the utilization of appropriate accounting methods to determine depreciation and required repairs

    c. Examination of financial situations as a reflection of changing conditions

    d. Management over the financial condition in compliance with the budget

2. Revenue:

    a. Calculation

        (1) of each revenue item by specified periods

        (2) of each expenditure or loss by specified periods

        (3) of profits and loss

        (4) of revenue from segregated capital items in the statements and financial records

    b. Protection

        (1) of revenue to ensure the receipt and correct accounting of each item

        (2) against incurring or paying of improper items

    c. Examination of the consequences of departmental operations during stated periods and the comparison of results between various periods of time

    d. Management over revenue and expenditure items and operating effects in compliance with the budget

The functions of accounting are executed through a system of accounts, records, procedures, and statements. The accounts are the means by which necessary data are collected for the preparation of accounting statements which are the formal summaries used for administering the enterprise. Statements are the bases of policy formulation and substantive managerial action. Thus, the functions of accounting are enacted by means of recording transactions, verification of records by audit, operation of internal control methods, preparation of fiscal and operating statements, examination of statements, and budgeting of operations and financial condition.

Governmental accounting is based on the same concepts and practices as is private or commercial accounting. The orientation, however, is quite different because of the problems that governmental agencies encounter. A governmental agency is established for the benefit of the citizens, and sources of funds are vastly different between public and private enterprises. The benefits of citizens are received at cost. A governmental unit, through legislative action, installs funds and appropriations and requires strict accountability of its personnel.

Accurate and complete accounting records and auditing procedures in governmental administration are necessary for a number of reasons, chiefly the pervasive requirements of the law:

> There is no phase of financial activity which, in some manner or other, is not controlled and directed by the law. The law determines the manner in

which money received is to be allocated to specific funds for expenditure, the law dictates, through formally adopted budgets, the purposes for which money may be spent. The routine requirements for controlling money received and its deposit (are) many times formally stated in the law. The duties and responsibilities of administrative officials are stated in the law. The submission of claims by vendors for payment and the manner of approval by government officials is another phase of financial activity which is subject to legal requirements. The foregoing are only a few of the ways in which legal mandates directly or indirectly influence the fiscal operations of local government units.[4]

Other reasons for thorough systems of accounting and auditing are to make financial transactions of a permanent record; to guarantee that public funds have been received and disbursed according to proper legal authorization and restrictions; to fix responsibility definitely on authorized individuals and bodies; and to facilitate the transaction of public business generally.

Internal control is essential in any accounting system. In public administration, the disposition of monies by two or more persons may be checked by correlated records designed in such a manner that the accuracy of one is entirely dependent on the accuracy of the other. Thus, more than one employee is involved to serve as a check against attempted collusion, misrepresentation, or dishonest practice, and accurate and verifiable records are readily available concerning the daily transactions and their results.

Accounting also indicates the financial condition of the system and its operating services during a specific fiscal period as well as the day-to-day position of the department with regard to the receipt of various revenues, and the kind and amount of services engendered as a result of the appropriation of funds.

Accounting Records

Financial statements contain information taken directly from the accounting records which consequently should be designed in such form as to enable this to be done without additional computations. In other words, the classification of accounts, the terminology used in the accounts, and other details should conform to the requirements of the statements. A distinction should be made between memorandum records, which any employee or executive might find expedient in the conduct of his work, and official records. The former are mere aids to administration. Official records register the official transactions of the city and must be of standard form and accurate. A falsification of them may constitute a crime. All entries are part of the official records which become instruments for internal control.

[4] George W. Lafferty, "Influence of Law on the Independent Auditor in the Examination of Local Government Accounts," *Journal of Accountancy*, Vol. XC, No. 2 (August, 1950), p. 122.

Cost Accounting

Cost accounting is the analysis of costs for services produced. Therefore it may be defined as a system of accounting that attempts to evaluate the benefits of services received by the public in terms of the cost of measurable units. Cost accounting is used as a basis for determining fees to be charged for services. It facilitates the evaluation of the efficiency of departmental activities and actually promotes it. Cost accounting is utilized in the preparation of budgets for those departmental services that can be estimated in terms of measurable units. Accurate cost accounting is valuable in determining the feasibility of constructing facilities with the agency's own labor force or through contractual means.

Analysis of unit cost data is of special interest in observing a proper balance between different phases of a department activity. Such data may reveal that too little is being expended for supplies in proportion to the expenditure for supervision; or that a highly expensive activity is being maintained in one quarter to the detriment of an inexpensive yet extremely desirable service elsewhere.

The customary accounts compiled by a central financial office cannot supply the essential information required for a thorough system of cost accounting. It is necessary to install systems of field reporting that will show personnel services, supervision, materials, supplies, equipment, and overhead which are applicable to separate jobs.[5] Such field records usually cannot be handled easily by the general accounting and auditing department of the city, but they can profitably be assembled in each department or bureau concerned.

For routine, continuous operations, cost checks can be made from time to time by sampling. The cost of separate items of expense in an operation may be computed and compared with the cost of rendering such a service at similar recreational centers.

Auditing

Auditing is an official examination and verification of accounts to determine whether or not an agency has spent or is spending appropriated funds in accordance with the budget. It has a deterring effect upon misuse, but it reveals evidence only after an act has been committed. Auditing relates to the collection and disbursement of money, the certification of its deposit, the payment of funds for contracts, and the receipt of the goods and services for which the money was used. An internal audit is made systematically by designated employees of the department or city; an external audit is usually made by an outside agency, such as a state auditing bureau or a private firm of auditors.

[5] Carl H. Chatters and Irving Tenner, *Municipal and Governmental Accounting* (Englewood Cliffs, N.J.: Prentice-Hall, Inc., 1941), pp. 227–273.

The accuracy of an internal audit is assured by the control of all financial stationery and by the assignment of auditing duties to persons other than those charged directly with the duty of making invoices, or charges, or collecting money. An internal audit also includes an inventory of all supplies in the central storeroom and a check of the supplies received on purchase and of withdrawals by requisition.

The financial stationery used by recreational service departments consists largely of numbered receipts (in duplicate or triplicate) bound in books or pads, and numbered admission tickets. The tickets should be numbered serially in rolls or released by recording ticket machines. The stationery used by employees at the operating center is released to them on receipt and they are required to account for all numbers recorded thereon. The supply of numbered tickets is kept under lock and key and in charge of a responsible employee.

Control

Control is also called *concurrent auditing*. It is an appraisal procedure that takes place prior to the expenditure of public funds or during the process of spending money. Control acts as an administrative check since it not only inquires into the correctness of expenditure, but also into whether the policy guiding the expenditure is wise.

In public work, a pre-audit of disbursements and receipts and a post-audit of all transactions are necessary. The pre-audit of disbursements checks original documents, such as invoices, receipts of deliveries of commodities, payrolls, and purchase orders, to ensure that each expenditure is made by proper authority and in accordance with law. The pre-audit of income checks duplicate receipts and other evidences of the collection of funds to determine the proper amounts to be deposited in the treasury.

Control has the distinct advantage over the post-audit in that it greatly assists in the minimization of possible invalid expenditures for purposes not consistent with the legal instrument dictating the allocation of public funds. In other words, it helps to alleviate the problem of unauthorized shifting of appropriations.[6]

ACCOUNTS AND FUNDS

Since the principal municipal accounting functions are usually performed by an agency other than the recreational service department, it is sufficient for our purposes to indicate the nature of some of the accounts and statements compiled by the auditor or comptroller and their respective value to the recreational service system. These records vary considerably, but the definitions and procedures indicated are fundamentally those followed in cities both large and small.

[6] James C. Charlesworth, *Governmental Administration* (New York: Harper & Brothers, 1951), pp. 344–345.

The term *account* indicates a descriptive heading under which money transactions that are similar as to purpose, object, and source are recorded. Examples are: salaries account, supplies account, insurance account, and utilities account.

A *fund*, in the public accounting sense, consists of monies intended by law for a particular purpose which must be accounted for separately. The several governmental operations of a city are usually grouped, for accounting purposes, under a general fund. Other funds of a small city include a special assessment fund, trust account fund, sinking fund, bond fund, and sometimes a utility fund for public utilities. Large cities have more elaborate fund designations. The separate funds are usually designated by the city charter and sometimes the governing boards are empowered to set up special funds. The recreational service department operations are most frequently included in the general fund except when certain outlays are financed from bond funds. When departments are granted a fixed annual revenue based on a millage tax or a tax allocation of the different functions. It can be readily seen that if the majority of real property, a special fund is established.

Municipal finance officers do not recommend special funds for the customary separate governmental operations of cities. This view is taken in part to simplify the accounting procedure, and in part to enable current resources of the city to be adjusted more finely to the variable needs of the different functions. It can be readily seen that if the majority of departments had special funds, the power of adjusting the total resources of the city to its variable needs would be diminished.

Accounting Terms

Appropriation is the amount of money, based on the budget, set aside in an account and authorized to be expended during the year for a particular purpose. The appropriation is legally considered a legislative act. Appropriations for the year are officially made when the budget is approved by the governing body. Thereafter, throughout the year additional appropriations may be made by the governing body by official legislative enactment.

Expenditure is the amount of money disbursed when payment has been made by the treasurer or other designated official of the city. No order may be executed calling for an expenditure until money is set aside in an account to consummate the transaction.

Encumbrance is a commitment of money for expenditures against an appropriation.

Capital outlay is an expenditure of money for property which has more or less permanent use and value, such as land, improvements to land, buildings, and permanent equipment (not supplies), and fixtures.

Revenue receipt is a monetary addition to assets, if it does not incur some obligation that must be met at some future date, and if it is available for expenditure by the appropriating body.

Non-revenue receipt is an amount of money received that either incurs an obligation that must be met at some future date or changes the form of an asset from property to cash and therefore decreases the amount and value of property. Money received from loans, sale of bonds, sale of property purchased from capital funds, and proceeds from insurance adjustments are examples of non-revenue receipts.

Contractual service is a service performed on order under agreement with outside organizations for a fixed fee.

Fixed charge is a financial obligation of a generally recurring nature incurred at a fixed rate and appearing as overhead in the operation of the department. Fixed charges comprise agency contributions to employee retirement funds, insurance, judgments, rentals of land and buildings, and interest on current loans.

Debt service is an expenditure for the retirement of a debt and for interest on the debt.

STATEMENTS

The statements required for a proper understanding of the financial transactions of a public enterprise dictate the kinds of records and accounts that must be kept. The three most important statements are: (1) a statement of operations, comprised of appropriations, encumbrances, expenditures, and appropriation balances; (2) a statement of revenues; and (3) a balance sheet. These represent only the basic statements required by the modern city and are those used most frequently to reflect the nature, status, and extent of operations of governmental agencies.

Statement of Operations

From the standpoint of control of expenditures and interpretation of the cost of conducting the operations of the department, the statement of operations is indispensable. It separates the expenditures for operations from those for capital outlays. Operations expenditures are classified according to the principal areas of expenditure, such as personal services; contractual services, materials, and supplies; fixed charges and current obligations; and their respective subdivisions. The statement usually shows in successive columns the annual appropriation for each object, the actual expenditures to date, the encumbrances outstanding as of that date, the total expenditures and encumbrances, the unencumbered balance of appropriations, and the percentage of appropriations unencumbered. When a city follows the practice of making a monthly or quarterly allotment of the annual appropriation for each area, the statement is elaborated to show actual expenditures and encumbrances against each cumulative allotment as of the date of the report.

Statements of operations are rendered by the auditor monthly and a final statement is rendered at the end of the year. In many cities there is a lapse of several weeks between the end of any month and the time when a statement for that month is available. The longer this lapse, the less valuable is the statement for control purposes. A statement may reveal a condition resulting in too rapid an expenditure of a given yearly appropriation and, if this condition is not revealed promptly, remedial measures are delayed.

Each municipal activity that is conducted wholly or largely out of revenues received from its own operations should be covered by its own supplementary or detailed operating statement. If the activity is routine, a seasonal or annual statement should suffice. The statement should show: (1) the cost of rendering the services, segregated according to the classification of objects of expenditure used by the auditor; (2) a proper allocation of general administrative expense or other overhead, chargeable to each separate facility; (3) the total operating cost for the time period; (4) the receipts of the total period segregated according to source; (5) the net profit or loss; (6) the total units of service, if the activity is susceptible to statistical treatment; and (7) the net cost per unit of service.

Charges against any operating unit of a fair portion of the general administration cost or other overhead may be computed according to the rates which the attendance at any unit bears to the total attendance of the department, or according to a purely arbitrary schedule based on opinions of the administrative staff. If the latter method is used, it should be a fixed schedule and should not vary month by month. As far as possible, services should be charged directly to the operating unit.

In compiling operating statements for public work, except public utilities, it is not customary to charge depreciation or interest on capital investment. But the fact that depreciation reserves are not built up for the governmental functions of cities should not be permitted to cause indifference to the relative capital costs of providing public services of variable types.

Statement of Revenues

The statement of revenues is prepared by the auditor monthly and at the end of the fiscal year. It is a cumulative record of receipts classified by sources for each department. The statement should show in successive columns: (1) the estimated total revenues for the year; (2) the estimated and actual revenues for the current month; (3) excess over or under the revenue budget estimate for the month; (4) the estimated cumulative total to the end of the current month; (5) the actual cumulative revenues to the end of the current month; (6) the cumulative excess or deficit; and (7) the balance required to meet the estimate for the year.

A statement of this kind enables a department to keep a month-by-month record of the revenue-producing operations and to adjust operations to actual conditions. An extraordinary deficit in revenues may justify a request for an additional appropriation before the end of the fiscal year, or it may require a curtailment of service.

Many cities do not render consolidated monthly revenue statements in sufficient detail, or render them too late to be of immediate value. Many do not classify the sources of revenue so as to permit the use of the statements to control the various revenue-producing activities offered by a recreational service department. In these cases the department finds it expedient to keep its own memorandum statements.

Balance Sheet

A separate balance sheet for each fund and a consolidated balance sheet of all funds are also prepared. These statements do not reveal the operations for a given period of time but show the nature and amount of assets and liabilities of the different funds and their relationship to each other. Because these balance sheets indicate the financial condition of a city at a given time, they are of interest to all department heads, since they reveal the credit standing of the city and its ability to finance improvements and additions from its current sale of bonds. Long-range planning for public recreational services (acquisition of lands, provision of buildings, structures, and other improvements) requires consideration of the financial facts revealed in the balance sheet.

One of the municipal balance sheets will deal with the capital fund and show the value of various types of properties. These properties will usually be carried at their original cost. The balance sheet will show additions that have been made to the recreational properties during the year. In most cities the public recreational service problem is largely the addition of properties and equipment, which may be organized for recreational purposes, to the physical assets of the city. The balance sheet is of interest then in indicating what progress is being made in this direction year by year.

The balance sheet and the property accounts on which it is based should also be used to interpret the relative capital cost of providing for different types of recreational services. The cost of conducting public recreational services has been considered primarily from the standpoint of the annual cost of operations, but the investment required to make the operations possible is also important. Consideration of the capital cost of a given recreational facility in relation to the services made possible thereby might indicate that capital funds should be expended on facilities that can be used all during the year rather than on those that can be of service only during a particular season.

COLLECTION OF REVENUES

Revenues from operations of a recreational service system are collected at the several recreational centers and facilities, and at the central office of the department. In many cases the amounts collected are too small to justify setting up a complicated and complex system of receipting and accounting. Nevertheless, systematic accounting is necessary in order to discourage dishonest practice and to avoid public criticism.

Collection at Recreational Centers

Cash payments at uniform rates are made for admission to recreational facilities, such as swimming pools, stadiums, and tennis courts. The participation of two employees in this type of transaction is recommended: one accepts the price of admission and gives the purchaser a numbered ticket, the other employee accepts and cancels the numbered ticket either by punching it or by tearing it. If the amount of business is large enough, mechanical ticket machines which record the number of tickets dispensed may be installed. Turnstiles automatically recording the number who pass through them provide a means whereby the number of persons admitted may be checked against the tickets sold.

In small establishments where the amount of business does not justify the use of two employees, the cash register is an acceptable device for checking receipts. The theory of the cash register is that the patron is interested in seeing that his payment is recorded. If cash registers are used, they should be placed so that the recorded payment will be easily visible not only to the patron, but also to others close by. The register should record the amount of each admission and the number of admissions on a printed tape.

Some types of payments for services can be collected in coin meters. Meters governing electrical switches are used for illumination of tennis courts. Gas and electric coin meters are used for stoves at picnic places and hot water meters are installed at camping grounds. The use of counterfeit coins is largely prevented by intricate mechanical devices. Tampering with meters and actual destruction of them to steal their contents may be deterred by frequent removal of their contents at irregular intervals.

Miscellaneous payments may be made for the use of recreational facilities. These payments should be on permits issued in advance on which the amount to be collected is plainly shown. If the permits can be obtained in the central office, further inconvenience is avoided. If not, the employee at the center where the permit is issued should use a numbered receipt in triplicate; one copy is given to the payee, the second is sent with the consolidated remittances to the office, and the third is retained as the employee's record. Only carbon-copy receipts should be used for this purpose and they should be kept in bound books. The book of numbered receipts should be issued from the central office and employees should account for all numbers.

For miscellaneous payments of small amounts, the tear-off receipt is best. The detached receipt given the purchaser and the remaining stub both indicate the amount of the transaction. Receipts are bound and numbered in books.

Collection at a Central Office

When practicable, payments should be required to be made at the central office of the department. Certain fees, such as seasonal playing privileges on tennis courts, entry fees in city-wide tournaments, camp fees, and the like, may reasonably be expected to be made at the central office. If there is sufficient business to warrant it, it is preferable to have two employees participate in these transactions; one issues the permit or another form indicative of the privilege purchased and the other accepts the payment and issues a receipt. Here again numbered receipts must be used.

Publication of Standard Fees

All rates of fees collected by a municipal agency should be regularly approved by the proper authority. These rates should be posted in conspicuous places or printed on the permit forms or tickets. This practice prevents overcharging or undercharging for services.

Safeguarding and Transmitting Collections

Collections made at the central office are customarily deposited daily by the treasurer, but often collections are made too late for bank deposits and must remain overnight in the office. Proper safes or other equipment must be provided at the central office for the protection of such monies. It is more difficult to safeguard and transmit collections made at field centers. In the case of small sums the director is sometimes permitted to make weekly deposits at the central office. Ordinarily, unless safes are provided, it is inadvisable to leave money in drawers or elsewhere in the centers, for this encourages theft. Employees should not deposit public funds in personal bank accounts. Burglary insurance should be carried, if the amount of the collection warrants, and all employees who handle considerable funds should be under bond. If collections are of sufficient amount they may be picked up daily by bonded messengers; however, they are usually so small that daily transmittal is not practical. Ingenious devices must be resorted to. In large cities the funds are sometimes deposited in neighborhood banks; cashiers checks or money orders are then purchased and transmitted by mail. Or, small safes may be hidden in concrete floors.

CONTROL OF "PRIVATE" FUNDS

The program of the public recreational service department includes many private organizations or groups that raise funds in various ways to sustain their own activities. These funds may be raised by dues, assessments against members, donations, collections, ticket sales, fees for admission to events, and sale of refreshments. The groups vary from informal children's clubs to highly organized adult groups.

Safeguarding the funds of these organizations presents a difficult problem to the recreational service department. To the degree that these groups are publicly organized and connected with or sponsored by the recreational service department, the department must assume some supervisory responsibility over their finances to ensure the proper use of funds and to remove the possibility of dishonesty. Some adult groups are sufficiently well-organized to be fully entrusted with the control of their own finances, subject to regulations acceptable to the recreational service department (such as filing monthly or annual reports with the department). Others require closer supervision. The extent to which control should be exercised over the finances of such groups is a moot point. On the one hand, it is plain that the monies are not public funds and consequently they cannot be deposited in the city treasury. If so deposited it would be difficult to disburse them for private purposes. On the other hand, if they are not subject to supervision, the possibilities of misuse or of allegations of fraud are multiplied.

Some departments disclaim any responsibility or concern for such funds and, to avoid any difficulty, prohibit fund-raising activities of all kinds by affiliated groups. This practice has some merit, but it limits the scope of the program of the department. Nearly all departments prohibit employees from accepting personal responsibility for the monies of participating groups. Some departments set up quasi-public organizations, controlled by the department representatives, to act as a depository for the so-called "private" funds and to disburse them according to the expressed wishes of the several groups to which they belong. This appears to be the best answer to the problem. When such agencies are established, their procedure should be according to approved accounting practice and their records should be regularly audited and open to inspection at all times.

Selected References

Brigham, E. F.: *Financial Management and Planning in Local Government* (New York: The Dryden Press), 1977.

Higgins, R. C.: *Financial Management: Theory and Applications* (Chicago: Ill.: Science Research Associates), 1977.

McConkey, D. D. and R. Vanderweele: *Financial Management by Objectives* (Englewood Cliffs, N.J.: Prentice-Hall, Inc.), 1976.

McKean, R. N.: *Public Spending* (New York: McGraw-Hill Book Company), 1968.

Maxwell, J. A.: *Financing State and Local Governments, 3d ed.* (Washington, D.C.: The Brookings Institution), 1977.

Schall, L. D. and C. W. Halez: *Introduction to Financial Management* (New York: McGraw-Hill Book Company), 1977.

Snyder, J. C.: *Fiscal Management and Planning in Local Government* (Lexington, Mass.: Lexington Books), 1977.

Shoup, C. S.: *Public Finance* (Chicago, Ill.: Aldine Publishing Company), 1969.

Rabinowitz, A.: *Municipal Bond Finance and Administration* (New York: John Wiley & Sons, Inc.), 1969.

Recreation and Youth Services Planning Council: *Policies and Practices in Charging for the Use of Recreation Resources by The Los Angeles Unified School District and The Los Angeles Department of Recreation and Parks* (Los Angeles, Calif.: The Council), 1976.

CHAPTER 20

Budgeting Administration

The technical intricacies of budgeting almost never receive the attention of the mass media even when public attention is focused upon national, state, or local presentations of the executive budget to the respective legislatures. Usually, public interest is directed to several controversial items and on those projects which represent radical or significant departures from typical government policy. The media and the public may be concerned with why more funding is recommended for some programs and curtailment of others, but they seldom inquire as to how such decisions are made and the kinds of information used on which to base budget formulations and governmental decisions. Consequently, there appear to be few public matters that are more untranslatable for the ordinary citizen than the methods used for determining program expenditures. Nevertheless, the policies and programs of every agency are very much an outcome of the procedures utilized for collecting and analyzing the spending requests made by administrators and their subordinates at every level. The fact that a great deal of the budget making process is conducted in a give-and-take atmosphere of trade-offs and desired policy implementation as opposed to or in accord with political decisions cannot diminish the importance of the process. The business of budgeting is inextricably tied to complex accounting and administrative techniques which are vital for professionals to understand.

As the public sector has developed in size and scope, there has also grown an increasingly concerned public about the sufficiency, effectiveness, and efficiency of the methods employed for determining public expenditures. In the past three decades, broadly based attempts have been made to improve the budgetary process used within the public sector. In the 1950s the concept of performance budgeting was put forward.

459

During the 1960s the concept of PPBS was developed. The objective of performance budgeting was to inform budget makers more completely concerning the work and services of a given agency. PPBS has a considerably broader purpose—the utilization of the budget process for analyzing the goals and predictable results of public programs, and for assessing the degree to which programs actually achieve the objectives they are designed to satisfy.

Budgetary Uses

The budget has as many uses as there are users. It is a vital factor of the economic, political, and administrative machinery of every modern government. Especially during the last thirty years, budgeting practice has been endowed with a variety of administrative applications directly related to the control of agency spending, the management of public activities, and the direction of agency objectives. Every budget improvement transforms the uses to which the budget is put, and it is these applications that are most pertinent to the achievement or failure of the innovation, the method of implementation, and the attitudes of those concerned with the daily function of budgeting.

Line-item budgets reflect a concentration on expenditure control. Control is the process of applying strict limitations and enforcing the conditions set forth in the budget document. It demands compliance to the allocations imposed by centralized authorities. The performance budget was developed for efficient managerial activities. Management concerns the use of budgetary authority to gain economical and effective utilization of personnel and other resources necessary for the conduct of the agency. Performance budgeting focuses on agency production; that is, what is being performed, for what price, and the comparison between actual performance and budgeted objectives. In PPBS, the budget process is looked upon as an instrument of policy and program planning. Planning deals with the methods by which public objectives are determined as well as the appraisal of alternative programs. In order to make maximum use of the budget for planning purposes, central authorities require information concerning the objectives and effectiveness of programs. Additionally, information concerning multiyear expenditures and of the connection between spending and public benefits must also be known. The planning orientation emphasizes the pre-preparation of the budget, or the analysis of policy prior to the submission of budget estimates.

The budget, as a financial plan, specifies the fiscal requirements of the jurisdiction for a particular period—typically a year—and in offering this picture provides an equalized relationship between estimated future expenditures and anticipated revenue. The budget, in a very real sense, focuses attention on intelligent policy decisions as well as effective management. The budgetary process is closely identified with every phase of planning, from the original concept and formulation of objectives and goals to the selections of priorities for immediate practice. It is concerned with the operation of current enterprise; without it the consequences of operations cannot be determined. It sets forth the manner in which monetary resources are allocated among competing requirements and how effectively such monies are utilized. In significant ways the budget of local government, particularly that of the recreational service department, is the fundamental instrument for identifying the major purposes of the system and achieving public policy.

THE BUDGET FORM

The principle activities and elements of the municipal budget may be presented in the following list: (a) It determines the rate of local taxes and the aims to which the revenues of taxation shall be allocated. The municipal family has many claims upon its limited financial resources and for this reason circumspection and precise analysis are vital if the community is to receive the greatest benefits from its taxes. All local public services must be weighed and compared so that the people shall be served effectively, efficiently, and economically. Establishment of priorities in the face of competing intangibles is one of the most difficult annual problems confronting municipal government. This is probably true of all government at every level. Current municipal policy and practice, the influence of pressure groups and public opinion, the intent of politicians, and the ability to invoke sympathy for the budgetary request by various department executives in justifying their proposals, all have a role in the budget procedure. The ability to verbalize intelligently and well may sometimes have a greater effect than the mechanical analysis of mathematics would infer. As Gladstone is reported to have stated, "Budgets are not merely affairs of arithmetic, but in a thousand ways go to the root of prosperity of individuals, the relation of classes, and the strength of kingdoms." The attractiveness of presentation and the fulfillment of social goals as well as costs play a part in levying taxes. (b) The budget is the means by which short- and long-term policies are executed. It brings the various operations of the municipality under examination, it assists the authorized legal body to forecast, it enables them to review current policy, and it affords a method by which equity of services and development of the community may be achieved. (c) As a plan of financial action, the adopted budget becomes the authorization of all expenditures included within the document for the purposes described. It is the prescription by which public funds will be dispersed, not exceeding the allotted amount indicated, under the different headings provided. (d) The budget becomes the means for certifying that the monies of the municipality are actually spent in the manner that has been prescribed, and for underwriting any changes which unforeseen exigencies force upon the community during the operation of the fiscal year. (e) Ultimately, the budget should attempt to secure the type of administration that affords the most beneficial services possible and be the instrument of appraisal in comparing objectives with actual achievement.

Control

The recreational service department budget is a managerial tool for fiscal policy and financial administration. The budget reflects and shapes the system's economic capacity to perform and maintain those services deemed essential for its existence in the community. The departmental activity described in the budget will mirror the estimated recreational requirements of the community and the projected action by the system responsible for meeting its needs. Budgetary control is concerned with the functions of collecting, analyzing, and categorizing data; recording such data in a prescribed manner; and presenting them to the governing body for approval in compliance with relevant policies.

The budget format is such that it is intelligible to those who read it. To facilitate understanding of the needs which its estimates attempt to satisfy, the budget is divided into specific parts. It should contain the following subdivisions and headings:

1. A general statement giving the major financial aims which the department executive hopes to achieve during the approaching fiscal year. This statement is made in terms of recreational service needs throughout the community and points out particular projects which are vital to the provision of such service. The statement may indicate the number of new facilities to be developed and constructed, employment of additional personnel, purchase of new equipment, specific programs to be initiated, and the general aims of the system.
2. A schedule of estimated revenues from various sources available to the operating department. This may include fees, charges, rentals, leases, concessions, grants-in-aid expected, probable donations, or retail sales which the department collects during its operational year.
3. A detailed itemization of expenditures in terms of functions and objects, or by performance or program.
4. A balanced statement for each separate fund which the recreational service department maintains and administers.

The recreational service system budget cannot perform its proper functions unless it is based upon a well-formulated plan of departmental activity. The budget is but an instrument designed to effectuate a plan of service. Thus, the plan of service is a carefully worked out program for providing the public the service that it requires within the limitations defined by available and anticipated revenue.

The Financial Plan

The budget, as a fiscal plan, has three elements which must be present. It must strike a balance between revenue and receipts, be inclusive of all the financial requirements of the system, and incorporate annual requests for appropriations. In theory, a budget should correctly reflect and match anticipated revenue and expected expenditures. In practice, such a precise balance may be attained by recreational service departments only when contingencies impinging upon modern government can be offset by either accurate forecasts or the luxury of taking in a larger amount of income than was anticipated. In some instances, the department may actually show an estimated surplus of income. Practically speaking, however, most departments tend to count upon contingency funds by which they plan to offset required emergency expenditures which were not foreseen. Unlike a profit making organization or business within the private sector of society, it is not the projection of public recreational service systems to become profit-making enterprises for the municipality. The service performed by the system is as necessary to the health and well-being of the community as are other public services. It is not generally observed that municipal functions, such as fire and police protection, public health, public works, or civilian defense, forecast anticipated revenues to balance expenditures. Normally, the expenditures of departments are equal to the anticipated amount of revenue taken in by taxes, fines, licenses, and/or forfeitures of various kinds. It has only been within the past 20 years that covetous eyes have viewed the public recreational service department as a municipal profit-making enterprise and have thus demanded that the system pay its own way. That this is an error of philosophy cannot be denied. As a political expediency it is surely a devastating piece of business because the essential reasons for the existence of the public recreational system will become subordinated to the profit motive. Eventually, the tax-paying public will begin to question the reasons why additional payments, after taxes, must be made to enjoy the services for which they are already paying through those same taxes. Nevertheless, there are legitimate sources of revenue which the public recreational service department may utilize. To the extent that these are readily forecastable, a balanced budget may be generated.

Inclusiveness indicates that the budget comprehends all revenue and all expenditures of the municipality, and, hence, the department. It signifies that the budget incorporates all the financial requirements of the local government and its several departments. It is a definitive statement that means that all monetary requirements are in their appropriate relation to each other, so that a budgetary balance may be struck. Except for these public recreational service departments which administer earmarked or special funds separate from the common or general fund of the municipality, most departments pay their expenses from a general fund through a system of checks, vouchers, and receipts. In this way all money received by the municipality is paid into a single fund and all expenditures are disbursed from this fund. In order for the financial plan to be practical and comprehensive every item of revenue and expense is listed. This makes more convenient and controllable the entire monetary process of local government.

The concept of regular voting of the budget safeguards the public purse because it requires that monetary disbursement for a given year must be met out of income for the year, and revenue must not be left to accrue from year to year. This really means that revenue and expenditure should be equal in every year.

FORMULATION OF THE BUDGET

The initiation of the budget involves the preparation and collation of estimates, both revenue and expenditure, the review and revision of such estimates, and the development of the financial plan. The work of gathering the estimates and compiling the data required for the preparation of the budget necessitates a staff whose size is directly associated with the size of the government. This staff is considered adequate when there are permanent municipal employees, as well as political figures, who are directly responsible for the actual performance of the financial system of the government. To such a staff may be added the officers employed within the public recreational service department (or other municipal agencies) who have responsibility for the development of the financial plan of the particular department.

The information necessary in the development of a financial plan is as varied and extensive as are the functions and responsibilities of the municipality. It involves current jurisdictional policy; forms of taxation and other sources of revenue; the discharge of existing financial obligations or the assumption of new financial obligations. It touches every phase of community life insofar as such aspects may have some connection with the income and outgo of community economics. The information thus generated comprises quite specifically the immediate fiscal needs of the local government, sources of all revenue, expenditures due to payments and purchases, and all cost data indicating functional performance and probable trends. From the facts and supportive documentation the budget process is systematically worked out and financial plans for individual departments are finally expressed as a budget for the municipality.

Budgets must be devised and considered several months in advance of the fiscal year to which they apply because of the involved procedure which is usually prescribed and also because the final budget estimate is the basis for determining the revenue-raising plan and the tax rate for the year. The tax rate must be fixed before the tax bills may be computed. A time schedule is stated for submission of department estimates to the budgetary authority of the municipality, for transmittal of the recommended budget to the chief governing body, and for its adoption by that body. This may be the body politic as in the case of town meeting communities, a duly elected finance board or commission, a mayor-council form, or other extant corporate bodies who have authority to adopt the financial plan. The adoption of the budget is by local ordinance, which requires time for publication, hearings, and debate. If the city operates on a fiscal year commencing July 1st, it is not uncommon for preliminary department estimates to be submitted as early as January. These estimates, after careful study, tabulation, and comparison, may be found to be in excess of the estimated available revenue and are referred back to department heads for revision. In this process there is a good deal of give and take. Compromise is not unknown. Further revision may also be necessary when all budgets have been submitted by the budget-making authority to the chief governing body. These revisions may be influenced by public opinion, departmental propaganda, the mass media, or other vociferous groups as they manifest interest during the period of consideration.

The preparation of the budget theoretically proceeds in the following order:

January to March. The process of budgeting is initiated in order that preliminary estimates may be culled to provide the basis upon which the departmental program requirements will be transformed into budgetary figures. During this time the finance officer makes preliminary estimates of the coming year. If the size of the department does not warrant an accountant, the superintendent, his assistant, or some other designated employee performs this assignment. Although such estimates leave a wide margin for error, the prior commitments or obligations contracted by the department provide a fairly reliable platform on which to build. After such estimates are gathered the accountant for the department confers with the line and staff executives and discusses preliminary figures.

March to April. The accountant confers with the chief executive officer of the department (Superintendent) after preliminary construction of the departmental estimates have been made. At this time a tentative ceiling for the system's expenditures is conceived as relayed to the Superintendent by higher authority. The ceiling figure is transmitted to the line and staff administrators as their basis for preparing final estimates.

April to May. During this period the line and staff administrators adapt their estimates to the superintendent's ceiling figures. They not only submit a budget that stays within the limits imposed by the superintendent, but they also forward for his consideration any items that are over the restricted figure for further scrutiny. Detailed analyses for personal services and other items are prepared.

May to June. The detailed estimates from the various divisions and sections of the department are compiled and reviewed by the accountant or superintendent. Appropriation propositions are considered and the budget document is developed. There is a detailed review of the document and the divisional administrators are called upon to defend or justify their estimates and proposal for expenditures.

16

June to July. After internal departmental hearings and reviews have taken place to determine the rationale for expenditures, the final budget document is compiled, edited, and submitted to the fiscal officers of the municipality for their inspection, amendment, and approval.

In the first year of operation of a newly established department there would be limited budget-making preliminary procedure. Either the department estimates the expenditure needs for its operation or the governing authority simply appropriates a certain sum, which may or may not be adequate, based upon a specific per capita figure. If the department finds it cannot operate effectively on such an appropriation, contingency funds might be available for use. In those instances where the monetary allocation to the department falls short, the recreational service to the citizenry must, of necessity, also fall short. This will be reflected in the following budget message which the department prepares. In any event, the budget process for the second year of operation would begin during the first year of establishment. Estimates would most probably be borne out by the third year of operation. There is greater probability that more valid comparisons between expectations and accomplishments would also be available.

The formulation of plans for raising revenues from taxation for the support of public work is a duty performed by financial officers and departments of the municipality and does not directly concern the superintendent of recreational service. The raising of direct revenues from sources attributable to recreational and related services is, necessarily, an immediate concern of the executive in charge of recreational services and particularly so if these revenues are credited to a specified recreational service fund and not deposited in the general fund of the city.

The Budget of Revenues

The revenue budget is typically considered to be the estimated income that will supply the necessary financial resources for the local government to perform its varied services. It is the most significant because it is the medium for fixing the amount of the tax rate. The revenue budget should not in itself be used as the instrument for determining new policy, such as the inauguration of new services, expansion of current programs, or the development of capital projects. All policy decisions influencing the budget should have been settled prior to its adoption, although operation of such services guided by new policy cannot be activated until budgetary allocation is made and authorized.

Even if the revenue budget is not the means for establishing new policy, it most assuredly gives effect to it. It is through the budget that local government contracts or enlarges borrowing and spending according to prevailing economic concepts. Factually, a rational long-term policy can scarcely be attained unless there is a concomitant budgetary management and advanced planning. A municipality may carry out its intent to acquire potential recreational land, develop recreational centers and other facilities, repair and otherwise maintain present recreational places without borrowing by carefully planning for revenue budgeting over several years. A good revenue budgeting procedure is quite valuable to local government in the formation of policy. It permits a guide for subsequent work to be performed as well as a means of control. There is a need for a methodical approach in compiling and assessing data which in turn encourages a sense of responsibility. The budget also requires all of the line agencies of the municipality and the officials who have been charged with the responsibility to review their aims and objectives, at least once during the year, and, perhaps more importantly, the methods by which they hope to achieve goals. Finally, the practice of budgeting not only assists in administrative functions, it is extremely helpful in educating both municipal officers and the public in understanding the programs and performances undertaken as well as the financial implications of whatever policy is in effect.

A budget is concerned as much with revenues as with expenditures, because all budgets must balance. The budgeting expenditures may not exceed the budgeted revenues. A balanced budget in the popular sense is one in which the expenditures allowed may be cared for from tax and operating revenues without the necessity of borrowing. If the tax and operating revenues are insufficient to finance estimated expenditures, the source of additional funds must be shown. Borrowing is not of direct concern to the recreational service department; it as well as the determination of the tax rate is a function of the fiscal officers of the city and the local governing body.

Operating revenues are earnings resulting from fees, charges for special recreational or related services, income from sales of commodities, services, income from concessions, and the like. In the whole scheme of municipal finance these do not bulk large, but from the standpoint of the departmental operation and control they are of great importance. Currently the trend is to produce more revenue as a result of fees and charges in a wide range of commodities, rentals, instruction, or use than has heretofore been done. Many public recreational service departments are getting into business operations in order to offset insufficient support received through tax base sources. For these reasons, it is quite as necessary to maintain control over such practices and to regulate operations which produce revenues as it is to control expenditures. Eventually, there may be produced a violent public reaction to the continuation of user fees and charges, although other legitimate sources of revenue for amenities will continue to flourish.

The total anticipated revenues are built up from specific detail in the same way that total expenditures are computed. It is necessary to analyze each operation which produces revenues and to estimate probable returns. These vary by seasons and are responsive to changes in operations. They are also subject to public whims which are often inexplicable. Past experience may be the best guide. For this purpose it is advisable to keep week-to-week, if not day-to-day, memorandum records of income from each operation with notations of factors which might have a bearing on the operations.

New services for which fees are levied are instituted from time to time, and sometimes the amount charged for established services is also changed. A study of the fee structure and probable patronage is helpful in arriving at proper estimates of revenues. Reasonable goals of accomplishment should be worked out in advance for each operation. These are helpful because if the actual income falls below what seemed to be a realistic goal, the executive is likely to investigate the operation to discover if something might not be done to improve the condition.

Departments which are granted the revenue accruing from a fixed tax allocation of so many cents per hundred dollars of assessed valuation are more concerned with the revenues budget than those which go directly to the local governing body for their appropriations. The former must present a budget of expenditures which is within the amount of the anticipated tax revenues from the tax allocation estimated by the fiscal officers of the city. This estimate takes into account possible tax delinquencies and credits from deferred tax payments of previous years.

FORM OF BUDGET ESTIMATE

After discussion of revenue budgeting, consideration must be given to long-term capital and the annual capital budget. It has been determined that periods of from 3 to 5 years are significant enough to provide realistic bases for the development of capital projects. Beyond the 5-year figure, estimates and projections no longer have meaning, but become wishes. All capital programs should comprehend the capital expenditures which are projected. Thus, the ordered plan of capital programs can be utilized to determine borrowing policy. Plans comprising the capital program must be adequately classified. Thus, plans being developed, plans underway, plans approved by the local authority, plans awaiting approval should illustrate the annual estimated cost of the program. A comprehensive report to the local authority should make perfectly clear the demands which long range programs will make upon the financial resources of the community.

Annual capital estimates concern a single year and incorporate expenditures on projects underway and plans which will be undertaken during the forthcoming year. To be of maximum benefit, the annual capital budget should define the result of each program on revenue in the current and first complete year. Annual capital budgets are worthwhile because they force attention of the local authority on those plans already fulfilled, and focus attention on those plans contemplated for immediate development. Although it is likely that most projects will be well advanced that inclusion is almost a foregone conclusion, a finance commission attempting to retrench may have to suggest deletions or postponements—a most painful task.

The budget estimate is usually submitted to the budget-making authority on columnar sheets showing: (1) the expenditures to date in the current year; (2) the expenditures in each of the two preceding years; (3) estimated expenditures as at the close of the current year; and (4) estimated expenditures for the coming year.

Detail sheets or supporting schedules showing how the several estimates are built up should accompany the department budget. For example, the detail sheet for "Services, Personal" should show under "Salaries and Wages, Regular": (1) the classification of position; (2) the names of incumbents; (3) ordinances fixing salaries; (4) the compensation for the current year; and (5) the compensation for the coming year. Wherever practicable, unit costs of all items enumerated in the budget should be shown together with the number of units that make up the total request.

The Functions and Objects Budget

A municipality performs several kinds of services which may be differentiated as to function. The classification of functions of the government is reflected in the organization of departments. The work of a department usually entails a single major function which often consists of two or more subordinate functions. For example, the major function of a recreational service department is provision for public recreational experience through planned and spontaneous activities conducted at public recreational or ancillary places. The subordinate functions may include operation of eating places, parking lots at beaches, or the maintenance of a nursery for public park beautification. It is desirable that expenditures be differentiated according to subordinate functions for which they are made.

Under each major function of the city and under each subordinate function of the several departments, expenditures are made for similar objects: i.e., personal services, supplies, materials, equipment, and purchase of property. A high degree of standardization in the classification of objects of expenditure is possible and is urged by all authorities. This enables comparisons of expenditures for like objects to be made between departments and between subordinate functions within departments, and often reveals inequalities in salaries paid for similar services and in prices paid for the same commodity.

The budget classification of expenditures should, if possible, parallel the classification of accounts used by the city comptroller or auditor. For the purpose of making and controlling a department budget within the department itself, it is often desirable to classify expenditures in more detail than is required by the fiscal officer of the city.

A simple expenditure classification that is already in use in more or less modified form in a number of cities is as follows:

Expenditure Classification

1000.   Services, Personal
        1100.   Salaries and Wages, Regular
        1200.   Salaries and Wages, Temporary
        1300.   Other compensations

2000.   Service, Contractual
        2100.   Communication and Transportation
                2110.   Postage
                2120.   Telephone and Telegraph
                2130.   Freight and Express
                2140.   Traveling Expenses
                2150.   Hired Vehicles
        2200.   Subsistence, Care, and Support
                2210.   Subsistence and Support of Persons
                2220.   Subsistence and Care of Animals
                2230.   Storage and Care of Vehicles
        2300.   Printing, Binding, and Public Relations
                2310.   Printing
                2320.   Typing and Mimeographing
                2330.   Binding
                2340.   Public Relations
                2350.   Engraving and Stamping
                2360.   Lithographing
                2370.   Photographing and Blue-Printing
                2380.   Publication of Notices
        2400.   Heat, Light, Power, and Water
                2410.   Furnishing Heat
                2420.   Furnishing Light and Power
                2430.   Furnishing Water
        2500.   Repairs
                2510.   Repairs to Equipment
                2520.   Repairs to Buildings and Other Structures
        2600.   Custodial, Cleaning, and Other Services
                2610.   Custodial Supplies

3000.   Commodities
        3110.   Office
        3120.   Food
                3121.   Food for Persons
                3122.   Food for Animals

3130. Fuels and Lubricants
    3131. Coals
    3132. Oil, Gas, and Other Fuels
    3133. Lubricating Oils
3140. Institutional
    3141. Clothing and Household
    3142. Laundry and Cleaning
    3143. Refrigeration
    3144. Surgical and Medical
    3145. General
3150. Park and Recreational
3160. Horticultural and Zoological
3170. Playgrounds and Centers
3180. Beaches and Camps
3190. General
3200. Materials
    3210. Building
    3220. Road
    3230. General
3300. Repairs
    3310. Parts of Equipment
    3320. Parts of Structure

4000. Current Charges
    4100. Rents
        4110. Buildings and Offices
        4120. Equipment
    4200. Insurance
        4210. Buildings and Structures
        4220. Stores
        4230. Equipment and Apparatus
        4240. Official Bonds
        4250. Employee Liability
    4300. Refunds, Awards, Indemnities
    4400. Registrations and Subscriptions
    4500. Taxes

5000. Current Obligations
    5100. Interest
    5200. Pensions and Retirement
    5300. Grants and Subsidies

6000. Properties
    6100. Equipment
        6110. Office
        6120. Furniture and Fixtures
        6130. Instruments and Apparatus
        6140. Tools
        6150. Recreational and Park
        6160. Motor Vehicles
        6170. Nursery
        6180. Animals
        6190. General

6200.   Buildings and Improvements
        6210.   Buildings and Fixed Equipment
        6220.   Walks and Pavements
        6230.   Sewers and Drains
        6240.   Roads
        6250.   Bridges
        6260.   Trees and Shrubs
6300.   Land

7000.   Debt Payments
    7100.   Serial Bonds
    7200.   Sinking Fund Installments

The code numbers which appear opposite each segregation in the classification of expenditures are for convenient identification of each item. For example, in the classification given above a requisition for postage would have noted upon it the number 2110. This would indicate that it is classified as a contractual service because it is in the 2000 series, and is classified under *communication and transportation* because it is in the 100 series. If it is to be charged to a particular place, further elaboration of the code may be made by using the unit digit, or by adding letters.

Quarterly Estimates

To prevent premature dissipation of funds and resultant embarrassment toward the close of the year, expenditures under the several segregations should be estimated by quarters or by months and only that portion of the total budget should be made available as is estimated to be required for that part of the year. The quarterly or monthly "split" should be based upon the work program. The several parts estimated for each quarter or months will not necessarily be equal, but will be adjusted to the seasonal requirements of the department. Quarterly or monthly estimates should not be exceeded without explanation, and over-drafts should be made up in subsequent periods.

Budget Savings

Adoption of the budget should not necessarily commit a department to actual expenditure for the items which were used as a basis for determining the amount of funds required. Conditions may alter the necessity for a certain expenditure, and if any expenditure proves to be unnecessary, funds set aside for it represent a saving. If a contemplated expenditure should prove unnecessary or should be deferred, the funds originally appropriated for it should not become available for an item that failed of approval when the budget was first drawn up, nor should such funds be used to meet a need not initially anticipated without the approval of the higher executive authority.

At the end of the fiscal year unexpended balances usually exist in several segregations. These balances arise either because certain expenditures were not made, or because the actual cost of certain work or commodities proved to be less than was estimated.

The superintendent of recreational service would probably prefer to be permitted to expend funds as he saw fit with no curbs except the injunction not to exceed a specific total for his department. With municipal government becoming increasingly centralized, however, financial control has come to rest with the chief executive of the municipality rather than with department heads. Accepted theories of municipal government assign to an elected or otherwise authorized body—usually the city council or finance commission—the responsibility for determining how the city funds shall be spent and for conducting the affairs of government within the available income. Some measure of responsibility must be assigned by the chief executive officer and the governing body to department heads and other subordinate officers, but final control of expenditures must not be relinquished. Likewise, control must be retained without hampering good and convenient administration. The budget plan, if wisely administered, accomplishes both these objectives.

Flexibility in the Budget

Good administration requires a budget that is flexible so that minor adjustments may be made without delay and difficulty. The appropriating body should adopt a budget differentiated only by departments and principal objects within the departments. This permits the chief executive officer, who is responsible for budgetary control, to make minor adjustments throughout the year so long as the total for any principal object is not exceeded.

There has been a resurgence of highly detailed budget documents as a means of insuring expenditure of funds for specific purposes for which the money was originally intended. Responsibility was assigned to one or a few responsible executives who were held strictly accountable for carrying out the plans of the appropriating body. Occasionally the total appropriation for a principal object will prove insufficient to accomplish the program of work contemplated under that object. Relief in such a contingency is usually afforded by the judicious transfer of funds, by authority of the chief executive, from an unassigned appropriation made for contingencies when the original budget appropriation ordinance was passed, or from an "unappropriated balance." The latter is the difference between the total amount appropriated and the total estimated revenue.

Control of Expenditures

The budget has too often been regarded merely as an instrument for obtaining appropriations, to be filed away and forgotten once appropriations are secured. Actually, it should be considered a controlling financial plan for accomplishing a program of work and departments should be held responsible for completion of the work indicated under the estimates. Failure to complete such work should be excused only under the most stringent circumstances. (In many communities a work program based upon the approved budget is drawn up after the appropriations have been made.) The work program of a recreational service department may include, among other things, the number of recreational centers to be maintained and operated, periods and hours during which they are to be supervised, recreational activities to be initiated and conducted, improvements to be added, supplies to be consumed, and contracts to be entered into. During the year, and especially at the end of the year, the actual accomplishments of the department should be checked against the work program to encourage adherence to a plan and assist in making more accurate the estimates for subsequent years by comparing actual costs with estimated costs.

Authorization of Expenditures

When the budget has been finally adopted, the auditor, comptroller, or other designated finance officer sets up in an expenditure register all appropriations by principal objects. Expenditures of all kinds, as specific authorization for them is formally requested, are entered in this register against their proper appropriation. When an expenditure is requested, only its estimated cost can be entered; when the actual cost becomes known, a correction can be made. The requested expenditures are said to "encumber" the appropriation. An *unencumbered balance* is carried forward for each segregation of the appropriation, from which it can easily be seen what part of an appropriation remains to carry the department for the rest of the financial year.

Since the auditor's expenditure register will check expenditures only against principal objects, the superintendent of the department should establish a departmental register in which expenditures are differentiated by subordinate objects or segregations, and by centers or activities to which they apply. Similarly, the Director of a center, if it is of sufficient size and importance, should have his own expenditure register to guide him in management. This process should be carried on as far down the ladder of administration as practicable. One of the difficulties in the administration of a large organization is that the higher executives are inclined to think too much in terms of cost, and those in charge of operating units too much in terms of needs. Sharing by all administrators in the procedure of budgetary control aids in bringing about a more balanced consideration of both costs and needs.

An essential budgetary principle is that no estimate may be exceeded without authorization. To exceed the total department appropriation or the total estimated for the few principal objects should require the approval of the chief executive, usually the mayor or city manager. To exceed subordinate segregations should require the approval of the departmental executive.

Selected References

Babunakis, M.: *Budgets: An Analytical and Procedural Handbook for Government and Non-Profit Organizations* (Westport, Conn.: Greenwood Press, Inc.), 1976.

Golembiewski, R. T. and J. Rabin, Eds.: *Public Budgeting and Finance: Readings in Theory and Practice* (Itasca, Ill.: Peacock Publishers), 1975.

Lee, R. D. and R. W. Johnson: *Public Budgeting Systems* (Baltimore, Md.: University Park Press), 1977.

CHAPTER 21

Budget Types and Formats

The necessity for having an effective budgetary system is increasingly clear insofar as governmental administration is concerned. All public institutions must cope with an environment in which the allocation of resources offers a continual contest between increasing demands and service costs along with a diminished capability to pay for such services. Budgets have tended to reflect the economic condition of society and have followed the economic thinking of those officials who have been charged with the responsibility for administering the funds which have been allocated by legislative enactment. Thus, budget formats have consistently followed particular intentions of budget officers.

When budgeting officials decided that central office administration was required for controlling expenditures, an object budget was introduced. This was useful to prevent administrative abuses by listing all objects of expense. Unfortunately, objects budgets also hampered innovative thinking and stiffled administrative ingenuity. In 1935, Function and Objects budgets were introduced as officials began thinking in terms of management instead of controlling. The intent of the functions and objects budget was to assess work efficiency. This was to be performed by relating costs to functions and determining them by object categories. This budgetary system has been in effect since that time and still survives. By 1961, it was time for a change. Budget officials felt that the social need for planning had arrived. The program budget was developed with the intent of utilizing the budget for policy making. Costs were assigned to programs with emphasis on program accounting, objectives, and internal analysis. It was from this format that Planning, Programming, Budgeting Systems were developed. A decade later, the economic disaster of recession had gripped the United States. The desire for retrenchment became the chief measure by which politicians and conservative economists could shape public services. All expense items had to be justified every time a budget was presented. Moreover, zero-base budgets (ZBB) were formulated with the idea of negative or decremental budgeting. Additionally, a major premise of ZBB is to ask what the result would be of not performing the function under review. There is a request for alternative "packages" of services providing more or less of the functions being justified. This chapter presents all of the above named formats together with positive and negative characteristics associated with them. It also provides a method for combining two or more of the budget types in a stepover manipulation which lessens the trauma when one of the budgets is phased out and another brought in.

PLANNING-PROGRAMMING-BUDGETING SYSTEMS (PPBS)

The function of PPBS provides policymakers with the ability to assess the costs and benefits of disparate spending plans. Thus, its chief stress is on expenditure aggregates, and specifics are generated only as they tend to develop a comprehension of the complete budget or of fringe alternatives among competing programs. This arrangement focuses attention on a planned grouping of data into modes that enable easier comparisons among alternative spending proposals. PPBS utilizes four basic practices: (1) Budget alternatives are to be made more exactly insofar as public objectives are concerned instead of needed resources for agency activities and operations; (2) the multiyear costs and effects of public programs are estimated, not just the subsequent year; (3) structured inquiry is mandatory for various means of achieving public purposes, not only based on the sole method supported in the budget estimates; (4) evaluation is undertaken to determine the benefits of agency expenditures.

In the PPB system, the budget is attenuated from single to multiyear length, expenditures are arranged into program categories, new methods for planning and analysis are insinuated into the budget process, and the information network is prepared to incorporate the expanded functions of budgeting and to connect the program, organizational, and budgetary accounts. PPBS attempts to mix an analytic thrust into budgeting by accommodating those with a knowledge of systems analysis in policy making positions as well as by moving the budget process closer to central planning and program development activities. Essentially, PPBS classifications deal with the basic purpose or mission of the agency. They are joined to the process of decision making and policy implementation through the allocation of agency resources. It is this emphasis on the systematic appraisal of alternatives and deciding what activities should be authorized which characterizes PPBS.

The Superintendent is nominally charged with responsibility for budget preparation within the recreational service department. The superintendent, the assistant superintendent, and the administrative staff made up of divisional supervisors set initial guidelines and make fundamental choices. Other personnel are also involved; most financial plans are first developed in consequence of financial requests from operational sections of the system. New ideas, innovative programming, or the necessity for expanded facilities or even new facilities originally come from within the department. Such activities in combination become programs or projects. These investments in time, money, material and personnel are translated at the departmental level into coherent strategies and performance. Programs are scrutinized, reassessed, and finalized at the departmental level for submission to the authorizing body of the municipality.

Essentially, the procedure followed is described as budgeting up the ladder. It is affected by awareness of administration attitudes, philosophy, and interests. These may be indicated by formal policy statements or in other ways. The process is influenced by devoted partisanship during the early stages when divisional administrators make their presentation. This requires program review and appraisal. The budget of any department should encompass and stimulate continuous analysis of problems of resource allocation among competing needs and programs. Thus all factors in the budgetary process should combine to formulate departmental aims that are consistent with municipal goals and aspirations, translate aims into program and performance, obtain authorization for proposed programs, execute authorized programs, and evaluate performance in relation to established goals.

To have meaning and reliability plans must be observed in terms of basic purpose. The most prevalent weakness in up-the-ladder budgeting is found in the tendency of each administrative unit to maintain is traditional activities without change, while attempting to expand its operations. Empire building is not unknown within departments. Such self- for identifying and accomplishing clearly defined quantitative objectives. The form of the system concentrates on alternative possibilities for consistency with departmental and municipal policy.

The thrust of planning and attaining logical ends in local government of all kinds has heightened interest in program budgeting. It is a method for identifying and accomplishing clearly defined quantitative objectives. The form of the system concentrates on alternative possibilities for achieving objectives, and allows constant comparison of results with expenditures incurred in the process. It offers an intelligent approach in relating resources to aims and is an instrument for honing administrative judgment in planning and making decisions.

Form of the Budgetary Process

PPBS conceives a special connection between planning and budgeting, one that does not reflect the ordinary budget process. In actuality, planning comes before budgeting. Such planning necessity is in direct contrast to the operational procedure normally used in a ladder sequence, that is, where subordinate levels develop their requests without existing fiscal or program direction from above. The basis of PPBS is that planning is mandatory from the beginning, or it will never develop at all; after the estimates have been put forward and when specialists are trying to meet administrative schedules, it will be futile to be concerned with mission, forecasts, and program alternatives.

To consider the planning function, two accommodations would be required in the budgetary schedule. First, the budget process would have to be initiated earlier—in a preview stage; during this time incipient policy analysis could be transacted. In this preparatory period, detailed classification of particular programs and questions would be undertaken. Every program and budget group would not have to be analyzed; only those that appear to provide the most appropriate consequences for analysis and action should be included. The initial reviews could be structured discussions attended by the chief executive and his principal assistants, or *ad hoc* deliberations between central office and middle management personnel. The precise development of the initial review is not terribly significant, but what is vital is that any discussion at this period should center on major budget questions and not on specific estimates. Even prior to these reviews, middle management and central office staffs would denote potential issues and prepare briefs outlining possible alternatives. Subsequent to the policy discussions, some of the projected items might be passed over, while others would be thoroughly scrutinized in preparation for the next level of budget, program, and policy decisions.

The second adjustment to be made in the budget calendar is a shorter allocation of time to budget estimation. As long as budget estimation continues to take up more than half of the budget year, there will never be enough time provided for policy proposals and analysis. Any reduction of time given over to estimation will undoubtedly rely upon the utilization of electronic data processing so as to exclude almost all of the manual work involved in budget estimation.

The Program Budget

The program budget is designed to offer information according to the objectives for which the recreational service department was established. There will still be a reliance upon classification of objects and functions for control and management purposes, but this may be easily undertaken if the stepover or transposition method is employed (Tables 21-1 and 21-2).

An operational PPBS requires a highly diversified and particularized information supply. The needs of control and management cannot be content with a planning-only basis. PPBS adapts this many faceted budget problem by means of a stepover or transposition organization, whereby program categories are rendered into the other informational arrangements as well as *vice versa*. In the technical sense, transposition is relatively easy. It can be performed by developing inclusive cost and activity codes and by automating the account system. However, even without automation, this stepover concept is simple enough to explain.

To total the multitude of line items of the objects budget or even the summaries of its operational segregations into their program-element consignments or costs, it is required to make appropriations, and some of them may be relatively capricious. The significant features of the stepover are (1) to have the two documents balance regardless of the size of the categories, and (2) to make sure that the decision-makers and reviewing authorities have the ability to define the following year's objects

TABLE 21—1   PROGRAM BUDGET STRUCTURE

Routine Program

Code

001 Art
002 Camping and Nature Oriented Activities
003 Crafts
004 Dance
005 Dramatics
006 Education
007 Hobbies
008 Motor Skills (sports, games, exercise)
009 Music
010 Service Activities (Volunteering)
011 Social Activities
012 Special Events

Administrative Services

Code

100 Central Office Coordination
101 Plant Maintenance and Operation
102 Concessions
103 Data Processing
104 Transportation
105 Supplies, Materials, Equipment
106 Central Administration
107 Facility Management
108 Media Resources
109 Professional and Technical Services

TABLE 21—2 FUNCTIONS AND OBJECTS BUDGET STRUCTURE

Functions and Objects Budget	Current Allocations
1000. Services, Personnel	
1100. Salaries and Wages, Regular	$186,000
1200. Salaries and Wages, Temporary	350,000
1300. Other compensations	15,000
2000. Service, Contractual	
2100. Communication and Transportation	
2110. Postage	500
2120. Telephone and Telegraph	4,000
2130. Freight and Express	2,000
2140. Traveling Expenses	1,000
2150. Hired Vehicles	800
2200. Subsistence, Care, and Support	
2210. Subsistence and Support of Persons	300
2220. Subsistence and Care of Animals	45,000
2230. Storage and Care of Vehicles	15,000
2300. Printing, Binding, and Public Relations	
2310. Printing	500
2320. Typing and Mimeographing	2,500
2330. Binding	300
2340. Public Relations	10,000
2350. Engraving and Stamping	150
2360. Lithographing	50
2370. Photographing and Blue-printing	850
2380. Publication of Notices	600
2400. Heat, Light, Power, and Water	
2410. Furnishing Heat	8,000
2420. Furnishing Light and Power	14,000
2430. Furnishing Water	500
2500. Repairs	
2510. Repairs to Equipment	1,800
2520. Repairs to Buildings and Other Structures	9,850
2600. Custodial, Cleaning, and Other Services	
2610. Custodial Supplies	22,000
3000. Commodities	
3110. Office	7,500
3120. Food	
3121. Food for Persons	150
3122. Food for Animals	8,750
3130. Fuels and Lubricants	
3131. Coals	13,000
3132. Oil, Gas, and Other Fuels	6,550
3133. Lubricating Oils	800
3140. Institutional	
3141. Clothing and Househlod	650
3142. Laundry and Cleaning	500
3143. Refrigeration	350
3144. Surgical and Medical	700
3145. General	250
3150. Park and Recreational	24,566
3160. Horticultural and Zoological	22,500
3170. Playgrounds and Centers	7,500
3180. Beaches and Camps	8,000
3190. General	750

TABLE 21—2 (Continued)

Functions and Objects Budget	Current Allocations
3200. Materials	
3210. Building	1,800
3220. Road	22,750
3230. General	1,500
3300. Repairs	
3310. Parts and Equipment	12,750
3320. Parts of Structures	6,500
4000. Current Charges	
4100. Rents	
4110. Buildings and Offices	22,250
4120. Equipment	750
4200. Insurance	
4210. Buildings and Structures	15,000
4220. Stores	5,000
4230. Equipment and Apparatus	7,500
4240. Official Bonds	8,550
4250. Employees' Liability	122,000
4300. Refunds, Awards, Indemnities	250
4400. Registration and Subscriptions	1,500
4500. Taxes	3,500
5000. Current Obligations	
5100. Interest	1,800
5200. Pensions and Retirement	27,350
5300. Grants and Subsidies	200
6000. Properties	
6100. Equipment	
6110. Office	7,800
6120. Furniture and Fixtures	2,650
6130. Instruments and Apparatus	3,860
6140. Tools	7,590
6150. Recreational and Park	42,750
6160. Motor Vehicles	2,750
6170. Nursery	3,240
6180. Animals	250
6190. General	150
6200. Buildings and improvements	
6210. Buildings and Fixed Equipment	17,500
6220. Walks and Pavements	7,250
6230. Sewers and Drains	3,750
6240. Roads	14,750
6250. Bridges	2,850
6260. Trees and Shrubs	17,470
6300. Land	37,500
7000. Debt Payments	
7100. Serial Bonds	1,800
7200. Sinking Fund Installments	650

TABLE 21—3 STEPOVER BUDGET—FUNCTIONS AND OBJECTS TO PROGRAM

	Staff	Services	Commodities	Current Charges	Current Oblig.	Properties	Debt.	Total
Art	$ 13,500.00	$ 1,966.66	$ 4,294.18	$ 8,463.50	$	$ 2,378.63	$	$ 30,602.97
Camping	16,000.00	1,966.66	11,294.18	8,463.50		3,938.95		41,633.29
Crafts	27,000.00	1,966.66	5,710.84	8,463.50		6,842.73		49,983.73
Dance	12,500.00	1,966.66	4,294.18	8,463.50				27,224.34
Dramatics	12,000.00	1,966.66	4,294.18	8,463.50				26,724.34
Education	28,500.00	1,966.66	4,294.18	8,463.50				43,224.34
Hobbies	2,000.00	1,966.66	738.63	8,463.50				13,168.79
Motor Skills	52,500.00	1,966.66	6,710.84	8,463.50		4,386.77		74,027.77
Music	15,800.00	1,966.66	4,294.18	8,463.50		2,427.03		32,951.37
Service Act.	500.00	1,966.66	738.63	8,463.50				11,668.79
Social Act.	1,900.00	1,966.66	738.63	8,463.50				13,068.79
Special Events	15,000.00	1,966.66	5,722.20	8,463.50		6,345.91		37,498.27
Central Office	24,000.00	6,107.07	7,613.63	8,463.50	29,350.00		2,450.00	77,984.20
Plant & Main.	113,000.00	25,113.65	58,313.61	8,463.50		104,138.48		309,029.24
Concessions	34,000.00	1,263.68	1,530.29	8,463.50		2,833.58		48,091.05
Data Proc.	13,000.00	3,800.00	1,530.29	8,463.50		2,651.50		29,445.29
Transportation	8,800.00	15,413.68	7,030.29	8,463.50		5,321.25		45,028.72
Supplies, Matr.		1,850.00	1,530.29	8,463.50		2,920.04		14,763.83
Central Admin.	55,000.00	2,928.00	1,580.29	8,463.50				67,971.79
Facility Manag.	65,000.00	1,450.00	113.63	8,463.50				75,027.13
Media Resourc.	10,800.00	12,260.00	113.63	8,463.50				31,637.13
Prof. & Tech.	13,200.00	914.00	213.63					14,327.63
Spec. Fac.	65,000.00	8,750.00	22,986.72	8,463.50		11,413.75		116,613.97
	$599,000.00	$103,450.00	$155,681.15	$186,197.00	$29,350.00	$155,598.62	$2,450.00	$1,231,726.77

budget in program terms and to identify next year's program budget in line-item terms (Table 21-3).

Utilization of the stepover permits conversion of information in existing records and reports into that desired for program planning. It allows program decisions to be translated into procedures currently in use for managing, authorizing, regulating, recording, and communicating operations. If the administrative methods used in any of these elements are unsatisfactory or insufficient for the purpose, they should be enhanced, despite the absence of PPBS. Whatever happens, the program budget needs to acquire its information from contemporary relationships and the current administrative records and practices as well as relying on them for the initiation of the programs.

PPBS technique of decision making incorporates a systems-analysis capacity with which the resource and cost meanings of program possibilities and their anticipated outcomes may be projected, studied, and compared. When a system-analysis faculty is absent or is incompetent, it should be established or improved, since analysis is the chief aspect of this approach to administrative decisions. A broad array of procedures is utilized in these program analyses, including statistics, modeling, gaming, simulation, operations analysis, and econometrics. Both the resource-cost facet and the benefit-effectiveness facet of program outcomes are analyzed.

Although quantification is looked for wherever possible, many factors are not susceptible to quantitative measurement. Under such circumstances, qualitative analysis is necessary. In each instance, whether the analysis is qualitative, quantitative, or a combination of both, there needs to be an exact definition of the problem, the casting of alternative solutions, and an attempt to determine the cost and effectiveness of each alternative.

The system of program budgeting is closely allied to techniques such as cost-benefit and cost-effectiveness analyses. Cost-benefit analyses provide the agency with the means for comparing the resources deployed on a particular project (expenditures) with the consequences (economic benefits) probably forthcoming from it. Cost-effectiveness analyses are formulated to determine the extent to which resources apportioned to a specific project under each of several possible alternatives actually contribute to the accomplishment of the project. In this manner a variety of means for attaining the goal may be compared.

Program analysis is not restricted to preconceived alternatives; generation of new possibilities is essential to the process. It is reasonable to assume that the analysis of one or more alternatives will develop other, more attractive possibilities, whose cost-effectiveness may become preferable to the original propositions. The analysis function of PPBS must not be understood only as the application of a collection of explicit analytical techniques to a problem. The process is much more facile and delicate, and requires inventiveness by both administrators and analysts and decision-makers.

PPBS deals with information and dissemination. The accounting and associated statistical-reporting systems denote information for all functions of the organization. Therefore, there is a need for a continuous flow of information detailing how resources are employed and the operational techniques taken in the initiation of the programs.

Even though the accounting and statistical reports are undertaken insofar as operations in the current calendar, the reporting mandate requires and supplies particular identification of current activities in terms of influence in both the latter part of the current year and the subsequent years of the multiyear plan.

Recording, reporting, and publishing is a significant feature of PPBS. These attributes of the system provide for (a) accounting for appropriated funds, (b) recognizing and assessing movement toward stated objectives (c) projecting for the future based upon knowledge gained from analysis of the past, (d) accounting practices can be made more understandable and therefore usable by decision-makers, and (e) a flood of data is now produced and can easily be adapted to any reporting system.

Rationale for Program Budgeting

The major reason for program budgeting is that it offers a routinized, systematic technique for the improvement of decisions regarding the allocation of scarce resources. Choices must be made between demands for service and the limited available resources concerning performance outcomes, quantity, and time of services provided.

Program budgeting has been formulated to consider these questions and place the propositions on a new footing. It does this by mandating specific recognition of all activities—continual or newly established—in relation to programs related to explicit ends. This permits the chief executve to take steps with regard to the entire organization instead of basing actions on the relatively restricted views of individuals or operating elements. The thrust of this new procedure is to plan for both short and long range future factors, and to decide what should be done.

Program budgeting enables the decision-makers to plan in terms of recognized costs. When a department's plans require more resources than it has at its disposal, planning allows for consideration of several alternatives which offer the means whereby resources and objectives are compared realistically. Any department that cannot carry the costs of its objectives should be prepared to change those objectives; unless there is no concern for the wasting or misusing of its substance. Resource debates inject reality into planning.

Every possible alternative should be introduced and analyzed at the planning level. Resource considerations must be regarded in totality. Fairly accurate estimates should be utilized to assist in the investigation of many possibilities in a relatively short period of time. The basis of program budgeting is developing many alternatives so that a complete range of relevant propositions can be tested for probable acceptance.

From the array of considered proposals, the most attractive are chosen and they are examined in a less aggregative but not completely detailed form. This is the essence of programming. It is at this stage that activities are identified and practicality is demonstrated in terms of capability, resource requirements, and propitiousness of each of the alternatives. The choice is associated with a budget-like process because the final budget decisions define the apportionment of resources during the next immediate year and encumber funds for subsequent years.

To establish a single program necessitates decisions on practicality, resource demands, and opportunity. However, data used for programming are never as detailed as next year's budget. The budget is a schedule of operations and a legal instrument. Because of this, it must supply great detail for items such as staffing, material, equipment, and allocation of such resources to the various departmental units. The amount of detail required is such that it submerges decision-making and renders useless a process intended to facilitate choice among alternatives.

Another reason for the establishment of program budgeting is that it supplies a basis for adoption between applicable and practical alternatives, a selection that occurs at the termination of programming. At that juncture the issues concerned have been cleared up. The executive can exercise whatever experience and knowledge he has and bring it to bear in a suitable and intelligent manner as he determines what must be done. Once decision packages have been finalized, the elaboration of technique in carrying out the enterprise follows closely. This is the point when performance budgeting, management by objectives, work estimation, and other procedures for the improvement of efficiency come to the fore. In program budgeting all attention, at this point, is on annual allocation of funds for the subsequent step to be activated in a sequence that has been painstakingly set by the policy-makers. Even more significant will be the orientation of the sequence, and the range to be included in the following year will have been determined after the analysis of a number of possibilities for the department.

This really means that program budgeting is not formulated to augment efficiency in the day-to-day performance of operations, nor is it established to increase administrative control over the expenditure of funds. Rather, it recognizes the fact that money can be wasted by wrong performance. Fundamentally, program budgeting is directly concerned with the decision-making process. It calls for continuous examination of program outcomes and for the identification and organization of programs and objectives.

As Novick has written:

> There are a great many different names now used to describe the techniques that make up program budgeting, the planning-programming-budgeting system (or PPBS), and it is likely that many other names will be used in the future. The significance of all of this is that the techniques of program budgeting are being tried, modified, and embodied into the decision making processes of business and government. Although the pace of innovation inevitably fluctuates, the direction is clear. Program budgeting is being implemented throughout Western Society and will continue to develop.[1]

PERFORMANCE BUDGETING

In the progressive refinement of budgetary procedure by municipal finance officers there has come into practice a technique termed performance budgeting. It is basically a method whereby money is budgeted toward accomplishment of specific measureable units of performance. This requires the preliminary development of a system of units of accomplishment for each of the functions to be performed with estimates based upon prior experience of the cost of accomplishing a single unit. It then becomes a matter of simple arithmetic to estimate how many units of accomplishment it is desired to achieve during the budget year and the amount of money necessary to achieve this total. During the year the estimated performance operates as a discipline upon the administrators of the function by providing incentive toward efficient performance and improved economical operation.

The performance budget permits the administration to interpret to the public what service is to be rendered during the budget year rather than solely how much money is to be spent. It also helps in the interpretation to the public of the relative cost of different types of services, thus rendering more intelligent the pressures brought to bear upon public officers for improved and expanded services. When fees are to be charged for special services, it provides a basis for the assessment of a fee commensurable with the actual cost of rendering the service.

Performance budgeting does not preclude budgeting according to a classification of functions, subfunctions, and objects of expenditures. It merely complements the conventional system and aids in better estimating programs of work and of accounting for the outcome of expenditures.

Detailed Description of Functions and Activities

One of the elements of a performance budgeting system is a detailed description of the functions, subfunctions, activities, and subactivities of

[1] David Novick, *Current Practice in Program Budgeting (PPBS)*. (New York: Crane, Russak & Company, 1973), p. vi.

the jurisdiction or department. In a comprehensive recreational service system these might be stated as follows:

1. Administration and business management
2. Construction, planning, and development
3. Maintenance of recreational places
4. Operation of playgrounds
5. Operation of pools and beaches
6. Operation of camps, golf links, parks and other recreational facilities.

This breakdown of function obviously is not a detailed one; each could be further subdivided.

Work Units by Functions and Activities

Another element is the development of appropriate units of work measurement for the activities and subactivities and the systematic recording of them day by day. It is relatively simple to break down into measurable units the work of a street maintenance crew, a rubbish collection squad, meter readers, typists, receptionists, or cashiers. But the work done by employees who render service to persons is more difficult to describe in meaningful work units. The director of a playground or center performs various services in amounts which vary according to daily needs. Recreationists also have difficulty in expressing units of their service in any meaningful way. Class enrollment may be suggested as one unit, but conducting such classes may be only incidental to the basic core of the recreationist's responsibility whose service might well be his physical presence to supervise people and to preserve order even on days when there were no classes. To measure his work by class enrollment would be similar to measuring the work of the policeman on the beat by the number of arrests made, when his duty might best be measured by the lack of arrests—in other words, by the influence of his presence in preventing conduct requiring arrest.

Work units can more easily be developed in maintenance functions, but even these must be applied and interpreted with caution. Formulae may be developed as to how many square feet of space one ground caretaker should maintain satisfactorily, assuming a normal division of the space into grassed area, asphalt walks, and play apparatus. This sounds very simple, but local parks may vary in size from ½ acre to 20 acres. Moreover, the space devoted to the several elements varies greatly. The most complicating element is the wear and tear resulting from use. Greater use requires more service.

Preparation of Work Programs

An additional element is the preparation of departmental work programs and budget estimates applicable to the programs all in accordance with standard forms and instruction. The work program might be stated in terms of the following:

1. Parks maintained (acres)
2. Playgrounds maintained (acres)
3. Buildings maintained (square feet)
4. Beaches maintained (acres)
5. Camp operation (camper days)
6. Playgrounds operated (visitor attendance)
7. Swimming pools operated (total attendance)
8. Beach lifeguard stations manned
10. Special structures or facilities (paid admissions or attendance)

Delegation of Budget Formulation and Responsibility

Performance budgeting encourages delegation of authority and responsibility down the administrative ladder. The proposed budget is a compilation of units of performance translated into costs and consolidated by activities and functions. It seems to have the effect of promoting cost consciousness among those who participate in it, especially line supervisors. Cost consciousness is a valuable attribute to develop among recreational service personnel, for it promotes employee cooperation toward greater productivity in the use of the employees' time and may permit savings to be applied to the range of services. Performance budgeting, on the other hand, provides top administration with more effective means than previously to control the activities of all divisions. This is, of course, one of the reasons for its development. The drive to introduce performance budgeting in a city comes not from separate department administrators or the performers within the division of a department, but from top city administration and from legislative bodies who make the appropriations.

Superintendents of departments and divisions, being human, prefer situations in which they may exercise their own judgments. In the past, the budgeting process seemed to have two purposes: to procure as much money as possible and to permit the preparation of a work program after the money was appropriated. Often there was little correspondence between the purposes for which the money was procured and those for which the money was eventually used. Occasionally a particularly appealing program was submitted year after year to procure budget allocations. The program was never carried out and the funds were used for other purposes. Performance budgeting, when linked with periodic reporting and checking of performance with the budgeted work program, renders such procedures impracticable.

Budgeting for Service Betterments and Capital Improvments

Allotments for service innovations and capital improvements must be considered separately from the budgeting of funds for continuation of established services. Suppose, for example, it was found in the public interest to offer fireworks at a dozen parks both to discourage the use of fireworks in the street and to provide public entertainment. The pyrotechnical displays might be provided by donations, but the presence of supervisory and maintenance staff would be required and probably (since fireworks are usually set off on holidays) on time-and-a-half pay. Presumably, under the performance budget, the staff is already assigned to capacity on other days, hour by hour. This innovation, then, would represent a considerable additional cost. It would have to be studied months before the event and would have to be included in the budget. Recreational activities and the needs and habits of people, or events to which program adaptations should be made, cannot be predicted and planned with the exactitude desired by strict adherence to the performance budgeting system.

Park and Recreational Service administrators traditionally have been effective in the creation of architectural effects, horticultural displays, and pleasing vistas in the parks. Most of these creations have been accomplished without formal plans and specifications. Personnel and materials budgeted to maintenance were used for capital improvements. Use of personnel in this manner is inevitably prohibited by the performance budgeting technique. A budget request for an extra crew to be used at the artistic whim of the park superintendent receives cold treatment when it competes with "practical" proposals involving prosaic and established service functions or activities or critically needed capital improvements such as bridges and storm sewers.

Zero-Base Budgeting (ZBB)

Zero-base budgeting, or ZBB, is a politician's dream and a recreationist's nightmare. It is a method by which any politician can slough off responsibilities for recreational program enlargement, space acquisition, or facility improvement by demanding basic justification for having public recreational service not once, but each year that budget making time comes around. Moreover, in an era with steadily rising costs and where taxpayers are continuously called upon to foot the bills for more governmental services, ZBB is the perfect ploy. On the one hand ZBB may be used to either reduce or seriously impair a recreational service department's ability to perform its functions; while, if citizens demand the service, it is a means to proclaim piously that the politician is merely satisfying citizen requests. In either event, the politician can assume a statesman-like position and deny responsibility for budget cuts or raises in recreational service or any other local function. In this way, the politician is assured the best of all possible worlds.

What is zero-base budgeting and why should it lend itself to the machinations of politicians? Presumably, the system is the most radical method to bring rapidly increasing budgets under control. Until ZBB was introduced, budget planners were able to take each year's allocation as a starting point to determine how much more or less money to request for the year ahead. Under ZBB, departmental officials have to begin as though the department and its program had never existed, justify its existence, and consider how much money, if any, each element of the program should have. This affects both the program and all other administrative operations of the agency in question.

At this time, tax-payers are increasingly unhappy about funding many of the local government functions formerly taken for granted, including school systems, fire, police, and sanitation departments. How much less inclined will they be to support public recreational service which, unfortunately, many citizens consider to be a frill and not the real necessity it is? Some of the blame may be attached to public recreational service departments for not doing a better job in educating the public to its own needs and presenting themselves in a better light (see Chap. 9). However, the contemporary economic climate is not at all conducive to the continued support of many governmental services. People are very willing to forego services, particularly when they cannot see the direct benefit to themselves or where they view such services as being essentially for the poor or minority groups residing within the community. Surely there may be some validity to deny local government services to the community on the part of an individual who sees taxes rising and who is on a fixed income, but much lack of public support stems from a misunderstanding about public recreational service and its functions. Zero-base budgeting may be a handy tool to apply to poorly conceived or operated governmental agencies, but in the present economic environment it also places soundly conceived and well-run programs in jeopardy.

ZBB in Operation.   Initially, budget planners and any other departmental managers must determine the objectives of the department and its various units. Performance standards are then established and the services which the department, through its program, is designed to deliver are defined. The next procedure is to identify decision units for which managers will prepare specific budget plans. The development of a park, playground, or other recreational facility, for example, might be one decision unit.

Presumably, the department executive will investigate alternative means to achieve the objectives which have been established, then select the most attractive and weigh different levels of spending and performance. The department executive, or his designated representative, will prepare budget plans or decision packages for two or more spending levels. One level is the minimum that would permit a department to continue on any meaningful basis. Another package might show monetary increments, personnel, and materials that would be required to match current performance and objectives. Additional packages would estimate funds, personnel, and materials that would be necessary for other performance levels, either higher or lower.

Among the questions which officials must answer are: (1) What would happen if this activity were not performed at all? (2) Can the elimination of this activity be measured in terms of impact on the public? (3) What would happen if the activity were reduced to a lower level of performance, instead of being entirely eliminated?

Decision Package Promotion. First the various departmental middle managers rank the packages or spending levels. These plans are then sent to upper echelon managers who consolidate decision packages for all units under their immediate supervision into a single ranking list. Final decisions on spending and performance levels are made by the chief executive of the department. The end product is the consolidated ranking of packages forming the basis for expenditure estimates that the department sends to whatever board, commission, or authority allocates money to the department.

Implementing ZBB. In order to derive value from zero-base budgeting the following procedures should be followed so that a budget document can be prepared:

1. Develop a program structure which clearly delineates all operational personnel and supportive operations.
2. Design a chart of accounts which would include codes for functions, objects, facilities, and programs.
3. Prepare a summary budget which would indicate current units and objects-of-expense.
4. Justify the decision package with program descriptions, benefits, alternatives, objectives, and direct costs.
5. Show various funding levels in terms of preferred, minimum, or reduced levels.
6. Determine the priorities of the decision package spending levels.
7. Consolidate decision packages through higher administrative echelon's.
8. Prepare the budget document with supportive displays of program cost, priorities, savings, and other possibilities.

This approach is based upon the requirement that all administrative functionaries with the department will be involved. Although the chief executive will play the key leadership role, it is obvious that all assistant administrators and middle management officials must assist in determining evaluation standards, rank the competing decision packages, and project the impact of reduced funding levels.

Benefits of ZBB. Zero-base budgeting is supposed to develop the following benefits:

1. Concentrate the budget process on a comprehensive analysis of needs and objectives.
2. Require administrators at all levels to appraise the cost/benefits of their operations.
3. Integrate planning and budgeting into a single process.
4. Incorporate management input in planning and budgeting at all levels of departmental operation.
5. Reduce costs of departmental operations while offering more efficient and effective service.

Deficiencies of ZBB. There are several drawbacks to zero-base budgeting, among them are:

1. Generation of tremendous amounts of information and paper.
2. Initial conversion to ZBB usually requires more time, effort, personnel, and money.
3. Competition within the department could produce internal squabbling, waste of time, and destroy cooperation.
4. Evaluation of governmental services is still a crude procedure.
5. Reduction of departmental personnel morale and increased tension between city financial authorities and recreationists.
6. Inevitable discrepancies between promised political rhetoric and governmental service reality.

Ideally, ZBB should provide administrators with the kind of information necessary to evaluate decision packages. As Pyhrr has written ZBB requires:

> . . . a statement of the goals of the activity, the program by which the goals are to be achieved, the benefits expected from the program, the alternatives to the program, the consequences of *not* approving the package, and the expenditures of funds and personnel the activity requires.[2]

However, the avalanche of information which is developed by virtue of a complete justification process and the gaps which are produced insofar as decreasing services are concerned may be more wasteful of time, money, and effort than the proposed savings.[3] Elimination of needed recreational services, particularly to low-end socio-economic groups who probably depend upon the public function to a greater extent than do other populations, may be more costly to a given community because of behavioral breakdown and social deterioration. Municipal administrators have long been aware of the connection between sound public recreational service and insensitivity to specific group needs. It is always easy

[2] P. A. Pyhrr, "Zero-Base Budgeting," *Harvard Business Review*, (Nov.–Dec., 1970), p. 113.
[3] Robert N. Anthony, "Zero-Base Budgeting Is a Fraud," *The Wall Street Journal*, (Wednesday, April 27, 1977), p. 26.

to cut budgets. It is difficult to prevent frustration and dissolution among minority groups when they obtain fewer satisfying public services.

Selected References

Cutt, J.: *A Planning, Programming and Budgeting Manual: Resource Allocation in Public Sector Economics* (New York: Praeger Pubs.), 1974.

Layard, R., Ed.: *Cost-Benefit Analysis* (New York: Penguin Books, Inc.), 1975.

Mishan, E. J.: *Cost Benefit Analysis* (New York: Praeger Pubs), 1976.

Novick, D.: *Current Practice in Program Budgeting* (New York: Crane-Russak Co.), 1973.

Office of Management and Budget: "Zero-Base Budgeting," (Washington, D. C.: Federal Register), 1977.

Pyhrr, P. A.: *Zero-Base Budgeting: A Practical Management Tool for Evaluating Expenses* (New York: John Wiley & Sons, Inc.), 1973.

PART VI

ADMINISTRATIVE RESPONSIBILITY

CHAPTER 22

Public Planning for Recreational Service

Planning as a feature of government considers the entire range of federal-urban support—physical, economic, social, educational, and re-habilitation grant and/or loan programs—with state and local government financial involvement and private resource assistance. Comprehensive planning is concerned with ecology, eco-systems, and the consequence of expedient decisions. Master planning deals with improving the environment of whole communities, with particular emphasis on activities incorporating and developing from community-wide commitment, and exemplifying the growth of integrated planning within the community. It includes all sectors of the social system by encouraging interested laymen and professional persons to assume some responsibility for the orientation and progress of planning within the community and the greater region in which they live and are a part.

There is no more important device for the improvement of urban life than city planning. With few notable exceptions, American cities have been permitted to grow without consideration of the long-range needs, the ecological implications of short-range decisions, or the aesthetic co-ordination of the numerous parts which go to make up the whole city. The traditional right of the owner of private property to put it to whatever use he may choose, regardless of the effect of such use on adjoining properties and the welfare of the entire community, has been sustained to the point of wholesale destruction of material and human values in many communities. The imperative necessity of rebuilding, renovating, and refurbishing cities to meet changing conditions and needs invariably results in appalling expenditures which might have been avoided if attention had been given to the development of comprehensive plans through the process of planning. Public planning is based on the continuous scientific study of the long-range needs of a community or region and the orderly control of present and future development in accordance with those needs.

All aspects of planning have some bearing on the recreational interests of people in any modern community, but certain features directly concern public recreational service. Land must be acquired for neighborhood playgrounds and recreational centers in already developed residential areas where there is little vacant space. In sections not wholly built up sufficient areas must be preserved for public use. District recreational facilities, athletic fields and centers, need to be set up. New community subdivisions must be controlled in order to reserve sufficient open space for future recreational needs. Regional parks and wilderness areas must be acquired before land prices become prohibitive.

Planners advocate the careful plotting of a master plan for land use against which all proposed development of industries, highways, subdivisions, and properties for public use is checked. Such plans must be compulsory, with proper discretionary power for their modification assigned to an appropriate governmental agency. Recognition of the legality of zoning ordinances by the Supreme Court of the United States has made this step possible. Unfortunately, there has been a great deal of foot-dragging by local governments in the use of zoning laws for the betterment of the community. Too often, zoning has been used as a negative force rather than as the positive activity for which it was originally intended. Faltermayer observes:

> Zoning can produce good results if it is tied in with a city plan that aims to create an attractive environment and attempts to influence the location of new private construction in a positive way by the careful timing and placement of new highways, sewer lines, and rapid transit routes. Without this kind of implementation, it can often break down under pressure from developers. Even if it holds up, its effect is mainly negative, i.e., preventing unwanted types of buildings from being constructed. It cannot design a beautiful city or an attractive suburb any more than building codes can design a handsome house.[1]

Some states authorize the adoption of authoritative master plans by properly constituted planning bodies. Many cities have already adopted such plans, but static thinking either permits them to gather dust on high shelves or refuses to modify such plans as community conditions change.

ASPECTS OF PLANNING

The planning process may be considered to have three distinct phases each conducing to the logical development of some unified aims that

---

[1] Edmund K. Faltermayer, Redoing America (New York: Harper & Row, Publishers, Inc., 1968), p. 28.

will better the community or region in question. A plan must be the departure point for proposed public projects. Planning permits a wider utilization of private property and prevents encroachment of public regulation on private holdings. The planning process provides all local property owners with information as to how land may be used by them for maximum benefit to themselves and the community. A plan should be flexible; i.e., it should be devised so that modifications of environmental variables (whatever they may be) can be accounted for or be responsive to exigencies which arise. A well-conceived plan offers an analysis of pertinent facts, a deliberate set of guides, and the elasticity to rebound from a possible disadvantage and transform an emergency into an advantageous opportunity. Finally, a plan must maintain the more delicate land-use arrangements so that their benefits are not lost.

Planning for recreational service means the exploration of all possibilities for the development of those spaces and structures that will enhance the recreational services offered to the community. Therefore it involves the collection and examination of pertinent information so that a basis for issuing policies and executing programs may be carried out in designing and developing physical properties.

Planning is concerned with the accumulation of pertinent or refined information, the analysis of that information for categorization, the projection of alternative courses of action, and the appraisal of the consequences of diversified actions. The planning process produces a detailed construct about the socioeconomic, political, geographic, topographic, educational, cultural, ecological, and ethnic characteristics of the community in order to determine the most effective placement of physical facilities to meet the recreational needs of present and future residents. It considers the following elements:

1. The growth rate of the community and the major forces producing population increments and community expansion.
2. The economic base of the community—all activities producing wealth within the community and on which the economic health of the city is founded.
3. Population studies—the facts about age, sex, ethnic derivation, religion, education, social, cultural, vocational, and racial characteristics of people within the community. Such studies indicate population densities, needs, aspirations, and movements within the community.
4. Geopolitical boundaries—regional and metropolitan relationships, district and neighborhood relationships, topographic features, natural resources, and gateways and barriers to the potential expansion of the community. Traditions, mores, and personal attitudes may also be represented in surveys of this type.

5. Land use surveys—how land is utilized within a given community. The natural and physical resources and structures within the city for map projection. This information is particularly useful in locating traffic arteries, transportation and communication facilities, residential, commercial, industrial, and public land-use zones.

6. Financial factors—tax bases and rates, property value, outstanding bond issues and other loan situations, community revenues, and the probable ability of the community to sustain capital expenditures for a comprehensive physical recreational development as well as all other physical developments within the community.

Any plan developed for municipal use contains a synthesis of the foregoing topics and outlines the precise actions to be taken in systematically acquiring space, designing and constructing physical facilities, and enhancing recreational service within the community. The plan is composed of a priority schedule, the composite picture of the entire community and its resident population, complete maps and layouts for placement of needed spaces and structures, and the estimated costs for the proposed developments.

Fundamentals of Planning Procedure

Comprehensiveness is the major theme of planning. Although the term "plan" is used to denote a variety of schemes that do not reflect incorporation of all factors, the city plan is a reflection of every facet of the city or region under study. To be comprehensive a plan must be applicable to all land-use and circulation systems; cover the entire geographic area influenced by the shared problems of development; designed to satisfy the consequences of long-term operations; and include the basic procedures to analyze facts, formulate plans, and carry out the plans. Operational policies characterizing planning administration in recreational service have been formulated to assist recreationists in comprehensive planning.

1. Properties should be acquired in the path of community development, according to a logical plan of action, and prior to the actual need and ability of the community to develop them.

2. Properties for recreational service use in fully developed areas should be acquired as the opportunity presents itself and as a part of urban renewal.

3. Lands acquired for park purposes should be dedicated in perpetuity for public recreational use only. No other utilization should be permitted nor should they be allowed to be diverted to private use.

4. Public parks and other recreational facilities should be situated

in an equitable manner so that all citizens may have the opportunity to enjoy them.

5. Public park and other recreational facilities should be designed and constructed for appropriateness and attractiveness in the areas where they are located. Maintenance of such facilities and places is mandatory for cleanliness, safety, and continued use.

6. Facilities should be situated according to the most efficient use of land, convenience of the group or groups for which they are planned, safety of users, effectiveness of supervision, and attractiveness of appearance.

7. Recreational structures should provide the essential public conveniences and whatever is necessary and suitable for the public recreational program produced therein.

8. Buildings and grounds of the public school system should be designed for multipurpose use and made available to community groups when such use does not interfere with the established curriculum. In return, the facilities of public recreational service areas and structures should be made available to the public school system under reciprocal arrangements.

9. Recreational service spaces may be developed adjacent to public schools.

10. If certain neighborhoods of the community do not have schools, other recreational service spaces should be situated there to serve the needs of residents.

11. Duplication of areas and facilities should be avoided by official agreements incorporating public school buildings and grounds into the total recreational service program.

12. The use of public parks or other recreational facilities and the special outdoor structures situated within them should not be limited to daylight use only. Efficient illumination permits them to become more widely utilized thereby increasing the services provided by the same capital outlay. Lighting must be intelligently planned to encourage active participation rather than passive observation.

THE MASTER PLAN

The master plan is directed toward the rational management and guidance of the complex physical growth and modification of communities. It is a detailed policy statement and timetable for the implementation of physical recreational facilities and spaces. The plan considers what kinds of recreational places are required, where they will be placed so that the greatest number of people can be served by the financial resources available, what the community has in the way of present recreational places and how they are being utilized, and, finally, what additional areas are necessary for providing the most effective service.

A master plan is usually undertaken as a 25-year directive with subplans offered to permit flexibility and allow for any unexpected or rapidly changing factors that might influence population density, movement, or land-use patterns. The subsections of the master plan are:

The Five-Year Guide. This plan consists of an immediate appraisal of the community including past surveys of traffic arteries, public utilities, housing projects, and subdevelopments. The plan considers the necessity of developing facilities in accordance with any population increases within a five-year period. It is limited by its short-term view and relation to particular districts and/or neighborhoods. It attempts to accommodate relatively recent variables in line with the master plan by the provision of public recreational facilities and spaces in areas of population growth or where other factors influence the master plan.

The Three-Year Guide. This plan is initiated by population increases or decreases in one neighborhood within the community, and it specifically meets the needs of that neighborhood. This plan requires continuous study and analysis of the community in order to monitor the growth potential of populations, economic resources, and recreational needs in any given section of the community.

The One-Year Guide. This plan deals with the provision of recreational services and the development or renovation of facilities in densely populated areas of the community. It is basically oriented toward the satisfaction of current recreational place deficits within the heavily populated neighborhoods rather than with the acquisition of land or the development of new facilities in outlying sections. This is a plan of immediacy.

CITY AND MASTER PLANNING

All facts concerning the acquisition of land, structures, facilities, and the cost of carrying out a plan must be examined before a logical plan can be initiated. Although specific elements can be set forth to assist all cities in the formulation of a complete plan, the variables and complex problems of each city make a standard pattern inadvisable.

The problem of providing open spaces in the crowded districts of large cities must be approached not only from the standpoint of recreational needs, but in relation to the provision of essential conveniences for healthful living. Valiant efforts at slum clearance and construction of multiple-housing units are being made in many cities. The federal government provides attractive financial inducements to any city that will join with it in low-cost housing programs. In addition, the program of urban renewal, redevelopment, and beautification has helped to remove blighted areas and develop attractive living places in many communities.

Mandelker sums up federal assistance in relation to local planning procedures in this manner:

> With increasing federal assistance for local programs such as urban renewal, highways, and open land acquisition has come increasing recognition of the importance of placing these programs within the framework of a comprehensive plan. Federal legislation often requires that comprehensive planning precede project execution in these programs. As compared with state enabling legislation for planning, which is optional, federal legislation is mandatory, at least insofar as it governs the receipts of federal grants-in-aid.[2]

The high premium placed on open space in excessively congested areas calls for the adoption of extreme and unusual measures to provide recreational facilities and places. The establishment of playgrounds on house roofs and the blocking off of streets for play are examples of such measures. In the great multiple-housing projects in New York City, Cincinnati, Cleveland, Chicago, Philadelphia, Oakland, and elsewhere, provision is made for playgrounds and other recreational areas. Although space in these recreational areas is grossly inadequate by standards applicable to more favored neighborhoods, the condition is infinitely more satisfactory than that which formerly obtained. Most of the largest cities have slums and ghetto districts, but the problem of creating recreational areas in such districts must be regarded as peculiar to the neighborhoods making up the districts and inextricably interwoven with a wide range of related problems. In endeavoring to arrive at standards for general application to urban communities, it would be well to consider conditions that are not extraordinary or peculiar to areas of extreme congestion.

Acquisition and Improvement of Recreational Property

Acquisition of space for recreational activities is one of the most pressing problems any public department has to face. Without adequate land there can be no effective recreational service. The real issue lies not simply with acquiring space, but with the acquisition of suitable and properly situated areas throughout the community.

Transfer of land from one use to another within the confines of a city is another method. Parcels of land in public ownership may no longer be required for the purposes for which they were originally acquired, such as reservoirs, firehouses, corral or stable sites, space for storage of city engineering equipment, public school lands or buildings, or properties bequeathed to the city in past years. Many municipal recreational centers across the country are situated on such lands. A search should

---

[2] Reprinted from *Managing Our Urban Environment, Cases, Text, and Problems,* by Daniel R. Mandelker, copyright 1966, by The Bobbs-Merrill Company, Inc. Reprinted by permission. All rights reserved.

be made in the public records for such properties, and, if they are suit-able for public recreational purposes, the proper authorities should seek to transfer such lands to the control of the recreational service system. If possible, transfer should be made permanent by ordinance. If this is impractical, temporary transfer may be acceptable. Occasionally, private owners will accept other lands in exchange for lands better suited for public recreational use.

All property should be examined carefully before being accepted when an exchange is being made. Often, small odd-shaped pieces of land are a source of continuing expense without being of value. Sometimes they can be maintained as parks. Lots of a sufficient size and shape to accom-modate recreational activities can be profitably incorporated into the properties carried by the recreational service system.

Use of lands under lease or permit is rarely advisable when the need for the land is permanent. A long-term lease would not ordinarily be granted by private owners except at commercial rates. A short-term lease does not justify the costly improvements that might be necessary for successful operation. Operation under lease or permit encourages complacency which militates against the formulation of plans for a more permanent solution of the problem. If the lease or permit is granted by another governmental agency the situation is altered. Each proposal or project must be examined and judged on its own merits, but as a general rule the acceptance of lands on lease or permit is not to be encouraged.

Acquisition by donation, gift, bequest, and dedication may be made by presentation and recording of a proper deed of gift. Gifts also may be made by filing a subdivision map showing the area dedicated as park or playground, but some courts have ruled that the dedication must be officially accepted by the governing body of the city and must be recorded. Sometimes acceptance is implied by the city's use and improve-ment of the land.

The land is usually a private estate. Sometimes the incentive to deed such property to cities arises out of sentimental attachment and a dis-inclination to have the property broken up. Sometimes it is due to a philanthropic spirit. Sometimes the fact that such gifts are tax deductible is the inducement.

Lands acquired and dedicated for recreational purposes, specifically parks, may not be used for any other purposes. However, courts have been quite liberal in interpreting what constitutes park purposes and have held that airports, swimming pools, playgrounds, auditoriums, and stadiums are not inconsistent with park purposes. In many states, park lands, once dedicated, may not be sold unless the courts agree public necessity requires such sale.

Cities and other jurisdictions prefer to receive gifts in "fee simple," which is the unrestricted title to the land without conditions as to its use or future disposition. Public benefactors, however, usually write into the deeds various conditions and restrictions, such as the use to which the property may be put, the name by which it shall be called, and how it shall be improved and maintained. Reversionary clauses providing that if the conditions of the grant are not complied with the title shall revert to the donor or his heirs or assigns are also included. In their eagerness to accept lands for public benefit, officials have frequently erred in agreeing to all sorts of unreasonable and fanciful restrictions. No general rule can be formulated as to which restrictions are reasonable and which are not. Perhaps the only reasonable restriction is that land be used for recreational purposes only. Each situation must be judged according to its individual merit.

Everyone recognizes the fundamental importance of neighborhood and district recreational places yet the problem of providing them in the older sections of a city and of reserving proper spaces in new districts has been almost insurmountable. Not only has little progress been made in acquiring areas in built-up districts, but new sections continue to be opened and developed without adequate provision for recreational needs.

In already subdivided and developed districts, there seems to be no other answer but to purchase land—usually at high price—and to clear it of unsuitable buildings or other structures. Other expedients have been employed, but the problem will not be solved until sufficient funds are provided to permit cities to rebuild in a manner that will give every neighborhood and district recreational places to meet their needs. A complete range of federal grant programs provides financial assistance for planning, land acquisition, facility construction, staffing, and urban renewal, enabling communities to purchase property, develop it, build recreational structures, and, in some instances, actually employ personnel. The writing of proposed projects to be financed by such federal assistance has become a highly technical enterprise requiring an expertise unknown in too many communities. Nevertheless, many communities are undertaking the painful reappraisals necessary for the wealth of material required of grant proposals. The federal aid program may just be the best encouragement that planning ever received in this country. Certain methods are open to public recreational service departments for the acquisition of open spaces and for the acquisition of lands in completely developed neighborhoods or city areas.

Right of eminent domain is the legal power of any government to take lands or property required for public purposes. This right applies to the taking of land for parks and other recreational facilities as well as for other public functions. Properties so acquired must be taken by due process of law as set up in the particular state with adequate compensation given to the property owner.[3] Courts have held that the

[3] Leonard v. Autocar Sales and Service Company, 392 Ill. 182, 64 N.E. 2d 477.

finding of the properly constituted governmental body as to the public necessity for the acquisition is conclusive. The courts merely adjudicate the damages to be paid the owner.

Condemnation is the process by which governments exercise the right of eminent domain. The government, having ascertained that funds are available for the acquisition of a given property, officially finds that the same is required for public purposes and serves legal notice on the owner to this effect. The case is then argued before a civil court. Procedures vary among the several states, some provide trial by jury and some do not. Usually it is provided that appraisers be appointed by the court and that evidence be admissible as to the value of the property.

Condemnation is usually the best means of determining a fair price, but properties are frequently acquired by direct purchase in the open market. Owners sometimes prefer to negotiate directly without awaiting condemnation proceedings (often a year or more is required). Public departments typically prefer to handle purchases by condemnation rather than direct purchase because the price is then fixed by the court and criticism of the department is thereby avoided.

Excess condemnation is the condemnation of more land than is required for a given project. A public improvement such as a park, beach, or golf course frequently increases the value of adjoining property. Value is thus created by the public investment for the benefit of the owners of adjoining private property. It would seem that the improvement itself might be financed in whole or in part by the value thus created. City planners have advocated the use of excess condemnation in order that the excess land may be sold later at an enhanced price. Proceeds derived from the sale are applied to the cost of the public improvement.

Several states have passed legislation permitting the use of excess condemnation, but the method has not come into wide usage. The constitutionality of such legislation is questionable on the ground that the power of eminent domain can be applied only to land necessary for a public use.[4] If this method ultimately proves legal, it will be of value in connection with certain large district or regional parks and other recreational projects where enough land is involved to make the method practicable and where the nature of the recreational improvements assures enhancement of adjoining property values. As far as neighborhood areas are concerned, however, it is questionable whether the plan can be employed advantageously.

Direct purchase of recreational space is a more simple procedure than condemnation. It is also less expensive, for court and other incidental expenses concurrent with condemnation often run very high in relation

[4] McAuliffe & Burke Co. v. Boston Housing Authority, Mass., 133 N.E. 2d 493.

to the total award to the owner. Particularly is this true when the award is not great, as in the case of small properties acquired for neighborhood and district use. If the city or department representing the city is in a position to "shop" as a private individual would do, and especially when there are two or more areas from which to choose, a better bargain can be made by direct purchase than by condemnation. It is usually not advisable to reveal that the government is seeking the property lest owners raise the price. Thus, departments considering the purchase of land frequently obtain options in the names of private persons. Commissions to realty dealers are not legal expenditure in most places, but nothing prevents the seller from paying a commission to one who represents him in a transaction of this sort.

Because the annual budgets of most cities do not permit land purchases for recreational purposes, it is often proposed that property be bought on the partial payment plan, under which a portion of the purchase price is paid each year. (Most states consider this procedure illegal on the theory that an incumbent administration may not make a commitment to any policy or expenditure binding on a future administration.) Purchase through lease contracts is another way of distributing the cost over several years. For example, suppose a park required ten lots costing $10,000, and that only $2,000 could be budgeted for land purchase each year. Two lots are purchased the first year and a lease and option taken on the remaining eight lots with an agreement that lease rentals would apply to subsequent purchases. The following year two more lots are taken and so on until all are purchased.

City government has one advantage over private buyers in the acquisition of property by direct purchase: when it assumes title to a property, unpaid taxes may be canceled; the private buyer must assume the obligation. Occasionally, owners of desirable properties become delinquent in tax payments and the properties are legally "sold" to the state for nonpayment of taxes. Although technically the state possesses the property after a certain period of tax delinquency, the owner may redeem the property by paying the back taxes and appropriate penalties. It is rare that such properties are completely abandoned, particularly those large enough and suitably situated for public recreational purposes. A recreational service department would do well to investigate whether taxes are owed on any desirable properties, for advantageous deals may be made with the owners to acquire their equities. This procedure must bear careful investigation and most assuredly when tax delinquencies are numerous and values of unimproved real estate are low.

Most public recreational service systems do not have the power to conduct purchase transactions. These duties are performed by designated agents of the city or by a special department. Nevertheless, knowledge of how purchases are made and close liaison with the properly designated agents of the city often enable the superintendent of recreational service to secure advantages for his department.

Real estate subdivisional dedication might be a good method of acquisition, if some way could be found to require land to be dedicated for public recreational purposes as a condition to approval of subdivision plans. This is the manner in which dedication of necessary streets is obtained. Municipal statutes uniformly require approval of street plans and dedication of easements for street purposes before subdivided lands may be sold. The courts have generally upheld zoning ordinances that set up reasonable requirements with reference to streets. Similar legal authority to require the dedication of recreational areas has come into being during the past few years. State laws, particularly those concerning zoning powers, have widely endorsed the concept that necessitates the dedication of specific areas for public recreational purposes.[5]

Many real estate subdividers realize the value of parks and other recreational spaces in making a subdivision a desirable residential place and in the sales appeal such sites might make. Not a few subdividers have voluntarily set aside lands for park, play field, and playground purposes, particularly in the large and more expensive subdivisions. The subdividers continue to pay the taxes on about one-fourth of the areas, usually with the expectation of later deeding the property to the municipality. In a few cases the cost of maintenance was carried by the subdividers and the property owners of the subdivisions; in some instances associations of property owners maintained and operated the areas.

Dedication of areas in subdivisions would be more generally adopted if immediate improvement of an area could be assured and if cities could give binding guarantees that the dedicated areas would be maintained and supervised in a creditable manner. Cities are not usually able to undertake improvement and operation before the subdivision is completely built and populated; this process often requires several years during which the cost of operation more than equals the value of the dedicated land. If the land is taken over by the city before it is actually needed, the city not only incurs the cost of operating it during the period when there is little return in usefulness but it also loses the taxes that would be paid on the land if it remained in private ownership.

Ocean beaches and tide lands are rapidly becoming of vast importance to the recreational pursuits of the American people. The waters are used by millions each year for aquatic sports and the adjoining beaches for related activities. The tidelands, the lands lying seaward from the line of mean or ordinary high tide, are generally owned by the state.[6] Public

---

[5] Chrinko v. South Brunswick Township Planning Board, 77 N.J. Super. 594, 187 A. 2d 221 (1963).

[6] In New Jersey and some other states on the eastern seaboard, certain portions of the tidelands are in private ownership which derives from original grants made to private individuals or companies by the English Crown.

ownership, vested in the state as the sovereign power, is based on the English common law. The right of the public to use the tidelands and their waters for commerce, navigation, and fishing is traditional; however, their use for recreational experiences until recently has received scant recognition in the law, although it has not been held to be inconsistent with the traditional right. Owners of land adjacent to or abutting the waters of oceans, lakes, or rivers enjoy what is known as *riparian rights* consisting of the right of access to and the use of the said waters, also of ownership of accretions to the foreshore when caused by natural forces. The ownership of artificially induced accretions varies in different coastal states.

It should be pointed out that tidelands and tidewaters cannot be generally enjoyed for recreational purposes unless access is had to them across the adjoining upland beach. For this reason seacoast cities, counties, and states have recently undertaken to acquire long strips of ocean beach for recreational activities. The manner of acquisition has been the same as that for park or other recreational spaces.

Rivers and lakes are enjoyed by the public with the same rights of ownership as with ocean beaches, but non-navigable waterways are often held wholly in private ownership, subject to certain riparian rights of owners of property dependent thereon for water supply. Acquisition of some waterways for recreational purposes is now recognized as commendable public policy and may be accomplished in the same manner as park and other recreational lands are acquired.

REGIONALISM AND PLANNING

The multi-jurisdictional conflicts generated in and around urban sections of the nation continuously give rise to problems, the solutions of which are not capable of being handled at local levels of government. Moreover, there has been a startling increase in the number of inter-city, interstate, and supra-urban difficulties that preclude local resolution because they flow freely across the man-made boundaries and geopolitical lines designed to meet one- or two-century-old needs. Special jurisdictions dealing with one particular problem may have appeared to deal with that specific problem, but the conflicts initiated by the creation of special units have more than demonstrated the paucity of creating single-purpose governmental jurisdictions.[7]

Regional Government

What is required to control intra- and intercity problems of mushrooming proportions is a form of government that can integrate and

[7] Committee for Economic Development, *Modernizing Local Government* (New York: A Statement by the Research and Policy Committee. New York: Committee for Economic Development, 1966), p. 17.

coordinate all activities under one jurisdiction with the requisite authority to plan and carry out all the functions necessary to the on-going operations of communities and the well-being of the inhabitants. Regional government would certainly appear to be the answer to the increasing urbanization and suburbanization of the country. The growth of metropolitan areas and the infiltration of one metropolitan area into another to form a megalopolis require some ameliorative power to find logical solutions to the problems such congestion and incoherent separatism offer. Regional government is in operation in several places in the United States and Canada and is successful.

It is possible that the major urban centers will serve as the central core from which regions will grow and that regions will arise wherever common problems and other homogeneous factors are present. Geographic, economic, transportation networks, and certain social features may also conduce to the formation of a region. The explosive population increases, the consequences of population growth into urban agglomerates, the hardening of urban sprawl into strip cities, and the movement of people away from central cities to suburbs, along with the concomitant ills of megalopolis with none of the benefits which formerly accrued to citizens of cities foreshadows the need for an immediate change of jurisdictional form. Such a government may combine the territory and powers now held by all local jurisdictions and states. The disappearance of local governments and, perhaps, the states as anything but historic place-names may seem to some a rending of the traditional fabric of society. However, the traditional governmental forms have lost all semblance of control of problems which in no way can be termed local or even state-wide. Only a jurisdiction that can deal with problems that originate within and extra to the urban areas can operate if provided with the necessary powers. Traditional local government does not now have, nor will it have, the ability to deal effectively with the massive conflicts currently afflicting it, and it will be capable of even less effort as such problems continue to be generated in the future. No attempt will be made here to further explain the philosophy of regionalism as a governmental form. Specialists have devoted much time and effort in developing the concept of the regional government as an effective instrument of the body politic.[8] Of necessity, this section must deal with regional planning.

Regional planning should be considered as a scientific operation of a particular kind. Essentially directed to the future, it examines the relation between social purposes and areal configurations. Thus, regional planning may be defined as a process of devising and explaining social goals in the regulation of experiences concerning both city and extra-city

[8] John Friedmann and William Alonso (Eds.), *Regional Development and Planning* (Cambridge, Mass.: The M.I.T. Press, 1967), 721 pages.

spatial relationships. Thus, there is continuity between city and regional planning because both study the organization of space.

Regional planning has traditionally been concerned with economics and resource distribution. However, with the concept of regional planning incorporating the city as well as extra-city space, physical land use and configuration problems will also be investigated. Although regional planning developed from theories of economic location and focal sites, it must now encompass the analysis of human ecology, ekistics, urban land economics, and the aesthetics of design. Regional planning is a way of looking at spatial factors in relation to the social needs of people, thus, the contrast and parameters of land uses, provision and operation of public services, population density, and the shaping of the urban core.

The distinguishing features of a metropolitan region and planning functions for the region have been identified by John Friedmann, who states that:

> . . . it has one or more cores, or control centers. Second, it provides a complete and year-round habitat for man, a place for work and residence and the pursuit of leisure. Third, it generally includes areas in which some forms of intensive agriculture will be carried on chiefly to supply the region. Fourth, it represents a suitable unit area (location matrix) with respect to which investment decisions will be made. Planning for this new form of human settlement must be related to its several cores and proceed outward from these centers to a line where densities of interaction fall below a certain threshold level. At this invisible boundary, one metropolitan region may run into another (megalopolis) or yield to a rural periphery which is not yet fully integrated with any metropolitan center.
>
> City and regional planning approaches meet and merge in the metropolitan region. The task of the regional planner will be to state the ordering of control centers within the area, to identify the functions to be performed by each center, and to study the inter-regional effects of the expansion of metropolitan economies.[9]

PLANNING RECREATIONAL PLACES

City and regional planning have a common border in the metropolitan region. All the diverse forces that combine to produce the warp and woof of the urban fabric are reproduced in the region. For these reasons, recreational service planning incorporates elements of both the spatial relations, economics, political, social, cultural, and the population needs of city and region. Planning is concerned with the spaces and physical facilities necessary through which the program of recreational activities can be offered to accommodate participants. Planning systematically achieves an equitable distribution of recreational places throughout the entire metropolitan area. Land space and structures and their place-

[9] John Friedmann and William Alonso (Eds.), *Regional Development and Planning* (Cambridge, Mass.: The M.I.T. Press, 1967), p. 66.

ment are the foundation of the public recreational service system, for they provide the setting in which the community's recreational culture may express itself and flourish.

Spatial Factors

The amount of space provided for recreational purposes in any given metropolitan area depends on a variety of isolated and interrelated facts about population needs and demands. Among the facets of metropolitan existence that determine space allocation are:

1. Topography of the land. A varied topography offers opportunities for creation of interesting and useful parks on land that is unsuited to more utilitarian or commercial purposes.
2. Established land-use pattern of the city. Most cities have grown without adequate planning and are committed to land uses that render effective replanning costly and difficult.
3. Economy of the metropolitan area—city and region. The needs of people are substantially the same across the country, but their economic capacity to afford well-placed and adequate recreational areas and facilities varies. The poorer communities will have to be content with more modest recreational planning.
4. Distribution of schools and policy of the school district in the provision of space for schools and use of school resources for community recreational purposes. Many schools were established when little space was needed. Thus the environs of the schools have been built up and committed to such uses that expansion of school space has become prohibitive. Complementation of school space by land otherwise provided becomes imperative and can be had only at extraordinary cost.
5. Fortuitous possession of marginal lands that can be incorporated in the modern land-use program for recreational purposes.
6. Privately owned land made available for public uses, rendering it unnecessary to acquire alternative properties. Some cities and towns today are seeking legal ways to ensure continued maintenance of park-like areas in their present condition by acquisition of title and lease-back to owners under negotiated financial settlement.
7. Size of the metropolitan region in relation to congestion of population and peripheral development of recreational places. The amount of land owned by cities and towns for recreational services varies according to the population. Urban areas inevitably tend to develop extreme congestion near their centers, because the value of land becomes so great near the center that only multiple residential or commercial uses of land can be afforded. The typical result is

planning that favors small but intensively developed park and other recreational areas and facilities near the central city and greater dependence on mass transportation or other means to regional recreational complexes in peripheral areas.

8. Unwillingness or inability of city government to support the development of innovative recreational developments, e.g., linear recreational spaces, which might serve a more densely populated area with less land. Because the linear proposal would force a reappraisal of current land-use practices and require unpopular political decisions, linear developments languish. Nevertheless, some progressive communities are attempting a corridor approach to recreational planning with great success. Such linear schemes may represent a future wave in the design of recreational places.

Space Standards

A long-established minimum standard for the amount of publicly owned space that a municipality should have for recreational purposes is 1 acre per 100 persons. This has been promulgated by the National Park and Recreation Association and has achieved endorsement by the several professional societies composed of personnel in recreational service, city planning, public administration, and federal agencies. It has gained acceptance by its practical application.

Very few cities, particularly the urban giants, achieve this minimum standard. The amount of open space reported by cities in relation to population tends to decrease in proportion to the population increase. In reporting the area comprising their recreational service systems, cities include all spaces set aside for park or other recreational purposes whether developed or not, such as areas of marginal usefulness and those poorly located for effective park use.

For a city of 100,000 population to attain the standard of 1 acre per 100 people, the distribution might reasonably and hypothetically be as shown in Table 22-1. School recreational areas (excluding college grounds) supply 240 acres and municipal recreational areas supply 760 acres of the 1000-acre total.

Another, less definitive, standard often expressed by recreationists and city planners is 10 percent of the total area of the city. One thousand acres of open space for recreational purposes would thus accommodate a city with a total area of 10,000 acres, which is roughly 16 square miles. The size of cities, however, bears little relation to gross population; hence this type of space evaluation and comparison has little validity.

The hypothetical estimate of distribution of space from the standpoint of adequacy evaluation assumes that the yards or playgrounds of elementary schools are open and supervised during non-school hours, and that neighborhood parks, also supervised, are situated in vicinities with

TABLE 22—1   SPACE STANDARDS FOR CITY OF 100,000 POPULATION

NUMBER OF AREAS	TYPE OF AREA	AVERAGE (ACRES)	TOTAL (ACRES)
10	Elementary school yards	10	100
10	Neighborhood parks, play- grounds, and recreational centers	10	100
4	Junior high school play fields	20	80
2	High school athletic fields	30	60
5	Additional community parks	20	100
Various	Small parks, historic monuments, and institutional grounds	—	60
2	Regional parks	250	500
	Total	340	1000

no recreational areas furnished by existing schools. It is further assumed that school yards have landscaped areas, and that the junior and senior high school fields generally are open to the public for uses not conflicting with conventional school uses. The two regional parks of 250 acres are predicated on two 18-hole golf courses, aquatic areas (ocean or bay front, lakes, reservoirs, river banks), marginal land (gullies, cliffs, drainage basins), and forested areas.

A city of 100,000 population would be fortunate to have the amount of open area for recreational purposes set forth in the table, especially if the land was well distributed and all of it was usable. It must be assumed that the standard is applicable only to usable space. Few cities achieve the hypothetical standard; some report more than 1 acre per 100 population, but do not have the orderly distribution set forth in the hypothetical tabulation.

Space requirements have forced many cities to face up to the problem of acquiring land. When population density outstrips land acquisition, great cost is incurred in obtaining suitable property. Foresighted municipal administrators have requested that their city begin to acquire land prior to need.

Recreational properties are now being planned for more widespread and diversified use than formerly. Planning for outdoor areas is receiving more emphasis in that they are being planned for the whole population with special facilities adjusted to the needs and interests of all age groups. On the national, as well as state and local, scene many more citizens are demanding the use of outdoor spaces. Today's program comprises outdoor education, camping, nature study, conservation, ecology, cave and space exploration, scuba diving and undersea exploration, and other activities related to the natural sciences. Outdoor exhibits, demonstrations, entertainments, and spectacles are included for vicarious appreciation, and many sports, games, and other participant activities are fostered.

Placement and Development of Recreational Places

After land has been acquired in the most suitable places, recreational areas and facilities must be designed and developed. Recreational areas should be situated in the most densely populated sections of the community. This means distribution of properties from local neighborhood settings to regional complexes. Development of recreational facilities that may best meet the varied and diverse range of recreational experiences can be neighborhood, district, community, and regional in nature if linear spaces are provided. The linear recreational facility accommodates densely populated sections of cities with regional quality. Contained within the linear space may be the varied facility types of a scale to attract many people. Since the linear space can traverse an entire city and may continue beyond city limits, it may furnish the most efficient, economical, and effective space allocated to recreational purposes.

In any city planning endeavor, the neighborhood recreational facilities are distributed first in order to provide recreational service with maximum effect. It may be that the neighborhood recreational area, whether a pass-through park, playground, or vest-pocket park, can be the initial point from which a linear recreational development may be begun. If a corridor can be designed, with neighborhood facilities serving as emphasis spaces along the route, a more interesting and varied series of places may then be constructed for maximum use. A basic requirement for community-wide recreational service is that a recreational facility be situated within a quarter of a mile from every dwelling in any given community.

Neighborhood Recreational Centers. A community should ideally contain as many neighborhood playgrounds as it has neighborhoods. This means that it should have no fewer neighborhood playgrounds than it has elementary schools, since elementary schools are usually located with reference to neighborhood need and convenience. In large cities, elementary schools are situated so that they may be within convenient walking distance of the homes af all children. Although there is considerable transportation of children across neighborhood boundaries for school purposes, the fact remains that a neighborhood elementary school may be the best recreational center because of its advantageous placement. The number of playgrounds at the neighborhood level should probably exceed the number of elementary schools because children are required to attend school whereas they participate at playgrounds voluntarily. They will therefore travel further to school than to a playground.

If all elementary schools were designed for dual utilization, i.e., school and recreational purposes, and were equipped with adequate playgrounds, these facilities would be sufficient to serve the recreational needs of the children residing in the neighborhood of the schools. There would be no need for additional playgrounds for small children except in neighborhoods in which school-recreational centers do not exist. The elementary school building can also serve the recreational needs of youths and adults when competently supervised and programmed.

District Recreational Centers. The district recreational facility is intended to serve adolescents and adults. It may be termed an athletic center because it is primarily equipped for organized athletic sports, but it can serve as a social center as well. The people it is intended to serve are able and willing to travel further than the younger children to enjoy its benefits because of their greater freedom and capacity to travel and because of their desire for more highly organized activity. District recreational centers should serve an area of approximately three-quarters of a mile in all directions.

Community Recreational Park. The community recreational facility is almost always a park with open lawns, woodlands, shrubs, and other plantings. Interesting features of landscape or topography should be utilized in their natural state. Some parks may have certain areas set aside for formal gardens, arboretums, or other botanical sites. Usually, a wide range of facilities is offered within the park to provide for varied recreational activities. Generally, parks have sections for relaxation—strolling, sitting, and picnicking—and other areas designed for small children and older adults. Perhaps an outdoor theater or concert hall, zoological exhibit, natural trail, or aquatic facility is situated in it. Occasionally there are bridle paths, golf courses, and reflecting pools which add to the aesthetic enjoyment of the viewer. Shelters and public rest rooms are often placed within the park. The community recreational park usually serves the area within a radius of a least 1 mile. Its capacity to attract patronage depends not only on the quality and diversity of its installations but also on the transportation conveniences that serve it.

Regional Complex. The city will not be well equipped for recreational service unless it possesses a large regional reservation, preferably an area of interesting terrain with hills, lakes, streams, and woods. It should have at least one golf course, well-developed picnic trails, bridle paths, a swimming pool or two, and special landscaped or horticultural features.

The regional complex is usually on the outskirts of the city, consisting of acreage that is not wholly suited to other uses or is considered as submarginal land. Often such land is along a seashore, around a lake, or in a hilly area. Because of these factors its exact size need not be considered in relation to usable area per unit of population. Obviously an area intended for the use of the people of the entire city and/or region and equipped as indicated will be large. Two hundred and fifty acres may be accepted as a reasonable minimum size for a city of 100,000 population. There is no maximum size, particularly if the regional complex is to serve a metropolitan region.

SITE SELECTION

The selection of sites for parks rarely proceeds on the same basis as the selection of a site for a home or factory or school. In respect to these institutions there is a preconception of the kind of home, factory, or school for which the site is desired. A park or playground, on the other hand, is of variable dimensions and arrangement and can be adapted to equally variable site conditions.

Rarely does a city have enough capital funds for the acquisition of a number of ideally located parks or playgrounds at one time. Rarely, too, can it consider placement of a park on a site already improved for other purposes. Usually vacant, or largely vacant, land is selected, or, perhaps offered, and the park plan is adjusted to the site available.

Only in the largest and oldest cities has it been practicable to acquire sites for intown parks in already congested areas. This has been done in a few cases when the structures, usually homes, were obsolescent. Consolidation of enough house sites to constitute a park has been accomplished at tremendous cost. In such cases, also, the end result has been attained occasionally as part of overall urban rehabilitation or renewal.

So difficult has it been to procure adequate sites for parks and playgrounds that cities have been prone to accept, especially if offered as gifts, many sites that are ill suited to their functional purpose. Sites of this kind do not return to the citizens a fair share from the cost of their continued operation and maintenance. Sometimes in plotting a subdivision, especially on undulating or hilly terrain, odd parcels of land inadequate as building sites are donated to the city. Thereafter they become a constant charge for maintenance at public cost, when they should never have been approved at all. Unless such parcels can contribute toward a well-considered master plan of parks or playgrounds, they should not be accepted nor be permitted to exist without owner obligation to maintain them acceptably.

Neighborhood Recreational Sites

Planners should apply the following general rules at the neighborhood level to acceptance or rejection of sites, especially to the search for ideal sites:

1. If a site is to be selected for a neighborhood playground the first consideration should be whether the existing school has adequate

play space to serve both its own requirements and the needs of its neighborhood. If not, the best location for a municipal playground is adjacent to the school site, providing this property can be attained reasonably. If the school has adequate land, whether it is presently used to its fullest potential or not, the playground site should be selected in an area that may not be effectively served by an existing school.

2. A playground site adjacent to a school should be large enough to accommodate the conventional outdoor recreational activities, with consideration of the convenience of the school, the safety of users and neighbors, and the aesthetics of the neighborhood.

3. Since it is desirable to provide facilities on such a school-connected but city-owned playground for older children and adults, the area should be large enough to offer separation of groups with buffers to provide the segregation.

4. Every recreational facility should have park-like features, with grassed surface, shrubs, trees, and as much landscaping as the size of the site will permit.

5. The site should ideally be of sufficient size to include a building unless the school itself can be so appointed and operated.

6. Should a neighborhood site apart from a school be desired, it should be situated so as to serve a neighborhood considerably removed from the school, affording such a neighborhood services which are in some respects supplied by the school to its immediate environs. The same considerations affecting neighbors, safety, usable space, and landscape adornment would apply. Unless the neighborhood facility is limited to adult uses, it is advisable to design it to serve all ages. Demands and needs of the population of the neighborhood dictate the most logical uses of the site. Thus if there are no other places for the recreational activities of children and youth than such a park-playground, they will possess it. Consequently, it is well to determine the needs in advance and plan for them.

7. The site for a park-playground, especially when not attached to a school, should preferably be surrounded by streets. Improvement of the streets is as important to the park as to a homesite. If situated in a well-built-up neighborhood, where adjacent streets are not sufficient for parking, the site should have a parking lot (underground, if possible). The site should have sufficient level land to permit conventional games to be played on grassed surfaces and paved courts. Additional land for park-like treatment need not necessarily be level, in fact some undulation of terrain is advantageous.

8. A site must always be considered in relation to its soil both as to

fertility and suitability for recreational activities. Adequate drainage is also important.

9. Of paramount importance is convenient location. Ideally the park-playground should be situated in the center of a neighborhood with equal population on all sides, preferably surrounded by homes, several blocks deep, and improved in a manner equal to the yard improvements of its neighbors. If otherwise, it will tend to depress property values in its immediate environs. If properly planned, planted, and maintained, it will serve to enhance values in its neighborhood.

Community Park Sites

A community is a group of districts and must contain an enhanced or enlarged series of recreational spaces as well as essential neighborhood park and playground facilities. However, the community recreational site is intended to provide additional facilities that cannot be supplied in all districts. To serve its purpose well, it should be about 200 acres in area.

1. The site for the community recreational park should meet the requirements of a district park but should provide as much open space as can be afforded for its main function. Since it becomes, under good planning, the center of the community recreational life, it can hardly be too large. It is not intended to be regional in scope, attractions, or services.

2. It should be accessible to the people of the community by foot, bicycle, or mass transit system. Preferably, it should be surrounded by residential neighborhoods.

3. The site should be of such size and conformation as to permit the development of sports fields and courts, children's play apparatus, sylvan-like area for assembly and picnics, special unit for senior citizens' activities, swimming pool (outdoor or indoor), clubhouse, border and buffer landscaping, water features if practicable, interior parking lots, and the like.

4. Unique flora or geologic formations sometimes commend a site for selection as a community park, particularly if it has open land for functional development.

5. In a city composed of several communities, all community parks need not be similar in all respects. Community differences and adaptability of the sites to unique development indicate variable planning.

6. A high school property, although meeting some of the needs of the community park, rarely can satisfy all or most of the requirements. Juxtaposition of high school and community park is frequently advisable.

Regional Recreational Sites

More fortuitous than other recreational spaces or centers in their location, size, and natural resources are the regional recreational complexes. The public incentive to their initial acquisition usually arises because they are areas of extraordinary natural attraction or have previously been developed as large private estates. Frequently they are composed of submarginal land, that is, land unsuitable for homes or commercial uses. They are most likely to be situated on the periphery of intensive urban development, and often beyond the boundaries of a city. Although cities sometimes choose to acquire regional recreational complexes beyond their boundaries, counties and states or metropolitan districts are tending more and more to assume the responsibility for acquisition and operation of complexes.

FUNDAMENTALS OF RECREATIONAL DESIGN

Among the factors that guide the layout and design of recreational places are:

1. Functional use without waste or overcrowding.
2. Harmony or blending of all elements on any given piece of property for an overall coordinated complex.
3. Utilization of each site in terms of the main feature or facility to be located thereon.
4. Alternate uses of areas must be considered, and, where possible, multiple uses should be planned either at different seasons or during different hours of the day.
5. Facilities planned for night use should have as much illumination as required for efficient performance of the activity planned. Supplementary lighting of ancillary facilities (parking lots, sanitary conveniences, paths, and roads) should receive careful attention. Location of switch and fuse panels is important for control and economy.
6. Most direct access should be planned to those areas that are used by the largest number of patrons. The circulation of users of multiple facilities should be planned to avoid cross traffic or interference one with another.
7. Fencing may be utilized to define areas of play, maintain safe conditions, prevent interference of one activity with another, and facilitate control and supervision.
8. Placement of sports facilities should aid participant and spectator enjoyment. Orientation of facilities in relation to the path of the sun is important.
9. Terrain features should be utilized to add to the beauty and attractiveness of an activity area and unattractive vistas should

be screened from view by appropriate planting. Planting should be employed to break the force of prevailing wind and for shade.

10. Safety factors must be considered in the placement and orientation of recreational activities and in the selection of equipment and construction materials. Fire prevention and audience control measures must be considered.

11. Rest room facilities and services must be provided, including adequate sanitary units, water fountains, and parking areas.

12. Economy of space arrangement is important to promote efficient utilization of recreational facilities for sound management of public funds.

13. The recreational space and structures must be clean, well lighted, well ventilated, colorful, and of attractive appearance. They should add to the quality of the neighborhood and thus be considered an asset rather than a liability by neighbors.

Developmental Costs of an Adequate Recreational System

What is the cost of providing a city of 100,000 population with a system that would include all the necessary facilities for recreational opportunities? What is the annual cost of operating and maintaining it? It is impossible to estimate the costs exactly because:

1. Land and construction costs and operation and maintenance costs vary tremendously from city to city.

2. Exact specifications of what constitutes each unit do not exist.

3. No city builds all of its recreational system at one time or in one generation.

4. Each city dispenses with several features until, at opportune times, they are provided one by one.

5. Some of the facilities may be supplied and maintained by public benefactors or by privately financed agencies.

6. Cities that do not recognize the need for comprehensive planning may construct facilities or develop areas in response to special promotion, pressure, or vociferous minority demands, and thus provide one or more features at greatly enhanced, if not exorbitant, costs.

Nevertheless, if the recreational service system set forth in this chapter cannot be shown to be within the financial capacity of a hypothetical city of 100,000 people, it could hardly be justified as an adequate and practicable plan. Accordingly, all of its features have been itemized in Table 22-2 (although it is recognized that a community rarely will have so complete a system), and a rough estimate made of its costs. The estimated unit costs are based on averages among many cities and on experience in planning and administering the type of facilities included.

TABLE 22—2 SUGGESTED COMPREHENSIVE RECREATIONAL SERVICE SYSTEM FOR A CITY OF 100,000 POPULATION WITH ESTIMATED COSTS PER UNIT

	CAPITAL INVESTMENT	ANNUAL MAINTENANCE AND OPERATION
NEIGHBORHOOD RECREATIONAL CENTERS		
Land for 20 playgrounds:		
120 acres at $10,000	$1,200,000.00	
Improvements to land: grading, landscaping, fencing, play apparatus and equipment, wading pool, etc.		
20 grounds at $15,000	300,000.00	
Buildings: service building for playground and average of five rooms for group activities		
20 buildings at $25,000	500,000.00	
Operation: 20 centers at $6,000		$120,000.00
DISTRICT RECREATIONAL CENTERS		
Land for 4 district playgrounds: 120 acres at $5,000	$ 600,000.00	
Improvements to land: grading, landscaping, fencing, 8 tennis courts each, athletic equipment, etc.		
4 grounds at $30,000	120,000.00	
Buildings: field houses, gymnasium, small auditorium, club-rooms, service rooms		
4 at $200,000	800,000.00	
Swimming pools (outdoor): 2 at $145,000	290,000.00	
Operation of recreational centers: 4 at $18,000 (net cost)		$ 72,000.00
Operation of swimming pools (partly self-supporting):		
2 at $5,000 (net cost)		10,000.00
REGIONAL PARK AND RECREATIONAL COMPLEX		
Land: 200 acres at $1,500	300,000.00	
Improvements to land: landscaping, grading, park roads, athletic fields, 18 tennis courts, picnic grounds, trails, etc. (excluding special improvements listed below)	500,000.00	
Operation and maintenance (not including special facilities): ...		120,000.00
Golf course (self-supporting): 1	100,000.00	
Swimming pool (self-supporting): 1	165,000.00	
Stadium: 1	500,000.00	
SPECIAL FACILITIES		
Museum: 1	400,000.00	65,000.00
Public auditorium and exposition center: 1	2,250,000.00	135,000.00
Horticultural conservatory: 1	200,000.00	20,000.00
Zoological park: 1	750,000.00	200,000.00
General administrative overhead: computed at 5%		37,100.00
TOTALS	$8,975,000.00	$779,100.00
PER CAPITA TOTALS	89.75	7.79

TABLE 22-2 *(Continued)*

	CAPITAL INVESTMENT	ANNUAL MAINTENANCE AND OPERATION
Recapitulation		
Neighborhood and District Recreational Centers and Parks	$3,810,000.00	$202,000.00
Per capita	38.10	2.02
Regional Complex	1,565,000.00	120,000.00
Per capita	15.65	1.20
Special Facilities	3,600,000.00	420,000.00
Per capita	36.00	4.20
General administrative overhead (5%)		37,100.00
Per capita		0.37
TOTALS	$8,975,000.00	$779,100.00
PER CAPITA TOTALS	89.75	7.79

The schedule is presented to suggest the possible application of the advised standards to the problem of comprehensive planning, not to serve as a formula to be applied in any given case. It may prove helpful as an aid to better understanding of the whole problem of planning and financing public recreational service systems. It may also serve as a list against which elements of the comprehensive plan may be checked.

Relative Cost of Operation

Further light on the cost of operating the public recreational service system presented above may be derived from an interpretation of the cost in terms of the tax rate. Suppose the assessed valuation of the city were $300,000,000 or $3,000 per capita, which is a fair average for large cities. To yield an annual income of $779,100, which is the total cost of operation, it would be necessary for a tax to be levied at the rate of 77 cents per dollar. Although it is true that some of the facilities enumerated (public auditorium and exposition hall) might conceivably be provided and operated by the county or state government, a figure of $6 to $8 per capita for public recreational service system expenditures is considered quite adequate.

Whether American cities can afford the annual expenditure for the operation of their park and recreational service system and for the special facilities (museums, auditoriums, stadiums, art galleries) is no longer open to question. Financial support is available, and public recreational systems, being a part of the municipal family, are receiving greater support from the general municipal fund, or from tax dollars, than ever before.

Recreational Services to Be Rendered

Another interesting speculation suggested by the schedule of facilities and costs is the number of services such a system would make possible. A simple way of estimating this is to divide $779,100 (the total annual operating cost), by 9 cents (a fair average cost of individual services rendered by varied types of public recreational facilities). This gives a quotient of 86.5, which is an estimated total number of individual services or visits the system would produce. Considering this figure in relation to the population of the city, it means an average of 86 services or visits for each citizen or about one and one-half services per week. Some citizens will not claim any of the services and others, usually children and youth, will receive service almost daily.

These statistics are based on purely hypothetical situations. But they suggest that a public recreational service system with something of interest for all citizens and meeting the reasonable requirements of the modern community is not impossible of realization. On the contrary, with careful comprehensive planning it is quite readily attainable without imposing an excessive burden of taxation.

RECREATIONAL SURVEYS

The recreational survey is a product of research which cities, and to some extent counties, have found exceedingly helpful. Recreational surveys vary not only in subject matter and scope, but also in their immediate purpose. Some are intended as exhaustive compilations of relevant subject matter to serve as a reference guide for technical students; others are intended as a technical guide to the administrator; some are intended to inform the public; and still others are designed primarily as factual support for a definite recommended program.

An outline for a comprehensive recreational service survey of a city is given below. This type of survey provides a basis for planning physical facilities, spaces, program, and organization of a system to administer the public recreational service program.

Outline of a Comprehensive Recreational Service Survey

    A. *Geopolitical aspects*

        Topography and description of the physical nature of the city, including size, boundaries, street development, major traffic arteries, railways, industrial, commercial residential zones

        Method: City Engineer's maps, traffic surveys, public utility corporation files and maps, aerial photographs

    B. *Population statistics*

        Examination and analysis of the residential population: density of population by age, sex, race, and religion; distribution of population by occupation; distribution of population by economics; distribution of population by age, sex, racial, and ethnic groups

Method: U.S. Census, school enrollment, public utility corporation records, consular offices, foreign church records, parish and congregational records, chamber of commerce records, health, welfare, and other governmental records

C. *Social factors*

a. Social agencies: organization, finance, relationships, program; possible duplication and competition; unserved areas

b. Delinquency trends: problems, districts, kinds of offenses, remediableness

c. Public opinion concerning public recreational service

Method: Reports and records of the several social agencies, records of law enforcement agencies, records of school attendance officers and probation officers, interviews, analysis of news media, court records, juvenile or youth bureau records

D. *Economic factors*

Property and land valuation; housing; purchasing power; economic base definition; dependency; indigence and relief; unemployment; tax structures (tax rates, assessed valuation)

Method: Examination of records and reports of public housing and social work agencies; statistics of commercial and mercantile establishments, public utilities, chambers of commerce, U.S. Census Bureau, real estate bureaus, assessor's records, building permits, welfare department records, and the like

E. *Governmental factors*

a. Organization of city, county, or other governmental subdivisions

b. Organization of public agencies rendering recreational services

c. Policies, administrative practices, and program of public recreational service systems

d. Budgets of public agencies

e. Cost analysis of recreational services

Method: Examination of public records and reports, the city charter, interviews, and the like

F. *Physical resources for recreational service*

Analysis and description of areas and facilities available for public recreational activities, considered in relation to neighborhoods, districts, communities, metropolitan region

a. Recreational service system areas and facilities: neighborhood parks, playgrounds, and centers; district parks, play fields, and centers; community parks, athletic fields, and centers; regional complexes; golf courses; botanical gardens; marinas; auditoriums; stadiums; camp grounds; zoological parks

  b. Facilities and areas under school control; neighborhood school playgrounds; athletic fields of junior and senior high schools; gymnasiums; playrooms; auditoriums; music rooms; meeting rooms; science rooms; shops

  c. Facilities and areas under parochial school control

  d. Other community facilities: public libraries; other public lands, if any; public places for seasonal activities (beaches, winter sports); municipal auditorium, exposition hall, museums, art galleries

  e. Privately owned and institutional facilities: churches; lodge halls, clubrooms, youth-serving agency facilities; country clubs and facilities available for public recreational activity

  Method: Reports and records of the several agencies involved; original records derived from inspection, field trips, and investigation

G. *Evaluation of existing public recreational services*

  Park department (unless consolidated with recreational agency): policy concerning recreational use of areas and facilities; program of activities; extent of services

  Recreational service department: policies regarding promotion, organization, and supervision of activities; program; amount and quality of leadership; extent of services rendered

  Public school system: analysis of courses of study in relation to preparation for use in leisure; extracurricular program of activities and extent of participation; extent of use of school buildings and grounds for community recreational purposes and leadership provided for same; policies concerning extension of school services into the recreational service field

  Parochial school system (same as for public school system)

  Public library: policy concerning use of facility; program including forums, debates, classes; extent of services

  Churches: policies of individual churches concerning use of facilities; program including public discussions, forums, exhibits, classes; amount and quality of leadership; extent of services

  Group work agencies: Boy and Girl Scouts, Camp Fire Girls, Boys' Clubs, Settlements, Neighborhood Houses, YMCA, YWCA, YMHA, YWHA, and the like: program; facilities; membership; leadership

  Fraternal, benevolent, and protective organizations: number, type, and location; facilities; activities; membership

  Ethnic societies: number, type, and location; facilities; activities; membership

Commercial agencies: theaters, bowling centers, sports centers, dance halls, skating rinks, and the like: number, type, and location; facilities; measure of services

Method: Consult reports of several agencies; interviews, inspections, questionnaires, correspondence

H. *Recreational habits of the community*

Typical recreational patterns of various groups: elementary school boys and girls; middle and junior high school boys and girls; senior high school boys and girls; college and university students; employed teen-age boys and girls; men; women; family groups; racial groups; ethnic groups

Appraisal of status of community development in relation to special activities: athletics; music festivals, concerts, shows; art festivals, exhibits, competitions; drama festivals, pageants, productions, carnivals; civic life; special projects and events; traditional, historic, or commemorative events

Community traditions and mores affecting recreational activity

Method: Prepare schedules for selected groups to fill out, utilize communications media, interview leaders, investigate by contacting groups wherever found, consult transportation system representatives and the like

I. *Diagnosis of important recreational needs of community as revealed by this inquiry*

Space and facilities; supplies, materials, and equipment; programs and leadership; organization and administration; financial support

J. *Recommendations for program improvement, acquisition of space, and development of facilities*

The Perpetual Survey

Efficient administrators conduct continuous surveys concerning the work of their agencies. They have in mind all of the factors and information that affect the service and are continually adding to their fund of knowledge. Much relevant information comes to the administrator in the routine of his work. A survey file in which such data can be placed for later reference, properly classified and cross referenced for easy handling, is of practical value to the executive. Even though the information is never formally transcribed and rarely, if ever, published, it is of value to the superintendent as a basis for his own recommendations and public recreational planning administration. The data can be utilized to substantiate or justify administrative actions and policies if they are questioned. With these considerations in mind, some systems require the staff at various centers to make surveys of their immediate neighborhoods or districts and furnish outlines as a guide to the staff. There is little question that continuous analysis of the facts about the community's recreational service offering will afford valuable knowledge for the most effective planning possible.

Selected References

Bacon, E.: *Design of Cities* (New York: Penguin Books, Inc.), 1976.

Bannon, J. J.: *Leisure Resources: Its Comprehensive Planning* (Englewood Cliffs, N.J.: Prentice-Hall, Inc.), 1976.

Colang, G.: *Innovations for Future Cities* (New York: Praeger Publishers), 1976.

Dansereau, P. Ed.: *Challenge for Survival: Land, Air, and Water for Man in Megalopolis* (New York: Columbia University Press), 1970.

De Chiaru, J. and L. Koppelman: *Planning Design Criteria, 2d ed.* (New York: Van Nostrand Reinhold Company), 1975.

Hester, R. T., Jr., Ed.: *Neighborhood Spaces: User Needs and Design Responsibility* (New York: Dowden, Hutchinson and Ross, Inc.), 1975.

House, P. W. and E. R. Williams: *Planning and Conservation: The Frugal Society* (New York: Praeger Publishers), 1977.

Houghton-Evans, W.: *Planning Cities: Legacy and Portent* (New York: Beekman Publications, Inc.), 1976.

Jackson, J. N.: *Surveys for Town and Country Planning* (Westport, Conn.: Greenwood Press, Inc.), 1976.

McHarg, I.: *Design With Nature* (New York: Doubleday & Company), 1969.

Mumford, L.: *Urban Prospect* (New York: Harcourt, Brace & World, Inc.), 1969.

Olmstead, F. L.: *Public Parks and the Enlargement of Towns* (New York: Arno Press), 1970.

Osborn, F. J.: *Green-Belt Cities, 2d ed.* (New York: Schocken Books, Inc.), 1971.

Rosbach, R.: *The Provident Planner: A Blueprint for Homes, Communities, and Lifestyles* (New York: Wallace & Co.), 1976.

Shivers, J. S. and G. Hjelte: *Planning Recreational Places* (Cranbury, N.J.: Associated University Presses, Inc.), 1971.

Thomlinson, R.: *Urban Structures: The Social and Spatial Character of Cities* (New York: Random House), 1968.

CHAPTER 23

Maintenance Operation and Administration

The physical maintenance of recreational properties and equipment is one of the major concerns of public recreational service administration. This function is not always performed by personnel of the system. In many cities the recreational service system is responsible only for the activity program; maintenance is done by a separate department. The coordination of recreational activities with maintenance is difficult even when both functions are performed by a single department. The difficulty is increased sharply when coordination must be effected between two departments. The maintenance of all buildings, grounds, and facilities is subordinate to the activities program from the standpoint of the fundamental purposes of the system. In other words, the requirements of the program should dictate the kinds of facilities to be provided and, to some extent, the manner in which they are to be maintained. The recreational program is too often subordinated to details of maintenance with disastrous results. A recreational service system that does not control its own maintenance work is usually subjected to severe handicaps in bringing about the proper relationship between maintenance and program functions. Regardless of how a city is organized, however, the problem of detailed administration of maintenance and construction is fundamentally the same.

A department responsible for the maintenance of a system of recreational areas, structures, and other facilities located in different parts of the city views the problem of administration as having both local and general aspects. If only one recreational place is to be maintained, all duties of maintenance may be localized. In an extensive system certain maintenance duties may be economically and efficiently decentralized. In this chapter, routine maintenance refers to that performed by the

529

staff of a recreational center or place, and general maintenance refers to that performed by a staff organized to serve all units of the system.

ROUTINE MAINTENANCE

Routine maintenance consists of all indoor and outdoor janitorial and inspection duties. Indoor duties include the opening and closing of buildings and their rooms; sweeping, cleaning, scrubbing, and waxing; heating and ventilating; minor repairing and painting; and arranging furniture and equipment for indoor activities. Outdoor duties consist of collection and disposal of refuse; arranging equipment for outdoor activity programs; watering and marking fields and courts; minor grading of grounds; repair of walls, pipelines, and water fixtures; irrigating, cultivating, mowing, pruning, and fertilizing; and inspection of recreational equipment for wear or for hazards to users.

Care of Grounds

The objective of every recreational service system is to create an environment conducive to recreational experiences or activities. To achieve this objective, the smallest details of maintenance must be attended to because each step has a cumulative effect on the successful operation of the recreational program.

Since playgrounds and parks are looked on as havens of safety for children and adults, it is the responsibility of all departmental personnel to ascertain that no condition jeopardizing the health, safety, or welfare of participants or visitors exists. Any condition that might lead to injury of persons or damage to equipment or property should be remedied at the earliest possible time.

The department must supply the safest apparatus and equipment available, but such devices are not immune to wear or breakage, and require periodic inspection and, when necessary, servicing. Children's play areas should be serviced daily and the grounds should be level and free of objects that could result in injury. If immediate repairs cannot be made on faulty apparatus, it should be moved or closed to use.

Some of the hazards on playgrounds or other recreational places are dirty or unsanitary buildings and facilities; broken benches, windows, and park furniture; overflowing garbage and trash receptacles; cracked or damaged drinking fountains; and unsafe wading pools. These conditions may be remedied and, in most cases, prevented by systematically cleaning in a prescribed maintenance program and by repairing when necessary.

Insects can be controlled by judicious use of insecticides. Rodents can be treated with poisons, traps, and the elimination of conditions favorable for their breeding and existence. Toxic plants can be controlled by defoliants in amounts that destroy the noxious plants without endangering other growing things. Such herbicides must be used carefully to avoid ecological problems and to make certain that such materials are kept away from human beings and their pets.

Maintenance of Facilities

A number of places in every recreational service system receive constant use and require routine upkeep if they are to serve the public. Perhaps one of the most used places is the ball diamond. The intensive use it gets justifies full attention to the factors that can sustain it in good playing condition. The rubber on both homeplate and the pitcher's mound should be examined daily, for spikes can cut the rubber which might hinder the sliding or pitching activities by hooking into the rubber and injuring the player. Homeplate has a black margin that should be embedded below grade. All iron anchor pins at the bases should be slightly below grade, and the strap buckles should be placed under the sacks. The areas around homeplate and the pitcher's box should be hand-graded. The surface of the infield should be free of rocks, pebbles, or anything that may cause a ball to ricochet. All wire screening around the field should be free of holes and loose wire. The backstop should be kept in good repair so that there are no loose boards or splinters. All hose-bibs and waterboxes should be checked daily and broken lids replaced as soon as they are detected. The outfield should be kept free of holes. No trucks or heavy equipment should be permitted on any playing field unless there is an absolute necessity, and then only when the field is dry enough so that damage does not occur. Benches must have no loose, weak, or splintered boards, nor protruding nails or bolts.

Cement surface courts should be kept clean by sweeping and washing down at least once a week. All of the nets should be checked daily. The wire backstops should be free of holes and loose wire, and no shrubbery or vines should be permitted to grow inside the playing area. The pores of the cement surface sometimes become filled with material from players' shoes, creating a slippery, dangerous condition that can be remedied by scrubbing with trisodium phosphate, muriatic acid or, if the condition is extreme, sand blasting.

Horseshoe courts should be serviced according to the amount of play they receive. The boxes must be kept graded and moist. Stakes with burrs should be lifted and sent to the shop for grinding. The backboard must be solid and free of splinters.

Sand that is thrown or kicked out of children's play areas, playground, or sandbox should be shoveled back. When the sand is too dirty to clean by screening or raking, it should be removed and replaced with fresh sand. Dirty sand may be cleansed by sifting through a filtering material and washing.

Turfed areas present a challenge to the grounds keeper. Watering is, of course, the most important consideration, the frequency and amount depending on the type of grass, soil, weather, and other bionic factors. Not less than 3 inches of soil should be moist after a watering. Over-watering kills grass. Grass 4 to 5 inches in height will stand up better under play, retain resiliency, and hold moisture better than shorter grass. Grass should be mowed before watering and in a different pattern each time for a more finished look.

Watering of fields should be done as early as possible so the fields are playable at game time. After watering, all boxes should be checked for proper closure and hoses and sprinklers should be removed from the field. The sprinklers should be placed on racks, and the hoses should be drained and hung in tool sheds.

Perhaps the most difficult problem encountered by grounds keepers in maintaining playing fields is compactness of soil from heavy traffic. Watering is relatively ineffective due to lack of penetration, and bacterial growth, necessary to plant life, is hindered through sealing of the soil. Aeration may remedy the situation.

Weed control and edging in large areas are best done by spraying. For weed control on playing fields, 2-4-D and diesel oil are effective. For weeds growing through asphalt or cement, sodium arsenite is preferable, but extreme care must be taken in its application. Precise dosages must be determined and all directions adhered to to preserve ecological balance. No indiscriminate use of chemical substances should ever be a part of maintenance practice. Sodium arsenite or diesel oil may be used for lining playing fields, effecting a saving in lime and eliminating the ridge that usually builds up in the grass. Weed areas killed by sprays may present a fire hazard, which is best eliminated by controlled burning. Burning should only be done after consulting the local fire department or marshal, the regulations governing open burning, and securing the necessary permits. The permits will specify how and when the burning shall be done. When spraying is completed, the sprayer should be washed with detergent and rinsed with clear water.

Planting of shrubs and trees should have a definite purpose: wind-break, screening, canopy, partitioning or buffering, accentuation of archi-tectural features, landscape design. Each tree and shrub has a definite form of growth, and the natural shape of the plant should be maintained. Sometimes it is necessary to eliminate plants because they may have become a hazard, but this should be done only after the appropriate supervisor has been consulted for his approval.

Insect infestations are controlled by stomach poisons and contact sprays. The utilization of various insecticides should be rigidly controlled and all precautions undertaken to ensure that chemical damage to ani-mals and plants will not accrue. Care should be exercised in watering to keep the foliage dry.

Work on recreational areas should be scheduled on a routine basis. Schedules vary with different grounds and types of activities so flexibility and practicality are fundamental guides in devising them. A list of maintenance duties is posted on a work board by the director of the facility the day before the work is to be done. When large grounds have to be covered, it is advantageous to organize the crew to work sections, thus, all areas are allocated to particular individuals with concomitant responsibility for completion of tasks. When a center contains buildings and grounds, it is necessary to assign indoor and outdoor crews. Every member of the maintenance crew should be able to work any job on the grounds and provide assistance to his fellow workers when needed.

Time Schedule of Maintenance Workers

The daily cleaning of a recreational center is done most efficiently when it can be scheduled during the hours that the facility is not in use. Many systems require their maintenance workers to report early in the day so that their work may be completed before the afternoon crowds arrive. Beach cleaning crews sometimes report for work at 4 or 5 a.m. and complete their work before noon, working six and sometimes seven days per week during the summer season. Auditoriums are often cleaned at night. Some incidental cleaning and other work must often be done while activities are underway in the afternoon and evening, calling for varied schedules of hours for some workers. Each type of recreational facility has its own problem in this regard, and, for this reason, standardization of hours and duties for local maintenance workers throughout the system is inadvisable.

Truck Use

Trucking plays an important part in maintenance, and unless some thought is given to it, much time can be dissipated. Routing a truck properly cuts down unnecessary mileage. Trucks should drive around playing fields rather than across them. Speed in a park or on a playground should be as slow as possible, because no amount of time saved can justify injury to a client or damage to structures or equipment. The condition of the truck is the sole responsibility of the driver. Preventive maintenance should be practiced continually so that the truck is kept in a state of good repair and able to perform the work for which it was purchased.

Water Systems

Maintenance personnel who must water planted areas are responsible for and should be familiar with the care and operation of the water systems. Among the factors they must know are the location, type, and size of shut-offs, pipes, and connections, and the amount of water pressure available to each section. Personnel should use appropriate tools in the operation of water systems. Suitable wrenches or shut-off keys must be applied. Pliers or stilson wrenches should never be used to turn off any faucets, water hydrants, or gate valves. Inspections should be made to ensure that water boxes are closed and covered when not in use. Stand pipes should be clearly designated and marked so that they do not constitute a nuisance or hazard to walkers. Leaky or defective shut-off gates or valves must be reported to the supervisors responsible. Worn or broken leather washers on leaky faucets should be replaced. All sprinkler heads must be cleaned and kept in working order. Water lines must not be overloaded with too many sprinklers, which lowers the water pressure and makes the sprinklers ineffective or inoperable.

In order to minimize wastage and maximize growth, watering should be done when the soil is fairly dry. One or two deep waterings per week produce better results than several light waterings in the same period. Flower beds and tender shrubs are best watered in the mornings and/or evenings, in hot weather, and lawns should be given a thorough watering once or twice each week, depending on weather and local conditions.

Maintenance Tools

The proper care of tools and equipment utilized in a standard maintenance program of an entire recreational service system is mandatory. There is a definite safety advantage to the worker and his efforts are optimized in terms of effectiveness and protection from injury. Proper care and use of tools increase the length of useful service, promote efficiency, and guarantee economy.

Any tool or equipment having a wooden part should be inspected routinely to be sure that the piece is neither split nor splintered. The wood can be preserved by a coat of boiled linseed oil applied as a protective glaze, after first sanding the surface to remove any rough or splintery edges. Such a dressing used at 60-day intervals will extend indefinitely the period of useful service of tools or equipment thus maintained. The wood fiber is fed by the oil and enough will remain to harden on the surface and provide an excellent protection from water. Any wooden part that shows cracks or splits should be discarded. All tools should be thoroughly cleaned with an oily rag before they are stored at the end of the working day.

Gardening is much easier if the tools utilized are suitable. They should be stored on racks in a tool room. Proper tool maintenance and storage permit efficient handling and produce economies in time, effort, and tool replacement. All cultivating tools should be kept clean and sharp, wooden handles or parts treated with linseed oil, and nuts and bolts tightened and oiled. Garden hoses should not be exposed to the sun longer than necessary nor allowed to kink, and they should be drained prior to coiling.

Inspections of Areas and Facilities

Preventive maintenance requires a uniform inspection procedure to bring about the highest standards of recreational facility operation through the continual upgrading of physical plant by the use of appraisal methods. It is the responsibility of administrators at all levels to conduct regular inspections to ascertain the level of efficiency of the system of recreational facilities, structures, and grounds. The responsible personnel should conduct regular field inspections as part of their supervisory responsibilities and make corrections as required. All inspections made by personnel other than those of a specific recreational park, center, or other facility should be held by central office personnel. Administrative officers are responsible for the organization of formal inspections and for overseeing the establishment of routine inspection procedures.

Follow-up inspection is made by central office supervisors approximately 21 days after the formal inspection to determine the progress made by the facility administrator in correcting discrepancies noted in the inspection report.

Informal inspections may be carried out by any supervisor without notice. When inspections are being conducted, the inspector should report to the office of the facility director and inform him of his presence and be accompanied on the tour of inspection by the director or an appropriate designee, if practical.

A formal inspection is conducted at each active recreational area or facility within the system at least once every three months. The central office is responsible for setting up the schedule, and notification to each facility and area director should be provided at least ten days in advance of the inspection. Each quarterly inspection places special emphasis on a particular aspect of a park or other recreational facility operation. Major import is given to selected areas to be designated by the central office at the commencement of the inspection quarter, including accountability and maintenance; cleanliness; legibility and placement of signs; traffic patterns; emergency and safety equipment; and the like.

An inspecting team, including representatives of the various divisions of the department, is assembled by the responsible administrator. The administrator is the inspection team leader and is responsible not only for assembling the team, but also for team briefings and for developing the required reports. If at all possible without interfering with public recreational service, inspections should be carried out during the peak days and hours of operation.

Formal facility inspections are guided by written policy enacted by the department. Major areas for inspection are listed with sub-headings also provided. As particular items are inspected, they are checked off. Check-offs should not constitute the entire on-site inspection. During the course of the inspection, the inspector should make appropriate comments about items on the checklist. Any discrepancies should be identified by name, number, or other specific designation. All facilities should undergo inspection whether in operation or not, to determine proper security, cleanliness, and storage of equipment.

A formal inspection report should be forwarded to the facility director no later than one week after the facility has undergone inspection. It should detail whatever deficiencies are noted and any remedial activity to be taken. The report consists of a memorandum containing the inspector's comments. If the discrepancy is a repeat from a previous quarterly inspection within the same calendar year, the notation is to indicate it. Comments may be made on any checklist item, but unsatisfactory or superior ratings are explained in the memorandum on the inspection report.

Replies to facility inspection reports should be returned to the appropriate administrative office within seven days after the receipt of the report and all corrective actions taken should be explained therein. Responses to inspection discrepancies should indicate what action was taken and the date of completion. If the facility director disagrees with the inspection report, a justification is submitted by a memorandum attached to the inspection report when returned. All reasons for the exception are noted.

When the next administrative staff meeting is held after the quarterly inspection and when the various reports have been filed, there is a review of all unsatisfactory and/or superior ratings. Additional comments on the strengths or weaknesses of the facility operation are noted and maintained in the central files.

GENERAL MAINTENANCE

Every recreational center requires repair work, from time to time, that is beyond the ability or facilities of the maintenance staff. Either this work has to be let out to tradesmen and contractors or it must be done by department mechanics other than those regularly assigned to the center. Most departments choose to have such work performed by traveling department repairmen who are equipped with a light truck in which they carry the tools and supplies most likely to be required. They usually have a regular route bringing them to every center at least once each week. From the director of the center or from local maintenance workers, they ascertain what ordinary repairs are required and, if they have the necessary materials and tools, they proceed with the work. Extraordinary repairs or alterations are referred to the central office where they are given proper consideration. Each repairman is required to keep a record of his visits, the time spent at each job, and the work done. Costs of labor and materials are computed from the repairman's original record and are charged against the proper centers and budgetary accounts.

Maintenance Support

When it is necessary to secure maintenance support beyond the personnel or equipment of the recreational department, or when specialized projects call for special shop facilities, a central office record form is available so that the director of the recreational facility can initiate a work order. The several copies of the work order are forwarded to the proper review authorities for approval or reappraisal of the situation.

The project requiring specialized assistance should be described in concise terms, but in sufficient detail to enable all parties to understand and execute their respective roles. Diagrams may be utilized and attached to the official report form. The individual who originated the request or who is directly concerned and familiar with the project should be indicated as the person to contact for detail. When special requests are initiated, it is necessary to be aware that there is considerable time required to complete the work order. This period of delay is reflected in such variables as other priorities and the complexity of the request, as well as available men, materials, and/or other resources needed to complete the project.

Every effort must be made to anticipate specialized work projects that necessitate extraordinary maintenance support and they should be submitted at the end of the season for accomplishment prior to the opening of a facility or program the following season. If extensive materials or unusual supplies or equipment are needed for construction of the project, it may be necessary for these projects to be initiated as much as 18 months in advance so that consideration may be made in the budgetary process to secure the necessary materials.

On the satisfactory completion of a work order, the facility director forwards the original copy of the request for maintenance to the administrative section involved within 24 hours. Maintenance personnel check with the facility director or his designated representative at the completion of the project to inform him of the completion.

The section administrator charged with the responsibility for maintaining a control system reports the status of the work order requests on a bi-weekly basis. This report is published and circulated to the concerned supervisory personnel. It is the responsibility of the facility director to inform the administrative tracking section in every instance when an incompleted work order could affect the opening of a facility, program, or operations in an on-going program, so that appropriate expediting actions may be undertaken.

Maintenance support procedures should be followed for extraordinary situations except when an emergency arises. An emergency will be considered to be any condition that poses a hazard to persons or property, causes grave embarrassment, or threatens security. In such an event, the director of the facility involved or his appointed representative should call the responsible administrative unit advising of the situation. The necessary arrangements are undertaken immediately for the initiation of emergency actions concerning maintenance operations.

Nature of Repairs

Repairs normally call for mechanics with varied abilities. Some small painting jobs are done by repairmen but generally a large department requires enough painting to occupy the full time of one or more painters who travel from one job to the next. Many states require important plumbing and electrical repairs to be done by licensed plumbers and electricians in accordance with the codes governing such work. Special crews are also organized for pruning and spraying trees, especially if the department is responsible for maintenance of parkways and trees along streets.

Not infrequently an extraordinary repair requires the work of several men in order to be completed in the available time, as when a sidewalk must be dug up to get at a stopped sewer line, or a long section of fence blows down and needs to be replaced. To care for such emergencies, traveling crews are consolidated, extra laborers are employed, or the job is let out on contract.

Extra Help for Special Events

Every recreational service system has special events that necessitate maintenance work in addition to that handled by the ordinary crew on the premises. If bleachers need to be moved or built, temporary stages erected, ropes or cables stretched to control crowds, or stage properties moved, these needs are handled in the same manner as are extraordinary repairs.

The Central Shop

The central shop is a necessity in every system of recreational service: it is the headquarters for the supervisor of maintenance and for all centralized mechanical services; it is the place where materials required in maintenance are classified, stored, and prepared for delivery to the various recreational facilities and places; it is the site where seasonal equipment is put in order for the next use; and it is the place where tools and mechanical equipment are serviced.

Even the small department requires such a shop. Large departments must have elaborate central shop facilities and may have several shops consolidated at one location, including millwork and carpentry shop; painting shop; forge and machine shop; electrical shop; repair shop for keys, canvas goods, nets, play supplies; and a garage and automobile service shop. The garage is important even though automobiles and power equipment may be repaired by outsiders on contract. The storage, oiling, greasing, and routine servicing of department automobiles and trucks at the central shop contribute to longer life of the equipment, economical operation, and effective control.

Central Warehouse

Any department large enough to have a central shop also needs a central warehouse and storeroom for recreational supplies, materials, and equipment. Supplies are purchased in large quantities to obtain the advantage of lower prices from bulk or volume buying, and are then parceled out to centers on requisition. The dispensing of supplies from the storehouse requires careful control and accounting to keep proper cost records and prevent unauthorized use. The administration of the storehouse is not ordinarily a maintenance function, but is more properly related to the accounting division. The storeroom, however, is usually located at or adjacent to the central shop because it dispenses maintenance and construction supplies and is then accessible to transportation equipment used in delivery.

Costume Storage. Many departments assemble and manufacture numerous costumes for use in dramatic programs, which must be renovated, repaired, remade, and repacked. For convenience, the central costume storage and repair facilities should be situated at the central shop.

Horticultural Nursery

Still another central feature in a large department is the horticultural nursery. Many departments find it practicable to propagate their own shrubs and trees. In determining a suitable location for the nursery, consideration must be given to soil conditions, wind exposure, temperature, and sunlight.

CONSTRUCTION

The public recreational service department is concerned with the following types of construction:

1. Grading and paving of recreational and landscaped areas, roads, paths, and sidewalks
2. Installation of pipelines, water systems, sprinkler systems, sewer lines, septic tanks, and storm drains
3. Bridges in recreational areas
4. Installation of electrical illuminating systems for outdoor recreational areas

5. Manufacture and installation of fences, backstops, bleachers, and playground or other recreational area apparatus
6. Reinforced concrete swimming pools, wading pools, tennis courts, and similar structures
7. Frame, brick, and reinforced concrete buildings
8. Landscaping of areas
9. Manufacture of various types of equipment, apparatus, furniture, and fixtures
10. Manufacture and installation of piers, jettys, marina docks, and other marine facilities
11. Manufacture and installation of special facilities: shooting ranges for skeet, rifle, pistol, archery; picnic shelters, fireplaces, and lodges.

Contract Work Versus Force Account

In public work the question frequently arises as to whether the designing and construction shall be done by *force account*, that is, by persons already employed by the public department, or by private architects and contractors. Minor design and construction are almost always done by regular employees of the public department. In major construction, however, there is no uniform practice. Sometimes the structures are designed by personnel of the public departments and let out to contract; sometimes architects and engineers are engaged to make the design which is then executed by the public departments' personnel. So many variables influence the situation that a decision should be made only after deliberate consideration of all factors and with reference to each phase of the construction plan.

Electrical work and street illumination are handled on contract as are the construction of concrete walks and curbs and the dredging of lakes. Plumbing work, grading, paving, and landscaping, on the contrary, are done under force account. The procedure in each case is determined by whether the department has a continuously sufficient amount of work in any field to justify, develop, and maintain an efficient crew of workers of the type required. Even if a crew can be maintained, the wages of public employment and the prevailing wages in private employment, the condition of the construction industry, the relative efficiency of public and private employees in various crafts, the size of the project, the labor union situation and its effects on both private and public work, the time factor (emergency or routine situation), and similar matters must be considered.

Minor Construction

The recreational service department's staff of mechanics are also used for minor construction. Several of the larger recreational service system staffs do all of their own designing and construction except on the largest projects, such as building a stadium, public auditorium, or similar structure.

Letting Construction Contracts

Contract jobs are handled on a cost-plus basis or on a stipulated total bid. Contracts are let after bids on published specifications have been submitted and considered. Public agencies are usually required by law to accept the lowest responsible bidder. If the lowest bidder is not accepted, valid reasons indicating his lack of responsibility must be shown. If precautions are not taken in advance, incompetent or unreliable and irresponsible contractors may submit attractively low bids. The burden of proof of irresponsibility in cases of rejection is on the public department. To avoid this situation some departments first qualify contractors for bidding by having them fill out questionnaires stating their qualifications to do the work and giving reasonable evidence thereof, including financial ability, previous experience, quality of workmanship, and reliability. Only those who qualify are permitted to submit bids.

Plans and specifications need to be drawn in more complete detail for work let on contract than for work done under force account, not only to enable bidders to estimate their bids accurately, but also to ensure completion of all details of the work according to plan. Departments must, of course, employ inspectors to represent them on the job and check on faithful adherence to detailed specifications.

Designers

Every recreational service department that maintains its own facilities and does any construction can use the services of competent architectural draftsmen, topographic draftsmen, structural engineers, and landscape designers. Expertness in all these lines is rarely found in one person. A department with sufficient work to employ four draftsmen would do well to select them so that all of these special fields are represented.

Frequently the recreational service department calls on the city engineering or other departments for expert assistance in designing and supervising construction if not also in actual construction work.

Coordination of Design and Operation

One of the most difficult problems in construction is the coordination of design with operation. Designers are not usually familiar with the operational aspects of the agency and those skilled in operation are not adept in interpreting their needs to the designers. Regardless of whether designing is done on force account or on contract, every opportunity must be taken to have the designers become cognizant of the operating problems in relation to their design. Obviously, if the designing is done by the department staff, there is ample opportunity for the designers to become increasingly familiar with the operating requirements.

Manufacture of Equipment

Personnel of a construction and maintenance shop with equipment for repair may manufacture much of the equipment required in public recreational places. It is quite common practice for department maintenance workers to fabricate equipment such as bleachers, benches, desks, game tables, banquet tables, drinking fountains, shower mixing valves, filters, chlorinators, ladders, playground apparatus, tennis nets, marina docks, and similar structures or equipment. But mass-produced equipment can usually be bought more cheaply than it can be made by department mechanics. However, innovative equipment of the non-traditional, maintenance-oriented type usually found on most playgrounds may be best fabricated by force account. Until such time as playground equipment specifically and recreational equipment or structures generally are developed to meet the increasingly sophisticated demands of users, creative designers will be in high demand and should be utilized as part of the force.

MAINTENANCE WORKERS

There is as yet no standardization of titles for persons performing routine maintenance duties. The titles most frequently used are janitor, caretaker, custodian, grounds keeper, and gardener. Maintenance workers employed for routine work at recreational center buildings or other facilities are recruited from many different crafts and have a rating generally equal to that of semi-skilled laborers. Other titles normally utilized for maintenance workers indicate the type and level of skill nominally required for the position. Such employees are recruited from a specific trade market and their titles are well known. Thus, electricians, plumbers, and mechanics and the various specialties included therein are taken into consideration when the public department hires such personnel.

Supervision of Maintenance Workers

There should be some localized and responsible supervision of all the employees at each recreational facility or center. When two or more maintenance workers are employed at any recreational facility, the duties should be divided among them. One of the workers may be placed in charge of all the others without being relieved of routine work. Large parks and other recreational places with a number of maintenance workers frequently assign one to be the foreman.

When there is a facility director, he has responsibility for all personnel employed at the park, center, or area. Included in his authority will be maintenance personnel as well as program or other specialists operating at the facility. The maintenance employees should be subject to the instructions of the facility director insofar as the conditioning of the place for the program of activities is concerned.

If maintenance services are limited, a conflict sometimes arises as to the division of the time maintenance personnel are to spend in relation to duties dealing with the upkeep of the property and duties related to the facilitation of the program. The facility director must resolve this conflict. Because most recreationists lack experience in the mechanical trades, maintenance workers often require some supervision from the general maintenance supervisor. This supervision is important in the practical training of maintenance workers. Instructions by general supervisors to maintenance workers should always be given with the knowledge of the facility director who will have personal dealings with the maintenance force.

Maintenance Workers and Public Relations

Although the duties of maintenance workers are primarily concerned with physical maintenance of property, the workers often come into contact with the public. In the director's absence, the maintenance worker may be called on to maintain reasonable order, to answer inquiries courteously and intelligently, and to represent the department. He must present a creditable appearance consistent with the nature of the work he performs. Many departments prescribe a uniform for maintenance workers, which should be of a readily recognizable type, kept as neat and clean as the daily routine permits, and easily identify the worker either by a small name tag on right breast pocket or a distinctive decal or other emblem at breast pocket level or on the back of the uniform jacket.

Another important consideration is the moral attitude and conduct of maintenance workers. Their close contact with the public, and especially children and women, makes it doubly important that only persons with good reputations be employed. As a precautionary measure, some recreational service and public school departments require finger-printing and an investigation of previous records of all applicants, including transmittal of fingerprints to the Federal Bureau of Investigation at Washington, where a central index of all recorded crimes is kept. The Bureau furnishes confidential information on request to any public agency concerning records or files. The selection of routine local maintenance workers must be made with all these factors in mind.

In internal employee-department relations, the department has as much responsibility for maintaining good employee relations and morale in promoting loyalty and dependability as does the employee in performing competently and efficiently. Maintenance workers are sometimes called on to perform heroically in repairing damage or constructing innovative recreational apparatus. They discharge the daily routine of housekeeping and groundskeeping that is not as glamorous as that performed by recreationists in programming positions. In too many instances the work of the maintenance crew is taken for granted. That grounds are kept clean and centers are maintained in a manner conducive to attract participation, all but goes unnoticed because it is routine.

Public recreational service departments should recognize maintenance achievement on a periodic basis. Public presentation of certificates of award for maintenance, whether by scroll, plaque, banner, or other symbol, should be instituted by the department and given wide publicity throughout the system and to the public. For superior effort, monetary increments may be used as well as public ceremonies. Such distinctions may be made several times during the course of the year. Field inspections, carried out to determine any discrepancies between suggested standards of operational efficiency and actual practice, may be the basis on which awards are given for superior performance by maintenance personnel. Such awards can be based on:

1. Ability of the recreational facility to carry out its assigned mission
2. Size and complexity of the facility
3. Number of items inspected that meet the standards of the department
4. Efforts of maintenance personnel to correct any discrepancies prior to inspection
5. Promptness and vigor with which discrepancies are corrected
6. General morale of the staff judged by records, personnel turnover, or other criteria
7. Level of training of the maintenance staff in relation to their assigned tasks
8. Knowledge of maintenance staff of the general operation of the recreational facility and its programs
9. Public image presented by both personnel and the facilities
10. Efficiency in maintaining report deadlines and records
11. Efficiency in use of manpower assigned to the facility.

In whatever form or shape the recognition occurs, it does much to sustain employee morale, promote greater efficiency among workers, and promote loyal support for the department by the worker. Sound employee-department relations do much to stimulate good public relations as well. The demeanor of the worker reflects his goodwill and is almost always noticed by the public.

Selected References

Axler, B. H.: *Sanitation, Safety, and Maintenance Management* (Indianapolis, Ind.: Bobbs-Merrill Co., Inc.), 1974.

Conover, H. S.: *Grounds Maintenance Handbook, 3d. ed.* (New York: McGraw-Hill Book Company), 1976.

Corder, A. S.: *Maintenance Management Techniques* (New York: McGraw-Hill Book Company), 1978.

Higgins, L. R. and L. C. Morrow: *Maintenance Engineering Handbook, 3d. ed.* (Lexington, Mass.: Lexington Books), 1978.

Mann, L.: *Maintenance Management* (Lexington Mass.: Lexington Books), 1976.

Nathans, A. A.: *Maintenance for Camps and Other Outdoor Recreation Facilities* (New York: Association Press), 1968.

Sternloff, R. E. and R. Warren: *Park and Recreation Maintenance Management* (Boston, Mass.: Holbrook Press), 1977.

Stewart, H. V. M.: *Guide to Efficient Maintenance Management* (Chicago, Ill.: International Publications Service), 1963.

CHAPTER **24**

Program Administration and Practice

The problem of providing recreational experience to satisfy felt needs is one of great significance to the recreationist. As he gains comprehension of the problems of human behavior and human motivation, he must attempt to find activities that provide satisfaction and stimulation to participants. The activities a recreationist considers basic are those generally found to produce positive benefits. After comparing recreational experiences, the professional recreationist includes in his own program those appearing to have valuable outcomes.

ACTIVITY PROGRAM OF A RECREATIONAL SERVICE SYSTEM

The term *program,* as applied to a public recreational service system, includes the entire range of recreational activities for all ages on public grounds, areas, parks, and schools under various sponsorships. Many activities in the program are those public agencies organize, sponsor, and conduct, ranging from encouragement, promotion, and general oversight to face-to-face leadership. Other activities in the program are those sponsored by voluntary agencies desiring only the use of public facilities. Services performed by public agencies include the granting of a permit, the preparation of the place for the activity to proceed happily, assistance in the organization of groups, incidental instruction, protection from the incursion of others, or whatever may be required to enable the activity to succeed.

The whole program, for which facilities are customarily provided and which an agency organizes, promotes, and directs, requires the services of professional and volunteer leaders and consists of selected activities in the generic categories listed in the schedule of activities observed at a typical large park during one week in summer (see Table 24-1).

TABLE 24—1   SCHEDULED RECREATIONAL ACTIVITIES, AGE GROUP AND LEADERSHIP IN CITY PARKS

Typical Week, June 9—15

			AGE GROUP			LEADERSHIP	
		Children	Youth 15+	Adults	Professional (Department)	Self-Pro and Volunteer
MONDAY						
JUNE 9						
10:00—12:00	Tot Time	X			X	
10:00— 3:00	*Hollydale Senior Citizens			X		X
1:00— 3:00	Tot Time	X			X	
3:00— 5:00	Brownie Troop #1329	X				X
3:00— 5:00	Girl Scout Troop #89	X				X
3:00— 5:00	Girl Scout Troop #1418	X				X
3:30— 5:00	Creative Dance	X			X	
4:00— 5:00	*Baton	X	X		X	
6:00—10:00	South Gate TOPS Club	X	X		X	
6:30— 8:30	Boy Scout Troop #11	X				X
7:00—10:00	Women's Volleyball League			X	X	
7:00—10:00	South Gate Youth Band		X			X
7:00—10:00	South Gate Golf Club			X		X
7:00—10:30	Men's Chorus			X		X
7:00—10:30	Alanon Group			X		X
7:30—10:30	*Adult Round Dance			X	X	
7:30—10:30	Senior Citizens' Dance			X		X
TUESDAY						
JUNE 10						
9:00—12:00	Basic Arts and Still Life Class			X		X
10:00—12:00	Tot Time	X			X	
10:00—12:00	*Tot Time	X			X	
12:00— 2:00	South Gate Soroptimist Club Luncheon			X		X
1:00— 3:00	Tot Time	X			X	
1:00— 3:00	*Tot Time	X			X	
1:00— 4:00	Senior Citizens' Shuffleboard and Cards			X		X
3:00— 5:00	*Tap Dance	X			X	
3:30— 5:00	Junior Gourmet Club		X		X	
3:30— 5:00	Handicraft	X			X	
3:30— 5:00	Girls' Tumbling	X			X	
6:00— 7:00	Teenettes		X		X	
5:30—10:00	Firestone Retired Club			X		X
6:00—10:00	Better Weigh TOPS Club			X		X
7:00— 8:30	Paiute Indian Guides	X				X
7:00—10:00	Rythmettes (song)		X			X
7:00—10:00	Youth Band Parents			X		X
7:00—10:30	Songsters			X		X
7:15— 9:15	*Boy Scout Troop #485	X				X
7:30—10:30	Adult Round Dance			X	X	
WEDNESDAY						
JUNE 11						
8:00—12:00	Ladies Day — Golf			X	X	
9:00—12:00	"Good Morning" TOPS Club			X		X

TABLE 24–1   SCHEDULED RECREATIONAL ACTIVITIES, AGE GROUP AND LEADERSHIP IN CITY PARKS—(Continued)

		AGE GROUP			LEADERSHIP	
		Children	Youth 15+	Adults	Professional (Department)	Self-Pro and Volunteer
10:00–12:00	Tot Time	X			X	
10:00–12:00	*Tot Time	X			X	
10:00–12:00	Women's Volleyball	X			X	
10:00–12:00	*Women's Volleyball			X	X	
10:00– 4:00	Senior Citizens' Handicraft			X		X
12:00– 2:00	Rotary Club Luncheon			X		X
12:30– 2:30	Child Health Center	X				X
1:00– 3:00	Tot Time	X			X	
1:00– 3:00	*Tot Time	X			X	
3:00– 5:00	Brownie Troop #1515	X				X
3:30– 5:00	Hula Dance	X			X	
4:00– 5:00	*Boys' Tumbling	X			X	
4:00– 5:00	*Handicraft	X			X	
6:30– 8:30	Boy Scout Troop #11	X				X
6:30–10:00	Bees on Target TOPS Club			X		X
6:30–11:00	'49er Coin Club			X		X
7:00– 8:30	Seminole Indian Guides		X			X
7:00–10:00	Adult Table Tennis			X	X	
7:00–10:00	Adult Mixed Volleyball			X	X	
7:30– 9:30	Yoga Class			X	X	
7:30– 9:30	Dog Obedience Class			X	X	
7:30–10:30	Green Thumb Club			X		X
THURSDAY						
JUNE 12						
10:00–12:00	Tot Time	X			X	
10:00–12:00	*Tot Time	X			X	
12:00– 2:00	Kiwanis Club Luncheon			X		X
1:00– 3:00	Tot Time	X			X	
1:00– 3:00	*Tot Time	X			X	
3:00– 5:00	Ko-Ko-Ki-Wa-Can Camp Fire Girls	X				X
3:00– 5:00	5th Grade Camp Fire Girls	X				X
3:00– 5:00	Baton	X	X			X
3:30– 5:00	Drama	X	X		X	
3:30– 5:00	Boys' Tumbling	X			X	
4:00– 5:00	*Girls' Tumbling	X			X	
6:00–10:00	Keystone TOPS Club			X		X
7:00– 8:30	Girl Scout Troop #2010	X				X
7:00–10:00	Parks and Recreational Commission			X	X	
7:00–10:30	American Field Service Dinner		X	X		X
7:30– 9:00	Hopi Indian Guides	X				X
7:30–10:00	Mineral and Lapidary Board			X		X
7:30–10:00	Jobs Daughters Bethel #329 Parents			X		X
7:30–10:30	Business & Professional Women			X		X
7:30–10:30	Senior Citizens' Canasta			X		X
7:30–10:30	*Adult Square Dance Workshop			X	X	
7:30–10:30	City Employees Association			X		X

TABLE 24—1   SCHEDULED RECREATIONAL ACTIVITIES, AGE GROUP AND
LEADERSHIP IN CITY PARKS—(Continued)

		AGE GROUP		LEADERSHIP	
	Children	Youth 15+	Adults	Professional (Department)	Self-Pro and Volunteer
FRIDAY					
JUNE 13					
10:00–12:00 *Tot Time	X			X	
10:00– 1:00 Creative Design			X	X	
10:30–11:30 Tap Dance			X	X	
12:30– 3:00 Won O'Clock TOPS Club			X		X
1:00– 3:00 *Tot Time	X			X	
2:45– 5:00 Tap Dance	X			X	
3:30– 5:00 Pre-Teen Dance	X			X	
4:00– 5:00 *Junior Gourmet Club		X		X	
4:00– 5:00 Drill Team	X			X	
6:30– 8:30 Boy Scout Troop #11	X				X
6:30–11:30 Bridge Club			X		X
6:45–10:30 Southeast Horticulture Club			X		X
7:00–11:00 Woodman of the World Bingo			X		X
8:00–12:00 T.A.D.I.C. Dance		X			X
SATURDAY					
JUNE 14					
9:00–11:00 Tennis Instruction		X		X	
9:00–12:00 Youth Band		X			X
9:30–11:00 Archery Instruction		X		X	
9:30–11:00 Bryson Avenue Blue Birds	X				X
10:00–12:00 Girl Scout Troop #1154	X				X
10:00–12:00 Stanford Avenue Brownie Troop	X				X
10:30–12:30 O-Da-Ko Camp Fire Girls	X				X
12:30– 2:30 Family Reunion	X	X	X		X
1:00– 3:00 Cub Pack #459-C	X				X
2:00– 4:00 *Park & Recreational Dept. Show "Circus"	X				X
6:00–12:00 Bachelors 'N' Bachelorettes Square Dance		X		X	
7:30–10:30 Senior Citizens' Bingo			X		X
7:30–11:00 *Adult Square Dance			X		X
SUNDAY					
JUNE 15					
11:00– 3:00 1965 Royal Matrons & Royal Patrons Assn.			X		X
1:00– 5:00 Senior Citizens' Social and Shuffleboard			X		X
1:30– 5:30 Bachelors 'N' Bachelorettes Round Dance			X		X
2:00– 6:00 *Pre-Teen Square Dance	X			X	
2:30– 4:00 High School Baccalaureate		X		X	
3:00– 6:00 Game and Varmint Hunters			X		X
7:00–11:00 Adult Singles Club			X		X
TOTALS	54	17	56	52	67
GRAND TOTALS			127		119

* Locale Hollydale Park. All others Recreational Park.

Types of Activities at a Typical Park

On perusal of the activities listed in Table 24-1, it becomes apparent that they are but a few of the innumerable experiences that could occur at a park or other recreational place equipped to accommodate them. Quite a different list could be planned if the program were one that had sprung solely from the interests, skills, and enthusiasms of the recreationists assigned to the center. The fact is that activities are preeminently an expression of the interests of the people in the community. They represent the prevailing recreational culture of the community. This, naturally, raises the question whether the establishment should endeavor to provide for the activities the people want and sometimes demand, or whether it should present a program deemed to be best in the opinion of the leadership of the agency. In this respect the basic principles of recreational programming differ from the principles applying to the preparation of curricula of public schools. In the latter case the curriculum (program) is determined by educational experts on the basis of their judgment of what knowledge, skill, appreciations, and general competencies are necessary to prepare children and, of course, the whole population to serve the needs of the individual and society. The needs are considered in terms of good health, economic competence, family responsibility, civic service, spiritual inspiration, happy living, preparation for leisure, and the like. Decisions are greatly influenced by tradition and public demand, but practice over many years has developed standards. Recreational programming, on the other hand, begins with what the people want, but it does not default in exercising enlightened leadership to influence the selection of recreational activities and to guide the behavior of people in the direction of socially acceptable goals. This calls not only for adroit leadership, but also for highly qualified and inspired professional preparation of recreationists.

In the park previously referred to as typical, inquiry was made as to the leadership provided during a typical summer week. It was determined that, of 119 separate and distinct events or sessions or scheduled practices, 52 depended on professional leadership provided by the recreational service department and 76 depended on both professional and volunteer leadership supplied by a non-departmental agency. Another fact noted was that, of 127 separate activities, 54 were organized for children, 17 for teen-age clientele 15 years of age and older, and 56 for adults, including senior citizens. The table indicates the various breakdowns of time, activities offered, age group responding, and leadership provided.

Programs for children require a great deal of attention by recreationists and volunteer helpers. The older the clientele, the less personal attention is required, except that the highly organized competitive activities do not prosper without competent direction and organization. It may be necessary to make resource personnel available when instruction or other direct counseling is required so that participants gain full benefit from their performance. Teen-age clientele cultivate their own leadership if permitted to do so. Among adults competent leadership can always be recruited.

That activities for teen-agers are considerably in the minority is somewhat symptomatic of programs of all youth service agencies (see Appendix A). Except for the mass activities of high schools and extracurricular participation in seasonal sports, youth drop out of agency programs in numbers that are giving concern to the long-established agencies, owing partly to the fact that many young people, perhaps one third to one fourth, enter the employment market in part-time jobs. It is also due to the unprecedented mobility of this age group today. Recent studies indicate that half the teen-agers leave their home city for recreational purposes one or more times per week and that only a fourth do not own or have access to an automobile.

In organizing and promoting programs in public recreational centers, it is desirable to achieve a balanced program. Balance should be sought in the involvement of all age groups of both sexes, and in the distribution throughout the days and hours, day and evening, of the week. More particularly, there should be balance among the types of activities so that attractions and opportunities for recreational experience are available for all, with wide variation in recreational preferences and aptitudes, and degree of competence in participation. Balance also implies that groups of people standing in special need of recreational experience and leadership are not denied them.

Important as the function of leadership of people and programs at recreational centers may be, it must be appreciated that professional leadership is sparsely supplied. Public school teachers outnumber recreationists by 50 to one. The ratio in individual cities is about the same. If a public school offers a public recreational service daily and year round primarily out-of-doors with some community activities indoors, one to three recreationists are usually employed, some of them perhaps on a part-time basis. Custodial employees are additional. A municipal park is staffed more generously, usually because of longer hours devoted to the recreational program and to more facilities. Again the custodial and maintenance employees outnumber the recreationists. These observations emphasize the fact that recreational programs depend largely on volunteer leadership and that many activities in the program are directed by leadership provided by those using the public facilities by permit.

The foregoing generalities do not always apply, however. In a school system that has adopted the "community-school" plan (Flint, Michigan, New York City, and Chicago) in which the school directs the recreational

TABLE 24-2   PROFESSIONAL LEADERSHIP PERSONNEL—HOURS PER YEAR PER 1,000 POPULATION

Typical City—50,000 Population

COMMUNITY	SCHOOLS			PARKS*		TOTALS	
	POPULATION	HOURS	HOURS/YEAR/ 1000 POPULATION	HOURS	HOURS/YEAR/ 1000 POPULATION	HOURS	HOURS/YEAR/ 1000 POPULATION
COMMUNITY NO. 1 4 Elementary schools 1 High school 1 Tot lot	11,810	6,884	584	—	—	6,884	584
COMMUNITY NO. 2 2 Elementary schools 1 Junior high school 1 Tot lot	21,840	3,060	140	—	—	3,060	140
COMMUNITY NO. 3 2 Elementary schools 1 Park and pool	9,939	1,864	188	23,438	2,348	25,202	2,547
COMMUNITY NO. 4 1 Elementary school 1 Park 1 Tot lot	6,438	—	—	5,632	875	5,632	875
TOTALS RATIO	50,027	11,808	236/1000	29,070	581/1000	40,878	817/1000
PERCENT			29		71		100

* Two parks have professional supervision. Tot lots are supervised by volunteers.

program, in respect to activities requiring face-to-face leadership, employed personnel in the program division far exceeds those in similar programs in the public parks. This is not to say that the schools serve more of the public than do the parks, where participation is heavier in informal and mass activities with outside leadership.

Examination of the administration of public recreational service in the "typical city," as compiled in Table 24-2, reveals some interesting comparisons. The city is divided into four communities on the basis of several demographic factors (river, freeway, utility rights-of-way) that impede communication from one to another. The total professional leadership hours assigned by the schools and by the recreational service department were computed. Although there are 11 schools offering recreational programs and only two parks, the park programs provided 71 percent of the professional leadership hours and the schools 29 percent; the computation, it must be emphasized, was based on the hours per year per 1,000 population. Inequalities in the deployment of leadership in the four communities are also apparent. Community number three with one fifth of the population of the city has three fifths of the professional leadership. The deployment of leadership is allocated largely on the location of facilities. Inventory of space and facilities by the same communities revealed similar inequities between them. This has occurred because the city chose to develop a very large park of 90 acres in one community, believing that its service would be spread throughout the entire city of eight square miles. This proved to be only partially correct, for the community in which the park is situated enjoys three times the service in terms of enrollment and attendance in activities than two others, and ten times as much service as the fourth community. Had the city been properly planned, four community parks (recreational centers) would have been developed, one in each of the four communities, not necessarily as large as the 90-acre one.

School-Operated Recreational Programs

The preceding discussion concerned recreational programs taking place and conducted under various auspices at the public parks in a "typical city." Tables 24-3, 24-4, and 24-5 show the organization of recreational programs at elementary, junior, and senior high schools in the same city. The principal difference between the park programs and the school programs is that the latter contain activities, each under the leadership of school-employed personnel. In addition to the scheduled activities shown in the tables, hospitality is extended to other agencies in the city to conduct some of their programs on the school premises, more particularly indoors than on school playgrounds, which are already occupied by the schools' own activities.

TABLE 24–3   TYPICAL WEEKLY RECREATIONAL PROGRAM AT ELEMENTARY SCHOOL PLAYGROUNDS AFTER SCHOOL[1]

HOURS	MONDAY	TUESDAY	WEDNESDAY	THURSDAY	FRIDAY	SATURDAY
9–3	Regular School Day Program					10–12 Physical Recreational Activities: (Sports, apparatus, shuffleboard, marbles)
3–4[2]	Physical Recreational Activities: Apparatus, games of low organization, circle games, relays, basketball, dodgeball, jump rope, quiet games, indoor games, kickball, tetherball, shuffleboard, marbles, tournaments. Several activities for different age groups can be conducted at the same time					12–12:30 Lunch
4–5[2]	Arts and Crafts: Drawing, clay work, woodwork, copper work, puppetry, painting	Storytelling & Play Acting: Listening to stories, reading aloud, pantomime, plays	Music and Dancing: Singing, folk and square dancing, listening to music	Weekly Special Events:[3] Hobby show, handicraft exhibit, doll show, parties, bicycle activities, movies—scheduled films or other audiovisual materials		12:30–1 Quiet Games: Checkers, caroms 1–2:30 Arts and crafts: Choice of handicraft 2:30–4 Play Acting: Choice of music, dancing, storytelling 4–5:30 Physical Recreational Activities
	If specialists in these areas are available, they should visit the playground once a week to initiate and conduct these activities					
5:30–7:30	Seasonal Special Events:[3] Family Night—a special event for the children and parents held at least once during the summer; it may include father-and-son or mother-and-daughter nights, crafts display, open house, circus, watermelon feed, family barbecue					

[1] Playground centers are open on Sundays whenever need is apparent.

[2] The time schedule should be planned to meet the needs of the children. If sufficient leaders are available, it is recommended that all activities be offered concurrently, beginning at 3 p.m. and continuing throughout the afternoon.

[3] Some special events, such as play days, track meets, holiday festivals, school bus excursions, and pageants, require a rearrangement of the regular program for that particular day.

TABLE 24-4 TYPICAL WEEKLY RECREATIONAL PROGRAM AT JUNIOR HIGH SCHOOL PLAYGROUNDS DURING VACATIONS[1] AND SCHOOL DAYS

HOURS	MONDAY	TUESDAY	WEDNESDAY	THURSDAY	FRIDAY	SATURDAY
10–12	Physical Recreational Activities: Basketball, softball, volleyball, tetherball, handball, kickball, track, swimming, badminton, table tennis, quiet games					Physical Recreational Activities
12:30–1:30	Movies (Same time each week)	Quiet Games: Charades, checkers, chess, carams, cards, quiz games			Rollerskating (same day during alternate weeks)	Quiet Games
1:30–3	Arts and Crafts: Wood, metal, plastic, leather work, jewelry, model making, sewing, ceramics, painting				Weekly Special Events: Trips, tournaments, handicraft exhibits, bicycling, talent show	Choice of Arts and Crafts
3–4	Dancing and Music: Social, folk, square dancing, singing, listening to music	Clubs: Hobby, photo, music, art, book science	Dramatics: Puppetry, pantomime, plays	Clubs: Art, ceramics, library, stamps, charm		Dramatics: Puppetry, pantomime, plays
4–5	Physical Fitness Activity: Coaching events involving strength, endurance, agility, daily practice					
6:30–9	Family Night: Special event for children and parents at least once during summer, such as father-son night or picnic	Community Recreational Nights: Choice of activities, such as basketball, volleyball, quiet games, music, dramatics, clubs, arts and crafts			Fun Night or Dance	Team practice night for sports; choice of other activities

[1] The closing hour for centers varies according to the needs and desires of each community. Playground centers open on Sundays whenever community need is apparent. Use of facilities by families is encouraged. Junior high schools accommodate more varied programs, schools having gyms, larger grounds with turf, lights.

TABLE 24–5 TYPICAL WEEKLY AFTER-SCHOOL RECREATIONAL PROGRAM AT SENIOR HIGH SCHOOLS AND JUNIOR COLLEGES

HOURS	MONDAY	TUESDAY	WEDNESDAY	THURSDAY	FRIDAY	SATURDAY	SUNDAY
10–3	*School in Session*					(1) Physical fitness activities on field and in gym	Physical fitness activities on field and in gym
	No recreational programs except at social centers in junior colleges					Basketball, football, track and field events, volleyball, baseball, badminton	Basketball, football, track and field events, volleyball, baseball, badminton
							Many father-and-son activities; mother-and-daughter activities
5:30	*Interscholastic Athletics:*				Social recreational night		
	No recreational programs except in junior and senior high schools and for special groups in dramatics, music, and crafts at senior high schools						
6:30–10:30	*Community Recreational Hours:*				Sports night, fun night, or dance	(2) Special group use	Special group use
	Intramural physical recreational activities on fields and in gymnasiums					Church leagues	A.A.U. leagues
	Touch football, basketball, track and field events, baseball, volleyball, badminton, gymnastics, swimming, physical fitness activities					Industrial leagues	Church leagues

(1) All-city special events for boys and girls are held on Saturdays in the following: badminton, table tennis, chess, fly casting, fishing derbies, volleyball, rifle shooting, archery, golf, swimming, tennis, barber shop quartet singing, modern dance, shows, and other activities.

(2) Sports fitness centers operate on Saturday evening.

PROGRAM ORGANIZATION

Program is the fundamental reason for the public recreational service system. It represents the basic concept of recreational service. Citizens are attracted to the recreational place because they expect to be entertained, amused, satisfied, or otherwise be a part of the enjoyment, excitement, and social action that accrues to both spectator and participant. Planning is essential to programming. It is the development of many different activities into a combined schedule, integrated, supportive, and having some relationship regardless of the distinction drawn by categories or major classes of activity. It is the presentation of various activity forms, active and passive or in combination, in such a manner as to stimulate some participation. Functionally, program is everything occurring in a recreational context at, in, or on a recreational place. The program is viewed as a dramatic interplay of events in the routine course of human events. Such confrontations deal with peer relations, spontaneous activity or performance, modified behaviors, adherence to prearranged schedules, conformity to particular codes, individual adjustment to changing conditions, and the free exercise of the individual's desire to achieve as far as such activity does not infringe on the rights of anybody else. The program, then, is the coordinated effort of the recreational service system to organize, administer, guide, lead, direct, or offer resources so that people may lead more satisfying recreational lives. Programming, in the strictest sense, means those planned activities that the system sponsors, organizes, or for which it provides leadership. The program, on the other hand, is all those activities that can or may occur at a recreational place. They consist of spontaneous, organized, routine, special, recurring, or intermittent activities through which people seek recreational outlet and value.

The experiences that take place at public recreational facilities of various kinds are known as the public recreational program. What responsibility is accepted by public recreational service agencies in relation to this program? Is their responsibility limited to the provision of facilities and to the exercise of essential control, to the protection of public property, and to the regulation of the patrons' behavior? Or is it their responsibility to assume full control of the recreational program and to permit on the public recreational facilities only activities that they have organized and promoted in accordance with certain preconceived objectives? These are two extreme viewpoints and many adherents to either view can be found. The park movement in America was built on the former concept. The playground movement in its early stages was concerned primarily with the welfare of children and tended to conform to the latter view. Schools that assume limited responsibility for public recreational service usually start with the concept that the school program of recreational operation must be conducted by teachers or recreationists employed as teachers and that the program must be of a curricular and extracurricular nature designed to accomplish certain educational values.

Modern public recreational service systems generally take the middle course. The modern recreationist recognizes that certain types of facilities should be available for "free play" or unscheduled individual activities and for self-organized and self-directed group activities. He is also aware of the need for a certain amount of promotion and organization to multiply the number of activities and participants in the program and to make for greater efficiency and larger usefulness of the public facilities. He also appreciates the necessity for supervision of activities and the provision of positive leadership by recreationists so that educational, social, and cultural outcomes may be realized.

THE BALANCED PROGRAM

Activities permitted and conducted by the public recreational service agency are countless. However, they may be classified into large categories for easier understanding and practical grouping. The normal recreational life of children and adults includes selected activities from all these groups. Each major grouping contains an infinite variety of subcategories which can be profitably utilized to provide a continuing series of interesting, challenging, and new experiences to the participants. The tendency to emphasize one category to the exclusion of others is a frequent error in programming that must be avoided. The groups may be graded from simple elementary forms to complicated expert forms. The following recreational activities have usually served as the basis for a well-rounded public recreational program.

Arts and Crafts. The creative activities enable individuals to express themselves freely. These self-determining acts translate ego-centered involvement outward in a healthy process of self-realization. The individual is able to forget the normal restrictions of social custom and thereby answer a felt need for originality.

Music. The value of music to the individual varies from person to person. The effect that music has on the individual, either as a participant or as a spectator, illustrates its unique attraction. Whether music is listened to for the pure sensual pleasure of sound, for the aesthetic effect, for the rhythm produced, or whether the individual plays or sings himself, empathy and emotional release are apparently generated. There is hardly anyone who does not appreciate some form of music.

Motor Activities: Games, Sports, and Exercise. The enhancement of physical vigor, improvement of physiologic functioning, and release of hostility or sublimation of socially disapproved feelings through competitive experiences or individual acts in a social setting provide satisfaction. Although many people take part in gross motor activities for achievement and self-realization, significant behavior toward others is also developed. Activities include group and individual sports and games, team sports, calisthenics, and other competitive or non-competitive forms.

Social Activities. Social needs are satisfied when people have to meet, mix, "get along," or adjust. Social activities of a wide scope have a place in any program in which socially approved actions and good mental health are objectives. The relationships developed through social intercourse contribute to the maturity of individuals, the development of empathy, sympathy, catharsis, personal esteem, and self-expression.

Hobbies. Hobbies offer engrossing, stimulating, and sustaining interest in an activity usually not connected with vocational experience. Hobbies include any human activity. A hobby provides an outlet for creative self-expression, self-determination, and self-realization, and fulfills the need for gregariousness, since hobbyists come into contact with one another as they explore manifestations of their particular interest.

Dance. Dance in its many forms is popular since it deals with the universal and basic need for movement. It is a process of symbolic communication, expressing many sentiments as well as serving as a fulfillment of emotional and physical feeling. It satisfies ambivalent desires and may be one method by which human beings satisfy hostility urges in socially acceptable ways.

Drama. Drama is a form of communication through the human voice and body. As a communicative process it gives satisfaction by transmitting ideas and emotions and providing self-expression either vicariously or directly. The elements of catharsis and empathy are closely related to dramatic reproductions.

Social or Civic Service. Service is concerned with all activities normally associated with altruistic or humanitarian programs. Social service activities have long been utilized by recreationists to fill leisure productively whereas other forms of activity may not satisfy the human urge to extend sympathy or give aid. The release one obtains from wholeheartedly giving service to others, the exchange of too much self-concern for self-giving, results in a feeling of warm satisfaction. No other experience provides this sense of personal extension.

Education. All experiences are educational, whether or not the participant is conscious of learning. Some learning takes place in formal settings (school); other learning is informal (recreational activities). Although it is true that nearly all recreational activity results in some learning, there are specific educational aspects of recreational experiences. A formally organized class in baton twirling, social dancing, or fur-coat remodeling closely approximates a classroom situation. Adult classes offered by the public recreational service department are both educational and recreational. Even formal subject courses, taken during leisure, may be recreational.

Camping and Nature Study. Outdoor activities of many kinds belong in a well-balanced recreational program. One of the most requested and important is camping. Camping combines many skills and satisfactions. Wilderness camping, in particular, provides the participant with the exhilaration that comes from being close to unspoiled nature. There is need for some camping activity in every recreational program, because all people have a traditional attachment to nature and instinctively seek to refresh themselves after the artificial environment of urban living.

All these activities should be part of the balanced public recreational program, for each activity contributes its part to the overall program. It is important for the public recreational service agency to offer a comprehensive and balanced program.

PROBLEMS OF PROGRAMMING

The program is not an arbitrary measure imposed on people; it is planned, developed, and operated in response to their needs. In establishing a new program, it is desirable to offer a wide range of activities to discover where participant interest lies. By developing only the specific activities for which there is a distinct call, the agency does not run the risk of spreading itself too thinly. It also places its program on a firm groundwork of interested participants. Although this may be ideal for budgetary reasons, it does present a negative aspect as well: the program may become unimaginative and stagnant. Because a particular activity meets the needs of some individuals does not mean that the agency is fulfilling its full potential. There must, therefore, be constant evaluation and appraisal of the program. The department must continue to build and actually create demand by stimulating the interest of the public in new and varied activities. It must offer its constituents opportunities to grow recreationally; it must provide the means and the leadership to allow participants to find new wholesome methods of expression in leisure.

Each type of public recreational place presents its own peculiar problems in program organization and promotion. Some recreational places are established primarily for a single specialized recreational experience. The program at such places tends to become a matter of mere routine. The patrons desire only to be granted freedom to pursue their interests and enthusiasms with a minimum of interference. Program administration therefore consists primarily in arranging the physical facilities for efficient use, issuing permits for use, establishing regulations governing use, and promoting activities to ensure maximum participation. Programming administration on these recreational places may be in the organization of certain competitive events, staged shows, carnivals, or town barbecues.

Factors for Consideration

Some scheduled activities may require no special organization of players in advance and may be engaged in at the whim of the player. These undirected activities (or free play) tend to become a routine for certain regular attendants. Other activities, particularly group and team games, class meetings for instruction, or group participation, must be planned in advance and scheduled for a given time and place, usually taking place again and again, but according to schedule. Still other activities occur only once and require preparation for days and sometimes weeks in advance and terminate in a performance or demonstration. These are the eagerly anticipated spectacular events that sustain interest in the program.

Relative Value of Activities. The routine activities are of greatest value from the standpoint of development of the powers and skills of the individual, because they are repeated day after day and their effects are cumulative. Their developmental value increases in proportion to the frequency of their repetition. The special events are valuable chiefly because of the preparation and instruction required to make them possible, and because they sustain interest in a program that might otherwise tend to become commonplace and monotonous.

In planning the recreational program, care should be taken to observe a balance between routine, scheduled, and special projects. If only routine activities take place, the recreational program is dull, uninteresting, and lacking in novelty. If the program is dominated by scheduled events to the exclusion of freedom of choice, it tends to become regimented. Preparation for and staging of frequent special events under high pressure often remove much of the joy and spontaneity that should always be evident in recreational activity. By careful study of the recreational complex and the interests and needs of its patrons, a coordinated program involving all types of activities can be developed.

Patrons Involved. Some people prefer only to "drop in" at recreational centers or other facilities and participate informally as the whim strikes them, or they prefer not to take part in any scheduled contests or meetings. Others come only to attend special events either as performers or as spectators. Still others come only by appointment to meet in a regular class or play a scheduled game. Some parents permit their children to attend a recreational facility only when a scheduled event is to take place. At every center, playground, or other facility, a regular clientele is almost always present and ready for anything. The program should be planned to provide some attraction for all these potential patrons.

Patron Assistance in Program Planning. The participant-planning

19

technique is a process whereby interested individuals help to plan activities. The program does not develop in a vacuum; it is the product of selected ideas, directed interests, and self-stimulating experiences. Participant planning is necessary to the continuing success of the program. The ideas generated from such groups are essential for the development of future activities. The ideas of patrons are important and may even be highly significant to program outcomes. When potential participants have a hand in developing the program, they will feel, and rightly so, that the activities are theirs. They develop a closer feeling for and responsibility toward the program. As a result, they derive much greater value from their efforts, they find the activities more stimulating, and they bring new ideas and views to what might become mere professional routine. Recreationists should utilize participant planning in attempting to satisfy the recreational needs of the public.

Playground Programming Problems. Other types of recreational places (playgrounds and recreational centers) are established for participation in varied activities by patrons of all ages. Many of the activities desired are those calling for organized group participation. The playground and the recreational center are also distinguished from other specialized recreational places in that they have specific educational objectives, requiring program planning of a particular sort. Therefore the problem of program administration presented by playgrounds and recreational centers is unique, concerning primarily the centers with more or less complete indoor and outdoor facilities for a varied program for adult and child participation. The principles set forth, however, apply also to centers that are not so complete in their appointments.

Scheduled Activities

The activities schedule enumerates the activities provided by any given recreational center or playground. Among the possible activities are those termed informal routine, recurrent, and special events. All activities conducted or sponsored by the recreational service department staff are scheduled so that prospective participants may know when those of particular interest to them are to be available. Even free play activities are listed so that children's parents are made aware that their services may be enlisted for supervision.

Informal Routine Activities. It should be the objective of the recreationist to encourage and initiate as many informal routine activities as possible. Ideally the center should be so attractive and well-equipped as to appeal to boys and girls and men and women at all hours of the day. The customary equipment should include play apparatus; areas and supplies for athletics; a natural area; and a recreational building with materials and tools for indoor activities.

It must be remembered that routine activities are not all spontaneous;

many of them are planned by the recreationists in charge. But the planning must not be obvious. The most common criticism of recreational programs is that they are repetitious and monotonous. Interesting ways to use the equipment must be constantly invented and taught. New non-equipment games and events must be introduced; old games and events should be revived. The director should be constantly thinking of new stunts, new emphases, new variations to suggest and introduce so that the center comes to be thought of as a place where something new and different is going on all the time. The recreational center is a place at which to spend free time. Once there, however, patrons should find many incentives and invitations to do interesting things and experience new thrills in learning.

Recurrent Activities. Recurrent activities are engaged in by appointment and are usually group activities such as clubs, classes, and competitions in which so many members take part that a given time and place must be set aside for them. These activities are repeated on a daily, weekly, or monthly cycle until the schedule is completed, the season is concluded, or the program is finished.

Many of the scheduled activities are self-managed. When the courts, fields, gymnasiums, and meeting rooms are not required for staff-directed activities, they are usually made available to self-managing groups. Recreational facility directors should aim to organize as many groups of this kind as possible without entirely relinquishing such staff control as may be necessary. The development of an extensive program of adult recreational activities at any center requires this technique; otherwise the number of groups is limited by the size of the employed staff. Also, the educational value of the activity is often greatly enhanced when the group manages itself and participates in the selection of its own leadership.

Special Events. The special events at every recreational facility are the occasions that give "spice" to the program. They attract new patrons, discover new talent, provide an incentive to practice, give an ever-changing flavor or emphasis to the program, and create opportunity to secure some educational outcomes not otherwise possible. Their variety is endless and limited only by the imagination of the recreationist in charge and the participants who may assist in the planning. In general they fall into nine classes:

1. Demonstrations of skills learned
2. Exhibits of objects made or collected
3. Performances before an audience
4. Special contests
5. Mass group participation in any activity practiced primarily in small groups

6. Social occasions
7. Excursions to places of interest
8. Spectacular displays
9. Special instruction.

It is a common error in planning and staging special events at recreational centers to emulate too closely the standards of professional entertainment and to expect comparable performances. The recreational amateur theater cannot compete with professional theater or with other forms of commercial entertainment. Moreover, the objectives of professional entertainment are wholly different from those of the recreational program: the former caters to audience approval only, whereas the latter endeavors to provide satisfying experience for the performers. In recreational events the entertainment of the audience is desirable but secondary.

Special events should provide opportunities for as many as possible to participate. They must be truly representative of activities learned at the center and should be the incentive for days, if not weeks, of preparation. Such preparation, however, should not be arduous, but in the spirit of good recreational endeavor.

Programming

Every recreational center should have a daily, weekly, monthly, seasonal, and yearly program. The recreational center director will find it helpful to chart the program for the whole year, marking those events during the year (opening and closing of the school, holidays, thematic projects, historic events, and seasonal emphases) that will influence the program. The program for each month or season may be worked out in more detail as the year progresses.

The program for the week should be posted in a conspicuous place so that all may see it, become interested in its activities, and be free to suggest other stimulating experiences. The daily program is the recreationist's plan of work for the day. The director plans each day's work in advance, always including something new or interesting and never depending wholly on the inspiration of the moment. He may also avail himself of a lay planning committee for additional help in formulating the program.

Playgrounds formerly tended to overschedule activities. Each half hour was devoted to some scheduled practice or class activity and frequently to instruction. Such regimentation had its advantages in that it ensured emphasis on varied activities and kept the playground patrons informed as to when each activity was to take place, but it made insufficient allowance for novelty and for freedom of choice by participants. The playground took on a schoolroom atmosphere. Scheduled events should be the framework within which the program develops, but they should not preclude unscheduled activities.

It is inadvisable to prescribe the same program for all the centers and playgrounds in a public recreational system, although a coordinated series of events and some special activities may be observed throughout the system. These are set forth in a master program for the entire year, announced in advance. The program of each facility should be designed for and adapted to the needs, interests, traditions, and organizations of the neighborhood, the programs of other agencies, the completeness of the facility itself, the available professional leadership, and the skills, talents, and prior experiences of the people residing in the neighborhood. These factors vary greatly between any two recreational centers. The director of each facility should be given freedom to establish the program for his center with no more control from the central office of the department than seems necessary to ensure a well-balanced and varied program.

The program is only a plan. Numerous unforeseen situations may arise, which dictate necessity for a change in the program. To adhere blindly to prescribed or preconceived programs devitalizes the recreational facility and its activities. To arouse the new interests of people, to capture their transitory and changeable focus of attention, and to involve them in newly programmed events are a real test of the recreationist's discernment, leadership, and skill.

No recreationist can have at his fingertips at all times of the day all the information necessary to conduct a successful program. The individual director finds it helpful to build up—for his facility and for his own personal and professional use—a library containing materials on all phases of the activities that he organizes and conducts. The director who refers again and again to such material generally has the most diversified program.

The physical equipment and the planned activities are not the only attractions at the recreational center. The opportunity to meet others under congenial circumstances is one of the most compelling incentives to attendance. The program should be set up to provide happy social occasions. Similarly, the possibility of negative experience should be minimized. For example, if the use of the equipment is attended by bickering, if timid persons are imposed on by aggressive ones, if orderly persons are intimidated by rowdies, many prospective patrons will stay away. Definite supervision to prevent such obnoxious behavior is important.

PROGRAM CONTROL

Every recreational service department is faced with the problem of determining what policy will afford the most comprehensive program for the satisfaction of public recreational needs. Certain rules and regulations have to be established and enforced if the most effective service is to be provided and if good order and maximum utilization of program opportunities are to be engendered.

Intramural versus Intermural Activities

All recreational agencies must decide whether their own controlled program of activities should be conducted on an intermural or intramural basis. This problem arises more in connection with the athletic program than with other activities. The early playground systems proceeded on the theory that each center should have a representative team in each of the standard sports, which should compete in leagues and tournaments with similar representative teams from other playgrounds. To encourage wider participation, teams were organized according to age, weight, or other factors tending to equalize competition.

One of the results of this procedure was to cause recreational directors to confine their service largely to those skillful enough to qualify for places on the representative teams. The early days of the playground movement were characterized by an oversupply of physical education graduates whose preparation often focused on the coaching of athletic teams. Directors became coaches who were more interested in producing winning teams than in performing varied services for the larger numbers of participants who were not likely to become members of representative teams. The inherent weaknesses in the intermural plan led to its complete abandonment in many cities in favor of intramural competition. Winners of local contests were not matched with winners from other centers. The emphasis was placed instead on the organization of as many groups as possible at each center and on the organization of local schedules with enough groups to make competition interesting.

The present tendency is to combine both plans and derive the advantages of both. Intermural competition is limited to teams that have participated in a qualifying intramural schedule or tournament during a preliminary season at the home center. This encourages the participation of the largest number possible in the local preliminaries and, at the same time, takes advantage of the special stimulation provided by competition with representatives from other centers. Various means are employed to tone down the importance of the intermural competition to avoid the evils of overemphasis.

Awards

The granting of trophies or other awards of intrinsic value to winners of recreational competitions is now regarded as inimical to the development of good attitude by participants. It emphasizes winning rather than participation. It develops an attitude of unwillingness to participate if the prize is of insufficient value. It also discourages from entering competition those who have little or no chance to win. The present practice is to grant no awards or to present only awards of insignificant intrinsic value, such as ribbons or certificates. Group awards of plaques, cups, and banners are favored over individual awards since they emphasize group cooperation. The granting of inexpensive awards is justified on the ground that they serve as a permanent record of achievement and an incentive to participation and improvement.

Transportation

The intermural program conducted by some recreational agencies raises the problem of transportation of participants and recreationists. A successful program requires participants to keep appointments made for them. To ensure their arrival, it is often necessary to organize their transportation. If they are young, a director or volunteer worker must accompany and supervise them while traveling from one center to another. If a recreationist must travel with representative groups, his home center will be understaffed during his absence or a substitute must be employed. For a director to travel with a single team while a potentially large number of patrons at the home center remains unattended or insufficiently supervised is inefficient and indefensible. The cost of employing a substitute should be measured against the value derived from the program requiring the worker to travel.

Other problems also arise. Shall the department pay the cost of transporting participants, particularly children? If not, will the participants be able and willing to pay for their own transportation? Can volunteers be secured to transport them in privately owned automobiles? Should the director transport the participants in his own car? What liability attaches to the volunteer, the recreationist, the agency, or the city in the event of negligence resulting in accident and injury to those transported? If the worker leaves one center and goes to another to conduct an approved event is he "on duty" while en route? If he has transported some players, with or without authority, does liability in the event of accident or injury attach to the agency, to himself, or to both? These and similar questions are not significant in the small city, but in the large city they loom as major problems and the answers to them have much to do with the determination of policy concerning intermural activities.

The answers to these problems depend on the legal variables which exist from city to city and state to state. The policy governing the program of recreational activities and the administrative control of one of the largest departments of public recreational service is outlined below. It is unlikely that smaller departments will have to formulate so comprehensive a policy statement for the control of their activities. However, these statements may serve as guides for any department whose schedule of activities includes similar features.

A Recreational Director will be entitled to *adjusted time off* under the following conditions:

(1) When he works more than his scheduled hours in any one day.
(2) When he works on a holiday (except Saturday).
(3) When a holiday falls on his regular day off. Such times off shall be taken within the period of four months after the extra time worked. Adjusted time off will not be allowed unless the extra time worked was authorized in advance by the supervisor concerned, or was connected with regular or special activity planned for, and recorded in the current program for the center.

Time allowed for approved *off-ground* and *overnight trips.* The following regulations apply to time allowed directors for group or club activities off-grounds:

(1) Recreational Assistant relief up to six hours per month is available, when needed, to permit the director to be off ground with a group or club. This is in addition to the budgeted playground operation.
(2) If a director takes groups or clubs on outings on his or her day off, and if this is only a daytime function *not to be followed by an overnight period,* the director may be credited as working up to eight hours; provided the District Director and/or supervisor has given prior approval to the event.
(3) On overnight trips, credit up to eight hours will be allowed for overnight time. This is in addition to the work hours normally scheduled on the preceding day.

Activities Conducted Away From The Recreational Center

(a) Directors at all recreational centers schedule special activities away from the center itself. These include inter-playground and inter-district competitive events, department playdays, outings, visits to cultural events, trips to various camps, weekend camps, etc. While these special activities provide "spice" to the routine program, they should be scheduled with caution, because they take the Director away from his home center. The Director must always realize that his first responsibility is attention to the program of the recreational center.

(b) Activities scheduled away from the home center usually involve the transportation of youth and/or adults. Except for the rare furnishing of transportation by the department, the basic responsibility for such transportation rests with the patron, his parents, or responsible volunteers.

In many cases Directors use their own automobiles to transport patrons, although the department never has required that Directors use their own cars for this purpose.

Directors who do not have personal liability insurance are in a difficult position in case of an accident, and there is no legal way in which the City can relieve the Director of his personal responsibility.

(c) All directors who plan away-from-the-center events, not officially scheduled, shall make written application furnishing information as to the type of the event, date, hour, number in group, and names of volunteer leaders. This request is to be sent to the District Director for his recommendation and forwarded to the responsible Supervisor for approval. For each proposed absence away from the center, this specific permission must be secured *in writing* and in advance.

In order to schedule any activity away from the center, the group must number at least fifteen (15) and, where the group is of any appreciable size, it is advisable to have at least one adult for each ten (10) persons making up the traveling group.

(d) Directors are reminded that when children leave the recreational center, they must exercise good judgment in providing for the safety and well-being of the members of the group; this includes someone *remaining with the group* at all times.

(e) For any activity away from the center which includes the transportation of minors, the Director shall use the "Parents' Request Form" or some other notification, to the parent, of the intended trip, and secure permission from the parent or guardian for the minor to be included in the group. Under no condition shall Directors permit minors to make scheduled trips without specific parent's or guardian's permission, in writing. The "Parents' Request Form," referred to above, may be requisitioned from the shop.[1]

Parental Permission

Requesting a signed statement from parent or guardian of a minor participating in any body contact activity or in an intermural activity requiring transportation from one playground or center to another has two benefits: it improves public relations and it indicates that the departmental authorities are concerned with the welfare and safety of the minors. It also alleviates many problems that occur when minors are transported to distant facilities or when there is some inherent danger in the physical activity. Usually the parent is requested to fill out a form that gives permission for the child to participate in a given activity, especially if the activity occurs away from the neighborhood playground or center. This device is being increasingly utilized by administrators of public recreational service departments. If the agency does not not seek parental permission for out-of-neighborhood or off-center activities, it runs the risk of litigation as a consequence of tortious acts. Legally the parent cannot sign away the minor's constitutional right to sue, if the results justify suit; however, judicious utilization of the parental permission form may mitigate legal hazards that might accrue without the grant of consent.

Physical Examination

The physical activities of the recreational agency should contribute to the health of the participants. Physical fitness is one of the stated goals

---

[1] *Administrative Manual,* Department of Recreation and Parks, City of Los Angeles, California, 1958. Quoted by permission.

of the department in conducting such activities. The demands placed on
players in strenuous physical activity require that the player be adjudged
physically fit to participate, by competent medical authority, before he
engages in the activity. The agency should require medical examinations
for all persons participating in activities of a strenuous physical nature,
particularly, if these activities are individual, dual, or team competition
in leagues and tournaments. This examination should be mandatory for
minors and discretionary for adults. Such examinations should be administered prior to actual participation or as required during the activity.
Examinations for participation in departmental activities should preferably be performed by the individual's family physician. It is unlikely
that any department will employ a physician for this purpose. However,
the agency should point out that competent medical examination may
be administered at any free public clinic or health center. This examination may effectively restrain those who cannot tolerate extremes of
strenuous physical activity from seriously injuring themselves or impairing their capacity to enjoy normal participation in the future. By
requiring such an examination, the department also effectively reduces
possible liability suits resulting from athletic injury. Mandatory medical
examinations at least indicate that reasonable and prudent care was taken
to prevent undue strain on the individual.

Self-directed Groups

The program of every well-equipped recreational service agency includes many activities not directed by professional staff members of the
agency but which take place on agency-controlled property. These range
from entirely self-initiated and self-directed groups, which merely use the
public recreational facilities, to agency-formed groups conducted on a
self-managing basis. They are usually not children's groups but are composed of youth and adults, including athletic teams, athletic clubs, choral
societies, bands, orchestras, glee clubs, hobby clubs, drama groups, and
the like. If they are open to the general public with no restrictions save
interest in the activity and ability to participate on a comparatively
equal footing with other members, they are generally regarded as public
and not private groups. They are welcomed by recreational service departments and are freely granted the use of facilities. As a considered
policy this appears more and more to be a trend in public recreational
program development, especially in programs for older youth and adults.

In relation to group activities for youth and adults, the public recreational department becomes largely a service agency. It discovers common
interests around which groups may organize. It arranges meetings, schedules, demonstrations, and competition that provide incentives to group
participation. It often provides group leadership only in the initial stages,
seeking as rapidly as possible to put the group on a self-sustaining and

self-led basis. It may also provide technical or advisory guidance as requested or required by the group.

Athletics. Commercial enterprises and industrial organizations form a convenient unit around which to arrange teams and leagues. A letter is sent to the heads or personnel managers of such agencies advising them of the intention of the recreational service department to form an industrial or commercial league in the appropriate activity and suggesting that a representative of the firm be sent to an organization meeting. Representatives who attend this meeting discuss details of classification of teams, eligibility and playing rules, available facilities, entrance fees, expenses likely to be incurred, and the like. An executive committee is formed which assumes jurisdiction. Thereafter the representative of the recreational department draws up the schedule, assigns the places of competition, and assists the committee in the conduct of its league, all in accordance with regulations previously approved by the department. Thus a great volume of recreational activity is induced by a minimum amount of organizational services.

Music. The members of high school glee clubs about to graduate are canvassed to ascertain how many would desire to continue their musical experience after graduation. If a sufficient number indicate such a desire, a meeting is arranged at a public recreational center at which plans for the formation of a choral society are discussed. An organization is formed and a competent leader is chosen. Perhaps the department itself will provide a leader for a season while the group, which is self-governing, gradually assumes more and more of the expense of leadership until it becomes wholly self-managing.

Self-directed groups have a tendency to get beyond the control of the public recreational service department even though their activities take place on department facilities. To maintain a proper liaison between the groups and the department, it is often advisable to require a recreationist from the department either to be a member of the executive committee of the group or to hold an ex-officio position. Another plan that works well is to require all groups not under the immediate direction of the department to file their constitutions and bylaws for approval. Charters good for one year are issued to organizations that comply with departmental rules. On expiration of a charter, the status of the group may be reviewed and its privileges withdrawn, renewed, or modified.

Private Use of Public Facilities

The use of public facilities for recreational activities by private groups whose membership is exclusive is often permitted by recreational service departments if the facilities are not required by public groups. Permits usually set forth the regulations governing the use. Some departments charge for such permits, especially if the group wants to charge admission. The charge is determined by the cost of making the facilities available, the ability of the group to pay, and the purposes for which the proceeds are to be used. If the proceeds are to be used for public benefit, the charge is usually low; if the proceeds are to be used for private gain, the charge is determined on a commercial basis.

Private exploitation of the public and of public places for monetary gain must always be guarded against. Professional promoters organize teams, enter them in leagues, and endeavor to derive profit from collections at games. Private teachers give instruction at public recreational centers and charge for their services. Vendors of commodities solicit business in recreational areas. Promoters, in the name of charity, hold "benefit" performances which benefit no one but the promoter. These, and many ingenious forms of exploitation, must be constantly detected and prevented by reasonable regulations.

Non-recreational Use of Recreational Places

The use of public recreational places is often requested for purposes not of a recreational nature. Auditoriums in recreational centers are sometimes used for civic meetings, political gatherings, and religious services, and athletic fields for outdoor rallies of various kinds. A board or department in charge of recreational facilities should take the view that the facilities are intended by law for public recreational purposes and should develop a program that will keep them well-occupied by recreational activities. There will be occasions nevertheless when applications for non-recreational uses must receive respectful consideration. Then some fine distinctions must be drawn. A civic purpose must be such in fact as well as in name. Occasions organized for purposes of propaganda should be discouraged, if not prohibited. Political meetings should be permitted only if they are nonpartisan. Religious gatherings, if permitted by law in public tax-supported places, should be nondenominational or interdenominational. It is impossible to lay down rules of guidance that will serve all cases of non-recreational use of public recreational places. The best or most expedient rule in a given situation depends on the state and local laws involved, the interpretations of the laws, and local traditions and attitudes. Some departments find it advisable to limit non-recreational uses by establishing schedules of special charges for such use of the facilities.

PROGRAM SUPPLIES, MATERIALS, AND EQUIPMENT

The successful conduct of a recreational program requires not only suitable areas and structures but also supplies, materials, and equipment. Goods consumed in the maintenance of structures or operation of the program are termed *supplies. Materials* consist of all wood, metal, paper, sand, clay, liquids, and other goods that are formed into objects produced in program activities. More durable items, consisting of expendable goods utilized for maintenance or in the recreational program, are termed *equipment*. Articles are classified as equipment when they are considered to have a useful life of more than one year.

Supplies and equipment required in the maintenance of properties are usually furnished at agency expense. Supplies and materials used and consumed by participants in recreational activities present a problem. It is not advisable for a public recreational service agency to be lavish in the provision of such supplies and materials. In most states textbooks and other supplies are furnished at state expense to children in the public schools. This is justified because children are required by the state to attend school and, if all are to enjoy equal educational opportunities, essential supplies and materials must be provided for all. In public recreational service, however, participation is voluntary. Moreover, public recreational service budgets are still too low to allow generous furnishing of all goods required in the program. Practice is not uniform among recreational departments but the following general rules may be deduced.

Supplies, materials, and equipment should be furnished:

1. for group activities when the item in question is used by the whole group or groups (basketballs, tennis nets, baseball bats).
2. generously for children but sparingly, if at all, for adults.
3. for individual activities when failure to provide material would definitely render a highly important activity impossible to conduct (handicraft materials in very underprivileged neighborhoods).
4. for demonstration purposes in order to get an activity started but which, when under way, will be furnished by the participants (tonnettes or harmonicas to initiate interest in playing these instruments).
5. when the cost of supplying the activity is insignificant or relatively low (inexpensive handicraft materials for children).

Supplies, materials, and equipment should not be furnished as a general rule:

1. when the activity requires an item peculiarly adapted to individual use (fielder's glove, gymnasium shoes, musical instruments).
2. when the cost is high in relation to the use derived (tennis racquets, badminton shuttlecocks, fencing foils).
3. when the item is easily stolen (handballs, arrows, tennis balls, golf balls).
4. when tradition favors individual possession of articles (marbles, tops, roller skates).
5. when the article can easily be made by the participant (kites, model planes, cars, boats).

6. when the supplies are to be utilized elsewhere than at the public recreational place.

Inventories

The individual recreational facility, as well as the entire recreational system, must maintain an inventory of its supplies, materials, and equipment. Only with an inventory will the department be able to control the cost of issuance and replacement and be able to make cost analyses for accounting purposes and to justify budgetary requests.

A perpetual inventory is maintained at all centers in the system. If facilities are open for public use only seasonally, the inventory is taken at the beginning and end of the season. Notations of items used or delivered to the facility should be made on appropriate forms. A certain amount of loss through damage, wear, or theft is to be expected. The facility director, however, must make every reasonable effort to account for all items in his custody.

Check-out

A procedure for the issuance of supplies, materials, and equipment must be developed to ensure the return of loaned articles. It is advisable to establish a list or index of all supplies, materials, and equipment on hand at the recreational facility. If patrons using the facility are not registered, they should be required to produce some identification when any item is issued. The participant's name is checked off when he returns the item.

Although there is less danger of loss or theft on a small playground or at a center where the recreationist is acquainted with all of the patrons, there is great likelihood of loss in a large recreational center that is heavily patronized and where the recreationist cannot know all of the participants, particularly when the center is utilized by transients.

Responsibility for Supplies, Equipment, and Materials

Efficient operation and conduct of program call for systematized handling of supplies, materials, and equipment. Failure to provide the needed items may cause serious delay and unnecessary inconvenience. Materials, supplies, and equipment represent substantial costs and render imperative the avoidance of waste, loss, and damage.

Central Stores

Quite apart from the issuance or loan of supplies, material, and equipment to patrons are the establishment and maintenance of central stores or stocks. The following procedures are found to be efficacious:

1. A central stockroom should be established for all departmental supplies, materials, and equipment, for all areas.

2. Responsibility for the central stockroom should be lodged with one employee with complete authority to receive and issue items to the several divisions of the department.

3. Location of the stockroom should be convenient to all divisions and secure against unauthorized entry.

4. Stock must be organized to facilitate issuance. Items should be indexed by established code for easy reference and fast location.

5. Supplies should be issued only on written requisition as authorized by departmental policy. A record should be maintained that indicates all items issued and entries should be posted from a requisition file. The record indicates the date of issuance and the division, section, or office to which it was issued.

6. Ordering dates should be established and adequate stocks, based on the rate of consumption, should be maintained.

7. Periodic inspection of supplies, materials, and equipment should be made to determine whether they are being utilized in the proper manner.

A Sample Program

The program of a selected recreational and park complex in a large city is outlined below. It is cited to illustrate its comprehensive character, although the facilities, program, and leadership are more highly developed than in most recreational parks. The activities have been listed as informal routine activities, recurrent scheduled activities, or special events. The numerous items under the last two headings were copied from the weekly reports of the center. The routine activities were observed during several visits.

Alpha Recreational Center or Park

Area: 15 acres

Investment
Land	$100,000
Structures	200,000
Improvement to grounds	100,000
Total	$400,000

Operating budget
Total average yearly budget .... $ 35,000

Outdoor equipment
    Baseball diamond, lighted
    Soccer and football field (overlapping baseball diamond)
    Softball diamond, lighted
    Basketball, volleyball, and handball courts
    Four paved tennis courts, lighted
    Roque, horseshoe, pitch putt, and bowling green

Separate playground and appropriate apparatus
Garden, with corner suitable for outdoor drama
Picnic area
Croquet court
Conservation and day camping area (small)

Building

Multiple purpose auditorium with stage, serving also as gymnasium
Clubrooms (four)
Meeting rooms (two, with dividers)
Kitchen
Sanitary facilities
Arts and crafts room
Office and supply room

Staff

Senior recreational service director
Recreational service director
Assistant director
Part-time assistants
Custodian, gardener, laborer

Time schedule

Open daily the year round from 8 a.m. to 11:30 p.m.

Attendance

Average daily attendance, approximately 1,500
Gross yearly attendance, approximately 550,000
Informal routine activities may be carried on almost any day, depending on the season and weather.

Small Children	*Older Girls*	*Women*
Sandbox play	Informal athletic	Gymnastic class
Doll play	games	Fur-coat remodeling
Climbing	Tennis	Literary club
Swinging	Social activities	Ceramics class
Sliding	Twirling	Card games
Running	Dancing	Discussion group
Tag games	Informal singing	Home nursing class
Singing games	Drama group	Arts and crafts
Jumping rope	Cooking class	Sewing circle
Fantasy games	Arts and crafts	Observing and super-
Low organized athletics	Competitive sports	vising children
Relays		
Kite flying	*Older Boys*	*Men*
Collecting specimens	Sports and athletics	Checkers, chess, cards
Rhythm band activities	Arts and crafts	Sports and athletics
Storytelling	Dancing	Discussion groups
Quiet games	Club meeting	Arts and crafts
	Band practice	First aid class
	Table games	Furniture refinishing
	Conservation activities	League meeting

Scheduled activities may be carried on during any week.

Day	Small Children	Older Boys and Girls	Adults
Monday	Collectors club	Basketball league game	Stamp club Photography club Chess club Women's slimnastics
Tuesday	Rhythm class	Sea Scout troop Softball, baseball Band activities Gymnastics	Sports activities Social dancing Drama activities Book club Bridge club Sketching club
Wednesday	Brownies and Campfire Girls meeting	Twirling and dance classes Sports clinic	Ceramics Orchestra practice Bird-watching society Craft classes Table tennis tournament Open forum
Thursday	Story hour	Dance matinee League games Tumbling Archery	Drama club Square dancing Water safety class Scuba diving Conservation class Neighborhood council Night school class
Friday	Boy and Girl Scout meetings Tap dancing Folk dancing Singing	Radio club Judo club Hay rides Astronomy club	Service clubs Big Brother meeting Baby sitting pool Hobby clubs Machine trade class Industrial arts Gardening club Flower arranging
Saturday	Handicrafts Dramatization (informal)	Model building club Hiking club Track and field activities	Picnics Oil painting Older adult club Sports car club Volunteer class
Sunday	Outings	Sports	Sports

Special Events held during the year.

> January: gym circus; soccer, district play-off, class AAA; skating tournament
>
> February: arts and crafts exhibit; Valentine party; Washington's birthday celebration

March: kite-flying contest; Arbor Day observance; basketball finals, class AAA; community night

April: musical program by all music groups; children's picnic; women's gym club exhibit

May: May Day; district track and field meet; Boys' Week—father and son program; neighborhood flower show; Mother's Day program

June: baseball district finals, class AAA; fishing rodeo; bicycle races

July: marble tournament, finals; swimming meet; puppet show; weekly children's dramatic matinee

August: doll show; boys' week-end hike; horse show

September: annual art show; Labor Day program; model boat regatta

October: Hallowe'en children's party; Hallowe'en community celebration; junior museum exhibit

November: stamp exhibition; Thanksgiving Day program

December: Christmas; community Christmas program

Program Evaluation

Efficient administration must not only facilitate the formulation and conduct of a satisfactory recreational program but must constantly evaluate this program qualitatively and quantitatively. Qualitative evaluation is rarely possible in terms of objective measurements, but depends on appreciation of values, sense of fitness, awareness of clearly defined purposes, and subjective appraisal of performance and outcomes. Except in terms of personal interviews with a random sampling of the patrons who attend and participate in the program of activities, there is little that can be done to measure the program qualitatively. Qualitative evaluation of programs requires frequent visitation by supervisors to recreational facilities where observation may be made of the program in operation. Observations and evaluations by executives and program specialists should be the basis for counseling the program recreationists and for the issuance of written program material and instructions.

Quantitative evaluation can be more accurate. The "productivity" of a recreational center may be evaluated constantly by the inauguration of a reporting system of such factors as attendance of participants and observers, group activities, financial receipts, special events, and so forth. The total attendance of participants in the recreational program and of spectators is used to compare the work of separate facilities of recreational service departments. Departments compile attendance statistics to study recreational trends, to measure their progress year by year, and to use in public relations. The use of statistics as a means of program control and evaluation has possibilities that have not yet been fully realized. More effective use of statistics for such purposes requires greater refinement of methods of recording and reporting than has so far been achieved by most recreational service departments.

Municipal recreational service systems with various kinds of facilities should devise methods for recording and reporting attendance that are applicable to the several types and allow for adaptations to local conditions. For example, the director of a neighborhood playground with an attendance of not more than 100 in any half-day session can estimate rather accurately at the end of each session the number who were present. Directors of large neighborhood and district playgrounds, where attendance is dispersed over a large area, must be content with gross estimates.

The gross attendance at recreational facilities is of little value in program evaluation, but the attendance—particularly of participants—at scheduled activities and special events has immense value. Such attendance is directly related to the efficiency of recreationists in planning and conducting the activities and events. For this reason the system of reporting should provide for accurate statistics concerning events where attendance reflects planning, organization, and leadership. Among the activities at playgrounds and indoor recreational centers for which fairly accurate statistics may be reported are the recurrent scheduled activities such as classes under leadership; club meetings; team, dual, and individual competitions; musical and dramatic performances, rehearsals; tournaments; meets; excursions; and shows. The number of participants in special events may be reliably reported, but the number of spectators usually can only be estimated unless the events are held indoors or admission tickets are sold.

The forms used by a department to report activities should be carefully designed to provide for accurate reporting of those units of activity that lend themselves to more or less exact treatment. They should be consolidated for study by supervisors and by the superintendent and used as a basis for counseling recreationists, reformulating programs, and making administrative adjustments. Instructions should provide that records be made daily or at the conclusion of each activity. At the same time care must be taken that superfluous information is not requested and that the task of recording information does not become a burden to the staff and keep them from other essential duties.

Evaluation of the recreational program indicates whether the program has achieved its stated objectives. The recreational program has a great deal to commend it in terms of the positive aims inherent in the comprehensive experiences offered by the department. A list of its positive objectives includes social acceptability, enjoyment, health, skill development, participation, challenges, and opportunity. These significant outcomes that result from well-planned, well-directed, and inspired recreational programs may be appraised and demonstrated.

By questioning program meaning, some indication of worth may be ascertained. Thus, the following and other questions may be raised, the answers to which assist in the evaluative process:

1. Is there carry-over for participants in the program?
2. Does the individual secure a sense of achievement through his participation?
3. Does the individual experience a sense of social acceptability and responsibility through his participation in program activities?
4. Are individual differences in skill, maturity, aptitude, and intellect taken into consideration in formulating the program?
5. Is there opportunity for creative self-expression?
6. Does the activity promote public goodwill?
7. Does the activity discover and develop qualities of leadership?

A SYSTEMS APPROACH TO PROGRAM PLANNING AND DEVELOPMENT

The development of the comprehensive and varied program of activities that public recreational service departments organize and promote is particularly amenable to a systems procedure. As with all systems organization, it is necessary to develop a major purpose, decide on responsibility for implementation of the program, set up approval and control procedure, provide for feedback, tracking, and other adjustment mechanisms, and establish appraisal techniques that will eventuate in more satisfying experiences for clientele.

The chief aim of initiating a program planning and development procedure is the creation of a regularized process for the establishment of recreational activities throughout the public recreational service system; to assure the coordinated support of all staff divisions within the agency; and to establish standards of programming for the department.

Responsibility for Programming

It is the fundamental responsibility of the facility director to initiate and plan the activities sponsored or directly organized by the department and conducted at his facility. When activities of a specialized nature, requiring specialists not indigenous to the facility, are conducted at a given facility, the supervisor in charge of specialists presents his plans to the director of the facility for his review. The responsibility for submission for programming purposes is that of the facility director. The final responsibility for execution of the activity is that of the facility director, although the specialist personnel are expected to provide liaison and consultant support to the effort.

It is the responsibility of the administrator in charge of the program division of the department and all other supervisors to stimulate programming in both the unit containing specialist personnel and at the various facilities, and, with the assistance of the various supervisors, to evaluate the activities for future consideration. Activities initiated by personnel of the office of the department executive are executed by the facility director or the supervisor of specialist personnel if the activity warrants specialists.

The administrator in charge of the program division will, from time to time, establish programming concepts and procedures that are meant for community-wide implementation in all active recreational areas. The success of these programs depends, in large degree, on the uniformity of implementation at the various levels. If a facility director disagrees with the kind of activity recommended for implementation at his facility or believes that the procedure should be modified, a memorandum should be forwarded to the program division office, through the established activity development channels, requesting approval on the disagreement and justifying the circumstances calling for the exception to be made. Without a special exception, it is assumed that facility directors are automatically scheduling activities introduced in this manner and are following the set procedures for their implementation without deviation.

Approval of Activity

All activities requiring budgetary consideration, public information support, maintenance support, or materials, supplies, and/or equipment may not be conducted without the approval of the administrator in charge of the program division of the department. Activity ideas may be initiated at any level of the department. All activities for a facility must be submitted to the facility director for his approval. Activities approved by the facility director are forwarded to the general supervisor responsible for all facilities and personnel in the district or community for his approval. The recommendations of the general supervisor are then forwarded to the division office.

Activity concepts presented for the first time must receive approval from the divisional office.

All activities for which fees are to be charged must receive approval for such charges through the office of the executive of the department. All such fees are established by an appropriate directive governing such matters. Fees that have been established for specific activities may be waived at the request of the facility director in accordance with instructions detailed in the aforementioned directive and in conjunction with departmental policy.

In order to operate an activity successfully certain forms are to be submitted, within specified time limits, as determined by the projected date for the initiation of the activity.

Program Planning Sheet. An activity planning sheet is to be submitted for any activity requiring approval as described above. This form is to be submitted in sufficient time so that materials, supplies, equipment, personnel, and public information may be coordinated for best effect. For special events that require exceptional planning and large monetary outlay, a minimum of three months is considered adequate for submission of the planning sheets. In other extraordinary events or when comprehensive activities are involved so that the planning concerns a program, the appropriate sheets are to be submitted a minimum of nine months prior to the scheduled opening date of the program or event. All pertinent information concerning the purchase of materials, supplies, work orders, and necessary personnel should appear on the program planning sheets to allow for adequate review of the support items for the activity.

It is suggested that programs for the following year be planned at the end of the month in which they occur so that recent experience will be fresh in the minds of the planners. Programs submitted after the nine-month period will have to be weighed against the capabilities of the organization to meet the various support deadlines necessary to complete the program successfully.

Depending on the nature of the program, a special events planning sheet or an ongoing program planning sheet is filled out in triplicate for each program. All three copies of the planning sheet are approved by the facility director and forwarded to the appropriate supervisor for his review and approval.

Publicity Checklist.   A publicity checklist form must be submitted ten weeks prior to the start of the program. This form conveys the details of the public information needs of the program and is to be submitted through the review authority established in the section dealing with program approval.

Program Evaluation Form.   Within five working days after the completion of each program or special event, the person responsible for the operation of the program must submit a program evaluation form in duplicate. One is forwarded to the program division administrator by way of the responsible supervisor. When appropriate, comments of the supervisor are attached to this evaluation form. The second copy remains on file in the facility director's office or, in the case of a special event put through by the supervisor responsible for special activities, the specialist unit office. The information in this form is used in planning for future involvements of the division. When other line or staff supervisors visit a program and make evaluation comments, they should be sent, in the form of a memorandum, to the facility director with a carbon copy for the divisional administrator.

Board of Review

A board of review meeting is held monthly to pass on the various program submissions. The program division administrator establishes the schedule and chairs the meetings. The various programs or activities submitted for review are evaluated in accordance with the following criteria:

1. Needs of the service area where the program is projected
2. Availability of personnel with the specialized skills required to operate the program
3. Concurrence with the departmental conception of recreational service
4. Concurrence with departmental policies
5. Budgetary requirements
6. Equipment, materials, and supply requirements
7. Ability of other sections or divisions of the department to support the program.

To ascertain the capabilities of other sections or divisions involved to support a projected program or activity being reviewed, members of the affected section are invited to participate in the board of review meeting. In all cases requiring maintenance support beyond the capabilities of the staff of the facility, a representative of the maintenance division should be invited to attend.

As a designation of program or activity approval at the various levels, the program planning sheet should have blocks for approval signature of facility director or supervisor of special activity; supervisor of appropriate level (district, community, or general); and supporting division or section heads of the department. There should be a space for the stamp that indicates formal approval of the program. After all necessary conditions have been accomplished, the authority for formal approval of a program is delegated to the administrator of the program division.

Program Tracking

At the time formal program approval is given, the program is assigned a number to be used as a guide to follow up on all support items and to appear on any work orders and requests for materials or supplies connected with the program.

After action by the program division administrator in concurrence with the departmental executive, copies of the program planning sheets are distributed as follows: one copy is sent to the facility director to inform him of the disposition of the program; one copy is sent to the supervisor at the appropriate level; and one copy is kept on file in the program division office.

Master Calendar

All approved programs are listed on a master calendar to be issued quarterly by the program division. This master calendar covers all ongoing programs and special events taking place for a three-month period in all system facilities, and all activities operated by the program division staff on facilities outside of the system (schools or other public or private structures). The master calendar is issued twice; first as a preliminary listing and then as a final listing. The preliminary listing is issued nine months prior to the start of a quarter and has blocks for the signature of the facility director and appropriate level supervisor. The information on the master calendar is taken from the program planning sheets that have been submitted and approved.

On receipt of the preliminary master calendar, the facility director may add to, eliminate, or modify the information for his scheduled program of activities. However, all changes should be accompanied by a written explanation for the change. The facility director signs the preliminary master calendar after he has listed any changes and submits it to his supervisor. The supervisor approves the changes on the master calendar for each of the facilities in his jurisdiction and forwards the signed preliminary master calendar to the program division office. Preliminary master calendars should be returned to the program division office within two weeks after their receipt by the facility director.

On receipt of the reviewed preliminary master calendars, the program division administrator issues a permanent master calendar for each three-month period. Programs on this final master calendar have been fully approved.

Cancellation

Once programs have been posted on the master calendar they are not liable to cancellation or modification. However, an unusual circumstance might arise which could cause a request for cancellation after a program has been approved and listed. In such cases, an activity may be cancelled up to 90 days before the starting date of the activity. Such cancellation requests must be in writing, detailing the situation requiring cancellation, and must be approved by the facility director, the appropriate supervisor, and the program division administrator.

Cancellation of activities within 90 days of the starting date requires the approval of the superintendent of recreational service. Recommendation in this matter is made to the superintendent by the program division administrator.

Responsibilities of the Program Division Administrator

The following items on the program planning sheet are determined in the superintendent's office by the program division administrator (assistant superintendent of recreational service).

Publicity. The publicity materials listed on the program planning sheets should be requested by the initiator of the program or the facility director. However, the final determination of the material to be provided, and in what amounts, is made by the program division administrator, based on the budgetary allotment for publicity materials and the ability of the other divisions or affected sections to support the request for printing and posters.

It is also possible that many events at a facility can be combined into one overall printed brochure, or even into a community-wide seasonal brochure. The determination of what public information materials and the quantity is covered on the program planning sheet prior to its return to the facilities. In order to make a sensible determination, it is necessary for the facility directors to specify on the program planning sheets the plans for the distribution of the public information materials they request.

Correspondence. Determination for the responsibility in this area is made by the program division administrator, since the particular correspondence depends on the need of the activity or entire program and the significance of the program throughout the system.

Sponsorship. Department programs, when practical, should be operated in coordination and cooperation with the various local recreational interest groups. Departmental involvement with business organizations in the promotion of any activity is to be considered valuable to the extent that the emphasis remains on the activity and does not become a point of departure for commercial promotion.

Since there are many different levels of sponsorship and one might encroach on the other, determination of the nature of sponsorship and the designation of the sponsor is made by the program division administrator. If local sponsorship is sought or offered by local organizations, the facility director must first receive clearance through the office of the program division administrator.

Selected References

Auburn, M. and K. Buckman: *Drama Through Performance* (New York: Houghton, Mifflin Co.), 1977.

Batcheller, J.: *Music in Recreation and Leisure* (Dubuque, Iowa: Wm. C. Brown Company Publishers), 1976.

Business Communications Company: *Hobbies and Crafts* (Stanford, Conn.: BCC, Inc.), 1976.

Hyatt, R. W.: *Intramural Sports: Organization and Administration* (St. Louis, Mo.: The C. V. Mosby Company), 1977.

Kraus, R. K.: *Recreation Today: Program Planning and Leadership, 3d. ed.*: (Salt Lake City, Utah: Goodyear Publishing Co.), 1977.

Kujoth, J. S.: *Recreational Program Guide: Organizing Activities for School, Camps, Park, Playground or Children's Clubs* (Metuchen, N.J.: Scarecrow Press, Inc.), 1972.

Lauffer, A. and S. Gorodezky: *Volunteers* (Beverly Hill, Calif.: Sage Publications, Inc.), 1977.

Lucas, C.: *Recreational Activity Development for the Aging in Homes, Hospitals, and Nursing Homes* (Springfield, Ill.: Charles C Thomas), 1974.

Mitchell, V. A., and others: *Camp Counseling, 5th ed.* (Philadelphia, Pa.: W. B. Saunders Co.), 1977.

Ratcliffe, D. A., Ed.: *Nature Conservation, 2 vols.* (New Rochelle, N.Y.: Cambridge University Press), 1977.

Roth, C. D.: *Art of Making Puppets and Marionettes* (Radnor, Pa.: Chilton Book Co.), 1975.

Ruben, W.: *Gardening Indoors as a Hobby* (New York: Vantage Press), 1977.

Schlaich, J. and B. Dupont, Eds.: *Dance: The Art of Production* (St. Louis: The C. V. Mosby Company), 1977.

Shivers, J. S.: *Camping: Administration, Counseling, Programming* (Englewood Cliffs, N.J.: Prentice-Hall, Inc.), 1971.

Shivers, J. S. and C. R. Calder, Jr.: *Recreational Crafts* (New York: The McGraw-Hill Book Company), 1974.

Siks, G. B.: *Drama With Children* (New York: Harper & Row Publishers), 1977.

Singer, D. and J. Singer: *Partners in Play* (New York: Harper & Row Publishers), 1977.

Stengel, A. K. and A. M. Feeney: *Volunteer Training and Development Manual* (New York: Seabury Press, Inc.), 1976.

Wade, M.: *Games For Fun* (Nashville, Tenn.: Broadman Press), 1977.

Winter, T. F.: *Art and Craft of Ceramic Sculpture,* (New York: Halstead Press), 1974.

Ziegler, S.: *Service Project Ideas* (Cincinnati, Ohio: Standard Publishing Co.), 1977.

CHAPTER **25**

Evaluation of Recreational Services

Evaluation concerns the collection of factual information about any experience, concept, process, or thing. The information is then presented so that some judgment can be made. The judgment assumes that standards or criteria exist by which a factor may be measured. Thus, the value of one aspect, such as an experience, may be determined on some known basis—for example, its promise of social contact or lack of interpersonal relationship. The value of each of several possible experiences may be assessed by comparison. In one instance, the intensity of relationship or social contact made possible, in another by the relative superficiality, denial, or rejection of the individual in question. How effective an experience is can be judged on the basis of information received dealing with what the individual obtained from participation. The value of any experience may be gained from its impact upon the participant—that is, by the extent to which it, in itself or in comparison with other potential experiences, concludes in specifically desired changes in those having the experience.

Recreational activity, while not a complex process insofar as the individual is concerned, is, as a social institution, among the more complex procedures attempted within any sector of society. Recreational service becomes a complex process dealing with the selection of concepts, objectives, delivery systems, administration, and all of the ramified functions which have come to be identified with the provision of recreational service. Choices have to be made in the design and implementation of a recreational service program, and the effectiveness of the program must be carefully scrutinized. The process of evaluation is a constant function to which all facets of departmental system, organization, operation, and services must be submitted for study so that assessments can be made.

Evaluation is the continuous process of improving any enterprise by the application of information so that deliberate selection of alternatives can be made. By process is meant a specific and consistent activity comprising a variety of techniques and concerning several procedures. Evaluation is an ongoing process and should not be perceived only as a finalized comparison between some objective and actual performance. The sole reason for evaluating anything is its improvement. Whatever information is generated is utilized with the immediate end of making the recreational service better. This betterment may come in terms of program, administrative practices, personnel performance, facility planning, design, construction, or operation, and any other condition, situation, or factor involving the provision of recreational service. Unless improvement is the net result of evaluation, evaluation has not been performed realistically.

The application of intelligence is conceived not only in terms of intellectual command, but also as the gathering, analysis, and utility of information designed to identify the possible alternatives before any decisions can be reached. In this sense, intelligence is viewed as perspicacity as well as the means for diminishing ambiguity in achieving a correct choice of the alternatives which present themselves. Deliberate selection has to do with intentional choice directed toward monitoring operations so that their enhancement is forthcoming. Deliberate selection is based upon differentiated alternatives which accrue in response to information collected about the action that might be taken concerning some enterprise.

Alternatives are two or more diverse measures that could be performed in reaction to some condition needing modification. Enterprise improvement takes place only when current behaviors, activities, or operations are changed. There are at least three situations which might require desirable altered action; if there is evidence that (1) some unsatisfied need exists, (2) a problem exists, or (3) a favorable condition exists which should be exploited. Where there are limited resources, as is so often true of public recreational service agencies, priorities must be assigned and decisions made on the basis of available means. The focus of evaluation is to come to some decision about a number of alternatives based upon assessed values and benefits determined by careful analysis.

THE DETERMINATION OF OBJECTIVES

The process of evaluation is based upon information which permits a comparison between any entity being scrutinized and its proximity to the objective or objectives which have been pre-determined as achievable. The objectives of recreational service, regardless of their derivation and kind, can be shown to have a number of sources. As an instrument for the benefit of society, recreational service is responsive to the needs or demands of the society from which it originates. Whether recreationists seek out these needs and initiate programs to satisfy constituent requests or actually propagandize the potential clientele, thereby creating demand where none existed previously, recreational service has responded both as a mirror of the culture and as an advocate for new and expanded horizons.

Societal Needs

The inexorable weight of society has required the establishment of the field of recreational service—at least in the public sector—to fulfill certain functions which otherwise would not or could not have been accomplished by other sector enterprises. Now that public sector agencies have demonstrated the feasibility of providing specific recreational activities for which there is a steady demand, private entrepreneurs have moved into the provision of services for commercial gain. There would have been little in the way of private racquet clubs, ski resorts, camping facilities, sports clubs, and other private sector delivery services unless the public sector departments had not first shown the popularity of specific recreational activities.

Individual Needs

The need of individuals comprise a second source for objectives. The extent to which recreational service can supply experience, places, leadership, instruction, in order to meet the common needs of all people, or on the variants of these for individuals, who constitute the potential participants of each agency, must be faced by each department sooner or later. The law plays a significant role in the determination of objectives. Although some legislation is broad and generally calls upon public agencies to perform in certain ways so that minimum services of a recreational nature are provided, other statutes or codes may itemize and specifically demand that public or other agencies offer particular recreational services of a certain type and other relatively regulated conditions. The ability of social sector agencies to live up to demands placed upon them by law offers a real source by which objectives may be selected.

Authoritative Statements

Another source of objectives is found in the scholarly statements issued by a number of recognized authorities, professional associations, conferences, institutes, or commissions. The objectives of the field, whether broadly or narrowly construed, may be developed by scholars in the discipline and these writings, almost by default, may become the authority from which objectives for the field are defined.

From these varied sources, a number of objectives may be formulated which will serve as the goals achievable by the means available. Investigation of needs and decisions on those to which recreational service should provide for involve both systematic research and value judgments.

Among the many possibilities some choice must be made, essentially by assessment of the rationale and logic supporting the divergent alternatives. Study of the consequences of pertinent information and of its relevance to recreational service planning is a form of evaluation. Philosophical orientations, by their very nature, concern and compel consideration of values. If all of these factors are not involved in choosing objectives, the ones which have been omitted may nullify efforts at achieving the objectives. As with any objectives, there may be freedom of choice, but the accomplishment of goals will be determined by the ability to perform and the availability of resources to insure success.

Establishment of Objectives

Establishment of the on-going process of evaluation requires the development of well-defined objectives. Initially, consideration must be given to the items through which evaluation of the agency may be made. Additionally, objectives should be signified which set forth what the agency is attempting to accomplish and what its constituent personnel should achieve. Agency objectives will best be understood and accepted when there is cooperative effort on the part of all professional personnel at every level of the agency hierarchy. Neither the executive alone, nor supervisors alone, should set objectives to be reached. Objectives should be broadly stated. However, the wide latitude of objectives must be susceptible to singular means for enactment. Other objectives will inevitably grow out of an appraisal of participant performance. Evaluation can never be looked upon as something apart from the performance of professional services to people. It is an integral factor of what the recreationist does to make his function more effecitve. Evaluation of performance is as significant as performance itself.

In establishing objectives, a distinct set of responsibilities is readily apparent. These facets of the organization can be grouped in general as agency organization, jurisdiction, finance, administration, personnel, planning, programming, physical plant, land, public relations, coordination, participation, and policy making. Thus, 14 separate areas emerge as having need for evaluation. These may be stated as:

1. The implementation of recreational service having to do with the initiation and development of the agency.
2. Jurisdictional control, comprising the sphere of service within which the agency operates as well as the authority to organize and operate the agency.
3. Adequate financial support from whatever various sources are available to the agency.
4. Operational aspects for the administration of the agency.
5. Personnel standards, professional development, and management practices.

6. Planning for recreational services.
7. Programming recreational activities.
8. The development and maintenance of the physical plant including all structures and facilities.
9. The acquisition and preparation of land for inclusion within the recreational system which the agency operates.
10. The development of an on-going program of public relations.
11. The development of coordination between agencies for comprehensive and effective services.
12. The appraisal of the quality of participation and the number of users which the agency has.
13. The institution of policy to guide substantive behaviors and operations so that the most efficient and effective services will be provided to the agency's constituency.
14. Patron perceptions of recreational service.

Continual procedures designed to determine the value of the recreational service agency in the community are essential if the department is to realize its objectives in the provision of a comprehensive and balanced program of activities to meet the recreational needs of people. The idea of evaluating recreational agencies is not new. Everyone who has ever been to a recreational agency intuitively knows the good and bad aspects of the service received. Almost every layman fancies himself as expert on the subject of recreational service. After all, "Isn't recreational activity a subjective and personal matter?" Because evaluation continues uninterruptedly, it is absolutely necessary that its standards, devices, and techniques be understood. Methods must be developed for gathering facts so that judgments can be made as to how closely the recreational agency approximates its goals. Evaluation must be based upon reliable information and the sources of these facts need to be identified. Therefore, instruments or measuring devices that are accurate, consistently applicable to the areas undergoing evaluation, and easily administered by competent professionals are required.

EVALUATION AND INTEGRATION

Evaluation is or can be closely associated with every phase of the planning and operational elements of any recreational service agency. Because of this fact, it is desirable that the process become a cohesive force which assures that all activities fulfill and contribute to the goals of recreational service. Evaluation is both end-in-view and practice. As practice it includes studies and procedures designed to sustain or improve the quality of participation, methods of program presentation, professional personnel performance, and every aspect of agency operation. It is a process which discloses evidence of inadequacy, evidence of progress, and evidence of proximity to any ideal which has been selected as the agency's goal.

To the extent that evaluation is also an end, it is improvement which more nearly exemplifies its meaning. Evaluation includes both ends and means, for it permits a judgment that is reached concerning some person, place, or thing and it may also be described as a process for reaching judgments. How such judgments are reached and what ends they may serve is a proper study for any recreationist who is concerned with evaluation procedures. It must be understood from the outset that evaluation is a process of determining information about the degree to which recreational service objectives are achieved by the department. It should never be thought of as a mere collection of techniques, the total of which equal the process. Among the principles of evaluation which can effectively guide the evaluation process are those which deal with:

1. Identification and understanding of what has to be evaluated. No method of evaluation can be chosen or initiated until the objectives of evaluation have been clearly determined. The effectiveness of the evaluative process relies as much upon what is to be evaluated as it does upon the validity, realiability, and technical stability of the instruments employed.

2. Prior consideration should be given to the appropriateness of the evaluative technique chosen in terms of the aims to be served. Every evaluative technique has plus or minus factors in regard to gaining an understanding of what is being evaluated. Whichever technique is best fitted for the situation under examination should be utilized. It is not a question of which procedure to use, but which best meets the needs insofar as appropriateness is concerned.

3. An inclusive program of evaluation requires diverse techniques and instrumentalities if it is to be effective and valuable. No one evaluation technique is adequate for determining all of the significant products of recreational service. A variety of devices, including objective, subjective, and observational methods are required to evaluate the host of possibilities which are included in the outcome of any recreational program. A variety of techniques may be fruitful, particularly when any single instrument is relatively limited in scope. By combining several or many procedures there is a greater likelihood that a more accurate and adequate judgment will be able to be made.

4. Appropriate use of evaluation techniques requires complete understanding of both strengths and weaknesses of the procedures. Evaluation techniques can vary from quite precise instruments, (e.g., quantitatively based statistics dealing with participant use of departmental facilities) to highly subjective narrative reports. Of course there is always the possibility of incorrect analysis of evaluation results. Sometimes accuracy is imparted to instruments which are not precise enough. There should be

a recognition on the part of evaluators that most techniques are limited and should not be credited with qualities not possessed.

5. Evaluation is a process that has justification only to the extent to which the results are put to appropriate use. If evaluation were to be considered an exercise rather than a means for delivering better services, it would be better left undone. When evaluation is seen as a process for obtaining information upon which substantive decisions can be based for improved services in every phase of departmental operation, then the process has served its purpose. Implied in this rule is the concept that objectives are clearly defined prior to the initiation of the process; that the techniques utilized were appropriate for the purposes identified; that decisions would be guided in light of what the evaluation process elicited; and that the varied evaluative techniques employed are chosen on the basis of its value to improved departmental offerings, organization, and administration.

The following topics, standards, and recommendations are offered as an illustration of selected areas for examination, relative to items of information which any recreational service agency might want to evaluate.

Topic 1. Organization and Structure for Initiation of Recreational Service

Requirement

There should be a distribution of personnel for achieving a satisfactory recreational program through the division of duties, responsibilities and authority.

Recommendation

A department of public recreational service will be organized as a functional agency of the local, civil subdivision so as to enable it to perform the functions for which it was created.

In effect this will mean the allocation of financial support to competently staff the organization, provide operating expenses, capital expenditures, and long-range planning for maximum efficiency.

Detailed Development of the Recommendation

1. Initiation of the agency.
   a. Approach the managing authority or legal governmental body of community with factual information relevant to the need for setting up a service agency within the municipal family responsible for the provision of activities and experiences of a recreational nature.
   b. Supplement this effort with planned visitations to local civic, professional, business, fraternal, social, school, religious and other service agencies in order to indicate the value that the organization of a public department would have for the community.
   c. Utilize the mass media of communication for presentation of ideas to the general public concerning the initiation of a public agency and its values to them.
   d. Obtain a written statement guaranteeing the institution of the

20

agency against political machinations and indicating the specific responsibilities that the agency will have.

e. Attempt to establish the recreational agency as a municipal department.

2. Functions of the agency.

a. Here we are concerned with the reasons for which the agency was created. Thus there must be listed the specifics relating to the operations to be conducted by the agency. There will be included a statement giving unshared and primary responsibilities to the agency for the provision of recreational service in the community.

b. The agency should have the legal power to utilize any and all public structures, to house activities of a recreational nature, sponsored by the agency if such and where such activities do not interfere, hinder, or conflict with the principle purpose for which those structures were created.

c. The agency should employ only professionally prepared individuals in full-time positions; employ only competent individuals, preferably professionally prepared, in the special activities necessary for the performance of the program.

d. The agency should be the authority on the selection and placement and acquisition of such spaces, structures and facilities for the maximum utilization and effectiveness in terms of recreational service for the community.

Topic 2. Establishment of a Lay Advisory Committee or Board

Requirements

The necessity of having representation from the community-at-large mandates that interested citizens will be requested to serve on an advisory body the functions of which are to assist recreationists in the provision of recreational services.

Recommendation

A lay advisory committee or board will be appointed by the appropriate authority of the local legal sub-division. The advisory body will offer advice and counsel concerning the provision of public recreational services for the community in whatever ways that body finds is necessary to inform, suggest, or recommend to the professional executive of the department which will effectively permit the agency to successfully fulfill its manifold obligations in the community.

Detailed Development of the Recommendation

1. Formation of the Lay Advisory Committee or Board.

a. The lay advisory body should be formed by appropriate municipal authority.

2. Functions of the Lay Advisory Committee or Board.

a. Generally the lay advisory group will meet as often as is required to carry out their counseling functions.

b. The lay group will serve as a chief public relations device between the agency and its clientele.

c. The lay group shall offer whatever advice or counsel it deems necessary to the chief executive officer of the department insofar as the provision of recreational services are concerned. This may include activity suggestions, suggestions for new facilities, advocacy of certain community interests, instigation of citizen action groups having recreational concerns, participation in public hearings which may determine budgetary allocations for the department, advise on physical maintenance, cleanliness, attractiveness, and other related conditions of the recreational system, and any other program or property ideas which will be of benefit to the community and its population.

3. Organization of the lay advisory committee or board.

a. The advisory group will consist of a specific number of persons not to exceed seven and always an odd number.

b. Appointment to the advisory group shall be by direct authority from the office of the governing authority of the local legal subdivision.

c. Officers of the advisory group should be provided, i.e., Chairman, Vice-Chairman, Secretary (usually performed by a member of the professional staff). Advisory group members may either elect or select their own officers. However, in some instances the chairman may be appointed by the local governing authority of the community.

d. The departmental executive may also designate a professional staff person to serve as an ex-officio member of the group.

Topic. 3. Financial Support

Requirements

An appropriation equal to the amount needed for the full operation and administration of all recreational service should be made.

Depending upon the interest of the community, the economic status of the community, and present or anticipated recreational resources, areas, or facilities of a personal or physical nature, the fiscal amount appropriated would be whatever is available and appropriate to supply the recreational needs of the people in the community.

Recommendation

An annual appropriation made from the general subdivisional fund will be earmarked for recreational service operations. This sum depends upon the willingness and need of the citizens to pay for and receive recreational services.

Detailed Development of the Recommendation

1. General fund appropriations.

That money supplied from general taxes received from the community and appropriated out to the various municipal agencies for their current fiscal operations.

This appears to be the most uncomplicated and direct means for providing financial support to the recreational agency if the sum appropriated actually allows effective operation of the recreational service department.

Where the local legal authorities do not provide sufficient funds for the effective maintenance and administration of their service agency, it will be necessary to support whatever funds are made available so that services can be offered.

2. The recreational mill levy.

An amount of tax money stipulated by state law which may be

collected from the citizens of a community in order to operate a recreational service agency.

It is necessary for a popular referendum to take place in order to pass a mill levy which generally does not exceed three mills.

Upon the completion of the referendum and if the motion for a millage levy is passed, such monies as are collected will be utilized exclusively for the operation of the recreational agency.

The mill levy may be for a stipulated number of years or longer and may also be rescinded by popular vote.

The mill levy may be considered a vote of confidence, but it may also engender certain factional rivalries within the municipal family because other municipal agencies may look with disfavor upon the recreational department which appears to be receiving an inordinate share of comfort and security. Thus the levy must be used discriminately.

3. The bond issue.

A legal instrument indebting the community for a specified sum within a particular period of time.

It is utilized in the construction and development of large capital outlays for land acquisition, construction of buildings and purchase of expensive equipment.

Only passed by popular referendum.

4. Special assessments.

Those levies laid upon specific individuals for improvements within a particular area when such improvements affect only the residents of that area rather than the community at large.

5. Fees and charges.

Utilized to supplement any financial support appropriated to the agency.

Such fees and charges must never be utilized for profit making, nor should they be excessive, exorbitant or of such nature to prohibit individuals from entering into or participating in recreational activities sponsored by the recreational agency.

The fee and the charge must be used sparingly and may be justified only in terms of providing extraordinary services, or activities not possible under the appropriated funds for the operation of the agency.

Corollary—better to allow an individual to participate in a recreational activity than to omit him from that activity because he has not the monetary means for entrance.

For items over and above the appropriated amounts in the budget, but just for service, not for profit.

Topic 4. Administration of the Recreational Agency (process applicable to the management, direction and coordination of money, materials, and men in the achievement of stated goals)

Requirement

The management and control of all personnel and operations having as their objective the achievement of policy in accordance with a logical philosophy as decided upon by legal authority in serving the recreational needs of the people within the local jurisdiction.

Recommendation

The administrative processes for fulfillment or enforcement of public policy will be implemented for the facilitation and effective operation of the recreational agency's service functions.

Detailed Development of the Recommendation

1. Record keeping.

   The organization and maintenance of documents relating to the daily operational activities of the agency. Such documentation will be rendered most effective by the standardization of format, duplication of materials to be transmitted to the various concerned sections of the agency for action, the utilization of such forms as required, and the storage of these materials in repositories for current and future reference.

   Records will concern all aspects of the agency's operations, including financial, personnel, maintenance, program, supplies, architectural and engineering drawings and plans, policy statements, safety procedures and practices, correspondence, insurance, tax, various and sundry reports, and other legal papers which must be filed for reference.

   The maintenance of records and the operation of a filing system are necessary if the agency is to profit by its successes as well as its failures. The records of the agency serve as primary resources in the development of better activities, consistency of policy aims, and avoidance of duplication, and assists in the implementation of better services provided to the people.

   Records will help the professional development of personnel, assist in the in-service educational procedure, and indicate the progress or regression of individuals or groups being served by the agency.

2. Standard operating procedures.

   Those methods which have been found to be successful and appropriate in carrying out the varied functions for which the agency was created.

   Includes such routine devices as the daily inspection of materials, supplies, equipment and facilities of the agency, the routine aspects of personnel practice including vacations, leaves, transfers, employment and discharge, chain of command authorizations, staff meetings, the scheduling of activities, the priority policies, and other features of agency operation which become standardized for efficiency and economy.

   Standard operating procedures will never be applied to program activities. The program shall always be highly flexible and unique in every way that may be conceived to retain its uniqueness.

3. Office management.

   Concerned with the assignment of duties and responsibilities within the central office of the agency in order to more efficiently carry out the routine accumulation of paper work and to more speedily process the requests of the operational workers of the agency.

   Office management is basically concerned with the maintenance of records and the flow of work procedure from the time a request for supplies or information is brought into the office to the time the request is satisfactorily answered or fulfilled.

   It is further concerned with the acquisition and maintenance of specific office machines which may be used in the process of creating or formulating various reports, records of a personnel or financial nature, answering or writing correspondence, duplicating or printing, directing information outward to mass media of communication, to individuals, to the staff, and for the clerical work necessary in fulfilling the aforementioned tasks.

4. Work flow efficiency.

The processing of all material from a raw state to a finished state without duplication and in the most direct way possible.

It is concerned with correct placement of lighting, the optimum degree of heat and ventilation, the careful use of color, the sanitary effect of cleanliness, the correct placement of machinery, the identification of efficient personnel, their placement so that maximum productive potential may be achieved, and the speedy dispatch of paper work from start to finish without undue time loss or hesitency in the transmission of such material.

5. Maintenance.

Basically concerned with the upkeep of physical properties owned, operated, or utilized by the recreational agency.

It is divided into two aspects:

a. Interior housekeeping which includes cleanliness, attractiveness and supply inventories within the buildings themselves, i.e., window washing, illumination maintenance, proper heat, power and ventilation, floor cleanliness (sweeping, mopping and waxing where applicable), interior painting, furniture, sanitary facilities, and other services related to the preservation of the structure.

b. Exterior maintenance including grounds keeping, horticulture arrangements, i.e., lawns, shrubs, trees, and plants, road ways, walk ways, pavements, asphalt or composition surface areas, equipment utilized in the recreational program, i.e., playground, sports, fencing, exterior illumination, shelters, sanitary facilities, drinking fountains, and exteriors of buildings.

Maintenance may also be concerned with the repair, replacement, or construction of program aids, including certain pieces of equipment, signs, posters, markers, benches, litter baskets, and any other physical property or equipment utilized in the preservation of property.

Maintenance is generally concerned with the custodianship of buildings and the conservation of physical property.

Topic 5. Planning for Recreational Services

Requirement

A broad framework guiding future substantive actions and operations in the recreational agency. These principles are concerned with the development and accumulation of pertinent information, the analysis of that information for categorizing into classes for easy comprehension, the projection of alternate courses of action, and the appraisal of the consequences of such diversified courses.

Recommendation

The initiation of planning procedures to guide the development of the recreational agency and to enhance the functions of that agency, in order

to avoid the waste of duplication, inefficiency, and deficient concepts, will
be undertaken.

Detailed Development of the Recommendation

1. Analysis and research.

Is concerned with the collection of basic material and information
relating to current concepts of recreational programming, design, construction, and maintenance of structures and facilities, investigation
of comparative agencies, study of professional literature pertinent to
the field of recreational service for philosophy, principles, ethics and
practices, the examination of the collected data in order to determine
whether or not the agency is keeping abreast of current professional
concepts in each of the aforementioned areas, i.e., physical plant,
philosophy, program and practices.

Research may be carried on by statistical representation, survey,
i.e., questionnaire, public opinion polls, group meetings, or open
forums. Observation of activities in which people participate, inspection for supervisory purposes of such activities will be involved in this
analysis.

Research will attempt to determine whether or not the recreational
services provided for by the agency are adequate and effective in
meeting the needs of the agency's clientele and the population of the
wider community.

2. The master plan.

Is a detailed construct concerning the socioeconomic, political, geographic, demographic, and educational investigation of the community
in order to determine the most effective placement of physical recreational resources and the employment of competent, professionally prepared individuals to operate the activities afforded by such physical
resources to meet the potential population trends and recreational
needs of present and future residents of the community. Such a plan
must be coordinated with other institutional physical structures of the
community including the school system, other municipal agency services, i.e., police, fire, health, public works, streets, parks, parkways
and lighting developments.

The master plan is usually undertaken as a 25-year-directive.

Factors to consider:

a. the economic feasibility of such a master plan.
b. whether or not the community is interested.
c. demand upon the citizenry.
d. increased and more interesting activities.
e. is the community in on the planning procedures?
f. political institutions of the city
g. under what agency does the recreational department operate?
h. the population—its ethnic and constitutional makeup, the type of
people, and the classes within the population. Any atypical or
special populations who require greater assistance or facilitation.

3. The priority schedule.

A time table for the implementation of physical recreational facilities in accordance with the master plan.

The master plan is a policy statement but the priority schedule is a
time table for the construction of the facilities already laid out.

Takes into consideration what is most important, what is needed immediately for the greatest number of people, and what can be done for the amount of money available.

Then lay out the land acquired, first priority, insofar as what is needed. The acquirement of suitable land for recreational purposes has first priority. When the land has been obtained it must be planned appropriately in terms of open spaces, various facility emplacements, structures, access areas, and so on, so that community recreational needs may be met.

4. The five-year plan.

Consists of an immediate appraisal of the community which includes immediate past studies concerning traffic placements, water mains, sewer and lighting systems within recent periods of time.

The master plan is enacted in five-year segments. This permits flexibility and provides for adjustment to be made as population density fluctuates or movements are noted. It also allows for technological innovation, natural or man-made events which might occur thereby changing the variables which influence the plan.

This plan is conceived as carrying out the provision indicated in the master plan and is related to those community-wide and regional installations which typically enlarge the kinds and comprehensive services capable of being offered within the community.

5. The three-year plan.

Concerns the relationship of immediate population movement, takes into consideration the necessity of developing facilities in accordance with a population increase within the next three years. Only concerned with that three year period. It is, therefore, one of considerable limitation and restricted physical developments.

This plan is generally concerned with specific neighborhood developments rather than community developments. The content of the plan will therefore be oriented to several neighborhoods within the community which appear to be gaining in population and with the provision of facilities to accommodate that increase. The development of facilities will necessarily be curtailed to building structures, individual playgrounds, individual parks or other facilities rather than with complex installations.

6. The one-year short-term plan.

This plan will be initiated in terms of population increase for one neighborhood within the community. This plan, rather than concerning many aspects of the community, will be related to meeting the needs of the fastest growing neighborhood of the community and the provision of recreational services and facilities in that neighborhood. Such a facility will usually be the neighborhood playground or the renovation of an existing building for increased use.

This plan makes necessary a comprehensive look at the community in terms of individual neighborhoods so as to determine the growth potential in terms of population, economic resource, and recreational need in that area.

7. The emergency plan.

Concerned with the provision of recreational services and development or renovation of facilities in densely populated sections of the community. Concerned with meeting recreational deficits within heavily populated regions of the community rather than with the acquisition of land or development of new facilities in outlying regions.

The emergency plan, as its name implies, is concerned with meeting the urgent and immediate recreational needs caused by underdeveloped property or lack of adequate space and facilities.

Must be undertaken because of lack of foresight on the part of the administrators or governmental authorities to see the necessity of recreational planning in relation to the growth of the community.

Will never keep up with population growth, is inadequate to say the least, and is instigated as an expediency measure to affect demand.

Indicates that no master plan is available.

8. Spot surveys.

Are appraisals of the community taken at random which indicate whether or not the provision of recreational service is adequate and therefore meeting the needs of the citizens of the community. The spot survey may be made in terms of the questionnaire, personal interviews, or observation.

Its most useful function is to indicate whether or not the program and the facilities are adequate, well attended and well operated.

Topic 6. Personnel Standards

Requirement

Incumbents in recreational positions must have an educational and experiential preparation that will enable them to perform the essential work of serving the public's recreational needs.

Such personnel will be on a professional level combining qualities of competence, dedication, knowledge, and personal integrity to effectively function and carry on the duties and responsibilities of office.

Recommendation

Only such personnel will be employed on a full-time professional basis as can demonstrate their theoretical and practical knowledge and professional efficiency.

Minimum standards for entrance into the field of recreational service include graduation from an accredited college or university with major work in recreational learning and additional experience and educational preparation at the position level with attendant salary, duties, and responsibilities becoming higher, more difficult, and complex. Appointments to professional recreational service positions require minimum standards of education and experience. Such positions carry certain job specifications, duties, and functions. With progressively more responsibility, authority, and higher salary as tenure on the job lengthens, job pressures also mount. As the incumbent obtains more experience and is, consequently, given more authority and responsibility the complexities at this level of the organizational hierarchy become more intense.

Detailed Development of the Recommendation

1. Job analysis, specifications, and minimal qualifications.
2. Personnel salaries and step increments.
3. Professional experience, affiliation, and preparation.
4. In-service education.

5. Appointment, advancement, transfer, disciplinary actions, seniority, merit, work schedules, leaves, retirement, and other work practices.
6. Line and staff division of functions.

Topic 7. Program Standards

Requirement

The program of any recreational service agency consists of all those activities provided by the agency which meet the recreational needs of the constituent public. The program contains a balance of activities which is produced on a full-time, year-round basis in which all age, sex, racial, religious, economic, or social status groups and the individuals which make up these groups may participate according to their several respective abilities and experiences.

Recommendation

The program will contain a balance of activities featuring recreational living experiences that provide social, cultural, emotional, physical, and moral values for participating individuals.

The program will consist of the following activities which may be further subdivided.
1. Physical and athletic experiences.
    a. Individual, dual, group and team, competitive and noncompetitive activities.
    b. Games.
    c. Aquatics.
    d. Sports.
2. Dance and rhythmic experiences.
3. Art.
4. Crafts experiences.
5. Outdoor education and camping.
6. Dramatics.
7. Music.
8. Education.
9. Social.
10. Special project.
11. Service or volunteering.
12. Hobby.

Detailed Development of the Recommendation

1. Possible activities and the criteria for their selection. It is ridiculous to select activities on any basis other than considering the objectives of the activity as being measurable.

Some concepts are already inherent within the activity. They are not valid as criteria. The recreationist has to develop other forms of criteria for the activity.

Criteria in terms of activities that can be measured:
a. Social acceptability (Does it abide by the law?).
b. Enjoyment (by attitudinal survey).

It is up to the recreationist to find out if the person does enjoy the activity he's in. If he doesn't, the recreationist has to find out why and do something about it. The recreationist serves a leadership function and is not there just to provide. Some people go into an activity for reasons other than enjoyment, and the recreationist has to determine what those reasons are, the return factor and duration factor included.

c. Safety precautions.

With precaution no activity is dangerous. Human uniqueness is the factor, not the inherent danger of an activity.

d. Skill (by rate of return to the activity, perseverance in the activity, and achievement).

Is measurable and indicates whether or not the recreationist is performing the instruction obligations.

e. Participation (by number who participate and the quality of it).

Evaluation by number simply involves "how many" in terms of a number.

The worker's evaluation of the activity in terms of the intensity or extent of the individual's participation.

Selection of activities to be determined by geographical region, or climate.

2. Evaluation.

3. A balance of the full range of activities offered.

In terms of the twelve activities of the well-balanced and well-rounded program. There must be adequate presentation of all these activities.

4. Equal opportunity in terms of age, sex, race, social, economic status, handicap, or disability.

Topic 8. Recreational Spaces.

Requirement

Any land, water, or physical structure, space, or area, i.e., physical property, which may be utilized for recreational purposes or which has historic, aesthetic, scientific or scenic value should be acquired as part of the public's legacy in conserving the natural open, wooded, and water spaces for present and future utilization.

Recommendation

That all land which has historic, aesthetic, scientific, or scenic value which may be feasible to acquire and hold for public benefit will be so acquired and held; that all current space holdings will be carefully investigated in order to discover present and potential recreational use in terms of population movement, subdivisional development, arterial construction, or other land diminishing encroachments on the public domain.

Detailed Development of the Recommendation

1. Land acquisition.

Interested in acquiring sites for recreational purposes. These sites must be located in areas such that they are accessible for utilization and acquirable for the amount of money that the community has to spend. The land itself must not need too much development before it can be utilized.

Land acquisition is necessary if recreational services in the community are to keep pace with the growth of the community. It is not necessary if the community shows no growth over a period of time.

As people realize the possibilities in recreational activities and recreationists have education along these lines, the need arises for the acquiring of various spaces; the public wants to get these areas for their use. Much of this land must be inside the community, as well as all of the areas outside of the community, to take care of the newly educated public.

Utilized to conserve potential recreational space in the face of encroachment of all kinds and by anyone. Acquire the land and dedicate it in perpetuity before all of the many commercial and private organizations have moved in.

2. Nomenclature, size, site, and characteristics.

What the land is called—park, playground, reservation, refuge, conservation site, wilderness area and so on.

Size should range from 5000 square feet to several hundred acres within the community for any one area. Should have one acre of land for every 100 people.

Site should be well located, dry or able to be quickly drained, not needing to be cut or filled extensively, easily accessible, not dangerous, placed so it can be utilized by people who have necessity to use it.

Characteristics refer to topographic and terrain features, the characteristics of the land.

3. Land use patterns.

Examine zoning laws of the community to determine land use patterns. Where will transportation, industry, and schools be placed, so that one can tell where it will be more feasible and important to place recreational facilities, structures, areas?

Get the land dedicated in perpetuity by the public for the provision of recreational services. To fight encroachment—an aroused public is the best bet.

Topic 9. Recreational Structures

Requirement

Any physical structure designed and constructed in such a way as to serve primarily and directly as a center for recreational activity or which may have a secondary recreational potential (indirect value for recreational experience although the principal purpose is oriented towards some other endeavor).

Recommendation

Physical structures will be designed and constructed to primarily serve as functional recreational centers where feasible. When existing physical structures have been designed with some purpose other than recreational service as their main function, they should be utilized as supporting centers until such time as pertinent structures may be erected.

Detailed Development of the Recommendation

1. Primary structures.

Buildings constructed for functional recreational activities and experiences, e.g., pools, parks, zoos, centers, botanical gardens, and so on. These items may have secondary purposes also, but they are primarily designed for and used for recreational purposes.

2. Supportive structures.

Structures utilized primarily for purposes other than recreational purposes, e.g., schools (activities for learning experiences), hospitals (structures for medical and health services), churches (structures for religious purposes). These structures should be used for recreational service providing such use does not interfere with the purpose for which the structures were originally intended.

Topic 10. Recreational Facilities and Traffic Patterns.

Requirement

All facilities which may be utilized for some recreational purpose should be considered in an inverse priority order (highest to lowest), in terms of their primary purpose. Facilities and equipment may only be appraised in view of population size, density and actual usage involved, particularly expendable equipment.

Recommendation

Such facilities as are necessary to accommodate public usage within or around a specific community shall be built, maintained, and operated in accordance with enumerated supervisory processes, design details, and relationship of population to any single facility, i.e., density, and construction types in conformity with local zoning and inspection codes.

Topic 11. Public Relations and Recreational Service

Requirement

This is a procedure that serves as an information gatherer and distributor, i.e., reception and transmission of data. Its functions are those of the sounding board and analytic machine in defining the public's interests and desires and where the policies, plans, and services of the recreational agency may be interpreted.

This procedure utilizes many media—oral, visual, and physical—in reaching the public eye, ear, and taste. By the same token, there are many instruments for gathering and analyzing public demands and interests.

Recommendation

The inauguration of a specific section within the recreational agency (if the organization is large enough) or the delegation of the public relations function to one employee of the organization, i.e., a public relations specialist, for the gathering, dissemination, and interpretation of information concerning agency policy and service to the public and the collection, analysis, and assessment of the recreational needs of the public.

Detailed Development of the Recommendation

1. Transmission.
   a. Program.
   b. Evaluation of the program.
   c. Utilizing the mass means of communication.
   d. Listing of material via flyers, leaflets, brochures.
   e. Advertising gimmicks.
   f. Meetings, forums, discussion.
2. Reception.
   a. Suggestion boxes.
   b. Interviews.
   c. Conferences.
   d. Inventories.
   e. Check lists.
   f. Check sheets.

Topic 12. Coordinated Agencies for Service

Requirement

The public recreational service agency is uniquely equipped to serve as a clearing house and coordinating body which can effectively schedule, channel, and direct activities of a recreational nature by other social institutions of all types within the community.

Recommendation

The public recreational service department will initiate such action as required to effectively coordinate recreational activities of various kinds, presented and promoted by the several social institutions within the community. To this end the public recreational agency will organize a community agency council or other such designated committee, council, board, or conference which will plan, schedule, and coordinate recreational experiences and services within the community so as to avoid economic and material waste through duplication and competition for the same public by many different agencies.

Detailed Development of the Recommendation

1. Technical assistance.

Provided by any one agency whose personnel have the skill, knowledge or ability to perform or teach activities of a recreational nature which are necessary for the provision of recreational services within the community. Such technical knowledge may also be of a nature not primarily recreational, but which when applied will enhance recreational service, i.e., legal advice, accounting procedures, mechanical or other material.

2. Speakers bureau.

The coordinating agency will have a roster of names of personnel employed by the various agencies who have speaking ability and technical or special knowledge of one or more special areas and who may be utilized to communicate necessary information to various groups within the community relating to their specialization.

3. Scheduling.

The main function of the interagency body will be to coordinate activities and services in such a manner that each segment of the public shall be served, that each agency shall provide an optimum presentation depending upon the resources at its command, and that local traditions, mores, and laws shall be adhered to concerning such provision without duplication of such services.

4. Committee organization.

Shall concern the membership, make-up, in terms of the number of individuals who shall sit upon the council. It may be necessary to have a large council made up of several members of each agency which wishes to contribute preparations for the resolution of recreational problems and conflicts within the community.

The council may elect from its number a smaller group which may serve as an executive board with rotating membership so that each agency will have representation.

Said board to meet weekly as opposed to the monthly meetings of the council; set policy and make decisions regarding daily presentation of recreational activities within the community.

In the event that this set-up is not feasible, it may be that an inter-organization council, having as its membership the executives of contributing agencies within the community, shall meet periodically, not more than once a month and decide recreational policies, programs and presentations in and for the community.

5. Agendas.

Will consist of all pertinent problems relating to the provision of recreational services within the community. Proper subject for discussion at the council is any problem of a recreational nature, whether it be personnel, program, or physical property for resolution by that body.

The exercise of the veto shall be avoided and majority vote shall carry any measure and be binding on any representatives on the council.

6. Material analysis.

The council shall serve as a clearing house for the dissemination of information, new publications, and other professional materials relating to the most current techniques in the provision of recreational service to the community. Each member shall be obliged to share his knowledge and technical skills with other council members for maximum services of an optimum nature, thereby benefiting all citizens of said community.

7. Representation

Representation shall be derived through any voluntary request from any public, quasi-public, or private agency within the community having any concern with recreational activity.

Topic 13. Policy Establishment (The initiation of directives which serve as behavioral and operational guide-lines designed to ensure responsiveness to the recreational needs of the community on the part of the public department. Additionally, policy is instituted to forestall serious deficits or inadequacies in public recreational service by anticipating problems and/or foreseeing potential problematic situations or conditions)

Requirement

The institution of policy is necessary to make sure that the delivery of recreational services continues with maximum efficiency, effectiveness, and economy and in accordance with the underlying principles of the field. Furthermore, policies shall be written, formalized, and widely disseminated throughout the recreational service system both internally to all personnel and externally to all potential participants and users of the system's program or physical plant.

Recommendation

The development of written policies will be undertaken by appropriate authorities within the department in response to specific conditions which call for clarification or specification. Additionally, policies will be developed in anticipation of departmental property use by certain groups within the community as well as for guiding the behavior of potential participants within the various activities sponsored, controlled, or operated by the department.

Detailed Development of the Recommendation

1. Policy shall be made by the executive and transmitted throughout the department by means of policy books. These books will be of loose-leaf design to indicate the dynamic aspect of policy making.

TABLE 25—1. EVALUATIVE INSTRUMENT

Organization and Structure (30) (Options)	Maximum point score	Departmental score	Modifications needed and any comments
1. Legislation enacted to establish a department.	10		
2. Unshared responsibility for providing a service.	10		
3. The establishment as an independent municipal department.	10		
4. Established as a subordinate agency.	5		
5. Combination of tax-supported agencies.	5		
6. Provided as a quasi-public department	4		
7. Established as a combination of nontax supported agencies.	3		
8. Provided by a denominational agency.	3		
9. Provided only by private organizations.	1		
10. Provided only by commercial enterprise.	0		
Lay Advisory Board or Commission (50)			
1. Establishment of an advisory body to assist the departmental executive's understanding of community recreational needs.	15		
2. Composition of the advisory body.	5		
3. Terms of appointment.	5		
4. Number of members.	5		
5. Departmental staff member as secretary of the advisory body.	5		
6. Meetings of the advisory body.	5		
7. Officers.	2		
8. Essential function of the advisory body as community recreational advocates.	8		

Financial Support (100)
(Options)

1. From the general tax support appropriation.	25
2. Funds earmarked.	20
3. Bond issues for capital improvement.	15
4. Fees and charges appropriate to the situation.	5
5. Minimum operational budget $5.00 per capita.	10
Debit one point for each 25¢ under.	
Credit two points for each $1.00 over.	
6. Personnel appropriation—82%	15
Credit ½ point for every 1% over.	
Debit 1 point for every 5% under.	
7. Facilities maintenance—15%.	5
Debit 1 point for every 5% over.	
8. Expendable program items—3%.	5
9. Millage levy appropriation.	10
10. Special taxes.	5
11. Operational expenditures—75%.	5
Debit 1 point for every 5% under.	
12. Capital expenditures—25% (equipment).	2
Debit 1 point for every 5% over.	

Administration (80)

1. Written policy.	10
2. Budget-making procedures.	10
3. Day-to-day reports.	10
4. Basic operating records.	6
5. Overall scheduling of activities.	4
6. Standard Operating Procedures for purchasing.	4
7. Lay committee records.	5
8. Records and receipts.	8
9. File for unfilled requisitions.	2

TABLE 25–1. EVALUATIVE INSTRUMENT (Continued)

	Maximum point score	Departmental score	Modifications needed and any comments
Administration (80) *Continued*			
10. Classified expenditures record (all except capital equipment)	5		
11. Capital outlay record.	1		
12. Perpetual inventory.	5		
13. Nonappropriated funds record.	5		
14. Comprehensive filing system.	5		
Personnel Standards (250)			
1. Minimal educational qualifications.	25		
2. Position classification under either civil service or merit system.	25		
3. Listed personnel salary ranges and step increments.	25		
4. Written job analysis for each position.	20		
5. Experience required depending on job analysis.	15		
6. Written job description.	10		
7. Personnel practices.	25		
8. Recruitment programs.	10		
9. On the job educational practices.	10		
10. In-service educational program.	15		
11. Orientation of personnel.	5		
12. Retirement plans.	5		
13. Fringe benefits.	5		
14. Part-time functional workers as required.	5		
15. Line and staff organization	60		
a. Requirement for executive officer full time.	15		
b. General supervisory positions on full-time basis.	10		
c. Facilities director full-time at year-round facility.	10		

d. Full-time program leader. Also serve as director of playground or director of facilities.	10
e. Part-time functional worker as required.	5
f. Specialists or instructors for public activities.	10

Planning (50)
(Options)

1. *Comprehensive study of the community*	20
a. Physiographic factors.	3
b. Economic factors.	3
c. Community features and characteristics.	2
d. Recreational resources of a personal nature.	2
e. Recreational resources of a physical nature.	2
f. Current recreational services provided.	3
g. Population factors.	1
h. Population trends.	1
i. Metropolitan movement.	1
j. Housing data and subdivision growth.	1
k. Recent municipal studies.	1
2. *3-5 Year recreational projection*	10
a. History and location of community.	1
b. Local governmental structure.	1
c. Economic factors.	1
d. Current recreational services.	1
e. Physical recreational resources.	1
f. Recreational personnel duties and number.	1
g. Activities making up the recreational program.	1
h. Land acquisition.	1
i. Commercialized recreational services.	1
j. Community agencies performing any recreational services.	1

TABLE 25—1.   EVALUATIVE INSTRUMENT (Continued)

Planning (50) Continued (Options)	Maximum point score	Departmental score	Modifications needed and any comments
3. Property schedule			
a. Land acquisition	10		
b. Construction of facilities.	2		
c. Construction of permanent structures	2		
d. Construction of special areas.	2		
e. Construction for present emergency needs.	2		
4. Recreational surveys			
a. Factual data on outdoor physical resources.	10		
b. Factual data on indoor physical resources.	1		
c. Factual data on current recreational services.	1		
d. Factual data on operating recreational personnel.	1		
e. Density of population to be served.	1		
f. Characteristics of the population.	1		
g. Geopolitical boundaries	1		
h. Agency which administers recreational program.	1		
i. Probable resources which are available.	1		
j. Structures of a nonrecreational nature that can be utilized for recreational activities.	1		
Program (150)			
1. Criteria for selection of activities	50		
a. Social acceptability.			
b. Safety precautions necessary.			
c. Skill required.			
d. Participation required.			
e. Self-expressive.			

2. Balanced program   60
   a. Art.
   b. Crafts.
   c. Dance.
   d. Dramatics.
   e. Education.
   f. Hobbies.
   g. Music.
   h. Nature-oriented activities.
   i. Motor skills.
   j. Service activities.
   k. Social activities.
   l. Special events.
3. Equalized opportunity   40
   a. Sex differences.
   b. Age differences.
   c. Economic levels.
   d. Ethnic characteristics.
   e. Religious affiliation.
   f. Social status.
   g. Active participation.
   h. Passive participation.
   i. Homebound.
   j. Handicapped or disabled.

Recreational Spaces (80)

1. Land acquisition.   25
2. Nomenclature land use patterns.   20
3. Location of land in relation to population density.   20
4. Size of the land parcel.   10
5. Topographic characteristics.   5

TABLE 25–1. EVALUATIVE INSTRUMENT (Continued)

Recreational structures (60)	Maximum point score		Departmental score	Modifications needed and any comments
		1 for each:		
1. Municipal camp.	3	50,000 pop. or less		
2. Band shell.	1	80,000 pop. or less		
3. Shelter Houses.	2	3,200 pop. or less		
4. Recreational piers.	1	2,500 pop. or less		
5. Stadium of 1,500 seats or more.	1	50,000 pop. or less		
6. Gymnasium.	5	10,000 pop. or less		
7. Auditorium.	3	13,000 pop. or less		
8. Recreational centers (Neighborhood)	8	10,000 pop. or less		
9. Natatorium.	1	3% of pop.		
10. Outdoor Theater.	1	78,000 pop. or less		
11. Club rooms.	3	30,000 pop. or less		
12. Multi-purpose rooms (should hold 40 persons).	3	3,000 pop. or less		
13. Special activity rooms.	1	8,000 pop. or less		
14. Library.	1	100,000 pop. or less		
15. Field houses.	1	130,000 pop. or less		
16. Game room.	5	8,000 pop. or less		
17. Lounge.	2	8,000 pop. or less		
18. Bleachers.	3	2,500 pop. or less		
19. Pavillions.	2	2,300 pop. or less		
20. Maintenance and custodial operations.	5			

Geographical and topographic factors will affect evaluation of this section.

Recreational facilities (60)

	Item		Standard
1.	Playgrounds.	3	1 acre per 150 pop. or less
2.	Playfields.	3	1 acre per 150 pop. or less
3.	Parks.	3	1 acre per 100 pop. or less
4.	Arboretum.	1	1 for 180,000 pop. or less
5.	Zoo	1	1 per 2,500,000 or less
6.	Bathing beach.	1	1 per 3% pop. or less or 50,000 pop. or less where feasible
7.	Baseball diamond (lighted or unlighted)	2	1 per 8,000 pop. or less
8.	Softball diamond (lighted or unlighted)	2	1 per 2,500 pop. or less
9.	Tennis courts (indoor-outdoor) (lighted or unlighted)	2	1 per 2,000 pop. or less
10.	Basketball courts (indoor and outdoor)	2	1 per 10,000 pop. or less
11.	Football field (lighted or unlighted)	1	1 per 35,000 pop. or less
12.	Wading pools.	1	1 per 1% pop. or less
13.	Volleyball and badminton courts (indoor and outdoor).	1	1 court per 2,000 pop. or less
14.	Handball courts. (outdoor and indoor)	1	1 court per 75,000 pop. or less
15.	Archery range (indoor and outdoor)	1	1 per 25,000 pop. or less
16.	Rifle range (indoor and outdoor)	1	1 per 100,000 pop. or less
17.	Locker rooms, showers, toilet facilities.	2	1 per each gymnasium
18.	Trailways.	1	1 per 100,000 pop. or less
19.	Kitchen facility.	1	1 per every large recreational center (community center)
20.	Boccie courts.	½	1 per 250,000 pop. or less
21.	Bowling greens.	½	1 per 250,000 pop. or less
22.	Soccer and field hockey field	½	1 per 150,000 pop. or less
23.	Golf course	2	1 hole per 3,000 pop. or less
24.	Track field	1	1 per 150,000 pop. or less
25.	Marina (where feasible).	1	1 per 150,000 pop. or less
26.	Bicycle trails (where feasible).	1	1 per 10,000 pop. or less
27.	Picnic area.	2	1 per 2,000 pop. or less

TABLE 25—1. EVALUATIVE INSTRUMENT (Continued)

Recreational Facilities (60) Continued	Maximum point score	Departmental score	Modifications needed and any comments
28. Botanical gardens.	1 per 150,000 pop. or less		
29. Nature trail (where feasible).	1 per 10,000 pop. or less		
30. Skating rink (indoor and outdoor) (lighted or unlighted)	½ per 50,000 pop. or less		
31. Apparatus, equipment and supplies (as required).	5 For facilities as required		
32. Design. Indicates layout, functional use of space, safety features, supervisory features, availability of facility, accessibility of facility, architectural features of the layout, and functional use of space.	5		
33. Construction. Types of materials to be used, economical materials, materials that will blend in with a surrounding design all best suited for the purpose.	5		
34. Maintenance and Custodial Operation. Number of personnel necessary to maintain the facility, service inside and outside, and materials for this.	5		
Public Relations (40)			
1. Policy	10		
a. Community service attitude by staff personnel.			
b. Definite community relations program in effect.			
c. Periodic review of public relations.			
d. Community relations committee.			
e. One person responsible for public relations.			
f. Coping with possible areas of friction.			
g. Directing points of public conduct for good will.			
h. Staff members taking active part in community affairs.			

2. Facilities
   a. Open house held recently.
   b. Acceptable appearance of facility.
   c. Established plan for taking care of visitor's who just drop in.
   d. Printed material to be handed to all people.
   e. Encouragement of community members to visit the recreational agency and program.

3. Mass media for communications
   a. Do local community people know where to go for information?
   b. Know where to get adequate information.
   c. Avoidance of trivial news releases.
   d. News releases made without discrimination.
   e. Adherence to deadlines.
   f. Means of communication notified concerning events of interest to them.

4. Speakers bureau
   a. Procedure for handling requests for speaker.
   b. Visual aid assistance when needed for speaker.
   c. Available roster of staff members who can speak well on their specialization.
   d. Manuscript cleared through administration channels.

5. Technical assistance
   a. Agency acts as central coordinating agency for service.
   b. Agency furnishes technical assistance to other agencies or private individuals when requested.
   c. Specialists available to answer questions relative to their area.
   d. Facilities placed on priority basis for public and private uses.

10

5

5

5

TABLE 25–1. EVALUATIVE INSTRUMENT (Continued)

Public Relations (40) Continued	Maximum point score	Departmental score	Modifications needed and any comments
6. Community awareness	5		
a. Conducting of periodic public opinion polls.			
b. Citizen awareness of staff affiliation to the agency whenever they perform in the community.			
Coordinated Agencies (10) (Options)			
1. Board or committee of community service agencies.	5		
2. Recreational agency serves as coordinating body for community service agencies.	4		
3. Recreational agency serves as clearing house for scheduling recreational activities in the community.	2		
4. Recreational agency sets aside space so that community agencies may meet.	1		
5. Recreational agency provides technical and clerical assistance so that service agencies may operate and function effectively.	2		
6. Neighborhood committees or councils in operation sponsored by the recreational agency.	3		
7. Definite policy of cooperation between the recreational agency and other tax-supported agencies.	2		
8. The cooperating agencies act on the basis of long-range planning.	2		
9. Definite plan of cooperation between the recreational agency and all the non tax-supported recreational agencies.	1		
10. There is no coordination for recreational service in the community.	0		

Patron Perception of Recreational Service (100)

1. Establishment of on-going citizen monitoring program to determine effectiveness of the recreational service. — 25

2. Determination of knowledge of program offerings operated by the department. — 15

3. Determination of knowledge of recreational facilities available for use by citizens. — 10

4. Determination of knowledge of hours of activities scheduled by department. — 10

5. Determination of citizen's perception of personal safety at recreational areas or facilities. — 5

6. Determination of public relations program. — 10

7. Determination of attractiveness of facilities: — 15
   a. Heat, light, ventilation (when appropriate).
   b. Suitable interior decoration and appointments
   c. Suitable exterior plantings
   d. Maintenance and repair of facilities and areas
   e. Accessability to potential users

8. Determination of citizens' perception of attitudes of employees insofar as helpfulness or consideration is concerned. — 10

Selected References

Abt, C. C.: *Evaluation of Social Programs* (Beverly Hills, Calif.: Sage Publications, Inc.), 1977.

Atkinson, C. C., Jr.: *Evaluation in the Management of Human Services* (Chicago, Ill.: Academy Press Ltd.), 1977.

International City Management Association: *Measuring the Effectiveness of Basic Municipal Services* (Chicago, Ill.: International City Management Association), 1974.

Owens, T. R. and W. D. Evans: *Program Evaluation Skills for Busy Administrators* (Portland, Oregon: Northwest Regional Education Laboratory), 1977.

Provus, M.: *Discrepancy Evaluation* (Berkeley, Calif.: McCutchan Publishing Corporation), 1971.

Stufflebeam, D. I., and others: *Educational Evaluation and Decision Making* (Itasca, Ill.: F. E. Peacock Publishers, Inc.), 1971.

Guidelines for the Establishment of Teen Programs

The past may not be an effective guide for the present; it most certainly has limitations for planning the future. There appears to be considerable evidence that the traditional teen-age recreational programs do not serve a large segment of contemporary youth well. The kind of teen-age center contemplated in these guidelines can be an important factor in improving the behavior, as well as influencing the lives, of thousands of youth who frequent it. Traditional agencies created to serve the recreational needs of teen-agers must pioneer a new form of program administration, only partially comparable to teen-age centers as we have known them in the past and as we know them today.

SCOPE AND GOALS

The teen-age center is a comprehensive new institution with a program emphasizing involvement of youth. Operating with a permissive recreational philosophy and offering a program unrestricted by concepts of what is and what is not recreational, it should be an informal, leisure-educational institution organized and created specifically for the welfare of teen-agers.

The center's primary goal should be to aid its members to find out who they are, what they can do, and what they believe. It should be conceived and operated to orient youth to a changing society in which leisure and recreational experiences occupy a prominent place in determining the quality of life.

Such a center should be guided by a statement of goals stressing individual development and commanding a consensus of support among the members, the staff, and the community.

ADMINISTRATION

The operation of the program of the center should be directed by a board or council elected by the teen members of the center. This board should be guided by staff and adult advisors made up of parents and community leaders, especially selected for their rapport with youth, and charged with both advising the board or council on community standards and interpreting the activities of the teen center to the community.

Membership in the center should be open to young people 13 to 19 years of age without regard to place of residence. Activities should be open to members only, with limited guest privileges. The members should pay dues and receive a membership card. Rosters and mailing lists should be developed, and members should receive program schedules two or three times a year and special announcements occasionally.

The center should be open from mid-morning until 10:00 p.m. through the week, later on Friday nights, and all day Saturday including Saturday nights. It should experiment with activities on Sunday afternoons and evenings.

Police officers should be employed to help maintain order and control ingress and egress of members and others when the need for their help becomes apparent and during special events, such as dances. Otherwise officers would be available but not present.

PROGRAM

The central content of the program should be interaction of the members in social situations. Many activities should be for small groups, organized by the members with the aid of staff as needed. The program should include forums, informal classes, and discussion groups in addition to the more traditional recreational activities.

In this kind of center, the involvement of teen-agers is an essential ingredient. The emphasis should be on aiding the teens to formulate their own program, not on the teens aiding the staff to produce the programs that the latter have conceived.

Members should be encouraged to develop a sense of ownership and a feeling of pride, respect, responsibility, and dependability that ownership entails. Their wishes must be known to matter because they have decision-making power in making rules and in program design and execution.

The members and staff should seek a close working relationship with the local schools, law enforcement, other youth-serving agencies, service organizations, and all appropriate community groups.

Evaluation of the ongoing program and identification of the interests of the clientele should be regular activities of the staff, adult leaders, and members. Activities should be selected for the specific teen-agers the center seeks to serve and interpreted in terms of the culture they embrace. Special efforts should be made to identify and provide services for those teen-agers who are not participants.

PERSONNEL

The center should be staffed with a specially educated, experienced director and assistant director, supported by a suitable number of part-time personnel selected for their rapport with youth and their recreational skills. The staff should be mature, stable men and women who are themselves well oriented, know their own competencies, and are devoted to service to teen-agers. They should provide suitable adult models for the members—short on prescription, long on example, and adroit in leadership.

The center should seek to involve a large number of volunteer workers from among the members, their parents, and community residents. Volunteer roles should be defined to include a wide range of responsibility from incidental services to policy determination. Among the staff there should be indigenous personnel recruited from the clientele to be served.

All staff should be committed to the process of learning as they serve, for the special field in which they work is new and in a formative stage.

FACILITIES

The center should consist of a special purpose facility for the exclusive use of the members during the hours it is used as a teen center. The center should be designed to create an informal, residential environment encouraging interaction of the members in small groups. Essential in such an environment are comfortable chairs, adjustable lighting, comparatively small and attractively decorated rooms, availability of food and soft drinks, although discouraged, smoking privileges for those legally eligible, and music. It is important that the center have some features of special interest to teenagers readily available—billiard tables, television sets, record players or juke boxes, and slot racing are highly desirable.

Whether the facility is to be newly planned or a substantial remodeling job is contemplated, teen-age leaders among the potential clientele should be consulted and identified from the earliest planning stages. Consideration should be given to including such major components as: playing field, multipurpose room, snack bars, game rooms, and meeting rooms. A gymnasium and a swimming pool are highly desirable.

Index